ODYSSEYS HOME

Mapping African-Canadian Literature

George Elliott Clarke

UNIVERSITY OF TORONTO PRESS
Toronto Buffalo London

© George Elliott Clarke 2002
Published by University of Toronto Press Incorporated 2002
Toronto Buffalo London
Printed in Canada

ISBN 0-8020-4376-3 (cloth)
ISBN 0-8020-8191-6 (paper)

Printed on acid-free paper

National Library of Canada Cataloguing in Publication Data

Clarke, George Elliott, 1960–
    Odysseys home : mapping African-Canadian literature

    Includes bibliographical references and index.
    ISBN 0-8020-4376-3 (bound)   ISBN 0-8020-8191-6 (pbk.)

    1. Canadian literature (English) – Black-Canadian authors –
    History and criticism.   2. Canadian literature (English) –
    Black-Canadian authors – Bibliography.   I. Title.

    PS8089.5.B5C56 2002   C810.9'896071   C2002-901165-5
    PR9188.2.B57C56 2002

University of Toronto Press acknowledges the financial assistance to its publishing
program of the Canada Council for the Arts and the Ontario Arts Council.

University of Toronto Press acknowledges the financial support for its publishing
activities of the Government of Canada through the Book Publishing Industry
Development Program (BPIDP).

ODYSSEYS HOME

Mapping African-Canadian Literature

Odysseys Home: Mapping African-Canadian Literature is a pioneering study of African-Canadian literary creativity, laying the groundwork for future scholarly work in the field. Based on extensive excavations of archives and texts, this challenging collection of essays and reviews presents a history of African-Canadian literature and examines its debt to, and synthesis with, oral cultures. George Elliott Clarke identifies the literature's distinguishing characteristics, argues for its relevance to both African Diasporic and Canadian Studies, and critiques several of its key creators and texts.

Scholarly and sophisticated, the survey cites and interprets the works of several major African-Canadian writers, including André Alexis, Dionne Brand, Austin Clarke, Claire Harris, and M. NourbeSe Philip. In so doing, Clarke demonstrates that African-Canadian writers and critics explore the tensions that exist between notions of universalism and black nationalism, liberalism and conservatism. These tensions are revealed in the literature that Clarke argues to be – paradoxically – uniquely Canadian *and* proudly apart from a mainstream national identity.

Clarke has unearthed vital but previously unconsidered authors and has charted the relationship between African-Canadian literature and that of Africa, African America, and the Caribbean. In addition to the essays, Clarke has assembled a seminal and expansive bibliography of texts from both English and French Canada. This important resource will inevitably challenge and change future academic consideration of African-Canadian literature and its place on the international literary map of the African Diaspora.

GEORGE ELLIOTT CLARKE is an associate professor of English at the University of Toronto.

ITINERARY

ACKNOWLEDGMENTS

Three editors at University of Toronto Press have seen this project through from its first contracted inception in 1997 to its long-delayed reception in 2002. Emily Andrew, Jill McConkey, and Siobhan McMenemy were dexterously patient in guiding, and expertly gifted in sculpting, the manuscript of *Odysseys Home*. They were the most beneficent Muses imaginable, and Ms McConkey sifted through and structured the bibliography. I apologize to them for being too slow (sometimes) in accepting their cogent suggestions. I also wish to acknowledge here the brilliant interventions of copy editor Ken Lewis and managing editor Frances Mundy. Gentle reader, any felicities that you identify in this book are due to all of these editors' congenial contributions.

The late John Pengwyrne Matthews (1928–95), the quintessence of a scholar, guided my doctoral dissertation, written in June 1993, at Queen's University, Kingston, Ontario, and inspired my empirical bias in examining post-colonial – or, to use his preferred term, *Commonwealth* – literature. Whatever precise thinking I have done is thanks to his example. His work is the continuous breath of my essays.

Another prime scholar I must acknowledge here is John Fraser, Professor Emeritus of Dalhousie University, who taught me how to analyse poetry. His knowledge of good poetry and scrupulous scholarship set excruciatingly high standards. I find his opinions and judgments to be unhesitatingly correct and insistently rigorous. I pray that he will scrutinize this book with a spirit of dauntless generosity.

While teaching at Duke University, from 1994 to 1999, I was befriended by Arnold 'Ted' Davidson, a leading scholar of Canadian literature. His interest in Native Canadian literature stimulated my thinking about *alterity*. I still mourn his too-early death, from cancer, in January 1999.

During my year, 1998–99, as the Seagram's Visiting Chair in Canadian Studies at McGill University, historian Desmond Morton shared with me his thoughts, including the plain but profound notion that 'people in the past are different from us. They think differently.' The concept has haunted my own attempts to imagine how eighteenth- and nineteenth-century African Canadians considered – and wrote out – their identities and realities.

In the Department of English at the University of Toronto, my colleague Linda Hutcheon has been a stalwart influence. She examined the manuscript and offered greatly supportive, challenging, and constructive comments. As a renowned scholar of literary irony, she will espy all of my unintentionally ironic critiques!

The anonymous reviewers who perused this manuscript and rendered insightful critiques will find some, but not all, of their wisdom incorporated herein. They pointed out directions for me that I was not, in the end, always brave – or smart – enough to follow. But I admire their perspicacity and careful assessments of my arguments.

I owe 'debts' to several agencies, whose assistance sponsored the researching and writing of the essays gathered here. In chronological order, the Department of English at Queen's University permitted me a conference travel grant that assisted the revision of 'Toward a Conservative Modernity.' A grant from the Canadian Embassy in Washington, DC, funded the composition of 'The Birth and Rebirth of Africadian Literature.' The Canadian Studies Program and the African and African-American Studies Program at Duke University provided me with many travel grants that supported the research and composition of 'Clarke versus Clarke,' 'Africana Canadiana,' 'Liberalism and Its Discontents,' 'Contesting a Model Blackness,' and 'Must All Blackness Be American?' McGill University and Carleton University funded speaking engagements that necessitated the preparation of 'Treason of the Black Intellectuals?' The Comparative Literature Program at the University of South Carolina at Columbia instigated the writing of 'Canadian Biraciality and Its "Zebra" Poetics.' Finally, moneys granted me by the University of Toronto supported research forays to New Orleans, Barbados, Trinidad and Tobago, and to sites across Canada, including Winnipeg, Ottawa, Fredericton, and Halifax. These travels assisted, decisively, the revision of my bibliography, 'Africana Canadiana.'

An international community of scholars and artists also came to my aid, sharing a smorgasbord of tips and info tidbits with me. Janet Friskney, Christl Verduyn, Nahum Chandler, Joe Pivato, Kwame Dawes, Barry Cahill, Pearl Eintou Springer, Robert Edison Sandiford, Michelle Wright, Uzoma Essonwanne, Sherene Razack, Shireen Lewis, Djanet Sears, Charles R. Saunders, Richard Iton, and Clement Virgo were all generous with their time and their ideas. I appreciated all of our impromptu symposia.

My bibliography of African-Canadian literature, 'Africana Canadiana,' first published (in different form) in 1997 (*Canadian Ethnic Studies* 28.3 [1996]), was compiled with the assistance of numerous scholars. Dr Leslie Sanders and Dr Frank Birbalsingh, both of York University; Dr Enoch Padolsky of Carleton University; Dr Sheldon Taylor of *Akili*; Dr John Saillant of Brown University; Dr Jean-Richard Laforest of Éditions du CIDIHCA; Dr Lucie Lequin of Concordia University; Dr Jean Jonassaint of Duke University; Dr Keith Henry of SUNY–Buffalo; Dr Lorna M. Knight, once of the Canadian Literature Research Service at the National Library of Canada / Bibliothèque nationale du Canada (NLC-BNC); librarian Sandra Bell, also of the NLC-BNC; Bruce

Whiteman, once of McGill University's Rare Book Collection; Dawn Carter, once of Canadian Artists Network: Black Artists in Action; librarian Anne L. Smith of Livingstone College; writers Austin Clarke, Ashok Mathur, Richardo Keens-Douglas, Dany Laferrière, Tololwa Mollel, Pamela Mordecai, M. NourbeSe Philip, Robert Edison Sandiford, Olive Senior, Roger McTair, Roger R. Blenman, Lorena Gale, Hugh B. Jones, Hilary Russell, Mairuth Sarsfield, and Jan Carew; independent scholar Adrienne Shadd of Toronto; the late Lenny Johnston and his now widowed wife, Gwen (once owners and operators of historic Third World Books in Toronto); Itah Sadu of A Different Booklist in Toronto; Lisa Marshall of Expressions of the Diaspora Books of Ottawa; Paul Fehmiu Brown of Montreal; Natania Feuerwerker of Moncton; my former graduate student at Duke University, Ifeoma Nwankwo; and Jo-Ann Cleaver of *Canadian Ethnic Studies*: I am indebted to all of these individuals for their insights, identifications, and suggestions; only the errors are mine.

I must also salute the various library staffs who assisted me, at the Bibliothèque nationale du Québec (Montreal), the Legislative Library (Fredericton), the National Library of Barbados, the National Library of Canada, and the National Library of Trinidad and Tobago. Also helpful were the staff members of the libraries of the University of the West Indies at Cave Hill (Barbados), St Augustine (Trinidad), the Amistad Research Center at Tulane University (New Orleans), and the Public Archives of Nova Scotia.

The essays and reviews that comprise this volume first appeared in the following publications:

'Africana Canadiana: A Select Bibliography of Literature by African-Canadian Authors, 1785–2001, in English, French, and Translation.' First appeared as 'Africana Canadiana: A Primary Bibliography of Literature by African-Canadian Authors, 1785–1996, in English, French, and Translation.' *Canadian Ethnic Studies* 28.3 (1996): 106–209.
'Another Great Thing.' *Canadian Literature* 165 (Summer 2000): 139–40.
'The Birth and Rebirth of Africadian Literature.' In *Down East: Critical Essays on Contemporary Maritime Canadian Literature*. Ed. Wolfgang Hochbruck and James Taylor. Stuttgart: Wissenschaftlicher Verlag Trier, 1997. 55–80.
'Canadian Biraciality and Its "Zebra" Poetics.' Forthcoming in *Intertexts*.
'The Career of Black English in Nova Scotia: A Literary Sketch.' First appeared as 'The Career of Black English: A Literary Sketch.' In *The English Language in Nova Scotia*. Ed. Lilian Falk and Margaret Harry. Lockeport, NS: Roseway Publishing, 1999. 125–45.
'Clarke vs. Clarke: Tory Elitism in Austin Clarke's Short Fiction.' *West Coast Line* 22 (or 31/1; Spring/Summer 1997): 110–28.
'The Complex Face of Black Canada.' *McGill News* 77.4 (Winter 1997): 26–9.
'Contesting a Model Blackness: A Meditation on African-Canadian African Americanism, or the Structures of African-Canadianité.' *Essays on Canadian Writing* 63 (Spring 1998): 1–55.

'The Death and Rebirth of Africadian Nationalism.' *New Maritimes* 11.5 (1993): 20–8.

'Harris, Philip, Brand: Three Authors in Search of Literate Criticism.' *Journal of Canadian Studies* 35.1 (2000): 161–89.

'Liberalism and Its Discontents: Reading Black and White in Contemporary Québécois Texts.' *Journal of Canadian Studies* 31.3 (Autumn 1996): 59–77.

'Love Which Is Insight.' *Books in Canada* 24.1 (Feb. 1995): 32–3.

'Must All Blackness Be American? Locating Canada in Borden's "Tightrope Time," or Nationalizing Gilroy's *The Black Atlantic*.' *Canadian Ethnic Studies* 28.3 (1996): 56–71.

'No Language Is Neutral: Seizing English for Ourselves.' *The Word* [Toronto]: 5.2 (April 1996): 11.

'The Outraged Citizen-Poet Speaks Out.' *Globe and Mail* [Toronto], 28 March 1998, p. D17.

'A Primer of African-Canadian Literature.' *Books in Canada* 25.2 (March 1996): 5–7. Expanded and included as the Preface to 'Africana Canadiana' (see above) in *Canadian Ethnic Studies* 28.3 (1996): 106–20.

'Reading Ward's "Blind Man's Blues."' *Arc* 44 (Summer 2000): 50–2.

Review of *Black Islanders: Prince Edward Island's Historical Black Community*, by Jim Hornby. *Canadian Historical Review* 73.4 (Dec. 1992): 558–9.

Review of *Pourin' Down Rain*, by Cheryl Foggo. *Canadian Ethnic Studies* 23.3 (1991): 183–4.

Review of *'We're Rooted Here and They Can't Pull Us Up': Essays in African-Canadian Women's History*, by Peggy Bristow, coord., et al. *American Review of Canadian Studies* 25.1 (Spring 1995): 153–7.

'Syl Cheney-Coker's Nova Scotia, or the Limits of Pan-Africanism.' *Dalhousie Review* 77.2 (Summer 1997) [1999]: 283–96.

'Toward a Conservative Modernity: Cultural Nationalism in Contemporary Acadian and Africadian Poetry.' *Revue Frontenac / Frontenac Review* 9 (1992): 45–63.

'*Treason of the Black Intellectuals?* Working paper of the Third Annual Seagram Lecture presented on 4 November 1998. Montreal: McGill Institute for the Study of Canada, 1999.

'An Unprejudiced View of Two Africanadian Poets.' *Arc* 27 (1991): 73–81.

'Viewing African Canada.' *Canadian Literature* 160 (Spring 1999): 185–6.

I thank the editors and reviewers at these publications for their queries and clarifications of my ideas.

Finally, I want to express my deep thanks to my wife, Geeta Paray-Clarke, for all of her patience, encouragement, insight, and generosity. A published scholar of eighteenth-century French literature, she is the model of intellectual commitment and savvy exactitude. She is the unerring star that this book, with its halting judgments, but stumblingly pursues.

Toronto, Ontario
Nisan MMII

A Note on the Text

Playing upon the metaphor of *odyssey*, I have divided this book into three main parts. Following my introductory chapter, *Odysseys Home* opens with 'Sorties,' a section comprising twelve essays on African-Canadian writing and writers, the last of which is a 'motherhood' statement on the efflorescence of black literature ('Seizing English for Ourselves'). The next section, 'Incursions,' reprints a few germane scholarly reviews. The third section, 'Surveys,' contains two parts. The first part, 'A Primer of African-Canadian Literature,' sketches its history. The second part, 'Africana Canadiana,' is a fat – albeit provisional – bibliography. I hope that the three sections of *Odysseys Home* will provide a 'map' – both eccentric and tentative – for further explorations of the literature...

Despite variations in nomenclature among African Canadians, I feel comfortable using both *black* and *African-Canadian* in my essays.* The dominant tendency, in my work as well as in African-Canadian communities, follows an African-American trend:

> *Black* succeeded *Negro* as the major term of self-definition during the Black Power years. In the late 1980s, in the aftermath of a smaller cultural nationalist moment, *African American* superseded *black* as a preferred term of self-reference. On the cusp of the twenty-first century, *black* and *African American* are often used synonymously. (Martin 253)

James Walker also states that 'the label African Canadian is being used increasingly to include all Canadians of African descent, wherever they were born' ('Canada' 360). I prefer this term because, orthographically, it demands the dignity of two initial majuscules. In contrast, *Black* is almost always written *black*. (Admittedly, the word *black* has been so tragically minisculized in critical thinking, for decades, that no clear usage is possible now. I choose, however, to capitalize *Black* when it modifies nationality or language – as in 'Black Canadian' and 'Black English.')

I have edited my reviews and articles to standardize spellings, capitalization, and stylistic predilections. I must confess that I have modified all of my essays and reviews: there is no longer a harmony between the versions printed here and their first appearances in print. For one thing, I have lightly updated some passages to take into account – *or to counter* – some recent work in the field. I have striven to minimize the repetition of ideas and quotations. To avoid other instances of duplication, bibliographical data has been separated into two parts: African-Canadian authors and their books are listed in 'Africana Canadiana'; cited African-Canadian essays, short stories, and individual poems, along with all other cited authors and texts, appear in the general 'Works Cited' bibliography.

* Debates and disputes over *black* nomenclature are inexhaustible. For instance, Euro-Canadian Marxist-Leninist Sandra Smith wonders, 'Why is a black from Jamaica not seen as an ethnic Jamaican and a black from Trinidad as an ethnic Trinidadian, and a black from Halifax as a Haligonian?' (38). Her question exposes the instability of any 'racial' naming, for some 'blacks' will want to be called 'African,' others 'Caribbean,' and still others 'Québécois.' J. Paul Grayson and Deanna Williams, in their 1994 study *Racialization and Black Student Identity at York University,* found that 'being black' was not as much a factor in their subjects' self-definitions as 'particularly culture and/or origin' (15). They report that one male student identified with being 'African' because 'he believes that "there's more power in being identified as an African than being identified as a black"' (14). A Jamaican-born woman said, 'I was born in Jamaica and I'm proud of that fact ... I'll always be Jamaican' (15). Another student, a male, described himself as 'Canadian basically,' but had not given this identity much thought (15). And 'one rare individual stated that he liked to be called "African-Canadian because Africa is the first place I am from ..."' (15).

ODYSSEYS HOME

Mapping African-Canadian Literature

Embarkation:
Discovering African-Canadian Literature

Irresponsable, à cheval entre le Néant et l'Infini, je me mis à pleurer.

Frantz Fanon

I

When I was a child, in Halifax, Nova Scotia, in the early 1960s, I knew that I was 'Coloured' because my father sat me and my two brothers in front of a mirror, held up a bowl of brown sugar, and bade us consider the sugar and our reflections. He said that we were brown like brown sugar, but that some people who look like white sugar do not like 'Coloured' people – people like us. He taught us this lesson because three white boys, only a little older than our four-year-old, three-year-old, and two-year-old selves, had called us 'niggers' and thrown rocks at us. Gracious reader, rest assured that we had promptly returned fire, and I remember clearly shouting the word *niggers* back at our pale opponents. Although I was only four, I had already watched enough television shows to know that retaliation is a gesture of fundamental self-assertion. Perhaps I also already understood, however vaguely, that, to be black, at least in Nova Scotia, was to insist on a separate and proud identity. Yet, as a boy, I was less certain about my Nova Scotianness. Nothing in the province reflected me or mine save for the two dozen or so churches of the African United Baptist Association (AUBA). Official – tourist brochure – Nova Scotian culture consisted of kilted lasses doing Highland flings to ecstatic fiddle accompaniment, or of hardy, stolid fishermen – or sailors – perishing amid the heaving North Atlantic waves, or of 'folkloric' Acadians pining for exiled 'Evangeline' in their 'picturesque' villages. The exalted Nova Scotian culture of my youth was *not* Africville – that black hamlet occupied by the City of Halifax, *not* poor black schools that somehow still educated and graduated people's intellectuals, *not* a couple of dozen black communities, *not* magnificent black ministers and unparalleled black singers, *not* even the indefatigable black boxers.

But anomalies happened. I would travel to Toronto, and someone would ask me, 'What island are you from?' and I would answer, 'Cape Breton.' I would stroll down a street in Old Québec and hear someone playing bagpipes and I would weep, almost shamefully. I would walk along the shores of English Bay, in Vancouver, and I would feel that I was just too far away, too far away, from, from what? Well, a certain pleasure in house parties, the special joys of rye and ginger ale, the deep, soul sound of the singing of African Baptist choirs, the gabble and eloquence of Black English on Gotti'gen Street, at Whitney Pier, on New Road, in Three Mile Plains. When I first left home, in 1979, to study at the University of Waterloo, in Ontario, I was surprised to suffer an abject homesickness, for I considered myself a 'Baptist Marxist,' unsentimental and 'radical.' Thus, I began to read, finally, all of the black – and East Coast – history that I could. The development of this nascent compound of identities – 'Black' and Nova Scotian – was furthered by my discovery, in the Halifax North End Library during the summer before I left, of a pamphlet of poems titled *To My Someday Child*, published in Montréal, in 1975, by Bilongo Publishers, for Gloria Wesley-Daye. Reading the verse of this beautiful, big-afro'd, Black Nova Scotian woman, I was astonished that someone could use the same medium as Shakespeare and Milton, Toomer and Brooks, to speak of alleyways and seaweed, ferry boats and broken glass, rats and bagpipes – I mean, to sing our reality. Her little book shook me. Although I was still only beginning to understand it, Wesley-Daye was the first published writer I ever encountered who was able to articulate our unique culture. She proved to me that a world both 'Black' and Canadian existed, and that it was available for art.

By the time I published my first book of poetry, *Saltwater Spirituals and Deeper Blues*, in 1983, I was assuredly 'Black Nova Scotian.' However, in those days, the adjective 'black' was shorthand for 'Black American.' I knew I was Black Nova Scotian, yes, but I still considered Black America the Mecca of *true* 'blackness,' that is to say, of Motown, Malcolm X, and Martin Luther King, Jr, of collard greens and hamhocks, of 'projects' and 'soul.' I identified so completely with Black American ways – as I understood them (which was, really, as a mass of 'progressive' stereotypes – the Panthers, Angela, and Superfly) – that I went to Detroit, Michigan, in early 1982, and was hired to help organize authentic Black Americans in veritable slums. I decided, instead, to go to work for the Ontario Legislature as a researcher, mainly because the pay was better. To be truthful, though, I was also fearful of having to test my book knowledge of Black American culture and history against the merciless interrogation of, yes, 'the streets' – and the white American power structure.

But the temptation to identify holus-bolus with Black Americana was powerful. Malcolm X's speeches were just naturally 'icier' than anything John George Diefenbaker could muster. True, Pierre Elliott Trudeau was 'cool,' but even he had to pale when set beside Amiri Baraka. And Margaret Atwood's back-bacon, backwoods rhetoric was 'nowhere' once I heard Alice Walker. To my brothers, peers, and I, Canadian culture was otherworldly, a Xanadu of snow, mosquitoes, and tepid documentaries about fishermen and loggers. Moreover, from the time I was baptized 'Coloured,' I had imbibed Black American culture. When Malcolm X was shot dead in Harlem on Sunday, 21 February 1965, I had just turned five. But I remember that day because other black kids came running up to me to tell me what had happened to this strangely surnamed man. Of course, my parents mourned the assassination of Martin Luther King, Jr. His integrationist politics appealed to their generation, and they both practised a modicum of civil-rights activism in Halifax, inspired largely by King's example. (Like many Black Nova Scotians back then, they recognized one secular Trinity: JFK, RFK, MLK.) But my mother deplored any 'Uncle Tom'-ism, denouncing the Las Vegas 'Rat Packer' Sammy Davis, Jr, as 'nothing but a white man's monkey.' But Black U.S. cultural influences were usually irresistible for us. When James Brown brought his show to Montréal in 1970, my mother took the overnight train ride up from Halifax and brought me along. When Gordon Parks's landmark film, *Shaft*, was released, my brothers and I (and a couple of friends) hung around inside the theatre and watched it *three* times. (My parents figured out why that film was so popular with us when they saw it themselves: it was the nude scenes. *But* we also loved Richard Roundtree's bad-ass attitude.) We also admired Sidney Poitier, Harry Belafonte, Aretha Franklin, Otis Redding, and Bill Cosby. In fact, his *Cosby Kids* cartoons were ideal because their gritty settings – junkyards, alleyways, sites of sabre-toothed mongrels – were the genuine article to us black, working-class, North End kids. Throughout my teens, too, the music that demarcated us was *funk*, and it was not easily found in Halifax. Thus, our Black American cultural inclinations made us automatically subtle, subterranean, and 'subversive.' When I set about organizing a 'Black Student Union' at Queen Elizabeth High School in Halifax during 1977–8, the then-principal, noting the 'Black Power' fist drawn in black marker on the back of my jean jacket, declared, 'Your *American* ideas have no place here.'

So, I grew up 'Black (American) Nova Scotian,' really, and I remained such until I was hired by Duke University, in Durham, North Carolina, and moved there in 1994 to commence my professorship. During my years in the 'Upper South,' I adored biscuits and grits, the music issued by several black radio stations, and the able self-confidence of a strong black middle class, one that controlled its own bank and life insurance company. However, I also came to recognize that African America *is* its own pseudo-nation, not a 'sub-culture,' but a *sub-civilization* of the United States, and that it is, like the American mainstream, solely self-absorbed. To be 'Black' and Canadian in that setting was to suffer the erasure of *Canadian* as a legitimate expression of black identity. Naturally, the politics of this setting inspired me to begin thinking about a literature that could be termed 'African Canadian.' In 1991 and 1992, I published *Fire on the Water*, a two-volume anthology of Black Nova Scotian – or 'Africadian' – literature, and, in the introduction, attempted to sketch its history and 'poetics.' A pre-doctoral publication, it was unabashedly undisciplined guesswork, but it included Wesley-Daye (now Wesley-Desmond), and, though shaded by African-American theoretical concepts, it represented my first effort to think through the concept of a 'Black' and Canadian identity. In 1993, in my doctoral dissertation for the Department of English at Queen's University, in Kingston, Ontario, I compared the evolution of African-American and (white) English-Canadian poetry, a process which had me claiming congruencies between George Grant and Cornel West, Gwendolyn MacEwen and Gwendolyn Brooks. Here I was thinking about 'The Similarity of Margins' between African America and English-speaking Canada. However, I had yet to examine 'African-Canadian'[1] literature – or even to accept its existence.

While teaching at Duke University, however, I was asked to write an article on 'African and African-Canadian Literature,' and I took the summer of 1995 to do it. I soon found that the extant bibliographies were error-prone and ahistorical. While striving to compose an accurate bibliography to undergird a reasonable essay, I began to wonder, intensely, about the sources and structures of African-Canadian literature. *Odysseys Home* represents the fruit of that thinking. Its essays, composed mainly between 1995 and 2000, are responses to the revelation of the existence of a canon of texts dating back to 1785, inked in French and in English, and written by people of 'Negro,' African heritage from the Caribbean, the United States, South America, Europe, Africa, and Canada itself. (From an Afro-Canadacentric perspective, Africa, the Americas, and Europe are duchies of African-Canadian literature.)

II

The Academy is a microcosm of the secular, mundane world. It is, perhaps, a public square where some read books and take notes, some doze and loaf, some picnic and drink with students, some kiss and exchange sonnets, some pack firearms, some wear placards, and some lead protests, shouting through bullhorns. Entering this 'public square,' I may resemble one of the latter 'types,' I hope, with a dash of menace – like sugar – in my speech. I recognize, however, that academic and public intellectuals and orators and rhetoricians, in Canada, are primarily white, and whenever they use the words *we* and *nous*, they almost always refer to people of the same class, cultural background, and hue as themselves. I know I am a nominal African Baptist from a marginal black community, that's all; but I still claim the right to comment on anybody's literature. I feel a responsibility, too, to contest the erasure and silencing of black culture and history in Canada. I am weary of black people always being a subject only for sociologists, criminologists, and morticians, their scalpel eyes slicing into us, their shrapnel voices exploding our dreams, their heavy metal hands ripping into us – with a crabby penmanship that dates back to the Dark Ages. In their minds, we are supposedly too poor to even have history. Or they consider our writing mere carping, that so-called 'protest fiction [is] just another ghetto, a proletarian literature in blackface' (Pinckney 65). Or they classify us as 'exotica,' as symbols of liberal progress, of white paternalism, of black suffering, of feminist rage. Or they pretend that 'Black Canadian' literature consists of two or maybe three writers, and, if pressed, will struggle to name Austin Clarke and Dionne Brand. Yet, reading only a few writers does not suffice for accessing the excellent diversity of the literature. As the Italian-Canadian writer Antonio D'Alfonso witnesses, 'it is the succession of [writers], united by their interdependence, their concatenation, that engenders the [literary] tradition of any one country' (61).

Appearing as I am, at the haunted readying of this literature, one I have found by accident because I am a poet, I hear the ardent violence of pamphleteers and the sly violence of cheerleaders and also the special violence of poets. No wonder: For some, the idea of an 'African-Canadian literature' may seem as fraudulent as Clifford Irving's biography of Howard Hughes. For some, its canon may resemble some bizarre, inverse universe compared to the established realms of African-American and Afro-Caribbean literatures, a new-fangled province of letters glimmering phantasmally in the reflected light of these better-defined, more-floodlit canons. It is, granted, a project(ion) of the imagination. Never spoken of before the 1970s, it was not conceived as any coherent articulation of national culture(s). Rather, it was viewed as a provisional assembly of texts by 'Blacks in Canada,' that is to say, as a grab-bag of writings by people who 'happened to be Black' and 'happened to be in Canada' (in many cases, temporarily, as students, or workers, putting in time in Arctic limbo before returning to 'real life' somewhere else, somewhere warmer). In the first sketchy anthologies and bibliographies of 'West Indians in Canada' or of charmingly named 'Other' voices, a beautiful innocence colours questions of identity and belonging. The popular belief in those halcyon times was that 'Black writing in Canada' began with the publication of Austin Clarke's first novel in 1964, and the vivid black history was considered to have happened offshore. One said of African Canada what Ezra Pound once said of Roquefixade in Provence: 'Of this place there is nothing in the archives' (*Walking* 50). To read its seemingly 'instant' literature is, for some then, to encounter the absurd, the strange, the unusual, the 'too white' and the 'too black,' and to dread that one is reading exotic repetitions of previous black literature(s). From such a perspective, Dany Laferrière's novel *Comment faire l'amour avec un nègre sans se fatiguer* (1985) may resemble a two-decades-belated, Black Arts Movement novel from the fringes of Greenwich Village. The only remedy for such accidental misprisions is neither glad-handing nor grandstanding, but intelligence, or, rather, to quote Poundian Kay Davis, 'a piece of scholarship searching for order and light out of confusion' (26). What students of African-Canadian literature must do is counter amnesia, for those who do not research history are condemned to falsify it. For one thing, there were likely signs from the genesis of Canada that a black literature would form, but its existence could not become known until its creators began to articulate themselves consciously as a people – or peoples. James Walker asserts that 'to order events in a coherent narrative is necessarily to suggest their meaning; in effect, historians create history' ('*Race*' 37). To understand any culture, one must excavate its past.

My placard and my bullhorn communicate, I hope, my context, which is 'Afro,' 'Canuck,' 'Africadian,' and my aim, which is to avoid oblivion. I have entered the 'public square' that is the Academy because I accept that 'African-Canadian literature' exists and must needs be defined and, yes, defended. I abhor the general Euro-Canadian tendency to either surrender critical assessment to celebrate the manifestation of these unorthodox texts or to ignore, imperiously, their presence. To understand that African-Canadian literature exists, in the guise of a parliament of accents inhabited by long-appointed and recently elected 'members,' is to adopt, in the brilliant 'true crime' phrase of Scott Burnside and Alan Cairns, 'a clarity that facilitates criticism' (560). Our duty now is to eliminate (1) faulty parallels with African-American culture and literature; (2) misconstructions of the African-Canadian communities and their different histories; (3) culpable omissions; (4) self-interested canon formations; and (5) evacuations of research.

The pure problem I seek leave to address in *Odysseys Home* is that the Academy too often dismisses – or distorts perceptions of – those populations it can hold at its mercy, those whose histories parrot narratives of defeat. Thus, the study of African-Canadian literature, culture, and history too often reflects a master discourse of black inadequacy, inferiority, illegality, *et cetera*. Glancing at criticism of African-Canadian existence, one may say that, perhaps as a consequence of 'an imprisonment within an eccentric totality, a sort of private language has grown up within a professional circle,' to borrow an apt phrase from Martin Kayman (38). Black creativity in Canada is denounced with bellicose ignorance or rebuffed with bellowing ripostes. Some scholars promulgate aberrant interpretations that mock the facts they feed upon. Others compose lyrical operas of errors. African-Canadian scholar Peter Hudson observes that 'the absence of black literary production in the writing of Canadian cultural histories has created a critical wasteland for African Canadian literature' (Editor's 5). One illustration of accidental, critical destitution occurs when sociologist Frances Henry alleges, in 'Black Music from the Maritimes' (1974), that Black Nova Scotians lack a recognizably black popular musical tradition. Here one may espy a Pollyannish Pan-Africanism scornful of the panoply of cultural differences among people who share the same range of melanin on the racial palette. Thus, Black Nova Scotia is stripped of musical accomplishment because *two* of its beloved musics – country and old-time spirituals – do not correspond with those associated with Black America and the Caribbean. One sees here a reductive reading of *blackness* which cannot accommodate – or hear – the *different* blackness of Nova Scotia.[2] Yet, musical production in many categories has been an imperishable aspect of Africadian[3] culture. Out of impoverishment the dazzle of creativity, and, to cite Vincent Sherry, 'out of contradiction great art' (168).

To open Paul Gilroy's signal work, *The Black Atlantic: Modernity and Double Consciousness* (1993), is to confront, yet again, the blunt irrelevance of Canada to most gestures of diasporic inclusiveness. In his introductory essay, Gilroy adduces 'the image of ships in motion across the spaces between Europe,

America, Africa, and the Caribbean as a central organising symbol for this [theoretical] enterprise ...' (4). Canada, as subject space, is patently absent. He never registers it as a site of New World African enslavement, immigration, emigration, anti-racist struggle, and cultural imagination. For Gilroy, Canada seems merely a semi-European and semi-American projection requiring little consideration. His true passion is to position Britain, France, and Germany, and their Afro-minority populations, as counterweights to the African-American tendency to annex all black-white racial discourse for its own hegemonic purposes. Hence, his *Black Atlantic* is really a vast Bermuda Triangle into which Canada – read as British North America or Nouvelle-France or even as an American satellite – vanishes.

Yet Gilroy's evacuation of the possibility for any real Canadian blackness is nothing new. In 1973, Mercer Cook pointed out that 'we cannot be surprised that Africans and persons of African descent, exposed to racism in places as distant as Mali, Martinique, Mississippi, or Manhattan, Pretoria, Pittsburgh or Paris, should sometimes voice their protest in somewhat similar terms' (119). Naturally, Cook did not choose to include blacks in Montréal and Peterborough in his alliterative schema. Introducing *Black Atlantic Writers of the Eighteenth Century* (1995), Adam Potkay practises a like erasure. He refers to Black Loyalist – and early African-Canadian – writer Boston King and his *Memoirs* (1798), but positions him only as American and British (18n14). In their *magnum opus*, *Africana: The Encyclopedia of the African and African American Experience* (1999), editors Kwame Anthony Appiah and Henry Louis Gates, Jr, include article after article that excludes significant African-Canadian personages. Thus, in his entry on 'Literature, English Language, Caribbean,' Selwyn Cudjoe stresses the growth of interest in Caribbean anglophone authors in Britain, acknowledging that most of them 'had to go abroad (primarily to England) to achieve literary recognition and to gain a sympathetic audience' (1179). However, the watershed anglophone Caribbean emigration to Canada – specifically Toronto and other major Ontario cities – is omitted. Cudjoe cites Trinidadian-Canadian writers M. NourbeSe Philip and Dionne Brand and Jamaican-Canadian writers Olive Senior and 'Mikeda' [*sic*] Silvera (1179), but skips the breakthrough writers Austin Clarke and Jan Carew.[4] In his submission, Richard Watts notes the writing of Haitian-Canadian author Dany Laferrière and his Québec residency (1183), but neglects Gérard Étienne (who has lived in Nouveau-Brunswick) as well as another Québécois, the sci-fi writer Stanley Péan. Worse, *Africana* misses the distinguished U.S.-born poet and novelist Frederick Ward, just as it neglects the Ontario native and novelist Lawrence Hill and Africadian poet Maxine Tynes. Discussing 'Afro-Atlantic Culture,' J. Lorand Matory holds that the 'live dialogue between Africa and its American diaspora has produced, if not always harmony, then a set of new, hybrid discourses of self-expression and identity' (37). But Canada is dismissed from this dialogue, despite the relative unity of the Americas and American experience. Earl E. Fitz recognizes that 'English and French Canada, the United States, Spanish America, and Brazil [constitute] a community of literary cultures related to each other by virtue of their origins, their sundry interrelationships, and their sociopolitical, artistic, and intellectual evolutions' (xi). In a Gilroy-like move, Fitz 'whites out' the Caribbean from his 'map' of New World literary unity. Unfortunately, one could compile a rather substantial library of African-Atlantic materials witnessing the generic invisibility of Black Canada in black-oriented scholarship.[5] Indisputably, extra-Canadian, Afro-Atlantic literary critical discourse focuses on Afro-Caribbean and African-American writers, and touches only on those Canadian writers who can be seconded to one of these desired geographies. The result is that a swath of vital writers goes unremarked and unnoticed, while those few who garner attention have their Canadian ties either Americanized or airbrushed out of existence. There is more 'blackness' in African-Canadian literature than is dreamt of in the criticism.

Naysayers may ask, why should Canada be registered as a black (minority) space by scholars of the transatlantic African Diaspora? After all, Black Atlantic writers inhabit multiple subjectivities/identities because they range broadly, and may be annexed by American, British, Caribbean, and African literatures. What special claim can Canada and Canadian literature exert upon these writers and their works? The answer is, I think, that *blackness* possesses a Canadian dimension that is recognized by engaging with black cultural works located here or that address black existence here. Canadacentric research is necessary because the expansive cosmopolitanism of the African Diaspora cannot be understood without taking into account the creative ways in which *blackness* has managed to thrive in this predominantly white settler-state. Antiguan-Canadian performance poet Clifton Joseph, ruing his initial disparagement of 'indigenous' African-Canadian culture, affirms that he had to learn that 'the history is always there to be found/out-about, to learn, and to make; that ... there are areas of our history that need to be researched, recorded, and reclaimed' (20–1). Scrutiny of the Caribbean and its diaspora must shift, for instance, to the extent that scholars are able to contrast the effects of Canadian-based expatriation with the more loudly analysed American and British examples. Assuredly, too, literary critics, cultural studies intellectuals, and historians who wish to comment incisively on African-Canadian art and acts must assess its annals. For example, the foremost historian of Africa Canada, James Walker, notices the black 'cultural renaissance' that has flourished in Nova Scotia since the 1970s, but also asserts that 'elsewhere in Canada it is primarily immigrants such as Austin Clarke and Dionne Brand who are resurrecting the black literary tradition and weaving it into a Caribbean memory and the migratory experience' ('Canada' 365). His statement is questionable: no African-Canadian literary tradition need be 'resurrected,' but, rather, *respected* as the living art of a long-residenced people. Another, happier quotation from Walker is pertinent here. Discussing his study of Supreme Court of Canada cases addressing racial issues, he defines them as 'above all, Canadian stories: the heroes are unsung and the achievements undramatic, the approach is cautious and the demeanour always polite. Quintessentially Canadian, it might be said' ('*Race*' 11). Similarly, the canon and the criticism of African-Canadian literature may seem subdued, even sedate, read alongside African-American and Caribbean texts. African-Canadian history may *seem* lacklustre when set beside the glittering epics of African-American toil and jubilee and the sun-dazzled odes of Afro-Caribbean struggle and carnival. True, Halifax is not Harlem or Havana or Haiti, and Prairie black settlers did not play the shoot-'em-up role of U.S. 'Buffalo Soldiers.' Nevertheless, the scholar of this racial minority culture (of differing ethnic minorities) must be animated either by animus or *amore*. For my part, I choose to love African Canada, or, at least *Africadia* – its heartbreaking blues spirituals and liquor-broken guitarists, its scriptural pigtails and curried Bible, its seaweed-embroidered sedition ... Scholarship is, in the end, a version of humility. And then there is always, ah, 'the glamour of history' (Korn 7) for further motivation.[6]

The scholar is not called merely to celebrate, but to elaborate the condition of his or her subject(s). Thus, I attempt, herein, to popularize knowledge of how African-Canadian literature came into being, and to note how international – and Canadian – literary styles inform African-Canadian texts. Certainly, African-Canadian literature encompasses the new and the old, the come-from-away and the down-home, the urban and the rural, the pull of the regional and the equally irresistible seductions of African-American – and Afro-Caribbean – culture. In my work here, I aim to counter what Hudson terms 'the shallow readings of black writing by mapping the literary topos of Canada as a province of the African diaspora and exploring the space of African Canadian literature as a province of the imagination' (5).

In sounding African-Canadian literature, I have been guided by U.S. anthropologist Lawrence W. Levine's illuminating study *Black Culture and Black Consciousness* (1977), which insists that 'it is time for historians to expand their own consciousness by examining the consciousness of those they have hitherto ignored or neglected' (Preface ix).[7] To refuse to do so is to figure black cultures as 'an unending round of degradation and pathology' (Levine, Preface x–xi), which has been precisely the cliché-ridden and petty approach, too frequently, to the richness that is black literatures. To fathom African-Canadian literature, specifically, we must view its works holistically – analysing both folk creations (including self-published texts, community histories, and religious testaments) and those demanding a modicum of academic literacy. I do not mean here to romanticize 'the folk.' Like Levine, I know they 'are not historians' (389). Yet, they are surely 'the products and creators of a culture, and that culture includes a collective memory' (Levine 389). This 'collective memory' is manifested, I would add, in literary works that recall slavery, segregation, decolonization struggles, and the search for viable, independent economies.

In deciphering these works, however, one must not mute their orality. Vitally, Levine states that the oral tradition represents a kind of communal manifesto: 'through [a black storyteller's] entire performance the audience would comment, correct, laugh, respond, making the folktale as much of a communal experience as the spiritual or the sermon' (89). This social dimension of African diasporic *orature*[8] also appears in its literatures, where it assumes the form of song, sermon, story, and proverb. Examining anglophone Caribbean literature, then, Cudjoe confirms it is 'an offshoot of the African oral literary tradition (most island inhabitants come from West Africa) and shaped by its Asian and European roots' (1178). Furthermore, it originates in 'the proverbs, riddles, and *kheesas* (tales) of African and Indian literature respectively ...' (1178). African-American literature began with the 'African oral heritage, in which music and poetry were inexorably linked' (Hill, et al. 3). From these roots, along with 'Euro-American folk elements' and 'their own interpretations of biblical myth and typology, [early African Americans] created work songs, spirituals, and folktales' (Hill, et al. 3). African-Canadian literature springs also from *orature* and communal creativity. Black slaves and settlers in early Canada sang, preached, and told stories. (For examples, see my essay 'The Career of Black English in Nova Scotia,' pp. 86–106, below.) Studying New World African literature, then, one must appreciate the inseparable union of text and voice music – as in transcriptions of spirituals (or blues, rap, samba, soca, etc.). For instance, Levine notices that 'William Arms Fisher warned his readers that his attempts to reproduce the music of the spirituals he heard in the 1920s could not capture "the slurring and sliding of the voices, the interjected turns and "curls," the groans and sighs, the use even of quarter-tones, the mixture of keys, and the subtle rhythms"' (159). This New World African investment in voicing nearly untranscribable transformations of word into song justifies the use, by savvy anthologists, of song lyrics and *orature* in their compilations of black texts. Verily, the ghost of orality haunts most black writers.[9]

But the spectre of intellectual miscegenation spooks some critics of African-Canadian literature, for it stems from 'a cultural mosaic as diverse as any in the world, with substantial African, Caribbean, and African American contributions' (Walker, 'Canada' 365). In fact, the catholicity of Canadian *blackness* is so pronounced that Canada may be the perfect space for what Stuart Hall terms 'the recognition of the extraordinary diversity of subjective positions, social experiences, and cultural identities that compose the category "black" ...' (706). Because its makers borrow unapologetically, from Caribbean and American, but also British, French, and African source cultures to furbish their experiences as a section of the African Diaspora, some commentators deplore their flamboyant appropriations and blatant 'plagiarisms.' So, scholar Sarah-Jane Mathieu complains that a 1996 high school text 'strangely positions African Canadian history against the backdrop of the United States, as evidenced by such subtitles as "Voter Registration," "Let the Cities Burn," and "Black Power" ...' (169). Her frustration is palpable. However, the real fault here of authors Ken Alexander and Avis Glaze is not that they failed 'to originate or invent all or even most of the elements of their culture' (24), a process Levine thinks unnecessary, but that they failed to make 'these components become their own, embedded in their traditions, expressive of their world view and life style' (24), a process Levine deems the *sine qua non* of cultural originality. Following Levine's insight, I argue that African-Canadian culture and literature have domesticated – nationalized – their influences enough to create an aboriginal *blackness*, even if this mode of being remains difficult to define or categorize.[10]

III

Levine's social science scrupulosity is venerable, but my own critical approach is neither fundamentally sociological nor historical – though I prefer the wisdom of history to the statistics of sociology. (As for psychology, I prefer poetry.) Schooled in post-colonial[11] theory by Dr John Matthews (1928–95), a classical empiricist, I pledge allegiance to no *avant-garde* fashion. (I am a positivist [new] humanist – for better or for worse.) My foundational philosophical reference is the Canadian 'Red Tory' writer George Grant (1918–88), whose romantic adoration of Canadian sovereignty and nationalism, *Lament for a Nation* (1965), has helped shape my thinking about cultural particularity. Grant's defence of 'local cultures' supports, then, my defences of the existence of Africville, Nova Scotia (see 'Death and Rebirth of Africadian Nationalism,' pp. 288–96, below), and Africadian literature (see 'Toward a Conservative Modernity,' pp. 151–62) and underpins my analyses of the persistence of racism in Québécois literature (see 'Liberalism and Its Discontents,' pp. 163–81) and the promotion of classism in Austin Clarke's short stories (see 'Clarke vs Clarke,' pp. 238–52). Though I value Grant's would-be *progressive* conservatism, I am wary of its gravedigger, Heideggerian roots. I admire, too, the robust liberalism of the Canadian 'philosopher-king' Pierre Elliott Trudeau (1919–2000) that champions equality of individuals – but also of *some* communities (anglophones *vis-à-vis* francophones).[12] Moreover, I laud the ways in which French Jewish philosopher Julien Benda (1867–1956), whose work explicitly influenced Trudeau (and may have tacitly influenced Grant), reconciles the communal orientation of literature and the individualist impulses of writers (see 'Treason of the Black Intellectuals?' pp. 182–210). These writers have been important in guiding my thought, for I believe that the central ideological conflict in New World African writing is that of liberalism versus conservatism, or 'integration' versus nationalism. This basic binary opposition is nuanced, not absolute, for the underlying tension oscillates among individualist, assimilationist, and cultural-separateness yearnings. (This division is necessary because liberalism can either be passively or aggressively assimilationist, while nationalism can either be pacific, indulging in cultural assertion, or violently exclusivist/collectivist.) Truthfully, I think the clash between conservative nationalism and liberal individualism is best exemplified, in a Canadian context, by pitting Grant versus Trudeau, or, in an African-American context, by unleashing Malcolm X on Henry Louis Gates, Jr. As much as I am enthralled by these thinkers, however, I am also a devotee of Frantz Fanon, and his existentialist, psychoanalytical approach to the problem of black identity in a Eurocentric civilization. To be precise, I admire his (socialist) liberationist aesthetic that insists, 'Il n'y a pas de mission nègre; il n'y a pas de fardeau blanc' (*Peau* 187).

I also value his 'liberal' assertion: 'Je ne suis pas prisonnier de l'Histoire. Je ne dois pas y chercher le sens de ma destinée' (*Peau* 188). Yet, to the degree that Fanon can diagnose, almost insouciantly, the existence of a black 'inferiority complex' due to the 'interiorisation ou, mieux, épidermisation de cette infériorité' (*Peau* 10), he is also conservative. Given my intellectual *bricolage* of Grant, Trudeau, Fanon, *and* Malcolm X (the patron saint of these essays), I articulate a delicate duality. Fundamentally, I am enough of a liberal to accept that a writer may *wish* to write independently of communal identification. But I am also enough of a conservative to appreciate that no writer ever does *completely*.[13] Some writers – sometimes – wish to immerse themselves in a loudly romantic union with their *perceived* primary cultural heritage; others – sometimes – *wish* to be *pur et dur* universalists, to assert a romantic liberty of affiliation. D'Alfonso reads the dialectic thus: 'For ethnicity to have any value it must be collective, even if, in the end, it is the individual who will count most' (61). I believe that balance is all.[14] Identities shift. I maintain, however, that all assertions of cultural *difference* are conservative, though grounded in myth (the literary version of essentialism).[15]

To speak about an 'African-Canadian' literature, then, I must be 'essentialist' enough to believe that an entity describable as 'African Canada' exists, though 'there is no longer a single African Canadian community tradition ...' (Walker, 'Canada' 363). In fact, I hold that African Canada is a conglomeration of many cultures, a spectrum of ethnicities. That perception colours the essays gathered here. For instance, the old, indigenous, African-Canadian communities, mainly African-American in derivation and often rural, adopted a strong church-bias, so that their 'music, dance, folklore, even daily speech, became imbued with religious motifs' (Walker, 'Canada' 365). My essays 'Toward a Conservative Modernity' and 'The Birth and Rebirth of Africadian Literature' (pp. 107–25) discuss the influence of this religious impulse upon the development of Black Nova Scotian literature. The 'New Canadian' black communities, mainly of Caribbean origin (and then chiefly Jamaican or Haitian), recall a heroic heritage in which 'wherever slavery existed, self-liberation began' (Whitten 257). Caribbean cultures emerged from 'the dialectic between ... the darkening influences of white domination in the African diaspora and ... the illuminated creativity produced and reproduced in the eternal fires of black rebellion' (Whitten 257). However, they also confront the tensions between 'two nationalist ideologies of racial culture: *mestizaje* (racial mixture) and Négritude (blackness)' (Whitten 258). Addressing this reality, my essays 'Contesting a Model Blackness' (pp. 27–70), 'Treason of the Black Intellectuals?,' 'Canadian Biraciality and Its "Zebra" Poetics' (pp. 211–37), 'Harris, Philip, Brand' (pp. 253–74) assess the function of anglophone Afro-Caribbean – and African-American – rhetorics in African-Canadian literature. For its part, francophone African-Canadian literature possesses a tripartite inheritance, drawing from Africa, the Caribbean, and from the work of native-born francophones like Paul Fehmiu Brown, a self-described 'Afro-Acadien.' For Richard Watts, francophone Afro-Caribbean literature divides between that of

Haiti, with its 'nearly mono-ethnic population (95 percent of Haitians are of African descent, whereas the rest of the Francophone Caribbean is considerably more diverse)' (1182), and that from Martinique, Guadeloupe, and French Guiana, the 'overseas departments of France' (1183). Even so, French-speaking Caribbean writers espouse two major impulses: 'Négritude and Créolité' (Watts 1183). Négritude writers try, says Watts, 'to reconcile their African past with their Caribbean present ...' (1183). However, *Créolité* writers seek their identity 'in the Caribbean itself' (1183). In Canada, I think both tendencies crop up in the works of Laferrière and Étienne, but it is Laferrière's astringent satire *Comment faire l'amour avec un nègre sans se fatiguer* (1985) which is a prime subject of my essay 'Liberalism and Its Discontents.' I also endeavour to feel out French-Canadian thought in my essays 'Treason of the Black Intellectuals?' and 'Toward a Conservative Modernity.' Finally, the import of African-American literature for African-Canadian literature is the subject of both 'Contesting a Model Blackness' and 'Must All Blackness Be American?' (pp. 71–85).

In all of these essays, I assume a modicum of *essentialism*, so that I am enabled – empowered – to discuss 'Africadian' and 'African-Canadian' literature with a fair (or black?) conviction that 'Africadians' and 'African Canadians' have *some* corporeal, 'real' existence. For, if these peoples do not have some coherency in the world, this book is so much nothing. I bear in mind Trinidadian-Canadian sociologist Sherene H. Razack's criticism of 'the ways in which essentialist constructs mask relations of power,' but also her acknowledgment that 'it is not clear ... that talking about culture in an essentialist way is always a bad thing' (21). Ultimately, I concur with Matory: 'Not all cultural legacies are continuous and none is primordial' (41). African-Canadian culture and literature cannot be sourced at any single cultural influence or moment. For one thing, they reflect 'the powerful role of the European-dominated Atlantic political economy in creating the conditions of the black Atlantic dialogue over collective identity' (Matory 38). African Canada is, then, a fragmented collective, one fissured by religious, ethnic, class, and length-of-residency differences. And few African Canadians express black nationalism that is not merely a nostalgic yearning for homelands in Africa, the Caribbean, or the southern United States. I accept the infallible contingency of black identities, but to surrender to this point does not void cultural nationalism.

Primarily the invention of German philosopher Johann Gottfried Herder (1744–1803), nationalism insists, writes Anthony Appiah, that 'peoples (or, as they were often called, nations) ... were the central actors of world history' and that 'their identities were expressed largely in language, in literature, and in folk culture' ('Pan-Africanism' 1485). Nationalism has thus served to *particularize* literary scholarship, so that 'from its inception, literary history, like the collection of folk culture, served the ends of nation building' (Appiah, 'Race' 1579). In African America, then, 'such intellectual pioneers as W.E.B. Du Bois from the latter nineteenth century on attempted to articulate a racial tradition of black letters as a natural expression of the Herderian view of the nation as identified above all else with its expression in "poesy"' (Appiah, 'Race' 1579). This vision flowers now in the contemporary academic movement, championed by Gates, Houston Baker, Jr, Nellie Y. McKay, et al., 'to argue for the recognition of an African American tradition of writing, with its own major texts, which can be studied as an independent canon' (Appiah, 'Race' 1580). According to Appiah, 'some of those who make such claims ... have been motivated largely by a black nationalism that is, in part, a response to racism; others have argued for the recognition of a black canon because they have identified formal features in the writings of black authors that derive from a self-conscious awareness of black literary predecessors and African or African American folk traditions' ('Race' 1580). In my mind, both positions originate in the nationalistic need to define African-American specificity in reference to a larger Anglo-Saxon and Euro-American literature which, bare decades ago, denied even the idea of African-American literacy, let alone the existence of a literature meriting scrutiny.[16] In addition, the thrust for Black Studies in the American academy, beginning in the 1960s, and its fruition in the issuance of institutional instruments like *The Norton Anthology of African American Literature* (1997), edited by Gates and McKay, and *The Oxford Companion to African American Literature* (1997), edited by William Andrews, has inspired similar canonizing energies in African-Canadian literature and culture. (However, the examples of Québécois, Franco-Ontarien, Acadien, and English-Canadian cultural nationalism in scholarship are also significant here.[17]) Thus the issue of an African-Canadian canon is, like that 'of an African American canon ... inevitably a political one' (Appiah, 'Race' 1580), for it bares the antinomian presence of cultural nationalism.[18]

Nevertheless, *blackness* remains an absolutely relative epistemology. The 'Canadian species' is not identical to the 'American,' and neither is the same as the 'Caribbean.' The structural conditions of each 'region' of blackness impinge upon its theorization and definition. Thus, some African Canadians call themselves *Black* to signal their affiliation with some larger African universe; but others call themselves *African*, choosing to accent their ancestral heritage. Some add the adjective *Canadian*, to express a Canadian identity modified by 'blackness.' Others identify with an ex-colonial heritage – either 'British' or 'Français.' Still others ask to be classed solely as *Canadian*. The oft-cited 'lack of unity' among African Canadians is, then, the result of the instability of *black-as-signifier chez nous*. Here the diversity of black communities proves that '"black" is essentially a politically and *culturally constructed* category, which cannot be grounded in a set of fixed transcultural or transcendental racial categories and which therefore has no guarantees in Nature' (Hall 706). In Canada, some are born black, some acquire blackness, and others have blackness thrust upon them.

Given that *blackness* is so undefined and indefinable, one potential objection to my essays is that they group human beings on the specious – and spurious – grounds of shared 'race,' a matter of a chance apportioning of pigmentation and melanin.[19] Appiah notes, reasonably, that 'such classifications as *Negro*,

Caucasian, and *Mongoloid* are of no importance for biological purposes' ('Race' 1576). Cultures are constantly deploying or redeploying subjectivities in either recognizably classic or startlingly fresh garbs. Yet, five centuries of Eurocentric imperialism have made it impossible for those of us descending from Africa, Asia, Oceania, Aboriginal Australia, and Aboriginal America to act as if we are pure, raceless beings. Then again, we confront the global complex of a white supremacist capitalism that vigorously *races* and erases whole populations – as it so wills. That racial identities 'are founded on mistaken beliefs does not deprive them of their power to shape people's attitudes and behavior' (Appiah, 'Ethnicity' 705) is a fact the liberal ideal of racelessness ignores. Who does not know that the 'Negro' peoples still struggle against the historical white racist construction of the black person as 'noble savage and violent avenger' (Hall 707)? (Frankly, black people in Canada have been defined and shaped, to some extent, by Eurocentric Canadian racism.[20] The country has long sniffed after what Jewish-Canadian poet A.M. Klein dubs 'the body-odour of race' [308].) Being pragmatic, I understand that even where post-colonial writers claim to be 'Indian,' 'African,' or 'Greek,' they are not 'Indian, African or Greek writers but Indo-Canadian, Afro-American or Greek-Australian writers' (Vevaina, 125). I also laud Appiah's proviso that 'discussion of some of the literary ramifications of the idea of race can proceed while accepting the essential unreality of races and the falsehood of most of what is believed about them' ('Race' 1576). This spirit is the one in which my own judgments – combative and contradictory – are offered in *Odysseys Home.*

Notes

1 'African Canadian' refers to persons and expressive cultures, located in or derived from Canada, possessing, to some degree, an ancestral connection to sub-Saharan Africa. The phrase encompasses, then, recent immigrants to Canada from the United States, the Caribbean, South America, and Africa itself, as well as the indigenous, Africa-descended community.

2 Henry's accidentally condemnatory scholarship, also displayed in her book *Forgotten Canadians: The Blacks of Nova Scotia* (1973), was rebuked by Black Nova Scotian popular historian Pearleen Oliver in a 1981 report to members of the African United Baptist Association (AUBA) of Nova Scotia:

> During the Spring and early summer I had the opportunity to talk with groups of University students on the Black people of Nova Scotia. It distressed me to learn that they were using as their information, the book, THE FORGOTTEN CANADIANS, THE BLACK PEOPLE OF NOVA SCOTIA [sic], written and published eight years ago by Francis [sic] Henry. This very-negative book on the Black people of Nova Scotia, is being used in Universities across North America. This book stigmatizes two of our communities, e.g., Sunnyville (called Vale Haven) and Cherry Brook (called Far Town). ('Report' 32)

Oliver must have been thoroughly scandalized by Henry's work, for the AUBA comments rarely on secular cultural matters. Sadly, though, Henry is no singular offender against comprehensive research. In her defence, too, one must recognize that she was hoping to highlight the dismal deprivations that African Nova Scotians had suffered. In contrast, Robin Winks's *The Blacks in Canada: A History* (1970), though a treasure trove of information, reads, at times, like a compendium of racial slurs. According to Winks, then, the Black refugees were so 'disorganized, pathetic, and intimidated' that they 'unwittingly fanned the sparks of a more conscious, more organized, white racism than Nova Scotia had known ...' (114). Time after time, Winks blames blacks for white racism. His scholarship evinces, here and there, the creepiest and subtlest – and supplest – forms of racialist thinking. It would be unwise to grant Winks's interpretations the same credibility that one must grant his facts.

3 René Dionne declares, in *La Littérature régionale aux confins de l'histoire et de la géographie* (1993), that 'une littérature régionale proclame son emancipation en adoptant un nom spécifique qui affirme le caractère distinct du groupe ...' (39). In accord with this 'emancipatory' strategy, I term Black Nova Scotia *Africadia* and its people and cultural works *Africadian*. A fusion of *Africa* and *cadie*, the Mi'kmaq term for 'abounding in' (and the probable cognate of the French toponym *Acadie* [Acadia]), *Africadia(n)* serves to stress the long history of Africans in Maritime Canada. *Black Nova Scotian, Afro-Nova Scotian, 'Scotian,* and *African-Nova Scotian* are other popular terms denoting the Africadian populace. While these labels have their merits and their defenders, I think they obscure the long residency of Africans in Nova Scotia, the first of whom, Mathieu da Costa, settled at Port-Royal, Acadie, with Samuel de Champlain in 1605. Another term, *Afro-Acadiens*, denotes Black Acadiens. See Loic Vennin 16–17.

   Throughout *Odysseys Home*, I use four other terms to refer to persons of African descent. *New World Africans*, a phrase I have borrowed from M. NourbeSe Philip, refers to all persons of African descent in the Americas. *African Canadian* covers *all* Canadians of Negro/African heritage, whether they have arrived here from the United States, the Caribbean, South America, Europe, or Africa itself; the term also applies to all those born in Canada. *African American* applies to those black people whose homeland is the United States; likewise, *African* [or *Afro-*] *Caribbean* denotes those whose homelands are in the Caribbean archipelago. Finally, I use *black* as a generic term distinguishing peoples and cultures of African descent from those of either Asian or European descent. See NourbeSe Philip, *She Tries Her Tongue, Her Silence Softly Breaks* (13), and my *Fire on the Water: An Anthology of Black Nova Scotian Writing*, vol. 1 [9].

4 Increasingly, it seems collections and anthologies of Caribbean literature efface any knowledge of the exiled, expatriate, and emigrant Afro-Caribbean communities in Canada. For instance, *The Routledge Reader in Caribbean Literature* (1996), edited by Alison Donnell and Sarah Lawson Welsh, includes only two African-Canadian writers – Louise Bennett (originally of Jamaica) and H.D. Carberry (a Québec native who grew up in the West Indies) – but their Canadian connections are never stated.

5 The identical damnation faces virtually all Euro-Canadian treatments of Canadian history and culture, which pretend that African Canadians do not exist, that they have never existed, or that they began to appear about the same time that Pierre Elliott Trudeau became prime minister in 1968. Peter Hudson charges that this latter sense 'has lead [sic] to the perception that black [Canadian] writing, minstreling the pioneer mythologies of survival, simply records the struggle of (West Indian) immigrants against a cold, white, bitterly racist Canada' ('Editor's Note' 5).

6 But the scholar of this literature must bear in mind Hayden White's thought that 'we require a history that will educate us to discontinuity more than ever before; for discontinuity, disruption, and chaos is our lot' (50). Moreover, we do not write history; we write, rather, an allegory of our present. We only and *must* imagine we can imagine the past. To cite Marianne Korn, 'historical truth is not necessarily fact to be received, simple and unchanged, unmediated into the [present] century' (8). *But nobody don't know how to struggle who don't know they history.*

7 Levine's call for a comprehensive inquiry into black cultural productivity is echoed in Norman Whitten's 1999 article 'Blackness in Latin America and the Caribbean: An Interpretation.' Here he complains that 'black culture in the Americas is viewed as unrefined, inchoate, fragmented, and static, studied only to find "Africanisms" as scattered traits, reinterpretations, or syncretisms that suggest a bit of Africa retained and an enormous amount of "culture lost"' (260). To correct this negative perspective, scholars must recognize a 'sophisticated, existential, experiential, and adaptable black culture, in which entwined processes of tradition, history, and modernity spur ever higher levels of black civilization ...' (260). My own view is that the marginalized always possess residual knowledge, interests, perspectives, ideas, theories, philosophies, theologies, and literatures unimagined by their external examiners. Furthermore, black populations which have been censored or marred by insufficiently attentive scholarship reserve the right, I think, to exercise their own redactions and establish their own visions. This expectation is just, for the formation and dissemination of ontological knowledge, that is to say, of identities and images, enunciates social relations of power, subjugation, and resistance.

8 This coinage for 'oral literature' appears in Chinweizu, Onwuchekwa Jemie, and Ihechuckwu Madubuike, *The Decolonisation of African Literature*, vol. 1 (1983).

9 This 'haunting' is mandated by the deep steeping of black cultures in *orature* and the equally profound prejudice against the 'spoken' and 'sung,' ostensibly literary, text in Eurocentric cultures. No less an authority than Ezra Pound wagers that 'poems made to be sung must be judged by a standard very different from that whereby we judge a poem made to be spoken or read' (*Walking* 84). In an Afrocentrist context, however, there is a need for a poetry of frank immediacy, a poetry of Malcolm Xian 'messages to the grassroots.' There is also the sense that Eurocentric standards of 'elocution' and 'grammar' are the detritus of colonialism and the offal of slavery. In her analysis of the theories of Frantz Fanon, Renate Zahar affirms that 'The European language, which has developed in an altogether

different historical context, cannot adequately express the experience of the colonized [or the enslaved], which is nourished from the sources of his own history' (47). The animus between the imposed European tongue and the repressed 'African' ones continues, perhaps, in our era. A basic dislike for 'Black English' may be the true reason for the distaste for black oral forms, such as 'Dub' poetry, in the pallid warrens of the Academy. But the 'black' canons, all of 'em, represent writers who shift registers religiously from Standard English *polis* to Black English pulpit. These writers appreciate that, to quote Vincent Sherry, 'the material of live speech is unmade and remade in the process of writing poetry: the sounding of the word gives way to the incisions of the pen or typewriter, tools to be hung with the chisel and rock axe' (191).

10 Reviewing *Towards Freedom: The African Canadian Experience* (1996), authored by Alexander and Glaze, Mathieu deplores the 'Americacentric' nature of their text, for she insists that African Canada 'is decidedly different' from African America (169). Mathieu outlines three major distinctions between the African-Canadian and African-American experiences:

> For the most part, Black Canadians came to this country of their own free will and lived under a unique social and political regime informed by linguistic politics unparalleled in the United States. Though a convincing argument can be made that defacto Jim Crow rule prospered in Canada, African Canadians' lives were not circumscribed by the same battery of laws as their southern brethren. Furthermore, the arrival of West Indian and African migrants and their pre-dominance in post–1960 Black Canadian affairs – at times even defining the meaning of Blackness in Canada – is unmatched in the United States. (169)

While Mathieu does not pay enough attention to regionalism, ethnicity, and official multiculturalism and the ways they help to define and differentiate Canadian blackness, her rejection of unthinking Pan-Americanism is sound. (See my article 'Contesting a Model Blackness ...,' pp. 27–70, below). Furthermore, African-Canadian literature often satirizes its African-American cousin, with Darius James's outlandish romp *Negrophobia* (1992) proving an impish example.

11 My conception of 'post-colonial' is informed by the definition crafted by Bill Ashcroft, Gareth Griffiths, and Helen Tiffin in *The Empire Writes Back: Theory and Practice in Post-Colonial Literatures* (1989): 'We use the term ... to cover all the culture affected by the imperial process from the moment of colonization to the present day' (2). The resultant literatures 'emerged in their present form out of the experi-ence of colonization and asserted themselves by foregrounding the tension with the imperial power, and by emphasizing their differences from the assumptions of the imperial centre' (2). African-Canadian writing represents a post-colonial literature within the still larger post-colonial literature of Canada. It is one more site where, in the terms of Italian-Canadian intellectual Antonio D'Alfonso, 'the very notion of [monocultural national] tradition is being positively challenged ... by the arrival of massive minority collectivities' (60). Thus, 'post-colonial' is still a useful term, so long as we are cognizant of the bloodshed and intellectual warfare over 'standards' and canons that it masks. The practitioners of post-colonial studies must always

choose between the definitions and philosophies of the (ex-)master and those of the (ex-)slave. Hence, the field seethes with unexpunged – even unexamined – cultural nationalisms and imperialisms of every breed.

12 By *liberalism*, I mean an ideology that exalts 'liberty,' the freedom of the individual, of markets, equality, small-is-good government, experimentation, and the erosion of prejudices. In stark contrast, by *nationalism*, I mean a *conservative* ideology that privileges 'order,' the primacy of communities, regulation of markets, preservation of cultural differences, interventionist (even expansive) government, stability, and the special status of the parochial. I do not, in this book, engage the fine discriminations proposed by a host of philosophers, from Stephen Toulmin to Charles Taylor. Rather, my conception of these ideas owes much to Grant, who argues that 'the choice between internationalism and nationalism is the same choice as that between liberalism and conservatism' (*Lament* 86). I also appreciate his idea that conservatism *qua* nationalism seeks 'to protect the public good against private freedom' (*Lament* 70), while liberalism denies 'any conception of good that imposes limits on human freedom' (*Lament* 56). Burton Hatlen divides liberals helpfully into two groups: 'economic liberals' who argue against 'any attempt to restrict the operation of the "free" market or to meliorate the radical transformations [wrought by] the operation of this market' and "cultural liberals": theorists who have vigorously argued for the principle of personal self-gratification as the only legitimate rule of human conduct' (146). Opposing them are both Burkean conservatives (like Grant) and Marxian socialists who 'give voice to a hunger for the "beloved community," a community founded on mutual trust rather than mutual exploitation, the kind of community which the liberal celebration of the autonomous individual has eroded' (147). Hatlen's thinking is, I think, strikingly akin to Grant's.

13 The blessing of contradiction is that it teases out the crucial issue in globalization: when does the desire to retain or promote a specific 'native' cultural tradition become 'fascistic' or 'racialist'? Or, rather, how can conservative group nationalism accommodate the liberal insistence on inalienable individual rights? In other words, how can a group determine its *difference* from others, while still accommodating *difference* within itself? Given such creative tensions, Stuart Hall states correctly that 'difference, like representation, is also a slippery, and therefore contested, concept. There is the "difference" that makes a radical and unbridgeable separation; and there is a "difference" that is positional, conditional, and conjunctural ...' (707). Thus, a disempowered group's essentialism – or nationalism – may be progressive when viewed in relation to an oppressor group's essentialism displayed plainly as gun-barrel conservatism or camouflaged as grinning liberalism. One is always caught 'between a turn to the left and a slide to the right' (Sherry 46).

As for contradiction, it is productively omnipresent. For James Walker, for instance, the history of African-Canadian culture exhibits two warring polarities: 'The original pioneers possessed the energy of those who had crossed a continent for their freedom, and an abiding faith that English Canadian institutions would fulfill the promise of equality. This often contradictory combination has reverberated through the development of black Canadian culture' ('Canada' 365). All post-colonial subjects are doomed to pursue such dialectics.

14 Yet, I favour 'conservatism,' for this philosophy allows for the existence of black community, whereas liberalism often bulldozes difference – a fact proven by the extirpation of the historic African-Canadian community of Africville, Nova Scotia, in the 1960s, to produce 'integration.' (See my article 'The Death and Rebirth of Africadian Nationalism.') Moreover, Walker suggests that a brand of conservatism is a norm for African Canadians, finding that, while we lack a single unified culture, 'the Canadian traditions of mutual support and cooperative promotion of community rights still prevails [sic]' ('Canada' 363). I also endorse the Canadian political economist and humourist Stephen Leacock: 'To avoid all error as to the point of view [in my writings], let me say in commencing that I am a Liberal Conservative, or, if you will, a Conservative Liberal with a strong dash of sympathy with the Socialist idea, a friend of Labour, and a believer in Progressive Radicalism' (quoted in Spadoni xxii).

15 Cultural *difference* can be constructed on the basis of language use and, most importantly, on the basis of historical – racial or religious – experience. And when all else fails, there is always economic difference. When the demand for oneness (unity) is coupled with a demand for sameness (homogeneity), cultural self-assertion moves toward cultural tyranny.

16 Echoing August Meier, James Clyde Sellman concludes that 'African Americans continue to view Black Nationalism with an essential ambivalence' (257). However, he also posits that 'nationalist assumptions inform the daily actions and choices of many African Americans' (255). In contrast, few African Canadians would see themselves unproblematically in Waldo Martin's depiction of the African-American community as embracing a 'black consciousness' characterized by a 'sense of Negro nationhood, of cultural uniqueness, of historical distinctiveness, increasingly contribut[ing] to a race-based brand of cultural nationalism that emphasize[s] the importance of an affirmative Negro identity' (253).

17 John Ralston Saul spies 'an almost Third World aggressivity [in Canadian literature] which is rarely found in the literatures of Europe and the United States' (426).

18 Thus, Benedict Anderson records that two eighteenth-century inventions – 'the novel and the newspaper' – provided 'the technical means for re-presenting the *kind* of imagined community that is the nation' (25). Literature, media, and the academy are all instruments of and for nationalist consciousness.

19 By 'race,' I mean, generally, any combination of conventions – cultural, linguistic, biological – which distinguish or differentiate one group of human beings from another. In *Odysseys Home*, I apply the term to summon up the indefinite categories of 'black' (connoting Negroid African descent) and 'white' (connoting Caucasoid European descent). Though many of the texts I discuss in this book invest *black* and *white* with essentialist or ethnocentric content, *I* do not presume that they carry such meanings. In my view, the old, discrete – indiscreet – categories must be broken down.

20 Walker asserts that, in Canada, 'it was thought that some "races" bore characteristics that were unsuitable as foundation stock for the fledgling Dominion of Canada'

('*Race*' 14). In particular, 'Black people were labelled as total aliens, incapable of adjusting to the physical conditions of British North America, unable to assimilate or even associate with Anglo-Canadians, suitable only for unskilled labouring and service employment ...' ('*Race*' 249). To overcome this *Canadian* racism, then, African Canadians learned that they had to engage in '*Canadian* struggle' (Walker, '*Race*' 309).

PART ONE

SORTIES

Contesting a Model Blackness:
A Meditation on African-Canadian African-Americanism, or the Structures of African-Canadianité

For John P. Matthews (1928–1995)[1]

Preamble

As a youth, when I desired to flaunt my blackness in the *très* white citadel of Halifax, Nova Scotia, I wielded African-American culture. I blasted Parliament-Funkadelic jams in the hallways of my high school, and I found it both comforting and *exciting* to shout out lines from Amiri Baraka and Carolyn M. Rodgers in my *bourgeois*, British-identified English class. I reviled Halifax, my native city, for it failed, I worried, to provide an 'authentic' black experience. We had no seditious civil rights agitation, for school segregation had been velvetly abolished by the provincial government between 1954 and the mid-1960s. There was no righteously destabilizing Black Power activism, for our provincial community of less than 30,000 souls was too small and too conservative to tolerate more than casually militant rhetoric. Consequently, I absorbed as much African-American music and letters as possible. Yet, I was dismissively ignorant of the 1783-established, local black culture that shaped me, where gospel and country music were, at times, preferred over blues, jazz, soul, and funk, and where the Bible and British poetry were required reading, though Langston Hughes was an acceptable afterthought. My own 'Baptist Marxist' commitment to a sassy, Malcolm X–styled blackness was complicated by my equally strong indulgence of the muscular intellectualism of the liberal Canadian prime minister Pierre Elliott Trudeau (whose tenure lasted from 1968 to 1984). Still, there was a 'blackness' about my culture, albeit of a more tentative nature than its bolder African-American counterpart. This paper is, then, an effort to elaborate some aspects of African-Canadian literary blackness, primarily in light of its ambivalent relationship to African-American culture. But it is also, perhaps, what the late scholar John Matthews believed a 'cultural history' to be, namely, 'a history of gropings towards self-identification' (8).

I. The Contours of African-Canadian African-Americanism

While an imperishable and ineluctable Pan-Africanism prods African Canadians, especially anglophones, to adopt African-American role models, modes of discourse, and aesthetic agendas, this adoption is never pure, never without a degree of implicit and deforming violence.[2] For African Canadians can never escape the situation of their blackness, whatever their adherence to potent, transnational Afrocentrisms, within the Canadian contexts of regional, ethnic, and linguistic 'Balkanization' and the perpetual erasure of their cultures from the public sphere. Yet, despite its indisputable beauty, Black America offers no easy refuge, for it addresses African-Canadian culture with attitudes of either hegemonic dismissal or peremptory annexation (practising the same vigorous chauvinism that mainstream America enacts toward Canada).[3] I think it is important to trace these visions, for they have coaxed and coerced the articulation of African Canada's own multiple identities. It is impossible to conceive of Black Canada without the sobering boundary that the United States supplies. If Canada itself is a residual America, old-line Black Canadians form a kind of lost colony of African America. The American Revolution, the War of 1812, and abolitionist agitation forged the first major African-Canadian populations. To revise a Mexican proverb, the African-Canadian dilemma is that we are so far from Africa, so close to the United States. Hence, African-American blackness has been and is a model blackness, a way of conceiving and organizing African-Canadian existence. Perversely, though, we will always veer away from it, only to return to it, relentlessly, with unstinting vengeance.

The latter assertion mandates some elaboration, for a classical African-American discourse on Canada, constructing the nation as the Promised Land, or *Canaan*, for fugitive African Americans, has existed since the passage of the iniquitous U.S. Fugitive Slave Law of 1850. This conception of Canada as a wilderness of true Brits, staunchly antithetical to the vicious Simon Legrees of the Republic, is a venerable archetype in African-American thought. Witness Rev. Dr Martin Luther King's 1967 panegyric on the theme:

> Over and above any kinship of U.S. citizens and Canadians as North Americans there is a singular historical relationship between American Negroes and Canadians.
>
> Canada is not merely a neighbour to Negroes. Deep in our history of struggle for freedom Canada was the north star. The Negro slave, denied education, dehumanized, imprisoned on cruel plantations, knew that far to the north a land existed where a fugitive slave if he survived the horrors of the journey could find freedom. The legendary underground railroad started in the south and ended in Canada. The freedom road links us together. Our spirituals, now so widely admired around the world, were often codes. We sang of 'heaven' that awaited us and the slave masters listened in innocence, not realizing that we were not speaking of the hereafter. Heaven was the word for Canada and the Negro sang of the hope that his escape on the underground railroad would carry him there. One of our spirituals, 'Follow the Drinking Gourd,' in its disguised lyrics contained directions for escape. The gourd was the big dipper, and the north star to which its handle pointed gave the celestial map that directed the flight to the Canadian border.
>
> So standing to-day in Canada I am linked with the history of my people and its unity with your past. (1)[4]

Like King, Malcolm X, the African-American nationalist orator, exempts Canada from prejudice: 'As far as I am concerned, Mississippi is anywhere south of the Canadian border' (*Autobiography* 417). One of the first African-American feature films, the silent *Within Our Gates* (1920), directed by Oscar Micheaux, names Indian Head, Saskatchewan, as the birthplace of the 'African-Canadian' African-American hero, a surveyor, Conrad Drebert. Drebert's origins suggest that his forebears were not just fugitives from slavery, but actual pioneers, or homesteaders (as was Micheaux himself). Intriguingly, Drebert's love interest in the film is the Acadien-surnamed, light-skinned, black woman, Sylvia Landry. In *Liberating Voices: Oral Tradition in African American Literature* (1991), African-American scholar Gayl Jones promotes the 'Canadian English' (10) of Margaret Laurence as a standard for African-American recuperations of oral-based, literary modes:

> In Margaret Laurence's prose ... we see the need for asserting identity through language. This applies to a nation's need to name its own songs, themes, and character in its own distinct language, and to a person's need to say, this is who I am (or in collective oral traditions, as are most by implication, 'this is who we are'). And by discussing [Laurence] we move closer to the motives of the African American writer and many other minority and Third World writers in their usually more manifest and deliberate use of oral traditions and folklore to achieve and assert a distinctive aesthetic and literary voice. (7)

African-American poet Gloria C. Oden writes deliberately in the manner of the Americo-Nova Scotian poet Elizabeth Bishop (see my letter 'Addendum to Bartlett' [2000]), while her 'brother' experimental poet, C.S. Giscombe, treats his relationship to his Canadian ancestry in his book *Into and Out of Dislocation* (2000). Jazz saxophonist Donald Byrd provides this bucolic perspective on Canada:

> Living across the river from Canada as a kid, I used to go down and sit and look at Windsor, Ontario. Windsor represented Europe to me ... For black people, you see, Canada was a place that treated you better than America, the North. For my father Detroit was better than the South, to me born in the North, Canada was better ... Canada represented for me something foreign, exotic, that was not the United States. (Quoted in Ursula Davis 102)

Marvin X (Marvin E. Jackmon), who fled to Canada in 1967 to evade service in Vietnam, thought it a haven at first: 'I departed from the United States ... to preserve my life and liberty, and to pursue happiness' (quoted in Thomas 179).

Black U.S. idealizations of Canada stem from the abolitionist propaganda of the 1850s, promulgated by writers like Mary Ann Shadd, who became, though born in the United States, Canada's first female newspaper editor and its first major black female writer.[5] In her stridently pro-Canada pamphlet *A Plea for Emigration; or, Notes of Canada West*, published in Detroit in 1852, Shadd essays 'to set forth the advantage of a residence in a country, in which chattel slavery is not tolerated, and prejudice of *color* has no existence whatever ...' (16). She declares that 'the colored subjects of her Majesty in the Canada are, in general, in good circumstances, that is, there are few cases of positive destitution to be found among those permanently settled' (30–1). Sounding precociously like a Canadian nationalist, Shadd alleges that, in Canada West (Ontario), 'there is more independent thought and free expression than among Americans' (34). If 'there is an aristocracy of birth' in the colony, it is at least 'not of skin, as with Americans' (35). Fugitive settler Mary Jane Robinson, writing to a friend in New York, proffers this idyllic sentiment: 'Come to a land of liberty and freedom, where the coloured man is not despised nor a deaf ear turned to them. This is the place to live and to enjoy the comforts of life' (quoted in Bristow 75). N.D. Hopewell, in an open letter (to African Americans) published in the *Provincial Freeman* (a Canada West–based, abolitionist newspaper edited by Shadd), also glorifies Canada:

> My dear relations and friends, in keeping with my promise to many of you, when husband and I made up our minds to leave the country of whips and tears – the country of Fugitive Slave Bill and blood hounds, for this the Canaan of the Colored people, I now take my pen to write to you – I say my pen, because I own something, and have learned to write since I left my native state. Here, I own myself, at least, and the pen is mine, and not old Mistress's. (Quoted in Bristow 123)

Mary Bibb, a teacher in Windsor, Canada West, states, in an 1853 letter, that she began a school for black children 'for the benefit of those who had recently arrived in the province from Republican oppression' (quoted in Cooper 151).

Not only do such opinions anticipate subsequent African-American romanticizations of Canada,[6] they also dovetail with a major Euro-Canadian resourcing of African-American culture, namely, to buttress Canadian wishful moral superiority *vis-à-vis* Euro-American culture. Michael Eldridge, an American scholar, recognizes Canada's 'disingenuous liberal smugness towards the US about its historical treatment of racial minorities' (171). American historian Robin W. Winks agrees that 'Canadians [have] tended to view their neighbours in the midst of their racial dilemma with a certain air of moral superiority, as Canadians often have done when the United States has tripped over its own egalitarian rhetoric' (471). *Certes*, such attitudes are legion. In an 1836 narrative, Thomas Chandler Haliburton bids a Nova Scotian squire, debating with the Yankee Sam Slick, to scorn a rank inconsistency in the U.S. Declaration of Independence: The proud claim that 'all men are created equal' demands the humbling modifier 'white,' for America 'tolerates domestic slavery in its worst and most forbidding form' (*Clockmaker* [1st Series] 176). In his semi-autobiographical novel *Les Enfances de Fanny* (1951), Eugène Seers's narrator sympathizes with the position of African Americans in Boston's Roxbury:

Roxbury est laborieux et pauvre, mais ne se compte pas malheureux. On y entend plus d'éclats de rire que dans le Back-Bay haut-huppé. Les danses, les fréquents 'parties,' disent la joie de vivre, si dure que la vie soit souvent. Il ne s'attriste qu'en songeant au poids étrange dont l'opprime l'accident de sa peau plus brune que les autres. (52).

The narrator denounces white Anglo-Saxon American racism (though he ignores his own ethnocentrism): 'L'expansion continue de la race noire crée un problème ardu, inquiétant, pour l'Amérique anglo-saxonne, en punition d'un crime ancien contre la dignité humaine' (52).[7] Theatrically, Pierre Vallières's *Nègres blancs d'Amérique* (1968) portrays Anglo-oppressed Québécois as 'les nègres blancs':

La lutte de libération entreprise par les Noirs américains n'en suscite pas moins un intérêt croissant parmi la population canadienne-française, car les travailleurs du Québec ont conscience de leur condition de nègres d'exploités, de citoyens de seconde classe ... N'ont-ils pas, tout comme les Noirs américains, été importés pour servir de main-d'oeuvre à bon marché dans le Nouveau Monde? Ce qui les différencie: uniquement la couleur de la peau et le continent d'origine. (26)

Canadian poet Raymond Souster decries American racism and its creation of ghettos in his apocalyptic *Howl*-like poem 'Death Chant for Mr. Johnson's America,' written on 5 April 1968, the day following King's assassination:

America
tonight fiery candles of the black man's mass burn crimson
  in the skies of Washington, Chicago, tributes from the
  ghettos to your Gandhi struck down by bullet of hate, the
  Gun used again to work out history... (69)

Popular Canadian usage of African-American experience tends to paint Canada as a tolerant 'Peaceable Kingdom' in contrast to the blood-splattered, gun-slinging, lynch-'em-high Republic. Scarcer are works like Michael Ondaatje's *Coming through Slaughter* (1976), a novel fictionalizing the life of jazz inventor Buddy Bolden, and George Bowering's poem 'Pharaoh Sanders, in the Flesh' (1991), which imagine African-American existence in almost purely aesthetic terms. (Ondaatje's Bolden *never* addresses either 'race' or racism. Bowering's persona mentions 'my Kanadian white face,' but gives no 'race' or 'colour' to the African-American saxophonist [17].)
  Crucially, the pro-Canada view of some African-American intellectuals has its dissenters. Even Byrd, after praising Canada as an imagined 'better place,' confesses that 'later on I found out otherwise' (quoted in Ursula Davis 102). In 1960 African-American novelist Richard Wright wrote Oliver Swan to decline to participate

in a Canadian Broadcasting Corporation program of contributors to Richard Grossman's [sic] book, *The God That Failed* (reminiscences of former Communists), because Canada is part of the British Commonwealth and Western World: 'The Western World must make up its mind as to whether it hates colored people more than it hates Communists, or does it hate Communists more than it hates colored people ...' (Quoted in Margolis 110)

African-American (and African-Canadian) abolitionist author Samuel Ring-gold Ward excoriated Haliburton's pro-slavery georgics, branding him a 'malignant enemy of the Negro' (261).[8] In 'Blake; or, The Huts of America' (1859, 1861–2), a novel published in serial form, African-American writer Martin R. Delany (who was also the first African-Canadian novelist) raps Canadian racism:

> [The newly arrived escaped slave] little knew the unnatural feelings and course pursued toward his race by many Canadians ... He little knew that while according to fundamental British Law and constitutional rights, all persons are equal in the realm; yet by a systematic course of policy and artifice, his race with few exceptions in some parts, excepting the Eastern Province [Québec], is excluded from the enjoyment and practical exercise of every right ... He little knew the facts, and as little expected to find such a state of things in the long talked of and much loved Canada by the slaves. (209)

In *Soul on Fire* (1969), a novel by Clarence Farmer, the 'ofay Canadian,' Raymond Sears, of Rumford, Ontario, is slain in Harlem by a black who equates his victim's Canadian identity with Anglo-Saxon racism. Farmer, an African American, also debunks Canadian claims of racial rectitude: 'there were no niggers in Canada, therefore no nigger problem' (27). An exposé of the racial politics of the Canadian Football League, LaVerne Barnes's *The Plastic Orgasm* (1971), reports the relief of one ex-pat football player's anonymous African-American wife to be 'back here in Chicago' (67). The woman attacks Euro-Canadian racial hypocrisy:

> And my children. They were real curiosities up there. There were no black people where we lived, and white people were always coming up patting the kids' heads and smiling. But I remember how long it took us to find a place to live. Those same smiling faces didn't know whether they wanted Negroes living right next to them. (67)

In *Another Country* (1960), novelist James Baldwin conjures a minor character, 'the Canadian-born poet, Lorenzo, moon-faced, with much curly hair,' who 'had an open, boyish grin ... even though he was beginning to be rather old for a boy' (256). Lorenzo happens to be writing '"a long poem ... , you know, Romeo and Juliet today, only she's black and he's white ... "' (257). Although the subject of his poetry shadows the plot of Baldwin's fiction, Lorenzo is a figure of futility. Ishmael Reed's novel *Flight to Canada* (1976), a satirical, surrealistic, anachronistic imagining of the American Civil War, wills a proudly slashing critique of Canada. The novel dreams Canada both as a hallowed space of deliverance *and* as a U.S. puppet-state with its own tawdry racisms.[9] An exchange among the protagonist, Quickskill, and his companions, Carpenter and Quaw Quaw, all newly landed in Niagara Falls, Ontario, establishes this perspective:

> 'But what about St. Catherine's [St. Catharines, Ontario]? William Wells Brown told me that he'd gotten a number of slaves across to St. Catherine's, where they found rewarding careers.'
>
> 'Let me show you downtown St. Catherine's,' Carpenter said, removing a photo from his wallet. It looked like any American strip near any American airport; it could have been downtown San Mateo. Neon signs with clashing letters advertising hamburgers, used-car lots with the customary banners, coffee joints where you had to stand up and take your java from wax cups.
>
> 'It looks so aesthetically unsatisfying.'
>
> 'You can say that again, Quaw Quaw,' Quickskill said.
>
> 'Man, they got a group up here called the Western Guard, make the Klan look like statesmen. Vigilantes harass fugitive slaves, and the slaves have to send their children to schools where their presence is subject to catcalls and harassment. Don't go any farther [into Canada], especially with her [the Amerindian Quaw Quaw]. They beat up Chinamen and Pakastani [*sic*] in the streets. West Indians they shoot.' (160)

Later in the conversation, Carpenter recites economic statistics proving that 'Man, Americans own Canada. They just permit Canadians to operate it for them. They needs a Castro up here bad' (161). With *Flight to Canada*, Reed backs Lloyd W. Brown's 1970 finding that 'on the rare occasions on which Canada has been a topic of Black literature, the tendency among these writers has been to view her as an extension of the United States, not only in a racial context, but in the social experience as a whole' (321). Brown is correct, but his theory does not apply to those writers, such as Mary Shadd, who emphasize Canada's Britishness to demarcate it positively from the United States – and to agitate for African-American immigration.

Ultimately, the African-American narrative scribing Canada as a potential refuge remains intact. One reason for its longevity is that, even though major African-American emigrations to British North America / Canada occurred in 1783 (the Black Loyalists), 1812–15 (the Black Refugees), 1850–65 (the fugitives), and at the turn of the twentieth century (the Prairie settlers), these out-migrations have no legacy in African-American culture. The flight of slaves to Canada is hymned, but those who chose to live out their fates north of the 49th Parallel, rather than return to the United States, have been excised from African-American consciousness. They are the *damnés* of African-American culture. Strikingly, for example, the thousands of African Americans who landed in Nova Scotia between 1760 (as slaves of the New England planters) and 1815 (as refugees freed by the War of 1812) fell promptly into a kind of limbo (and their writers fell instantly out of the nascent African-American canon). They vanished from African-American historiography while hardly registering in that of Canada. And their disappearance from African-American history has had particular consequences for African Americans.

For one thing, African-American scholars have tended to regard African Canadians as a failed version of themselves, or as a warning to others who may tumble beyond the precincts of the contiguous – and *holy* – forty-eight states. Howard McCurdy, a black member of the Canadian Parliament from 1984 to 1993, doubts that African-American leaders 'will ever see Canadian Blacks other than as just marginal' (quoted in Foster, *Place* 152). To African-American anthropologist Arthur Huff Fauset, collecting folklore in Nova Scotia in the mid-1920s, his Africadian respondents 'live for all the world like planta-tion folk, in their rickety cabins (not log cabins), off to themselves, with reli-gious customs and even habits of living distinctly their own ...' (viii). Fauset was perturbed to find that Africadians spurned the Joel Chandler Harris–promoted Uncle Remus tales, which he identified with *echt*-African-American culture: 'Throughout the province I found this reticence of the Negroes to tell a story if they feel it is below their level, or shall I say, dignity? I seemed to detect a disdainful attitude toward telling tales which put them in the role of minstrels, let us say' (ix). For Fauset, African-Canadian culture was a pallid extension of his own. Thus, he could only scrutinize it through the blinkered lens of African-American norms.

Some African-American intellectuals have simply erased the existence of a separate culture. Eddy L. Harris, despite swerving into Nova Scotia on his journalistic motorcycle odyssey, missed the Africadian presence.[10] Henry Louis Gates, Jr, intervening in a 1993 controversy over the production of the U.S. musical *Show Boat* (1927) in Canada, gave a public lecture in Toronto in which, states African-Canadian scholar Rinaldo Walcott, '[he] entirely evacuated the notion of historical difference, collapsing the two nations [Canada and the United States]' (26). While averring that Black British scholar Paul Gilroy omits Canada from his *The Black Atlantic* (1993), an account of transatlantic black connections, Eldridge deems Canada merely 'a distinct segment of *Afro-America*' (171). Lorenzo Thomas, in his biographical article on Marvin X, dis-cusses the poet's flight to Canada in 1967, but does not cite his engagements there with the pioneering African-Canadian writer Austin Clarke (179–82). Common, too, are instances of naïve omission, such as Mae G. Henderson's 1996 proviso that the spur for the erection of Black Studies programs in the 1960s was the entry into colleges and universities of 'black students – from the U.S., Africa, and the Caribbean' (65).[11] To sum up, as African-Canadian writer André Alexis observes, 'Canada is *often* invisible in American writing, black Canada even more so ...' ('Borrowed' 17).

African Canadians also suffer the implacable truth that, as an officially 'vis-ible minority,' they are, in fact, largely invisible in Canadian public affairs.

Canadian historian James Walker determines that, in the past, 'Blacks were out of sight and out of mind for most white Canadians, an "invisible" minority despite their physical distinction, occupying the unskilled and service employment ranks and living a separate existence' (*West* 22). African-Canadian writer Cecil Foster insists that African Canadians see 'virtually no reflection of ourselves in the mainstream media and popular culture ...' (*Place* 30). Responding to this invisibility, Carol Talbot jokes, in her memoir *Growing Up Black in Canada* (1984), 'the term "visible minority" is a misnomer' (16). Likewise, Adrienne Shadd asks, 'What is the impact of this kind of invisibility (note the irony here!) of being a nonentity in your own country?' (10). The perpetual, white denial of Canada's own history of slavery, segregation, and anti-black discrimination accents black invisibility. Adrienne Shadd records a salient fact in this regard:

> When nineteenth-century Quebec historian François Garneau decided to write Histoire du Canada (1846), he deliberately suppressed the fact that slavery existed in New France, leading the public to believe that the 'peculiar institution' never tainted our soil. Even though the fourth edition of his work was changed in 1882, the misinformation of a generation had effectively taken place, with a quite lasting impact to this day. (9)

Naturally, most anglophone histories of Canada also gloss over its slave past. Winks records that a 'standard account of Ontario's history published in 1898 concluded that Canadians could "claim the proud distinction for their flag ... that it has never floated over legalized slavery"' (472). Therefore, as African-Canadian scholar David Sealy notices, it is possible for 'an English professor at a Canadian university [to tell] her students that when she was emigrating to Canada, friends in Sweden told her that Canada was better than the US because "there are no blacks in Canada"' ('Talking' 12). Preston Chase, a native Black Ontarian, alerts us that 'coming out of the Detroit tunnel and turning left on Wyandotte [in Windsor, Ontario], you reached the neighbourhood first and the first response people got [from U.S. visitors] was shock that there were coloured people living in Canada' (9). Adrienne Shadd finds that the constant obliteration of blacks from 'the Canadian psyche' renders 'the very concept of a "Black" or "African-" Canadian ... in the public perception – a contradiction in terms' (10). In a 1972 article, African-Canadian playwright Lennox Brown charges that 'there is no substantial Black culture in Canada'(8).[12] For Brown, 'Black culture in Canada was born in the cradle of Whiteness' (6). Indeed, the early black settlements in the Maritimes, Ontario, and the Prairie provinces 'were firmly based on the White pillars of the Protestant-Puritan ethic, whose white imagery recurs bitterly like the whiteness of the Canadian winters: *hard work, thrift, prudence, industry, discipline, sobriety, frugality, Godliness, piety*' (6). Eldridge blames dub poet-performer Lillian Allen's hobbled international success on 'something like the Canadian "climate"' (174), by which he seems to mean both 'the absence in Canada of a relatively large and coherent market for *homegrown* black musics' (173) and the prevalence of a 'poignantly square [i.e., white] idea of soul' (174). For her part, African-Canadian writer M. NourbeSe Philip instances a sense of suppression within the Canadian milieu: 'A Jamaican artist described to me how her colours became more muted and sombre when she painted here in Canada' (*Frontiers* 29). Talbot reinforces this sense of repression: 'To be a black child in Canadian society, even in *my* generation was a painful experience. The positive vibrations and the wholesome warmth of family and church could not counterbalance the forces of the dominant white world' (80). In reality, the insistent pressure to assimilate, emigrate, or to accept a marginalized position is acute in Canada, where people of African descent account for roughly 3 per cent of the population. (In contrast, African Americans number 13 per cent of the American whole.) This point is momentous. Winks feels that 'white Canadians could afford to be indifferent to their fellow blacks, and for the most part they were' (482). Alexis snipes that 'it sometimes feels as if no one, black or white, has yet accepted the fact and history of our [African-Canadian] presence, as if we thought black people were an American phenomenon that has somehow crept north, or an African one that has migrated' ('Borrowed' 18). Sealy says, 'Whenever anti-racist political activity emerged among black Canadians, it was read as part of the Americanization of Canada, something which Canadians have always been actively resisting' ('Talking' 15). In a strange 1971 statement exemplifying such attitudes, American historian Eugene Genovese identifies the 1969 black West Indian student revolt at Sir George Williams University (now Concordia University) in Montréal with the American New Left (v). He chastizes the students for their alleged 'demagogic manipulation of the real oppression suffered by black people' and their 'reactionary nihilism' (vi).[13] Foster suspects that 'too often, the rest of Canada tries to treat Canadian Blacks are [*sic*] if they were an offshoot from what they see on television in Los Angeles, New York, Chicago or Detroit' (*Place* 13). Given its perpetual campaign against these forms of erasure, African-Canadian literature occupies the contested space between the Euro-Canadian reluctance to accept an African presence and the African-American insistence on reading Canadian blackness as a lighter – and lesser – shade of its own.[14] The sumptuous dilemma of African-Canadian literature is that it is caught between two national(ist) pincer movements of exclusion.

To further compromise the position of African-Canadian culture, however, I reiterate that it derives a substantial portion of its identity from African-American culture. For instance, in 1912 the African United Baptist Association of Nova Scotia planned to invite African-American leader Booker T. Washington (1856–1915) to lecture in the province (*Minutes* [1911–12] 15).[15] Talbot recalls being 'way up in the northern bush scrabbling for literature on Martin Luther King, the Black Muslims, and the Civil Rights Movements in the States' (51). Her father, though, 'was sometimes to be found quietly listening to jazz, a black church programme from Detroit, or to [African-American] artists like Billy Ekstein [*sic*] and Nat King Cole' (57). Even in the diets of Southwestern

Ontario blacks, Talbot detects 'a down-south (U.S.) influence here' (61). For Foster, 'the reality for many blacks in Canada may be closer to what they see in the streets of New York or Los Angeles than what many people assume as being their reality' ('Long' 21). Antiguan-Canadian writer Althea Prince recollects that, in the 1960s, 'the things that Malcolm X and Elijah Mohammed [*sic*] had spoken about were happening in the United States, but the experiences I was having in Canada were similar' (*Being* 31). Prince also remembers that 'from the United States (the country my [British] textbooks had scornfully decried as spawned by a "dangerous rebellion"), came the language, analysis, and praxis of another rebellion. The Black Power Movement ...' (*Being* 31). Of course, African-American styles are popular with many African-Canadian youth (as they are with most youth). Alexis worries that 'the language used by [Toronto] black [Caribbean-born] activist Dudley Laws ... is laced with Americanisms' ('Borrowed' 18).

Undeniably, too, African-American texts enter into and inform African-Canadian texts with hegemonic regularity. Clarke's clutch of short stories treating the economic struggle of black (that is to say, 'immigrant') males in Toronto, *Nine Men Who Laughed* (1986), is a conscious 'riff' on Richard Wright's *Eight Men* (1961), 'a diverse collection of short pieces connected only by a tentative exploration of black masculinity' (Gilroy 155). While the hero of Wright's story 'The Man Who Was Almost a Man' escapes Southern peonage by leaping aboard a north-bound freight train (26), the hero of Clarke's equivalent tale, 'Canadian Experience,' surrenders to racism by leaping *in front of* a Toronto subway train (51). Wright's signature novel *Native Son* (1940) is slyly cited in the title of Trinidad-Canadian writer David Woods's lyric miscellany *Native Song* (1990). But so is 'Song of the Son,' a poem included in Jean Toomer's classic prose *cum* poetry pastiche, *Cane* (1923). The bleak, acidic voice that dominates Woods's lyrics echoes Toomer's brooding, corrosive narrator. A strophe from Woods's poem 'Bidii (The Flight)' –

I prefer to say –
A black soul – bloated by torture,
Folds as a sickly child
Under the weight of its oppressor's eyes (18)

– recalls a passage in Toomer's 'Prayer':

My body is opaque to the soul.
Driven of the spirit, long have I sought to temper it unto the spirit's longing,
But my mind, too, is opaque to the soul.
A closed lid is my soul's flesh-eye. (70)

Woods also shares with Toomer an interest in like motifs: the soul 'calling' for instruction, the eyes demanding 'vision,' the people's dreams being stifled by oppression. Too, the title of Woods's cover painting, *Cain*, signifies on, not only Toomer's book, but a common Africadian surname (Kane, or Cane) as well as the Genesis story of Cain and Abel. In turn, Foster defers to Richard Wright when he describes an African-Canadian murderer as 'a Bigger Thomas' (*Place* 222), alluding to Wright's most notorious protagonist. Africadian playwright Walter Borden transforms Lorraine Hansberry's vaunted, African-American, classic play, *A Raisin in the Sun* (1959), into a meditation on value and identity in his one-man drama 'Tightrope Time' (1986).[16] African-American influence is also registered in Jamaican-Canadian poet Allen Forbes's reworking of Irish bard W.B. Yeats's poem 'The Second Coming' (1921). Forbes employs 'vernacular I borrowed from a thin Southern US memoir written about the same time [as Yeats's poem]' (59) to create 'De Secon Comin' (1996), his version of Yeats's oracular, pessimistic masterpiece:

> Turnin an turnin de wide nin gyre
> De falcn caan hear de falcner;
> Tings dey fall apart, de cenner caan hole;
> Mere anarchys loosed pon de hole worl
> De blud-dimmind tide loost, an evy were
> De sirmoney er incense s drown;
> De bes lack convexion, while de wors critters
> Ar fuller pashnit tenstee (59)

Mairuth Sarsfield's novel about black life in Montréal in the 1940s calls up African-American poet Langston Hughes in its title, *No Crystal Stair* (1997), and lines from his poem 'Mother to Son' (1922, 1926) appear in the text (12, 178). Other African-American celebrities parade through the book, including union organizer A. Phillip Randolph (22), boxer Joe Louis (72), and entertainers Lena Horne (72), Josephine Baker (76), Paul Robeson (76), Cab Calloway (77), Redd Foxx (80), Sammy Davis, Jr (80), and others. Jamaican-Canadian poet and playwright Ahdri Zhina Mandiela mentions *five* African-American writers in the introduction to her play *dark diaspora ... in dub* (1991): Audre Lorde, Nikki Giovanni, Sonia Sanchez, Alice Walker, and Ntozake Shange (viii).[17]

Given the constant African-Canadian appropriations – and frank thefts – of African-American culture, it seems that the former seldom differentiate themselves from the latter. Canadian historian Allen B. Robertson complains, then, that 'when Black History Month is celebrated in Nova Scotia ... it is Martin Luther King and Malcolm X who appear on the [publicity] posters, not [Black Nova Scotian heroes and heroines] Viola Desmond, Carrie Best, the Reverend William Oliver or Victoria Cross recipient William Hall' ('Book' 158). Alexis moans that 'despite Caribana [the annual Caribbean-Canadian Toronto street festival], I'm surprised by how often we talk of [African-American subjects like] B-ball and B-boys, homeboys and rap, and how seldom cricket and ca-

lypso, pogey [unemployment insurance] and projects [government employment schemes]' ('Borrowed' 18).[18] Sealy notes that 'three young black Canadian women from Toronto journey[ed] to the Gullah Islands off the Carolina
coast, site of Julie Dash's *Daughters of the Dust* [1991], as if conducting a pilgrimage to the site of the enactment of their black femaleness' ('Talking' 12).
Pace these examples, African Canadians appear blithely acquiescent to the
forces of a homogenizing African-Americanism.

Yet, one culture's borrowings of ideas, personalities, and goods from another culture can serve to structure its own sense of itself, as well as to objec-
tify the source culture. Hence, African-Canadian appropriations of African
Americana enact a version of Edward Said's Orientalism: that is to say, Black
America is, for Black Canada, an exotic *Other*. African Canadians construct
their own *African-Americanism* to suit their own cultural and psychological
needs. Two close parallels in social circumstances between Black Canada and
Black America enable this transubstantiation. First, both cultures share histories of slavery, colonialism, and segregation.[19] Secondly, they both constitute
black minorities within white majoritarian (and white supremacist) contexts.
Thus Winks acknowledges that 'many characteristics of American Negro life
... are to be found in Canada' (470). And African-American scholar Houston
Baker, Jr, also speaks to African Canadians when he perceives that the root
dynamic or problem for our intellectuals 'is that of the black man in a white
country, of the black author writing for a white public; and many thousands
have perished in the resulting flood of emotions' (*Afro* 48). When African
Canadians read African-American culture, then, they look enviously upon an
enviable record of noble striving ('movin' on up'), of baptisms of fire, steel,
and blood, of the self-conscious construction of a *civilization* (political mastery
of some cities and regions, backed with an astonishingly pervasive influence
over *global* popular culture styles, argots, and modes of thought) amid an
often still-ruddy oppression.[20] For African Canadians, *African America* signifies
resistance, vitality, joy, 'nation,' community, grace, art, pride, clout, spirituality, and *soul*.[21] It is a cluster of attractive qualities we crave for ourselves.

II. The Determinants of African-Canadianité

W.E.B. Du Bois's historic 1903 formulation of 'double consciousness,' this specific condition of African-American selfhood, identifies African Americans as
a select race in the world:

> After the Egyptian and Indian, the Greek and Roman, the Teuton and Mongolian,
> the Negro is a sort of seventh son, born with a veil, and gifted with second-sight
> in this *American* world, – a world which yields him no true self-consciousness, but
> only lets him see himself through the revelation of the other world. It is a peculiar
> sensation, this double-consciousness, the sense of always looking at one's self
> through the eyes of others ... One ever feels his two-ness, – an *American*, a Negro;

two souls, two thoughts, two unreconciled strivings; two warring ideals in one
dark body, whose dogged strength alone keeps it from being torn asunder. The
history of the *American Negro* is the history of this strife – this longing to attain
self-conscious manhood, to merge his double self into a better and truer self. (5,
my italics)[22]

The very structure of African-American thought is embedded within an
Americanist notion of global Manifest Destiny, and this fact carries profound
ramifications for African Canadians. Even so, Du Bois's conception applies
meaningfully to us, for we also exhibit a divided being. Tussling with our own
'double consciousness,' African Canadians question whether the 'Canadian'
half of the epithet 'African-Canadian' is merely a convenience referring to our
geographic residency, or whether it hints at an identity. Is it possible to think
of the hyphen as an ampersand, or is it really a double-edged minus sign? Is
an 'African Canadian' always more black than Canadian? (Or, as Winks asks,
are 'they Negro Canadians or Canadian Negroes' [483]?) Yet, the African-
Canadian consciousness is not simply dualistic. We are divided severally; we
are not just 'black' and Canadian, but also adherents to a region, speakers of
an 'official' language (either English or French), disciples of heterogeneous
faiths, and related to a particular ethnicity (or 'national' group), all of which
shape our identities.[23] African Canadians possess, then, not merely 'double
consciousness,' but what I will call poly-consciousness. Foster verifies that 'in
Canada, [black] consciousness has many more layers [than the U.S. variety]'
(*Place* 15). Anthony Joyette, once an editor of anglophone Canada's only black
literary journal, *Kola*, divines that 'the environment in Canada is a transition of
attitudes from a post-colonial tradition to multi-ethnic values, in which both
French and English Canada are part of the collective psyche' (5). At bottom,
the constant challenges to African-Canadian identity create fissures and dis-
junctures in the culture that make it what it is – as fraught with indefinition as
Canada itself. For Black Swiss photographer Simon Njami, Canadian space
instils a 'Schizophrénie compliquée qui pousse à l'oubli de soi en même temps
qu'elle renvoie sans cesse sur soi' ('Canada' 4). Talbot affirms the efficacy of
Njami's reading: 'Canadians have a long-term identity crisis ... Nobody seems
to know who they are. Some are not even sure of who they were. Others are
not too sure of who they want to be' (93). Blacks are also 'victims of this kind
of cultural confusion' (94). Hear Philip:

I carry a Canadian passport: I, therefore, am Canadian. How am I a Canadian,
though, above and beyond the narrow legalistic definition of being the bearer of a
Canadian passport; and does the racism of Canadian society present an absolute
barrier to those of us who are differently coloured ever belonging? Because that is,
in fact, what we are speaking about – how to belong – not only in the legal and
civic sense of carrying a Canadian passport, but also in another sense of feeling at
'home' and at ease. It is only in belonging that we will eventually become Canadian. (*Frontiers* 16)

Diane Jacobs's poem 'On Becoming Black Canadian' (1996) identifies a like instability of identity:

My little white friends made it clear
I could not really be Canadian because I was Black.
In college I didn't have worth with Blacks if
    I was *just* Canadian.
But I was accepted if I described myself as a
    Black Canadian of West Indian heritage.
Though the me inside didn't change.

Strangely it was in the U. S. A.
    that I truly became a Black Canadian.
In an attempt to rebut American Blacks' assumption
    that being Canadian was an aberration.
That Canadian Blacks had no history. (71–2)

Talbot recognizes that 'most of my existence in this Canadian society has been a lonely odyssey from "coloured" through "negro" to "black"' (79). Tellingly, she brackets her racial signifiers with quotation marks, thus substantiating a neat difference between African-Canadian and African-American culture. If 'blackness' must be read in Canada as an elusive, even illusory, quality, in the United States, it is spirit that has put on flesh. I cite here Baker's suggestively pseudo-religious call for a critical poetics based on 'an informed *faith* in Afro-American *spirit* work – in the ceaseless ... poetic flow of an *impulse* that both unifies Afro-American life and history and makes them coherent' (*Afro* 88, my italics). The pentecostal religiosity of Baker's terminology is radically less possible in Canada.[24] Then, too, Du Bois's articulation of an African-American 'soul' exemplifies his culture's sense of itself. In Canada, such certainty is rare. One cannot avoid the hypothesis that, in Canada, few *know* what *blackness* is, but in the United States, few have any doubt.

Revealingly, 43 per cent of African Canadians did not identify themselves as 'Black' in the 1991 Canadian census. Walton O. (Wally) Boxhill of the Treasury Board Secretariat discloses that 'some Haitians called themselves French, and some Jamaicans called themselves British, so they were counted as people of European origin' (*The Spectrum*, 'Census' 1). This position is explicable, for, as the 1996 census indicates, of the 573,860 Black Canadians listed, 54.5 per cent were immigrants, while less than half, some 42 per cent, were born in Canada; another 3.5 per cent were non-permanent residents (*Black to Business* 14). Clearly, the maintenance of ethnic and 'homeland' bonds reduces the primacy of racial identification. Because of their varying allegiances, then, African-Canadian writers wrestle with ideas of blackness. As Lloyd Brown finds, 'the ambivalence which Canada's ambiguous image inspires among Blacks not only emphasizes the contradictions of the Canadian's racial values, but also reveals the emotional complexities of the Black man's nascent self-awareness ...' ('Beneath'

325). Consequently, *In Black and White,* a hefty, Christian interrogation of the infamous 1995 homicide trial of Orenthal James Simpson (an African-American sports celebrity accused of murdering two European-Americans), the author, I. Jing-Shin (the pseudonym of Hugh B. Jones), argues that the word *black* is a reactionary misnomer:

> While he misappropriated 'whiteness' for himself, the 'white' man called you an evil name ... If you challenge him by adopting the name 'black' you are playing the same evil game, and playing it ... to no good end. So then! – Can you really gain revenge by being 'black' in apposition to being 'white'? No! (116)

Toronto-born novelist Lawrence Hill, in his 1994 essay 'Zebra: Growing Up Black and White in Canada,' also articulates a complex deconstruction of racial categories and the resultant ambiguity of Black Canadian identity:

> Even as a boy, I sensed that terms such as 'mulatto,' 'half-Black' and 'part Black' denied my fullness as a person ... And ... a person like me couldn't be all white [*sic*] and not Black, or all Black and not White, unless society imposed one colour on me.
>   I didn't grow up under apartheid, or slavery, or racial segregation ... That meant periods of ambiguity. It meant confusion. It meant anxiety. (47)

In a significant anecdote, Hill fleshes out the effect of 'ambiguity,' 'confusion,' and 'anxiety' (recurrent words in African-Canadian literature) on his life. On a sojourn in Niger with six white Québécois, Hill eschewed their company because 'that summer, with an intensity that I had never anticipated, I wanted to be Black! Welcomed and loved as a brother' (46). Ironically, though, the Niger 'appeared to see me as White' (46). When he fell ill, it was the Québécois 'who slept on the floor by my hospital bed, carried me to the toilet, and fed me when I could eat again' (46–7). He left hospital, as he says, 'a changed man' (47). Anthony Bansfield rejects this romanticized ideal of the racially amicable Québécois. Introducing his anthology *The N'x Step: Hochelaga and the Diasporic African Poets: A Collection of Performance Poetry by a Montreal-based Black Writers Group* (1995), Bansfield asks, 'Is there such a thing as Black Quebecois? Being born in Quebec doesn't get over the Aryan-like concept of "pure laine," old-family Quebecois' (5). In his 1995 poem 'Mystory,' the Jamaican–Nova Scotian Robin Browne voices an agonizing self-doubt:

> Being Black
> Being afraid of being Black
> School dances: writhing pits of
> Apart-hate
> Paralysed by tension, I dance ...
> Like a White boy

I imagine Black eyes stabbing, gashing
Tearing up my soul papers

* * *

Who am I?
Who are my brothers and sisters? (9, his ellipsis)

Ambiguity haunts Marvin X's 1967 interview with Clarke, '*Black Man in a White Land*,' in which Clarke discourses under the Nation of Islam-inspired pseudonym of Ali Kamal Al Kadir Sudan. Here Clarke proposes that 'the Canadian black man is obsessed with an irrational Negritude: he hates the white man partly because it is fashionable to hate him' (3). States Clarke: 'His external moral freedom is directly related to the CANADIAN BLACK ATTITUDE derived from the Black-White clashes in America' (2). The African-Canadian sense of racial identity is, really, specious: 'Because of his relative security from experiences of racial embarrassment, he tends to be silent and ambivalent, therefore deceitful in his identity with the Muslims and the Black Power Movement in America' (2–3). Clarke's 1973 essay 'Some Speculations as to the Absence of Racialistic Vindictiveness in West Indian Literature' implicates black nationalism with Americanism:

> It seems that the West Indian writer, a man from a society ostensibly free of the worst pathologies of racialism, a man from a society into which Black nationalism had to be imported from American Blacks (like most other attitudes and fashions and styles – styles of living included), could do nothing more than couch his literary expression in the pathology of self-identity and crisis, personal crisis ... (180)

African Americans who settle in Canada develop a like dissociation of sensibility. Willa R. Dallard, a farmwife who was born in Alabama in 1897 but raised in pioneer-era Alberta, recalls in her 1978 memoir that it was upon entering western Canada for the first time that 'I began to learn what it is like to be a negro in a white world' (2). In his maudlin suite of poems *Studies in Black and White* (1966), Dave Pinson, exorcizing his doomed amour for a *pure laine* Québécoise, allows,

> How completely strange it must have seemed to others
> As we walked arm in arm on Ste. Catherine, Peel,
>   or *la rue de la Montagne*,
> Where you often remarked, 'Everybody look you, look me,'
>   followed by the inevitable, '*Pourquoi?*'
> Everybody stares at us ... Why???
> Because we were too complete, and yet, so incomprehensible. (21, his ellipsis)

A crisis ensues when the persona asks his lover to accept him in marriage: '"Mother wouldn't like because ..." and you pointed to my skin' (22, his ellipsis). Vainly, the persona can only cry, with atrocious sentimentality, 'If again I seem bitter, God, forgive me this time / For not having been born French ...' (24, his ellipsis). In a 1990 essay, Rita Shelton Deverell recalls growing up in a black section of Houston, Texas, where 'we knew exactly who we were. We were Negroes' (21). Living now where 'not only are most of the people white, but snow covers the ground five months of the year' (25), Deverell relies upon her black majoritarian upbringing to steel her against the subtle workings of Canadian racism. She relates this anecdote:

> In the fall of 1984 I went to audition for a television drama to be produced by the Canadian Broadcasting Corporation (CBC). The casting call sent out through the actors' union advised me that two 40-year-old women were required by the script.
> Being 39 and a woman and an actress, I booked an audition. In the studio the following dialogue took place between me and the producer/director:
> DIRECTOR: I'm so glad you've come, and I would have you read these parts, but these people are white.
> Me: Are you sure?
> DIRECTOR: Yes – and so is the writer. (25–6)

Deverell goes on to observe that 'had I not grown up Negro in Houston I might not understand this incident for the simple racism that it is ... The security of living in an all-black world, in an isolated society, provides the strength to fight through to another Renaissance, and the knowledge that in intellectual isolation the soul and the mind die' (26). Canada is a location where, in distinction to the United States, blackness is threatened with psychological evisceration.

African Canadians of Caribbean heritage are not immune to such ontological probings. Despite the Great Exodus of Caribbean nationals to Canada after 1955, their relationship to both African-American and Euro-Canadian culture is as complicated as that experienced by their indigenous African-Canadian compatriots. Warns Philip: 'The great Canadian void either swallows you whole, or you come out the other side the stronger for it' (*Frontiers* 45). That 'void' is a sink-hole of anti-'Coloured' racism, which, when expressed against Caribbean-heritage peoples, assumes an 'imperialistic' aspect. In 1972 the Trinidad-born Lennox Brown opined that 'Canada is no country for a playwright let alone a black one' (Chintoh 28). For Clarke, confusion pertains to being a West Indian abroad:

> Whether or not the West Indian can see his 'predicament' at all, he is at the same time an exile, an escapist, an immigrant, and he has become imbued ... with the respective radicalism or Black nationalism of the time and place of his sojourn. It is, therefore, from these West Indians living in Canada, Britain, France, and the United States that the literature takes on, in varying degrees of their attachment to

the Black consciousness of their new locations, the quality of racialistic vindictive-ness. ('Some' 184–5)

Clarke seems to feel that this 'racialistic vindictiveness' is an artificial quality, a reaction to displacement within a white majority context. Analysing Clarke's fiction, Lloyd Brown locates a sense of ambiguity in the Canadian landscape itself: 'To be more precise, the snow-white landscape which [a Clarke hero] sometimes sees as the symbol of Canadian negrophobia becomes, on other occasions, the reflection of [that character's] own white, anti-black impulses' (325–6). Clarke and other Caribbean-Canadian writers must address an alien-ation originating in the association of blackness, in Canada, with an indelible foreignness.

One of the strongest markers of the specificity of African-Canadian experi-ence is a question that, though innocuous in the United States, attracts, in Canada, indignant rebuff from Black Canadians. In Dany Laferrière's *Comment faire l'amour avec un nègre sans se fatiguer* (1985), the protagonist, Vieux, greet-ing his lover, Miz Littérature, at a Montréal bar, reacts thus when her friend asks him, 'Where do you come from?' ('Tu viens d'où?'):

À chaque fois qu'on me demande ce genre de question, comme ça, sans prévenir, sans qu'il ait été question, auparavant, du *National Geographic* references, je sens monter en moi unirrésistible désir de meurtre ...
    – Tu viens de quel pays? me redemande-t-elle.
    – Le jeudi soir, je viens de Madagascar. (106)

In his novel *Some Great Thing* (1992), Hill stages this exchange between an inept journalist and the protagonist, Mahatma Grafton:

'I mean, I know you're black,' Chuck said, 'but from where? You're not from Pakistan?'
    'Do I look like I'm from Pakistan?' (10)

Sealy notices that 'young black students at York University, born and raised in the Toronto area, are constantly questioned as to their island of origin' ('Talk-ing' 12).[25]

Even though Canadian realities promote a racial ambivalence, they also stimulate, for many African Canadians, a compensating black nationalism. This nationalism enacts a counter-influence to the pervasive identification of Canada as a northern, white, wanna-be empire, a pseudo-imperial self-image which reduces blackness to the status of problematic and pitiable *Other*. But while African-Canadian cultural nationalism makes common cause with Afri-can-American symbols, styles, leaders, and ideas, it also deviates from them sharply. When *Showboat*, the progressive American musical by Oscar Hammerstein and Jerome Kern, opened in Toronto in 1993, it sustained vocif-erous opposition from members of the African-Canadian intelligentsia. Fêted in the United States for portraying blacks 'as characterful individuals rather than racial stereotypes' (Kellner 322), *Showboat* was vilified as racist, American cultural imperialism by its African-Canadian opponents. For instance, rejecting the argument of Euro-Canadian feminist Judy Rebick that 'a lot of Black people in the States [support *Showboat*],' African-Canadian law student Kiké Roach yields this assertion: 'As far as *Showboat* goes, we're living in Canada, and we have a different Black population here, one that comes from majority countries in the Caribbean and Africa, so we have a different relationship to and understanding of the issues' (77). Philip accentuates this reading: 'Surely the fact that Canadian Blacks strongly opposed the production of *Showboat*, while there has been nary an oppositional whisper from the United States, suggests that there are some very marked differences between the two populations' ('Blackness' 2). Similarly, Samuel Clemens's *Huckleberry Finn* (1884), a likely African-American-influenced, American classic, runs into trouble in Hill's *Some Great Thing*. The book is banned from a Winnipeg, Manitoba, high school after a '15-year-old girl of Jamaican origin – had cried in class after being made to read aloud a section about the runaway slave character "Nigger Jim"' (141). In *No Crystal Stair*, Sarsfield's heroine, Pippa, impugns Clemens's *Tom Sawyer* (1876) for using 'the word "nigger" ... over and over again' (17). Talbot remarks that 'by the time I was old enough to read [Harriet Beecher Stowe's *Uncle Tom's Cabin* (1852)], I had already learned how to read *Tom Sawyer* and *Huckleberry Finn* in a tuned-off [*sic*] state of mind' (15). Treating Alice Walker's *The Color Purple* (1984), Philip castigates the novel's alleged reinforcement of stereotypes: 'There are, however, reasons why the book was a "suitable" choice for the Pulitzer Prize: none of the stereotypes assigned to American Blacks – male (loutish brutes with a predilection to rape) or female (passive and mule-like) were successfully challenged' (*Frontiers* 206). McCurdy, critiquing African-American leader Jesse Jackson, announces, 'I do not like having American black leadership coming to Canada as saviours ...' (quoted in Foster, *Place* 152). The effort by some African-Canadian cultural nationalists in Toronto in the mid-1990s to set up black-focused schools was scotched by the ultimate unimportability of American models:

> But even then, we recognized that the Detroit model [for Black-focused schools] would have little use in Canada, if only because we do not have the geographical concentrations of Blacks to allow us to virtually elect a black school board and set up black schools. We do not have the concentration, money or votes to set up a similar system in Canada. (Foster, *Place* 132)

As these examples indicate, there is a Canadianness about African-Canadian culture that cannot be subsumed under the banners of an 'imperial' African Americanism.

To go further, a structural metaphor for the steadily beleaguered status of Canadian blackness is suggested – appropriately – by a Glissantian reading of the Caribbean. To cite Debra L. Anderson's *Decolonizing the Text: Glissantian*

Readings in Caribbean and African-American Literatures (1995), 'the concept of [Glissant's] Antillanité is ... the ongoing search for a Caribbean identity – a search rooted in Caribbean reality, or rather in the questioning of this reality ...' (29). Glissant's understanding of the situation of the Caribbean is richly applicable to African Canada. Certainly, his emphasis on heterogeneity is suggestive. But it is the quality of indefinition that African-Canadianizes Glissant. I sound Anderson again: 'If it is difficult to define Antillanité, this difficulty arises from the "undeniable reality" of the complex historical, cultural, geographic, and linguistic specificities of the Caribbean ...' (29). A similar complexity configures the fractious African-Canadian identity. For one thing, African Canada replicates a Caribbean-like diversity. Discussing Caribbean-Canadian writers, then, Canadian scholar J. Edward Chamberlin asserts that, given their heritage of struggle with 'the imperial languages of Europe ... Canada must feel at least a little bit like home. It shares [the Caribbean's] preoccupation with language ... ' ('Canadian' 8). When James Walker writes that 'even within any specific West Indian territory there exists a medley of ethnic types and heritages' (*West* 3), he could just as easily be describing African Canada. Indeed, no truly 'national' black organization exists in Canada (save those representing nationalities, such as the Jamaican-Canadian Association), nor are any fully bilingual. Furthermore, there has been – and there is – no 'national figure to whom Negroes can turn,' no 'effective national leadership,' and 'no genuinely national [black] newspaper' (Winks 474, 475). Too, as Joyette acknowledges, 'there is a conspicuous absence of a Black Canadian school of thought, or a critical perspective of the art of Black Canadians' (5). This reality conjures up Glissant's notion that, says Anderson, 'the greatest threat for the Caribbean resides in the balkanization of these islands when, in fact, they share a common history as well as common economic, social and cultural realities ...' (30). Startlingly, 'Balkanization' is a pronounced metaphor for African Canadians. According to Winks, 'Canada had fragmented [the black] ...' (483). Problematically, the heterogeneity that defines African-Canadianité also threatens its coherence. Reacting to this tendency, writers often invoke the unifying spirit of history. This rhetorical *glissade* supports the Glissantian sense that 'the isolation of the Caribbean islands that impedes the awakening of a collective consciousness is inextricably embedded in Caribbean history, or rather, ... the "non-history" of the Caribbean ...' (Anderson 30). Similarly, African-Canadian anthologists intone the mantra of the need for, or flatly declare the existence of, a 'collective consciousness.' In *Canada in Us Now: The First* [sic] *Anthology of Black Poetry and Prose in Canada* (1976), editor Harold Head feels, 'This anthology is representative of the collective consciousness of people in the act of liberating themselves ...' (7). Introducing *Voices: Canadian Writers of African Descent* (1992), editor Ayanna Black posits that African Canadians 'write out of a collective African consciousness ...' (xi).[26] But *angst* persists, a fear that African Canada lays claim to only a spectral history. Here one can compare Glissant's concern *vis-à-vis* Martinique that 'this lack of a collective consciousness and the nonhistory of Martinique has serious implications for the literary production of Martinique ...' (Anderson 32). Echoing this fear, Philip argues that, 'working in Canada as an "Afrosporic" writer, I am very aware of the absence of a tradition of Black writing as it exists in England or the U.S.' (*Frontiers* 45).[27] Glissant's Antillanité accords with what I will term *African-Canadianité*, a condition that involves a constant self-questioning of the grounds of identity.

It is useful here to register Anderson's fine discrimination among the terms 'negritude,' 'Africanité' (a species of Pan-Africanism), and 'Antillanité' to reinforce the appropriateness of *African-Canadianité* as a *sign* for African-Canadian culture:

> Negritude reclaims the humanity and wholeness of the oppressed and shattered black self through a return to a mythical unified Africa (values, cultures, and traditions) and a rejection of the dominant system of white / Occidental values. Likewise, Africanité attempts to unify the many African cultures, languages, histories and peoples by negating their diversity. Antillanité, however, unites the Caribbean islands through their shared history while recognizing their diversities. Antillanité does not, and cannot, exclude, deny or reject the different ethnic components – African, European, Indian or Lebanese – of Caribbean realities. (44n6)

Because African Canadians constitute an *archipelago* of blackness (our black communities reside in disparate parts of the nation), the term Antillanité – or, rather, African-Canadianité – is archly suited to this reality. While no one can deny the impressive relevance of *négritude* and Pan-Africanism for many African Canadians, African-Canadianité marks the hegemony of heterogeneity, an attribute that African Canadians share with other communities in Canada. Indeed, an essential eclecticism also engulfs Latin Canadians, as Dominican-Canadian musician Papo Ross explains: 'In other countries, you either play merengue *or* salsa. Here, we have no choice because the Latin community is so mixed. We have to work together and play all the styles' (quoted in Jennings 12). A similar catholicity defines every black community in Canada. Bansfield numbers the Montréal black community in these terms:

> The Caribbean is represented by those from the English-speaking islands, by a huge Haitian community, and by immigrants from Spanish-speaking areas like Dominican Republic and Cuba. Continental Africans from francophone countries form another element ... At clubs like Balatou or Keur Samba, Cameroonian and Togolese share dancefloor space with Trinidadian and Scotian. On the courts of Concordia's Victoria Gym, Zairois and Senegalese take ally-oop [*sic*] passes from American and St. Lucian. (5)

Walker sees that 'while there is no single community, identity, or culture among African Canadians, it is surely significant that in recent census questionnaires, when Canadians have been invited to designate their own ethnicity in a variety of fashions (including continent, region, or country of origin), the largest number, and a majority of the younger people, have chosen to identify as "black Canadian"' ('Canada' 365). But this affirmation in no way detracts from the kaleidoscopic nature of African-Canadian identity. Angela Lee finds that the heritage of the contributors to a 1995 *Canadian Theatre Review* issue on African-Canadian theatre 'ranges from the continental African, the indigenous American and Canadian, the Caribbean, the Haitian and points in between' (3). The March 1996 edition of *The Afro News* of Vancouver lists such upcoming Calgary events as a Panorama Steelband sponsored by the Canada / St Lucia Friendship Society, a Jamaican Food Festival and Dance, and a St Vincent and the Grenadines Dance (5). Rinaldo Walcott sees, then, that 'the multiplicities of blackness in Canada collide in ways that are instructive for current diasporic theorizing' (29). The variegated composition of the African-Canadian polity marks an imposing difference from the more homogeneous African-American 'nation.'[28] As Foster attests, 'this mix [of ethnicities] represents the uniqueness of Canada's black population' (*Place* 18).[29]

III. A Model Blackness and Its Revisionists

As Matthews's 1962 study of the development of Canadian and Australian poetry suggests, no foreign influence enters a country without undergoing adaptation or change suitable to the new environment.[30] Hence, the specific constraints of African-Canadian life – its heterogeneity, the scant population, its perpetual marginalization within white majority discourses – in a word, its African-Canadianité – means that the powerful African-American influence upon it must itself be adjusted. Canada is an American space that warps Americanité. Remarkably, an African-Canadian sensibility may be articulated at the very point where it seems to vanish: at the moment when African-American texts seem to possess African-Canadian ones. If this is so, the model blackness that is African America, that is to say, the fount of racial discourse, engenders a new blackness, one that may prefer to be encased in quotation marks. Yet, the model blackness that African-Canadian writers contest is not easily countermanded. An analysis of its structures is in order here, for they help to determine the nationalist and racial attitudes that appear in African-Canadian literature.

In the Winter 1996 issue of the journal *Callaloo*, two critical essays disrupt the apparent mission of British Cultural Studies luminaries – such as Gilroy and Stuart Hall – to dislodge Black Studies and, by extension, African-American Studies, in the name of a beautiful anti-essentialism. In her entry, Mae G. Henderson advises, 'I am less concerned about the displacement of African American hegemony in black diasporic studies than I am by the erasure of a historical genealogy for black cultural studies that extends back ... to the African American critique of politics and culture formally inaugurated by W.E.B. DuBois ...' (63). Henderson is moved to 'insist that the emergent project of black cultural studies be situated in the context of Black Studies' (64), for 'Black Studies draws upon a tradition that derives in large part from black

American writers and scholars' (64). Henderson even adopts a colleague's witty riposte to insurgent Brits: 'we must not only look to Birmingham, *England*, but to Birmingham, *Alabama*, as a site of historical struggle and contestation – a site whose academic counterpart we still find in Black Studies programs across the country' (65). One can almost feel envy, or repulsion, cascading through her words. Next, Henderson plumps for her own scholarship – and that of her contemporaries, '[Houston] Baker and [Henry Louis] Gates' (65) – as exemplifying an *engagé* 'vernacularization of theory' (65).[31] In her essay, Wahneema Lubiano cites the writings of African-American folklorist and author Zora Neale Hurston as 'only one site that offers fecund possibilities for cultural studies theorists to "discover" a pre-existing body of [African-American] work with similar imperative with regard to readings of "everyday life" and "style" as subversion' (72).[32] These two essays forward, nakedly, African-American struggle and thought as the salient *avant-garde* for such work. African America emerges as a 'model' blackness – a dream of *négritude* or Africanité – around which all others may coalesce. Grandly, this argument urges an investment in the 'Americocentricity' (Gilroy 191) that Canadians are wont to rue, that 'Manifest Destiny' that *lovingly* appropriates the world for its own interests.

Though I confess that, being African Canadian, I risk producing yet another version of our African-Americanism, it is time for me to spell out six principles of African-American blackness. (1) *African-American blackness is internationalist*. Note that James Baldwin 'saw the [U.S.] civil rights struggle as a worldwide struggle, not just as a matter of national politics ...' (Ursula Davis 23). Richard Wright argued that 'the history of the Negro in America is the history of America written in vivid and bloody terms; it is the history of Western Man writ small' (*White* 109). King believed that 'the American Negro of 1967 ... may be the vanguard in a prolonged struggle that may change the shape of the world, as billions of deprived shake and transform the earth in their quest for life, freedom, and justice' (10). (2) *African-American blackness is revolutionary*. King specifies that 'the first man to die in the American Revolution was a Negro seaman, Crispus Attucks,' whose death rang the death knell of 'the institution of absolute monarchy' (10). As a university student, Du Bois admired the imperialism of Otto von Bismarck as an example of 'the kind of thing that American Negroes must do, marching forth with strength and determination under trained leadership' (*Dusk* 32). U.S. intellectual Stanley Aronowitz believes that 'no oppressed people in human history has more thoroughly embraced the leading features of modernity than American blacks' (234). (3) *African-American blackness actuates principled, defensive violence*. Witness the tactics of the Maoist-styled Black Panther Party or the apocalyptic rhetoric of Marcus Garvey and Malcolm X. Gus John advises that the Black Panther Party provided British blacks with 'models of resistance linked to a continuity of struggle' (quoted in Walmsley 155). For Du Bois, the struggle of 'the American black man' to enter 'modern civilization here in America' on equal terms with whites is 'the last great battle of the West' (*Black* 703). In waging this struggle, Du Bois notes, 'black folk, after all, have little to lose, but *Civilization* has all' (*Black* 703, my italics). (4) *African-American blackness licenses non-violent, mass mobilization.* The Civil Rights Movement of 1956–68, as led by King, the 1964 Nobel Peace Prize laureate, is the best example here. But other boycotts, crusades, and the mass promulgation of key ideas fit within this category. African-American scholar Clyde Taylor casts the Million Man March of (principally) African-American males, on Washington, D.C., on 16 October 1995, as 'a mass do-it-yourself happening, a free-form collective performance' ('One' 88). Chastising March critics, Baker asks, 'Did they believe they could stand tall for black redemption, and simultaneously distance themselves from the only *mass* message being seriously listened to by black people in the United States?' ('America's' 72). (5) *African-American blackness is territorial.* Gilroy pillories 'the great ethnocentric canon of African-American literature' (186). For Marvin X, Canada was dandy, but the United States was *sweeter*, at least in terms of action. Thus, X decided 'he could not remain an exile if he wanted to work for the betterment of his people's condition' (Thomas 182). African-American scholar Robert F. Reid-Pharr perceives that 'King's "I Have a Dream" speech [1963] receives much of its force from the evocation of an ethos that is at once Christian and American nationalist, supporting ... a liberal integrationist agenda that insists upon the expansiveness – and expansion – of the nation' (42). Notably, the Nation of Islam, under the leadership of Elijah Muhummad, maintained, for decades, a call for land to set up an independent black state within the continental United States. (6) *African-American blackness is influential.* British writer Anne Walmsley asserts that 'Malcolm X's visit [to London, in February 1965], like Martin Luther King's a few months earlier [in December 1964], had a profound effect on Caribbean people in Britain at a time when they were feeling increasingly pressured and unwelcome in Britain' (28). Gilroy points out that 'the role of external meanings around blackness, drawn in particular from black America, became important in the elaboration of a connective culture which drew these different "national" [Caribbean] groups [in Britain] together into a new pattern ...' (82). Chamberlin credits Du Bois's *Souls of Black Folk* as a source for the concept of *négritude* developed by 'Léon Damas from French Guiana and the Senegalese writer and politician Léopold Senghor' (*Come* 50). Chamberlin also confirms that the 'black power movement in its most familiar form was American ...' (*Come* 54). African-American blackness is, assuredly, a model blackness. But not for all, at least, not all the time.

The fine 'choreopoem' *for colored girls who have considered suicide / when the rainbow is enuf* (1977), written by African-American playwright Ntozake Shange (b. Paulette Williams), proves the case. Though African-Canadian playwright Ahdri Zinha Mandiela uses Shange's work as a model for her own choreopoem, *dark diaspora ... in dub* (1991), she revises it wilfully. This manoeuvre may seem peculiar, or ungrateful, for Mandiela *approves* the revolutionary *summons* of Shange's drama:

then the 80's: a different ilk of speaking out – the black woman's voice, heard only
before in spaces "for colored girls ..." Shange's "mistresspiece" had set the tone.
newly-opened ears were forced to hear black women's voices decrying our shame-
less struggles and celebrating our near triumphs. (viii, her ellipsis)

Too, Mandiela pays Shange the outright compliment of echoing the latter's
work in her very fabrication. The text of *for colored girls* features black and
white photographs of African-American women performers in skirts and tops.
Mandiela follows suit in *dark diaspora*, printing black and white photographs
of her performers wearing African-print skirts and high-necked tops. Shange's
text consists of twenty dramatic poems; Mandiela's work admits twenty-one.
Shange's play is dedicated to *'the spirits of my grandma* / viola benzena murray
owens / *and my great aunt* / effie owens josey' [vii]; Mandiela's play is 'for
your *aunt vida*' (n.p.). Shange's cast demands seven women, named after pris-
matic colours; Mandiela enlists a 'cast of characters,' ranging in number from
seven to fifteen to fifty. Shange provides a single, untitled preface, describing
the genesis of her play; Mandiela offers two separate forewords: 'about this
dub' narrates its politics; 'evolution of this dub' delineates its origins and
development. While Shange's 'choreopoem' enacts a tour of African-American
women's consciousness, with its performers recounting experiences such as
abortion, rape, domestic violence, and formations of community, Mandiela's
play limns a single black female consciousness whose voice can be represented by either one speaker and several dancers or by multiple speakers and
dancers. Her characters depict an internal voice, with dancers dramatizing
abstract representations of a state of mind. Mandiela feels that her play explores 'the present day psyche of the black diaspora which revels in the surety
of being: "afrikan by instinct," and heir to a specific legacy of joy, pain, hopes
& a continual driving force' (vii). In contrast, Shange's introduction stresses
her intention 'to explore the realities of seven different kinds of women ... the
women were to be nameless & assume hegemony as dictated by the fullness of
their lives' (xvii). Shange's introductory poem foregrounds feminism:

> my work
> attempts to ferret out
> what I know & touch
> in a woman's body ...
>
> i discuss the simple reality
> of ...
> looking out the window
> with a woman's eyes.
> we must learn our common symbols,
> preen them
> and share them with the world. [i]

Shange names, as her foremothers, a liberal pantheon: 'from Isis to Marie Laurencin, Zora Neale Hurtson [*sic*] to Kathe Kollwitz, Anna May Wong to Calamity Jane' (xv). Swerving from Shange's insistence on sharing 'common symbols ... with the world,' Mandiela desires to speak for 'the scatterlings of the world's descendants of afrikan origin' (vii). Hence, her heroine 'speaks from her immediately familiar heritage, the Caribbean: "sugar & spice & parboiled rice"' (viii). Shange strives for a universal feminism, but Mandiela accents a contrastingly out-of-fashion Pan-Africanism. In a 1995 interview with Angela Lee, Mandiela discloses a fierce commitment to specifically black theatre:

> the 80s for me saw the last of afrikan peoples in the diaspora exploring our own: township theatre in south africa; exploration of carnival style theatre by amah harris at theatre in the rough/ toronto; the popular works of a company like sistren in jamaica ... not since shange's *'colored girls'* & musicals like [vinette] carroll's *'your arm's too short'* have we seen anything outside of the 'regular' on or off-broadway mould in america; none of these kinds of activities are happening within our afrikan communities now ... no introspection or coccooning of our fragile selves in these hostile environments of the diaspora. ('ahdri' 8)

Though both plays review the experiences of black women, Shange's work is *generally* American, while Mandiela's is focused on the African diaspora.

Nevertheless, Shange is conscious of her women characters as *black*. The author twins racial and gender consciousness: 'With the acceptance of the ethnicity of my thighs & backside, came a clearer understanding of my voice as a woman & as a poet' (xv). Irrefutably, the drama is constructed around the motif of 'a young black girl's growing up, her triumphs & errors, our struggle to become all that is forbidden by our environment, all that is forfeited by our gender, all that we have forgotten' (xxi). Despite such conscious overtures to blackness, the centre of gravity in Shange's play is women's experience. Audaciously, even ingeniously, she presents contemporary, urban, African-American female lives as *models* of global female experience. Veering from this blueprint, *dark diaspora* foregrounds its adoration of Jamaican English – 'reclaimed in the work of poets like oku onuora [Orlando Wong] – emerging in the mid to late 70s' (x) – and its interest in expanding 'the literary tradition of *dub* poetry – by producing an integrated stage script composed entirely from *dub* poems – as well as to present a totally new stage experience: *dub theatre*' (x). Mandiela emphasizes this concern in her 1995 interview with Makeda Silvera: 'Mother tongue, being Jamaican, gives me a definite perspective on language, both written and oral use. Even when I write in English, I think I conceptualize in Jamaican. It seems to yield more precise symbols, hence crisper, more descriptive images' ('Interview' 82). Mandiela's nationalist language reconstruction and Pan-Africanist enthusiasms imply no rejection of feminism, however. She accepts 'the choice of a black woman as main character ... not mine; simply the heart/beat of the "dark diaspora ..."'; her charted course: as is and once again recorded in my mind/words' (x, her ellipses). Fundamentally, Mandiela follows her idol, Shange, in utilizing the black female body as emblem, but for nationalist and Pan-Africanist, not universalist and feminist, purposes.

Though Shange's text is an opening to the world, a nationalist ripple scores her work. In the first poem, 'dark phrases,' uttered by the lady in brown, race nationalism appears: 'dark phrases of womanhood ... / distraught laughter fallin / over a black girl's shoulder' (1). In 'Toussaint,' the lady in brown exalts her girlhood worship of the leader of the Haitian Revolution, Toussaint L'Ouverture (1743?–1803), and her discovery of the incarnation of his spirit in a neighbourhood boy, Toussaint Jones (26–32). Here Shange domesticates Pan-Africanism for American interests. Likewise, Mandiela is not obsessed solely with blackness. Her lyric 'for my sister whose/heart/broke against a poem' issues a cosmopolitan utterance:

it's easy to fall in: love
holds like a grave
our bodies/mesh: wire
& lace/from dust/to dawn ...
kisses flower from a snap–
ped nail as my mind swims
in the sweat of your fingers/even
then the musk of rhymes seep on–
to my tongue/i spit blood
thinking again it's just: ink
residue from your pen
but this time my heart is a well.

and your pen is dry (22)

Nationalist and feminist themes conjoin, in the end, in both Shange and Mandiela, although their emphases are opposite.

But a signal rupture occurs at the level of language. Throughout *for colored girls*, Shange, perhaps foreseeing vernacularized – or mass-centred – theories of African-American literature, sings realistic experiences in a tongue redolent of the blues, of jazz, of funk; a pop discourse, culled from the streets, the Sound of Young America (as Motown Records once billed its popularization of *soul* music). This speaker evinces a convincing *vox populi*:

i want my stuff back / my rhythms & my voice / open
my mouth / & let me talk ya outta / throwin my shit
in the sewar [sic] ... / now you cant have me
less i give me away / & i was doin all that / til ya run
off on a good thing / who is this you left me wit /
some simple bitch widda bad attitude / i wants my
things ... / i want my calloused feet & quik
language back in my mouth ... (53)

This is recollected Whitman and Hughes, the quintessence of the American populist tradition put to good use. Mandiela's language, diction, and tone are seldom this personal. See, for instance, 'afrikan by instinct':

> enter: the caribbean/see/we
> afrikan/by instinct/here
> *l'ouverture* roam free/here/
> against poverty/here
> shackles without keys/here:
> a different slavery? here/check
> here/check/check/check
> by air/by boat
> *fidel's* big 'c'
> then *mobay/ja.*/visit my auntie
> /cousin/dead grannie/rise *nanny*:
> afrikan spirit in *garvey*
> one god/one aim/one ancestry. (43)

Despite the familial references, Mandiela prefers to present abstract slogans, not personalized depictions of pain and oppression. While Shange's work is steeped in the African-American vernacular and in urbanity, Mandiela's work utilizes a mixture of standard and 'real' English and finds its strength in its poetry rather than its referentiality. In a word, Mandiela resists realism.

While Shange's play concludes – like a traditional comedy – with the 'marrying together' of a pacific, unified, female community chanting the mantra of 'i found god in myself / & i loved her / i loved her fiercely' (67), Mandiela's play ends with a flourish of Pan-Africanist utterances:

> viva! *mandela*/chanting arms
> *garvey* forever/chanting arms
> say it/say it/say it
> say it loud/i'm black
> & i'm proud/say it loud
> black black black
> black/gay gay gay/hey
> say it loud/come what may
> we're here to stay/
> rally round/*jah! rastafari*
> a luta continua ...
> sanctions now/sanctions now/
> by any means necessary/we shall overcome/
> our will be done today/
> after 50 eons of black tracks/
> better mus come!
> chanting arms

chanting arms
chanting arms
chanting (52–3)

Mandiela's predilection for intellectual abstraction manifests her *African-Canadianité*, for Canadian poets have tended to value an 'academic' as opposed to a 'popular' ideal of poetics. According to Matthews, 'academic poetry refers to that based directly upon sophisticated ... models of the central [British] tradition, whether the theory and practice of such poetry had university associations ... or not ...' (113). Contrarily, 'popular poetry refers to that of folk-literature and to literary adaptations of it, based upon less sophisticated models of the central tradition' (113). Importantly, Mandiela's verse, though largely accessible, enacts a post-modern elusiveness: 'this flower / bloomed to pollen pus / borne of back /-lashing and unconstructed / promises / trapped in the dew of twilight / passion / who is my lover? now' (7). Mandiela revises Shange's *for colored girls*, dispensing with a definable, 'real' setting to dramatize, instead, the negotiation of interiority, that is to say, of identity. Mandiela's verse is 'concerned with,' to borrow from Matthews's critique of mid-century Canadian 'socialist' poets, 'recording universal [black] experience, with little reference to the local [Canadian] scene' (149). Her work is, to sound Matthews's terminology again, 'a cerebral poetry, intellectual in conception ...' (148). This finding represents, as the Florida-born, African-Canadian actor Celeste Insell (who has lived in Canada since 1971) insists, a psychological difference between African-American and African-Canadian plays:

> There is a greater feeling of potential external violence in plays written by African Americans, as contrasted to the more internal violence taking place within African-Canadian protagonists. In many plays written by African Canadians, there is often a sense that the central characters are experiencing a kind of slow madness as a result of confusion. What could be expressed more openly with the support of a strong Black community, has had to be said less directly in the latter context. Therefore, the writing becomes more symbolic, more poetic and we must decipher the images to really understand what is being said. (39)

The 'violence' to which Insell bears witness compares well with what Njami spies in the work of African-Canadian photographers: the passage of 'a well-founded construction ... through a violent process of deconstruction, of destruction and the dismantling of unquestioned truths' (*Traces* [4]). 'African-Canadian plays,' Insell insists, 'constantly deal with problems of identity and isolation' (39). Mandiela's *dark diaspora* plays out these Canadian divergences from African-American theatre.

Intriguingly, a Vancouver, B.C., African-Canadian women's theatre group (one to which Insell belongs) has also practised a *virage* from Shange's text, a reaction based on a felt African-Canadian nationalism. Here is Siobhan R.K. Barker's instructive confession:

There has been much emphasis placed on the assertions of the African-American right to cultural identity while very little has been expressed regarding their neighbours to the north ... For African-Canadian women, prior to confronting those issues offending her American sisters, she must first tackle her omission from dramatic presentations ... *Images of Whole* is focused on the creation of theatre that is specific to the experiences of African-Canadian women ... The three women currently involved – Liza Huget, Celeste Insell and myself, Siobhan Barker – met when all were cast in [a Canadian] production of Ntozake Shange's choreopoem *for colored girls who have considered suicide / when the rainbow is enuf*. As any performer does in taking on a role, we tried to be as true as possible to Shange's vision and text while bringing as much of ourselves to the American characters which to some degree remained alien to us. Our African-Canadian voices were not heard through the African-American mouths of Shange's characters. Our story had still gone untold and we began searching individually for performance opportunities that would be representative of our African-Canadian heritage and indicative of our presence in Canadian society. (15)

Barker opines that Shange's play 'is as complete a picture as has ever been offered of the Black woman's experiences' (15). Yet, 'despite its universality in broaching such issues as emotional and physical rape and seeing oneself as exploited and unappreciated, it is merely a slice of a section – the African-American section' (15). Barker proceeds to a vigorous defence of African-Canadian culture:

It is not enough to have a multitude of americanizations dictating how our Canadian reality is shaped in juxtaposition. There is an African-Canadian history wherein lives the reality of the African-Canadian woman which calls out time and time again in the hopes that her voice will grow loud enough and not give way until it is recognized and heard. (16)

'Understanding the black reality in Canada must start with the recognition that Canada's black population ...' writes Foster, 'isn't a carbon copy of the African-American population south of the border' (*Place* 13). Lee supports this position, finding that 'unlike "Black Theatre" in the United States, this concept in the Canadian context has not become a movement completely born of self-confirmation ...' (3). It is up to artists, or so Barker implies, to satisfy 'the need for specificity to the Canadian, and particularly the African-Canadian women's experiences' (16). Joyette senses that African-Canadian writers are 'establishing an aesthetic that distinctly speaks of and for Canadians of African descent' (5). This aesthetic 'will help to explain and define the complexity of various literary forms found in the Black Canadian diaspora' (5).

Mandiela's work proves that such an aesthetic – or understanding – exists. Her play dramatizes the deliberate reconstruction of imported African-American forms, to quote Gilroy, 'in novel patterns that do not respect their originators' proprietary claims or the boundaries of discrete nation states and the supposedly natural political communities they express or simply contain' (98–9). Her text performs a 'deformation' or 'reformation' of the African-American original.[33] She even exalts her own Jamaican-Canadian brand of poetry over African-American forms: 'Dub poetry's form is not very different from some African American musical and lyrical styling, yet there is an in-the-pocket groove thing which dub poetry excels in more precisely than other forms' ('Interview' 83).

In addition to such annunciations of innate *différence*, African-Canadian writers also indulge in critiques of American society, avowing a typical Canuck anti-Americanism. This tendency has a long history. Peggy Bristow reminds us that nineteenth-century black British North American settlers 'were concerned about the possibility of republican ideas taking hold in British North America' (124). In his unusual pamphlet, *'Black Man in a White Land,'* Clarke, writing as Ali Sudan, claims that 'Canada is an American satellite' (*Black* 5). His anti-Americanism resurfaces in his 1992 pamphlet, *Public Enemies: Police Violence and Black Youth*, where he claims that Toronto is 'still *north* of the border of America and of racism' (18, his italics). Attempting to adapt his 1996 play about a May 1992 riot in Toronto, *Riot* (1997), for the screen, Andrew Moodie was angered when it began to metamorphose into 'a carbon copy of any inner-city [U.S.] youth flick made in the past 20 years: *Boyz in the Annex'* (22). In *Native Song*, Woods paints this image of an 'ugly' African American – or, rather, of a Canadian 'playing' at being one:

He got the latest American tapes
And talks in the latest American slang,
He got imported suits from New York
And his cologne can leave you in a trance. (42)

For her part, Philip adopts an anti-technological and defensive nationalism reminiscent of the thought of Canadian nationalist philosopher George P. Grant:

Strangely enough, in the Caribbean, in these islands that are predominantly African, the links *appear* weaker, the flight from Africa manifesting itself in either a profound erasure and silencing or a submerging under a growing Americanism through the uncritical absorption of CNN news, *Santa Barbara*, *Knots Landing*, and *Dallas*. (*Frontiers* 11)

This Grantian touch is real, for, in a 1995 article, 'Signifying Nothing,' Philip declares that 'the profound changes [Americanization] that had begun in Canada in the sixties had more to do with the fundamental reorganization of the Canadian political system that George C. [*sic*] Grant described in his brilliant and prescient work, *Lament for a Nation* [1965]' ('Signifying' 8). Philip colludes further with Grantian thought by basing her opposition to *Showboat* on its being a 'blatant exercise in cultural imperialism' ('Blackness' 3). Grant locates the power of American liberal capitalism in its faith in technology; Philip agrees:

> Technology – the god that rules the world with a savage unforgivingness, putting to shame any Old Testament god. Technology that inspires hubris in its makers and believers who, believing, bomb indiscriminately. They believed they could bomb Viet Nam out of existence; they found instead a poor 'Third World' country that defied that technology ... Technology had reckoned without the human spirit. Emotive, meaningless words perhaps – the human spirit – but aren't we just machines, meaningless machines without it? (*Frontiers* 250)

Presumably, she has read Grant's *Technology and Empire* (1969) with some closeness, perhaps even the passage where he argues that 'the ruthlessness and banal callousness of what has been done in Vietnam might lead one to see North American events as solely self-interested nihilism of a greedy techno logical empire' (26). (Moreover, Philip's critiques of U.S. culture ask implicitly a question that Euro-Canadian scholar Diana Brydon puts explicitly, 'why should Black U.S. imperialism be any more palatable than White U.S. imperialism?' [3]). Grantian thought also seems to tinge McCurdy's House of Commons speech of 5 July 1988 against the Canada-U.S. Free Trade Agreement Implementation Act (Bill C–130):

> Madam Speaker, I should not have thought it possible that over a century of struggle of this nation to maintain its independence would end with the fulfill- ment of the American notion of a manifest destiny within the House of Commons of Canada ... The future of this country does not reside in becoming part of the continental divine mission of the United States ... I do not want the cities of Canada to look like Detroit, New York, or Chicago with a market oriented phi- losophy ... Let us retain our independence. (17153–4)

Understandably, an anti-U.S., anti-modern posture colours Dionne Brand's volume of poems on the Grenada Crisis and U.S.-led invasion of 1983, *Chronicles of the Hostile Sun* (1984):

> I am walking on the rock of
> a beach in Barbados
> looking to where Grenada was
> now, the flight of an american bomber
> leaves the mark of a rapist in the room. (39)

The pseudonymous Jing-Shin raises this rhetorical, anti-U.S. question: 'How can any "white-supremacist" state with a history of enslaving men, putting others in concentration camps in time of war, and which extends through its generations the execrable human trait of racial discrimination claim justice for all its citizens, when, in times past and even now but to a lesser degree, it practices racial discrimination against peoples that are not of their preferred culture or skin colour?' (310). Like invective infuses many African-Canadian texts.

The writings of African Canadians are also connected to mainstream Canadian culture; in terms of opposition, *oui*, but also in terms of affinity. Pinson, in the dedication to his book, thanks poet Irving Layton for 'fanning' his 'flame' of poetry [4]. Maxine Tynes dedicates poems to singer and writer Leonard Cohen ('Phillips Square 18/08/83,' in *Borrowed* 31–2), singer Rita MacNeil ('Becoming Rita,' in *Borrowed* 30), painter Christopher Pratt ('The Bay,' in *Borrowed* 65), writer Margaret Atwood ('Addendum,' in *Woman* 42), and singer Joni Mitchell ('Joni Mitchell Again,' in *Woman* 55). Alexis confesses his inability to 'describe the emotion I felt reading *The Stone Angel, Fifth Business, The Apprenticeship of Duddy Kravitz, The Luck of Ginger Coffey, Who Has Seen the Wind*, and *Surfacing*. It was like discovering that half my soul was shared by Margaret Laurence' ('Borrowed' 20). Allen divulges her 'love' for the poetry of *avant-garde* figure bp Nichol and her admiration for the 'revolutionary' fearlessness of Atwood (quoted in Dawes, '360 Degrees' 89, 90). Though the existence of an 'African-Canadian people' cannot be *dogmatically* asserted, readings of the literature suggest that no alternative is viable, for African-Canadian writers understand themselves to be Canadian.[34] Indeed, the debts and homages that African Canadians have paid to mainstream Canadian literature and art are numerous. African-Canadian writer Peter Hudson asserts that 'themes of survival and victimization in the hostile, frozen North have receded from the Canadian literary imagination, but African Canadian literature still finds itself awkwardly tethered to it' (Editor's 5). Black Canadian intellectuals are shaped just as much by the broad cultural and socio-political currents of the nation as they are by their irrevocable engagement with the thought and art of offshore African-heritage intellectuals. It is time that scholars began to recognize this Canadianness, rather than presuming that it does not exist.[35]

To move toward a conclusion of this essay, I must affirm explicitly African-American scholar Nahum Dimitri Chandler's sage proposition that to harry African-American Studies for its supposed essentialism 'naively implies that a non-essentialist discourse or position can be produced' (79). Chandler's understanding that it may never be possible to advance a non-essentialist discourse, coupled with Baker's reading that the texts of early twentieth-century African-American leaders marked 'a field of possibilities for an emergent Afro-American *national* enterprise' (*Modernism* 71), is pertinent here. Chandler's position implies, like that of Baker, that creators and scholars of literature always forge a national identity. Indeed, as Matthews determines, 'it is difficult to separate nationalism from the search for a native tradition' (49). Thus, one significance of African-Canadian culture's *veerings* from its African-American influences is that its writers draft, thereby, 'a tradition which will be different from both the English and American traditions of writing and literature by Black writers' (Philip, *Frontiers* 45).[36] One may expect, then, that African-Canadian demonstrations of 'mastery of form' and 'deformation of mastery' (to employ two phrases from Baker)[37] will be practised increasingly upon African-American – as well as Euro-Canadian – models.[38] Nevertheless, this 'national(ist)' African-Canadian literature will be rent – as it must be – by regionalism as well as by ethnic and linguistic differences. *Mais, c'est le dilemme canadien.* The result is not a model, perhaps, but a *modal,* 'blackness': an *African-Canadianité.*

Postscript and Prelude

To scrutinize the paradoxical and often parasitical relationship between African-Canadian texts and their innocent, oblivious, African-American precursors is *not*, however, to indulge some soft-headed thesis that 'African-Canadian texts evolve directly out of African-American ones,' the argument that Canadian scholar Richard Almonte feels that I urge. Says Almonte: 'Clarke proposes that "African-Canadian literature" ... is produced through a process whereby Canadian writers signify on African-American texts and writers' (Introduction 17). Almonte exaggerates my position, which is *not* that all African-Canadian literature derives from African-American source texts, but, merely, that one cannot access African-Canadian literature without taking into account the remarkable tendency of many of its creators to deliberately, deliriously, parrot/parody Black U.S. intertexts. This procedure *is* one, but only *one*, aspect of African-Canadianité, although its practice is second nature to the culture. Almonte's own work proves this tendency. Introducing his annotated edition of Thomas Smallwood's *A Narrative of Thomas Smallwood (Coloured Man)* (1851, 2000), Almonte alleges that 'the slave narrative is a literary genre of the United States' and that 'Smallwood's *Narrative*, as the sole example of a slave narrative written and published in Canada, contests this American cultural hegemony' (Introduction 16). Both statements are factually incorrect.[39] As well, Almonte's own terms position Smallwood – quite unfairly, really – as an African-Canadian imitator of a *supposedly* African-American form. (Almonte forgets, unlike Oswald Ducrot and Tzvetan Todorov, that 'every text is absorption and transformation of a multiplicity of other texts' [quoted in Bernstein 20].) True: Smallwood's self-consciously intellectualized text, sugared with quotations from British and American abolitionist poets and orators, may owe debts to African-American writers David Walker (whose fiery *Appeal* of 1829 led pro-slavery forces to put a price on his head) and the escaped slave Frederick Douglass. However, Smallwood refers twice to Caesar (29, 34) and styles himself, obliquely, as a type of Julius Caesar, a 'great' man beset by 'slander' and 'treachery.' He also stresses an academic orientation, damning slavery as an 'abyss of intellectual darkness' (35) because it has 'robbed the world of the intellectual part that God designed they [Africans] should perform in creation' (41). His ideological – nay, Miltonic – concern is fraud: plagiarism, deceit, embezzlement. Thus, his *Narrative* is a *j'accuse*, one whose recurrent words are 'treachery' and its cognates, applied both to 'my own colour ... [who] through envy and for the sake of filthy lucre, were trying to betray me' (52) and to the white 'slave-holders' and their agents (52). In this sense, too, Smallwood's text is archetypally *Canadian*, given its Shadd-like[40] boosting of Canada – 'the British dominions' (53) – as the Douglassian 'north star' realm of *real* liberty (38) versus the hypocritical land of 'democratic and Christian slavery' (38).

Commendable is Almonte's frustration regarding the reiterated obsessions of African Canadians around African-American culture. However, annoyance should not blind the scholar to the truth that *even* out-and-out Black Canadian 'imitations' keep resulting in Black Canadian originality. Sealy states that he resists, virtuously perhaps, 'viewing Black Canadian life as either a repetition of Black American life, Black African life or Black Caribbean life' ('Canadianizing' 91). But the matter to be addressed is not elementary iteration, but calculated repetition insisting upon a *signifying* difference. (See James A. Snead, 'Repetition As a Figure of Black Culture' [1990]). The insight is vision. Let us hear Antiguan-Canadian dub poet Clifton Joseph here: '[In Toronto, in the 1970s, we Caribbean-born youth] knew we were not black/americans, even though we imitated them in dress, speech & pop-ular [sic] culture' (19). One more excellent example of this pattern of radical adherence to – and deviation from – African-American sources occurs in the only published play authored by Africadian poet Walter Borden ...

Notes

1 This paper arose from a presentation at the plenary session of the Association of Canadian College and University Teachers of English and of the Association for Canadian and Québécois Literature, during the Congress of Learned Societies, at Memorial University, St John's, Newfoundland, on 1 June 1997. I am indebted to several individuals whose questions served to clarify its focus. I dedicate it, though, to the memory of Professor John Pengwyrne Matthews (1928–95), an Australian-born, Canadian authority on what he preferred to call Commonwealth Literature, and whose classic text, *Tradition in Exile: A Comparative Study of Social Influences on the Development of Australian and Canadian Poetry in the Nineteenth Century* (1962), anchors my ideas. Still, I alone am responsible for the flaws.

2 This paper deals with the issue of African-American influence and its role in shaping an African-Canadian 'aesthetic.' But the Caribbean has also been influential for many African-Canadian writers, where, in fact, most were born. To draft a full history of African-Canadian literature, it will be necessary to examine not only the Black Power and Black Arts Movements of the United States, but also the London-based Caribbean Artists Movement (CAM), 1966–72. Its members 'sought to discover their own aesthetic and to chart new directions for their arts and culture; to become acquainted with their history; to rehabilitate their Amerindian inheritance and to reinstate their African roots; to reestablish links with the "folk" through incorporating the peoples' language and musical rhythms in Caribbean literature; to reassert their own tradition in the face of the dominant tradition' (Walmsley xvii). This movement engaged expatriate African-Canadian writers John

Hearne and Alma Norman as well as several Caribbean nationals who later emigrated to Canada, including writers Louise Bennett, Honor Ford-Smith, Roger McTair, Samuel Selvon, and Olive Senior. Most importantly, the ideas of Caribbean writers and intellectuals like Lloyd Best, Edward Kamau Brathwaite, Stokeley Carmichael (who visited Montréal in March 1967 and both Montréal and Halifax in October 1968), Stuart Hall, Wilson Harris, C.L.R. James, John La Rose, Marina Maxwell, Kenneth Ramchand, Walter Rodney (who visited Montréal in October 1968), and Andrew Salkey received wide dissemination among the aforementioned figures as well as among writers, such as Austin Clarke and Jan Carew, who were already landed in Canada. In addition, some of the aforementioned writers were published in the crucial CAM journal, *Savacou*, while others were undoubtedly influenced by it. In short, some CAM ideas likely mark some African-Canadian writers of Caribbean descent. For an exhaustive discussion of the CAM, see Anne Walmsley, *The Caribbean Artists Movement, 1966–72: A Literary and Cultural History* (1992). Furthermore, attention must be paid to how Euro-Canadian racism, when promulgated explicitly against Caribbean-originated Canadians, becomes exposed to international condemnation. Thus, in 1977, in an interview with the Caribbean-based *Caribbean Contact* newspaper, Edward W. Scott, then head of the World Council of Churches and archbishop of the Anglican Church of Canada, found himself asserting the role of church-led, anti-racist activity in Canada. 'Referring to the very sensitive area of racial discrimination against West Indians and other non-white immigrant communities in Canada, Archbishop Scott said that the churches were quite active in ensuring that the Canadian government respects its own human rights law, and that both "structured and individual cases of racial discrimination were dealt with effectively"' ('WCC's' 24). Finally, a comprehensive history of contemporary African-Canadian literature would have to treat Garveyism, Jamaican politics, reggae, 'dub' poetry, and Rastafarianism (see Chamberlin, *Come* 55–7), Bajan calypso, the Cuban Revolution, the February 1970 revolt in Trinidad, Mas, steelband, the *Haiti Littéraire* movement, the 1986 Haitian revolution, the assaults on Caribbean immigration to Britain in the 1960s and 1970s, the 1968 First Cultural Congress of Havana, the 1968 Congress of Black Writers in Montréal, Jamaica's Carifesta '72, as well as the struggle against *apartheid* in South Africa, the struggle for the decolonization of other African countries, and the waging of civil wars in Ethiopia and Somalia.

3 Fascinatingly, African-Canadian and African-American culture both mirror – and dissent from – their respective majoritarian influences. Thus, African America regards Black Canadians in much the same way that America regards Canadians in general, that is, as kinder, gentler, but also as less interesting versions of themselves. Yet, as American historian Robin W. Winks notes, 'Canada did differ in profound ways from the United States; and consequently Canada's reception of the Negro, and the Negro's place in Canadian society, differed from the Negro's place in American society' (482). This knowledge accesses the articulation of a more-or-less recognizably African-Canadian ethos. Yet, Winks falls into an interpretative abyss when he urges that 'at each stage of his development, [the Canadian Negro] seemed to be perhaps a generation behind his American counterparts; and on the

whole he did not seem to have shown the cumulative pride, energy, enterprise, and courage that the catalog of individual acts of defiance would lead one to expect' (473). Winks's reading of African-Canadian history exhibits, purely, a small-*l* liberal, American bias. I would need an entire book to amend – one by one – his false precepts. He cannot appreciate the true import of being 'part of a border-crossings culture in which Canadian and American fact and feeling meet, contradict, or confirm each other in most complex and subtle ways' (1), to lift a phrase from Canadian poet Peter Sanger. Yet, African-Canadian 'progress' must be read against Canadian cultural norms, not American ones.

4 King even praised Canada for its role in helping to end McCarthyism in the United States: 'CBC Radio produced a satire of extraordinary brilliance on McCarthyism titled *The Investigator*, which was recorded and widely circulated in the United States with devastating effect' (25).

5 The first African-Canadian woman writer was likely Susana (Susannah) Smith, a U.S.-born ex-slave, who emigrated, with other Black Loyalists, to Nova Scotia in 1783, and then to Sierra Leone in 1792. Once there, she addressed a brief letter to the superintendent of the Sierra Leone colony, John Clarkson, requesting 'Sope' for her family. This humble document may be considered the first expression of African-Canadian literature. See my Introduction to *Eyeing the North Star: Directions in African-Canadian Literature* (xiv).

6 For instance, African-American novelist Richard Wright, who lived for two months in 1945 on Île d'Orléans, Québec (Dorsinville 9; Winks 462–3), espoused a Rousseauesque adoration of Québécois peasants. For him, this 'Catholic culture' practised 'a close, organic, intimate, mainly rural, way of life' (*White* 106). He felt that 'the Negro, like everybody else in America, came originally from a simple, organic way of life, such as I saw in French Quebec' (*White* 108).

7 Seers's solution for racism – the assimilation of African Americans via mass miscegenation – is itself racist. See my article 'Liberalism and Its Discontents: Reading Black and White in Contemporary Québécois Texts' (pp. 163–81, below).

8 In his 2000 essay '"Treason in the Fort": Blackness and Canadian Literature," Richard Almonte claims that Haliburton, in his 1836 sketch 'The White Nigger,' stages a 'condemnation of American slavery' (20). Almonte's misreading of Haliburton is instructive of a general Euro-Canadian tendency to associate slavery and segregation (and the practice of racism itself) only with the United States. Indeed, though Haliburton allows one character, the Squire, to attack American slavery, his true target is the then extant Nova Scotia custom of selling poor whites into servitude at annual auctions. Haliburton asserts that black slaves are better treated than poor whites. Thus, bleeding-heart abolitionists such as the Squire, who are quick to shed tears over the plight of U.S. slaves but who ignore the degradation of the poor whites of Nova Scotia, are just so many hypocrites. (See my article 'White Niggers, Black Slaves: Slavery, Race and Class in T.C. Haliburton's *The Clockmaker*' [1994], especially pages 34–5.) Almonte also charges that I fail to set 'Haliburton's portrayals [of black characters] ... in the larger context of early Canadian literature' (20). But he is guilty here of another misreading. In my article

'White Niggers, Black Slaves,' cited above, I mention Joseph-Octave Plessis, Joseph Howe, Lord Durham, and Samuel Ringgold Ward. In another article, 'Must We Burn Haliburton?' (1997), I refer to Durham, Ward, James Beaven, Thomas McCullough, John William Robertson, and Egerton Ryerson, as well as a complex of socio-political thought regarding 'race' in Haliburton's era.

9 Afua P. Cooper describes this reality succinctly: 'Canada had styled itself as a haven for the oppressed, those Blacks who had fled the United States because of slavery and virulent racism. But on coming to Canada, many Blacks found that the only difference between the new country and the old was that in the new country the law protected ex-fugitives from re-enslavement' (153). In Canada, blacks were free from slavery, but not from white racism. Thus, Susanna Moodie records the lynching of a black man, Tom Smith, who had dared to marry a white woman in Upper Canada (Ontario) in 'The Charivari' chapter in her memoir *Roughing It in the Bush* (1852). Generations later, Carol Talbot, in her memoir *Growing Up Black in Canada* (1984), judges that 'Canadian white people, born and bred in the imperialist, monarchical, colonial traditions of Europe, are masters at keeping the necessary distance to maintain the status quo. Meanwhile they [have] also learned ways to make themselves appear as benefactors' (21).

10 The fifth chapter of Harris's travelogue *cum* meditation on Southern African-American history announces his intention 'to have a peaceful, perfect time watching the whales in Nova Scotia' and eating 'fresh lobsters' (67). Presumably, he visited the province, for he says he was 'harassed and practically strip-searched by U.S. Customs on my return from Canada' (70). But he either did not encounter black people in Nova Scotia or, if he did, decided that their presence was accidental, or that they were also vacationing African Americans like himself.

11 How speedily Henderson has forgotten John F. Bayliss's 1973 comment that 'teachers, scholars, and students must strive for an internationalizing of Black Studies courses ... By internationalizing I mean, first, the dispassionate study of Black literature by all. Second, I mean *the study of Black literatures other than American* (especially African and West Indian writing in English and French) ...' (78, my italics). Too, as Rinaldo Walcott underlines, at least one Black Canadian, namely, Austin Clarke, played a role in the development of 'black studies programs and politics from the late 1960s to the 1970s at Yale, Brandeis, Duke and the University of Texas at Austin' (*Rude* 154n19).

12 Here Brown performs his own erasure of African-Canadian culture. For a critique of his position, see my Introduction, *Eyeing*, xx–xxi.

13 Winks thinks that 'the thoughtless, needless, and frustrated destruction of the twentieth century's symbol of quantification, the ultimate equality – Sir George Williams University's computer center' is a 'turning point' in African-Canadian history (478), that is to say, the end of an alleged era of passive suffering and the advent of a new one of witless aggression. But it is possible that the Sir George Williams incident served, along with the FLQ Crisis of October 1970, to spark the federal Government to promulgate, in October 1971, an affirmative policy of official multiculturalism. For black perspectives on the Sir George Williams

incident, see Dennis Forsythe, ed., *Let the Niggers Burn! The Sir George Williams University Affair and Its Caribbean Aftermath* (Montréal: Our Generation Press / Black Rose Books, 1971).

14 In his article 'Borrowed Blackness' (1995), Alexis suspects that, from a proprietary African-American vantage, 'black Canadians [are] not Black enough' (17).

15 Winks charges that 'in Canada Negroes continued to subscribe to Booker T. Washington's nonmilitant, essentially separatist, precepts long after W.E.B. DuBois had begun to move his fellow American Negroes toward militancy' (473). Winks fails, though, to consider that the African Baptist Association's proposal was, in 1912, *radical*, nor does he note that the same body, in 1920, circulated a sermon on race consciousness. Then again, 'revolution,' when it comes to Canada, loses its *r*.

16 For a full analysis of Borden's audacious revision of Hansberry, see my following article, 'Must All Blackness Be American? Locating Canada in Borden's "Tightrope Time," or Nationalizing Gilroy's *The Black Atlantic.*'

17 Elsewhere, Mandiela insists that 'there are five poets of all the hundreds of works which I've read which I can concretely connect with influencing my work, either through style, form or content. Of the five, two are women: [Jamaican Canadian] Miss Louise Bennett and [African American] Mari Evans.' See 'An Interview with Ahdri Zhina Mandiela: The True Rhythm of the Language,' in *The Other Woman: Women of Colour in Contemporary Canadian Literature* (1995), ed. Makeda Silvera (90). Despite Mandiela's omission of Shange from this list – an omission and a list that African-Canadian historian Afua Cooper misses in her discussion of the play (see Cooper 'Redemption' 441–4) – the African-American playwright must be named, for reasons I will clarify later in this essay.

18 Alexis's comment reveals a deep 'anxiety of influence' but also an utter allegiance to a monolithic 'Canadianness' that has no time for 'homeboys' and rap music, but should embrace 'cricket' and 'calypso,' though these aspects of Canadian culture are Caribbean in popularity, and so practised more in Ontario than in any other part of the country. Thus, their 'Pan-Canadianness' is just as questionable as that of 'homeboy' and rap music. Even the term *pogey* – a supposed marker of Canadianness – is not universally employed in Canada.

19 Both cultures even share significant personages: the slave liberator Harriet Tubman lived for eight years in Canada West. African-American writer Frances Ellen Harper, 'a Black U.S. abolitionist, visited Toronto, and Mary Ann Shadd Cary met with Harper during one of the former's lecture tours in the United States' (Bristow 126). William Wells Brown, 'an ardent abolitionist, ... undertook a tour of the Black settlements of Canada West' in 1861–2 (Cooper 169n72). The parents of Malcolm X – Earl Little and Louise Langdon Norton – met in Montréal in 1918 and were married there in 1919 (Carew, *Ghosts* x). Many African Canadians moved stateside to pursue their arts, including New Brunswick native and landscape painter Edward Mitchell Bannister (1828–1901), Ontario-born composer R. Nathaniel Dett (1882–1943), Canada West–born novelist Amelia Johnson (1858–1922), and Ontario-born actor Richard Harrison (1864–1935).

20 'If the Negro in Canada were to have any power, politically, economically, or socially, given his minor presence numerically,' Winks prescribes, 'he would have

had to unite with the far greater body of Negroes in the United States,' an act that Winks admits was not possible (481). Even so, African Canadians have adopted select African-American influences – from Garveyism to black Marxism – and *adapted* them to suit our own needs. Thus, Winks is wrong to charge that Black Canadians 'remained cut off from the broad Negro story unfolding on the continent' (481). No: *one* story unfolded in the United States; a different – but associated – one unfolded in Canada.

21 Though African Canadians may conceive of African America as a string of such adjectives, it would be a gross error to believe that African America may be *reduced* to any such monomaniacal description. As Keith Byerman says of African-American literature, 'if it has ever been possible to talk about African American fiction as a homogeneous, ideologically-based body of work, it certainly is not possible anymore' (1). African Americans are various, but share a variety of essentialist perspectives.

22 Du Bois's statement lays bare the abiding Americanness of African-American thought. Time has not withered its forceful truth. Writing almost a century after Du Bois, scholar Waldo Martin is certain that '[African-American] consciousness as a unique people evolved simultaneously with the notion that they, like whites or Caucasians, were not only a race, but inherently American as well. These two allegiances – to the Negro race and the American nation – have decisively shaped Black Consciousness in its various modes' (253), or, one should say, its various *American* moods. Martin's apparent indebtedness to Du Bois is inevitable given that '*The Souls of Black Folk* (1903) stands as the preeminent text of modern African American cultural consciousness' (McHenry 1173). Finally, he accepts Du Bois's own reckoning that African Americans constitute the 'advance guard of the Negro people' (quoted in Appiah, 'Pan-Africanism' 1485). Then there is the fascinating formulation of art critic Cedric Dover that 'American Negro' art is 'American art, but it is also Negro art. For Negroes are Americans – and Negroes' (15).

23 Paul Gilroy admits that British blackness, like its American cousin, depends upon a bifurcation of identity: 'Striving to be both European and black requires some specific forms of double consciousness' (1). To be African-Canadian is, however, to allow for an almost continuous splintering of identity.

24 The Africadian community in Nova Scotia may be an exception here. Its literary history has been so pronouncedly fostered by African Baptism that a Bakerian spirituality should animate its criticism. See my Introduction to *Fire on the Water: An Anthology of Black Nova Scotian Writing*, vol. 1, 11–29.

25 Adrienne Shadd also observes that, though her roots in Ontario extend back for six generations, she is asked, regularly, to identify her origins (10). Her skin colour marks her as an automatic 'immigrant,' Other, in Canada, a nation which likes to imagine itself as *white*, without ever having to be impolite enough to bluntly say so.

26 In a 1997 article, Alexis notes that 'in the black Canadian community ... it's pretty common these days to hear some version of the idea that black people, Africans as well as members of the "black Diaspora," have both a shared history of oppression at the hands of Europeans, and a shared consciousness based on that oppression; that there is a global African culture to which black people have access' ('Cross-

roads' 34). Alexis denounces such nationalist leanings. See also my Introduction, *Eyeing*, xix.

27 Philip is imperceiverant of the existence of early African-Canadian texts, from Mary Shadd's publication of 1852 to Pearleen Oliver's of 1953.

28 I am mindful of the diversity of cultures (especially urban/rural, Northern/ Southern, as well as immigrant/native) that exists within the African-American polity. Yet, Clyde Taylor's thought that, at the Million Man March of October 1995, he encountered 'a sweeping diversity within a core identity' ('One' 100) yields a capsule definition of *the* African-American sensibility.

29 But it also hampers projects to encourage black unity. Instructively, in March 1997, the effort of Québec's black leaders to form a caucus faced an immediate obstacle in terms of whether it would 'include the entire Black community or only the English' (*The Spectrum*, 'Caucus' 8). Foster notes that 'instead of having one voice, the Canadian black community has always relied on many voices speaking out on issues, sometimes some of them not even in harmony' (*Place* 57). The multiplicity of identities that defines African-Canadianité renders the invocation of a 'national' project a risky task. Characteristically, Winks puts the matter more negatively: 'The Canadian Negro ... [has been] divided, withdrawn, without a substantial body of shared historical experiences ...' (477). His prose is always only one step removed from propaganda.

30 Matthews presents his vivid thesis in this passage:

> No single institution imported from England and transplanted to Canadian soil survived the journey unchanged ... To a greater or lesser degree the country worked its own change upon them. The whole social histories of Canada and Australia are records of the introduction of outside influences and institutions, and of the adaptations that were wrought upon them to make them suitable to the new environment. (65)

Regardless of the fears of cultural nationalists and liberal cosmopolitans alike, a 'foreign' influence will always experience a transforming domestication in its new environment. For instance, rap music is an African-American invention, but it cannot sound the same in its Torontonian and Haligonian variations.

31 Such 'vernacularizations' will be tough to produce for African-Canadian literature, given the presence of multiple dialects – in English and French – among African Canadians. Ian Pringle's 1983 analysis of Canadian English is eminently applicable to African-Canadian discourses: 'For Canadian English doesn't really exist: it is still coming into existence. Or rather, there are an undetermined number of Canadian Englishes – and perhaps thousands of them' (119). Any Bakeresque, vernacularized theory produced for African Canadians will have to be polyphonous to be legitimate.

32 The comparable Hurston figure in Canada was, arguably, Arthur Huff Fauset. However, his account of Africadian folk culture almost dismisses its existence. For him, Black Canadians were bleached-out 'souls on ice.'

33 In *Modernism and the Harlem Renaissance* (1987), Baker finds that African-American 'discursive modernism' or, rather, *renaissancism* (his neologism), consists of 'the blending ... of class and mass – *poetic* mastery discovered as a function of deforma-tive *folk* sound ...' (93). Hence, African-American artistic achievement depends on

both 'mastery of form' and 'deformation of mastery' (50). African-American artistry demands both rigorous fidelity to the execution of 'master' forms (such as the sonnet), and, contrarily, the assertion of a devious deviance from European/ American forms/norms. Vengefully, Mandiela 'deforms' Shange, her African-American model.

34 Simon Njami emphasizes this point in his introduction to the 1997 *Revue Noire* issue on 'African Canada': 'La nationalité, l'identité [des artistes], s'aquéraient par la présence, l'occupation de sol. Ils étaient tous Canadiens, parce qu'ils vivaient tous au Canada. Mais qu'était dès lors le Canada, si ce n'est un assemblage hétéroclyte de gens autonomes qui chacun à sa manière, tentaient de recompenser les pièces éparpillées de leurs histoires?' ('Canada' 4). *Oui*, and this is perhaps the only useful definition: an African-Canadian artist is one who takes this identity for himself or herself (or one who has it imposed upon him or her by an interested scholar).

35 This must be done even where artists and writers deny any influence from Canadian society. Foster alleges that 'many' Black Canadian poets 'do not consider their writings to be part of a Canadian tradition that reveres a Margaret Atwood, Robertson Davies or Alice Munro. Rather, they lay claim to a proud tradition that produced international names like Derek Walcott and Bob Marley ...' (*Place* 117). Still, these writers also engage with Canadian dialects, media, and political and educational systems, all of which *must* also colour their voices and their ideas. For the record, then, Alexis has expressed a debt to both Atwood and Davies ('Borrowed' 20), while Allen favours Nichol and Atwood (quoted in Dawes, '360 Degrees' 89, 90). Because of the imbrication of African-Canadian intellectuals with *generic* Canadian concepts and precepts, one cannot credit David Sealy's thought that 'notions of Blackness' in Canada are only 'directly connected to the history of race talk and radicalized discourse in Canada' and *not* also 'constructions of the so-called "French-English problem," "regional problems," "multy-culty" discourse, "the vertical mosaic" or "the just society"' ('Canadianizing' 97). For a further discussion of this point, see my article 'Treason of the Black Intellectuals?' (pp. 182–210, below).

36 It must be said, though, that a different tradition *already* exists – and has existed – since the origins of the community.

37 See note 33, above.

38 Because African America is a privileged *Other* for African Canada, African-Canadian writers must create their identity out of partial strife with it. They must answer to the injunction that Chandler formulates: 'no identity can acquire its coherence without [a] constitutive detour through the other' ('Figure' 259).

39 The 'slave narrative' is actually the first Pan-African literary form. It is not solely a relic of U.S. slavery. Considering *only* English texts, there are West Indian, migratory 'Black Loyalist,' and Afro-British types. (See, for instance, *The History of Mary Prince: A West Indian Slave, Related by Herself*, published in London and Edinburgh in 1831, which narrates the author's enslavement in the West Indies and her escape to freedom in England in 1828.) Furthermore, in British North America and in Nouvelle-France, those twin early forms of Canada, the slave narrative 'inhabits' legal documents such as the defence statement of Marie-Josèphe Angélique, who

was executed for arson in Montréal in 1734. Her recorded testimony is a *de facto* slave autobiography. (See Marcel Trudel, *L'Ésclavage au Canada français* [Montréal: Les Éditions de l'horizon, 1960], 92–5.) Arguably, then, slave narratives are not absent from Canadian literature; rather, their presence goes undetected because they assume an un-American *form*. To extend my refutation of Almonte, I note that Smallwood's *Narrative* was *not* 'the only ex-slave narrative to be written and published in Canada' (Almonte, *Narrative*, back cover). Other examples include that of John William Robertson, who issued his *The Book of the Bible against Slavery* in Halifax, Nova Scotia, in 1854, while Jim Henson had his story chronicled by John Frost Jr (writing under the pseudonym of Glenelg) in 1888 and published in Toronto in 1889 as *Broken Shackles*. William H.H. Johnson of Vancouver, B.C., published his narrative, *The Life of Wm. H.H. Johnson: From 1839–1900, and The New Race*, also known as *The Horrors of Slavery*, in 1904.

40 In his 2000 article '"Who is she and what is she to you?": Mary Ann Shadd Cary and the (Im)possibility of Black/Canadian Studies,' Rinaldo Walcott arrives at 'one conclusion' that 'we need Mary Ann Shadd [Cary], now more than ever' (30), and then states it thrice more (39, 45, 46) – as if iteration nullifies argument. When he does venture a reason for Shadd's relevance as a primary black (Canadian) woman intellectual, he cites her 'self-assured Black Canadian presence' (39), which is fine, but it nixes his idea that she sits 'in-between' Canada and the United States (33). Though Walcott muses hesitantly on Shadd's 1852 publication, *A Plea for Emigration; or, Notes of Canada West*, he misses her espousal of a black nationalism – or Pan-Africanism – that flouts the notion that Shadd 'spoke and acted from political conviction, desire and commitment – not from nationalistic yearning or desire' (45).

Must All Blackness Be American?
Locating Canada in Borden's 'Tightrope Time,' or Nationalizing Gilroy's The Black Atlantic

For Blair Arnold States (1959–2001)[1]

Preface

As I suggested in 'Contesting a Model Blackness,' a primary ontological co-nundrum to confront the analyst of African-Canadian literature is as obvious as it is invidious: How Canadian is it? The question is insidious, but it cannot be peremptorily dismissed, for the literature is awash in African-American and Caribbean influences. These 'presences' are so palpable, so pervasive, that the literature may seldom seem 'Canadian' (whatever that means) at all. This essay explores, then, the supposed alterity of African-Canadian literature, given its bold-faced absorption of African-American literary modes and models. Yet, it also scrutinizes the manner in which one specific writer, Walter M. Borden, produces *African-Canadianité* within his text, chiefly, by revising an African-American mentor. I conclude by reading Paul Gilroy's thesis, *The Black Atlantic: Modernity and Double Consciousness* (1993), in the light of Borden's post-colonial practice, to examine the points where Gilroy's pronounced anti-nationalism fails to be practicable.

I

Until the onset of major black immigration from the Caribbean Basin in the mid-1950s, European Canadians imagined African Canadians as once-and-always Americans. In a 1956 magazine article, Edna Staebler ventures that some Black Nova Scotians 'had a broad Southern accent' (quoted in Dillard, 'History' 517), even though the last considerable migration of African Americans to Nova Scotia occurred during the War of 1812. Two generations later, the U.S.-born, Canadian literary scholar Leslie Sanders charges that 'the Canadian literary and media establishment ... too often chooses to read race through the American situation ...' (2). If Canadians have viewed blacks as misplaced Americans, African Americans have tended to annex African Canadians within their dominant cultural matrix. Thus, in his biography of the great African-American intellectual W.E.B. Du Bois, historian David Levering Lewis asserts, with admirable aplomb, that Du Bois's Cambridge, Massachusetts, landlords, John and Mary Taylor, were 'African-Americans originally from Nova Scotia' (84). African-American film historian Donald Bogle remarks that Oscar Micheaux's silent feature *The Brute* (1920) 'featured boxer Sam Langford' (xvii), but Bogle overlooks Langford's Nova Scotian nativity. The Canadian backgrounds of painters Robert Duncanson and Edward M. Bannister are granted in Cedric Dover's *American Negro Art* (1960), but they remain strictly 'American Negroes' (25, 27, 11). The erasures continue. The 1996 Filmakers Library catalogue lists Africadian Sylvia Hamilton's National Film Board of Canada documentary *Speak It! From the Heart of Black Nova Scotia* (1993) under the rubric 'African-American Studies' (2). At other times, African Americans reject African Canadians as representing some aberrant version of *blackness*. Thus, U.S. historian Robin Winks tells us that 'Reverend Wilton R. Boone, who came from Massachusetts, returned there because he found the customs of the country [African Baptist Nova Scotia] too different to accept' (346).

These bold denials of what I term *African-Canadianité* illuminate the dynamic dilemma of African-Canadian culture. Euro-Canadian critics often consider it as *Other*, while African-American (and Caribbean) critics read it – unabashedly – as a bastard version of their own. To complicate matters further, African Canadians often utilize African-American texts and historical-cultural icons to define African-Canadian experience (which can seduce the unwary into believing that no uniquely African-Canadian perspective exists).[2] Examples are legion. In the pages of the *Atlantic Advocate*, a black community newspaper issued in Halifax, Nova Scotia, between 1915 and 1917, one finds the poetry of African-American writer Paul Laurence Dunbar juxtaposed with surveys of race progress in the United States. In October 1968, Stokeley Carmichael (Kwame Turé), the charismatic Black Power orator, toured Halifax, unnerving whites and inspiring blacks to adopt militant stances, a process intensified by the visit, the following month, of two members of the radical, U.S.-based Black Panther Party.[3] Spectacularly, in Toronto, in May 1992, black youths rioted in sympathy with those who had taken to the streets in Los Angeles. Awad El Karim M. Ibrahim reports, in his 2000 sociological study '"Hey, ain't I Black too?": The Politics of Becoming Black,' that 'a group of continental *francophone African* youths, living in a metropolitan city in southwestern Ontario' (111, my italics), in the latter 1990s, demonstrated 'an *identification* with and a *desire* for North American Blackness' (111, his italics). Remarkably, the youths articulate a *specific* interest in *African-American* cultural styles. One stresses that 'Black Canadian youths are influenced by the *Afro-Americans*' because of popular culture (124); another announces, bluntly, 'We identify ourselves more with the Blacks of America' (125).

Too, most African-Canadian writers, whether native-born or immigrant, eye African-American culture with envy and desire. Novelist Cecil Foster, a Barbados native, defends the attractiveness of African-American culture for African Canadians, stressing that, if Black Canadian artists have developed African-American sensibilities in place of a strong Canadian consciousness, well, *c'est la vie*:

Also, I do not have any problem whatsoever in laying claim to black icons from any place in the world. I feel they are all common property and we can use them ... Should I disown a Martin Luther King or a Malcolm X? Other cultures don't. English writers – even those who are living here in Canada – can deal with Chaucer and the pre-Chaucerian writers, and Shakespeare. ('Long' 21)

Rejecting interviewer Donna Nurse's argument that 'African-American culture fails to reflect accurately the black Canadian experience,' Foster insists that 'the reality for many blacks in Canada may be closer to what they see in the streets of New York or Los Angeles than what many people assume as being their reality' ('Long' 21). Given the gravitational attractiveness of Black America and the repellent force of frequently racist Anglo-Canadian (and Québécois *de souche*) nationalisms, African-Canadian writers feel themselves caught between the Scylla of an essentially U.S.-tinctured cultural nationalism and the Charybdis of their marginalization within Canadian cultural discourses that perceive them as 'alien.'[4] Hence, African-Canadian writers are forced to question the extent and relevance of their Canadianness (that notoriously inexpressible quality).

Yet, African Canadians cannot avoid assimilating African-American influences, for both African Canada and African America were forged in the crucible of the slave trade, an enterprise the British aided, abetted, and affirmed, then suppressed, then finally abolished in 1833. Before the American Revolution, New World Africans – both slaves and freeborn – were probably traded (or migrated) up and down the Atlantic coast, given the existence of New World African English in both the American South and Nova Scotia.[5] Linguist J.L. Dillard confirms that 'the literary evidence ... provides a clear picture of a continuum of eighteenth, nineteenth, and twentieth century Black English from the American South to Nova Scotia, with no great break in such places as New York City, Boston and Connecticut ...' ('History' 517).[6] Thus, both African Canada and African America originated in the working out of the global fate of the British Empire; both arose (with the exception of communities situated in Hispanic and francophone locales) in a colonial, English milieu.[7]

Certainly, anglophone African Canada can trace its origins to the arrival, following the American Revolution, of roughly 3,400 African Americans (or 'Anglo-Africans,' to use the nineteenth-century term). These Black Loyalists opposed the Revolution, supported Britain, and, in the aftermath of the republican victory, were accorded refuge in Nova Scotia and New Brunswick. Significantly, those who did not come as the chattel of white Loyalists, but as free persons – the majority – did so because they rejected a Revolution waged to secure a theoretically egalitarian society which still promised to oppress people of African (and First Nations) ancestry. Another 2,000 African Americans were settled in Maritime Canada following the War of 1812, while tens of thousands of others found asylum in Montréal, southern Ontario, and even Saltspring Island, British Columbia, in the years between the passage of the Fugitive Slave Law (1850) and the end of the American Civil War (1865). African Canada was created, then, by the struggle to extinguish slavery – both in British North

America (where it had 'withered away' by the early 1800s, while still remain-ing legal) and the United States – and to secure a free 'homeland' for blacks. It is, then, a kind of inchoate, New World version of Liberia, the African 'Canaan' or 'free state' organized by anti-slavery African Americans.

Too, African Canada and African America share a history of marginality that has impinged on the constructions of their literatures. Both entities resist the fugues of racial erasure indulged in by mainstream Canadian and Ameri-can critics. African-American *and* African-Canadian writers create 'texts that are double-voiced in the sense that their literary antecedents are both white and black [texts], but also modes of figuration lifted from the black vernacular tradition' (Gates, *Signifying* xxiii). For both *états* – African Canada and African America – the development of usable identities, in the face of strong, countervailing, imperial(ist) influences, has driven their histories. Close read-ings of African-Canadian literature can spotlight, moreover, the manner in which post-colonial theory can be applied to ever-smaller units of 'mass' iden-tity. For one thing, ethnic texts are, writes Joseph Pivato, 'on the periphery of this North American margin,' Canada, which 'is itself marginal' from 'the perspective of the literary traditions of Europe ...' (*Echo* 44). Hence, as Canada seeks to establish its difference from the United States, so does Québec con-front English Canada, and so do, in turn, Haïtian emigrés challenge the domi-nant Québécois culture.

II

This constant regression of post-colonial politics, its shrinkage about each par-ticularity, also governs the construction of African-Canadian literature. This point is underlined by a contemporary Africadian drama, 'Tightrope Time: Ain't Nuthin' More Than Some Itty Bitty Madness between Twilight and Dawn' (1986), by Walter M. Borden (b. 1942), an Africadian poet and actor of African-American descent. Borden proves himself to be a deft, post-colonial exploiter of the 'parent' culture of African America, one who engenders a Canadian *différence* (that race-conflicted, native sensibility), even while he confiscates significant African-American intertexts. In Borden, one finds, as does Margery Fee in her analysis of Australian/Aboriginal literary duality, 'the use of repeti-tion to effect a reversal ... [T]hrough signifying, power relations are changed through the signifier's clever (mis)use of someone else's words' (18–19). Borden pursues a tradition in which Canadian writers strive 'to forge new meanings out of foreign links and foreign chains' (Trehearne 320).

A truly one-man show, 'Tightrope Time' was selected to represent Canada at the International Multicultural Festival in Amsterdam in 1987. Composed of two acts (of fourteen and nine scenes respectively), the drama's printed text of 1986 includes a dozen photographs of Borden playing each of the drama's twelve characters. (In order of appearance, they are the Host, the Old Man, the Minister of Justice, the Minister of Health and Welfare, the Child, the Old Woman, the Pastor, the Minister of Defence, the Minister of the Interior, Adie,

Ethiopia [a 'drag queen'], and Chuck.) 'Tightrope Time' does not stage a single protagonist, but rather a *bizarrerie* of speakers delivering a pot-pourri of monologues, blending song, poetry, and prose. This *bigarré* semi-musical, blending Jacques Brel *chansons*, African-American spirituals and blues, Top 40 pop (circa 1978), and other music, is unified, though, by recurrent discussions of identity and consciousness. These overarching interests are broached and buttressed by felicitously utilized, African-American interpolations.

Principally, Borden sounds the work of celebrated playwright Lorraine Hansberry (1931–65), both directly and indirectly. Hansberry's best-known work, *A Raisin in the Sun* (1959), treats the desire of the Younger family to escape the claustrophobic poverty of their apartment, where *'the sole natural light the family may enjoy in the course of a day is only that which fights its way through [a] little window'* (12, her italics). Borden bypasses this limited setting to explore, instead, 'the mansions of my mind' (13). Hansberry regards the move from a blighted apartment to a hitherto segregated suburban neighbourhood as illustrative of the progressive amelioration of the Youngers' and, allegorically, the African-American, condition. Borden evades such plain social realism, however, opting instead for intellectual abstractions. His difference is enunciated at once. *A Raisin in the Sun* opens with the preparation of a breakfast of fried eggs, but 'Tightrope Time' debuts with the Host's *recollection* of a like breakfast as he launches into a philosophical revery. Borden's first, indirect allusion to Hansberry's work stresses, then, not the nobility-versus-indignity it privileges, but rather the casualness of causality:

Born on some forgotten *FRY*day,
That's *FRY*day with a '*y*,'
Not *FRI*day with an '*i*,'
At half past discontent,
Mama sat down on life's sidewalk,
Spread her legs
And pushed one ain't-no-problem time;
And spewed me there
Where *MAYBE-YOU-WILL-CHILE BOULEVARD*
Cuts across *MAYBE-YOU-WON'T CHILE AVENUE*,
And Indifference sauntered by
To serve as midwife,
To wrap me in my soul and say:
You are Nature's love-chile –
And Freedom is your father. (14)

Borden's speaker is disengaged from active, socio-political struggle; rather, he emphasizes, in an almost neo-Neo-Platonist manner, the 'many mansions / in the complex of my mind' (13). The gallery of speakers in 'Tightrope Time' depicts a multiply divided consciousness. The function of the Host is, in fact, to provide the cranial space – a cabinet of Dr Borden, if one likes – in which the motley'd monologuers can assemble. If Hansberry promotes laudable black bourgeois aspiration, Borden expresses a kind of quixotic black psychoanalysis. If Hansberry may be related to the liberal 'uplift' slogans of the early twentieth-century African-American leader Booker T. Washington, Borden seems closer to the existentialist *cum* Freudian stance of Frantz Fanon.

Borden imports Hansberry directly into his work in 1.2, where he rechristens the 'Hermit' – a character from an early draft of *Raisin*[8] – as the 'Old Man.' Save for this single – and signal – alteration, Borden reprints Hansberry's speech for the 'Hermit' with uncompromised fidelity: 'And so, to escape time, I threw my watch away. I even made a ceremony of it. I was on a train over a bridge ... and I held it out the door and dropped it' (Borden 16; Hansberry, *Be* 3). The arty speech that Hansberry omitted from her most successful play is precisely (or perversely) the one that Borden feels compelled to use in his own.[9] Tellingly, rather than appropriating a discourse from the finished, realist version of *Raisin*, Borden cribs Hansberry's more philosophical musing on time. Even as he honours Hansberry, Borden dissents from her dramaturgy, scribing a metaphysical stance to her more physical focus on place and race.

Yet, Borden's predilection for ideas over ideals manifests his *Canadian* sensibility, for Canadian poets have often mingled the 'Aesthetic' with 'committed and realistic poetry' (Trehearne 314). The result is what Québécois literary scholar Clément Moisan calls 'strange and esoteric poetry' (30), and what Anglo-Québécois critic Louis Dudek names as 'poetry ... almost surrealist in its contortions, and well-nigh private in its subjectivity' (161). Indeed, 'its metaphysical searchings and symbolic profundities cannot hope for a contact with ... "the common reader"' (Dudek 161). For Norman Newton, Canadian poetry stresses 'a fondness for ornate and colourful language' (8). Anglo-Canadian poetry tends to exalt the absurd and the abstract – even when the poets themselves believe they are being plain and down-to-earth. In Anglo-Canadian poetry, the 'vernacular' is interpreted by professors of literature. Accordingly, Borden's verse, though accessible, ransacks the Byzantine lexicon of Beat cant as often as it does that of black populist directness: 'let emptiness come sneak into my solitude / & ravage all my dreams / & bittersweet rememberings of yesterday / when all my thoughts were young as innocence itself / & love & understanding flowed from me like *MAN-AH* was completely in control' (62). Suitably then, Borden opts to read Hansberry in academicist terms.[10] He closes his use of her Hermit (his Old Man), then, by calling for the playing of a song, 'The Old Folk,' recorded by Brel, accompanied by the sound of a clock ticking '*in syncopation with the music*' (16, his italics). These absurdist touches are Borden's invention. Hence, 'Tightrope Time' enacts a revisioning of Hansberry's *Raisin*, dismissing her 'realism' and ghetto setting to dramatize, instead, the unreal 'inscape' of identity.

Borden's adoption of Hansberry's Hermit hints, too, that 'Tightrope Time' is only tangentially about 'race'; or, rather, that it avoids dissecting 'race' in any stock sociological-empirical fashion. For instance, the Old Man's pentultimate speech in 1.2 turns, not on explicit concerns about 'race' or racism, but, instead, on one concrete and two abstract nouns – *piece(s)*, *time*, and *value* – a trinity of tropes that presides over the play: 'I am afraid men invent time*PIECES* [time*pieces*]; they do not invent time. We may give time its dimensions and meaning;[,] we may make it worthless or important or absurd or crucial. But,[ ] ultimately,[ ] I am afraid it has a value of its own' (Borden 16; Hansberry, *Be* 4). Borden absorbs Hansberry's academic musings and terms, detecting in them corollaries for his interests. This fact is clarified by his use of the word(s) *piece(s)*. Though the term occurs in contexts that can allude to Hansberry, they are wholly Borden's own. In 1.4, the Minister of Health and Welfare relates that his dream 'dried up, just like that raisin in the sun' (24), a clear reference to Hansberry as well as to African-American poet Langston Hughes (1902– 67);[11] then the Minister continues on to assert that 'painful thoughts rummage through / the few last pieces of my heart' (24) and that he seeks 'bits and pieces of love / that I have known' (25). Borden shifts from the specific concerns of both Hansberry and Hughes to anatomize alienation. In fact, the African Americans are sounded only after the Minister declares that 'this celebration is not so much an historical documentation of the quest of a people for a place in the Nova Scotian or indeed the Canadian mosaic, as it is an illumination of the resiliency of the human spirit' (22). An abstract universalism takes precedence, thus, over African-American utterance – even though, paradoxically, Hansberry herself is the source of the notion of 'the resiliency of ... this thing called the human spirit' (Borden 80; Hansberry, *Be* 256). This pattern recurs in 1.4, where Hansberry is again directly quoted. This time, Borden seizes a passage from Hansberry's *The Sign in Sidney Brustein's Window* (1964), uttered by Brustein, a white ex-fighter for social justice, who feels compelled to re-enter the fray:

> I care. I care about it all. It takes too much energy *not* to care. Yesterday, I counted twenty-six gray hairs on the top of my head all from trying *not* to care ... The *why* of why we are here is an intrigue for adolescents; the *how* is what must command the living. Which is why I have lately become an insurgent again. (Borden 25; Hansberry, *Be* xvi)

Just as Hansberry's Brustein continues to struggle for social liberation, so does Borden's Minister of Health and Welfare, this Canadian liberal, decide to shore pieces – of love, of heart – against his potential ruin. Borden's transference of words written for a Euro-American character to the mouth of a Black Canadian, is, once again, a universalist gesture. His audacious reconfiguration of Hansberry's words accents their innate universality. Racial identities are collapsed within his enveloping view that 'the human spirit has no special resting place. It will find a lodging wherever it is received' (22). Thus, Borden dislodges Hansberry from an easy essentialism or empty liberalism, choosing to use her words to gird his interest in the 'mansions of the mind,' that is to say, the multiple addresses where 'the human spirit' may dwell.

Toward the conclusion of the play, Borden utilizes the term *pieces* one last time, citing Hansberry's rhetorical question '*Life?*' and her reply, 'Ask those who have tasted of it in pieces rationed out by enemies' (Borden 80; Hansberry,

Be 256; their italics). Ironically, 'Tightrope Time' is itself just such a *piece* of theatre, just such a *'PIECE OF RESISTANCE'* (62, his italics), to use an epithet that Borden ascribes to Ethiopia, his transvestite character, for it flouts both racism and homophobia.

This last point necessitates a brief examination of Borden's use of *value*, another term that he teases from Hansberry, his putative precursor. His assault on prejudice is predicated upon its reduction of the worth of human beings. When Borden utilizes (with slight amendments) Hansberry's comment that time 'has a value of its own' (Borden 16; Hansberry, *Be* 4), he lets it follow the Host's act of satiric self-evaluation:

> I read the other day
> That, on the open market,
> I'm worth about five ninety,
> Allowing for inflation.
> But that's alright –
> I'd hate to think
> That I was priced beyond accessibility. (13)

To Hansberry's insight that time possesses its own value, independent of socially imposed, ideological criteria, Borden adds the body. He goes on to besiege racial (and, thus, physical) devaluations throughout his play:

> A second glance, however,
> Reveals a flaw in pigmentation,
> So, regretfully, you must look for me
> in the *reduced for clearance* section. (13)

In 1.7, the Host recalls a childhood incident in which his mixed-race heritage resulted in his receiving a 'high' – but unsought and racially inflected – e/ valuation:

> i knew that there was something wrong
> the day i watched my living room become
> an auction block
> [and a visitor]
>   ... called my blue eyes,
>   honey hair and
>   mellow/yellow presence
> *A WONDERMENT*! (30, his italics)

Throughout 'Tightrope Time,' Borden juxtaposes 'face' value and 'soul value,' specifying that the oppressed are those 'who have no place / the ones who have no face' (32), whose value, then, is little. They are *'CHEAP GOODS'* (34, his italics) to be bought up by Death. In 1.10, the Host remembers an Old Woman who spent her days *'puttin the pieces together'* of a patchwork quilt (36, his italics), and whose speech reiterates the connections between time and value. The Old Woman notes that *'the young folks'* are *'wastin' all that precious time / at tryin' to be what other folkses want'* (38, his italics). The loss of time, of life, is affiliated with trying to live according to false notions of one's worth. The Minister of the Interior, in 1.14, restores value, lustre, to *blackness* by producing a roster of worthies whom, he alleges, have been wrongly claimed to be white, including Queen Charlotte Sophia (the spouse of King George III), the Queen of Sheba, Ludwig von Beethoven, and Charles XIV of Sweden, to name but a few (55–6). Poetically, Borden 'borrows back' these 'credits to the race.'

Not only does Borden rescue the devalued black body, he also redeems that of the homosexual. If act 1 centres – albeit usually obliquely – on 'race,' act 2 considers sexuality – the repressed side of black self-consciousness. Here Borden revalues, in order, Adie, a female prostitute; Ethiopia, a Queer transvestite; and Chuck, a hustler. Ethiopia disparages hypocritical, bourgeois sexual mores, declaiming, *'& HAPPY DAYS / unsanitized for early primetime viewing / meant more than suckin' lollipops out back behind some diner / but no one really thought that we was fuckin' up / TRADITION / cuz / no one saw / no decrease in / the surplus population'* (62, his italics). Chuck augments the currency of his Queer body by coupling coitus with money:

I don't fuck for I.O.U.'s
   for Master Charge
   or Visa
Just hard old cash ... (66)

In a sense, here, Borden conducts a radical raid on Hansberry, for he drafts her voice, that is to say, her insight into *value*, for a liberatory movement for which it was not, perhaps, primordially intended.

The most ostentatious broadside against devaluation in act 2 speaks, though, to 'race.' At the conclusion of 2.7, a 'tired and beaten' black mother, whose innocent son has been slain by a paranoid white man,

Slowly turn[s] the pages
Of some book,
And look[s] at all the faces
Of those selected few
Thought worthy of being voted
As the Mother of the Year ...
Worthy
Because of all her suffering...

And she tently [*sic*] [takes] a pencil
And mark[s] the letter X
Beside the picture of
Rose Kennedy! (77)

The passage is a damning indictment of self-devaluation – the manner in which oppression replicates itself.

While Hansberry becomes a useful means of debuting the motifs of fragmentation (*piece*[*s*]), time, and value, Borden domesticates or nationalizes her work, wresting it from its African-American context and recasting it in Canadian terms. For instance, he transforms her sentence 'O, the things that we have learned in this unkind house that we have to tell the world about' (Borden 79; Hansberry, *Be* 256) from a commission to young African-American writers to tell of the African-American experience into a commission to *all* to practise humane behaviour. Specifically, he translates her metaphor for a racist America, that 'unkind house,' into a metaphor for the 'cage' that is the self-imprisoned consciousness (Borden 79). The resistance valued by Borden is not achieved merely by denouncing social ills, but also by refusing any facile quotation of Hansberry. He changes the name of one of her characters, alters, by proxy, the race of another, and quarantines her more abstract, less social realist, work. By recontextualizing her work to suit his own needs, Borden renders Hansberry a 'Canadian' writer.

III

Borden's reforms of Hansberry, his major African-American influence, must be read in the context of an intra-racial post-coloniality. Certainly, his emphasis on 'piecing together' his patchwork drama reinforces Paul Gilroy's notion that 'even where African-American forms are borrowed and set to work in new locations they have often been deliberately reconstructed in novel patterns that do not respect their originators' proprietary claims ...' (98). Moreover, Borden's post-coloniality, *vis-à-vis* African-American texts, pushes him to adopt a contestatory stance, for this is the condition of the ex-centric writer. No matter how deep lies the commitment to imitate the 'parent' culture, any 'imitation' must always be different – and critical – because of its temporal lateness, its automatic status as 'post.' Max Dorsinville maintains that all emerging literatures suffer a similar condition of lateness. Yet, his notion that postcolonial writers are merely 'indigenous writers hypnotized by the cult of metropolitan "models"' (*Caliban* 201) is contestable. The standard practice of these writers – which Borden's (mis)use of Hansberry illustrates – is to revise original influences or intertexts. (Cogent here is Trehearne's proviso that 'Influence' can be a 'dependence' 'avidly sought, a life-giving transfusion of order and authority when no such order [is] provided by the [native] environment, or by the present means of mastering it' [8].) In other words, Borden does not – and cannot – read Hansberry in the same way as would an African American. His acts of quotation represent not, then, abject capitulation to metropolitan forces (Halifax succumbing – finally – to New York City), but (im)polite subversion; his 'lateness' is a marginal position that permits radical reinterpretation of the 'original' source. Eyed from this perspective, the margin is a timedevoid centre in which literary forms and movements coexist in democratic chaos; it becomes a location where the neoclassical can jar against the surreal, the sonnet clang against the haiku, and dead authors possess the living. Thus, Borden's text can be read as exemplifying the ability of temporally 'late' Canadian writers to adapt a variety of European and American forms and influences to their unique contexts – of environment, history, and language, including different forms of English. 'Tightrope Time' testifies to such hybridity or *bricolage*. This peripherally situated text becomes a homeplace where African-American literature – in its northern, existentialist exile – is assimilated, domesticated, into a Canadian context. Borden's relationship to Hansberry affirms, too, Harold Bloom's thesis regarding, as Stephen Sicari puts it, 'an Oedipal struggle between a great precursor poet and his follower' (38). If 'the later poet looks for (and discovers) places where the precursor fails to communicate to a [contemporary] reader ... and requires "updating" by the [contemporary] poet' (Sicari 221n6), then Borden amends Hansberry similarly, translating her (African-)American obsessions into (African-)Canadian ones. He observes, wryly, that 'Black folks always seem to get those / Hand-me-down revisions!' (72). Borden's rewriting of Hansberry demands a theory of post-colonial 'placement' and 'displacement,' one which recognizes that the supposed recipient of meaning (the 'colonial') can instead become its bestower (the resister, the newly subjectivized).

Gilroy himself needs to tussle more muscularly with this imperial-colonial dialectic. He argues that texts like that of Borden represent the 'unashamedly hybrid character ... of black Atlantic cultures,' which thus confound 'any simplistic (essentialist or anti-essentialist) understanding of the relationship between racial identity and racial non-identity' (99). He forgets, though, that cultural nationalism never entirely evaporates, even when techniques of 'creolisation, métissage, mestizaje, and hybridity' (3) are in play, as in Borden. *Au contraire*, it is exactly the use of forms of *bricolage* that allows new understandings of the native (or post-colonial) culture to be articulated. When Borden reads Hansberry (and Hughes and James Weldon Johnson)[12] into his own Canadian text, his *Africadianité* is not reified but reinforced.

Borden's practice serves to highlight, then, a few of the *a priori* aporias in Gilroy's vaunted text, *The Black Atlantic* (1993), which undertakes, like 'Tightrope Time,' to dissent from 'Americocentricity' (Gilroy 191). The notion that authentic *blackness* – or *Africanité* – is implicated, ontologically and epistemologically, with some subtle sense of 100 per cent Americanism challenges all other would-be national(ist) versions of *blackness*. Gilroy attempts to dismantle the 'U.S. first' conception of 'blackness' by constructing a 'transcultural, international formation [called] the black Atlantic' (4), which consists of African communities in the United States, the Caribbean, Britain, and Africa. While Gilroy omits Canada (this gap in his map replicates a suspiciously 'Americocentric' blindness), his 'Pan-Atlanticism' is intended as a panacea for the 'ever-present danger' of 'ethnic absolutism' (5), or larval nationalism, especially 'the easy claims of African-American exceptionalism' (4). Yet, Gilroy's project is fraught with contradiction. His very formulation, 'the black Atlantic,' resurrects a Pan-Africanism that almost dare not speak its name. As well, his decentring of African-American culture is intended to shift attention to the Caribbean-British contributions to Pan-African culture. Fundamentally, then, Gilroy, like Borden, poses this question: Must all blackness be American? But Gilroy's attempt to naysay this interrogative, while simultaneously vetoing cultural nationalism, scores his project with irrepressible self-negations.

Blatantly, Gilroy ups old-fashioned nationalism when he announces that 'the dependence of blacks in Britain on black cultures produced in the new world has recently begun to change' (86). He relishes 'the current popularity of [pop music acts] Jazzie B and Soul II Soul, Maxi Priest, Caron Wheeler, Monie Love, the Young Disciples, and others in the United States' because it confirms that during the 1980s 'black British cultures ceased to simply mimic or reproduce wholesale forms, styles, and genres which had been lovingly borrowed, respectfully stolen, or brazenly highjacked [sic] from blacks elsewhere' (86). This inchoately neo-nativist pronouncement denies the truth that, as Borden's work demonstrates, utterances of 'un-American' *blackness* often represent deliberate 'deformations' or reformulations of African-American cultural productions (which Gilroy admits when he treats the 'hybridity' of black Atlantic cultures).[13]

In addition, Gilroy's effort to dispense with African-American parochialism is complicated by his decision to focus his analyses on African-American writers and intellectuals, namely, Frederick Douglass, Martin Robinson Delany (who may also be classified as African-Canadian), Du Bois, Richard Wright, James Baldwin, and Toni Morrison. Though Gilroy essays, valiantly, to set these figures in a Pan-Atlantic context, he nevertheless succumbs to ideas that, once again, Americanize blackness. For example, Gilroy lauds Richard Wright's insight that 'the word Negro in America means something not racial or biological, but something *purely social*, something made in the United States' (quoted in Gilroy 149, his italics), seeing in it an 'anti-essentialist conception of racial identity' (149). But if the Negro is, as Wright thought, 'America's metaphor' (quoted in Gilroy 149), then is not all *blackness* (i.e., *négritude*) deemed American? If so, then (an American) essentialism lives. Gilroy even urges that 'in Wright's mature position, the Negro is no longer just America's metaphor but rather a central symbol in the psychological, cultural, and political systems of the West as a whole' (159). An American conception of *blackness* is made to dominate the entire Occident, thus situating U.S. definitions at the centre of diasporic African experience, the very fate that Gilroy had sallied forth to avoid. The only possible counterweight to this *de facto* dictatorship of influence is precisely the cultural nationalism that Gilroy, haphazardly and haplessly, both disparages and embraces, but that Borden, quietly, consistently – 'Canadianly' – employs.

Despite the blithe assurance of some liberal theorists that the post-national Brave New World Order has arrived, Gilroy's infuriatingly mercurial struggle to displace 'Americocentrism' with his dream of 'the black Atlantic' demonstrates that nationalism persists. For one thing, as Elizabeth Alexander sees, 'there is a place for a bottom line, and the bottom line ... argues that different groups possess sometimes subconscious collective memories which are frequently forged and maintained through a "storytelling tradition," however difficult that may be to pin down, as well as through individual experience' (94). Though the scholarly voodoo of the notion of 'collective memories' is regrettable, Alexander reveals a strong reason for the continued vibrancy of 'tradition,' of group identities, namely, the primacy of shared (narrative) experience as the locus of 'national' feeling. Pivato concurs with this precept, urging 'the history of this century demonstrates that a distinctive culture is vital to the life of a people; it survives beyond language, beyond geography and beyond political states' (*Echo* 252). What one must seek is the lyricism of cultural difference, not the mere prose of cultural diversity.[14] Consequently, the canon of 'African-Canadian literature' emerges when a writer or a critic declares his or her membership in that tradition. Such new canons are also created, though, through acts of resistive appropriation – the mandatory practice of Borden, the muddled practice of Gilroy. This fate cannot be evaded.[15] All narrative pursues an original identity, and poetry declares it.

This declaration can be heard within the basic lineaments of a language. It sounds even within the history of Black English in Nova Scotia – or 'Africadia' ...

Notes

1 This paper was first read on the occasion of the 13th Biennial Meeting of the Association for Canadian Studies in the United States, in Seattle, Washington, on 16 November 1995. I am indebted to Professor Joseph Pivato and to Professor Arnold 'Ted' Davidson (1936–99) for their suggestions for revisions. I dedicate this essay to the memory of Blair Arnold States, my cousin and mixed-race Africadian, who could 'pass' for white, but was *culturally* black, who was Canadian, but also profoundly African-American in his orientations.

2 André Alexis believes that 'black Canadians have yet to elaborate a culture strong enough to help evaluate the foreignness of foreign [i.e., American] ideas' ('Borrowed' 20). Yet, this presumed instance of Americanization is simplistic: though African-American culture enjoys wide currency among African Canadians, they – we – remain a distinct group.

3 See Bridglal Pachai 247–9.

4 Joseph Pivato observes, that 'Canadian [thematic criticism] has not been open to ethnic texts since it cannot accommodate them into such national myths as the two solitudes, the ellipse with two centres, or the garrison' (*Echo* 72).

5 Dillard also states that 'slaves were transferred from one place to another, as from Nova Scotia to Surinam ... quite freely in the eighteenth century' ('History' 513). Before the American Revolution, then, there was likely a good measure of black travel – voluntary and involuntary – between the Thirteen Colonies and Nova Scotia.

6 In his study of the ways in which francophone African youth in Franco-Ontarian high schools 'become Blacks' (111), Awad Ibrahim demonstrates that many of his subjects 'articulated their identification with Black America through the re/citation of rap [music] linguistic styles' (125). They even eschewed the 'highly valued symbolic capital' of *'le français parisien* (Parisian French)' (122) in favour of 'Black Stylized English' (119), a way of saying, argues Ibrahim, '"I too am Black"' (119). His study illustrates, then, the steady circulation of specifically *African-American*-styled English among black newcomers to Canada, despite their francophone and direct-from-Africa backgrounds. In this new sense, too, Dillard's 'continuum' of North American Black English continues ...

7 Philip Brian Harper urges that while 'the situation of black Americans [cannot] be posited unproblematically as a colonial one, its historical sine qua non – the slave trade – can certainly be considered as a manifestation of the colonizing impulse' (253n26).

8 See Hansberry, *To Be Young, Gifted and Black*, 3–4.

9 Hansberry considered her work 'genuine realism,' which she defined as depicting 'not only what *is* but what is *possible* ... because that is part of reality too.' She also speculated that 'ours [i.e., black theatre] ... will be a theatre *primarily* of emotion' (*Be* 211, 228). Hansberry's adoration of realism and empiricism explains her omission of the Hermit's unrealistic speech from *Raisin*, but this fact also throws into even starker relief Borden's inclusion of the discourse in his play and his employment of expressionist theatrical techniques and devices.

10 I refer here to John Matthews's theory that Canadian poetry prefers 'Academic' over 'Popular' modes of discourse. See my article 'Contesting a Model Blackness' (pp. 27–70, above), particularly Part III.

11 Hansberry reproduces Hughes's famous poem 'Harlem' (1951) as an epigraph to *Raisin in the Sun* (whose title is derived from a line in the poem) and also in a 1964 letter to the editor of the *New York Times* in support of the civil rights movement (*Be* 20–1). (To read a copy of the poem, see *The Langston Hughes Reader: The Selected Writings of Langston Hughes* [1958], p. 123.) Borden also reproduces the poem in its entirety, using its hint of menace to preface the Minister of Justice's discussion of the demise of his 'dream,' which 'had something to do with my trying, in quite a humble way, to make this world a better place in which to work – and play' (22, 24).

12 Borden reprints the whole of 'The Prodigal Son,' a sermon-poem by African-American poet James Weldon Johnson (1871–1938), in 1.11, and accords this piece to the Pastor. Borden is largely faithful to Johnson's text, but he introduces a few alterations. He increases the stanza breaks, thus yielding sixteen stanzas to Johnson's thirteen. He confers extra articles, pronouns, adverbs, and adjectives upon some lines. For instance, Johnson's line 'That great city of Babylon' (23) becomes, in Borden's treatment, 'That great, great city of Babylon' (44). Likewise, Johnson's line 'And he went to feeding swine' (24) is transformed by Borden to read, 'And he went down to feeding swine' (44). Such relatively minor redactions are accompanied by three ampler interventions by Borden. Johnson's 'stopped' (23) becomes 'passed' in 'And he passed a passer-by and he said' (Borden 44).

Johnson's 'you've' (25) becomes the more idiomatic 'you' in 'Today you got the strength of a bull in your neck' (Borden 44). Dramatically, Borden affixes two new lines to the conclusion of the penultimate stanza of Johnson's poem:

You'll have a hand-to-hand struggle with bony Death,
And Death is bound to win,
Make no mistake about it;
Old bony Death is bound to win. (Borden 45, my italics)

Borden's revisions of Johnson's already speakerly text intensify its oratorical power. Moreover, the line 'In my father's house are many mansions' (Johnson 24; Borden 45) accents Borden's strategy of presenting the psyche as the 'Host' of various speakers. See Borden 43–5; Johnson 21–5.

13 Thus, Gilroy's text is an anthology of antitheses. His wilful pleasure in the success of Black British art adumbrates a vision of the resistive workings of cultural nationalism that he seeks, elsewhere, to undercut.

14 Sneja Gunew distinguishes between *difference* and *diversity* in a vital passage in her foreword to Pivato's *Echo: Essays on Other Literatures* (1994):

Like Homi Bhabha, my sympathies have always been with *cultural difference* as distinct from *cultural diversity*: an insistence on the untranslatability or incommensurability of cultural difference. For me, this is most clearly apparent in my own studies of Aboriginal epistemologies. I am trying to hear and acknowledge the difference rather than attempting to equate it with known elements in more familiar epistemologies. To put it another way, it is the opposite of the old humanist assumption that all human experience is essentially the same. (20–21)

15 The construction of any particular artistic tradition requires, as well, the articulation of nationalism, even if merely *naïf*.

The Career of Black English in Nova Scotia: A Literary Sketch

For Geraldine Elizabeth Clarke (1939–2000)[1]

Rehearsal

Like too many minority tongues globally, the speech of the majority of Africadians has long been 'buked and scorned, repressed and suppressed, and denigrated as *dialect, lingo, bad* or *broken* English, and *yink-yank*. Their *accent* has been labelled *American* and *Southern*. Their grammar has been treated as foreign, substandard, and deviant. Yet, their speech is as Nova Scotian as that of the province's white majority. *Black* English has flourished in the province for three centuries. Recently, it has emerged as a vivacious literary and performance form in consonance with the popular efflorescence termed the Africadian Cultural Renaissance, which began to attract public notice in 1983.

To understand the career of Black English in Nova Scotia, that is to say, its two-century-long ascent from a position of abysmal disparagement to one of almost accepted respectability, one must examine its origins. First associated with the slave trade, it was later treated as a comic deviance by white Nova Scotian authors and performers and by white author-visitors to the province. Due, in part, to these parodies, the tongue was eschewed by educated, middle-class Africadians. Instead, it became the sole property of the poor and illiterate, who succoured it in their lore and in their soul songs. Still, some *bourgeois* Africadians retained enough of a working knowledge and appreciation of the tongue to maintain their own sense of racial consciousness and black solidarity. Now the language is experiencing a resurgence as a major artistic instrument for Africadian performers and writers. Clearly, one cannot separate the reception of Black English in Nova Scotia from the treatment of Black Nova Scotians – or Africadians – by the majority culture. Whenever a people is oppressed, their tongue is likewise impugned. Whenever a people experience liberation or lived improvements in their circumstances, their tongue likewise flourishes.

The Genealogy of Black English

The variety of Black English spoken in Nova Scotia is one first forged and shaped in the fierce furnace of the slave trade. African-American linguist J.L.

Dillard states that 'American Black English can be traced to a creolized version of English based upon a pidgin spoken by slaves; it probably came from the West Coast of Africa ...' (*Black* 6).[2] Dillard also asserts that 'African languages survived in the New World for a time,' and he notes that scholar David Dalby 'has documented the widespread use of Wolof, which seems to have a special *lingua franca* status among West African languages, in the [original] thirteen [American] colonies' (*Black* 74).[3]

Dillard theorizes that this imagined common African language allowed slaves deported from polyglot West Africa to the Caribbean islands and the mainland Americas to converse with each other while learning, simultaneously, the rudiments of their Euro-American masters' tongues, mainly Portuguese, French, Spanish, and English. Though based on European languages, these pidgin varieties – which permit speakers of various nationalities to communicate in a kind of Babel or Esperanto-style language – were established, says Dillard, 'through African resources' (*Black* 83). The English version, which Dillard terms 'West African Pidgin English' (*Black* 83), was likely used, he thinks, wherever slavery was practised in British North America – from Mississippi to Prince Edward Island.

Recent research, particularly that spearheaded by Shana Poplack and Sali Tagliamonte, disputes the Dillard hypothesis of a creole origin for what they call African American Vernacular English (AAVE) and African Nova Scotian English (ANSE). Rather, along with other linguists, they hold that, in Poplack's words, 'AAVE originated as English, but as the African American community solidified, it innovated specific features,' including 'the spread of *ain't* to past-tense contexts' (27). Applying this theory to ANSE, Poplack notes that Tagliamonte and Jennifer Smith have found that the 'non-concord *was* in African Nova Scotian English' descends from 'the erstwhile [northern] British English model to which [it was] exposed' (11).

While Dillard plumps for an Afrocentric origin for New World African English, Poplack, Tagliamonte, et al., cite early models of Modern English as the primary influence on the origin of AAVE and ANSE. In my own view, the two theories may be linked by the slave experience of violence, both corporeal and intellectual. If Poplack is right that early forms of New World African English 'differ systematically from creoles and, in one case, African languages' and that their grammatical structures 'were already present in the English that the Africans first acquired' (27), then virtual suppression, if not annihilation, of the African linguistic base was the basis for later linguistic hybridity.

One may speculate that Anglo–North American slaves were compelled to learn a rudimentary English to increase their 'value' for their masters and improve their ability to prosecute their commanded tasks. Trinidadian-Canadian poet M. NourbeSe Philip describes this 'education' with merciless political realism:

> To speak another language is to enter another consciousness. Africans in the New World were forced to enter another consciousness, that of their masters, while

simultaneously being excluded from their own ... [L]anguage was one of the most important sites of struggle between the Old World and the New World. The outcome of this struggle was the almost absolute destruction and obliteration of African languages. ('Absence' 15)

Dillard stresses that Africans in British America did not just adopt the speech of their masters. They transformed it; they Africanized it; they made it theirs.[4] They used it as a means to negotiate their way through a hostile white society and to construct a somewhat protective community among each other. Philip cites this revolutionary act:

In the vortex of New World slavery, the African forged new and different words, developed strategies to impress her experience on the language. The formal standard language was subverted, turned upside down, inside out, and even sometimes erased. Nouns became strangers to verbs and vice versa; tonal accentuation took the place of several words at a time; rhythms held sway ... The havoc that the African wreaked upon the English language is, in fact, the metaphorical equivalent of the havoc that coming to the New World represented for the African. ('Absence' 17–18)[5]

The shotgun wedding between West African languages and English fostered a new, distinctive English: Black English or New World African English. Dillard asserts that early Black English took two forms: West African Pidgin English and 'Plantation Creole' – the actual anglicized language spoken by the masses of agricultural slaves (*Black* 85). These forms were contemporaneous (*Black* 85). Poplack retorts that 'the grammatical core of contemporary AAVE developed from an English base' and that the many 'grammatical distinctions between contemporary varieties of AAVE and American and British English are relatively recent developments,' that is, post–U.S. Civil War (1). Nevertheless, it is incontestable that 'Negro' tongues had to adapt English for literally 'home' usage, all over North America, and with varying degrees of innovation and regional colouration.

Black English among the Bluenoses

The situation was no different in Nova Scotia. Dillard finds that 'with its long seacoast, Nova Scotia has been a more likely place for the use of the [West African] Pidgin English of the maritime slave trade ... than inland Canada' ('History' 508). C.B. Fergusson, a provincial archivist, reports the presence of sixteen black slaves in Halifax in 1750 (1), all of whom probably spoke a version of Black English.

The use of West African day-names for slaves yields further evidence of the historical presence of Black English in Nova Scotia. Dillard points to the prevalence of such names as '*Quaco*, "male born on Wednesday" and *Quashee*, "male born on Sunday,"' in records published by Fergusson ('West' 258). 'Phoebe,' a female slave name that also appears in the work of Fergusson, is likely an English corruption of 'Phibba,' a day-name for a female born on a Friday (Dillard 'West' 259). Such distortions inspired further creativity by slavemasters. 'Believing that some of the slave women were named for the goddess of the moon,' Dillard writes, 'the whites apparently proceeded to the next logical step (to them) and gave names like *Caesar* ... and *Scipio*' ('West' 259). Such Romanized names were commonplace for Africadians. In his history 'The Black Population of the County of Annapolis,' Frederick Wheelock Harris reports that 'fanciful names were bestowed upon their servants [slaves] by their masters such as Cato, Pompey, Jupiter, ... for the men, while we find names like ... Sylla, ... Phoebe, ... and Venus given to the women' (61). Famed nineteenth-century Nova Scotian author Thomas Chandler Haliburton includes an Africadian character named 'Scip,' presumably a short form of 'Scipio,' in an 1838 *Clockmaker* sketch, 'Slavery.' In other cases, slaves received English versions of West African day-names. Proof appears in a runaway slave advertisement placed in a Halifax newspaper during the 1770s: 'Ran away from her master, John Rock, on Monday, the 18th day of August last, a negro girl named *Thursday* ...'[6]

The existence of the day-names, like that of the *blackened* European languages, underscores 'the great amount of African culture which remains, iceberg-like, below the surface of the Europeanized Americas' (Dillard, 'West' 260). Thus, the day-name 'Quasheba,' denoting a female born on a Sunday (Dillard, 'West' 259), probably survives in Black Nova Scotia – or Africadia – as 'Sheba.' Moreover, while 'the African use of reduplicated names' lives on in America in such forms as 'Bus Bus' for 'Boston,' 'She She' for 'Sheila,' and Leelee' for 'Lisa' (Dillard, 'West' 260–1), Africadians employ similar monikers. I have heard the names 'Bun Bun' (accorded a man) and 'Lee Lee' (accorded a woman). The persistence of such naming practices suggests the rootedness of Africanized English in Nova Scotia.

Then again, the approximately 3,400 African Americans who entered Nova Scotia as Black Loyalists in 1783, as well as a further 2,000 who arrived as Black Refugees during the War of 1812, were primarily of southern United States origins and brought with them the already well-established naming traditions, accents, and grammatical patterns of their class. Here the research of Tagliamonte and Jennifer Smith is important, for, in keeping with the thesis that British English is the primary source of New World African English, they point out that the immigrant Black Americans arrived from locales, mainly in the South, where northern British white settlers were predominant (163). In his Introduction to *The Black Loyalist Directory* (1995), historian Graham Russell Hodges notes that the majority of Black Loyalists hailed from Virginia and South Carolina (xix). Anthropologist Frances Henry states that the Black Refugee immigrants decamped from 'Virginia and Maryland' ('Black' 12–13). Thus, Nova Scotian Africanized English – or Africadian English – owes some of its colouration to its southern U.S. heritage. Tagliamonte and Smith wager that this Southern heritage predisposed 'African Nova Scotian English enclaves' to retain 'conservative features of northern varieties of British English' so that they 'closely resemble a northern Scottish fishing town' in sound (163). All theories aside, the Loyalists and Refugees entered a colony where slavery had been practised since the founding of Halifax in 1749. Nova Scotian Black English was first established, then, by the African-American slaves transported to the province by their New England Planter owners. Given this lengthy history in the province, Black English is as Nova Scotian as blueberry grunt.

Black English, White Mischief

While the Black Loyalist colonization of Nova Scotia cemented the presence of Africadian English, the later arrivals of Black Refugees and, before 1861, of fugitive U.S. slaves *via* what might be termed the 'Submarine Route' expanded the language's popularity. The downside of this upsurge in usage was that this reformed English became the butt of racist humour. It is a sour irony that the most spacious evidence for the use of Africadian English in the nineteenth century is found in the pages of white authors who abused it for 'comic' purposes. These authors, especially Haliburton, reflected their era's thinking, which 'heard' Black English as a harlequin, piebald, patchwork English – all motley and muddle. African-American literary critic Henry Louis Gates, Jr states that 'the *spoken* language of black people had become an object of parody at least since 1769 when *The Padlock* appeared on the American stage, including among its cast of characters a West Indian slave called Mungo,' whose language was 'represented by a caricature that signifies the difference that separated white from black' (*Figures* 6). African-American writer Gayl Jones points out that 'the containment [or the restriction to dialect] of the black voice seems the prerequisite of parallel freeings of voice in European American literary traditions ...' (164). In other words, white writers – Nova Scotian, British, and American alike – utilized a bastardized English, signified by a reliance on a baroquely bizarre orthography – to highlight the supposed superiority of their own 'Standard' speech and writing. Their texts are rendered thus almost 'recalcitrant to philology,' to pinch a phrase from Richard Sieburth (viii). In her critical work *Playing in the Dark: Whiteness and the Literary Imagination* (1992), African-American novelist Toni Morrison notes 'how the dialogue of black characters [in white-authored texts] is construed as an alien, estranging dialect made deliberately unintelligible by spellings contrived to disfamiliarize [*sic*] it ...' (52). Frantz Fanon also emphasizes the segregating usage of 'dialect,' observing that 'le faire parler petit-nègre, c'est l'attacher à son image, l'engluer, l'imprisoner, victime éternelle d'une essence, d'un *apparaître* dont il n'est pas le responsable' (29).[7]

White distortion of Black English served another purpose, however. It permitted white writers to assume a black mask, thereby enabling the bruiting of le risqué et l'outré. In effect, the white use of Africanized English constituted, frequently, literary blackface. Morrison sustains this point:

In minstrelsy, a layer of blackness applied to a white face released it from law. Just as entertainers, through or by association with blackface, could render permissible topics that otherwise would have been taboo, so American writers were able to employ an imagined Africanist persona to articulate and imaginatively act out the forbidden in American culture. (66)

According to folklorist Neil V. Rosenberg, this early form of pop culture 'began in the 1840s with white American performers who carefully studied black performing arts,' which they then 'endeavoured to present as authentically as they could ...' (142). Songs, in particular, were a popular currency. V.L.O. Chittick suggests that the minstrel songs that spice up Haliburton's work 'were carried to his attention ... [by] the spring-time Nova Scotian visitations of the travelling American circus, with its coloured entertainers' (177). The minstrel show, 'with its blend of eccentric costumes, blackface makeup, and a musical ensemble that included fiddles, banjos, tambourines, and bones' (Abrahams 131), was an early form of mass entertainment. In adulterated guise, it survives in country and western music (which has retained the African-originated 'banjo' and some of the dance steps and instrumental techniques created by slaves).[8] In blackface form, it is still popular in the rural Maritimes (Hornby 85). Haliburton's career coincided, importantly, with the rise of blackface minstrelsy. Wilf Carter (Montana Slim) decided to become a country and western singer after he saw a travelling *Uncle Tom's Cabin* show in the Annapolis Valley in the 1910s (Beaton and Pedersen 2). Nearly two centuries ago, too, a ready audience existed for this pop culture – even in literature.

Robert Cantwell feels that 'the racial attitudes symbolized by blackface placed the performer, whatever his background or temperament, among his audiences, not among the people he parodied' (265). A white performer – or writer – could demonstrate, then, his or her kinship *with other whites* by mimicking the speech of blacks. He or she played a kind of ideological tar baby that absorbed and cancelled within his or her identity, the possibility for positive recognition of African difference. Haliburton falls into this troupe, for he spent his career as a satirical Socrates, using ascerbic humour to promote 'the greater empire of the British peoples, a world-wide Anglo-Saxon unity' (Logan 25). His use of Africanized English always relates to issues significant to his Anglo-American readers. Always, too, he disdains black people.

Haliburton is, nevertheless, a crucial interpreter of nineteenth-century Africadian English. Dillard cites Haliburton's writings as evidence of 'the existence of Black English all the way from the American South, by way of Boston and Connecticut, to Halifax, Nova Scotia' (*Black* 103). In 1850, a French reviewer, Émile Montegut, praised Haliburton's books, 'badly composed yet full of excellent pages, made colourful with American dialect, provincial English, and the jargon of Negroes, fishermen and seamen' (72). In her 1956 study of Haliburton's use of various types of English, including 'Negro Lingo,' Swedish scholar Elna Bengtsson declares America 'a conglomeration of different nationalities, all mangling the English language in different ways. Haliburton ... would not have been Haliburton, had he not utilized this to create comic effects' (45). More precisely, Haliburton's work showcases the minstrelization of Africadian English.

A typical instance of Haliburtonian Africadian English appears in 'Slavery,' the aforementioned 1838 sketch in Haliburton's *The Clockmaker; or, The Sayings and Doings of Samuel Slick, of Slickville*, a work issued in three separate and distinct 'Series' between 1836 and 1840. In this excerpt, Haliburton's hero (and frequent authorial mouthpiece), Sam Slick, stopping at an inn between Kentville and Wilmot, meets Scip, an escaped slave who yearns – incredibly, ignobly – to return to slavery:

> Oh, Massa Sammy! Massa Sammy! Oh, my Gor! – only tink old Scippy see you once more? How you do, Massa Sammy? Gor Ormighty bless you! How you do? ... Oh Massa Sam, you no recollect Old Scip, – Massa 'Siah's nigger boy? How's Massa Sy, and Missey Sy, and all our children, and all our folks to our house to home? De dear little lily, de sweet little booty, de little missy baby. Oh, how I do lub 'em all! ... How is dat black villain, dat Cato? ... I hope dey cowskin him well – I grad of dat, – oh Gor! dat is good. (97–8)[9]

Scip's speech contains items that descend either from West African Pidgin English or early forms of British English, including 'Massa,' 'Gor,' and negation with 'no' ('you no recollect').[10] Nevertheless, his speech is cartoonishly as distorted as the self-indulgent notion that he would like to return to slavery.

In a Third Series *Clockmaker* sketch, 'The Black Brother' (1840), Haliburton's representation of a minister's speech includes snatches of songs borrowed from minstrel shows (Chittick 178–9):

> De Raccoon ginn to scratch and bite,
> I hitty once wid all my might,
> I bungy eye and spile his sight,
>   Oh, *Ise* de child to fight.

> But I is a new man now wid de ungenerate heart, and only fight old Scratch, old Adam, or old sin, but not a brudder in de flesh – no naber I ain't goin' get mad no more.

> For little childer neber let
>   De angry passions rise,
> Your little hands were neber made
>   To tear each oder's eyes.

> Nothin' else save him from catchin' it, for I is de boy dat could do it ... Temper, him werry trong, and say cuss him, bung up both he eye, and put in de dead lite ... (49)

Chittick wagers that Sam Slick's 'repertoire in song was acquired mainly from what he could have heard on the contemporary vaudeville stage, so-called music-hall "ballads" of the sort feaured in "black-face" minstrel shows' (177). Too, because Haliburton was, for many years, a circuit-judge, he would have met Africadian servants, witnesses, and defendants. He could have gleaned some of his impressions of Africadian English by attending to their speech, but always with an inclination to mockery.

Another mid-nineteenth-century white writer who had occasion to mutilate, imitate, or transcribe Africadian English was Frederick S. Cozzens, an American writer who spent a month touring the province. In *Acadia; or, A Month with the Blue Noses* (1859), Cozzens holds forth on the Africadians he encounters in his travels. To him, they are figures of pity and of comedy: their 'very language was pregnant with mirth' (43). Cozzens gives this account of a conversation between himself and Mrs William Deer, who, with her husband, kept an inn near Preston:

'And which place do you like the best – this or Maryland?'
    'Why, I never had no such work to do at home as I have to do here, grubbin' up old stumps and stones; dem isn't women's work. When I was home, I only had to wait on misses, and work was light and easy.'
    ... 'But why,' said I, 'do you prefer Nova Scotia to Maryland? ...'
    'Oh!' replied Mrs. Deer, 'de difference is, dat when I work here, I work for myself, and when I was working at home, I was working for other people.' (64–5)

Though Cozzens attempts to make Mrs Deer sound ridiculous, she makes him sound silly instead: her sensible reply implies her moral dispute with slavery. Like Haliburton, bereft of any patina of African history, gifted only with clichés, Cozzens is reduced to barking prejudices.

White writers like Haliburton and Cozzens were not the only authors to attempt to incorporate – or exploit – the *sound* of Africadian English. John William Robertson, a fugitive slave who had escaped by boat from Virginia to Nova Scotia, utilized it in his fire-and-brimstone pamphlet *The Book of the Bible against Slavery* (1854). Like many other escaped slaves, Robertson, though barely literate, felt he had to testify in print against oppression, so as to speed slavery's abolition. Certainly, the slave narrative was a fearsome weapon in the arsenal of anti-slavery forces. If their language – like Robertson's – was rough, so be it: relative crudeness verified authenticity.

While it is likely that 'fugitive slaves did not leave their plantation dialects behind them' (Dillard, 'History' 515), it is also likely that they retained a sense of the structures of their dialects. For instance, while Robertson's narrative reflects a superficial knowledge of Standard English, his grammar exhibits his deeper, original schooling in orality. To be precise, his syntax seems to follow his speech, not some print model:

... but I knowed one thing that God has declared unto all men, I desire the righ-
teousness which is of the law ... Under divine Providence I proceeded to the sea
side, and I saw the sky was darkened and clouded for rain, but I felt that heaven
was shining in my heart, saying away, and I made up my mind ... The wind being
light, was not twenty miles from home when the day broke, and wind rose to a
hurricane, but as the sun rose the wind blowing very hard indeed. (*Book* 4)

Robertson's use of a comfortably oral-oriented grammar inaugurated an influential style for other Africadian texts.

Robertson's impassioned polemic was not prominent enough, though, to
prevent Black English in Nova Scotia from becoming associated with the
'blackface' English of writers like Haliburton and Cozzens. These scribers of
black 'dialect' failed to produce works that could be described as '"revelatory
of interior lives" as well as society, history, landscape, and language' (Gayl
Jones 32), but they did succeed in helping to promulgate supercilious – but
vicious – stereotypes. Haliburton reveals nothing profound about his Scip, for
instance, but he does create a Negrophobe-comforting caricature, a 'straw'
black man, in a burlesque of scholarship.

Mass versus Class

These stereotypes served to suppress Africadian English. While it remained
the public tongue of most Africadians, it was seldom spoken by the élite, a
group consisting principally of teachers and ministers of the African United
Baptist Association (*né* African Baptist Association), an Africadian religious
organization formally constituted at Granville Mountain in 1854. Two petite
collections of church-sung hymns and spirituals, published respectively by
Rev. F.R. Langford and Rev. W.N. States in 1882 and 1903, attest to this fact,
for the texts are printed in Standard English.[11] Yet, the ministers' congregations could not have sung these songs in Standard English, for Africadians did
not receive formal schooling – or indoctrination – in majority-group English
until well into the twentieth century.[12] Furthermore, spirituals epitomized oral
art. Blyden Jackson terms them 'the epic verse of black America' through
which 'an African ethnicity speaks ... in their incremental leading lines, their
choral iterations, and their call-and-response chants' (314). Their inherent *blackness* would have frustrated renditions in Standard English.

Hence, the ministers' decisions to print their hymnals in mainstream English highlights Dillard's insight that social class membership is the surpass-
ing determinant of whether an African American – or Africadian, in this case –
will speak Black English or Standard English. Generally, the more educated –
or, perhaps, the more assimilated into 'white' society – one is, the less likely
one is to speak Black English, the tongue of the mass of African North Americans (a collectivity defined by economic struggle as well as racial discrimination). Dillard opines that 'it is true that the economically disadvantaged Blacks

of today are primarily members of the unassimilated group ... It is the members of this undervalued culture who are the basic population for a study of Black English' (*Black* 231–2).[13] This class division in black community speech was surely exacerbated by the clownish – nay, oafish – and reductive deformation of Black English by white writers, but it has always existed.

Dillard theorizes that 'there were three language groups among the slaves': 'those who learned the English of their masters' (a *relatively* 'good' English); 'the great mass of native-born field workers, who spoke Plantation Creole' (or Early Modern Black English); and 'recent imports from Africa,' who spoke West African Pidgin English (*Black* 98). Consequently, Dillard states, 'the differentiation of varieties of English used by Black speakers [was] based most probably upon social factors within the slave community ...' (*Black* 86). Because Black English is not a geographically determined dialect, but rather a 'sociolect' or 'social dialect' (Dillard, 'History' 507), that is, the language of a specific, class-constructed group, the class distinction in its use persists. (In addition, the urban versus rural dynamic/dialectic functions so that the rural 'folk' are viewed as 'authentic' if 'illiterate,' while urbanites are classed as 'sophisticated' if also 'alienated.')

This division between folk and élite speakers is pronounced in any marginal or colonized community. Commenting on this phenomenon as it affected colonized Martinique, Fanon remarks that 'le Noir Antillais sera d'autant plus blanc, c'est-à-dire se rapprochera d'autant plus du véritable homme, qu'il aura fait sienne la langue française' (16). A colonized person pursues this sort of psychological *cum* linguistic 'lactification' (Fanon 40) because of his or her sense of inferiority 'du fait de la mise au tombeau de l'originalité culturelle locale': 'Le colonisé se sera d'autant plus échappé de sa brousse qu'il aura fait siennes les valeurs culturelles de la métropole. Il sera d'autant plus blanc qu'il aura rejeté sa noirceur, sa brousse' (Fanon 16). For some Africadians, then, suppression of Black English and 'mastery' of Massa's English inspired assimilationist hopes. E. Franklin Frazier's critique of the education of the African-American middle-class is also relevant to its Africadian counterpart: 'students were taught to speak English correctly and thus avoid the ungrammatical speech and dialect of the Negro masses' (71). For some members of the élite, the Africadian vernacular must have seemed irredeemably invested with the vulgar and the uncouth.

This association had repercussions for the career of literary Black English in Nova Scotia. Bluntly, it disappeared for generations, not to re-emerge until the 1970s. The reason was, as I have written elsewhere, 'the progenitors of [early twentieth-century] Africadian literature were mainly ministers. Indeed, they produced and propagated all the literature that mattered – petitions, songs, newsletters, histories, speeches, and sermons' (Introduction, *Fire* 17). Combined with 'Africadian culture's puritanical streak (a natural feature of an ecclesiastic community),' this fact 'militated against the publication of tales that could be considered lewd, rude, or crude' (Introduction, *Fire* 16). In brief, the Africadian religious élite was not about to exalt Africadian English, even if many of its disciples used the tongue.[14]

The Survival of Africadian English

Africadian literature published between the turn of the century and the mid-1970s was written principally in Standard English. The glorious exception was *Folklore from Nova Scotia*, a 1931 compendium of lore collected, mainly from blacks, from around the province. Although the compiler, Arthur Huff Fauset, a pioneering African-American anthropologist, seems not to have understood the bowdlerizing effect of the African Baptist faith,[15] his collection is a treasury of *circa* 1920s Africadian English and lore. Fauset's informants demonstrate an inimitable authenticity. Here is a part of 'Cinderella,' as told by Caroline Reddick, then aged eighty-seven, of New Glasgow:

> There was a rich Lord's son at the party an' he fell in love with her. He danced mostly with her. He wouldn't pay any attention t'others. She had a foot about six inches long, an' glass slippers. 'Twasn't no other lady there with glass slippers. He laughed an' talked, an' squashed with her. All the others jealous, wonder why he stay with that strange girl. The music was so sweet that Cindy forgot, an she stayed overtime. (5)

Fauset – and others – might criticize Reddick's story for its lack of originality. But its true vivacity resides in the vivid movement of its verbs ('laughed an' talked, an' squashed') and in their imagism ('squashed'), in casual exaggeration ('a foot about six inches long'), in the lively excision of parts of speech ('All the others jealous, wonder why'), in the personalization of story ('Cinderella' as 'Cindy'), and in repetition ('glass slipper' and 'stay'). Thanks to Reddick's inventive adjustments, a hoary story attains a startling vivacity. A similar ingenuity characterizes the 'trickster tale' that Ned Brown, then aged sixty, of Dartmouth, told:

> Rabbit came in man's house of a bluff to warm himself. The man knowed what he was up to, an' said to him, 'If you come in to warm yourself, when the cold comes I'll throw you out into the snow.' Rabbit said, 'Oh, don't do dat.' Man said, 'I will.' ... Den de man got mad, an' he throwed him out, Rabbit all the time hollerin', 'For God's sake, whatever you do, don't put me out of a frosty night.' After he throwed him out, Rabbit said, 'Ho, ho, I was bred an' born in de snow, didn' you know dat?' (46)

As in Reddick's 'speech-act,' Brown seizes our attention by axeing articles ('came in man's house'), mutating verbs ('knowed' and 'throwed' for 'knew' and 'threw'), utilizing repetition ('warm,' 'snow,' and 'throw'), and juxtaposing contradictory commands ('don't do' and 'do, don't'). Brown's story also establishes that such forms as 'dat' have a history in Africadia, for the word also occurs in the texts of Haliburton and Cozzens.

The Renaissance of Africadian English

The type of folk speech surveyed by Fauset is the basis for all of the innovative literature which characterizes the contemporary Africadian Cultural Renaissance. Although they probably do not know Fauset's work, such writers as Frederick Ward (b. 1937), Walter Borden (b. 1942), Charles R. Saunders (b. 1946), Goria Wesley-Desmond (b. 1948), Maxine Tynes (b. 1949), George Boyd (b. 1952), and David Woods (b. 1959) revel in the moods and music of Africadian English. Yet, they also move fluently between the demands of Standard English and the delights of their black idiom.

Previous Africadian writers, by privileging Standard English, gave voice, as did early African-American writers, to the 'literate elite, whereas folklore is the expression of the mass,' to use the terms of Donald A. Petesch (130). From this perspective, to become a writer was 'a way of leaving the black mass' (Petesch 130). Such writers were perhaps unaware that 'if there is no such a thing as a Negro writer or a body of Negro Literature, then, it follows, there is or can be no such thing as a Negro psychology or a distinctly Negro sociology, or a Negro political theory or a particular kind of Negro cultural theory ...' (Cruse 247). The 'Renaissance' generation differs. While they have been described as forming 'part of the indigenous Black Nova Scotian middle class' (Mannette, 'Revelation' 4), these writers, for the most part, embrace Black English.

Their recuperation of the tongue can be related, in fact, to the revolutionary use of oral traditions in emergent, once marginalized literatures. Gayl Jones believes that contemporary African-American literature demonstrates 'the movement from the restrictive forms (inheritors of self-doubt, self-repudiation, and the minstrel tradition) to the liberation of voice and freer personalities in more intricate texts' (178). The same process is under way in Africadian literature. This literary assertion of the vitality of Africadian English is essential, for, to cite Gayl Jones again, 'the foundation of every literary tradition is oral,' whether it is audible or inaudible in the text (3). The specific experience of Africadians cannot be named accurately until it is named in their unique tongue. The return of Africadian writers to the vernacular, then, reflects the 'nation's need to name its own songs, themes, and character in its own distinct language' (Gayl Jones 7). This measure also represents an effort to reclaim the collective memory or history, for the '... lack of history and literature ... is a result of the "amnesie culturelle" which,' according to Sylvia Söderlind, 'is symptomatic of the experience of colonization ...' (92) and, I would add, of marginalization.

If 'the revolutionary's difficult task' is to restore memory and language 'to the people' (Söderlind 92), *Riverlisp: Black Memories* (1974), a collection of stories and poems by Ward, seems to accomplish this act. Inspired in part by conversations that Ward had with exiles from Africville, the 150-year-old North End Halifax Africadian village which the City bulldozed into ruins between 1964 and 1970, the text builds on the original orality of writers like Robertson and the Africadians interviewed by Fauset:

When Grandma Snooks spoken'd you see'd

a sleeping bee
cuddled in a tear drop
hidden hind a elephant's ear
... cause she talk'd in them parable kind of vissions [*sic*] to show her meanings:
'Fuss is round all beautiful-ness. When you's in trouble boy, you just seeks that
inner place   you got it!   we all's got it!'

But Micah Koch's *inner place* was all fuss too. He'd seen Miss Purella Munificance.

Dear sweet Purella Munificance the huckster man on his produce wagon, put
light to your meaning so we can understand huckster man be thinking on your
continence he sing the painter's brush strokes of your mouth; a low soft soothing:
ahhhh sound of the sea bird, leaning on the air! ... (36)

Ward is a consummate artist in Africadian English, one who infuses poetry
with music. He even disorients the expected placement of contractions: where
one expects to read 'we's all,' Ward offers 'we all's.' He deploys white space,
rather than punctuation, to set off phrases as if they were musical – or verse –
stanzas. Repetition ('meaning,' 'fuss,' 'huckster,' 'inner place'), sudden out-
breaks of lyric, coinages ('beautiful-ness'), onomatopoeia ('ahhhh'), alliteration
(sussing out sibilants), and original orthography ('vissions') are all plotted and
arranged to create a text that practically demands to be sung – at the precise
moment that it is also visualized. Ward marvels at the pictorial power of the
music of black speech; he revels in its jazzy sinuosity.

    While Ward's work achieves a kind of aural magic realism, Saunders steeps
his rendition of the speech of Africvillers in realism. Written after he had
interviewed several ex-Africville residents, Saunders's 1989 narrative, 'A Visit
to Africville: Summer, 1959,' is resonantly audible prose:

We used to get coal that fell off the hoppers and the tender. In the wintertime, you
need every piece of coal you can get to heat your house. No more of that, with
these growlin' diesel engines. Steam engines sounded friendly; these diesel engines sound like they want to kill you. And they go too doggone fast. Can't
complain too much about the trains, though. Plenty of our menfolk worked as
Pullman porters ... Kept those sleepin' cars cleaner than the Sheraton hotel. They'd
come home in their uniforms with the shiny brass buttons, and they'd be like
heroes comin' back from a war. (5)

Saunders's text accumulates a heartbreakingly lovely poetic density, with its
perspicacious parallelisms (juxtaposing 'steam' and 'diesel' engines and Pullman porters with war heroes), repetitions ('get,' 'coal,' 'steam,' 'diesel,' 'engines,' and 'come'), sharp comparison ('cleaner than the Sheraton hotel'), and
similes ('like they want to kill you' and 'like heroes'). Saunders frames rich
reminiscences with a lush orature.

Tynes prefers to use Standard English. Nevertheless, the grammatical texture of her texts often possesses the nappy silkiness of Africadian English. In stories such as 'For Tea and Not for Service' (1990), she offers snippets of Africadian speech: 'Celie doesn't remember the afternoon ending, or how she got out of there. But she does remember the warm and secret hug from Dora as she put Celie into her coat; and that hot, breathy whisper into Celie's collar, 'I knows 'em, child. I knows 'em too well' (*Borrowed* 88).

But there is also a reliance upon the active, perhaps orally derived verb 'put' (not the conventional 'helped'), an emphasis on the sensuous ('hot, breathy whisper'), and the implicit recognition that black speech often conspires to be 'warm and secret,' to deliver hidden knowledge and private wisdom.

Woods's first book of poems, *Native Song* (1990), includes an unrhymed couplet, indebted to Ward, that edges toward the status of song. Titled 'Love,' it seeks to replicate the *resonance* of an Africadian voice:

'I love that girl so much,
My hair getting kinkier' (51)

Yet, the poem trifles hardly with grammar. Though the second line omits the auxiliary verb *is*, its tonal *blackness* depends more on the idea of 'kinkier' than it does on syntax or orthography. Woods's poem proves that ideational content is as important a signifier of an Africadian *voice* as pronunciation or grammar.

Borden's play-in-poetry 'Tightrope Time' (1986) further establishes the Renaissance of Africadian English. A precise juggler of rhythm, diction, and imagery, Borden, a professional actor and former teacher, turns Africadian English into a performance art:

... and don't go blabbin' about your father;
he was walkin' in the devil's shoes
before he left his mama's tit,
and be [sic] the time that he was twelve years old,
every girl in this here country
knowed the colour of his drawers.

and that same old fool come in my face
and had the nerve to say:
my boy will be a real man;
yeah – steady, fast and deadly;
and true's i'm sittin' in this chair,
a chill went through my bones –

well Doodle Boy roared down that road
and drove hisself to hell.
and wrapped hisself around that tree
and took some young folks with his. (39–40)

Borden evokes a believable folk voice by deploying homely conceits ('walkin' in the devil's shoes / before he left his mama's tit' and 'every girl in this here country / knowed the colour of his drawers'), an unusual contraction (of 'as' in 'true's'), East Coast coinages ('hisself'), a nickname ('Doodle Boy'), and foreshadowing ('devil's shoes' prefacing the drive 'to hell'). This text, assigned to an old black woman in Borden's play, condenses a life – from boy to youth – into an Ecclesiastes-like proverb.

For Borden, Woods, Tynes, Saunders, Ward, and other Africadian writers, Africadian English has become a specific element of their self-expression.[16] They are writers who are 'easy in their bones, at home ... with the black mass, the traditional source of black strength' (Petesch 131). They combine the techniques of formal literary writing with the *echt*-expressiveness of folk grammar and diction. They strive 'to keep the deep structure, the movement, the kinetic energy, the tone and pitch, the slides and glissandos of the demotic within a tradition that is primarily page-bound ...' (Philip 'Absence' 23). Indeed, 'the *righteous* recital of a poem or story, the *proper* enactment of a play, the *soulful* utterance of speech or song' are crucial to the Africadian sensibility (George Elliott Clarke, Introduction, *Fire* 25).[17] Africadian writers share, then, a similar rhetorical style based not so much on grammar as on rhythm, one marked by biblically cadenced phrases and sentences and by the usage of such techniques as repetition, catalogues, and parallelism. Additionally, Africadian texts exhibit such characteristics as the 'multiple-voice, complex metrical patterns' that Roger Abrahams identifies in classical African-American culture (xviii).

A Polemical Apocalypse

Black English has had a long career in Nova Scotia. Though it arrived in chains and suffered persecution for its perceived 'perversity,' it survived and flowered in the utterance of those who had no hope of, and perhaps even less interest in, assimilating into the white Nova Scotian middle class. It will continue to flourish 'perhaps because of the aloofness of the white population from the Black,' to cite Dillard (*Black* 114). Given this 'aloofness,' Africadian English will not be fade out. Nor should it. Its writers *gotta* remember, with the Italian-Canadian critic Antonio D'Alfonso, that 'any new language entails ... its set of burdens on the minority writer' (59). Worse *and* better yet, 'every word an ethnic writer positions on a piece of paper is therefore laden with ideology, whether he or she likes it or not' (59). The challenge facing Africadian authors is to disorient the central Standard English orientation of English-Canadian literature, by voicing their own *distinctive* English (while staving off the mass-merchandised African-American varieties). Analysing the works of Ezra Pound and Wyndham Lewis, Vincent Sherry argues that 'voice infects the printed literature of a democratic state,' but 'an aristocratic society tends to reverse this tendency: to influence and improve the material of speech by imposing a page-based standard of usage upon it' (100). Africadian writers must fight against this aristocratic 'rage for the page,' to let the *vox populi* out, to let it sing and shout. To paraphrase Maureen N. Eke, their task is to 'indigenize' English, thus Africadianizing it 'and transforming its functionality' (103).[18]

While we Africadians will continue, in increasing numbers, to learn Standard English, that education must not be won at the expense of our own native, stunning, and bluesy tongue. We must prize the old Africadian proverb 'All I gotta do is stay black and die.' Can I get an 'amen'?

'Frozen in time, something that is "becoming" appears as if it already "is,"' Walker attests ('*Race*' 320). It would be a mistake to view Africadian literature as cultural work that is finished. It is still evolving, and its 'is' *is* bound up with a tradition of orality, one reinforced, unhappily, by a history of desperate deprivation. I maintain that, like the career of Black English in Nova Scotia, Africadian literature has had two beginnings, a point my next essay affirms.

Notes

1 This paper was written in 1992 in response to a request from Saint Mary's University professors Lillian Falk and Margaret Harry for an essay on Africadian English. Because I am no linguist, I would never have attempted to canvass the topic if not for their urging. I dedicate this essay to Geraldine Elizabeth Clarke, who bestowed upon me my maternal – Africadian – tongue.

2 'American Black English' is the immediate ancestral tongue of Africadians, for they are mainly descended from African Americans who entered Nova Scotia, in the thousands, in the two major migrations of 1783 and 1812–15. Nevertheless, as discussed later in the essay, some linguists think that 'Black' English itself derives essentially from 'lost' forms of British English.

3 Dillard cites two works by Dalby: (1) 'The African Element in Black American English' (1972); and (2) *Black through White: Patterns of Communication in Africa and the New World* (1969). However, Dalby's thesis has met with fatal objections. The simplest one is that Wolof is a minority tongue, and so it could not have constituted a *lingua franca*. Yet, even if slaves held no African language in common, they may still have shared similar syntactical and grammatical approaches to assimilating and modifying the European tongues imposed upon them.

4 Poplack, too, feels that 'contemporary AAVE is the result of evolution, by its own unique internal logic,' although he traces its source to Britain, not Africa (27). He does not explain, however, what happened to the African languages the forcibly transplanted Africans must have known. It does not seem credible that they could have been so perfectly obliterated that *nothing* of their flavour survived to tart the taste of the new tongue the exiled Africans were *driven* to learn.

5 The nineteenth-century African-American novelist Charles W. Chesnutt reports another instance of 'havoc.' In his novel *The House behind the Cedars* (1900), Chesnutt observes that 'the current Southern speech ... was rarely without a touch

of it. The corruption of the white people's speech was one element – only one – of the Negro's unconscious revenge for his own debasement' (10). If one accepts Chesnutt's thesis, the celebrated 'Dixie' accent is African in derivation.

I must also register here the closeness of Philip's description of Diasporic African linguistic evolution to Black British writer David Dabydeen's analysis of Creole:

> In the 'Preface' to *Slave Song* (1984), I state that the creole language is angry, crude, energetic ... Words are spat from the mouth like live squibs, not pronounced with elocution. English diction is cut up ..., the splintering making the language more barbaric. Soft vowel sounds are habitually converted ... If one has learnt and used Queen's English for some years, the return to creole is painful, almost nauseous, for the language is uncomfortably raw. One has to shed one's protective sheath of abstracts and let the tongue move freely in blood again. (61)

Dabydeen's appreciation of the violence of *Other*-language 'adoption' may be *une source* for Philip's own articulation of the experience.

6 This notice is discussed in J.J. Stewart, 'Early Journalism in Nova Scotia' (113).

7 One objection to the Poplack theory for the genealogy of New World African English is that, if early African American English and early Africadian English arose primarily from Standard English, it should not have seemed so 'comic' and alien to British and British-descended writers ... One must wonder why they did not recognize the 'echo' of their own English in that uttered by blacks. In any event, the duty of determining the correctness of linguistic theory merits this aside from Ezra Pound: 'it is work for encyclopedists or else it isn't' (*Walking* 7).

8 Cantwell treats the relationship between contemporary white country music and dances and slave music and dances and between country music and blackface minstrelsy in *Bluegrass Breakdown* (124, 255–65). See also Abrahams, *Singing the Master* (102).

9 'Cato' is another example of a romantic, Romanized slave name.

10 I am indebted to Dillard for my information on these forms. In his history of Black English in Nova Scotia, Dillard includes a list of 'the characteristic structures of Pidgin English.' The forms that I identify appear in Dillard's list – with the minor difference that his *'Gar'* is rendered as 'Gor' here. See Dillard, 'History' 508–9. While I bear in mind that Poplack, Tagliamonte, and Smith challenge Dillard's view, they provide no literary evidence for their theory, while Dillard supports his with frequent citing of literary texts.

11 Rev. F.R. Langford published *A Call from Zion: Jubilee Songs and Old Revival Hymns* in Weymouth in 1882. Rev. Wellington Naey States published *Hymns Sung at the Services* in Halifax in 1903.

12 According to historian Colin A. Thomson, at the end of the nineteenth century, 'thousands of ... Blacks remained illiterate or taught themselves the rudiments of reading and arithemtic [sic]' (9). Thomson also states that 'attendance at black schools was often poor' (8). It was not until the mid-1950s that major efforts were undertaken – at the behest of Africadian leaders like Rev. William Pearly Oliver, Pearleen Oliver, and B.A. Husbands – to end segregation in schooling, to provide a basic education for Africadian adults, and to provide incentives to Africadian

youths to remain in school. See my article 'The Birth and Rebirth of Africadian Literature' (pp. 107–25, below) for a further discussion of the educational deprivation Africadians endured.

13 As discussed in 'Must All Blackness Be American?' sociologist Awad Ibrahim reports that black, African-born, Franco-Ontarian students tend to cast aside their prestigious 'Parisian French' (122) in favour of adopting *The talk* (119, his italics), or 'Black Stylized English' (119). Thus, these 'African youths enter the realm of becoming Black' (119). In spite of their often middle-class and quasi–*foreign language* backgrounds, these youths feel that one way to model an imagined *African Americanité* is to adopt a 'Pop' Black English, using 'rap lyrics, syntax, and morphology' (127).

14 In his 1895 *History of the Coloured Baptists of Nova Scotia*, Rev. Peter E. McKerrow reports that, when Rev. James Thomas prayed at public ceremonies such as waterside baptisms, 'there was nothing too high, too low, or too broad, but he could find language to meet the case ...' (*McKerrow* 31). Perhaps Africadian English served as one of Thomas's apt 'languages.'

15 In my Introduction to *Fire on the Water: An Anthology of Black Nova Scotian Writing*, Vol. 1 (1991), I argue that 'Fauset failed to appreciate that a radical religious culture would repress its seemingly vulgar constituents' (16). I also assert that 'Fauset was exasperated by the refusal of some of his informants to recite material that they felt was beneath their dignity' (16).

16 For the works of other writers, please consult my edited anthology, *Fire on the Water: An Anthology of Black Nova Scotian Writing*, vol. 2 (1992). See especially the work of Raymond L. Parker (b. 1936) and George Boyd (b. 1952). In Volume 1 of *Fire on the Water* (1991), see the writings of Grace May Lawrence (b. 1928), whose work, though ostensibly in Standard English, betrays a Black English 'sensibility.' For further types of transcribed Africadian English, see the Black Cultural Centre for Nova Scotia's two-volume collection, *Traditional Lifetime Stories: A Collection of Black Memories* (1987–90). Two recent films also feature Africadian English. See the National Film Board (NFB) production *Black Mother, Black Daughter* (1990), directed by Claire Prieto and Sylvia Hamilton, and another NFB production, *Remember Africville* (1991), directed by Shelagh Mackenzie. For musicked Africadian English, sample the compact disc compilation by the Black Cultural Centre for Nova Scotia and the Canadian Broadcasting Corporation, *Lord You Brought Me a Mighty Long Way: An African Nova Scotian Musical Journey* (1997), particularly the songs of William Riley (c.1856–1943).

17 I knew, while living in Halifax in the mid-1980s, Cynthia Chandler, an Africadian woman who recited her rhymed compositions from memory. A true community poet of the black North End, she loved to wear stocking-caps year-round and declaim – on the spot – topical, political, and comic poems.

18 Of course, all African-Canadian writers should feel a similar impulse, to impose Jamaican, 'Bajan,' Haitian, Nigerian, 'Trini,' and even *Dee-troit* accents on Canadian literature. See, for instance, Antiguan-Canadian writer Althea Prince's interest in 'African-Caribbean Voice' and 'Elder Voice Lineage' (*Being* 89–91). As usual, M.

NourbeSe Philip, sums up the issue facing black writers nicely, in the conclusion of her poem 'Meditations on the Declension of Beauty by the Girl with the Flying Cheek-bones':

> If not in yours
>   In whose
> In whose language
>   Am I
> If not in yours
>   Beautiful (93–4)

Peter Hudson points out that the language of one Jamaican-Canadian subject represents 'the use of performativity, non-English syntax, neologisms and vernacular lexicons, and code- or register-switching that is typical of black Canadians, especially those of Caribbean descent' ('Primitive' 194). Hudson also declares that 'many black Canadians shift between the languages of the Caribbean and "standard" English according to context. Among younger black Canadians the vernaculars of African Americans are added to the mix' ('Primitive' 194). If these speakers restrict themselves to employing only Caribbean registers, they may access a palette of five. Alfred Jean-Baptist lists the varieties of Caribbean English available as 'Creole,' 'Erudite,' 'Foreign,' 'Rasta,' and 'Standard.' See his *Caribbean English and the Literacy Tutor: Tutor's Kit* (1995, 36–45).

Appendix: Toward a Glossary of Africadian English

To prepare a thorough glossary of Africadian English, extensive field research is required. Only a few terms are canvassed here. This glossary omits both slang and such commonly used English words as *banjo, bozo, buckaroo, gumbo, jazz, juba, okay, okra, tabby, tote,* and *voodoo,* all of which are of definite or strongly suspected African origin (Dillard, *Black* 118–19). Many of the words and phrases listed below have been in use for several generations.

ashy: Describes the grey film on dry black (or brown) skin.
Association: The annual third-Sunday-in-August gathering of members of the African United Baptist Association and their families and friends to worship Christ, enjoy fellowship, and celebrate homecomings.
Aunt Jemima: a black female who acts 'white' or curries favour with whites.
aya: sugar. (Gerald Taylor, a former executive director of the now-defunct Black United Front of Nova Scotia, reported this usage to me in 1986.)
big-feeling: proud, vain.
black: an intensifier, as in 'Mind your own black business!'
blue (-black): Describes a dark-skinned black person.
buried: to be totally immersed in water during a baptism. The term arises from the phrase 'buried in the likeness of Christ.'

clip: to strike or hit; to cut (hair).

crack: to strike or hit.

cream and molasses: Describes a person of black and white ancestry. (See Marion Robertson, *The Chestnut Pipe*, 213.)

cross-eyed: angry.

crying doll: an infant.

cut [one's] eyes: to cast a quick, mean look.

derasifying: good, tasty, delicious.

dirty [one's] knees: to kneel and pray.

drag: a horse-drawn, plank-platform on wooden runners. (See Raymond L. Parker, *Beyond the Dark Horizon*, 62.)

dried up; dry: Describes a person who is boring or old or strict or simply unpleasant. Can also apply to things and places.

exhorters: lay preachers. (See Willard Parker Clayton, *Whatever Your Will, Lord*, 48.)

good-fisted: a good fighter or boxer.

greens: vegetables.

hamhocks: hog portions.

heavy-natured: lustful.

hotcomb: a heated steel comb used to straighten hair.

in service: working as a domestic in a stranger's home.

lick and lap: to make love.

little house: an outhouse.

Lucifer: a male lover. (See Grace May Lawrence et al., *Reflections to the Third Power*, 45.)

making pictures: telling stories; making someone believe something that isn't true. (See Fauset, *Folklore from Nova Scotia*, 11.)

mannish: Describes a boy who boldly or brashly pays others no mind.

mean-minded: mean, nasty.

miserable: Describes a mean-minded, no-count person.

nappy: Describes supposedly unkempt 'Negroid' hair.

New Road: an area of Preston.

niggerish: devilish.

nigger rig: a plain and simple, but useful invention.

no-count: no good.

num-nums: food.

oreo: a black who ignores other blacks, or who sides with whites or who acts 'white.'

out home: Usually used by an urban black to refer to the family homestead, usually located in a rural area. Can also be 'back home' or 'down home' (especially if one is living or travelling 'away').

padana: bread pudding. (See Marie Nightingale, *Out of Old Nova Scotia Kitchens*, 23.)

pasty-faced: a white or a light-skinned black.

picky: Describes supposedly unkempt 'Negroid' hair.

piss-ass: a nasty person.

pullin' (on): accosting or grabbing someone to try to coax him or her into sexual intimacies.

pup: an upstart.

Queen of Sheba: a vain girl or woman.

receive the right hand of fellowship: to be formally welcomed by a minister into membership in a Baptist church.

rubber-lipped: Describes supposedly too-fleshy lips.

run: to sleep around; to sleep with someone; to commit adultery.

seeker's bench: a place set aside in church, following the invitational hymn, for those seeking salvation. (See Clayton, 33.)

shakes: sexual intercourse.

showoff: a vain person.

shuck: to sham; to shirk or avoid labour or duty.

slack ass: Describes 'Caucasian' buttocks negatively.

slow as cold molasses: Describes a slow-moving person.

steel wool: a negative term for 'Negroid' hair.

stringy: a negative term for 'Caucasian' hair.

stuck-up: proud, vain.

suck [one's] teeth: to make a noise with the tongue and the teeth to express displeasure or anger.

sugar bowl: vagina.

sugar diabetes: diabetes.

sweet man: a male lover.

take the water: to be baptized.

talk black, sleep white: Describes a black person who espouses black equality or liberation (or both), but whose spouse or lover is white.

teehee: to laugh.

testify: to speak; to tell the truth; to bear witness.

two-faced: Describes a backstabber or hypocrite.

Uncle Tom: a black male who acts 'white' or who curries favour with whites.

uppity: proud, uncompromising, resistant.

upside [one's] head: the favourite spot for striking – or an unfortunate spot for being struck.

vanilla fudge [cookie]: a white person who sides with blacks or who acts 'black.'

what's [his/her] face?: what's [his/her] name?

womanish: Describes a girl who boldly or brashly pays others no mind.

yellow: a 'light'-skinned black. A 'high yellow' black has very light-complexioned skin.

yellow and white earth: cash. The term may derive from yellow and white gold. (See Lewis J. Poteet, *The Second South Shore Phrase Book*, 44.)

The Birth and Rebirth of Africadian Literature

For Portia May White (1911–68)[1]

Debut

An immediate distinction of Black Nova Scotian – or, to continue my use of my neologism, *Africadian* – literature is that it has had two, quite separate, annunciations – a first *and* second coming, so to speak. Nearly two centuries lapsed, moreover, before the original burgeoning was replenished by the second, a period I term the Africadian Renaissance. Though Africadian literature commenced in 1785, when John Marrant, an African-American Methodist missionary who lived in Nova Scotia from 1785 to 1789, published his popular *Narrative of the Lord's Wonderful Dealings with John Marrant, a Black*, a corpus of imaginative works did not begin to develop until 189 years later. Then, Frederick Ward published the first Africadian novel, *Riverlisp: Black Memories* (1974), a text followed in short order by Gloria Wesley-Daye's chapbook of modernist poems *To My Someday Child* (1975), and Peter B. Bailey's nationalist-nuanced collection *This Is My Song* (1975). This essay traces the conditions of Africadian literature's birth, abeyance, and rebirth, and speculates upon the reasons for its staggered development. It also attempts to declare the concerns of this now-emergent literature and its milieu, namely, Africadia – an ethnocultural archipelago consisting of several dozen Black Loyalist– and Black Refugee–settled communities (including some in and about the Halifax-Dartmouth metropolitan region), whose foundings date back to 1783 and 1815 respectively. Although my focus here is on African-Nova Scotia, I suspect that research will uncover similar evolutions for the 'indigenous' African-Canadian literatures of New Brunswick, Quebec, Ontario, the Prairies, and British Columbia.

I

Africadian literature was born in urgency. It originated as a rebuke to the American Revolution and its pure, internal contradiction, namely, chattel slavery. Thus, when the nearly 3,400 African Americans who supported the Crown during the Revolutionary War were exiled *post-bellum* to Nova Scotia in 1783, these Black Loyalists continued to castigate slavery and its tortures and to glorify the late conflict as having been a God-sent opportunity to escape a Sadean hell. These beliefs (along with a wish to tell of the miraculous intervention of Providence in their lives) animate the Black Loyalist texts of David George and Boston King. In George's 'An Account of the Life of Mr. David George' (1793), the *sign* 'Americans' becomes a synonym for *enslavers*: 'I was then about a mile from Savannah, when the Americans were coming towards it a second time. I wished my wife to escape, and to take care of herself and of the children, and let me die there' ('Account' 477). In contrast, as King's 'Memoirs of the Life of Boston King' (1798) illustrates, the British are viewed as liberators: 'The English had compassion upon us in the day of distress, and issued out a proclamation, importing, That all slaves should be free, who had taken refuge in the British lines ... ' ('Memoirs' 157). The Manichean division that George and King erect between the *signs* 'American' and 'British' communicates their hatred for slavery, that exquisitely Luciferian system. George's text bruits a catalogue of torments:

> My oldest sister was called Patty; I have seen her several times so whipped that her back has been all corruption, as though it would rot ... I also have been whipped many a time on my naked skin, and sometimes till the blood has run down over my waistband; but the greatest grief I then had was to see them whip my mother, and to hear her, on her knees, begging for mercy. ('Account' 473)

King reveals that he was beaten 'severely' by his master, on more than one occasion, for little cause ('Memoir' 106). Given such casual viciousness, both men cast their lot with the British. King rationalizes his decision thus: 'To escape [my master's] cruelty, I determined to go to Charles-Town, and throw myself into the hands of the English. They received me readily, and I began to feel the happiness of liberty ...' ('Memoir' 107). Once they have been delivered from the fledgling Republic *cum* slave state, George and King pursue two priorities – acquiring literacy and spiritual liberty. In his spiritual, not slave, narrative, Marrant worries only the latter precept. His work is not abolitionist, but rather mystical, an ideological echo of the New Light divine Henry Alline (1748–84), whose end-is-nigh religious revival of 1776 to 1783 catalyzed Nova Scotian disinterest in the American Revolution:

> What poor unbelieving creatures we are! though we are assured the Lord will supply all our needs. I was presently directed to a puddle of water very muddy, which some wild pigs had just left; I kneeled down, and asked the Lord to bless it to me, so I drank both mud and water mixed together, and being satisfied I returned the Lord thanks, and went on my way rejoicing. (*Narrative* 18)

Despite their differences, though, George, King, and Marrant embody classical Africadian literature and determine its persistent concerns: liberty, justice, and faith.

Early Africadian creativity was not limited to writing. Black Loyalist settlers must have embarked for Nova Scotia with a heritage of song, both secular and religious, for, as musicologist John Lovell reports, African Americans 'belonged to a singing tradition that was centuries old' (96). Some Africadians also engaged in carnivalesque festivities: historian T. Watson Smith records that the government of the white Loyalist settlement at Shelburne passed an ordinance in 1789 enacting 'that fifty handbills be printed immediately, forbidding negro dances and frolics in this town ...' (77). George and Marrant evince intimate acquaintance with music and popular religious song. George learned 'a hymn of that great writing man, [Isaac] Watts' ('Account' 476); Marrant 'in a twelve-month's time became master both of the violin and of the French-horn ...' (*Narrative* 9). As my previous essay suggests, *orature* – oral literature – and music have *flourished* in Africadia since its inception. But the same cannot be, no, it cannot be, unproblematically urged for written texts.

II

This peculiar truth creates for Africadia an unusual literary history, one whose existence depends upon a trio of texts published between 1785 and 1798 and another score or two issued between 1798 and 1974, all of which preface the relative outpouring of texts late in the twentieth century. Nineteenth-century works are rare, but number in their prize ranks John William Robertson's poetic slave narrative *The Book of the Bible against Slavery* (1854), the numinous revelation, in a *macédoine* of Queen's English and Black English, of his embarkation from bondage in Virginia and his attainment of liberty and literacy in Nova Scotia. The century's most important work, namely, Peter E. McKerrow's *A Brief History of the Coloured Baptists of Nova Scotia 1783–1895* (1895), appeared five years before its end. Notable early-to-mid-twentieth-century texts include Rev. Adam S. Green's published speech *The Future of the Canadian Negro* (1904); a choice anthology of folklore, *Folklore from Nova Scotia* (1931), compiled by the African-American anthropologist Arthur Huff Fauset after his mid-1920s field trip to the province; Rev. W.P. Oliver's impressionistic paper 'The Negro in Nova Scotia' (1949); and Pearleen Oliver's substantial chronicle *A Brief History of the Colored Baptists of Nova Scotia, 1782–1953* (1953).[2] Apart from these works, Africadian literary production between 1798 and 1974 is a mélange of African Baptist Association (ABA) and African United Baptist Association (AUBA) minutiae, chiefly Church minutes (which incorporate letters, sermons, circulars, reports, and brief treatises), Church-spawned booklets of spirituals and hymns, newspaper verse, journalism, petitions to governments, and other ana and ephemera. To seek, in this period, this 'Great Void,' plays, novels, or collections of poetry, short stories, or essays, is to face a *sfumato* blankness.

III

The issuance of so few texts between 1798 and 1974 indicates that Africadia endured a protracted cataclysm, one that required, not the generic modes of expression, but rather a Church-sponsored corpus of non-fiction and spiritual writings. The era posed a quintet of emergencies, of which the fifth – the doom of Africville (a historic Africadian community) in the late 1960s – precipitated the rebirth of Africadian literature. The literature's hiatus into silence was spurred, though, by the four *ur*-predicaments, which were, in order, the emigration of the Black Loyalist intellectual élite, including George and King, to Sierra Leone in 1792 (in quest of a more genuine liberty than was available to them in Nova Scotia); the *dégringolade* of the remaining Africadians into a diabolical poverty; their pointed disbarment from education; and the promulgation of anti-black stereotypes.

The first blow was the harshest. Historian James Walker posits that the voluntary self-exodus of 1,190 Black Loyalists to Sierra Leone meant 'social dislocation' for those who stayed behind: 'The black remnant of Nova Scotia was a decapitated community, having lost most of its teachers, preachers and other leaders ...' (*Black* 386). Writer Sylvia Hamilton concurs: 'Approximately two thousand Black Loyalists and an undetermined number of slaves were left scattered throughout Nova Scotia to fend for themselves against a white populace that was so clearly hostile' (29). Although the population loss was offset numerically by the landing of more than 2,000 Black Refugees from the War of 1812 in Nova Scotia between 1813 and 1815, a leadership deficit remained. This want weakened Africadia at a time when white Nova Scotian society was closing ranks against the 'Nova Africanae' in its midst. States Walker, 'the conditions, prejudices and insecurities that drove their brethren to Sierra Leone drove the Nova Scotian blacks into their own isolated society during the nineteenth century' (*Black* 396).

This isolation, geographically demarcated (most black settlements were located on the fringes of larger white towns and villages), enforced economic dependence upon white communities and employers, a context which assured poverty for most Africadians, for few white Nova Scotians scrupled to distinguish black colonists from slaves. Historian Colin A. Thomson confirms that 'the perpetuation of black economic marginality was linked with the fact that Nova Scotia was once a slave society' (15). Walker cites 'the telling resolution of the Nova Scotia assembly in 1815, defining all African people as "labourers and servants" ...' ('*Race*' 303). An 1841 petition, addressed to the Government of Nova Scotia, showcases the Africadian plight:

> Petitioners are Refugees ... or their descendants, being placed by Government out upon ten acre lots, of poor land, many of them including swamps and likewise entirely barren & unproductive, and none of them sufficient to yield subsistence for a family however skillfull and industrious, they have dragged on a miserable existence but few, if any of them, rising above the level of hopeless poverty.[3]

This state of subsistence persisted deep into the twentieth century. It fostered, says Africadian theologian Peter J. Paris, a condition of perpetual inequality: 'Deficient education, job insecurity, low social status in the white community have all contributed to a permanent structure of social and economic deprivation, housing discrimination and, for a very long while, no access to internal plumbing, sewerage, electricity and telephone lines' (18–19).[4] Conditions were so desperate that some Africadian settlements – such as Delaps Cove and Bear River – vanished as a result of the wholesale emigration of their populations to the United States (Boyd, *McKerrow* 3.25–3.27). Such voluntary removals were not 'simply a case of African Americans returning home, but of the Canadian-born moving to the cities of the American north in search of educational, cultural, and employment opportunities' (Walker, 'African' 144).[5] Certainly, Africadians could expect little justice or support at home. Popular historian Dean Jobb avers, 'There's no doubt blacks were treated as second-class citizens' in the 'opening decades of the twentieth century' (99):

> In many towns theatres had separate seating for blacks, and some restaurants and hotels were off limits ... In 1911 *Maclean's* magazine published an article that purported to describe the typical black section of a Nova Scotia town. 'White people pass it in fear ... It is the abode of little more than innocent shiftlessness, but such places are adapted to the breeding of vice and crime.' (99)

Of three black men sentenced to death by Nova Scotia courts in the 1930s, two – or two-thirds–went to the gallows. In his 1920 paper on Annapolis County Africadians, Frederick Wheelock Harris finds that 'the majority of them are still "hewers of wood and drawers of water." It would appear that the great hardships their ancestors have gone through have left their stamp on the generations that followed and crushed out the desire to rise to better condition' (67).

For Africadians, Nova Scotia was a virtual dystopia. They not only lived an epic indigence, they also suffered ramshackle, poorly staffed schools – when they had any at all. The 1811 Nova Scotia Public School Act alloted provincial moneys only to those communities which could erect a school and supply a teacher; thus, most black communities went begging. But even where schools were established, usually with government or religious order support, they reflected a principle of *de facto* and legal segregation, resulting in separate and grossly inferior schooling (George Elliott Clarke, 'Reading' 5–6). At the 24th Session of the ABA, held in 1877, McKerrow rendered this verdict on the educational status of Africadia:

> The condition of the people of colour in this province ... [is] deplorable, none worse throughout the Dominion, for although our votes are sought both in parliamental [sic] and civic elections, yet no recompense do we receive, but have to put up with the meanest of schoolhouses that the province can afford, which deserves the greatest censure from the educated world. (*Minutes* [1877] 8)

Decline persisted. By the end of the nineteenth century, Thomson says, 'thousands of ... Blacks remained illiterate or taught themselves the rudiments of reading ...' (9). Writing in 1904, African Baptist pastor Adam S. Green proclaims that 'slavery ... left its blight upon our fair province [Nova Scotia] in the illiterate and impoverished condition of the negro, and in the abnormal class-restrictions and prejudices to which he was and *is* subjected by white Canadians ... ' (quoted in *Fire* [vol. 1] 74). In his 1949 article 'The Negro in Nova Scotia,' W.P. Oliver sketches a scarcely improved picture of Africadian educational chances:

> Life in the distinct Negro community has not created a desire for education on the part of the people; attendance of children at school has not been considered an essential as the school has never been associated with the child's post-school life ... During the 135 years of their settlement here, there is a record of only nine Negro university graduates, and of these nine only three can really be called direct descendants of the early settlers ... (132)

In 1945 there were only twenty-five black teachers in Nova Scotia; in 1948, only fifteen or twenty of 8,000 black schoolchildren had reached high school (Clarke 'Reading' 6). Racial preferences blighted the laws pertaining to education, moreover, until 1954 when Nova Scotia struck racial references from education legislation and began to abolish segregated school districts in the 1960s (Winks 385–6). Segregation was diabolical. Walker reports that, even into the 1960s, Africadians had 'substantially lower educational qualifications' ('African' 164). In 1965, 83.8 per cent of Africadian adults in Three Mile Plains and Five Mile Plains reported having only an elementary school education (Connor and Marshall 38).[6]

Segregation's appeal depended to some extent upon the derogatory images of blacks in general and of Africadians in particular that white Nova Scotians imbibed through mass media – newspapers, magazines, novels, minstrel shows, plays, early film, and radio. These conceptions were ubiquitous. In *Down North and Up Along* (1900), American writer Margaret W. Morley opines that 'the negroes are not yet reconciled to the climate of Nova Scotia – small wonder that they are not! – and though many of them were born there, they sigh for the palms of the traditional land of their ancestors and have little zest for the fir-trees of the North' (144–5). Here too I must summon the spectre of Thomas Chandler Haliburton, that most eminent anglophone writer – and Negrophobe – of nineteenth-century British North America. In his 1829 history of Nova Scotia, Haliburton offers this assessment of the Black Refugees:

> At Preston and at Hammond Plains, in the neighbourhood of Halifax, there were settlements, composed wholly of Blacks, who experienced every winter all the misery incident to indolence and improvidence, and levied heavy contributions on the humanity of their more frugal neighbours. In some instances they have sighed for the roof of their master, and the pastimes and amusements they left behind them. (292)

No friend to Africadians, Haliburton utilizes outrageous terms of abuse in his satirical sketches. In 'The White Nigger,' an 1836 piece, Haliburton's protagonist, Sam Slick, states that he and his fellow Americans 'deal only in niggers, – and those thick skulled, crooked shanked, flat footed, long heeled, wooly headed gentlemen, don't seem fit for much else but slavery ...' (*Clockmaker* [First Series] 176). This Menippean rhetoric echoes the epithets of white Southern apologies for slavery (which Haliburton also defended).[7] Likewise, Frederick S. Cozzens, an American travel writer, practised this literature of 'humorous' disparagement. In *Acadia; or, A Month with the Blue Noses* (1859), Cozzens conceives Africadians as idiots. In this spirit, Cozzens reproduces this exchange between himself and William Deer, whose parents owned an inn near Preston: '"Bill, did you catch any trout?" It was some time before William could control himself enough to say, "Not a single one, sah"; and then he rolled over on his back, put his black paws up to his eyes, and twitched and jingled to his heart's content' (67). In his novel *Solo* (1923), written under the pseudonym Pierre Coalfleet, Frank Cyril Davison (1893–1960) uses, as one of his characters, a real-life Africadian resident of Hantsport, Nova Scotia, namely, Becky States. Historian Allen B. Robertson charges that 'in stereotypical language Coalfleet portrayed Becky States as a washerwoman and domestic,' seeing her in 'derogatory and derisive terms' (*Tide* 116).[8] The writings of social scientist Frances Henry demonstrate the influence of some of these invidious characterizations as late as the early 1970s. She asserts that the Black Refugees who landed in Nova Scotia following the War of 1812 were so degraded that they lost 'whatever folk culture' they had formerly possessed:

> From their arrival, penniless, demoralized, and products of an exceedingly brutalized slave system, these refugees became and continued to be wards of the state. They were untrained and ... they had, in the main, been field hands without the benefits of civilized domesticity ... The word 'miserable' is frequently applied to them and we may conclude that whatever folk culture they came with from Virginia and Maryland was quickly eroded and did not survive the gruelling period of adjustment to their new surroundings. ('Black' 12–13)

Such scholarship is practically an unblanching echo of Haliburton.[9] (One must even wonder what 'benefits of civilized domesticity' – i.e., household enslavement – the erstwhile 'chattel' had so churlishly foregone.)

Depleted intellectual leadership, poverty (and attendant outmigration), illiteracy, and anti-black stereotypes taxed Africadians ruinously. But they invented a versatile counterweight to their oppression: the African Baptist Association (ABA) and its successor (following the healing of a thirteen-year-long [1867–80] rift in the organization), the African United Baptist Association (AUBA) – the oldest and most prominent Africadian institution (a grouping of some two dozen churches). Founded in 1854 by Richard Preston (c.1791–1861), an escaped slave from Virginia and an evangelical heir of Alline and George, the genius of this black-focused church was that it incarnated the separatist and spiritually oriented ideology that, as Walker urges, Africadians had evolved by 1840:

In their peripheral society they produced their own leadership, developed their own religious style and nourished a belief that in separation they could best realise the salvation of their souls and the integrity of their group identity. For the black Nova Scotians the Promised Land became a realm of the spirit, a place where they could be themselves and find their own destiny even though engulfed by a society that denied them all other means of self-expression. (*Black* 396)

The importance of the creation of the ABA/AUBA cannot be exaggerated, for it incorporated, in Africadian form, the luminous properties of the New World African church:

[It] comprised a product constructed by the faith and devotion of an oppressed people diligently bent on building a world of their own: (a) a political space wherein they could experience the necessary conditions of human existence, namely freedom and equality; (b) a moral space wherein individuals could expect to be treated with respect and dignity befitting their nature as 'children of God'; (c) a socio-cultural space wherein the people could enjoy themselves, express their many and varied talents, and compete for social status; (d) a sacred space wherein the people could discover the ultimate source of meaning for their lives in the midst of their suffering and oppression. (Paris, *Moral* 3–4)

Nor can the insistence of ABA/AUBA adherents on their distinctiveness be downplayed, for, as historian Philip G.A. Griffin-Allwood admits, 'in 1887 the African Baptists decided to keep their separate identity within the [white Maritime Baptist] Convention, thus remaining essentailly [*sic*] separate while becoming partly integrated' (167).

Being the premiere institution and vehicle of communal expression in Africadia, the ABA/AUBA produced, sponsored, or sanctioned, in its first century, all the Africadian literature that was considered mandatory, and proscribed the sinful.[10] Its influence was pervasive enough that Africadian folk culture generated scant secular or anti-clerical material. When Fauset toured Nova Scotia, for instance, he was shamed to find 'whole groups of Negroes who had never heard of Brer Rabbit' (vii) – in the Uncle Remus tales popularized by author Joel Chandler Harris (1848–1908). He suspected that his respondents objected to this material.[11]

If the Church did not ordain such stances, certainly it did nothing to hinder them. Rather, it promoted its own vision of Africadian culture, one which eulogized Africadians as a God-favoured remnant who had triumphed over American slavery and survived British North American (and Canadian) prejudice. Its role, then, was messianic, a conviction revealed by Rev. James Thomas when he reports, writing in 1861, that Preston 'used to speak of [the ABA churches] rising up and taking a stand upon one common platform amongst the great nations of the earth' (*Minutes* [1861] 5). The 1911 AUBA minutes record Rev. M.B. Puryear's declaration that 'we are responsible for the salvation of Nova Sctia [*sic*]' (*Minutes* [1912] 3). For the Church, then, religion *was* culture; the *Spirit* rainbowed over every righteous instance of communal expression. Proof for this assertion appears in the manuscript minutes of the meeting of 6 May 1951 of District No. 4 of the AUBA, during which, writes secretary Mrs E. Cromwell, 'Mrs Anderson reviewed the history of the negro that we might understand the various type [*sic*] of music born of slavery' ('Minutes' [1956] n.p.). Significantly, this music – 'sorrowful song, jubilee and testimonial songs' – was interpreted as connoting the slaves' 'various moods in their love for Christ' ('Minutes' [1956] n.p.). Such evidence indicates that the supposed Great Void (1798–1974) in Africadian literature should be read, rather, as the Golden Age of its ecclesiastical heritage. The supreme Africadian epic poem of the era is the ABA/AUBA itself.

IV

The Great Void culminated in the late 1960s with the destruction of Africville, a rural, historic black enclave on the northern shore of the peninsula of Halifax. This final emergency saw the Church's collapse before the incursions of the modern state. Indeed, its defeat entailed the reduction of four hundred Church parishioners to public tenancy and the epochal demolition of Seaview United Baptist Church (founded in 1849 as Campbell Road Church). Too, in the undeniable crucifixion of Africville, Church leaders witnessed a graphic display of the power of the modern state – with its squads of social scientists, journalists, and police – to delegitimate Africadia's existence – and, thus, potentially, to annihilate the AUBA itself. Hence, in 1966, Deacon S.M. Jones, president of the AUBA Laymen, warned, apparently, a district meeting of the AUBA that 'the African Baptist Churches are going down-grade' and asked, rhetorically, 'if we should lose our churches by reneging our responsibilities, what will tie us together?' ('Minute Book' [1966] n.p.). In 1967, following the extirpation of Seaview United Baptist Church, Rev. W.P. Oliver delineated, scathingly, his hostility to the possibility of the further loss of Africadian communities:

> The Church is a social institution and exists because of communities. When communities disintegrate and are broken up, the church disappears. The community of Africville has been destroyed; its people dispersed; [*sic*] The Seaview Baptist Church will be no more ... Can the church serve its community? Will there be an African Baptist Association when the communities are dispersed? (*Minutes* [1968] 17–19)

The death of Africville alerted the Church that it faced a sly enemy in the modern state, a foe metonymized by W.P. Oliver as 'social scientists and psychologists' who 'move in and break up the power structure of our communities – more than that, our Association as a whole' (*Minutes* [1968] 17).

In an indelible dialectic, however, the cowing of the Church, that is to say, the public revelation of its weakness, also renewed and re-energized nationalistic forces. If 'the impotence of classical [i.e., religious-based] Africadian nationalism in the modern age was ... revealed by the confrontation between the bulldozers of "progress" and the frail, wooden walls of Seaview United Baptist Church,' its 'literal collapse ... was a signal, especially to the younger generation, that new values had to be asserted to preserve the collectivity against the corrosive effects of [empty] secularization and liberal individualism' (George Elliott Clarke 'Death' 26). These values included a heightened political awareness, that is, a *blackened* consciousness, and an attendant effort to reclaim Africadian history and to revivify and proclaim the beauties of Africadian culture. If all art is a cry for identity, that cry, for Africadians, became much more urgent after the martyrdom of Africville. Paradoxically, then, through its defeat on the Africville question, the Church mothered contemporary Africadian literature.

In the disaster's wake, two texts materialized that underscored the need to prevent the recurrence of 'another Africville' (a now popular Africadian slogan)[12]: *Africville: The Life and Death of a Canadian Black Community* (1974), authored by two Euro-Canadian sociologists, Donald H. Clairmont and Dennis William Magill, analyses the dynamics of the community's slow, painful dismemberment, while Frederick Ward's *Riverlisp: Black Memories* (1974), based in part on conversations with Africville relocatees, provides a prose coda to the lost community. In their work, Clairmont and Magill conclude that 'if the [Africville] relocation is framed in terms of the liberal-welfare model of planned social change ...' it can hardly be called a success and in none of the ... components of social policy does it signal new creative ways of intervening dramatically to alter radically the life opportunities of the poor and deprived' (258–9). Lyrically, Ward maps an imaginary community, Riverlisp, whose residents take as much pride in their settlement as had Africvillers in theirs: 'Nobody claim th [*sic*] woods and swamp hind em. I means, we all just goes there and uses em to hunt rabbit, take care of our wants, or whatever. We ain't on welfare here ... ' (13). *Africville* warned of what could happen to every black community in Nova Scotia if no struggle were undertaken to preserve their territory; *Riverlisp* promised that every black community was worth preserving. Both texts, in their different ways, awakened Africadians to the need to assert their cultural heritage, an impulse which motivates most post-Africville literary works.

Although the Africville debacle weakened the AUBA, thereby helping spur the issuance of Africadian literature *sans* the Church's imprimatur, other factors also wrought change. The cessation of legal segregation, the semi-mitigation of poverty and illiteracy, the adoption of human rights legislation, and the striking of publicly funded, secular and cultural nationalist, black advocacy groups, expanded the beleaguered Africadian *bourgeoisie* and increased the ranks of its professional artists. Sociologist J.A. Mannette classes these post-1974 artists and writers – including poets Maxine Tynes (b. 1949) and David Woods (b. 1959), writer-filmmaker Sylvia Hamilton (b. 1950), and other artists – as a relatively privileged, *arriviste* cadre:

[T]hey are part of the indigenous Black Nova Scotia middle class. They are educated; most have or are seeking, post-secondary academic training. They took
advantage of the spaces provided by a conjuncture of historical forces in the 1960s
and 1970s which propelled some Black people into upward mobility ... Most are
under forty years of age. Many are women. They tend to live in the Halifax metro
area. They are self-consciously Black. ('Revelation' 4)

Though Mannette fails to stress that blacks were not merely passive beneficiaries of social progress, but, rather, forced liberalizations to occur, her description is just. The new Africadian artist is a confident articulator of the communal culture, albeit in often staunchly individualist ways.

If, in 1960s Québec, 'a secular and urban-orientated liberalism took firm
root' in a formerly faith-based, conservative community (McNaught 274), a
radical transformation also occurred in Africadia. It was as if, after the bulldozers pushed Africville into the sea, rank-and-file Africadians sought to
strengthen their *nation*. Simultaneously, artists like Wesley-Daye sought to
publish, to utter themselves and their people into being, an effort she undertakes in *To My Someday Child*: 'You gave me these boundaries – / Of alley dirt
and fears, / I'm your product, / I'm your child, / Your back alley tramp!'
(quoted in *Fire*, vol. 2, 67). The outcome of the downfall of Africville was an
upsurge in *national* feeling, pride, which, in turn, demanded a combative
assertiveness. This reflex, engendered in the rubble of Africville, can be termed
the Africadian Renaissance.

V

It is impossible to divorce the Africadian Renaissance from nationalist thought.
Critic René Dionne writes that 'la littérature [marginale] trouve alors sa place
dans ce mouvement humain qu'est l'effort de développement régional; elle est
la conscience vivante d'une totalité nouvelle' (27). Moreover, a dream of nationalism has existed from the inception of the Africadian community, a fact
proven by the establishment and perpetuation of the ABA/AUBA. If Africadia,
this tiny, ecclesiastical state, was, classically, a community of believers, present-day Africadian cultural nationalism enacts the transubstantiation, not the
obliteration, of religious feeling, that profound emotion whose genealogy is
located in the myths of the collective.

From the instant of its annunciation in Africadian discourse, the term *renaissance* is linked to notions of a distinct collectivity. In a 1983 interview, Africadian
activist Burnley A. Jones cites the occurrence of 'a cultural and intellectual
renaissance' which he relates to 'the development of a black intellectual elite
for the first time in Nova Scotia' (Story 39–40).[13] Introducing George Borden's
Footprints – Images and Reflections (1993), W.P. Oliver cites 'an evolving renaissance from within the Black population of this seaside province,' that is to say,
'a new and novel reaction to dissatisfaction, replacing placards and rallies'

(Introduction iv). David Woods's poetic debut, *Native Song* (1990), was, according to its back-cover publicity, an addition 'to the bold chorus of Nova Scotia's Black Cultural Renaissance.'[14] The Africadian Renaissance exemplifies what African-American scholar Houston A. Baker, Jr, terms 'renaissancism,' that is to say, 'a *spirit* of nationalistic engagement that begins with intellectuals, artists, and spokespersons' (*Modernism* 91).

Replying to the clearance of Africville, this Africadian *renaissancism* seeks to reclaim Africadian history, for, as Mannette urges, 'the story of black Nova Scotians' is part of 'the "forbidden history" of this province' ('Strangers' 5). Africadian artists contest received notions of Nova Scotianness: 'The image of the Nova Scotian may be white and kilted but what is claimed by black people is a Nova Scotian identity' ('Strangers' 5). In his introductory note, then, to the program of the Neptune Theatre production of his unpublished play *Shine Boy* (1988), a history of Africadian pugilist George Dixon (1870–1909), George Boyd proclaims, 'my aim, with this play, is to resurrect him from obscurity; emancipate his voice and let the public know this was a great man, a man of which we all can truly be proud' (*Shine* n.p.). Not only do Africadian writers reconfigure history, they also resist their erasure from the canons imagined by their African-Canadian *confrères*. For example, Trinidadian-Canadian author M. NourbeSe Philip observes that, 'working in Canada as an "Afrosporic" writer, I am very aware of *the absence of a tradition of Black writing* as it exists in England or the U.S.' (*Frontiers* 45, my italics), a comment which misreads and pauperizes, albeit innocently, that very tradition. If Africadian literature is born and reborn in crisis, the perpetuity of this condition is determined in part by the constant effort of Africadian writers to attempt to breach the consciousnesses – and bibliographies – of extra-communal scholars and writers.

Thus, a pronounced attribute of contemporary Africadian writing is that, like many ex-centric discourses, it is 'une littérature engagée' (Dionne 40). Hence, W.P. Oliver finds that George Borden's poetry 'unmasks' the legacy of 'deprived education and training, rejected employment and benefits, denied services and recreation, withheld rewards and praises, injurious insults and dehumanizing humiliation' (Introduction v). The poet broods on 'problems and unfavourable changes, in order that those who follow after may not forget the mountain-like chain of obstacles which had to be surmounted' (Introduction v). In her poem 'Africville Spirit,' Tynes testifies, 'it is important to recognize / Black community and to own community and all Black experience' (60). In 'Cashiers at the Supermarket,' Tynes views afresh those who manage elementary market exchanges: 'Cashiers never look into your eyes. / They fondle and trade someone else's cash / for tomatoes and cauliflower' (25). In 'November Tea,' Hamilton mulls the poverty of the elderly:

On a chilly November morning
what does it feel like
when you're old

(when you're sixty-three)
to ask someone
not even half that
for twenty-five cents
to buy a cup of tea? (Quoted in Wallace, *Daughters* 48)

Africadian socio-political commentary is legion.

Though Africadian renaissancism debates public issues, it also articulates a specific sense of place, for 'home' is where self-identity is rooted. In her 1991 essay 'The "Home Place" in Modern Maritime Literature,' Gwendolyn Davies suggests that this locale 'emerges as a symbol of cultural continuity and psychological identification in the face of social fragmentation ...' (194). Davies also affirms that the 'home place' conveys 'an "intensified realization" of *self* ... in Maritime literature' (199). Similarly, African-American critic bell hooks, in 'Homeplace: A Site of Resistance,' accents the psychologically recuperative effects of the 'homeplace.' For hooks, it is 'that space where we return for renewal and self-recovery, where we can heal our wounds and become whole' (*Yearning* 49). In 'Dialogue #3: Old Man (to the Squatter),' Ward writes perceptively, 'You ain't a place. Africville is us ... Now go back ... and put you [*sic*] dwelling up again' (quoted in *Fire*, vol. 2, 19–20). In 'Native Song,' Woods lists Africadian communities like Weymouth Falls and Sunnyville as 'deep cradles of human love' (102).

If Africadian Renaissance literature is, to large extent, the disavowal of a perilous marginality, its strategies – as an English literature formed in the crucible of colonialism and slavery – mirror those of other post-colonial literatures.[15] It can be interpreted, then, in terms of two models of post-colonial theory that Bill Ashcroft, Gareth Griffiths, and Helen Tiffin expound in *The Empire Writes Back: Theory and Practice in Post-Colonial Literatures* (1989). First, it fits a 'regional' model, which eyes 'the distinctive features of the ... regional culture'; secondly, it fits a 'race-based' model, which identifies the elements that it shares with other diasporic African literatures (15). Being a 'regional' discourse, it contests the charges of provincialism that are often levelled against literatures produced by ex-centric regions. Dionne broaches this point in the context of French literature: 'en France, en effet, la littérature dite régionaliste ... a toujours été considérée comme inférieure, parce le particularisme qu'elle reflète, jugé de Paris, l'empêcherait d'atteindre à l'universalité dont ferait montre la grande littérature française' (12). Sallying against such damnations, Africadian writers reject 'the silencing and marginalizing of the post-colonial voice by the imperial centre,' through 'the abrogation of the imperial centre within the text; and the active appropriation of the language and culture of that centre' (Ashcroft et al. 83). See, in this regard, Tynes's 'Africville Spirit,' which declares, 'Tynes is a Black community name / and I am from this community; / this Maritime, Halifax, down home Nova Scotia Black community' (60). Tynes undercuts allegations of provinciality by foregrounding and mapping the vitality of her experience – according to the 'poetics' of the 'imperial' or metropolitan centre ('white' Nova Scotia or Toronto or New York City). Other Africadian writers perform likewise.

As well as being a 'regional' discourse, Africadian literature is also a 'racial' one. This point gilds its necessarily double-edged relationship to English. As Ashcroft, Griffiths, and Tiffin maintain, English was, for the slaves, 'a language of division imposed to facilitate exploitation' (27). The struggle between African tongues and the imposition of the Anglo-Saxon language was conducted, as I discuss in 'The Career of Black English in Nova Scotia,' throughout the English-colonized Americas, including Nova Scotia. The eradication of traditional African tongues issued in the making of a new English, the residue of havoc. This 'havoc' or sense of rupture in the traditional grammar, syntax, and literary meaning of English explains the inherent tension between the written and the spoken that disturbs African diasporic literatures. Ward is one Africadian writer who has demonstrably triumphed in employing this tension creatively. See his poem 'The Death of Lady Susuma':

> It were a quick and trembling-tickled *yes*,
> Hushed as though a hollowness neath ovals filled
> With finger presses and waved off by hen's down
> Tied at the hollowness's end in streamers – sing a
> Softness. (*Curing* 57)

The pronounced employment of what linguists Shana Poplack and Sali Tagliamonte term 'African Nova Scotian English (ANSE)' (301) is a signal aspect of the Africadian Renaissance. ANSE, 'a variety spoken by descendants of African American slaves who immigrated to Nova Scotia in the late 18th and early 19th centuries' (Poplack and Tagliamonte 301), resonates with distinctiveness – and marginalization:

> [*De facto* racial segregation in Nova Scotia] is largely unidirectional. Given the nature of the African Nova Scotian settlements, almost all residents must seek employment outside of the community, whereas there is little reason for strangers to enter. This has the double effect of preserving the appropriate conditions for use of the vernacular within the community, while at the same time rendering use of the standard infelicitous in this same context. (Poplack and Tagliamonte 333)

While the separateness of black communities makes retention of Africadian English possible, 'many speakers also control the standard pole of the English continuum' (Poplack and Tagliamonte 333). Ward and other Africadian writers play with this diglossic heritage, thus recuperating Africadian *orature* as a literary instrument.

History-oriented, *engagé*, home-centred, post-colonial, ex-centric, and diglossic, Africadian Renaissance (that is, post-Africville) literature resists any facile incorporation within the post-modern project of anti-nationalism and the concomitant engineering of a technology-driven, global 'free market' of goods, services, and intellectual property. Contemporary Africadian literature displays an anti-modern modernity,[16] a cultural form exhibiting what critic Clyde Taylor casts as 'the familiar African dilemma of needing to sift and mediate progressive directions from the options of tradition vs. techno-capitalism' ('We' 80). This 'Afro-modernity' undertakes 'the transformation of the best traditional values in the post-feudal context of industrial society, and the simultaneous extrication from the co-products of western industrialism: slavery, colonialism, and imperialism' ('We' 80). In other words, 'Afro-modernity' entails both a tenacious retention of the best values of the past *and* a rejection of the intolerant systems linked to technological expansionism. Woods voices this position in his poetry, which equates modernity with doom. In 'Preston,' 'A native-land ... / Moves with its own style / against the dint of the modern world'; in 'Bridgetown,' the speaker 'could not ... convince minds bent / on modernity, / Out of their own destruction'; in 'Les Negres,' 'modern lights reveal / Wrecked souls and lost souls'; and in 'Epitaph,' the race-traitor Kipoch 'is a modern type / He goes and serves willingly' (*Native* 13, 35, 60, 72). ·

The ghost of Africville lurks behind this *angst* regarding liberal modernity. Indeed, the community lives on – in its exiles and in its literature – 'as an indictment against racism, as a critique of technocratic, imposed approaches to social change, and as a celebration of community and the human spirit' (Clairmont, 'Moving' 76). Clearly, this opposition to the dangers posed by modernity – read as a homogenizing and erasing liberalism – must be conservative. When W.P. Oliver lances the euphemistically titled 'Africville Relocation' in 1967, he also skewers a fundamental tenet of liberal rhetoric – integration, which he views as an ideological threat to the survival of the AUBA and of black community:

I support those members of our Association who claim they are going to hold on to the African Baptist Association until they are sure of where they are going. I am not a racist or a separatist but with the breaking up of communities and the scattering of our people (integration they call it), I have seen too many furlorn [*sic*], rejected, churchless people, to take any other position. (*Minutes* [1968] 17)

If Oliver's posture seems regressive, what, then, is one to make of Ward? In *Riverlisp*, he authors this monologue – a transparent critique of the Africville Relocation and the feckless liberalism that produced it:

'We had our own school – education be important culture, you knows? – til year fore last when th government been cused of segregated schooling. Then they done tore our school down soon after that. When a group – *they* aint been down here to look in to see what happen since – anyway they cused them government gin of having schools for black peoples only. Well, th government say "AIN'T NONE SEGREGATION! they done be no segregation." They didnt say "Aint *NO* schooling at all for black folks" ... and some of our people moved out. Then last year come'd and th city, Ambrose City, started surveying and then we come'd like th Indians dispose ... something. Dispossess'd? Yer, that's right.' (14)

Ward's critique – with its wily juxtaposition of the fates of being 'dispose[d of]' and 'Dispossess'd' – recalls that of W.P. Oliver; both men denounce the threats of, in Oliver's words, 'Redevelopment' and the attendant use of black people as 'sociological guinea pigs' (*Minutes* [1968] 18). Interestingly, Oliver, an African Baptist leader, and Ward, a Bahà'i, make common cause against the reverse 'ethnic cleansing' – that is, denial of cultural difference – that liberal modernity implies. Furthermore, their dissent is religiously based. Like the classical French-Canadian nationalists who credit the '[Catholic] Church with its educational privileges [as being] the chief instrument by which an indigenous French culture has survived in North America' (Grant, *Lament* 80), they view the Black Church as a source of Africadian distinctiveness.

The presence of conservatism in contemporary Africadian literature is evinced in the agency granted to Africadian English, the emphasis given to history (events and personages), and the privileging of the mode of realism. Strikingly, too, the classical Africadian concerns – justice, liberty, faith – sung in the *ur*–texts of George, King, and Marrant, recur in contemporary Africadian texts in eulogies for Africville and in assertions of the existence of a unique identity and special history in a specific place.[17] Thus, the sensibilities of the African Baptist Church remain secreted within even 'secular' Africadian texts. For instance, George Borden's 'A Race Defaced' sounds the rhythms of Church oratory:

Wrenched
from their mother earth,
de-rooted
from source and substance,
stripped
corn-husk bare of pride and principle,
marketed
like garden produce. (3)

At the same time, the terms of his critique recall David George's narrative of the brutality of slavery ('Account' 473) and Robertson's breathtakingly searing *The Book of the Bible against Slavery*. One cannot cleave contemporary Africadian literature from its first flowering ...

The Africadian Renaissance is, despite its seeming, sassy newness, a secular recapitulation of the classical religious themes. The persistent desire to conserve vital group values has fostered a lingering, if subtle, religiosity, a subtext that continues to link the present writers of the *nation* with their ancestors. The two annunciations of Africadian literature, in the crises of the Loyalist Exile and the Africville Relocation, are identically conservative, religious, and nationalist.

A like religious conservatism animates those African Americans who, rather than remaining in Nova Scotia after their arrival in 1783, moved on to Sierra Leone in 1792, to live out a Pan-Africanist dream before Pan-Africanism had been dreamt of. Yet, despite their genealogical and historical connection to their compatriots who became Africadians, their inchoate Pan-Africanism failed to bridge the Atlantic. Indeed, neither Africadians nor Sierra Leoneans proved able to unite beyond the baldest sentimentality. Inhabiting different political states – and statuses – they could share little in common, and this truth also framed their literatures. 'Black' literature divides into 'national' enclaves. See, for instance, the work of Sierra Leonean writer Syl Cheney-Coker ...

Notes

1 The research I conducted for this paper was funded by the Canadian Embassy in Washington, DC. Portia May White, a contemporary of U.S. singer Marian Anderson, was a world-renowned, classically trained, Africadian contralto – and the First Diva of the African United Baptist Association of Nova Scotia.

2 A title – or titles – by Rev. Dr Edwin Howard Borden (the first Africadian to graduate from Acadia University, with a Bachelor of Arts degree, in 1892) should also be added to this list of major twentieth-century Africadian works. According to a 1994 newspaper article, Borden, who became a professor of German and ancient and modern languages and a significant interpreter of scripture, published several books. Because he spent his career in the United States (where he died in 1953), his scholarly endeavours have yet to be reclaimed for Africadians. See Donna Byard Sealey, 'Lone,' 18; and Colored, 215–17).

3 Petition of the Coloured People at Preston (1841).

4 Pearleen Oliver's discussion of the history of the community of Beechville foregrounds the typical problems encountered by Africadians during the Great Void (1798–1974):

> The community of Beechville, like all the Black communities of Nova Scotia, was settled with toil and tears ... The grant of land consisting of five thousand acres ... on the North West Arm [at Halifax] was granted to [Black Refugees] by Queen Victoria and was called 'Refugee Hill.' Their tenure on this land was of short duration. They were soon removed further back into the woods to the Chain Lake area. In the early twentieth century the City of Halifax desired this land for a water-shed area and the people of Beechville faced a second removal, and the present community of Beechville took shape. The Great Depression stalked the land and the people of Beechville suffered its damaging effects. The secret of their survival lay in their humble church It was their rock in a weary land and their shelter in a time of storm. ('Mini' n. pag.)

5 The extent and effects of the Africadian diaspora to the United States, especially New England, must not be underestimated. For one thing, the black community of Prince Edward Island virtually disappeared. See Jim Hornby, Black Islanders: Prince Edward Island's Historical Black Community (1991).

6 Blacks in Ontario also endured school segregation. Historian Claudette Knight reports that 'in the March 1857 edition of the *Provincial Freeman*, black editor H.F. Douglas condemned religious and educational segregation: "Separate schools and churches are nuisances that should be abated as soon as possible, they are dark and hateful relics of Yankee Negrophobia"' (265). At the conclusion of her essay on the matter, Knight says, 'The history of black education in mid-nineteenth-century Canada West establishes the presence of racism in the formation of Ontario's public education system' (274). The only 'good' thing that may come out of a separate school and a separate faith *is*, arguably, a separate literature, and one not 'inferior' but 'different.'

7 A fuller discussion of Haliburton's racialized politics and his deployment of racist caricatures is allowed in my articles 'White Niggers, Black Slaves: Slavery, Race and Class in T.C. Haliburton's *The Clockmaker*' (1994) and 'Must We Burn Haliburton?' (1997).

8 Robertson progresses on to postulate that, 'on closer examination' of the text, one can see that 'Coalfleet' is actually using States as a 'marginalized or outsider' character who voices 'emotional truth and unadorned folk wisdom untouched by the artificiality of social custom or advanced education' (*Tide* 116). In other words, perhaps, his Becky States signifies the primitive.

9 If Henry's argument were valid, it would not only eliminate Africadian folk culture, but that of any marginalized community. Her conclusions constitute only, to snatch a phrase from James J. Wilhelm, 'a pseudo-poetry of things' (105). Yet, her views are akin to those of American historian Robin W. Winks, whose own treatment of African-Canadian history is so negative that it borders on racism. For instance, he scruples to tell us that 'Samuel Ringgold Ward[,] "the original nigger" according to Wendell Phillips[,] ... was so black, the abolitionist maintained, that one could not see Ward when he shut his eyes' (265–6). Henry makes mistakes, but Winks's opinions sour and curdle scholarship.

10 Thus, at the 102nd Annual Meeting of the AUBA, Pearleen Oliver, the chair of the Social Service Committee, tabled a report condemning 'the widespread use of Crime Comics among our children and youth. We deeply feel the need of filling the minds of our children with wholesome literature and not with that which promotes crime and violence.' See the 1955 *Minutes of the African United Baptist Association of Nova Scotia* (47).

11 Perhaps some of these Africadian informants saw the Brer Rabbit stories for what Bernard Wolfe was to later view as 'les contes merveilleux ... pour la joie des tout-petits,' that is, as constituting just one more weapon in the arsenal of white, anti-black propaganda (quoted in Fanon, *Peau* 42).

12 Historian C. Mark Davis notes that 'it is not surprising that "Remember Africville" has become a rallying cry against all Black injustices in contemporary Nova Scotia' (151).

13 In his July 1983 *Atlantic Insight* article, 'Black Renaissance in the Arts,' in which he interviews Jones, journalist Alan Story himself uses the phrases 'current artistic awakening,' 'black cultural revolution,' and 'dynamic cultural movement' to denote the heightened artistic activity of Africadians (40–1). In 1987, Jones disputed

the use of the term 'renaissance,' positing that 'the current high level of Black cultural activity does not really represent a "renaissance," for that word denotes a "rebirth" which, in turn, implies a dearth, an absence, of something. The artistic activity represents not a "Harlem Renaissance" but more of a continuum.' See my 1992 article 'An Interview with Rocky Jones: The Politics of Passion' (29). Africadian journalist and writer Charles R. Saunders agrees with Jones:

> Beginning in the 1980s, the arts scene in Nova Scotia has witnessed a major increase in black participation. Informally known as a 'black renaissance,' the upsurge extends to all forms of artistic expression, from the visual to the dramatic ... Welcome as this growth in the quantity and quality of work has been, it is accompanied by an unfortunate side effect. Because previous black literary expression tended to be unheralded and unacknowledged, the current body of work has been perceived as a new development rather than the continuation of a long-established heritage. ('Standing' 12–13)

In my opinion, though, Africadian literature manifests both a long history and a recent blossoming.

14 The complete sentence runs thus: 'As David Woods now makes himself known across Canada through his work in drama as well as in poetry, Pottersfield Press is proud to add his *Native Song* to the bold chorus of Nova Scotia's Black Cultural Renaissance.' See Woods, *Native Song* (back cover).

15 These codes of discourse involve a series of binary relationships, namely 'the dialectic of self and Other, indigene and exile, language and place, slave and free, which is the matrix of post-colonial literatures ...' (Ashcroft et al. 173).

16 The term 'anti-modern' is borrowed from Erik Kristiansen's 1994 essay 'Time, Memory and Rural Transformation: Rereading History in the Fiction of Charles Bruce and Ernest Buckler.' Kristiansen urges that many Atlantic-Canadian writers offer 'critical assessments of modernity'; he defines 'anti-modernist' as representing an 'anti-capitalist, radical conservatism' (225). W.P. Oliver seems to have shared a similar outlook, for, as Kristiansen notes of Nova Scotian novelist Ernest Buckler, Oliver also had cause to believe that 'modernity simply and relentlessly bulldozes history, literally wiping it out of existence' (249). Africville's fate was a literalization of this metaphor.

17 W.P. Oliver went on to found, in 1983, the Black Cultural Centre for Nova Scotia, whose governing body is 'The Society for the *Protection* and *Preservation* of Black Culture in Nova Scotia' (my italics). Surely, this name reflects a general post-Africville concern for the future of a viable Africadian culture, a fate that continues to be coupled with that of the Church. Anne Johnson reminds us, in her preface to *Three Nova Scotian Black Churches*, that 'when a church falters or ceases to exist the community weakens' (n. pag.).

Syl Cheney-Coker's Nova Scotia, or the Limits of Pan-Africanism

For Kenule Saro-Wiwa (1941–95)[1]

Complaint

When scholars and writers have analysed the formation of Black Nova Scotia – or Africadia – between 1783 and 1815 and the establishment of Sierra Leone as a self-governing Crown Colony between 1787 and 1809, they have drawn distinctions injurious to Africadians. Yet, the first black settlers of Nova Scotia and the second-wave black settlers of Sierra Leone were, really, the same people. Both originated in the 3,400 or so African Americans, known as Black Loyalists, transported by Britain, from New York City to New Brunswick, Nova Scotia, Québec, England, and German states at the close of the American Revolutionary War in 1783. Within a decade of their landing in Nova Scotia, however, nearly a third of the Black Loyalists – some 1,200 people – sick of a nasty and hardscrabble colony, accepted the offer of the London-based Sierra Leone Company and its agent, Lieutenant John Clarkson, to be transported to the new 'Promised Land' of Sierra Leone.[2] In Sierra Leone, the ex–Black Loyalists became 'Nova Scotians,' while their African-American sistren and brethren who remained in Nova Scotia became 'caste-down' 'Negroes' and 'Coloureds': the invisible, unsung niggers of the diaspora. The Sierra Leone Nova Scotians formed eventually an élitist élite in their new country, while, in Nova Scotia, blacks became underemployed, poorly educated wards of the state. This arch distinction has played out significantly in the requisite historiography, but also literature, with the work of Sierra Leone poet Syl Cheney-Coker – particularly his novel *The Last Harmattan of Alusine Dunbar* (1990) – proving an ideal instance. No matter, then, the Pan-Africanist precept asserting that 'no black person is free until all are free, and that the liberation and unification of Africa is essential to the dignity of African people everywhere' (Moses 18).[3] National or nationalist identifications distinguish among black peoples to the point of asserting the superiority of some over others. Thus, Cheney-Coker's novel imagines an inimical Nova Scotia in order to explain the later decadence of Sierra Leone – or, in fictional guise, *Malagueta*. Paradoxically, though, Cheney-Coker's attacks on the repressive dictatorship(s) of his belovèd country reveal a heroic equality between the repressed black minority of Nova Scotia and the beleaguered Creoles of Sierra Leone. Before considering Cheney-Coker's novelization of the aforementioned division in treatments of Nova Scotian and Sierra Leonean Black Loyalists, we must trace its influential historiographical manifestations.

British historian Christopher Fyfe, narrating the exodus of the Nova Scotian settlers, informs us – in a tone reminiscent of the cautionary words about those who refused to heed Noah – that those who 'feared to embark [from Nova Scotia] ... remained in a life of abject poverty and humiliation (where their descendants survive today)' (1). In contrast, the Sierra Leone Nova Scotians enacted, by their decision to settle there, 'the first practical manifestation of Pan-Africanism' (2). In addition, their leaders fleshed out a winning, Romantic heroism. To effect their escape from the oppressive Maritime colonies of British North America, Richard Crankapone (or Corankeapon), Fyfe exults, 'led four men three hundred miles on foot from New Brunswick to Halifax through the snowy forests' (5). In choosing to escape to Sierra Leone, Fyfe concludes, 'the settlers had found a new home, better than what they left in Nova Scotia ... ' (19).[4] There is nothing particularly egregious in Fyfe's views and sentiments, for one should expect *the* major historian of Sierra Leone to wager that this country was a superior locale for its foundational settlers than the narrow North Atlantic peninsula they had fled. What is surprising, however, is that Fyfe's perspective has been the dominant reading of most historians.

For instance, introducing his *Black Loyalist Directory: African Americans in Exile after the American Revolution* (1996), American historian Graham Russell Hodges upholds the credo that the Black Loyalist 'exodusters' were wiser than their stay-at-home counterparts. They were, he argues, 'Black religious nationalists' who 'regarded the inevitable assimilation into white Nova Scotian sects as a dilution of their identity' (xxxiii). They were creditably more successful than Africadians: 'In Africa, black women developed leadership gained only by Rose Fortune [the first black policewoman in North America] in Nova Scotia' (xxxvi). In her essay collection *A Genealogy of Resistance* (1997), M. NourbeSe Philip celebrates 'stories of returnees. To Africa' (14), including that of the stalwart 'Loyalists of Nova Scotia who, fed up with the racism in Canada, deciding to go back. Back to Africa' (14). Elsewhere, Philip opines that those who returned to Sierra Leone were 'reconnecting with what should never have been severed' (23). In his majestic, magisterial account of the Black Loyalist odyssey in Nova Scotia and Sierra Leone, *The Black Loyalists: The Search for a Promised Land in Nova Scotia and Sierra Leone, 1783–1870* (1976), James Walker finds that 'the conditions, prejudices and insecurities that drove their brethren to Sierra Leone drove the Nova Scotian blacks into their own isolated society during the nineteenth century ...' (396). To this day, 'the blacks in Nova Scotia have remained a peripheral society, economically marginal and socially distinct ... Their victory has been in their endurance' (396). The Sierra Leone Nova Scotians savour, however, a distinctly positive fate: their descendants 'have played a leadership role in Sierra Leone right up to the present time' (396).

Walker also records their sentiment that 'the Black Loyalists who followed Thomas Peters and John Clarkson [to Sierra Leone] made the wiser choice in 1792' (397). Damningly, Africadians themselves agree with this assessment: 'One black student [in Halifax] exclaimed in 1971, "We all should have gone over there when we had the chance". He met no argument from his classmates' (Walker, *Black* 397). Even Africadian amateur historian Pearleen Oliver salutes the Sierra Leone exodus in her booklet *A Root and a Name* (1977): 'They came into Halifax with a mighty surge and Lieutenant [John] Clarkson, observing them, spoke of them as "the flower of the Black people"' (139). Oliver then iterates Clarkson's phrase to emphasize the exodus's romanticism: '[Black Loyalist Baptist leader] David George and the more than twelve hundred "flower of the Black people" took with them a bag of Nova Scotian soil which they ceremoniously planted in Sierra Leone' (*Root* 140). The Black Nova Scotians who elected not to go to Sierra Leone seem to have made an anti-romantic, if not foolish, choice, for they endured subsequently generations of poverty, powerlessness, and illiteracy.[5]

Admittedly, this city-mouse-versus-country-mouse historiography has served us well. It has illuminated the clear opportunities for 'Nova Scotian' agency and progress in the black majority state of Sierra Leone, while exposing the ill-usage and inclemencies to which Africadians were historically subjected as a highly visible and stigmatized minority in Nova Scotia's white-supremacist society. Moreover, a multitude of anecdotes and examples bears out the bleak repercussions of their anti-flight decision. When Sierra Leone achieved its independence from Britain in 1961, for instance, it boasted an indigenous black leadership, from its prime minister through to its civil servants and its political and professional class. In contrast, in Nova Scotia in 1961, the black minority was just beginning to benefit from the cessation of legal school segregation. But it was also soon to lose one of its historic communities, Africville, to an obliterating urban renewal *cum* social engineering plan implemented by the provincial capital, the City of Halifax. It would appear, then, that any objective comparison of Sierra Leone and Black Nova Scotia (Africadia) must conclude that the Black Loyalists who chose to remain in Nova Scotia in 1792 gambled badly.

It is time to examine the literary construction of Africadian inadequacy that Sierra Leone's premier poet, Syl Cheney-Coker, enunciates in his collections of poetry and in his novel *The Last Harmattan of Alusine Dunbar*. Valuably, Cheney-Coker's writings suggest that there are limits to Pan-Africanism, for the ideology of black internationalism cannot restrain the necessity for constructing the black national state (or being) as an approximation of paradise. In short, an ineluctable poetic dialectic leads Cheney-Coker to degrade Africadia to both exalt Sierra Leone and to explain its decline.

Creoles and Corruption

Born Syl Cheney Coker in Freetown, Sierra Leone, in 1945, Coker hyphenated, legally, his middle name and surname in 1970. A professor of English at the

University of Maiduguri, Nigeria, he holds degrees in English from the University of Oregon, University of California (Los Angeles), and the University of Wisconsin (Madison). Before entering the Academy, he worked as a drummer, radio producer, factory worker, stevedore, and as a journalist in both Sierra Leone and the United States. He took his first teaching position at the University of the Philippines, and he was a visiting writer in the International Writing Program at the University of Iowa in 1988.[6] Though his poems and fictions centre on his native land, Cheney-Coker has lived most of his adult life in exile from Sierra Leone. Perhaps because he is partly of Nova Scotian settler – that is to say, of Creole – or *Krio* – descent, Cheney-Coker alludes to Nova Scotia often, if obliquely, in his work. In his poetry, Nova Scotia is conflated with the epithet *Creole*; in his novel, the province is conflated with the sign *Canada*.

Cheney-Coker's stance toward Nova Scotia reflects his aesthetic, which is 'dictated,' he has said, 'by a nagging desire to understand the contradictions of the elements of my people' ('Cheney-Coker' 114). Influenced by the Marxist Chilean poet Pablo Neruda (1904–73), Cheney-Coker sees poetry as 'a return to the primordial beginning of the word, when the word was free of associated meaning, of metric clarity or purity' ('Cheney-Coker' 114). Less abstractly, he asserts that 'my poetry comes from the wellspring of a country, a world continually brutalized, and from the depths of my own suffering ...' ('Cheney-Coker' 114). His themes consist of 'his disgust with himself and what he calls his "foul genealogy"; his disillusion with the christian [*sic*] church; the betrayal of his love for a woman whom he had seen as a symbol of his committment [*sic*] to a Third World revolution; the suffering of his people as experienced through his own exile' (*Concerto*, back cover).[7] Thus, 'he sees his poetry as more Latin American than African' (*Concerto*, back cover). Not unexpectedly, then, Cheney-Coker dramatizes a reading of Nova Scotia intended to heighten the grandeur of the Sierra Leonean experiment and the tragedy of its real failure. In essence, Nova Scotia is, for him, a Hell, while Sierra Leone is a proto-Utopia stymied and stultified by its political and ethnic elites, particularly that class now termed *Creole*.

At this juncture, a brief discussion of the class and ethnic structure of Sierra Leone is advisable. When the nation became independent from Britain in 1961, it possessed a democratically elected parliament dominated by the Creoles, whose members – only 2 per cent of the population – 'controlled most of the major civil service and professional positions' of the state (Roberts [25]). Created by nineteenth-century intermarriages among Nova Scotians, Jamaican Maroons, and Africans liberated from slave ships by the British and landed in Sierra Leone, the Creoles were a group of 'westernized black settlers' (Cartwright 11). Later, they asserted their claim to be the natural, post-independence ruling class of Sierra Leone, repressing both the indigenous Temne and Mendi peoples. But this situation could not endure. For one thing, while the indigenous peoples are mainly Muslim or Animist in faith, the Creole group is predominantly Christian. Scholar J. Lorand Matory holds that while Creole and other 'repatriates from the African diaspora modeled their lifestyles on those of their Euro-American former masters ..., the Creole cultures they produced, including the forms of transatlantic racial identity that they propagated, became objects of both resentment and imitation by their indigenous neighbours ...' (38). Historian John R. Cartwright agrees that '[the Creoles'] very westernization ... set them apart from the indigenous tribesmen ...' (15). Then, 'under the impetus of tribal [sic] rivalry [between the Mendes and the Temnes], military rule entered the political arena' in the late 1960s (Roberts 250), resulting in the formation of Dr Siaka Probyn Stevens's All People's Congress (APC) one-party dictatorship and the decline of Creole power. Political scientist George O. Roberts notes that the APC grew, at first, with 'the support of dissatisfied or disenchanted Creole politicians' (101), but later 'managed to elevate tribal [sic] hostility to a high level' (182), thus inculcating 'a new hierarchy of Temne and Limba ..., with a clear expression of animosity toward the Mende and, to some extent, the Creoles for having been their "oppressors"' (183). Still, the APC maintained its governance by striking an alliance among the Temne, Limba, minority peoples, and Creoles.[8] It is this Creole complicity in dictatorship that Cheney-Coker assaults ferociously in his second and third books of poetry, *Concerto for an Exile* (1973) and *The Graveyard Also Has Teeth* (1974), issued jointly as *The Graveyard Also Has Teeth*, with *Concerto for an Exile* (1980). (His fourth book of poetry, *The Blood in the Desert's Eyes* [1990] also proffers a damned Sierra Leone, but in relatively few of the poems.) The unifying theme of his work is a belief that the Creoles have slid into decadence, interpreted as a mania for European culture and Christianity.

Cheney-Coker's concern is not just a matter of poetic licence, however, for historians and other writers have cited the Occidental orientation of the Creoles as a source of cultural conflict. According to Cartwright, the Creoles, as a dominant class, valued 'literacy in English, Christianity, and a marked attachment to English social values and to England as a spiritual home' (16). Too, they were 'sufficiently "westernized" to be set sharply apart from the [indigenous] people ..., and to act as spearheads of the Western cultural advance' (16). Even so, as the twentieth-century waxed, their status waned, and, claims Cartwright, 'the Creoles began to show that marked lack of self-assurance and self-esteem which became so obvious to observers in later years' (17). Supporting this reading, Sylvia Wynter, in her treatment of the work of Sierra Leonean poet Lemuel Johnson, views the Sierra Leonean capital, Freetown, as a symbol of Creole obeisance to white imperial power and, thus, to racial confusion:

> Freetown, Sierra Leone is a part of the continent of Africa. Yet, in part, it is also a Creole island, like an island in the Caribbean. The Creole experience is born out of the condition of exile; out of a Middle Passage of body and mind ... For Freetown was to be a monument to that great act of British/European philanthropy – by which the English, having enslaved the Africans for centuries, had accumulated enough wealth from their labor and sale to afford an exquisite frisson of conscience. (86)

The Original Sin of the Creoles was to accept an intolerably partial assimilation, not only in terms of a more-or-less phoney capital, Freetown, established by white guilt, but even in terms of their own souls, or so Wynter insists:

> The Cross of Christ was made of wood. The Cross of the Freetown Christian was an arrangement of genes: black skin, lips, eyes that existed to negate, perversely, the white skin of Christ. They took up their Cross and walked. They endured their passion – 'their hell in small places' – and proceeded to sweat in thick English flannels, to answer in Latin, to endure the incongruity of their passions, and to re-enact the Crucifixion not as tragedy but as farce. (87)

For Wynter and Johnson, the Creole allegiance to false gods and false ways rendered them false to themselves and false to Sierra Leone.

Likewise, Cheney-Coker attacks the Creole class with unadulterated vitriol that does not spare the author:

> I think of Sierra Leone
> and my madness torments me
> all my strange traditions
> the plantation blood in my veins
> my foul genealogy!
> I laugh at this Creole ancestry
> which gave me my negralized head
> all my polluted streams ...
>
> imagine my alcoholic head at dance
> but from what plantation
> and from what people my rum
> in my country the Creoles drink only
> Black and white with long sorrows
> hanging from their colonial faces! ('Hydropathy' 7, 8)

A critique is also rendered in 'Freetown':

> and I think of my brothers with 'black skin and white masks'
> (I myself am one *heh heh heh*)
> my sisters who plaster their skins with the white cosmetics
> to look whiter than the snows of Europe
> but listen to the sufferings of our hearts
> there are those who when they come to plead
> say make us Black Englishmen decorated Afro-Saxons
> Creole masters leading native races ('Freetown' 16)

The reference to Frantz Fanon's *Peau noire, masques blancs* (1952) – *Black Skin, White Masks* (1965) – is appropriate, for Cheney-Coker loathes the supposed attempt of Creole blacks to undergo a kind of 'lactification' (Fanon's term), to betray their own bodies, their own reality, and to 'ape' their former European oppressors:

> civic women lead the cotillion
> but the twenty yards of your gowns
> are dragged through the violent zero of riot
> mopping up the blood reeking of rape ('Cotillion' 12)

The poet voices an even more vehement class hatred in 'Absurdity':

> I am the beginning the running image
> and the foul progency [sic] of my race
> these strange Afro-Saxon negroes
> and for deceiving the world
> about our absurdity
> behold my negralized head in flames! (17)

His disgust with the decline of his country, from a locus of emancipation – founded by British philanthropist Granville Sharp – to a slough of privation, animates his 1974 poem 'He Falls, the Invertebrate Man':

> once I howled Africa trumpeting all my sorrow
> you were the witness Africa of that plantation madness
> you and I dancing to our fallen history
> here is the monument to my disgrace the ship hailing my chagrin
> and the four centuries of shame like a halo over the head of my country
>
> and how the angelic bell rings welcoming you Granville Sharpe [sic]
> the image of the passage I dare not name ...
> my luckless voyagers dumped on the spot where no grass
> has grown with propitious scions (91)

Cheney-Coker's rage spews forth in images of fire, garbage, putridity, volcanic eruptions, bloated corpses, storms, suicide – a repertoire of Blakean visions of Satanic decrepitude. But these grim tropes mirror what he terms 'my Nova Scotian madness my tree of agony' ('Concerto for an Exile' 20), that is, the fratricidal violence, Eurocentrism, and pervasive corruption of the Creole class. Certainly, his anger at Stevens's sanguinary régime is only equalled by his frustration at the ugly failure of his compatriots to end it. In 'Concerto for an Exile,' he mourns the 1971 Stevens-ordered executions of Brigadier-General John Ahmadu Bangura and other soldiers: 'away in Sierra Leone the boulevards of corpses / they shot them and slit their bellies for proof of their subversion' (20).[9] His poem 'Obelisk' personalizes the supposedly rotten Anglophilism of the Creole élite in terms of a Byronic self-indictment: 'I die to be posthumously rewarded / with an English grave with elephants dancing there!' (33) The poet seeks an un-Europeanized, un-Christianized *Africanité*, a version of purity, what Black British scholar Paul Gilroy dubs 'the ontological essentialist view ... often ... characterised by a brute pan-Africanism' (31). Tragically, Cheney-Coker's yearning for Romantic innocence can never quite be requited because his being is 'impure': he is a Creole. Occidentalized, his caste is fated to turn the proto-Utopic Sierra Leone into waste.

Protest against the betrayal of Sierra Leone by Europe-loving and lucre-besotted Creoles and complicitous Temne soldier-dictators receives expansive expression in Cheney-Coker's novel *The Last Harmattan of Alusine Dunbar*. Opening with the imminent execution of the brave leader of a failed *coup d'état*, General Tamba Masimiara, the novel is a magic realist, *roman à clef* account of the establishment and decline of Malagueta, a palimpsest for Sierra Leone. The novel reprises its slide from its first aspirations to glory as a province of freedom for repatriated Africans (Black Loyalists, Jamaican Maroons, and Liberated Africans) to its APC status as the bankrupt fiefdom of a Creole-backed, Temne *Duce*, his mercenaries, his military, and his foreign and transplanted business allies. The recurring reason for the implosion of Malagueta / Sierra Leone is the aristocratic pursuit of fanciful, Eurocentric values that deny the needs of the majority of the citizens:

> Modes of behaviour long abandoned in the factories and gutters of England were still being copied with diligence by the despicable lot who made up the middle and upper classes. They were men and women whose other passion was to drink tea in the afternoon in the ovens of their drawing rooms and parlours modelled on the antediluvian style of pre-abolition America while worrying about the cost of taking holidays in England. (xiii)

Cheney-Coker's fictional study of the prevailing plight of Creole Sierra Leone accords with the socio-political and poetic analyses advanced by Cartwright, Roberts, Johnson, and Wynter. His representation of a backward Europhilicism amongst the Creoles is affirmed by Roberts's insight that their 'Westernism is one that is conducive to the minimizing of communal adherence, and ... the dimunition [sic] of ethnic identity' (132). Thus, Cheney-Coker blames the 'new philosophy called Individualism' (*Last* 377), in part, for the degradation of Malagueta. It creates 'fratricidal worms' (*Last* 377).

To condemn the falling away of Stevens's régime from the communalism that Cheney-Coker prefers,[10] the author aligns its fictional *other* – contemporary Malagueta – with the historical American and British North American oppression that the founding Nova Scotian settlers had fled. Thus, the dour conditions that Black Loyalists suffered in Nova Scotia are contrasted with their reasonable expectations of establishing a free and satisfactory life in Malagueta (Sierra Leone). A Black Loyalist character, Phillis, recalls that in 'Canada ... de people same as white folks in America, but dey don't have no slaves, but ain't kind either 'cause dey done give us land ain't fit to grow nothing: marshland and swamp, and when de winter come, oh Lawd, it sure is cold!' (125). Another character, Thomas Bookerman, an image of the historical Black Loyalist leader Thomas Peters (c. 1738–92), remembers having been 'inspired by the irrefutable evidence of the exploitation of his people, now eking [sic] out a threadbare existence in the marshlands of Canada after the colonial war, he could dream anew of an exodus, of a country with an even more fearsome and turbulent mountain, where they could settle' (102). He persuades his fellow and sister Black Loyalists to abandon Canada, that is, Nova Scotia, in this speech: '"But what you 'fraid of, what is freedom, if you ain't willing to test it, wipe away de humiliation, dem tears from your eyes? You ain't never gon be men and women in dis place fit only for dead folk. All free men gotta go to a new place to become new people ..."' (103). Bookerman is a spiritual leader, a Baconian *philosophe*, believing that 'the universe was orderly, and man would cease to oppress man once he was free of his own fear' (104). He plans to found, in Malagueta, a society that is 'free, just and humane' (104). He sets out to form a black Eden, parcelling out the land and directing the construction of housing for a prize Black Loyalist–Nova Scotian capital: 'The town which they conceived was a beautiful one. It rose from the sea with its breath of moist and humid air, towards the rolling green hills and golden plateaux, overshadowed by the great forested mountains ...' (112). But the town idealizes more than physical beauty: 'What they had to uphold was not so much a vision but a present, the pillars, the structure of an organic world in which they had established some sort of order, with their own nameplates, and where they hoped to die in peace' (158). In defence of this freedom, Bookerman reminds his followers, 'You all know how we came here, why we here. Dis place ain't anything till we opened up dem roads and cleared de jungle, built schools and let de Christian folks build their church; so we ain't going to be lettin no one mess up wid us, least of all, no white men ...' (157). When Europeans arrive to colonize Malagueta for their own interests, Bookerman recounts the epic of the Nova Scotian exodus to stiffen the resistance of his settlers to the incursion of 'white men in flannels' (130):

> '[We left "Canada"] 'cause de king [George III] done lie to us; tell us to fight for him and he gon give us land, gon give us respect and we gon be safe. And we done believe him, but he gives us land ain't fit for man or animal. People dying there 'cause ain't nothin you kin do wid dat land: marshes, swamps, thorns, thistles and it's cold.[11] So we come here and make dis place real nice, and we got a little happiness, and our women ain't afraid no more people gon be taking their chillum.' (159)

Later, Bookerman and his nationalist compatriots destroy a European garrison – or 'slavehouse,' in Bookerman's lexicon (170) – 'out of the love for all men and women who had rejected tyranny and had been born free, and were determined to die free' (170). Thus, Bookerman plays Toussaint L'Ouverture.

Bookerman's model coup against imperialism inspires, some seven or eight generations later, General Tamba Masimiara's plotted coup against the tyrannous President Sanka Maru:

> ... he saw with the clarity of hindsight that Thomas Bookerman had not come all the way from Canada, with the invincible marks of his chains ... simply to get away from the bitter despair of broken promises; that if the one-eyed man [Bookerman] had attacked the garrison ... he had done so not to have Malagueta fall into the hands of a black president more despicable than the English pirate, but to add a few pages to the remarkable history of its people. (393–4)

Bookerman is the prototype of Masimiara. When he charges the British garrison, Bookerman regards his action, not 'as war ..., but as a legitimate act of expelling a pest' (217). Similarly, Masimiara acts *contra* an immoral black president, *contra* 'the most despicable government that the world had ever known' (396). Heading the military government that has driven out a criminal, civilian administration, Masimiara tells his aides, '... we can either screw up everything or try to save some of the good that this country was famous for' (384). Failing in his *Putsch* against Maru, Masimiara dies, 'proud that as a soldier he had not sought fame or glory, but had been prepared to die so that Malagueta could go on shining like a star' (396). Like Bookerman, Masimiara sacrifices himself in vain; he cannot create an enduring republic. Yet, because he is the spiritual reincarnation of Bookerman, his death unleashes supernatural forces that execute the literal downfall of Sanka Maru:

> ... he felt himself lifted out of the grandiloquent illusion of power, borne into space as if he were a dwarf, by a force too terrible to contemplate ..., as he came crashing down in the middle of a street so that when the dust had been cleared, his countrymen and women would see not the eyes of a dead general [Masimiara], but the paralysed wreck of Sanku [*sic*] Maru. (397)

The relationship between Bookerman and Masimiara even possesses an allegorical dimension, for Masimiara is the fictional representation of Brigadier-General Bangura (1930–71), and the president he confronts, Sanka Maru, represents the non-fictional dictator-president Stevens (1905–88).[12] Thus, Masimiara's actions reprise Bookerman's courageous struggle for liberty as well as Bangura's leadership of a coup that had allowed Stevens to take office. However, on the orders of Maru, Masimiara is arrested and 'hanged in the national prison' (*Last* 68), just as – in reality – Bangura was charged with 'attempted assassination of ... Stevens and other senior members of his cabinet' in 1971 (Roberts 137), convicted of treason, and hanged that same year (Abraham 40).[13] Cheney-Coker means for us to read the martyrdom of Masimiara-Bangura at the hands of the autocrat Maru-Stevens as signalling the defeat of the lustrous, state-founding dreams of Bookerman-Peters.

Refuting the efforts of Bookerman – and, later, Masimiara – to build a free and prosperous state, Malagueta is doomed to implode because of an original betrayal by those who should have known better, namely, the Nova Scotian settlers. It is their obsequious surrender to white flesh and white ideologies that engenders the two-century-long disintegration of Malagueta into abject dictatorship. Cheney-Coker's omniscient narrator predicts, early on, that 'the black people who would come from America ..., those bastards would hate one other [sic] in their parsimonious hearts' (30). They would already 'bear the signs of the adulteration of the blood' (69). They would be, like the exiled children of Israel in the desert, riotous followers of golden calves. Once they arrive in Malagueta, they act like 'a heterogeneous lot whose only semblance of common interest was their wish to get out of that land of unbearable cold [Canada] ... ' (112). Heterogeneity sparks religious strife: 'A great divide ... opened up between those who came to escape the intolerable loneliness and hardship in life in the New World and those who came to impose a most severe form of Christian rigidity and morality' (129). These differences widen when new arrivals – Africans liberated from slave ships and landed in Malagueta – bring 'a most heterogeneous note into the town' (167). Thus, the 'idea of one family in Malagueta' (138), the dream of communal unity ('we all like one family and we gon grow togeder, die here and we want to stick togeder' [138]), dies, split between those blacks 'who would be insurrectionists and patriots, and those who would place their destiny in the hands of the white men' (130). Given these depictions, Cheney-Coker follows Roberts, who points out that, in Sierra Leone, because of the strength of 'Westernism,' 'in place of homogeneity and its related affinity, there came into prominence heterogeneity and pluralism' (132). Exploiting division, the British impose their government upon Malagueta, but with the acquiescence of well-off blacks. This fact marks the capital Creole treason. Soon, Bookerman rues the appearance of 'newly minted black English men' (305):

> He viewed with contempt the beginnings of the rise of an oligarchy: men who only yesterday were shopkeepers with bad teeth and could barely read now ordered evening jackets in black Venetians and hopsacks; women who only yesterday were content to wear hand-me-downs and keep clean houses had taken to buying gold and parading in silk and brocade at church services. (213)

This initial mimicking of the luxurious and nation-smashing habits of the white *bourgeoisie* is carried to fresh extremes by the grandchildren of the settlers:

> The children of the noveau [sic] riche mixed with the few sons of the colonial administration in the grammar schools. Their expensive jackets and ties marked them out as belonging to a specail [sic] breed; they stood out like precious bulls: proud stubborn and opinionated ... If life had been an enigma for the children of

the old families, the new ones regarded it as a large dinner to be eaten at one go. (325)

While the Creole adoption of European clothing and arrogance is irritating, their adoption of European mates corrodes the nation, for the resultant families reject 'purer' black, or 'organic' African, values, aesthetics, and practices:

> Some of the grandchildren of the original founders of the town were indeed drawn into all kinds of marriages with the new rulers. They were so fascinated with the prospect of being accepted into the houses of the English that they went to the Notary Public and changed their names from African to 'Christian' ones so that the pronunciation would not break the jaws of the English when they met at parties ... To the strings of music played by a black band that had been trained to play 'classical music' they [black *bourgeois* youths] forced their unclassical bodies to respond to the torturous strains of the baptism from 'native' to 'civilised,' while the oestregen in their immature bodies multiplied with a vigorous sexuality. (325)

This self-oppressive situation stems from the original settlers' lack of pride in their venture. The anonymous narrator insists that 'they were ashamed in their hearts of hearts of being men and women without the fine graces, refined speeches and manners which not so long ago they had laughed at when practised by their spurious masters' (214). Yearning for European validation, they evolve a Eurocentrism that leaves them vulnerable to the plans of the first English governor, Captain David Hammerstone – the fictional image of the historical Lieutenant John Clarkson (1763–1828) – to stamp Malagueta with 'the permanence of English laws.' Thus, its blacks would become 'the messengers of the metaphysical transition – darkness to light, neo-paganism to classicism' – and admire 'the encyclopedic mind of the English' (259).[14] The Creole fascination with whiteness abolishes any opportunity for black self-discovery and self-rule.

The *bouleversement* of the old ways, the old beliefs, the old verities, botches black pride and black power. For Bookerman, these changes mean '"De idyll is over"' (217). Shortly then, he is exiled from Malagueta and imprisoned by its new rulers, but not before he states his horror at seeing the arrival of 'de day when de men of dis town gon talk 'bout going to share dere freedom wid some Englishfolk who ain't worth nuthin' (312). But it is the genie-like seer, Alusine Dunbar, who prophesies the true import of the Creole surrender of power and of self-respect: 'One age is about to end in Malagueta, a new reign without honour but with the embellishment of falsehood ... is about to begin ...' (304). Having lost their putative black republic, the settlers are soon victimized by the new white régime's anti-black laws. This point is marked by the construction, by the English, of a 'beautiful garden' surrounded by 'a one-foot-thick stone wall with a heavy iron gate at the entrance,' upon which is hung a sign reading, '"Africans and dogs not allowed"' (300).[15] The *Animal Farm*–like behaviour of the Creole *bourgeoisie*, who collude happily with its white rulers to keep 'Malaguetans of a certain class confined to the poor areas of the town' (351), also figures a loss of innocence. Yet, in time, the Creoles' comprador complicity redounds upon them. Soon, insultingly, the colonial régime invites 'the leaders of the people from the surrounding towns, which were now part of Malagueta, to sign a treaty which barred the great-grandchildren of the founders of Malagueta from ever owning land outside the area that Thomas Bookerman had painstakingly laid out' (369). In non-fiction, too, the Creoles found themselves 'despised by the British as a shabby caricature of Western culture [and] squeezed out of their commercial niche by the impact of the big European firms and the Lebanese [traders]' (who moved into Sierra Leone at the turn of the twentieth century) (Cartwright 17). In Cheney-Coker's novel, the degradation of the Malagueta Creoles – and of the state – is summed up by Masimiara: '... the president had turned the country into a joke, plundered it and shared the loot with his friends. When he wasn't doing that, he was inviting the Lebanese smugglers and others to "come here and dump your miseries, there is room for all of you"' (x). Hence, the country has become 'garbage': 'Everywhere you looked, you could see the dogshit and dead dogs where once there had been beds of violets and fountains in gardens with clear alabaster statues. The general felt something had to be done. Garbage has a way of producing more garbage' (x–xi). Illegality abounds: Maru has 'had one of the brightest lawyers ... write him a new constitution, which the compliant Congress ... readily passed,' thus making him 'President of the Republic, Commander-in-Chief of the Armed Forces, granting him more powers than he had hoped for' (389). To correct this state of affairs, Masimiara stages his unsuccessful coup. Even so, there is no solution but the unsatisfying, *deus ex machina* intervention of a supernatural deposing of Maru, an event that implies, in no way, the rehabilitation of the Creole class.

Cheney-Coker's fictional excavation of Sierra Leone's history unearths a tragedy. The heroic flight from Canada–Nova Scotia and the establishment of a free state concludes in dictatorship, greed, a Western orientation, and the formation of a sell-out oligarchy. Roberts puts the *dénouement* of Sierra Leone thus:

> It is quite surprising that an 'experiment' by Granville Sharp about 200 years ago (which sought to provide a community in which persons who had once been enslaved could attain the right of self-government and a democratic experience) would in 1978 become a bastion of one-party government with all its implied curtailment of individual rights and liberties. (274)

Once known as the 'Athens of West Africa' (Roberts 15), Sierra Leone had become, by 1982, when Roberts's *The Anguish of Third World Independence: The Sierra Leone Experience* appeared, a nation ruled by 'a coalition of constitutionally-ordained and authorized components of law and order carrying out illegal acts and condoning the violence perpetrated by the government' (184). Roberts finds this fate surprising:

> Despite the preponderence [*sic*] of one-party states in Africa today, the history of Sierra Leone, especially deriving from the emulation of British ideals of democracy by the Creole settlers, should evoke bewilderment as to the effective implementation and submission of Sierra Leoneans to a one-party state. (275)

Cheney-Coker is bewildered – better, shocked – by the eruption of tyranny. He lays the blame for the coming of dictatorship on the loss of communal solidarity, on the entry, into the state, of impure ideas – European political philosophy and Christianity – and of 'alien' peoples – Europeans and Arabs.[16] Arguably, his writing, certainly *The Last Harmattan of Alusine Dunbar*, strives to explain the downfall of the black, self-governing republic of which he, but also the Nova Scotian settlers of 1792, had dreamt.

Censoring Sierra Leone

Though Cheney-Coker rails at the dictatorship of Stevens and his Creole, Temne, and Limba supporters, his complaint has found no audience among Africadians, who continue to deem Sierra Leone a Shangri-La (when they think of it at all).[17] In the January 1982 edition of the *Black Express News*, of Halifax, Nova Scotia, Frank Merryman Parkinson of Freetown, Sierra Leone, presents an article sketching the contemporary history of his country. His surname suggests that he is Creole, but what is germane here is what he chose to say about his nation (or what his Africadian editors chose to print). Parkinson reports that 'in March 1967, Dr. Siaka Stevens was appointed Prime Minister after his opposition All Peoples Congress Party had won the general elections' (11). However, this tidy summation omits the discomfiting truth that Stevens's APC did not actually achieve power until three *coups d'état* had transpired. The first coup, led by Brigadier David Lansana (1922–75) on 22 March 1967, established martial law. Only twenty-three hours later, however, Lansana was overthrown by junior officers (colonels and majors) who then suspended the constitution, banned all political parties, and established a military government, the National Reconstruction Council. This government lasted thirteen months, until 18 April 1968, when it was, in turn, driven from power by a group of non-commissioned officers. Accepting their request to head a new National Interim Council, Brigadier-General Bangura led, for just over a week, 'the effective government of the country' (Abraham 40).[18] On 29 April 1968, Bangura relinquished control of the government to Stevens, thus restoring civilian rule.[19] But democracy soon surrendered to dictatorship, for Stevens's régime 'gradually created an atmosphere of ... fear, tension, and distrust' (Roberts 135). 'Within a year of its existence,' observes Roberts, '[Stevens's government] was able to convince Sierra Leoneans that personal ambition and interest in monopolizing power would supercede any concern for human rights, justice and equity' (135).

None of these disquieting details interrupts Parkinson's placid, bowdlerized account of Stevens's presidency. He asserts simply that 'the country became a Republic in April 1971, with Dr. Stevens as the first President' (11). Parkinson fails to note that Stevens's declaration of a republic ran counter to the platform on which he was elected.[20] Worse, Parkinson neglects to mention that, from 1968 to 1973, Stevens's program was one of sheer terror: 'Officially enacted detentions, arrests, harassments, and incarceration without proper trial became the order of the day, culminating in the atrocious behavior by government whereby a significant number of Sierra Leone [opposition party] politicians and sympathizers ... found themselves detained under very harsh and cruel conditions ...' (Roberts 135). Parkinson even ignores the public hangings in 1971 of Bangura and three other alleged traitors, as well as the public hangings, in 1975, of Brigadier David Lansana and seven other men convicted of treason, even though these actions traumatized Sierra Leone, fostering a paralyzing public 'numbness' and 'psychological helplessness' (Roberts 138). Parkinson's news bulletin, accompanied by a grandiose photograph of 'His Excellency, Dr. Siaka Stevens, G.C.R.S.L., D.C.L., President of the Republic of Sierra Leone,' in military regalia, offers a sanitized version of the Stevens's régime (11). For this reason, perhaps, some Africadian leaders, including Dr George F. McCurdy, then director of the Nova Scotia Human Rights Commission, decided to invite Stevens to visit Nova Scotia to participate in ceremonies marking the 1983 bicentennial of the arrival of the Black Loyalists. Once the Canadian media heard of the proposed invitation, however, controversy ensued, and Dr Stevens remained in Sierra Leone.[21] A potentially enriching intercourse between Nova Scotia and Sierra Leone, after nearly two hundred years of mutual disregard, thus halted, at least temporarily.[22]

Mirror Experiences?

Stevens's dictatorship managed to elude Africadian scrutiny, just as Sierra Leoneans have preferred to imagine the oppressive Nova Scotia of two centuries ago. Both peoples have been ignorant of each other, even though they share, to some extent, the same family tree. Too, despite Cheney-Coker's interest in juxtaposing black oppression in Nova Scotia with Creole debasement in Sierra Leone, Africadian and Sierra Leonean literatures narrate certain congruencies of experience. While Africadians have endured segregation and anti-black racism, Sierra Leoneans have suffered imperial, neocolonial, and dictatorial power relations that have made a mockery of their independence and bankrupted their state.[23] Two 'nations,' not one, emerged from the Black Loyalist exile of 1783: the black minority enclave of Africadia and the black majority, Creole- and Temne-dominated state of Sierra Leone. The main distinction between the two entities is that Africadians have never enjoyed control of the Nova Scotian government, while their ancestors, who ended up as Creoles in

Sierra Leone, came to exercise a measure of effective, albeit minority, power. To note their similarities is to revise the received wisdom that posits Africadians' inferiority *vis-à-vis* their Sierra Leonean cousins.

Spirituality is one point of equivalence. American historian Robin W. Winks, writing of the Black Refugees who arrived in Nova Scotia during the War of 1812, accepts as gospel the critical observations of Anglican catechist William Nisbett:

> Nisbett soon lost patience with his charges, writing that they were universally superstitious, mad, ridiculous, and given to 'monstrous absurdities, that they believe, and substitute in the place of Religion.' He was utterly opposed to their insistence on 'experiencing God'; and those, such as one William Redman, who twice told him of seeing a person before him on a cross whom he stabbed with a knife, drawing out blood and water, confounded him. Nisbett damned the Refugees for being 'indolent to an extreme, insensible to kindness, dishonest and untrue, so that notwithstanding all their pretenses to what they call spiritual experience, they lie in a deplorable state of moral degradation.' (138)

Winks states that most of these allegedly fanatical Refugees were 'Baptists before they came [to Nova Scotia]' (138). Though the Refugee Baptists were no doubt distinct from the John Marrant–inspired Huntingdonian Methodists and the David George–led Baptists who emigrated to Sierra Leone, they shared an attitude toward Christian expression that white commentators found both blasphemous and seditious. Thomas Jefferson blamed the failure of Sierra Leone self-government (1787–1809), for instance, on the 'fugitives from these [United] States during the Revolutionary War' who had 'by their idleness and turbulence ... kept the settlement in constant danger of dissolution, which could not have been prevented but for the aid of the [Jamaican] Maroon negroes from the West Indies ...' (quoted in Saillant 32). Despite their contradictory yoking, 'idleness and turbulence' were disruptive qualities that whites saw in both Africadians and Sierra Leone Nova Scotians. Sierra Leone governor Thomas Perronet Thompson charged that 'the Nova Scotians are roaring out hymns' (quoted in Saillant 31), while, back in Nova Scotia, the government of the Loyalist settlement at Shelburne bade constables arrest 'any black found gambling or dancing at night' (Jobb 99). In *The Last Harmattan of Alusine Dunbar*, Cheney-Coker describes a pioneer church of pitiless rectitude: '... the founders of the church would have a virtual veto over who would become members, and would turn away all those who might dare to break their sanction by placing sextons with the look of avenging angels at the door, under the cinquefoil of their achievement' (126). Likewise, the major Africadian church – the African (United) Baptist Association – established in 1854, has also been noted for its strictness. According to Winks, by the early years of the twentieth century, a few families controlled the church, creating 'an aristocracy of the faith, and often [holding it] to more than ordinarily frozen and conservative theological and social positions' (346).[24]

If Africadians and Sierra Leone Nova Scotians share certain religious expressivities, they also held – once – similar ideological views. Hodges feels that the Black Loyalists were 'the first mass group of emancipated African Americans' (xii) and practised a 'black republicanism' that resembled 'the artisan republicanism motivating the working classes of American cities in the postwar period' (xv).[25] Fyfe observes that Governor John Clarkson 'quickly learnt that freedom for them [the Black Loyalists] consisted above all in a secure title to a piece of land, to make them and their children independent, free to live lives of their own' (4). Fyfe also declares that 'like their former American owners, they believed they were entitled to inalienable rights – the rights they had been denied in slave-owning America ...' (6). These beliefs drove many Black Loyalists to abandon Nova Scotia for Sierra Leone. Yet, those who chose to remain behind could not have been innocent of ideology. Indeed, their brand of thought may simply have been more conservative than that of their departing fellows – a difference that would have coalesced around religion. Intriguingly, historian John Saillant asserts that 'Methodists, whether Calvinist or Arminian, were the most likely of the black Nova Scotians to emigrate' (23). Apparently, Methodist preacher John Marrant emphasized, in his tour of Nova Scotia, the persuasive black nationalist gospel of 'the providential restoration to Africa of a holy black community, bound by affection and the covenant of grace' (Saillant 9). Even so, the Baptist zealot, David George, carried off a goodly swath of his congregation to Sierra Leone. Still, one may speculate that the Baptist faith moved some Black Loyalists to endure privation and deprivation in Nova Scotia rather than to venture afield. Hodges asserts that George's 'highly democratic message, which taught that "a Baptist Church may arise and continue as a self-originating, self-governing body without any consent or approval from without," sparked many congregations ...' (xxvii). If it is true that 'George's strongly democratic methods created a lasting base for black religion in Nova Scotia' (Hodges xxvii), some Black Loyalists may have felt that they could practise their faith as easily in the province as in Sierra Leone. Africadian historian, lawyer, and activist Burnley ('Rocky') Jones affirms that '... the Black Baptist church was the only place where Blacks [in Nova Scotia] practiced democracy, embracing a democratic religion which allowed the hiring and firing of ministers and the electing of deacons' ('Uncrowned' 6). Conceivably, then, the blacks who chose to remain in Nova Scotia believed that they had already found their *spiritual* Promised Land (despite their objective – horrific – socio-economic conditions). Pearleen Oliver observes that, 'following the exodus of 1792 and for twenty years afterwards, only a few scattered communities of Blacks could be found in Nova Scotia' (*Root* 140). Significantly, though, 'these were located in the [Annapolis] Valley and in the Tracadie areas' (*Root* 140), that is to say, in some of the lushest (and most isolated) parts of the province. Feelings of religious independence, the possession of useable land allotments, and even a smidgen of landscape romanticism may have convinced some Black Loyalists, then, that they could realize their spiritual aspirations in Nova Scotia. Thus, a modicum of conservatism, if not blunt Toryism, may be ascribed to the Black Loyalists who spurned the exodus. Still, these stay-at-homes held no absolute monopoly on this position, for, as Saillant assesses, the Sierra Leone Nova Scotians 'remained influenced by a religiously-inspired antislavery thought that had little to do with the new liberal thought of the late eighteenth century concerning slavery, freedom, and commerce' (23). Simply put, Black Loyalist ideology may have had less to do with founding a republican state than with finding a free space for worship. For some, this space was Sierra Leone; for others, it was Nova Scotia.

The lay historiography of Pearleen Oliver lays bare this spiritual dimension of the Black Nova Scotian pilgrimage:

> When we meditate on our beginnings in this rugged province by the sea we catch glimpses of the difficulties, the hardships, the deprivations and the fears of our early ancestors. Forcibly uprooted from their African homeland, roughly and in-humanly transplanted to the fields of slavery in the United States, and a remnant escaping to Nova Scotia. This remnant found a new land, a new life, and a new name. (*Root* 143)

She stresses the unique history – the God-scribed history – of the Africadians, the Chosen Remnant who had found their Promised Land – of physical liberty and religious freedom – in Nova Scotia. She inks a standard nationalism. Oliver is, therefore, a precursor of Cheney-Coker. His protest against the fate of Sierra Leone–Malagueta stems from a nationalist fear that the pure sensi-bilities of the founders – Thomas Peters–Thomas Bookerman, and their allies – have been perverted by Eurocentrism, neocolonialism, and the incursions of aliens. The troublesome foreigners are mainly Arabs supposedly given to 'para-sitic breeding,' 'pugnacious competitiveness,' and 'Byzantine cunning' (*Last* 376, 377). Oliver would not support Cheney-Coker's literary racialism here, but her conservative insistence on the exceptionalism of Africadia finds an echo in Cheney-Coker's rendering of Sierra Leone:

> We are a strange people; our history, language, and culture are not to be confused with those of other English-speaking Africans.
>
> The admixture of English philanthropy and African exotica that has produced and shaped the Sierra Leone Creole is for me the makeup of any genuine Sierra Leonean literature. My 'Afro-Saxon' heritage has meant a lot for me ... and I hope it will convey something of the strangeness of my people to the reader. ('Cheyney-Coker' [*sic*] 156)

Oliver admires the heroism of the Loyalists and Refugees who comprise the founding members of the *African Baptist* realm of Africadia. Cheney-Coker, as we have already seen, trumpets the pioneering zeal of men like Bookerman-Peters, who 'found himself at the head of twelve hundred men, women and children ensconced inside their tents on the shoreline of a great ocean, looking at their new country [Malagueta–Sierra Leone]' (*Last* 101). Tory notions of race history guide both Oliver and Cheney-Coker. From opposite sides of the Atlantic, they reflect the separatist Black Loyalism that Walker depicts:

> As they regarded the more formalised white churches which had segregated them, they noticed that God did not seem to speak to those older churches in quite the same way as he did to them, the blacks. Inevitably, this produced a feeling of being closer to God, of being, in fact, a chosen people, an elite group of Christians whom God regularly visited and whose role it was to preserve the truth of the moment of salvation. (*Black* 78)

What was true for Africadians was also true for Nova Scotian Sierra Leoneans. Or, as Sierra Leonean J.B. Elliott told Walker, in an interview in Freetown, in June 1970, 'the Church is the solid rock for all Nova Scotian people' (*Black* 383).[26]

Given the links in religiosity and ideology between Africadians and Sierra Leone Nova Scotians, we must temper the facile – but dire – dichotomies that historians and writers wedge between the two groups. After all, the two polities claim the same first writers – Marrant (1755–91), David George (c.1743–1810), Boston King (c.1760–1802), and Susana Smith.[27] Moreover, despite their obeisance to British Christianity, the eighteenth-century Africadian and Sierra Leonean texts of Marrant, George, and King share the protest strategies that Keith A. Sandiford identifies in Afro-English writing of their era. They 'usurp certain of the slave master's hegemonic prerogatives' (11) and develop 'the individuated and inalienable consciousness' (152). Thus, although the historical Thomas Peters was barely literate, Cheney-Coker bids his alias, Thomas Bookerman, write a *History of the Founding of Malagueta* (*Last* 209). Arguably, this text replicates the Afro-English desire of the period to expropriate 'the symbolic system of language and its allied arts to reinvent themselves for themselves and to revise the discourse about Africa and Africans' (Sandiford 152). Bookerman's creator, Cheney-Coker, sets himself the same task in his writing, noting that 'a popular awareness of self and the creation of different modes of expression of our social and cultural needs seems to me to be the immediate task of the Sierra Leonean writer' ('Cheyney-Coker' [*sic*] 156). His *The Last Harmattan of Alusine Dunbar* epicizes Sierra Leone's history, while the popular historiography of Pearleen Oliver (and the history and fiction of other Africadian writers) seeks to epicize and lyricize Africadian experience.

The painful similarity between the descendants of the African Americans who journeyed only to Nova Scotia and those who went on to Sierra Leone is that both witnessed the collapse of their ancestors' original political dreams. Significantly, however, those who made their homes in Nova Scotia, though they became a castigated minority, did not have as far to fall. They began as generally illiterate, isolated, and impoverished workers and small farmers, and so they remained for nearly two centuries. In contrast, the Nova Scotian Sierra Leoneans saw their briefly realized dreams of living independently of white control in a black communitarian Eden disrupted, then destroyed, by the Sierra Leone Company's vision of them as 'a caste of workers in a Euro-African extension of the Atlantic economy' (Saillant 26). Ultimately, 'the [white] commercial and imperial forces prevailed over the [Nova Scotian] religious visionaries in Sierra Leone' (Saillant 33). From Cheney-Coker's perspective, this defeat destroyed black communalism, catalyzed class stratification, spawned the wilful treachery of élites, and assisted the eventual constitution of a neocolonial régime of thugs and thieves. Neither the Black Nova Scotians nor the Creole Sierra Leoneans can argue convincingly for the superiority of one over the other.

As the work of Cheney-Coker suggests, then, no authoritative Pan-Africanism can be articulated that disregards the cogency of local black adaptations to local black conditions. Indeed, the Black Loyalists in Sierra Leone lost control of a state; the Black Loyalists in Nova Scotia lost wealth, land, and population. Black Loyalism floundered in surrender to despotism in Sierra Leone, in segregated inequality in Nova Scotia. Neither destiny was ordained by some congenital defect in the people themselves; rather, both became trapped in disenfranchising power arrangements that severely limited their political options.[28] In mythologizing this history for his people, Cheney-Coker has painted Nova Scotia as a Hades ('fit only for dead folk' [*Last* 103]) and its Black Loyalist emigrés as apostles of paradise. So be it: such are the necessities of nationalist mythopoesis.[29] *Négritude*, as it turns out, may never be sufficient for building international black unity. Yet, the Black Loyalists on both sides of the Atlantic were enough alike that perhaps the only real difference between them was that the Africadians had no state to call their own, while the Sierra Leonean Nova Scotians, even as minority Creoles, were able to dominate (under white supervision) the power structure of Sierra Leone. To acquire a more precise understanding of this difference, and its cultural meaning, we must undertake a far more exacting study of Black Loyalism and black nationalism than we have thus far been able to produce.

Although Africadians control no state, they have managed to inaugurate a cultural renaissance with nationalist undertones. Here they follow *les Acadiens*, another Maritime minority – linguistic, rather than racial (for the most part) – who have striven of late to renew their literary tradition and strengthen their culture. For both Africadian and Acadian writers, nationalism – or conservatism – is a means to forge *progressive* cultural identities. Let us compare now their dual 'renaissances.'

Notes

1 This paper was first presented at the 'New Currents in the North Atlantic: Emerging Scholarship on Atlantic Canada – Atlantic Canada Workshop,' held at the Public Archives of Nova Scotia, in Halifax, Nova Scotia, on 16 August 1997. I am grateful to then–Saint Mary's University English professor Uzoma Essonwanne

and Africadian educator – and Sierra Leone resident – Wayn Hamilton for their critical readings of the paper. I dedicate this essay to Kenule Saro-Wiwa, the Ogoni writer and environmental activist who was executed by the Nigerian Government on 10 November 1995.

2 The colony had been organized in 1787 as a receiving station for indigent African Americans and Afro-Caribbeans who had found themselves free – and free to starve – in foggy, chilly London.

3 In his excellent study *The Golden Age of Black Nationalism, 1850–1925* (1978), Moses finds that 'Black nationalism differs from most other nationalisms in that its adherents are united neither by a common geography nor by a common language, but by the nebulous concept of racial unity' (17). Thus, it becomes 'impossible to speak of black nationalism without simultaneously speaking of Pan-Africanism' (17). Both ideologies seek to 'unify politically all ["the dark brown-skinned peoples whose ancestors lived in sub-Saharan Africa before the age of European expansionism" (17)] whether they are residents of African territories or descendants of those Africans who were dispersed by the slave trade' (17). Moses concludes that 'Pan-Africanism persists today as a movement of all African peoples throughout the world, who believe that all black people have interests in common' (18). Yet, as M. NourbeSe Philip states, it has had a brief history: 'The primary attachment of an Ashanti or Yoruba person during the heyday of slavery was to their ethnic group and not to Africa or to a Black brother or sisterhood ... The pan-African concept is a relatively modern concept, as is the pan-European concept, which today is still resisted by many within Europe' ('Other' 29).

4 Fyfe concludes the sentence by pointing out that the settlers failed to secure 'the kind of independence they had dreamed of, and had expressed their longing for in their letters and petitions' (19). Sierra Leone may have been 'better than' Nova Scotia, but in neither locale did the settlers win an unquestioned liberty.

5 Their drastic situation is outlined in my previous essay, 'The Birth and Rebirth of Africadian Literature.'

6 The biographical information is culled largely from Cheney-Coker's entry in *Contemporary Authors*, vol. 101 (114).

7 Reasonable autobiographical hypotheses may be gleaned from Cheney-Coker's poems in his *The Graveyard Also Has Teeth*, with *Concerto for an Exile* (1980). Many poems refer to an Argentine (or Latin American) lover. (See, for instance, 'Concerto for an Exile,' 20.) They suggest that his commitment to left-wing Latin American political struggles originates in a love affair with this Argentinian woman.

8 See Claude S. Phillips 211.

9 Cheney-Coker's poem evinces the fear inculcated by Siaka Stevens's use of execution-as-desecration:

> The passing of many years has yet to erase the pain and revultion [*sic*] experienced by those Sierra Leoneans who first saw, or were made to acknowledge, the public display of the corpses of 'ordinary political offenders.' And the fear and insecurity generated by that reality has deepened from year to year, to make the majority of Sierra Leoneans pathetically constrained, suspicious, insecure,

ingratiating, and a-political [sic] – making it easy for a revengeful and callous oligarchy to prescribe and enforce what it deems appropriate for Sierra Leoneans, in terms ... of their overt behavior. (Roberts 139)

10 Cheney-Coker declares that his politics are 'Decidedly Left.' See *Contemporary Authors*, vol. 101 (114).

11 In his *Memoirs* (1798), Black Loyalist Boston King relates the bitter conditions extant in Nova Scotia in the 1780s:

About this time the country was visited with dreadful famine, which not only prevailed in Burchtown [sic], but likewise at Chebucto, Annapolis, Digby, and other places. Many of the poor people were compelled to sell their best gowns for five pounds of flour, in order to support life. When they had parted with all their clothes, even to their blankets, several of them fell down dead in the streets, thro' hunger. Some killed and eat their dogs and cats; and poverty and distress prevailed on every side; so that to my great grief I was obliged to leave Burchtown, because I could get no employment ... (Quoted in *Fire*, vol. 1, 55)

12 Indeed, Maru is a former 'trade union leader' (*Last* 387), just as Stevens was an ex-labour union official (Roberts 103).

13 These horrifying events serve as Gothic inspirations for another Sierra Leonean poet, namely Lemuel Johnson. His lyric 'The Brigadier-General's Dance' is an unflinching response to the judicial assassination – nay, lynching – of Bangura and others at the behest of Stevens's tyranny. The poem cannot be cited here, but students of Sierra Leone or of Cheney-Coker should seek it out at their leisure.

14 The Creole fascination with all things British was, in history, a vicious irony, for, in Sierra Leone, 'official British collusion with slavery lasted longer than in any other African territory' (Chisholm 1708). In the aboriginal hinterland, reports Alistair Chisholm, 'the British allowed [a] slave economy to persist until 1928 ...' (1708).

15 The scene hearkens back to the stern moral of William Blake's allegorical poem 'The Garden of Love' (1794), which also dramatizes the promulgation of harsh regulations in a once-paradisal space:

I went to the Garden of Love,
And saw what I never had seen:
A chapel was built in the midst,
Where I used to play on the green.

And the gates of this chapel were shut,
And 'Thou shalt not' writ over the door;
So I turn'd to the Garden of Love,
That so many sweet flowers bore,

And I saw it was filled with graves,
And tomb-stones where flowers should be:
And Priests in black gowns were walking their rounds,
And binding with briars my joys & desires. (554)

Cheney-Coker's allusion to this poem suggests the complete reversal of the 'desires' of the founding 'Nova Scotian' settlers of Malagueta.

16 In *The Heart of the Matter* (1948), a novel set in post–Second World War, pre-Independence Sierra Leone, British author Graham Greene (1904–91) permits his character, Harris, to provide this demographic snapshot of 1940s Freetown: 'This is the original Tower of Babel ... West Indians, Africans, real Indians, Syrians, Englishmen, Scotsmen ... Irish priests, French priests, Alsatian priests' (14). Greene's depiction of an Anglo-imperially multiculturalized Sierra Leone is apt preface to Cheney-Coker's own.

17 One Africadian who possesses first-hand knowledge of Sierra Leone and who has long considered its connection to Black Nova Scotia is educator Wayn Hamilton, who lived in Sierra Leone on several occasions between 1989 and 1996. In his letter to me of 29 September 1997, Hamilton advises, 'We must ... remember that Nova Scotia is a distant world to the true Krio [Creole]' (1).

18 See 'Sierra Leone,' *Africa Year Book and Who's Who 1977*, 764–5.

19 Bangura's popular military government of 18–29 April 1968, his courtly restoration of civilian rule on 29 April 1968, his noble coup attempt against a dictatorial Stevens in March 1971, and his subsequent execution on 29 June 1971 are events Cheney-Coker describes heroically, albeit in *roman à clef* style. See the Prologue (vii–xvii), chapter 16 ('A Fatal Mistake,' 384–92), and Epilogue (393–8) of *The Last Harmattan of Alusine Dunbar* (1990).

20 Roberts notes that the 'irony' of Stevens's action 'is that the party which had won the [1967] election because it was against a Republican form of government, decided to reverse its posture' (251).

21 Siaka Stevens's dictatorship lasted until 1986, when he was succeeded to the leadership of his party by Major-General Joseph Momoh, who, after heading an elected government, was overthrown in a military coup in May 1992. Since then, Sierra Leone has suffered through a depressing cycle of coups, civil wars, and foreign military interventions that has left it one of the five poorest nations in the world. In July 1999, however, Sierra Leone president Ahmed Tejan Kabbah signed a peace accord with Revolutionary United Front leader Foday Sankoh, halting, temporarily, one phase of civil war. The post-colonial history of Sierra Leone exemplifies an African political pattern that scholar Frederick Cooper analyses ably: 'Postcolonial gatekeeper states were more knowledgeable than colonial ones, better able to forge relations of clientelism within their boundaries, but without coercive power coming from without they were extremely vulnerable to any attempt to contest access to the gate itself. Hence the cycle of coups and military governments that beset Africa shortly after decolonization ...' (582). Rob Nixon notes simply that 'the problem of competitive ethnicity is widespread in Africa ...' (110). Insightfully, too, he points out that 'a microminority' cannot 'influence national events, particularly in a society run on the principles of kleptocratic militarism' (116). Nixon describes the Ogoni people of Nigeria, but he could just as easily be citing the situation of the Creoles of Sierra Leone.

22 In a 1994 article, Africadian journalist and writer Charles Saunders reminds his readers that 'geographically, Nova Scotia and Sierra Leone are far apart. History,

however, is another matter. A common thread of ancestry ties the Canadian province to the West African nation' ('N.S.' 167). Written on the occasion of Africadian educator Wayn Hamilton's third departure for Sierra Leone, where, 'on his second trip, two years ago, he discovered another branch of his family in Freetown' ('N.S.' 167), Saunders's article makes the strange claim that 'the Sierra Leone government has remained remarkably stable since the country became independent in 1961' ('N.S.' 168).

It is worth noting here that Saunders, who is also a novelist, has not set any of his works in Sierra Leone, but his trio of fantasy-genre novels, featuring an African hero of Herculean strength, is set in an imaginary Africa. See his *Imaro* (1981), *Imaro II: The Quest for Cush* (1984), and *Imaro III: The Trail of Bohu* (1985).

While Nova Scotian and Sierra Leonean contact has been sporadic and sentimental, the connection between Sierra Leone and African America has been saccharine. Thus, during a 'highly public' 1986 visit to the U.S. Sea Coast Islands, then–Sierra Leone president Joseph Saidu Momoh cultivated an 'ahistorically specific tie' between the African-American *Gullah* people and the Sierra Leonean Creole (Matory 42). Momoh 'continued the American tradition of attributing [*Gullah*] islanders' linguistic distinctiveness' to their African roots, offering the similarities between their tongue and Sierra Leone Krio 'as proof' (Matory 42). Though the evidence for the relationship is 'highly ambiguous,' its cultivation reveals the triumph of an indulgent Pan-Africanism in fostering 'a complex politically, economically, and academically shaped dialogue' to serve as 'the grounds of a powerful new kinship – of a "family across the sea"' (Matory 42).

23 One reason for the socio-political problems that have plagued Sierra Leone (and other decolonizing African states) is that, as Frederick Cooper writes, 'the act of imagination that had made "development" the watchword of colonialism created its own standards: officials began with an imagined end-point – industrialization, European social relations, legislative institutions – rather than with the nature and dynamics of African societies themselves' (581). Thus, 'development efforts created more new points of conflict than they resolved ...' (581).

24 The similarities between Africadian and Sierra Leone Creole religion must not be overplayed. In his letter to me, Hamilton cautions that one must recognize 'the difference in the solemn, non-expressive and rigid rituals of services in Sierra Leone among the Krio's [*sic*] and by comparison the openness, emotional ... expressiveness of the Black Nova Scotian Church' (2).

25 Hodges's Introduction to *The Black Loyalist Directory* offers a fine summary of scholarship on the Black Loyalists. However, his argument that black republicanism resembled 'the ideology of artisan republicanism [which] included deep reverence for the lessons of the revolution, pride of community and trade, an inclination towards evangelical religion, and a powerful egalitarianism' (xv) is disputable. For one thing, as the *Directory* listings make clear, most of the Black Loyalists were not artisans but ex-plantation hands who had fled their *revolutionary* masters. Hodges seems to turn any black aspiration for liberty into a species of American republicanism, but much too cavalierly. He claims that those Black Loyalists who voyaged from New York to England 'arrived filled with republican

determination' (xxviii). But his proof is less than it seems. He states that 'a song ... popular among London blacks' in the 1780s – namely, 'Yankee Doodle; or the Negroes' Farewell to America' – captures their 'republican sensibility' (xxviii). Yet, the song's title suggests a satire of America's republican pretentions, and its lyrics proclaim England as the *true* fount of liberty:

> Den Hey! for old Englan' where Liberty reigns
> Where Negroe no beaten or loaded with chains
> And if Negroe return [to the U.S.] O! may he be bang'd
> Chain'd tortur'd & drowned – Or let him be hang'd. [Reproduced in Hodges]

If this is republicanism, it is a distinctly monarchical breed.

26 Yet, differences exist – inalienably. In his letter to me, Wayn Hamilton submits that 'Krio's [*sic*] would be a bit shocked at the "way" in which we [Africadians] conduct and "act out" our Sunday services. The original Krio churches carry on today in ways that are very, very similar to the [formality of the] British church services' (2).

27 Marrant published *A Narrative of the Lord's Wonderful Dealings with John Marrant, a Black*, in 1785. George's 'An Account of the Life of Mr. David George' appeared in the *Baptist Annual Register* in 1793. King's 'Memoirs of the Life of Boston King' appeared in the *Methodist Magazine* in 1798. In *'Our Children Free and Happy': Letters from Black Settlers in Africa in the 1790s* (1991), Fyfe reprints a letter from Nova Scotian emigré Susana – or Susannah – Smith, who penned a letter requesting 'Sope' for her family, in Sierra Leone, in 1792 (24). Fyfe cautions, though, that 'one cannot now tell' with absolute certainty whether Smith is [the letter's] actual author (69).

28 Frederick Cooper gives, as one cause of African political instability, this instance of political psychology: 'The anxieties – and the brittle repressiveness – of new African rulers reflected as much their appreciation and fear of the diverse move-ments they had ridden to power as their inability to confront the divisions in society that colonial regimes had encouraged' (582). Cooper insists successful decolonization movements 'drew together the poor peasant hemmed in by colonial agricultural policies, the well-off merchant feeling the heavy hand of the European import-export houses, the railway worker facing barriers to advancement, the literate clerk trapped in the racial hierarchy of a bureaucracy, the lawyer espousing constitutional justice ... ' (579). However, there was a built-in tendency to self-destruct, as occurred in Sierra Leone, for 'political parties both were constrained by regional and ethnic differences and cut across them' (579). Worse, 'the affiliations that defined an "ethnic group" changed in the course of political mobilizations' (579).

29 Perhaps one should not expect Sierra Leoneans to imagine a realistic Nova Scotia. Winks reports that 'those few Freetown Creoles who today are willing to discuss their vaguely held conceptions of life in Nova Scotia think most often of two facets of that life: the cold and the godly; for they are convinced that surely no Negroes could now remain in so bleak and forlorn a land ...' (77). The brute fact is, 'Nova Scotia is not remembered plain in Sierra Leone ...' (Winks 77).

Toward a Conservative Modernity: Cultural Nationalism in Contemporary Acadian and Africadian Poetry

For Arnold 'Ted' Davidson (1936–99)[1]

Introduction

The critique of modernity offered by conservative Canadian philosopher George Grant (1918–88) must be considered by those who would conserve a nationalist or regionalist poetic. If modernity (read by Grant as the cosmopolitan liberalism of international capitalism) dissolves nationalism and regional cultures, then the embracing of modern/post-modern[2] poetics by poets who issue from such cultures is imperilled. Significantly, the poets of *Acadie* and of Nova Scotia's Black Loyalist and Black Refugee–settled communities – an ethnocultural archipelago I term *Africadia* – confront modernity without even the buffer of a state to call their own (though Acadians in New Brunswick wield some political power). Interestingly, the challenges posed by modernity to the expression – and even the notion of expression – of the local and the particular are surveyed in two recent anthologies arising from the contemporary efflorescence of both Acadian and Africadian cultural nationalism and poetry. *Rêves inachevés: Anthologie de poésie acadienne contemporaine* (1990), edited by Fred Cogswell and Jo-Anne Elder, and *Fire on the Water: An Anthology of Black Nova Scotian Writing*, 2 volumes (1991–2), edited by myself, present works penned during the Acadian Renaissance and the Africadian Renaissance respectively. Though the Acadian confrontation with modernity has a longer literary history than its Africadian parallel, poets from both embattled minorities have attempted to conserve aspects of their peculiarities while simultaneously adopting and adapting a democratic and liberal poetic.

The risks of this project are prophesied in Grant's work. In *Lament for a Nation: The Defeat of Canadian Nationalism* (1965), Grant equates 'progressive modernity' (63) with a homogenizing liberalism which, valuing technique more than tradition, erodes particularisms. Grant puts his case with suave succinctness: 'Modern science makes all local cultures anachronistic. Where modern science has achieved its mastery, there is no place for local cultures' (54). Hence, English Canada, 'a local culture,' situated 'next to a society [the United States] that is the heart of modernity,' is fated to disappear as a nation (54). In

Technology and Empire: Perspectives on North America (1969), Grant assesses the impact of *la révolution tranquille* on Québécois, noting that 'their awakening to modernity, which seems to them an expression of independence, in fact leaves them wide open to conquest by a modernity which at its very heart is destructive of indigenous traditions' (67). Grant's critique frames modernity as an imperialist, technologically propelled, American creed. Hans Hauge suggests that, for Grant, 'americanization is another word for modernization' (65). This vision of modernity as a colonizing force, inimical to the sustained, independent existence of 'local cultures,' challenges not only the long-term viability of the polities of English-speaking Canada and Québec, but also the regional, Maritime cultures – and poetries – of Acadie and Africadia.

Maritime Anti-Modernism

If, as Grant states, 'the choice between internationalism and nationalism is the same choice as that between liberalism and conservatism' (*Lament* 86), Maritime poets have often opted for the latter and thus incurred the concomitant obscurity and marginalization. Gwendolyn Davies establishes this fact in her recovery of the 'Song Fishermen.' This literary 'School' comprised Romantic, deliberately regionalist, Nova Scotian poets of the late 1920s who rejected insurgent cosmopolitan modernism in favour of a local poetic privileging traditional verse forms, including ballads and sea chanties, and even the use of Gaelic (Davies 164). The conservative ethos of the 'Fishermen,' whose members included Charles G.D. Roberts (1860–1943), Bliss Carman (1861–1929), and Charles Bruce (1906–71), was articulated by the poet Andrew Merkel (1884–1954) in 1929:

> We are rather isolated down here in Nova Scotia ... The march of progress goes by us on the other side of the hill ... Let us not get too ambitious. Keep your eyes free from the glare of big cities and big reputations. Keep your mind free from the contemporary illusion which names every new thing a good thing, and turns its back on old things which have been proved in many thousand years of human blood and tears. (Quoted in Davies 168)

For their fidelity to 'old things,' this anti-modern group has been omitted – *qua* group – from most Canadian literary histories. Yet, the 'Fishermen' did what the regional perspective required, for, as Erik Kristiansen notes, 'anti-modern attitudes are peppered throughout Maritime literature' ('Time' [1990] 26).

Triumphant Secularism

Given the relative prejudice that Maritime poets in general have suffered for their dissent from modernity (or, perhaps, their dissenting modernity), it is somewhat disconcerting to open *Rêves* and find a happy disparagement of Acadian conservatism. Yet, in his introductory essay titled 'Une poésie qui est un acte,' Raoul Boudreau (b. 1949) savages Eddy Boudreau (1914–54), Napoléon Landry (1884–1956), and François-Moïse Lanteigne (1885–1964), 'les trois premiers poètes acadiens des années 50, dont la poésie ou religieuse, ou patriotique, ou les deux reste conformiste par la forme et par le fond' (*Rêves* 8). Boudreau assaults a conservative poetic vision based on *le pays* conceived as an ecclesiastical community:

> Cette poésie propose une vision théocentrique du monde et elle présente l'Acadie et les Acadiens comme le peuple élu de Dieu qui, par son indéfectible attachement à sa foi catholique malgré ses souffrances et ses misères, doit servir d'exemple aux peuples de la terre. Elle incite le plus souvent à la prière et à l'action de grâce, jamais à la révolte. (*Rêves* 8)

In this modern conception, religious nationalism is retrograde: it fosters a regressive poetic in both form and content. Boudreau seems to endorse a liberalism that is, as Grant noted of that of Québécois youth of the 1960s, 'openly anti-Catholic and even existentialist or Marxist' (*Lament* 80). Boudreau ignores Grant's caution that 'the old Church with its educational privileges has been the chief instrument by which an indigenous French culture has survived in North America' (*Lament* 81).

Instead, Boudreau lauds such epic and epochal moments of triumphant modernity as the founding of the Université de Moncton in 1963, an act which salvaged Acadie for the age of progress: '... l'Acadie sort brusquement du folklore du 19ᵉ siècle pour découvrir d'un seul coup le marxisme, la lutte des classes, les rapports de force et la contestation étudiante' (*Rêves* 9). Certainly, Sue Calhoun asserts that the establishment of the university, along with the 1960 election of Louis Robichaud (b. 1925), the first francophone premier of New Brunswick, resulted in the 'secularization' of Acadie (7).

This 'secularization' or, rather, liberalization/modernization also spawned a secular nationalism to replace the religious nationalism that had fallen from grace. It was characterized by 'refusing to accept the status quo, though it wasn't consciously thought out at the time, nor is it well articulated even today' (Calhoun 9). For Boudreau, this nationalism is defensive: the Acadian poet has 'une cause urgente à défendre, une culture à sauver du naufrage et à laquelle il s'identifie, et prendre la plume, c'est avant toute chose affirmer cela' (*Rêves* 12).

In *Unfinished Dreams: Contemporary Poetry of Acadie* (1990), the English version of *Rêves*, Boudreau quotes Alain Masson (b. 1944) on the peril which Acadian writers felt they faced (but have since learned how to overcome):

> The truth is that there is a cruel dyssemmetry: on one side, there is New Brunswick, administrative subdivision of a cultural empire of which the capitals are New York and Hollywood; on the other side, there is a small nation whose *survival is threatened by this empire*, but who has learned how to give itself a cultural life all its own. (Quoted in *Dreams* xxi, author's italics)

This 1986 sounding of cautious success is complemented by Masson's 1974 comment, quoted by Boudreau in *Rêves*, declaring the liberation of Acadian writers from any literary heritage: 'Il n'existe pas de patrimoine littéraire en Acadie; la littérature est un projet. Paradoxalement, l'écrivain acadien se trouve ainsi placé de plein-pied [*sic*] avec l'universalité' (quoted in *Rêves* 15). Both comments represent the troubled victory of secular nationalism. The Acadian writer has mastered the defence of his or her identity amid what the Québec nationalist historian Henri Bourassa (1868–1952) termed 'cette mer immense de l'américanisme saxonisant' (49). Now, he or she is free to invent his or her literature at will within the empire of 'l'universalité.' The two positions are nastily polar. Masson would bake his cake as a literary universalist – disregarding the Acadian poetic tradition – but he would sell it as an Acadian nationalist.

Masson would have at least one customer however – M. Boudreau, who would slice off the nationalist icing to consume the cosmopolitan content and savour the international flavour. Boudreau condemns, in fact, the nostalgia of contemporary Acadian poets for the secular nationalism of the early 1970s – the first phase of the Acadian Renaissance – as a kind of modern folklore: 'pour beaucoup de lecteurs, à l'intérieur et à l'extérieur, l'image de l'Acadien pleurnichant est rassurante, et l'exotisme est si rentable littérairement ...' (*Rêves* 18). In the post-modern present, Acadian poetry, liberated from nationalist yearning, is '[e]n phase avec les courants mondiaux de la littérature' (*Rêves* 18). In the brave new Acadie, '[l]' Acadien joue de sa francité pour résister à l'Amérique et il joue de son américanité pour résister à l'hégémonie de la culture française' (*Rêves* 18). Boudreau continues on to note, with seductive aplomb, '[c]ertes, cela ne va pas sans risques dont l'avenir nous dira l'ampleur' (*Rêves* 18–19). Freedom is the watchword:

> Ignorant presque tout de la métrique du vers français dont ils ne préoccupent guère, les poètes acadiens bouleversent, parfois même inconsciemment, les règles de leur art. En ce qui concerne la langue, ils se donnent la liberté d'écrire, à un moment ou l'autre, en bon français, en mauvais français, en *chiac* [Acadian dialect] ou même en anglais. (*Rêves* 15)

With this comment, the conservative poetic tradition of Acadie seems buried for good: the Acadian poet, liberated from the past and fearless of assimilation, is free to write as he or she pleases – *même en anglais*!

Such *de facto* assimilationism would be the logical result of Masson's and Boudreau's flirtation with a variant of Québec's then–opposition leader Robert Bourassa's 1969 program, 'American technology, French culture,' which sought, in an aphorism, to combine a liberal belief in technique with a conservative idea of culture (Grant, Introduction ix). Ultimately, Grant warns, one cannot have it both ways: the conservative wish to sustain particularity must surrender before the will to individual and technological liberty.

However, Boudreau perpetuates the attempt to fuse these two notions warring within the bosom of a single poetic. Despite his liberal vision of Acadian literature as 'une contre-littérature inventant un nouveau code auquel il serait vain d'appliquer des critères anciens' (*Rêves* 19), he reverts to a conservative, almost religious, nationalism to assert its importance:

> ... aucune autre n'a eu un tel impact sur le tissu même de la conscience collective d'un peuple; aucune autre n'a été chargée d'une telle responsabilité; aucune autre n'a joui d'une telle liberté dans l'élaboration d'un projet littéraire qui se confondait avec un projet d'existence. (*Rêves* 20)

Within only a few pages of castigating some poets for bemoaning a lost nationalism, Boudreau himself emerges as a nationalist. His split consciousness is an apt metaphor for contemporary Acadian poetry ...

Africadian poets have also attempted to articulate their particularity in the face of modernity. Descended from the ranks of the 3,400 Black Loyalists who came to Nova Scotia in 1783 to escape the slavery-licensing, fledgling United States, they share with Acadian poets a literary tradition which has its genesis in a conservative religious nationalism. Peter E. McKerrow (1841–1907), an early Africadian historian, gives voice to the genesis of this sensibility in his chronicle of the establishment of the 'Coloured Baptists of Nova Scotia':

> The close of the American war brought scores of coloured people: men, women and children, from the United States, and among them many Baptists, whom when enquired how they got their religion, would frankly tell you, in the forests, behind the stone walls, in the cane brakes, in the cotton fields, and in the rice swamps. (Quoted in *Fire*, vol. 1, 65)

This nascent religious nationalism was consolidated in 1854 with the formation of the African Baptist Association (ABA), an independent association of Africadian Baptist churches. The wish to maintain this symbol of particularity was so strong, explains Africadian historian Frank Boyd (b. 1943), that when, in 1887, a motion was discussed to dissolve the ABA in favour of association with the white Maritime Baptist Convention, it was soundly defeated. 'African Baptists wanted to maintain their identity through continued separatism' (Boyd v). If Acadia, a particularity defined by language (and religion), is, as the back-cover blurb of *Unfinished Dreams* insists, 'a country which exists in the imagination and words of its people,' Africadia – a particularity defined by race and religion – is a community of believers. Accordingly, W.P. Oliver (1912–89) writes that 'the church has been the centre of Negro culture and every phase of his life has been influenced by it. It stands today as the unifying force in the lives of the people throughout the province' ('Negro' 130).

Like pre-modern Acadian literature, pre-modern Africadian literature reflected the Church, an institution which was, in essence, argues U.S. historian

Robin W. Winks, 'the Negro aristocracy of the Province' (346–7). A similar conservative nationalism dominated pre-modern Acadie (Calhoun 7). More-over, just as Acadie and its poets converted to modernity, so did Africadia and its poets. However, Africadian modernity was not marked by the founding of a university or the election of a premier. Rather, it was heralded by the bull-dozers of 'progress' destroying the Seaview United Baptist Church and the entire community of Africville (an Africadian village on the outskirts of Nova Scotia's capital, Halifax) at the close of the 1960s to engineer 'integration' and engender urban development. The failure of the ABA to protect 150-year-old Africville and its church fostered a defensive, apparently secular, nationalism. Thus, sociologist Donald Clairmont claims, 'Africville has become central in the new black consciousness in Nova Scotia' ('Moving' 74). As a result of the Africville debacle and the proliferation of secular self-help, political, and pro-fessional organizations, modernity came to Africadia. Literature left the Church – now called the AUBA (African United Baptist Association) – and took to the streets. Acadienne sociologist J.A. Mannette registers 'the rise' in the 1970s and 1980s of 'the "Black Renaissance," an explosion of music, writing, art and community consciousness' ('My' 59).

Africadian Religious Nationalism

Africadian poets have formed the vanguard of the current Africadian Cultural Renaissance. Along with other Africadian artists, they 'delineate black initia-tives and black decisions on how to live black in a white society' (Mannette, 'Revelation' 3). Thus, 'black artists are publicly expressing Nova Scotian black-ness in a black voice' (Mannette, 'Revelation' 8).

The inscription of this identity is accompanied by an explicitly anti-modern stance which recalls the conservatism of the 'Song Fishermen' without, how-ever, reproducing that group's formalism. In 'Epitaph,' then, Africadian poet David Woods (b. 1959) describes a black traitor as 'a modern type' (145). Hence, though Africadians share the same tongue as the 'American empire,' they continue to explore a dissenting modernity. This critique arises from a conservatism that persists in the culture, which is largely African-American in origin. According to Frank Boyd,

> there are a number of continuities between Afro-Nova Scotians and Afro-Ameri-cans, South and North, especially in their religious and social organizations: the African Baptist churches which Afro-Nova Scotians established are denomination-ally typical of the South, from which regions Afro-Nova Scotians derived ... (Boyd xxiv)

African-American religious practice stresses, writes African-American politi-cal scientist Charles P. Henry, 'faith, collectivism, suffering, and authori-tarianism' (62). Hence, it opposes the liberal ideal of 'possessive individualism' (Charles Henry 107). These African-American religious practices and political attitudes survive, albeit somewhat altered, in Africadia.

Cross-Cultural Conservatism

The African-American *cum* Africadian religious vision mirrors Grant's recollection of an English-Canadian nationalism that, based upon British conservatism, 'expressed itself in the use of public control in the political and economic spheres' (*Lament* 71). In fact, 'Canadians have been much more willing than Americans to use governmental control over economic life to protect the public good against private freedom' (*Lament* 71). African-American theologian Cornel West seems to echo Grant when he states that 'the modern world has been primarily about the power of big business, about the expansive possibilities of science and technology' ('Cornel' 45). Finally, West's dream of a black nationalism that would stress '[p]reservation of Black cultural integrity, acknowledgement of Black cultural distinctiveness' ('Cornel' 47) resembles Grant's memory of old-school, English-Canadian nationalism.

This implicit alliance between Canadian Red Toryism and African-American social democratic principles validates the notion that 'group identification can serve as a basis for radical as well as conservative political consciousness' (Charles Henry 15). Group identification *and* a politic rooted, like that of African America, in a 'black church tradition that blends sacred and secular vision' (Charles Henry 107) animate Africadian poets.

The major difference between Acadian and Africadian poetry lies in the latter's relative hesitancy – thus far – to repudiate religion as the opiate of the poets. But, then again, perhaps Boudreau is too hasty in proclaiming the victory of a post-nationalist, post-religious poetic, while I am too hasty in asserting the triumph of a nationalist, quasi-religious poetic for Africadians. Let us compare 'mythologies.'

Insurgent Religiosity

Boudreau describes Acadian poet Herménégilde Chiasson (b. 1946) as a 'poète fondateur de la poésie acadienne moderne' (*Rêves* 11). Along with his fellow nationalist poets of the early 1970s – Raymond LeBlanc (b. 1945) and Guy Arsenault (b. 1954) – Chiasson created work that is 'à coup sûr un acte et un événement' (*Rêves* 12). His prose poem 'Rouge' is a lyrical nationalist plaint:

> Acadie, mon trop bel amour violé, toi que je ne prendrais jamais dans les draps blancs, les draps que tu as déchirés pour t'en faire des drapeaux blancs comme des champs de neige que tu as vendus comme tes vieux poteaux de clotûres ... tes vieilles chimères, blancs comme une vieille robe de mariée qui parle à crédit pour dire des choses qu'il faut payer comptant, qui emprunte ses privilèges en croyant gagner ses droits ... Arrache ta robe bleue, mets-toi des étoiles rouges sur les seins,

enfonce-toi dans la mer, la mer rouge qui va s'ouvrir comme pour la fuite en Égypte; la mer nous appartient, c'est vrai, toute la mer nous appartient parce que nous ne pouvons pas la vendre, parce que personne ne peut l'acheter. (50–1)

Chiasson cries for his adored country in the tones of a betrayed lover. Though his nationalism arises from secularization, the process by which a nation sells its soul to market forces, Chiasson laments this reality. One hears in 'Rouge' the moan of Grant's melancholy: 'We find ourselves like fish left on the shores of a drying lake. The element necessary to our existence has passed away' (*Lament* 4). M. Darrol Bryant casts Grant's *Lament* as a 'meditation,' a religious form both 'reflective and reflexive' (112). Hence, 'Rouge' can also be considered, in Bryant's term, a 'meditative-lament' (118). Thus, Chiasson's poem, despite its modern appearance, recapitulates a classical, religious form to mourn – like Jeremiah – political immorality that endangers the existence of the nation.

Chiasson's 'Eugénie Melanson' also falls into the category of a religious lament. His comparison of Eugénie with Evangeline (the heroine of Henry Wadsworth Longfellow's sentimental epic *Evangeline: A Tale of Acadia* [1847], treating the expulsion of the Acadians in 1755) echoes the tone of the writer of Lamentations:

Tu étais la plus belle, pourtant
Quand tu te déguisais en Évangéline pour pouvoir recréer avec des Gabriels de parade les dates mémorables d'un passé sans gloire, englouti dans les rêves et les poèmes d'antan que tu n'avais jamais lus. (47)

Chiasson concludes his long poem on an aptly bitter note:

Tu t'endormis
Tu t'endormis en rêvant
Tu t'endormis en rêvant à des nouvelles déportations. (49)

Lamentations sound a similarly caustic impression of Jerusalem: 'How doth the city sit solitary, that was full of people! how is she become a widow! she that was great among the nations, and princess among the provinces, how is she become tributary' (Lam. 1:1). Despite his (post-)modernist intentions, a religious, biblical rhetoric infuses the poetry of Chiasson.

In contrast, Frederick Ward (b. 1937) seeks to cheer Africadians to assert their right to be, and, in his poem 'Dialogue #3: Old Man (to the Squatter),' to actually set about to rebuild the abolished community of Africville. He posits a positive, hopeful nationalism:

... You ain't a place. Africville is us. When we go to git a job, what they ask us? Where we from ... and if we say we from Africville, *we are Africville!* And we don't git no job. It ain't no place, son: It was their purpose to git rid of us and you believed they done it – could do it! You think they destroyed something. They ain't. They took away the place. But it come'd round, though. Now that culture come'd round. They don't just go out there and find anybody to talk about Africville, they run find us, show us off – them that'll still talk, cause we Africville. NOT-NO-SHACK-ON-NO-KNOLL. That ain't the purpose ... fer whilst your edifice is foregone destroyed, its splinters will cry out: *We still here!* Think on it, son ... Now go back ... and put you [*sic*] dwelling up again. (Quoted in *Fire*, vol. 2, 19–20)

Nevertheless, this vision is also conservative. Like Grant, Ward seems to reject a modern liberalism that must 'undermine all particularisms' (Grant *Technology* 69). His poem, published in 1983, is a premonition of the current intellectual rehabilitation of Africville performed 'as an indictment against racism, as a critique of technocratic, imposed approaches to social change, and as a celebration of community and the human spirit' (Clairmont, 'Moving' 74).

Ward's poem is 'Red Toryish' – not just in content, but in form. Though flamboyantly modernist, it conserves two traditional elements of African-American – and Africadian – culture: 'the Black Christian tradition of preaching and the Black musical tradition of performance' (West, 'Dilemma' 136). Ward does not share Boudreau's fetishistic suspicion of the folkloric, but rather integrates the choice tongue (a species of Black English) of Africadians with Standard English to produce his poem's preacherly performance. His poem conserves the African-American and Africadian sermonic tradition. Church influence continues to be felt in Africadian literature *despite* the collision with modernity.

In 'Consecrated Ground' (1996), a teleplay by George Boyd (b. 1952), which delineates the destruction of Africville, the drama is the clash between the African Baptist communal vision of 'the good' and the secularist welfare preached by the City of Halifax. When Clancy, a white social worker, suggests to Clarice, a church woman, that Africville has no 'holy' land, she replies, 'Africville is already consecrated ground ... It's your bulldozers that ... that's desecratin' the land, tearin' up people's lives. You and your machine's desecratin' their souls' (26). Clarice's insistence on the spiritual integrity of her homeland finds a rejoinder in the poem 'Avoir un pays,' by Calixte Duguay (b. 1939), in which his persona lusts for the tabernacle of an actual state: 'Dire mon Acadie / Comme on dit ma Chine ... / Et sentir dans ses entrailles / Palpiter ... / Et des frissons d'appartenance' (93).

Another instance of the persistence of an informal, shadowy religiosity occurs in the openly nationalist poem 'The Profile of Africa' by Africadian poet Maxine Tynes (b. 1949): 'we wear our skin like a flag / we share our colour like a blanket' (quoted in *Fire*, vol. 2, 74). Likewise, the aggressively modern verse of Acadian poet Dyane Léger (b. 1954), particularly her long poem 'Lesbiennes latentes,' cannot avoid traces of religious imagery and the expression of love in tones and rhythms that may refer/defer to a sermonic tradition: 'Il n'est pas intéressé à lire une description du mort et encore moins par une description de fleurs, de pleurs et de prières; il veut vivre tes émotions fortes, tes états d'âme!' (167).

A radical reading of African-American literary modernism, a reading applicable to the Africadian variety, construes it as a conservative and nationalist instrument. Literary theorist Houston A. Baker, Jr, defines African-American modernism as 'renaissancism,' that is, 'a *spirit* of nationalistic engagement' (*Modernism* 91). This nationalist modernism seeks to integrate the black oral and folk tradition with modern literary practice: '[O]ur modernity consists, finally, not in tumbling towers or bursts in the violet air, but in a sounding renaissancism where a blues [i.e., folk or popular or communal] reason may yet prevail ...' (*Modernism* 106). No wonder. For Baker, 'Afro-America [is] a physical enterprise – a real country in the known world' (*Afro* 176). Though Baker's nationalist modernity is innovative, Boudreau posits, unconsciously, a like view in his essay.

Raymond Guy LeBlanc is a poet who represents a kind of Acadian 'renaissancism.' His 'Je suis acadien' enacts the same folk/vernacular (in this case, *chiac*) *cum* literary fusion that Ward achieves:

> Je jure en anglais tous mes goddams de bâtard
> Et souvent les fuck it me remontent à la gorge
> Avec des Jesus Christ projetés contre le windshield
> Saignant medium-rare
>
> ...
>
> Je suis acadien
> Ce qui signifie
> Multiplié fourré dispersé acheté aliéné vendu révolté
> Homme déchiré vers l'avenir (144–5)

Moreover, LeBlanc's seemingly secular nationalism encodes, again, a lament, a folkloric blues. Its concluding line expresses no hopeful yearning for a paradisal future, but rather a fear for what may come.

In her discussion of Québécois novelist Hubert Aquin's *Trou de mémoire* (1968), Sylvia Söderlind asserts that Aquin uses a vernacular full of anglicisms and colloquialisms to emphasize the homelessness or non-territoriality of the metropolitan French language in Québec (92–3). Her sense that Aquin's *joual* – the folk-form of Québécois French – performs a phatic, territorial function (93) provides a way of reading the *chiac* utilized by LeBlanc. This point stresses the vindication of the folkloric that Baker's concept of 'renaissancism' demands. Furthermore, such inscribing of the vernacular would seem to represent a conservative defence of 'local culture.' The interest of Baker and LeBlanc in defining a populist modernism recalls the early efforts of the 'Song Fishermen' to construct a regional poetic. Too, if LeBlanc's radicalism is, like that of Aquin, 'religious and aesthetic before it is political' (Söderlind 107), it hints that a nationalist poet must always return, even if chorused by curses, to the precincts of faith.

Africadian poet George Borden (b. 1935) sounds an irreligiosity that chases that of LeBlanc. His poem 'To My Children I Bequeath' treats Africadian history as a chronicle of oppressions and deprivations:

> To my children
> I bequeath:
> my Baptist religion –
> for which I had no choice
> but received it second-hand
> from those who ruled my life.
> ...
> To my children
> I bequeath:
> my tar-paper mansion ...
> my over-crowded bedroom ...
> my hand-me-down wardrobe ...
> my probation officer ...
> my high-blood pressure ...
> my hate ...
> my anguish ...
> my despair ... (166)

Like LeBlanc, Borden expresses a secular nationalism that shades into the blues, the spiritual of the dispossessed. The title of his first book of poems, *Canaan Odyssey* (1988), suggests that, like LeBlanc in *Cri de terre* (1986), Borden is seeking to articulate the experience of a particularity.

Conclusion

The poets of both Africadia and Acadia have pursued a demonstrably similar poetic. Thus, pronouncedly secular Africadian and Acadian poets can write in ways that echo religious traditions. Though Boudreau has argued for the internationalism of contemporary Acadian poetry, the poets themselves have continued to speak from a sense of their particularity. Not surprisingly, then, Boudreau has had to articulate a nationalist ethos in order to insist upon the specificity of Acadian poetry. Indeed, the poets of both cultures, despite their embrace of aspects of liberal modernity, continue to espouse a conservatizing nationalism. They attempt to nationalize modernity, to conservatize liberalism, to convert secularism. They want to grant themselves the liberty to speak, to sing, their nations, to preserve the local within the universal, the provincial within the cosmopolitan. Hence, the cryptically religious nationalism of Ward and Chiasson and the deceptively secular nationalism of Borden and LeBlanc both require a conservative poetic, despite the 'liberal,' that is, non-traditional, forms of their poems. It might appear, then, that Grant's thesis has been disproved.

However, Grant insists upon the 'impossibility of conservatism in our era' (*Lament* 69). Because 'science produces such a dynamic society[,] it is impossible to conserve anything for very long' (*Lament* 67). Hence, those who seek to act conservatively, that is, nationalistically, tend to 'harness the nationalist spirit to technological planning' (*Lament* 45); in poetic terms, they express their nationalism through modern technique, believing all others to be outmoded. Yet, the issue of whether Africadian and Acadian poets will be able to sustain their particularisms beyond the present will depend, ultimately, upon their abilities to conserve their respective religious and folk traditions ...

Of course, the quarrel between liberalism and nationalism is not just confined to the literary and political expression of Acadiens and Africadians. It is also a feature of English-Canadian and Québécois literatures and social practices. In the case of French-speaking Québec (a majority francophone culture within its own 'borders' and a minority culture within anglophone and Hispanic North America), the competition between the two stances pervades the society, issuing in instructive usages of 'black' and 'white' racial metaphors in the literary and political spheres ...

Notes

1 This paper was first read at a meeting of the Southwest Association for Canadian Studies Conference at Southwestern Louisiana University, in Lafayette, Louisiana, in February 1993. I am grateful to Lisette Boily for her helpful interventions. I dedicate this essay to the late Arnold 'Ted' Davidson, who was a Research Professor of English, specializing in contemporary Canadian literature, at Duke University, Durham, North Carolina. Known widely for his pioneering studies of Margaret Atwood and Joy Kogawa, Davidson also wrote thoughtful and feeling works on Western Canadian fiction and First Nations literature.

2 Silvio Gaggi observes that 'although one can describe postmodern concerns as different from modern concerns, one can also find roots for postmodernism in the early part of the century and even in the earlier part of the humanist epoch' (21). Gaggi also finds that, in contemporary arts and literature, 'modernism is not entirely rejected, but is found to fall short of its ambitious and sometimes utopian aims' (21). Hence, one can read post-modernism as a self-conscious extension of modernism. This tendency is likely for emerging literatures, such as those of Acadia and Africadia, whose writers confront simultaneously the early and later versions of modernism and, therefore, cannot maintain rigid distinctions between the two varieties. Italian-Canadian writer Antonio D'Alfonso proposes that an 'ethnic tradition does not limit itself to only one national tradition nor to one country,' while 'the postmodern phenomenon ... is ultimately an extension of nationalism' (62). In my view, however, no matter how much, for example, an Italian-Canadian writer may refer to Italian-American culture or Italian culture *de souche*, clandestine Canadianism will assert itself.

Liberalism and Its Discontents:
Reading Black and White in Contemporary Québécois Texts

For Gérard Étienne (1936–)[1]

The question of race is increasingly a concern of literature.

Terrence Craig, *Racial Attitudes in English-Canadian Fiction*, 21

I

In their wry, picaresque travelogue *Two Innocents in Red China* (1968), co-authors Jacques Hébert (b. 1923) and Pierre Elliott Trudeau (1919–2000) record the latter's quip that 'Chinese Marxists are like Quebec collegians. On questions of religion and sex, they lose their sang-froid' (141). This incisive jest may also be applied to the Québécois intelligentsia, demonstrably if one adds *race* to M. Trudeau's taxonomy of disconcerting discourses. Indubitably, since 1945, Québécois intellectuals have frequently inked white/black racial metaphors to dramatize the polar conflict between liberalism and nationalism that annexes all serious political discourse in *le bel état putatif*.[2] I seek, here, to identify how these metaphors clarify and contradict the liberal *cum* nationalist ideologies of several Québécois thinkers – principally, Suzanne Lantagne (b. 1957), Dany Laferrière (b. 1953), Eugène Seers (1865–1945), and Michel Garneau (b. 1939). Importantly, their depictions of 'black' and 'white' disrupt the triumph of liberalism, the incipient terminus of the chronology of philosophical evolution proposed in Francis Fukuyama's famed 1989 essay 'The End of History?'

To elucidate the nature of the challenge that these writers pose, perhaps unwittingly, to partisans of liberalism, I must delineate the elements of the clash between the two surviving post–Cold War ideologies (a contest with solemn consequences for Québec). Fukuyama finds that victorious liberalism entails 'the universalization of Western liberal democracy as the final form of human government' (4). The content of this 'universal homogenous state' is, he summarizes, 'liberal democracy in the political sphere combined with easy access to VCRs and stereos in the economic' (8). In this 'post-historical period there will be neither art nor philosophy, just the perpetual caretaking of the museum of human history' and 'the endless solving of technical problems, environmental concerns, and the satisfaction of consumer demands' (18). Fukuyama's formidable, Utopian, and millenarian liberalism is complemented in Canada by the strict, aggressive thought of Trudeau. In *Federalism and the French Canadians* (1968), his central, cardinal text, Trudeau judges nationalism a *gauche* irrationality, parading in the guises of 'chauvinism, racism, jingoism, and all manner of crusades, where right reasoning and thought are reduced to rudimentary proportions' (175). This eschewal of nationalism – and *de facto* liberation of capitalist individualism – the *Zeitgeist* blessed by Fukuyama and Trudeau, is opposed by the conservative vision of George Grant (1918–88). In his incendiary defence of nationalism, *Lament for a Nation* (1965), Grant agrees that the erasure of national differences is the aim of classic liberalism. He dubs it 'the perfect ideology for capitalism,' for it 'demolishes those taboos that restrain expansion' (47). He advises that 'the classical philosophers asserted that a universal and homogeneous state would be a tyranny' (*Lament* 96), that is, 'a society destructive of human excellence' (*Lament* 86). Grant insists, then, that only those who dread this threat 'can assert consistently that parochial nationalisms are to be fought for' (*Lament* 85–6). Writing in 1994, Québec nationalist Pierre Vallières (b. 1937) follows Grant in repudiating liberal triumphalism:

La réconciliation du peuple et du capital est impossible lorsque celui-ci multiplie les inégalités, augmente le chômage, désindustrialise des pans entiers de l'économie, provoque le démantèlement des services publics, détruit l'environnement, etc. Tous ces problèmes ne peuvent être résolus par le libre-échange et la 'globalisation de l'économie.' (99)

Announcements of the demise of nationalism seem egregiously premature.

The appearance of racialized metaphors in Québécois literature illumines, I urge, this oscillation between nationalist (collectivist-conservative) and liberal (individualist-universalist) ideologies, to utilize Grantian grammar, which is the contrapuntal tension inherent in all post-colonial literatures. Truly, Seers, Garneau, Laferrière, and Lantagne engage 'race' in ways that re-inscribe romanticized or demonic constructions of the racial Other, even as they interrogate such reductive visions. In other words, the black-white trope functions in their texts to delineate notions of unfettered liberality *and* unplumbed anxieties *vis-à-vis* assimilation. African-American novelist Toni Morrison's insight into the use of black characters by American writers is, thus, applicable to these authors:

Through the simple expedient of demonizing and reifying the range of color on a palette, [blackness] makes it possible [for writers] to say and not say, to inscribe and erase, to escape and engage, to act out and act on, to historicize and render timeless. It provides a way of contemplating chaos and civilization, desire and fear, and a mechanism for testing the problems and blessings of freedom. (7)

My selected Québécois writers work with notions of 'blackness' to achieve similar ends, even deploying, at times, deplorable racial imaginings.

In making this statement, however, I do not mean to tarnish Québec. I recognize that English-Canadian writers have produced a bracing canon of sanguinely racist texts. For example, as discussed in my previous essays, Thomas Chandler Haliburton, the definitive writer of nineteenth-century British North America, mongered derogatory caricatures of Africadians.[3] Terrence Craig reveals that John Murray Gibbon, the first president of the Canadian Authors' Association, 'consistently displayed,' in his writings, 'a vehemently anti-Semitic attitude as well as ... sympathy for eugenics' (46). Pervasive anti-Orientalisms in Hilda G. Howard's novel *The Writing on the Wall* (1921) provoke Craig to label it 'the most racist book in Canadian fiction' (51). James Walker reminds us that Magistrate Emily Murphy published, in 1922, *The Black Candle*, a book containing articles attacking primarily 'the Chinese opium user' ('*Race*' 111). Murphy also savaged '"blackamoors" or "gen'lemen of color," and their most heinous crime was the entrapment of white women into addiction and prostitution' ('*Race*' 111). Walker also tells us that 'Mrs. Isobel Graham, described as a "Manitoban suffragist," wrote in the *Grain Growers' Guide* of 3 May 1911 that [immigrant black men would inevitably commit atrocities] against white Canadian women, and warned that lynching and even burning at the stake would become necessary' ('*Race*' 127). Laura Fairburn's 1994 novel *Endless Bay* drafts a Mi'kmaq character who seems a psychotic Heathcliff.[4] Craig stresses that racism has always shaded Canadian fiction, 'whether as a mild form of xenophobia, or in one of the more fanatical forms of group-hatred such as anti-Semitism' (139).[5] English Canadians cannot feel morally superior to francophones when it comes to their treatment – and depiction – of minorities.

Nevertheless, I survey Québec in this paper for two reasons: first, the nationalist *versus* liberal debate is sumptuously acute in this locale; secondly, Québécois writers have made steady political use of racialized metaphor – festively so during *la révolution tranquille*. Thus, Vallières parallels, in his splenetic *cri-du-coeur*, *White Niggers of America* (1971), the mutual marginality of blackness and proletarianized *francité* in North America: 'The liberation struggle launched by the American blacks ... arouses growing interest among the French-Canadian population, for the workers of Quebec are aware of their condition as niggers, exploited men, second-class citizens' (21). Vallières asks rhetorically, 'Were [Québécois] not *imported*, like the American blacks to serve as cheap labour in the New World?' (21). Sébastien Joachim reports that the Québécois narrator of the 1965 novel *Journal d'un hobo* likens his compatriots to Jews and blacks: '[Vancouver] manque de *Juifs* et de *Nègres*. C'est peut-être aussi bien, ces deux races ont des complexes et présentent des problèmes *comme nous*' (quoted in Joachim 238). *Circa* 1968, Michèle Lalonde (b. 1937) composed 'Speak White,' a conjoining of the felt experiences of Québécois and black oppressions that Québécois critic Jean Royer terms 'le poème-étendard de la poésie du pays' (85): 'speak white / tell us again about Freedom and Democracy / nous savons que liberté est un mot noir' (quoted in Royer 85). In Hubert Aquin's anti-colonial allegory *Trou de mémoire* (1968), 'un Noir est au centre de l'intrigue' (Joachim 238). Because of this long-standing linking of black and Québécois subjectivities, one can read white-black tropes as accounts of the ongoing liberalist-nationalist rivalry, both within Québec and in the world.

II

In both Seers's *Les Enfances de Fanny* (1951), or *Fanny* (1974) (the title of Raymond Y. Chamberlain's English translation), and Laferrière's *Comment faire l'amour avec un nègre sans se fatiguer* (1985), or *How to Make Love to a Negro* (1987) (the title of David Homel's English version), the male protagonist is an immigrant-exile of racial minority status. Seers (who wrote under the pseudonym of Louis Dantin) presents the pseudo-autobiographical Donat Sylvain, a white Québécois artist who has settled in Boston and taken Fanny Lewis, an African-American woman, as his lover. Contrastingly, Laferrière sketches the yearnings and acts of Vieux, an equally pseudo-autobiographical Haitian refugee in Montréal (a demi-America), who desires the capitalist salvations of white women, lucre, and fame.[6] Lantagne's short story 'Histoire noire' (1995) narrates the bleak encounter between a white woman and an African immigrant. *Héliotropes* (1994), a drama by Garneau, depicts a multiracial group of prostitutes and a black male pianist. These texts declare, credibly, both a liberal openness to others – the alien, the exotic – *and* a nationalist or ethnocentric resistance to the same.

Of this textual quartet, however, only Laferrière's work is situated in Québec; Seers's novel and Garneau's play are grounded in the United States. Lantagne's narrative locates itself in a generic Canadian city. Still, the salient commonality of these texts is their engagement with the tradition of racialized metaphor adumbrated above. Therefore, I must challenge Max Dorsinville's curious submission, in *Caliban without Prospero: Essay on Québec and Black Literature* (1974), that 'it is in the early sixties ... that the figure of the Black man, as symbol, image and myth, emerges in the French-Canadian consciousness' (10). Two earlier forms of metaphoricized blackness repay scrutiny.

Québec's superlative *fin-de-siècle* poet Émile Nélligan (1879–1941) manipulates blackness-as-metaphor in his *circa* 1899 poem 'Le Perroquet.' Nélligan portrays a 'pauvre négresse,' resident of a 'coin hideux,' who fancies that her parrot embodies 'l'âme de son amant,' a presumably white sailor who had told her that his being would inhabit the bird (111). This 'crédule enfant d'Afrique' thus countenances the parrot's mocking utterance, 'Ha! Ha! Ha! Gula, mes amours!' but perishes, eventually, of 'la rancoeur' (111–12). Blackness signifies, in this late *symboliste* poem, indigence, gullibility, and pathos. Whiteness is construed, by its exact invisibility, as a positive opposite, manifesting the kinds of virtues

Frantz Fanon catalogues in *Peau noire, masques blancs* (1952): 'On est blanc comme on est riche, comme on est beau, comme on est intelligent' (43).

Nélligan's friend and editor, Seers, in 'Chanson javanaise,' a poem of contemporaneous provenance with *Les Enfances de Fanny*, hallows blackness as the *sign* of impassioned being. In this poem, which recalls both Nélligan and Charles Baudelaire, a white sailor is granted succour and love by 'c'te grande fill' d'Afrique,' a Gauguin-like woman with 'les bras ballants / N'ayant sur les seins et les hanches / Que sa court' chemise des dimanches' (140). She is a *National Geographic* earth goddess, a 'chaude fleur d'Afrique' (144), and her history admits the usual, fevered atavism:

> 'Quand j'pens', dit-ell', que pour ma fête,
> Chaque année, on coupait vingt têtes,
> Et qu'tout l'mond' battait du tom-tom:
> Et m'v'là plus coulée qu'l'oncle Tom! ...' (142)

Seers's lyric supports the finding of Joachim that 'la foule africaine, c'est toujours la horde primitive à l'état pur' (95). Seers concocts a Manichean polarity in which blackness marks, to cite Fanon again, 'une fusion totale avec le monde, une compréhension sympathique de la terre, une perte de mon moi au coeur du cosmos ...' (38). It implies the exotic, the sexual, and the savage, a series of associations that Marxist *philosophe* Herbert Marcuse also accepts, linking 'black, violent, orgiastic' (42). Like, essentialist fantasies mar Seers's novel.

In contemporary Québécois literature, too, blackness evokes licence, force, and transgressive sexuality. Suzanne Pellerin promulgates these forbidding representations in her unhesitantly nationalist poem 'La Cité des interdits' (1994).[7] Privileging a nurturing darkness over daylight, this lyric depicts a white female speaker, 'fille de Piaf et [Juliette] Gréco' (44), who attacks 'la nouvelle race aryenne' (44) and 'la cité aux phallus de béton' (46) represented by 'deux Anglos blancs' (44). Their city is a sexless, commercial desert of 'pâles mutants / Le corps désinfecté, le coeur déshydratée / Steak frites, verre de lait et condom' (44) and 'La passion plasmifiée ... / Le sexe muselé par mille interdits' (44). The speaker spurns this *plat* whiteness, stating, 'Je me réfugie dans le noir / À la recherche des sources de la vie' (44). Not only is *blackness* qualitatively superior to the culture of the white Anglos, they merit destruction: the speaker dreams of shattering their porcelain hearts (46). Pellerin perpetuates the cliché, *à la* Marcuse, that blackness signals 'a desublimated, sensuous form of frightening immediacy, moving, electrifying the body, and the soul materialized in the body' (Marcuse 52). This 'liberating,' opulent blackness is an unabashed repetition of the civilized white's 'nostalgie irrationnelle d'époques extraordinaires de licence sexuelle, de scènes orgiaques, de viols non sanctionnés, d'incestes non réprimés' (Fanon 135), a longing projected onto the black. In Nélligan, Seers, and Pellerin (in spite of her progressive politics), blackness is affianced to the sexual, 'comme si,' as Haitian-Canadian writer Gérard Étienne alleges, 'la sexualité était le seul critère existentiel de l'homme ou de la femme noirs, comme si nous ne vivions et ne respirions que par la sexualité, que le nègre et la négresse sont des bêtes toujours en rut' (*Question* 148).

As this overview attests, Québécois writers have often metaphoricized race, using it, as in the work of Vallières and Pellerin, to allegorize French-English relations. Québec politicians lend further credence to the territorial, self-applicability of this trope. Queried about his reticence in defending bilingualism during the 1972 federal election campaign, for instance, Trudeau delivered, reportedly, the following analogy:

> He would in effect have been telling people they had to vote for him to prove they weren't bigots ... and he likened that to a black man asking a white woman to go out with him and insisting that a refusal could only be due to his colour. The woman might have 101 reasons for refusing, just as people might have 101 reasons for voting against him ... and he hadn't wanted to distort the issue. (Radwanski 261)

The separatist Québec *premier ministre* René Lévesque (1922–87) also delighted in politicizing blackness. He characterized the first francophone prime minister, Sir Wilfrid Laurier (1841–1919), as 'a black king' (quoted in Grant, *Lament* 77) and the third, Trudeau, as 'our Negro King in a sports jacket' (quoted in Sullivan 302).[8] Lévesque viewed these liberals as Québécois marionettes within the federal system. Yet, Trudeau, too, utilized this spectacular metaphor, condemning Québec independence as a 'form of African tribalism that even the Negro kings don't want for themselves' (quoted in Vastel 134). He denounced the idea of a Québec leader or lieutenant within the federal Liberal party caucus in equally clear terms: 'The concept of a Quebec lieutenant is really the black Negro king theory translated into the federal field' (quoted in Sullivan 122). Trudeau parades an extended analysis of this notion in *Federalism and the French Canadians*:

> ... in politics, Anglo-Canadian nationalism took on the form of what André Laurendeau has so admirably named the 'cannibal-king' theory (théorie du roi-nègre). Economically, this nationalism has been expressed essentially in treating the French Canadian as *un cochon de payant*. Sometimes, magnanimously, they would go as far as putting a few straw men on boards of directors. These men invariably had two things in common: first, they were never bright enough or strong enough to rise to the top, and second, they were always sufficiently 'representative' to grovel for the cannibal-king's favours and flatter the vanity of their fellow-tribesmen. (163)

No doubt should exist as to the potency of blackness as racialized metaphor for both liberals and nationalists in Québécois political and literary discourse.[9]

Assuredly, Lantagne's saturnine *conte* 'Histoire noire' sketches an actual 'Negro' King, that is, 'un noir' named 'King,' who is just as abject a figure as the mythological rulers conjured by Laurendeau, Lévesque, and Trudeau. This

Negro 'King' lives up to Lantagne's single-white-female narrator's expectations – or, more accurately, her prejudices. King is purely farcical – a fantastic
puppet – as weak and pitiable as those in Québécois political lore. Lantagne's
narrative welcomes the unwelcome, value-laden, binary opposition that Fanon
excoriates, the supposition that 'le péché est nègre comme la vertu est blanche'
(*Peau* 114). To the anonymous protagonist, then, King embodies soul, the earth,
the flesh – in other words, to turn to Fanon, 'l'instincte sexuel (non éduqué)'
(*Peau* 145). The narrator confesses such beliefs when, after having arrived,
'saoule dans [un] bar, avec une copine, pour danser avec n'importe quel Noir
chaud et sexy' (19), she revels, while dancing with King, in an Anaïs Nin–like
sensuality:

> Mon esprit divaguait, je laissais mon corps danser tout seul, je fermais les yeux et
> King me faisait bouger. La musique résonnait contre ma poitrine, les autres
> danseurs se perdaient dans une espèce de chaud brouillard; j'avais de l'écho dans
> la tête, des bourdonnements dans les oreilles, un voile épais devant les yeux, les
> jambes souples et le ventre comme un volcan. (19–20)

This lush evocation is chased by a chain of verbs supported by the eroticized
repetition of the first-person direct and indirect object: 'Mon partenaire noir
me suivait..., me tenait, me provoquait, me manipulait, me consolait, me
regardait, m'embrassait, me serrait, me faisait rire et fondre, me prenait...' (20).
Decadent, the speaker perceives King only as a bestower of pleasure. She
disregards, cavalierly, his cultural identity, presuming that he is 'probablement
zoulou, ou quelque chose comme ça' (19). She rejects 'un Blanc' as a potential
partner, for 'il regarderait autour, serait légèrement mal à l'aise et surtout ne
saurait pas quoi faire de ses deux mains' (20). She prefers 'ces hommes-là me
parlent avec leur chair' (20). Like Pellerin, she espouses blackness as the source
of sex-gaiety.

Yet, if the first half of this two-paragraph-long story locates the narrator in a
primeval paradise of the senses, a site of 'chaleur' and bliss, the remainder
portrays her fall into the cold, sordid, capitalistic world that she had sought,
through mere *jouissance*, to obliterate. This *chute* commences as soon as the
music stops. In the end, King is reduced to a man whose name seems 'une
vraie farce' (19). The narrator accompanies King home for 'une chic aventure
bien perverse' (20), an expectation which Fanon would attribute to the myth
that black men keep 'la porte impalpable qui donne sur le royaume des Sabbats,
des Bacchanales, des sensations sexuelles hallucinantes' (*Peau* 145). But the
affair decays into debacle. King declines to purchase condoms; the narrator
prevails. He requests money, she feels insulted. At King's 'correct mais laid'
apartment block, his 'triste réalité,' the narrator fears, while showering, that he
will filch cash from her purse (21). Epiphanically, 'la vie avait,' the narrator
discovers at this moment, 'un visage sans masque' (21). The once-charming
King, 'maintenant qu'il savait qu'il pourrait enfoncer son queue quelque part,
il ne faisait plus le beau ...' (21). Now 'lui, le roi,' is 'conscient d'être pitoyable
au milieu de ses guenilles' (21). The speaker's disillusionment conjures a spiri-

tual panic: 'La crudité de cette rencontre m'est apparue dans toute sa plénitude. Je n'étais pas devant un vide spirituel qui conduit à l'illumination, mais devant un effroyable trou sans fond et infiniment glacial' (22). Completing the picture of King's corrupted state, the narrator notes, after they have made love, that King possesses 'un sexe décevant pour un Noir' (22), thus reinforcing a stereotype – 'le nègre est appréhendé avec un membre effarant' (Fanon 145) – even as it is eviscerated. Once King falls asleep, the narrator steals away, after checking her billfold, 'dans l'hiver noir' (20), the polar negation of the bar's 'chaud brouillard' (20).

'Histoire noire' is a black comedy, one replete with images of black holes, a black winter, a conspicuously ridiculous black, and even an atmosphere of black shirts, that is, of a faint fascism. This possibility exists as a result of the narrator's fascination for the body, her mania for cleanliness, and her resolute adherence to regressively narrow racial beliefs. King is the reincarnated 'négresse' of Nélligan, a slave to indigence and failure. Worse, he is a potential thief, semi-impotent, a *faux* man. The narrator fucks him but experiences a glacial dark night of the soul.[10] Her tryst with alterity leaves her trapped agonizingly in the prison of herself – and in the mercenary dystopia of late capitalism. Lantagne's story enacts a collision between whiteness and blackness, one that sullies both. 'Histoire noire' bodes ill for the consummation of multiculturalism in Québec.[11]

I suspect, though, that Lantagne immerses her readers in the *merde* of ethnocentrism as a riposte to the misogynist and racial positions struck – satirically – in Laferrière's consideration of the cruising bar milieu in *How to Make Love to a Negro*. There is a leaven of humour in Laferrière that Lantagne lacks, but his work patents her spendthrift way with racial stereotypes. If Lantagne's King administers squalor, Laferrière's hero, Vieux, rules, with his nominally Islamic chum, Bouba, a slummy Montréal apartment. Lantagne's narrator *drague les hommes noirs*, but Laferrière's narrator dragoons white women. Lantagne's barfly heroine denigrates white men as sexually maladroit, and Laferrière's hero concurs:

> Streaming bodies. Eighteen-carat ebony. Ivory teeth. Reggae music. Combustion. Black fusion. A white/black couple practically copulating on the dance floor. Atomic shockwaves ... 'Sexually, the white man is dead. Completely demoralized. Look at them [the black-white couple] dancing. Do you know any white man who could keep up with that madness?' (*How* 93)

If Lantagne envisions such dancefloor unions as a pseudo-tropical event, Laferrière agrees: 'It's like moving into Amazon humidity. Bodies running with sweat. You need a machete to cut through this jungle of arms, legs, sexes and mingling smells. Spicy sensuality' (*How* 94). Like Lantagne, Laferrière grounds his narrative upon the notion that, to sound Fanon, 'c'est ... qu'avec le nègre commence le cycle du *biologique*' (*Peau* 133). For both writers, the African denotes the physical, the earthy, the sexual.[12]

Neither, however, adheres to this construction entirely. Lantagne's heroine casts King as the key to orgasm, then recants, thus refusing the very narrative that Vieux validates, ironically, in a mock interview with Miz Bombardier: 'She was beside herself. She had found her African. Her primitive' (*How* 112). Laferrière's hero is hedonistic, but his copulations generate finely honed dissertations. Indeed, Laferrière produces a laid-back, bohemian atmosphere in which titillating, liberal coitus occurs between the *déclassé* black narrator and his *bourgeois* white partners, but, as in Sade, it is the commentary – a steady, pseudo-black nationalist riff on North America society – that is paramount. Vieux and Bouba are, as Vieux admits, 'two blacks in a filthy apartment ..., philosophizing their heads off about Beauty in the wee hours' (*How* 30), but his emphasis is on the act of cogitation. The text details tantalizing indulgences of reading, eating, drinking, fucking, sleeping, and barhopping, but it is more than an 'erotico-satiric' novel (Homel 8). Rather, Laferrière showcases a potent Negro King, a Haitian-Canadian *roi soleil*, whose ideology is written out in sperm.

Significantly, Vieux's subjugation of white women is putative reprisal for the sins of their imperialist ancestors:

> This Judeo-Christian girl is my Africa. A girl born for power. So what is she doing at the end of my black rod? ... I want to fuck her subconscious ... I catch a glimpse of my oiled thighs (coconut oil) against this white body. I take her white breasts firmly in my hands. The light down on her white marble body. I want to fuck her identity. Pursue the racial question to the heart of her being ... (*How* 60–1)

When Vieux enters Miz Literature's posh home for a tryst, he experiences an agreeable sensation of racial and class transgression: 'This house breathes calm, tranquillity, order. The order of the pillagers of Africa' (*How* 76). In this *haute-bourgeois* oasis, he will 'fuck the daughter of these haughty diplomats who once whacked us with their sticks' (*How* 76). An unarticulated revenge fantasy also spans the abrupt transition between Vieux's musings on American slavery – 'Black bodies shining sensual, beaten by the cruel wind of the Deep South' (*How* 78) – and his presumption of 'Black desire obsessed with pubescent white flesh' (*How* 78).

Vieux never expresses love for the white women he takes. Instead, their bodies attract a Sadean glamorization: 'My sex celebrates your golden hair, your pink clitoris, your forbidden vagina, your white belly, your bowed neck, your Anglo-Saxon mouth' (*How* 61). The unacknowledged inspiration for the rapacious violence of such portraiture is likely the African-American essayist (and confessed ex-rapist) Eldridge Cleaver (1935–98), whose 1968 poem 'To a White Girl' telegraphs Laferrière's compulsions:

> I love you
> Because you're white,
> Not because you're charming

Or bright.
Your whiteness
Is a silky thread
Snaking through my thoughts
In redhot patterns
Of lust and desire.

I hate you
Because you're white.
...
You're my Moby Dick,
White Witch,
Symbol of the rope and hanging tree,
Of the burning cross ... (25–6)

Vieux moans a hymn of sexual vengeance against white women. He declares, 'Put black vengeance and white guilt together in the same bed and you had a night to remember!' (*How* 18) His incessant, sacerdotal, but ironic citing of *The Glorious Qur'an* underlines his dissident vision of the Caucasian Occident (marked by the 'sign' *America*) as a citadel of '"evil-doers"' (*How* 104, 115) and 'infidels' (*How* 24, 99), an empire whose women, as in any total war or crusade, are *fair* – pale and proper – game. Vieux's penis is a weapon, one wielded in a manner that knights, even as it skewers, the brand of sexist racism endorsed by a writer like Michel Cournot: 'L'épée du Noir est une épée. Quand il a passé ta femme à son fil, elle a senti quelque chose' (quoted in Fanon, *Peau* 139). Sexuality is, for Laferrière's Vieux, a continuation of *jihad* by other means.

Homel observes that 'one critic went after Laferrière for making all his white women English-speaking' (Homel 8). Of course, the critic was wrong. Vieux lusts after the British-born, but now *French*, actress Jane Birkin (*How* 86), and he lusts after a white Québécoise film star, imagining, 'Carole Laure, slave to a Negro. Why not?' (*How* 24). Since Vieux perceives Miz Literature as his 'slave' (*How* 35), his dreams of lording it over Laure are likely rooted in the same race-sex *chiaroscuro* that defines his 'hookings up' with anglophone women. He exclaims, 'I want Carole Laure! I demand Carole Laure! Bring me Carole Laure!' (*How* 89) Plainly, Vieux's attitude toward white women, whether English or French, iterates the ambivalence that marks the conclusion of Cleaver's poem:

Loving you thus
And hating you so,
My heart is torn in two.
Crucified. (26)

However, Vieux's ambivalence is not one of love-and-hate, but rather of desire-and-repulsion. White women are targets for the settling of scores, but they are also potential allies in Vieux's attempted seizure of the riches – economic, cultural, sexual – of the white-majority states of Amérique du Nord. As Haitian-Québécois writer Michel Adam (b. 1945) posits in his 1976 poem 'Femme blanche,' the white woman is '[un] cheval de troie / d'hommes noirs / dans les pâles / citadelles' (26). Miz Literature and Miz Sophisticated Lady serve in precisely this capacity for Vieux. Yet, they remain pawns in a cold, unholy war of attrition, one which Vieux means to wage on both sides of Québec's linguistic divide and on both sides of the 49th Parallel.

Affirming that Laferrière subjects Québec to glancing criticism in his 1994 text *Chronique de la dérive douce*, nationalist Québécois critic Renaud Longchamps takes the author to task: 'Il serait déplacé aussie de signifier à Monsieur Laferrière que ne l'avons pas invité à cracher dans notre sauce blanche ..., nous lui demanderons bien respecteusement de se la fermer' (17). Irritated by Laferrière's question 'pourquoi les Blancs ont-ils toujours la même réaction devant le racisme?' (quoted in Longchamps 17), Longchamps answers, with a *soupçon* of ethnocentrism, 'Nous aurons la politesse de ne pas lui demander la sienne, ni à son peuple' (17). Longchamps accuses Laferrière of craving 'à l'universelle gloire américaine et à la vaisselle d'or du couchant' (17) and of seeking to profit 'du meilleur des deux mondes [Québec and the United States], comme le dernier des trafiquants mohawks' (17). He even draws a line in the snow, so to speak, between 'le peuple québécois,' who love their 'pays' in 'tous ses états,' and Laferrière, the *so*-ungrateful immigrant (17).[13] His tone is acerbic, but the value of Longchamps's nasty critique is that it teases out the gnashing of nationalisms, Québécois (and white Anglo) *versus* black, which lurks within Laferrière's vision of Québec/North America.

Crucially, references to black nationalist icons pervade Laferrière's work. Though few black women appear in *How to Make Love to a Negro*, Vieux catalogues an Afrocentric, religio-historical figure – 'the Egyptian princess Taiah' (15) – and vital cultural signifiers – Ella Fitzgerald (69), Bessie Smith (70, 77), and Tina Turner (74). The text is rife with allusions to jazz performers, Fanon, and Cleaver,[14] and the 'blackest' cult figure of them all, Malcolm X (74).

Despite his nationalist moods, however, Vieux is an avowed individualist. His joust with white society will be won on egocentric and economic grounds. The typewriter that will make his fortune becomes – like his penis – a 'terrorist machine' (*How* 46). In addition, Vieux avers that 'to be a traitor is every writer's destiny' (*How* 113). The novel concludes, not with a communal call to arms, but with a truly U.S.-style declaration of pragmatic self-interest: 'My novel is a handsome hunk of hope. My only chance. *Take it*' (*How* 117). At this point, one should imagine a welling up of strings, perhaps laid over a funky, disco beat.

How to Make Love to a Negro rehearses the nationalist-versus-liberal dilemma, assuming, finally, a provisional position on the side of capitalist individualism. Vieux's ideology remains, though, as unstable as his sex-race dichotomies: he ignores the issue of whether he is first or foremost Haitian, Québécois, or American, or a tripartite fusion of these identities. And his adoption of a *dépaysé* persona has import. His narrative settles 'neither into clearly postcolonial counter-discursive subversion nor into neo-colonial submission,' to quote Daniel Coleman (53). Hence, the book both 'exposes and ridicules the discursive system that produces the racist stereotypes which degrade men of African ancestry, and it recycles and recommodifies those very stereotypes in the process' (Coleman 53). Vieux's attempt to mock racism by fucking white women and living off the proceeds of his accounts of his encounters endorses, paradoxically, the grotesque, Cournotesque rhetoric that casts black men as pimps.

Like Laferrière, Seers employs racialized tropes to accent individuality. Unlike Laferrière and Lantagne, though, Seers wields his metaphors with a blithe, unfinessed innocence. In *Fanny*, he ransacks the dark romantic diction of Baudelaire to limn the adoration that a Québécois artist, Donat Sylvain, feels for Fanny Lewis (*née* Johnston), his widowed black housekeeper:

> Her body was a precious jewel-box of mirages and symbols. The color of her skin reflected golden bees, rare orchids, polished wood, ripe chestnuts, fine topaz, delicate coffee, the shimmering brilliance of insects' wings, the down on the breasts of birds. (141)

While Laferrière borrows from Sade to sing his white female characters, Seers turns, not only to the *symbolistes*, but also, perhaps, to French *négritude* poets.[15] Unfortunately, the tropes of this Québécois author who exiled himself to the United States and married an African-American woman are just as confining as those of the Haitian author who exiled himself to North America and semi-married Québec. When Fanny first appears as a tomboy of twelve years of age, Seers demystifies her mixed-race heritage:

> [Her] maternal grandmother had been a slave, the favorite slave, it was said, of the planter Johnston, which no doubt explained why both [Fanny and her older sister, Linda] had delicate brown complexions and thinner, more refined features than are commonly found in their race. (*Fanny* 10)

The historical act of rape, or of coerced sexual intercourse, has had the happy consequence of infusing in Fanny and her sister enough of the right genetic material to render them more palatable to the Eurocentric eye than their darker-skinned compatriots. (It is the memory of exactly such presumedly criminal fornications that motivates Vieux, like some hip, black Nosferatu, to stalk Montréal's young white *bourgeoises*.) Perhaps, too, they are even closer to virtue, which, for the dour Lantagne and the excitable Longchamps, is a decidedly white quality. Fanny is, then, a brand of 'Tragic Mulatto': her Caucasian genes 'refine' her features, but her veins tap 'the exuberant sap of the jungle' (*Fanny* 10). She is torn between two worlds: the white, rarefied sphere of Donat and the black, earthy sphere of her friends and family in Roxbury, a black section of Boston. Donat is liberal, deeming Fanny 'simply a woman, distinguished solely by the rare qualities that he would have admired in a person of any color' (*Fanny* 142). However, his antagonist, Charlie Ross, is a lay black nationalist who, at the melodramatic climax, asks that Fanny quit Donat, 'this white man,' and 'come back with us, with your own kind' (*Fanny* 177).

Seers attempts to complicate the racial formula. Donat loves Fanny and he is, politically, a progressive. Still, he envisions her as 'an *enfant sauvage* fresh from the jungle with the perfume of her virginal nature still around her' (*Fanny* 142–3). A New World Carmen, her heart is 'primitive' (*Fanny* 143). Like Seers's contemporaneous 'javanaise,' she is 'natural,' 'spontaneous,' and an emblem of vitality: 'She had taught him how to live again on his own original soil' (143). She is a siren who cancels inhibitions: 'He would caress her like a man transported, with the almost sacrilegious headiness of one entering forbidden realms' (*Fanny* 142). Seers markets the standard, Western *tchotchkes* that assign naturalness, spontaneity, and emotion to blackness.[16]

Contradictorily, though, blackness remains an imperilled quality. Seers's black male characters are all failures. Worse still, after having harboured a unrequited love for Fanny since boyhood, Charlie causes her death. His innate unworthiness is signalled, though, by his 'gross lips' (*Fanny* 13).[17] The historical African-American divine Father Divine (1880?–1965), granted a cameo turn in the novel (chapter 26), resembles a spiritual Maurice Duplessis (1890–1959) – the authoritarian Québec premier of the Depression and post–Second World War years – 'a naive and neighborly god who had taken the image of his creatures to move among them, dispensing his gifts in just exchange for their veneration, satisfied with himself and with his universe' (*Fanny* 104).[18] Though black self-expression fills Donat 'with increased respect for the mind and the aesthetic sensibilities of black people' (*Fanny* 151), he deems U.S. playwright Marc Connelly's 'black' musical *Green Pastures* (1930) 'a transformation into popular drama of all of biblical history, as naive black people might conceive it' (*Fanny* 150).[19] For her part, Fanny is both strong and weak, an incongruity that metaphoricizes her bi-racial status. In addition, she sacrifices her own happiness whenever circumstance requires, and her death is that of a saint: 'Emaciated, almost ethereal, even in defeat Fanny's body kept its indestructible youth. Her face had taken on a new, purer beauty, the reflection of her virginal soul' (*Fanny* 185). This death scene mirrors the conclusion of Henry Wadsworth Longfellow's narrative poem *Evangeline: A Tale of Acadie* (1847), a work which Fanny knew in part (*Fanny* 128). As Fanny faces her 'ultimate trial' (*Fanny* 185), she incarnates 'devotion and selfless renunciation' (*Fanny* 183) and 'patience and tranquil resignation' (*Fanny* 185). Likewise, in *Evangeline*, the eponymous heroine exhibits 'patience and abnegation of self, and devotion to others, / ... the lesson a life of trial and sorrow had taught her' (84). The theme of *Evangeline* – defined by Fanny as the separation of two lovers by fate (*Fanny* 128), and encapsulated in Seers's 'Chanson javanaise' ('J' comprends ton sort, mon p'tit spahi, / T'es comm' moi, la chanç' t'a trahi' [142]) – becomes that of his novel. Fanny is a black Evangeline separated from her true lover by traitorous fate. Problematically, though, her blackness seems to evaporate as she dies.

Startlingly, this etherealization of blackness concretizes the hard-edged liberalism that composes Seers's racial judgments. Indeed, the omniscient narrator hints that the final solution to racism is assimilation: 'Already in certain areas there are more "blond Africans" than Negroes who hardly show a trace of their ancestry, suggesting for some later date an automatic and highly ironic solution to the "black problem"' (*Fanny* 167). Seers's liberalism is almost as negative as Lantagne's chequebook ethnocentrism. If blackness is, for her, irremediably black, for him, it must be – easily – lactified.

Placed against the texts of Lantagne, Laferrière, and Seers, Garneau's 1994 verse-play *Héliotropes* is unquestionably progressive. Set in a bordello in early twentieth-century America, the era of ragtime, the play presents a rainbow coalition of prostitutes – Léola ('noire'), Cléopha ('chocolat'), Eugenia ('high yella'), and Blossom ('blanche et blonde'). The queans are bossed by Martha Jane – the fortyish, white madame, and her mature, white, mute, adopted pianist-daughter, Janey O. When a black Scott Joplin–like 'Compositeur' steps into this world, precipitating a moral emergency, the drama becomes a racialized *salon au bordel*. Martha Jane worries that, if she permits the composer to stay, her white male clientèle will melt away because 'les nègres ça les rend fous' (45). Blossom and Cléopha concur, observing, in sequence, that 'ils aiment bien les négresses / les hommes blancs / c'est pour ça / qu'ils n'aiment pas les nègres' (46). Sexual jealousy is here, as it is in Laferrière and Seers, the progenitor of racism. Then again, sexual relations in literature are always an amplification of hierarchies.

The Compositeur determines to remain, though, for he is won by the artistry of Janey O, who plays his music with 'dignité' (41). Thus, he argues his case, ridiculing, for instance, the stereotype that 'une musique écrite par un nègre / soit sans profondeur / et que sa joie / soit seulement naive / une joie pas trop intelligente' (40). He likens himself to legendary piano composers – Alessandro Scarlatti, Ludwig von Beethoven, and Frédéric Chopin, for he has also inherited 'un vocabulaire / et j'organise mon héritage [that of the bordello where he learned to play piano] / pour en tirer le plus de beauté possible' (44). By making this claim, the Compositeur disputes Marcuse's racial-romanticist opposition of blackness to European art, the hallucination that 'the soul is black ...; it is no longer in Beethoven, Schubert, but in the blues, in jazz ...' (42).

Ultimately, the Compositeur proposes a liberal basis for his induction into this little society, namely, recognition of his talent, his art. Furthermore, as Eugenia sees, he is 'un beau nègre' (41). His union with the household would manifest, then, a new aesthetic: 'Kinship of the beautiful, the divine, the poetic ...' (Marcuse 34). Janey O's performance of the Compositeur's music manifests this integrationist ethic: 'elle est blanche / et joue de la musique / noire' (59). Too, while the Compositeur has sought 'dignité' (41) and 'beauté' (44), the women value 'intégrité' (14). *Héliotropes* is, then, a liberal manifesto, positing

'Beauté, Dignité, Intégrité' against the yahoo ideology of the white males who invade the bordello at dusk.

Unswayed by the Compositeur's discourse on art, Martha Jane (a character based on the mid-nineteenth-century American frontierswoman Calamity Jane, born Martha Jane Canary [1852–1903]) brandishes a revolver and threatens to shoot him (48–9). Soon, though, she is won over, and allows the Compositeur to join her domicile. She concedes for three reasons: (1) his music does not seem 'très nègre' (53), a judgment exalting technique over cultural authenticity; (2) he is as much 'un orphélin' and 'un bébé' as the prostitutes (79), and thus her matriarchy is affirmed; and (3) he is dying of syphilis (79), an argument that sacks the social liberalism that *Héliotropes* appears to extol. No serious liberalization is needed to accommodate the Compositeur, for he is not long for this *demi-monde*, anyway. The *dénouement* expresses, as in Seers, an insouciant disrespect for the legitimacy of cultural difference.

While Pellerin manipulates racialized imagery to vandalize the dessicated, unnatural city of *les maudits anglais*, Lantagne uses like imagery to attack the liberal fantasy that capitalism produces tolerance. Laferrière mouths the credos of individualism, but lobs black nationalist barbs at European–North America. Seers champions a bleached, reified blackness, that is, a benign assimilationism. Garneau's gold-hearted matriarchy welcomes an outsider only because he has exploitable skills (the *sine qua non* of any liberal immigration policy). In the end, these writers depict varying levels of anxiety, or discomfort, in regards to the dream of the open society, *la cité libre*. They strive to be good liberals, but their liberalism unleashes, finally, a pugnacious and repugnant ethnocentrism.

III

The works of Lantagne, Laferrière, Seers, and Garneau controvert the propaganda that nationalism has ceased to influence Québécois literature. This implicit dissent is fruitful, for several critics have sought to cleanse the literature of its 'embarrassing' eruptions of nationalism. In 1970, John Glassco argued that nationalism harmed the work of Québécois poets: they seemed 'too often preoccupied by political ... ideas, by the one incandescent ideal of a beleagured Québec – and it is a truism that politics and nationalism have somehow never managed to make really good poetry' (xix). Dorsinville opined, in 1974, that Québécois and Black American writers had jointly moved beyond regressive theories of nationalism. They had attained a stage in their cultural evolution 'where the universal is reached through descent into the self, or through overture towards other selves' (*Caliban* 210–11), a strategic definition of cultural maturity that rendered nationalism, *per se*, *passé*. In his introduction to the Fall 1994 special issue of *International Poetry Review* (*Voices of Quebec*, which includes Pellerin's poem), Roch Smith follows Dorsinville's evolutionary conceit. If, twenty years before, Québécois poets had been slaves to nationalist thinking (a supposition which actually questions Dorsinville's universalist finding of that year), now there are poems that do not betray 'specifically Québécois origins' (8). Others represent an 'opening to the world' (13); still others share 'the self-reflexive preoccupation with words' that is 'a feature of the modern esthetic in much of ... Western literature' (7). Contemporary Québec poetry has eliminated fatal, ugly nationalism. In his unpublished paper 'Quebec Culture and Its American Moods,' Pierre Nepveu adopts like reasoning. He claims that the 'white negroes of America' metaphor adopted by some Québécois in the 1960s to '*assert* our marginality, to claim, in a statement that was both poetic and political, that we belonged to the America of the oppressed, of the unrecognized, of the unnoticed' (15), has 'become obsolete' (17). Nepveu speculates that this fate was inevitable, for Québécois 'were ... hoping (without always admitting it) to become sort of French-speaking yankees' (18). He finds that this metaphor implied that 'our poetry would be, in the French language, a form of jazz, the equivalent of the rythm [*sic*] and musical idiom practiced by John Coltrane and Miles Davies [*sic*]' (16). But, he also states that the 'white negro' trope carries 'some sort of anti-intellectualism' (19), an argument which aligns blackness with intellectual turpitude.[20]

What Dorsinville, Smith, and Nepveu agree upon, however, is their weariness of history, of, that is to say, the constant Shakespeareanization of liberal versus nationalist tensions. Their solution is to declare, *à la* Fukuyama, the victory of liberalism, to find solace in this brand of arbitrary, Nixonian sorcery. Yet, Dorsinville's hope that nationalism would die out was wishful thinking. Smith's thesis is also erroneous, for national feeling persists in Pellerin and Lantagne (and subsists in Garneau). Nepveu's sallies against the 'white negro' metaphor are not fully thought through.[21]

Though liberalism prophesies the withering away of history, the texts of Lantagne, Laferrière, Seers, and Garneau show, magnanimously, that there is no escape from its impress. History is, to quote Hardial Bains, 'the kind of irresistible force which does not leave anything alone' (19). Rather, one is left only with the eternal, sadomasochistic ecstasy of contradiction. I suspect this dialectic lives, for, as Mao Zedong maintains, 'the struggle of opposites is ceaseless, it goes on both when the opposites are coexisting and when they are transforming themselves into each other ...' (72). Thus, liberal versus nationalist toing-and-froing will remain unresolved. Québécois writers, like *all* postcolonial writers, will continue to oscillate between nationalism and liberalism, producing, perhaps frequently, disturbingly *louche* racial constructions. To conclude, history ain't history yet ... Witness, in this regard, the philosophical disputes among black intellectuals ...

Notes

1 This essay emerged from two presentations – one given before the annual meeting of the Association for Canadian and Québécois Literature at Université du Québec

à Montréal, on 2 June 1995, and the other at the Windy Pines Colloquium on Race and Ethnicity in Canadian Literature, organized by Professor Christl Verduyn, then of Trent University, near Peterborough, Ontario, on 25 August 1995. I am grateful to all those who contributed suggestions for revisions. I dedicate this essay, though, to Gérard Étienne, the great Haitian-Canadian writer.

2 See 'Embarkation,' above, note 12.

3 For an analysis of Haliburton's use of racist caricature, see my article 'Must We Burn Haliburton?' (1997).

4 In this astonishingly inept book, Fairburn narrates the desires of Montréal grad student Rhea Northway, who, bored with marriage and dreaming of fame, abandons her repulsive husband, Jeff, and absconds to northern Cape Breton to research the life of an obscure, nineteenth-century writer. There Rhea indulges in an exploitative fling with a fellow student – Abelard Hearn, her 'Mi'kmaq lover' (136). She is a callous manipulatrix:

> I toyed with the possibility of using Abelard ... Literary history justified small sins. Abelard might be hurt, I accepted that ... (109)

Abelard remains a cypher. His behaviour is senseless, his speech reproduces gangster clichés ('And if you don't change your mind, there are ways of persuading you' [160]), he possesses, puckishly, 'the disturbing knack of appearing out of nowhere' (85), and he commits suicide when Rhea betrays his love. *Endless Bay* recycles a rather damnable brew of white paranoia and sexual attraction for the dark Other.

5 Craig adds that 'racism is the theme of many non-fiction works as well ...' (139n1). James Walker records that Lionel Groulx, who taught Canadian history at the Université de Montréal, conceived of it as 'a contest between "races": on the one side "a stock that is more princely than any on earth. We are of a divine race, we are the sons of God"; on the other "barbarians," aliences, the forces of cosmopolitanism and "hermaphroditism"' ('Race' 141). In his study *The Race Question in Canada* (1907), the French scholar André Siegfried announces that 'in the first place, and above all, ["what may be called the Canadian problem"] is a racial problem' (14). Siegfried refers primarily to an Anglo-Saxon and Gallic rivalry, but this style of 'racial' thinking influenced European-Canadian popular conceptions of 'colour' and 'culture.'

6 In his book *Masculine Migrations: Reading the Postcolonial Male in 'New Canadian' Narratives* (1998), Daniel Coleman observes that 'the narrator of the French original is regularly referred to as "Vieux" (the colloquial for "man," as in "Cool, man!")' (172n1). Like Coleman, I have decided to use Laferrière's name for his protagonist, rather than Homel's 'anonymous.'

7 Pellerin's title may allude to Québec playwright Dominic Champagne's *pièce, La cité interdite* (1992), which addresses the October Crisis of 1970.

8 It may be objected that the usage of the 'Negro king' metaphor is not racial, but merely an accurate allusion to the manner in which Britain conducted its imperial policy in sub-Saharan Africa. I would maintain, though, that the opprobrium evinced by the phrase is directly related to the innate inferiority implied by 'Negro' and its synonyms. In other words, it is defensible to read 'Negro king' as a palimpsest for 'nigger.'

9 In February 1996, a federal Liberal politician, M. Stéphane Dion, managed to rankle
   the editors of *Afrique Tribune*, a Montréal-based, African-Québécois, biweekly
   journal. Scorning the idea of Québec sovereignty, Dion warned, 'Si une telle idée
   devait mener le monde, elle ferait exploser l'Afrique et l'Asie et mettrait à mal
   l'Europe' (quoted in *Afrique Tribune* [16]). The journal editorialized, 'Curieux tout
   de même que pour une des rares fois que le continent africain surgit dans le debat,
   il ait été associé à une explosion alors que l'Europe serait simplement à *mal* sous la
   même menace' ([16]). In 1996, it was not as easy to posit the backwardness of
   Africans as it was in 1968 ...
10 Lantagne's evocation of this dark, wintry, existential crisis illuminates a similar,
   more ludic, passage in Québécois author Anne Dandurand's novel *The Cracks*
   (1992):
     I'm experiencing the tundra of the soul, much worse than the other, geographic
     tundra.
       Readers, I beg you to console me, grant me the Caribbean of kindness, an
     Africa of goodness, a super-nova of human warmth, relieve me of this black hole
     I'm foundering in, help! (115)
   Dandurand's protagonist also utilizes racial conventions. She sums up her Ugandan 'ex' as 'the most rigid prick of my entire past, the sexual technique of a pile-
   driver and a heart whose size was in keeping with my thin little figure' (22).
11 Incidentally, Lantagne's text debuted amid a flurry of ugly statements by
   Québécois politicos on the status of non–*pur laine* ethnicities in *la belle province*. First
   published in the autumn 1994 edition of *Nuit blanche*, 'Histoire noire' was in
   Québec bookstores when then-deputy premier Bernard Landry charged, on
   29 October 1994, that 'it's not healthy that democracy in Montreal is completely at
   the mercy of the ethnic communities' vote ...' See Julie Barlow (4).
12 Some critics of Laferrière paid fealty to this stereotype. For instance, Étienne recalls
   that, in response to Laferrière's work, 'un grand critique littéraire patenté de *La
   Presse*, dans son compte rendu, avoue le plus candidement du monde que, dans
   certains clubs de la ville [Montréal], "les Blanches courent après le sexe des nègres"
   (citation de mémoire)' (*Question* 148).
13 While bearing in mind that writers' critiques of their critics are suspect, I must
   mention that, in a conversation I had with Laferrière in Antigonish, Nova Scotia,
   on Friday, 8 March 1996, he informed me that Longchamps's comments reflect –
   I paraphrase – the ignorance of someone who has not travelled widely.
14 Laferrière's sentence 'Look, Mamma, says the Young White Girl, look at the Cut
   [*sic*] Negro' (*How* 17) echoes Fanon's voicing of white reactions to the image of a
   black: 'Regarde le nègre! ... Maman, un nègre! ...' (*Peau* 93). His phrase 'Soul on fire'
   (*How* 74) refers, ironically, to Cleaver's *Soul on Ice*.
15 The latter possibility cannot be discounted, for Seers knew Haitian poets. He even
   planned to publish *Les Enfances de Fanny*, in serial form, in a Haitian newspaper.
   See R. Dion-Levesque 1–2.
16 I wonder what the supposedly Negrophilic Seers would have thought of the early
   African-American poet Phillis Wheatley, whose lyric 'An Answer to the *Rebus*, by
   the Author of These Poems' celebrates the 1760 conquest of Québec by British
   forces:

Quebec now vanquish'd must obey,
She too must annual tribute pay
To *Britain* of immortal fame,
And add new glory to her name. (124)

I also wonder whether Seers knew that slavery had flourished on the soil of Nouvelle-France. Perhaps he would have found salutary the play *Angélique* (2000), penned by Afro-Québécoise Lorena Gale, who reimagines the history of Marie-Josèphe Angélique, a black woman slave executed for arson in Montréal in 1734. In her final speech, Angélique foresees a Montréal 'swarming with ebony' (75).

17 According to Joachim, white authorial depictions of blacks' supposed 'grosses lèvres' connote 'animalité, viscosité, mobilité, humidité (rampance), rétractilité, laideur' (60).

18 Father Divine, who was born George Baker, reversed the white male and black female coupling of Donat and Fanny as well as the white Canadian male and African-American female marriage of Seers and his bride by marrying, in 1946, a twenty-one-year-old white Canadian woman. One of his disciples, she was known as 'Sweet Angel' and, later, 'Mother Divine.' ('Divine' 605). Their wedding is one more instance of African-American and Canadian interaction (see my article 'Contesting a Model Blackness,' pp. 27–70, above), plus an inversion of the racial-sexual interests of Seers's Donat.

19 Here Donat's sentiments dovetail with those of Mayotte Capécia, the Martiniquaise author who found *Green Pastures* (or *Verts Pâturages*) a shock: 'Comment imaginer Dieu sous les traits d'un nègre? Ce n'est pas ainsi que je me représente le paradis' (quoted in Fanon, *Peau* 43). Interestingly, both Seers (white) and Capécia (black) desired, ultimately, a whitened blackness.

20 In a *published* version of his paper 'Quebec Culture and Its American Moods,' Nepveu clarifies his disgust with the 'white negro' metaphor. In 'Le Poème québécois de l'Amérique' (1998), Nepveu specifies that his quarrel is with those writers who 'occulter' or 'magnifier notre rapport foncièrement ambigu à la culture blanche américaine' (190). In such hands, the idea of '"nègre blanc" est une création hybride burlesque' which contributes to evacuation, through 'la dérision,' of 'le problème de l'âme et de l'intériorité, en somme la question du sujet' (190). The 'white negro' metaphor supports an at-large discourse of evasion, so that Québécois identity is reduced to a 'certaine clownerie, en imitant les visages de l'Amérique, en multipliant les postures, en rêvant aux stars du ciel hollywoodien' (190). In other words, a phoney whiteness, a phoney *Americanité*. But Nepveu's argument is still problematic. His 'notre' seems reserved for white Québécois, so blackness constitutes an illegitimate status.

21 Yves Préfontaine (b. 1937), a nationalist Québécois poet, hosted a Radio-Canada jazz program, and has held civil service posts with the *péquiste* government of Québec (91–2). He has also written poetry on the African-American jazz artist John Coltrane (1926–67): 'Coltrane-my-friend-pure-negative-of-my-snow-white-photo / misery of ebony as in the Stravinsky concerto / for petty bourgeois figuring their fractions in guilt / on the Stock Market of horror' (53). Arguably playing a 'white negro,' he enacts a romanticization of blackness, but he is not anti-intellectual.

Treason of the Black Intellectuals?

For Burnley A. ('Rocky') Jones (1937–)[1]

Preamble

Because analysis often originates in pain, the feeling of crisis lashing the flesh, this essay – a combination of accusation and confession – commences with three anecdotes illustrative of the agonies that have provoked its being. First, in the summer of 1979, in Halifax, Nova Scotia, during a provincial black youth conference I had helped to plan, a young, male representative of the Toronto-based Black Youth Community Action Project, frustrated by our joyously disorganized, anarchic proceedings, rose up and exclaimed, 'There are too many mulattoes here.' His allegation shocked me, for he was, if not Mulatto himself, then, certainly, of mixed-race descent. But his words also stung me, for, though my parents are of African, Negro heritage, my late mother was part Mi'kmaq; thus, my pigmentation is, to use a phrase she coined, 'tantalizingly tan,' not beautifully black. (For some folks, then, my thought *be* as suspect as my colour.) This incident marked one treason of a black intellectual: the refusal of that young Torontonian to extend solidarity to all self-identifying children of the African Diaspora, not just to those whose gene pools had not been 'adulterated' by *some* admixture. My second proof of arguable treason transpired in Toronto, in July 1997. Following a dramatic reading of my verse-play *Beatrice Chancy* (pub. 1999), which treats slavery in early nineteenth-century Nova Scotia, a Mulatto-looking poet, renowned in Toronto, looked me flat in my ochre eyes and said, damningly, 'It's a mulatto play.' I remain mystified as to the identity of the target of her imprecation, whether it was the mixed-race heroine of the tragedy or me. Perhaps she meant to denounce both author and character. Her act of treason lay in her implication that the mixed-race reality, whatever it is, cannot be reasonably interrogated or critiqued by any truly black-oriented artist or intellectual.[2] My third case of implicit race treason unfolded in Ottawa, Ontario, at Carleton University, where, during the summer of 1997, I was researching the MacOdrum Library's holdings of African-Canadian titles. One afternoon there, I overheard a conversation between a fortyish white woman and a twenty-something black woman, in which the former assured the latter, with unequivocal ease, that white Canadians respect Caribbean-born blacks, but not the Canadian-born variety, for the first are combative, while the second are passive. In this episode of black intellectual treason, neither the black student nor I disputed the white woman's supercilious claims. Here my own silence was the rankest treason.

Yet, these charges of treason are facile, even glib. After all, the archetypal young black man who castigated the corrupting influences of 'mulattoes' was adhering to a Garveyite ideal of blackness: he was voicing a black nationalism that eliminates those who lack the right portion of melanin. Ditto for the middle-class Marxist poet, who was likely the captive of her reading of the Trinidadian intellectual C.L.R. James's reading of the Haitian Revolution, one which casts mixed-race blacks as pernicious aristocrats-in-a-hurry and as devious, Kerenskyite, reactionary defenders of the slaveholding status quo.[3] (Call this the Toussaint-L'Ouverture-position, in honour of the god of those wannabe black nationalists who suspect mixed-race blacks of being congenital traitors.) Lastly, the young black woman who failed to challenge her interlocutor's claim alleging the inferiority of indigenous African Canadians was likely respecting that timeless black *bourgeois* vision which counsels prudent silence in the face of any white aggression. Thus, for her, nothing momentous was at stake in the white woman's 'rap.' In defence of all of these alleged traitors, I stress that their positions are eminently politic: all of them relate to one species of nationalism or another.

This fact reveals a devilish norm: the necessary attractiveness of nationalism for any minority that feels itself downtrodden and disrespected. Canadians understand this truth. Impressive examples of this defensive thinking are vividly visible in Québec, where both the francophone majority and the anglophone minority define themselves as embattled communities. Witness Josée Legault's alarmist 1992 catalogue of these 'threatening' traits of the so-called 'Anglos-Québécois': 'La langue anglaise, la domination économique des anglophones, de même que leur culture politique propre, qu'ils considéraient supérieure à celle des francophones, étaient au coeur même de leur identité collective' (58). In reaction, some English-speaking Quebeckers, especially the impassioned *partitionistes*, feel that they must defend the English language in Québec by, as Charles Taylor disdainfully puts it, 'speaking of fundamental rights to such things as commercial signage in the language of one's choice' (176). But the entirety of English-speaking Canada images itself as a squeezed minority – culturally and economically – *vis-à-vis* the 'Great Satan' to the south, a sentiment accorded baritone expression in George Grant's cataclysmic polemic, *Lament for a Nation: The Defeat of Canadian Nationalism* (1965). Given these compelling, domestic models of combative minorities, it is natural that Black Canadian intellectuals should agree that nationalism is a prerequisite for *la survivance du peuple noir*, as well as for our political empowerment and prosperity.[4]

Thus, a never-quite-vanquished nationalism remains a poignantly unavoidable source for frictions between the articulation of group identities – those

persistent fictions – and individual negotiations of either more-or-less orthodox cultural allegiance or cosmopolitan openness (even assimilationism). For
most minority entities, then, a measure of cultural nationalism – or group
unity – has been a prize element of their steady existences as quote-unquote
communities. The hazard of nationalism – its tendency to decay into fallacious
myths, misty romanticisms, and blood-rite fascisms – persists, then, despite
the globally swaddling and homogenizing embrace of IBM and Coca-Cola.

Black intellectuals possess no immunity against the potentially toxic allure
of nationalism. Rather, we are notorious for being either 'too' doctrinairely
race-conscious, or nation-conscious (consider Malcolm X), or for not being
conscious 'enough' (consider Rev. Dr Martin Luther King, Jr). In fact, no medi-
tative scholarship of African-Canadian culture and literature can refuse to
limn the contours of its nationalism. To begin, African-Canadian intellectuals
and cultural nationalists must interrogate the complication that Canada's only
legitimized nationalisms emanate from the cultural institutions of the federal
state; the cultural, economic, and political state apparatus of Québec; and –
though with less effective power – the cultural, economic, and political organs
of The First Nations. Whether we like it or not, black nationalisms in Canada
must be either domestic-oriented or alien. If rooted in Candian realities, they
may exercise some provenance. If not, their backers will face the same condemnation lodged by African-American thinker Harold Cruse (b. 1916) against
his peers in *The Crisis of the Negro Intellectual* (1967): 'If an army on the battle-
field were conducted the way the Negro movement is in America, its general
staff would be beset with mutinies among its troops, sacked by higher authority for incompetence, investigated for suspected sabotage and quite probably
shot for treason' (415). Can African-Canadian intellectuals avoid the paralyzing confusions that Cruse lists for our African-American counterparts?: 'The
Afro-American nationalists cannot make up their minds whether they want to
emigrate, separate, migrate, or simply sit still in the ghettoes admiring each
other during the quiet lulls between uprisings' (441).

I

This essay takes as its incitement the work of the first twentieth-century intellectual to accuse others of treason: enter the French Jewish philosopher Julien
Benda (1867–1956). Benda assumed political consciousness during the dirty,
anti-Semitic Dreyfus Affair, a scandal that became the target of his first philosophical publication, *Dialogues à Byzance* (1898). From the first, Benda was
animated by a reasoned and beneficent anti-racism – or anti-nationalism. Suitably, then, his polemical monograph *La Trahison des clercs* (1927), translated by
Richard Aldington and published, in Britain, as *The Great Betrayal* (1928) and,
in the United States, as *The Treason of the Intellectuals* (1928), is an unforgiving
indictment of race-identified European intellectuals. Benda flays those who, in
the 1920s, became slavish disciples of nationalism and sycophantic defenders
of its dictatorial proponents, including Benito Mussolini (1883–1945) in Italy

and Maurice Barrès (1862–1923) in France. Benda's arch nemesis is, as he warns us from his first page, 'those passions termed political, owing to which men rise up against other men, the chief of which are racial passions, class passions and national passions' (1). He denounces 'this desire of the "clerk" [or intellectual] to feel himself determined by his race and to remain fixed to his native soil to the extent that it becomes in him a political attitude, a nationalist provocation' (48). Benda is most vexed by those scholars and writers who act as cheerleaders for their race or ethnicity. His example is one 'German master' who feels that 'a true German historian ... should especially tell those facts which conduce to the grandeur of Germany' (55). Benda asks us to disparage those who would claim that 'this universal is a mere phantom, that there exist only particular truths' (77). Examples of such 'truths' are those he enumerates in a quotation from Barrès: 'Lorrain truths, Provençal truths, Brittany truths, the harmony of which in the course of centuries constitutes what is beneficial, respectable, *true in France* ...' (77). For Benda, intellectual nationalists like Barrès, Mussolini, Rudyard Kipling (1865–1936), Gabriel D'Annunzio (1863–1938), and 'the immense majority of German thinkers' (60) resemble Macbeth's Weird Sisters: they stir a cauldron bubbling tyranny and hysteria. These defrocked clerics 'have praised the efforts of men to feel conscious of themselves in their nation and race, to the extent that this distinguishes them from others and opposes them to others, and have made them ashamed of every aspiration to feel conscious of themselves as men in the general sense and in the sense of rising above ethnical aims' (60–1). *Touché*.

Given Benda's ferocious indictment of the violence-prone illogicality – or profanity – of nationalism, it is reasonable that, some thirty-five years after Benda's broadside appeared, Pierre Elliott Trudeau annexed (*nationalized*) Benda for his own French-Canadian – and linguistic 'Mulatto' – intellectual interests. Included in his historic work *Le Fédéralisme et la société canadienne-française* (1967), his scalding – scandalous – essay 'Nouvelle trahison des clercs' (1962), or, in Patricia Claxton's translation, 'New Treason of the Intellectuals' (1968), renews Benda. In this *Cité libre*–originated document, Trudeau trounces Québec politicos and *philosophes* for 'throwing themselves headlong – intellectually and spiritually – into purely escapist pursuits' (168): that is, the 'self-deluding passion' (168), the fantasy of nationalism, the desire to transform Québec into a veritable nation-state, an independent country based on a racialized collective. Instinctively, Trudeau resists – and resents – this tendency, for, with Benda, he declares 'a nationalistic movement is by nature intolerant, discriminatory, and, when all is said and done, totalitarian' (169). Dangerously, it leads to sterile dreaming and passivity. Trudeau tells Québécois that 'Anglo-Canadians have been strong by virtue only of our weakness. This is true not only at Ottawa, but even at Quebec, a veritable charnel-house where half our rights have been wasted by decay and decrepitude and the rest devoured by the maggots of political cynicism and the pestilence of corruption' (167). In one excoriating quip, Trudeau exorcizes the rationale for nationalism: 'It is not the concept of *nation* that is retrograde; it is the idea that the nation must necessarily be sovereign' (151), especially that nation which is based on race – or language – as opposed to 'ethnic complexity' (153). Always petty, nationalism 'can find no room above itself in its scale of values for truth, liberty, and life itself' (157); worse, its intelligentsia becomes 'propagandists for the nation and the propaganda is a lie' (157). At this juncture, Trudeau quotes French historian Ernest Renan's rejoinder to nationalism, that 'man is bound neither to his language nor to his race; he is bound only to himself because he is a free agent, or in other words a moral being' (159). Here Trudeau displays his debt to Benda, who uses the same quotation from Renan in *Treason* (47). Renanesque diction also structures Trudeau's later essay 'The Values of a Just Society' (1990). Here he gives the liberal view of humans as beings 'not coercible by any ancestral tradition, being vassals neither to their race, nor to their religion, nor to their condition of birth, nor to their collective history' (364). Their mutual desire to spoonfeed hemlock to shifty intellectuals is driven by a hatred for all nationalism from Benda and a special loathing for Québec nationalism from Trudeau.[5]

Trudeau and Benda are no lonely white apostles of anti-nationalism. Some black intellectuals also dread the lustre of the nationalist dream. African-American writer, folk singer, and political activist Julius Lester, in *Fallen Pieces of the Broken Sky* (1990), complains that a vision of black exceptionalism 'correlates collective identity with intellectual and emotional perception and comes dangerously close to equating biology with human values' (246). North of the 49th Parallel, African-Canadian writer André Alexis lodges a like charge. 'In the black Canadian community, ... it's pretty common these days to hear some version of the idea that black people, African, as well as members of the "black Diaspora," have both a shared history of oppression at the hands of Europeans, and a shared consciousness based on that oppression; that there is a global African culture to which black people have access' ('Crossroads' 34). Alexis explains that this incorrigibly mystical notion of a global black connectedness 'follows from Afrocentrism, a distant cousin of Negritude, [thus allowing] black Canadians [to feel] they have a special, racial insight into the culture of black Americans or Africans or Haitians that transcends local language and culture' (34). Alexis foregrounds his distrust of the accuracy of such claims, including the associated assertion that 'African, black American and black Canadian cultures are subgroups of Black Culture' (34). One hears, in Alexis, an echo of Trudeau, particularly in his dismissal of the 'magic' and 'mysticism' in which nationalism enjoys dressing itself. But Alexis also traces Trudeau by mauling ethnic nationalism.[6] Controversially, then, in his 1995 article 'Borrowed Blackness,' Alexis submits that 'there's an absence I feel at the heart of much black Canadian art. I miss hearing black Canadians speak *from* Canada' (20).[7] Triumphantly, Alexis annihilates black nationalism based on shared history and replaces it with a Pan-Canadian nationalism emanating from nineteenth-century, quasi-Herderian ideas combining soil and consciousness. Although Trudeau would spurn the *naïf* Herderianism in Alexis's lament, he himself noted that previous politicians had 'deplored the absence of a pan-

Canadian national feeling' ('Values' 376). Trudeau attempted to repair this fault by erecting Canadianism upon the celebration of and adherence to abstractions like justice and freedom and strategic symbols such as the Charter of Rights and Freedoms. Thus, Trudeau enshrines the Charter in 'the grand tradition of the 1789 Declaration of the Rights of Man and the Citizen and the 1791 Bill of Rights of the United States of America' ('Values' 363). A tad egotistically, he casts the Charter as 'a new beginning for the Canadian nation' that strengthens 'the country's unity by basing the sovereignty of the Canadian people on a set of values common to all, and in particular on the notion of equality among all Canadians' ('Values' 363). Alexis would 'save' the Black Canadian intellectual by having him or her embrace icons of Canadiana, while Trudeau would 'save' the French-Canadian intellectual by asking him or her to swoon over federalism and the constitution (*circa* 1982).

These views are vulnerable to critique. Thus, in his *Black Like Who? Writing Black Canada* (1997), Rinaldo Walcott broadsides Alexis for de-emphasizing blackness and luxuriating in Pan-Canadianism. Nevertheless, Walcott himself obeys a shibboleth of liberalism: 'Nation-centred discourse can only be a trap that prohibits black folks from sharing "common feeling," especially when common actions and practices of domination seem to present themselves time and again in different spaces/places/nations' (136). Against big nation chauvinism – in this case, Alexis's version of Canada's – Walcott would like to set a catholic Pan-Africanism. Even so, Walcott weirdly – painfully – ends up backtracking toward Alexis's position, proclaiming that 'thinking carefully about a *Canadian* grammar for black might help us to avoid the painful and disappointing moments of an essentialized blackness' (139, my italics). Yet, he fails to notice that Alexis's 'Borrowed Blackness' article yearns – despite its explicit Euro-Canadamania – to articulate a 'Canadian grammar for black.'

But where Trudeau (*pace* Benda) and Alexis (*pace* Trudeau) decry the treasonous obtuseness and irrationality of bare-faced nationalists, Walcott seems to fear – in open denial of his universalist desires – that black nationalism remains a weak phenomenon. Commenting on writers Dionne Brand and M. NourbeSe Philip, he posits that they 'make us perform, and in our performance acknowledge, that blackness cannot constitute Canadian-ness in contemporary nation-state narratives' (113). Yet, this attitude is one Alexis rejects; he seeks to harmonize blackness and Canadianness. When Walcott declares that 'Black Canadian is a counter-narrative or utterance that calls into question the very conditions of nation-bound identity at the same time as national discourses attempt to render blackness outside the nation' (120), he seems both anti-nationalist, *à la* Trudeau, and nationalist, *à la* Alexis. Walcott insists on 'Black Canadian' as a preordained disruptive identity. Still, his definition omits the troublesome Canadianism to which Alexis subscribes. Certainly, Walcott never addresses Alexis's adamant refusal to look anywhere else for his identity than in his own backyard.[8] Worse, Walcott frustrates his own later summons to 'black Canadian artists and critics ... to articulate a grammar of black that is located within Canada's various regions, both urban and rural'

(148). In contrast, Alexis's position – like Trudeau's – could be described as a kind of Booker T. Washingtonism – that is to say, self-reliance, or finding one's identity, not in past history or a lost culture but in current socio-economic realities. This stance forces Walcott to disparage Alexis for not being Afrocentric enough; that is to say, for committing a kind of treason against blackness. Sensing Alexis's basic conservative liberalism, Walcott drums him out of a Pan-Africanist consensus, declaring that Alexis's 'refusal to seriously engage the conditions of black diasporic identifications is puzzling' (135).[9] Walcott stresses that 'black people in Canada can and do identify with black people in the Caribbean, Brazil, South Africa, America, and the rest of the world; and such identifications are valid. These identifications are the stuff of which the conditions for a nomadology of blackness is [sic] constituted' (135). There is no space here for Alexis's Canadacentrism, given Walcott's assertion that black people in Canada identify with other black people around the globe.[10] One must be wary, however, of drawing any defining lines around *blackness*: the concept is too malleable for containment. *Blackness* is not just skin colour, but a polysemous consciousness.

The temptation to draw such lines is irresistible, though, and Rinaldo Walcott offers a stark example. He opens *Black Like Who?* by declaring that the terms 'African-Canadian and African-American carry with them a particular connotation which is very much related to distancing oneself from the black urban poor and working class' (xiv).[11] To use *African Canadian* is, then, tantamount to playing an Uncle Tom or an Aunt Jemima, that is to say, *un vendu*. For Walcott, the privileged term is *black* – and not even with a majuscule B. Perilously, Walcott's allocation of black as belonging to those who prefer *black* over those who prefer *African Canadian* or *African American* is pure proof that Benda is right that 'our age is indeed the age of the intellectual organization of political hatreds' (21).[12] If, as Benda states, 'neither Pius XIV nor Napoleon apparently thought of using literary criticism in support of the social system in which they believed' (57), Walcott surely does. Count him among those (post-)modern scribes who proudly cry, 'We are not in the least the servants of spiritual things; we are the servants of material things, of a political party, of a nation. Only, instead of serving it with the sword, we serve it with the pen. We are *the spiritual militia of the material*' (Benda 57). Perversely, by stooping to an unexamined, facile black nationalism and Pan-Africanism, to support his reading of certain African-Canadian writers *into* or *out of* an African (or black) aesthetic, which is, treacherously (perhaps just lazily), never defined, Walcott is a capital candidate for the charge of treason.

Before anyone erects a gallows, however, I must recognize that Walcott's zigzags underscore the problem nagging this essay, namely, the question of the relationship between blackness and Canadianness, I mean, whether any fusion (rather than confusion) can be negotiated between the Scylla of one and the Charybdis of the other. It is far too easy to emphasize one identity to the near-exclusion of the other, so that Alexis stumps for 'Canadianness,' while Walcott plumps for 'blackness.' Paradoxically though, this disjuncture is where

African Canadians live out their lives. Our history is nothing less than the problem of the definition of our identity. Hence, at the conclusion of *The Blacks in Canada: A History* (1970), American historian Robin Winks asserts that 'Canada might now [in the 1970s] give cause to a younger generation to answer the fundamental question, were they Negro Canadians or Canadian Negroes?' (483). Or: were they blacks who happened to be Canadian or were they Canadians who happened to be black? The distinction is determinative, with a critic like Walcott staking out the first perspective and a writer like Alexis taking the latter.[13]

Even so, no analysis of African-Canadian literary nationalism will proceed far that is only interested in painstakingly isolating 'black' elements in texts, for the 'Canadian' influence and context must also be scrutinized. Canadian literary scholar Enoch Padolsky posits that 'in order to obtain credibility on issues of Canadian differences (such as ethnicity, multiculturalism, and race relations), [post-colonial theorists] will have to engage the "language and political analyses" developed locally and nationally in Canada over a number of decades, and test their insights in the cauldron of "Canadian history and politics"' ('Olga' 27). Padolsky's neo-nationalist assertion is applicable immediately. Trudeau states that 'Anglo-Canadian nationalism produced, inevitably, French-Canadian nationalism' ('New' 163), and it is equally true that, as African-American scholar Wilson Jeremiah Moses reports, 'black nationalism [may] be seen as a byproduct of the slavery experience' (16) and as 'largely a reaction to attitudes of white supremacy' (25). Because French-Canadian and black nationalisms are defensive and reactive in origin, they also seek, at least from a liberal perspective, to crush diverse bodies of people into a single, homogeneous, monolithic mass, thus suffocating the vitality of difference. Hence, Trudeau, sparring with Québécois nationalism, declares that 'Quebec is not a *nation*. It's a multi*national* entity whose government should govern for the good of every citizen, not just one linguistic group or religious group' (*Essential* 105). In fact, 'a province is not a nation but a mix of diverse people, differentiated by religion, culture, and mother tongue' (*Memoirs* 73). To paraphrase Trudeau, then, a 'race' is not a nation 'but a mix of diverse people.' African-Canadian scholar David Sealy supports this insight, noting 'discussions that centre on African authenticity or African personality elide the diversity of Black diasporic histories, and with it "the diverse ways in which Black diasporic subjects have selectively appropriated, incorporated, European ideologies, culture, and institutions, alongside an 'African' heritage"' ('Canadianizing' 91). Sealy knows that 'the search for an originary univocal "Black" source precludes the plurivocality of "blackness"' ('Canadianizing' 91).

The danger of the provincialist – or racialist – approach to nationalism is the wish of its proponents to fetishize the nation, often with negatively ironic results. Trudeau suggests as much in the analysis of French-Canadian nationalism that he forwards in his 1956 essay 'The Asbestos Strike.' For him, 'to oppose a surrounding world that was English-speaking, Protestant, democratic, materialistic, commercial, and later industrial, [French-Canadian nationalism] created a system of defence which put a premium on all the contrary forces: the French language, Catholicism, authoritarianism, idealism, rural life, and later the return to the land' (43–4). Trudeau theorizes that this nationalism overcompensated for marginality and tipped Québec society into a folkish fascism, a *Kitsch* corporatism, which made a virtue of perceived backwardness. Yet, black nationalism, in its Romantic guise, also indulges in authoritarianism and racial stereotypes. As the nineteenth-century ideology developed, Moses writes, 'an authoritarian collectivist ideal was evolved, a belief that all black people could and should act unanimously under the leadership of one powerful man or group of men, who would guide the race by virtue of superior knowledge or divine authority towards the goal of civilization' (21). Not only was this nationalism dictatorial, it complemented the Rousseauesque fantasy that 'nature had actually been kinder to the sensitive gentle African than to the stolid, frigid European' (Moses 25). While classic Québécois nationalism venerates Louis Hémon's agrarian romance *Maria Chapdelaine* (1914) and the folk figure Ti-Jean, standard black nationalist mythologies allot passion, sensuality, naturalness, and warmth to blacks, thus reinforcing clichés and, most mischievously, promoting anti-intellectualism. See, for instance, Eldridge Cleaver's *Soul on Ice* (1968) and its hype about blacks 'personifying the Body and [being] thereby in closer communion with their biological roots than [white] Americans, [and] provid[ing] the saving link, the bridge between man's biology and man's machines' (186). Such hallucinations can be debilitating, helping to channel creative energies into wasteful escapism. Cruse depicts the risks of racial romanticism nicely:

> The mere fact of self-identification, of the ideology of pro-blackness, the glorification of the black skin, the idealization of everything African, the return to the natural quality of African hairstyles, the rediscovery of black female beauty, or the adoption of African tribal dress – all of these phases and moods signify a return to the root origins of self which can also be made into protective mystiques. If these black mystiques are suffused with contempt for, a hatred and a rejection of, everything white, instead of being channeled into positive trends of action, such mystiques are capable of veering off into dangerous nihilistic fantasies of black supremacy that have little to do with the actualities of the real world. In this world of fantasy there will be a pecking order of blackness – 'I am more black and more pure than thou' – in which case the enemy ceases to be whiteness but other less black breeds. (439–40)

If *péquistes* are hazardous, so are *noiristes*. Cruse charges that 'the readiness of most Black Nationalist trends, to lean heavily on the African past and the African image, is nothing but a convenient cover-up for an inability to come to terms with the complex demands of the American [I will add "or Canadian"] reality' (554). Cultural nationalism is desirable, however, for 'the basic impulse behind all creativity is national or ethnic-group identity ...' (Cruse 221).

The contradiction between disavowal of racialist nationalism and the assertion of cultural 'authenticity' is the matrix of – national – art, including African-Canadian literature.

II

Djanet Sears's Governor General's Literary Award–winning drama, *Harlem Duet* (1997), shouts out a principal black nationalist theme: the corrosive effect of black-white union on black identity and unity. In one speech, Her – an emblem of black womanhood – mourns Him's love for a white woman:

> Once upon a time, there was a man who wanted to find a magic spell in order to become White. After much research and investigation, he came across an ancient ritual from the caverns of knowledge of a psychic. 'The only way to become White,' the psychic said, 'was to enter the Whiteness.' And when he found his ice queen, his alabaster goddess, he fucked her. Her on his dick. He [was] one with her, for a single shivering moment became ... her. Her and her Whiteness. (91)

Worrisomely, Sears replicates Cleaver's sexist racial archetypes, primarily his sketch of the 'Ultrafeminine' (the white woman) and the 'Supermasculine Menial' (the black man), and for his express purpose: to lobby for black, heterosexual solidarity (Cleaver 163–75). But Sears also recalls Frantz Fanon's argument, in *Black Skin, White Masks* (1965) – the translation of his *Peau noire, masques blancs* (1952) – that the black man who loves a white woman also loves white civilization.[14] Pushed just a little, such sentiments slide toward fascism.

Yet, I would not accuse Sears of that, or even of Benda-defined treason, for her work complicates allegations of either liberalism or nationalism. One chief value of her play is that it stages actual cultural debates occurring in Black Canadian communities, thereby dodging both cant and rant. Hear this dialogue between an anachronistic Othello (Shakespeare's Othello, but before he marries Desdemona) and Billie (who is, in this play, Othello's first – and black – wife):

> OTHELLO: When I was growing up ... in a time of Black pride – it was something to say you were Black. Before that, I'd say ... My family would say we're Cuban ... It takes a long time to work through some of those things. I am a member of the human race.
>
> BILLIE: Oh, that's a switch. What happened to all that J.A. Rogers stuff you were pushing. Blacks created the world, Blacks are the progenitors of European civilization, gloriana ... Constantly trying to prove you're as good, no, better than White people. White people are always the line for you, aren't they? The rule ... the margin ... the variable of control. We are Black. Whatever we do is Black.
>
> OTHELLO: I'm so tired of this race shit, Billie. There are alternatives –

BILLIE: Like what? Oh yes, White.

OTHELLO: Oh, don't be so –

BILLIE: Isn't that really what not acting Black, or feeling Black means.

OTHELLO: Liberation has no colour.

BILLIE: But progress is going to White schools ... proving we're as good as Whites ... like some holy grail ... all that we're taught in those White schools. All that is in us. Our success is Whiteness. We religiously seek to have what they have. Access to the White man's world. The White man's job.

OTHELLO: That's economics.

BILLIE: White economics.

OTHELLO: God! Black women always –

BILLIE: No. Don't even go there ...

OTHELLO: I ... You ... Forget it!

BILLIE: *(Quietly at first.)* Yes, you can forget it, can't you. I don't have that ... that luxury. When I go into a store, I always know when I'm being watched. I can feel it. They want to see if I'm gonna slip some of their stuff into my pockets. When someone doesn't serve me, I think it's because I'm Black. When a clerk won't put the change into my held-out hand, I think it's because I'm Black. When I hear about a crime, any crime, I pray to God the person who they think did it isn't Black. I'm even suspicious of the word Black. Who called us Black anyway? It's not a country, it's not a racial category, it's not even the colour of my skin. And don't give me this content of one's character B.S. I'm sorry ... I am sorry ... I had a dream. A dream that one day a Black man and a Black woman might find ... [...] Let's ... Can we just get this over with? (55–6)

Sears's dialogue shifts between liberal and nationalist perspectives, with Othello taking the universalist and individualist liberal positions and Billie adopting black pride and separatist rhetoric. (Billie lampoons, suavely, the integrationist stance of King's famous 'I Have a Dream' speech of 28 August 1963.) Both characters *are* intellectually treasonous: Othello, because he wants to abandon 'blackness'; Billie, because she assumes an essentialist black identity. But what saves this play from falling into the trap of treason is its scrupulous fidelity to a 'black-bottom' empirical realism. The dialogue between Billie and Othello echoes conversation that can be (over)heard in *any* intra-black community debate about race and belonging in Canada. Sears narrates the tussle between, in African-American philosopher Cornel West's apt phrasing, the philosophical 'alternatives of meretricious pseudo-cosmopolitanism and tendentious, cathartic provincialism' ('Dilemma' 135). Truly, Sears has turned her gaze 'as firmly and in a sense disinterestedly as possible on concrete human behaviour,' to lift a phrase from Canadian literary scholar John Fraser (*Violence* 116). Read as 'protest' art, *Harlem Duet* succeeds in performing the task that Fraser sets such work: that it 'see both the ridiculous or evil aspects of the [ideas] under attack and their strengths – that is, not to reduce them, for the sake of propaganda or of one's peace of mind, to the merely ludicrous or grotesque' (*Violence* 139). Sears dramatizes two persistent black political positions, without ridiculing either of them, though she seems to endorse Billie's race pride over Othello's integrationist (or assimilationist) dream. Although Sears writes specifically as a black playwright for a black audience,[15] her cultural nationalism never impedes her ability to present the liberal position, with an emphasis – really – on sympathy. Like Cruse, she knows that 'when the Negro creative artist turns his back on the imperatives of the ethnic culture *he is also turning his back on ethnic politics, ethnic economics, in fact, on practically the entire range of problems inherent in the inner-group reality of Negro existence*' (296, his italics). Yet, Sears's cultural nationalism is balanced; she allows a liberal viewpoint its full weight.[16] Still, the question of the position of black identity (or consciousness) *vis-à-vis* Canadian or American identity is never raised, though the play is set in Harlem and Billie is Canadian by birth. *Harlem Duet* might appear to confirm Alexis's worries about the suspected Americanization of African Canadians, a fear that participates in white English-Canadian nationalism.

III

Sears's writing proves that no nastily anti-nationalist position can find credence among African-Canadian intellectuals. We contest the anti-nationalism of Benda and Trudeau. Our thought is more in concert with that of the late political philosopher George Grant – the most eloquent English-Canadian critic of Trudeau's anti-nationalism. In *Lament for a Nation* (1965), Grant warns that liberalism, if taken to its logical conclusion, would result in the disappearance of Canada as an independent state: 'The belief in Canada's continued existence has always appealed against universalism' (85). Ignoring such criticisms, Trudeau maintains that nationalisms must wither in the truly liberal society. In 'New Treason of the Intellectuals,' he prophesizes:

> In Canada, ... there is, or will be, a Canadian nation in so far as the ethnic communities succeed in exorcising their own respective nationalisms. If, then, a Canadian nationalism does take form, it will have to be exorcised in its turn, and the Canadian nation will be asked to yield a part of its sovereignty to a higher authority, just as is asked today of the French-Canadian and English-Canadian nations. (155 fn)

This view boasts few adherents among African-Canadian intellectuals, and it chafes against Grant's Tory-starched nationalism. In a 1970 passage, Grant dubs Trudeau 'our "show-biz" technocrat' (Introduction viii). In a 1974 letter, Grant labels him 'a kind of Canadian Kennedy – a shallow politician who makes people think this vulgar society has a slick patina to it' ('Pierre' 103). Grant's lacerating comments arise from his sense that Trudeau's support for 'universalism in a Canadian setting means integration into a smooth functioning continental system' ('Pierre' 104). Principally, Trudeau was, for Grant, a glitzy Trojan horse, importing corrosive Americanizations into Canadian political administration and the style of public life.[17]

Ironically, Grant, like Trudeau, honours Benda's Platonism, though Grant
steers Platonism to a defence of nationalism.[18] Vitally, Benda and Grant are
classical humanists. Benda deplores 'political passions rendered universal, coherent, homogeneous, permanent, preponderant' (7); elsewhere, he claims that
'political passions show a degree of universality, of coherence, of homoge-
neousness, of precision, of continuity, of preponderance ...' (22). His statements reveal a Platonist abhorrence of passion over reason, but also an abhorrence of the *universality* of passions. Grant, likewise, hates the thrust toward
universalism, remonstrating that 'the universal and homogeneous state is the
pinnacle of political striving. "Universal" implies a world-wide state, which
would eliminate the curse of war among nations; "homogeneous" means that
all men would be equal, and war among classes would be eliminated' (*Lament*
53). For Grant, 'the masses and the philosophers [or *clerks*] have both agreed
that this universal and egalitarian state is the goal of historical striving' (*Lament* 53). For him, the treason of the intellectuals is their abandonment of
cultural particularities for the dream of a unified, global, liberal-capitalist state.
In union with 'classical philosophers,' Grant suspects that 'the universal state
will be a tyranny' (*Lament* 85–6). Hence, he defends Canadian nationalism as
one small obstacle to the erection of such a global state. For Benda, though, the
impulse to create the universal state represents, not the destruction of nationalism, but rather its transmutation into what he calls 'this imperialism of the
species' (162). When Grant critiques the idea of 'the world-wide and uniform
society' (*Lament* 54), when he writes, disparagingly, that 'man will conquer
man and perfect himself' (*Lament* 54), thus rejecting God, he chases Benda,
who has already raised the alarm. At the conclusion of *Treason*, Benda writes
(in language that licenses Grant's), 'It is Man, and not the nation or the class,
whom Nietzsche, Sorel, Bergson extol in his genius for making himself master
of the world' (162). Benda warns that 'the abolition of the national spirit with
its appetites and its arrogance' and its transformation into universalism would
mean the reconstitution of nationalism in 'its supreme form, the nation being
called Man and the enemy God' (163). Benda fears that this state would be a
de-spiritualized Hell:

> Thereafter, humanity would be unified in one immense army, one immense fac-
> tory, would be aware only of heroisms, disciplines, inventions, would denounce
> all free and disinterested activity, would long cease to situate the good outside the
> real world, would have no God but itself and its desires, and would achieve great
> things; by which I mean that it would attain to a really grandiose control over the
> matter surrounding it, to a really joyous consciousness of its power and its gran-
> deur. And History will smile to think that this is the species for which Socrates
> and Jesus Christ died. (163)

The problem for Benda is not nationalism *per se*, but rather the international-
ization of materialism. Here Grant again makes common cause with Benda.
Although he feels that nationalism serves to impede impieties, that is to say,
the globalization of greed, pride, lust, and the scientific dismissal of the eternal

and the spiritual, Grant, like Benda, dreads the outcome of this secular struggle between universal materialism and 'true' spirituality. Appropriately, then, Grant (*Lament* 89) cites the identical quotation from the German philosopher Friedrich Hegel (1770–1831) – 'Die Weltgeschichte ist das Weltgericht' (World history is world judgment) – as does Benda (93). Grant voices, like his philosophical forebear, the pessimistic expectation that international disputes will continue to degenerate into blood-curdling wars. The conclusion of *Lament for a Nation* echoes Benda too closely for coincidence. Grant remarks, 'Those who loved the older traditions of Canada may be allowed to lament what has been lost' (96). He goes on to state that 'it is also possible to live in the ancient faith, which asserts that changes in the world, even if they be recognized more as a loss than a gain, take place within an eternal order that is not affected by their taking place' (97). Both comments reprise the wisdom of Benda. That philosopher, quoting Italian historian Francesco Guicciardini (1483–1540), allows that 'a citizen who witnesses the end of his country cannot feel so distressed at her misfortune with so much reason as he would lament his own ruin' (44). Benda also sees that 'above their nations there exists a development of a superior kind, by which they will be swept away like all other things' (44). He recognizes, like Grant, that 'the ancients, so completely the adorers of their States, nevertheless placed them beneath Fate' (44). Arguably, Grant is a better acolyte of Benda than Trudeau, for he shares with Benda a crucially religious impulse; that is to say, an enmity for materialism. Trudeau, while agreeing with Benda's anti-nationalism, essays to combat nationalism by affirming a secular or material or pragmatic universality. But Benda suspects that this program will only internationalize nationalism, thus worsening it, and Grant feels similarly. Thus, Grant attacks what he terms 'the American Empire' (*Lament* 5) as 'the heart of modernity' (*Lament* 54), while Benda rejects any role for the intellectual as a complicit ally of imperialism: 'It remains to determine whether the function of "clerks" is to secure empires' (39). In the end, Benda provides no *praxis* for eliminating nationalism. He asks, merely, that intellectuals strive for a spiritual universalism, or humanitarianism, 'to set up a corporation whose sole cult is that of justice and of truth' (41), avoiding any crippling allegiance to their states or to the things of this world. Grant believes, contrastingly, that a dedication to the local, the particular, the nation, is one way of accessing the good. Still, their exalting of the ancients over the modern philosophers (that is to say, their faith in a supreme and eternal order) unites Benda and Grant in opposing the functionalism that a Trudeau must endorse. Thus, Trudeau read Benda for his attack on nationalism, while ignoring his anti-universalism; Grant read Benda with the reverse emphasis, thus permitting a defence of nationalism.

IV

Not surprisingly then, nationalism – especially of the cultural variety – remains viable, a fact Black Canadian intellectuals flesh out. Hence, Trinidadian-Canadian writer M. NourbeSe Philip has acknowledged in print her appreciation of Grant's *Lament for a Nation*.[19] Moreover, her attack on the 1993 production of the American musical *Showboat* in North York, Ontario, reflected her espousal of a Grantian opposition to the 'wholesale importation of American culture to launch, with the assistance of public funds, the opening of a multi-million-dollar civic center. In Toronto!' ('Blackness' 2). In addition, Philip grounds her observations of African-Canadian culture in an obvious black nationalism or Pan-Africanism (with a touch of Garvey in the margins). Hence, she does not hesitate – treasonously – to advance totalizing visions of black life. In her essay collection *Frontiers* (1992), Philip admonishes her black readers: '... to forget that what we now *appear* to share – education, religion, dress, legal institutions – are really tombstones erected on the graves of African customs, culture and languages, is simply to collude in our own erasure, our own obliteration' (19). Benda would be mortified by Philip's open strengthening of black 'national passions' by accenting 'the determination of the peoples to be conscious of *their past* ..., and to vibrate with "centuries-old" aspirations, with attachments to "historical" rights' (Benda 16). Philip stirs up, in short, a dangerous 'Romantic patriotism' (Benda 16). Like Philip, Trinidadian-Canadian poet and novelist Dionne Brand articulates an up-front nationalism, declaring,

> All Black people here have a memory, whether they know it or not, whether they like it or not, whether they remember it or not, and in that memory are such words as land, sea, whip, work, rape, coffle, sing, sweat, release, days ... without ... this ... pain ... coming ... We know ... have a sense ... hold a look in our eyes ... about it ... have to fight every day for our humanity ... redeem it every day. (*Bread* 22)

Again, Brand deviates from Benda; she feels herself – resolutely – 'determined by [her] race' and remains 'fixed to [her] native soil to the extent that it becomes in [her] a political attitude, a nationalist provocation' (Benda 48). Brand even speaks of seeking 'a Black woman country' (*Bread* 130). Benda – *and* Trudeau – would have a fit.

I admit it *is* troubling to read in Philip, for instance, blunt annunciations of the existence in black dance of 'African traditions of movement,' or the presence of 'the African aesthetic in painting, sculpture, or the plastic arts' (*Frontiers* 112), *but only because their Africanness is never defined.* There is not enough scrutiny articulated to lift such declarations from the domain of sentimentality and romanticism into the realm of objective knowledge. Likewise, when Brand concludes that Toronto's Bathurst Street subway station, in the 1970s, represented 'the nexus from which we all radiated, the portals through which we all passed, passing from Negroes into Blacks, from passive into revolutionary' (*Bread* 70), she is blithe, but also inexact. Her 'we' enacts a warm gesture of inclusion for immigrant blacks, but excludes simultaneously the history of indigenous African Canadians. Worse, her charge that there is 'no forgiveness from racial history' (*Bread* 71) appeals to an undefined race feeling, the inkling that this passion should be the basis for revolutionary action.[20] A similar primicry arises with Barbadian-Canadian writer Cecil Foster, who also lays claim to privileged access into the souls of black folk. Recalling the conclusion of his interview with an African-Canadian activist lawyer, he reports that 'suddenly, it appears that I have penetrated the darkness. She lets more of her real self show through. In the end, this is what it really means to be black' (*Place* 97). Here Foster relies upon the hoary stereotype of emotional spontaneity to authenticate his interviewee as black.[21] Too many African-Canadian intellectuals peddle received ideas of blackness, despite the calls for universalism (and Pan-Canadianism) that emanate from other quarters of the political and cultural 'strivers.'

This peddling *is* treason, especially if we apply the severe standards, the exacting Platonist measure of Benda, to Philip, Brand, Foster, and several other African-Canadian writers, who exhort blacks 'to feel conscious of themselves in what makes them distinct from others' (Benda 64). Hauled before the court of Trudeau, they would also face condemnation, for they have become 'propagandists for the [black] nation and the propaganda is a lie' ('New' 157). But they would also face indictment from Alexis, who stresses, in 'Crossroads,' that 'the insistence on racial connection to Black Culture makes race something of an aesthetic category, fetishizing "blackness" as it manifests itself in song, movement, and poetry' (33). Anxiously, Alexis observes that 'it doesn't take much imagination to see where that road leads' (34–5); yes, to a series of damaging queries:

Who's more black? Who speaks deepest for the diaspora? For Africa? (35)

In 'Borrowed Blackness,' Alexis claims that 'I have the distinct impression that black Torontonians identify more passionately with America, not simply with black American culture but with black intellectual assumptions as well' (18). In his critique of the perceived treason of African-Canadian intellectuals, Alexis (*pace* Benda) questions the efficacy of their racial nationalism and the strength of their Canadian patriotism (*pace* Trudeau), but he also sides with Grant in demanding a – nationalist – attentiveness to Canadian space. Alexis summons African-Canadian artists to 'sing, dance or write Canada for ourselves, to define our own terrain and situation' ('Borrowed' 17) and to produce 'writing that is conscious of Canada, writing that speaks not just about situation, or about the earth, but rather *from* the earth' ('Borrowed' 20). So, one must parry parochial Pan-Africanisms or reductive black nationalisms with a pristine, vigorous, Black Canadian or African-Canadian nationalism, if one likes. If Black Canadian intellectuals would only imbibe white-authored, canonical, Anglo-Canadian texts such as Margaret Laurence's *The Stone Angel* (1964), they may also discover, like Alexis, that one half of their souls is 'shared by Margaret Laurence' ('Borrowed' 20).

It is tempting to sneer at Alexis's Pan-Canadian sensibility, his cultural Canadian nationalism, and Foster is quick to do so, charging that 'many [Caribbean-Canadian youths] do not consider their writings to be part of a Canadian tradition that reveres a Margaret Atwood, Robertson Davies, or Alice Munro' (*Place* 117). Instead, says Foster, 'they lay claim to a proud tradition that produced international names like Derek Walcott and Bob Marley, some of the voices of the extended Caribbean society – a community that nurtures them in Canada' (*Place* 117). Like Alexis, though, Foster is partly right, but mainly wrong, for when African-Canadian artists and writers have discussed their influences, they reveal a sustained interaction with European-Canadian culture. Consider African-Canadian film director Clement Virgo. His *Rude* (1995) sounds, at times, the conscious meditation on mass media pioneered by Atom Egoyan. Even Foster is not committed to the idea of a hermetic black tradition, for he feels that 'when we seek isolation, we do little to improve our lot' (*Place* 309). African-Canadian culture is – as its hyphen suggests – already a synthesis: the dreamers of reaction, who seek either a pure, pristine, unhyphenated Canadianism or a spic-and-span Africanism, are too late. White racists may scream their adoration of the 'Great White North,' while 'African' racialists scheme to repatriate all black people to (Sub-Saharan) Africa. But it is now impossible to understand Canadian blackness or black Canadianness without accounting for both African-Canadian cultural production and history and the ways in which blackness and Canadianness have already blended (and are blending). It is the duty of African-Canadian intellectuals to undertake this work. Thus, they will effect a coalition between Malcolm X, say, and Trudeau, by subjecting racial romanticism to an adoringly pitiless scrutiny.

For this reason, one must challenge Rinaldo Walcott's unthoughtful proviso that Black Canadian intellectuals 'can begin to refuse the seductions of "firstness" and engage in critique, dialogue and debate, which are always much more sustaining than celebrations of originality' (xiv). This utterance pauperizes the value of research, specifically of historical inquiry. Yet, those who do not interrogate history are fated to imbibe half-truths. One must treat the objective realities of the African settlement of Canada, *via* slavery, resistance to slavery, pioneering, homesteading, and the twentieth-century experiences of labour and professional immigration, as well as fluxes of refugees escaping civil wars, invasions, famines, and other species of disaster. To refuse to inquire into the history of the formation of the African-Canadian people is to opt for bewilderment, confusion, a veritable intellectual treason once again.

I lay this charge, however, against Walcott's *Black Like Who?* It disdains any grappling with the broad philosophies, socio-political and economic forces, and cultural *données* that touch all Canadians, no matter their race, gender, class, political orientations, religious beliefs, ethnicity, sexual orientations, or language. This decisive ignorance leads Walcott into varieties of nationalist error. In examining Brand's first novel, *In Another Place, Not Here* (1996), Walcott opines that one of the two protagonists, Elizete, 'struggles to survive in the context of a hostile land' (46), a theme that could have been lifted straight from

Atwood's *Survival: A Thematic Guide to Canadian Literature* (1972). Yet, only a few paragraphs later, Walcott insists that Brand's novel moves 'beyond the discourse and literary tropes of "roughing it in the bush" and "survival" in a barren landscape' (47). Does Walcott think that Atwood's thesis applies to Brand or not? The question is pertinent, for, in his reading of Stephen Williams's film *Soul Survivor* (1995), Walcott states that the sole interest of the film's protagonist, Tyrone, 'is to survive' (130). Is Atwood applicable here as well?

Then there is the problem of African-Canadian conservatism to address, a condition of thought that Walcott never deigns to consider, though he alleges that Virgo's *Rude* is 'locked within a socio-religious narrative steeped in the politics of conversion, [but failing] to register [a] politics of transfiguration' (68–9). Walcott does not ask why Virgo should have opted for a 'conservative' trajectory. Nor does he question the employment of a 'conservative voice-over' in Williams's *Soul Survivor* (132). Yet, conservatism has always influenced African-Canadian life.[22] Winks chronicles instance after instance of these tendencies. Before the rebellion of 1837–38, 'William Lyon Mackenzie, its Upper Canadian leader, noted that Negro settlers were "opposed to every species of reform in the civil institutions of the colony," that they were "extravagantly loyal," and that they were prepared to "uphold all the abuses of government and support those who profit by them"' (149). In the British Columbia election of 1860, African Canadians 'voted unanimously for [conservative, Hudson Bay Company] men rather than for reformers' (282). Later that century, Alfred Shadd twice ran unsuccessfully for office as a member of the Conservative party (302). The *Provincial Freeman*, an Upper Canada, black, abolitionist newspaper, supported the Conservative party after 1856, 'likening the reform party of George Brown ... to the Locofocos in the U.S.: "*Clear Grit*, Reform and Radical ... are words that belong to the vocabulary of Yankeedom"' (396). An early African-Canadian newspaper, the *True Royalist*, 'while intended for Negroes,' says Winks, 'contained little news that was racial, rather discussing dissension within the church and preaching political conservatism and obedience to the queen' (397). In the 1920s, the Montreal Negro Conservative League was founded, reports Winks, 'to support the Tory party' (458). In addition, the first African Canadian elected to the House of Commons (in 1968), Lincoln Alexander, belonged to the Progressive Conservative party. Nor are African-Canadian intellectuals of Caribbean heritage immune to Toryism. Barbadian-Canadian novelist Austin C. Clarke stood as a Progressive Conservative party candidate in the 1977 Ontario provincial election. Cruse notes that 'West Indians are essentially conservatives fashioned in the British mold' (119).[23] Too, the communitarian tendencies in African-Canadian culture reflect a conservative inclination. Tending to this facet of black nationalism, Moses reveals that 'the old patterns of [racial] mythology have not died easily because they have continued to serve as an inspiration for the black masses among whom the traditional black nationalist longings are still strong' (29). Given the persistent conservative leanings – or nationalist longings – among black intellectuals, it is astonishing that Walcott never engages the ideology.[24]

Walcott's attempt to refute Alexis's 'Borrowed Blackness' polemic is hampered by his facile resort to nationalist assertion. He claims that Alexis's short stories are 'representative of a black Canadianness constituted from various fragments of the nation, usually seen as outside blackness' (137), thus conscripting Alexis into a nebulous nationalism. But Walcott has no evidence to support the ambition – even though wisps of blackness score the generally non-black-specific fictions featured in Alexis's *Despair, and Other Stories of Ottawa* (1994). A remarkable instance of racialization occurs in 'The Night Piece.' The story's terminal sentence, 'He went looking for the Soucouyant' (43), could easily be read as 'He went looking for Trinidad.' I say this because the story – which treats a blood-sucking night *piece* (or, in slang, *piece of ass*), or Soucouyant (a Trinidadian 'vampire') – represents the Canadianization of a Trinidadian legend. Importantly, 'The Night Piece' rehearses the identity tensions of the partially assimilated – or Canadianized – immigrant, in this case, the fifteen-year-old protagonist, Michael. At an Ottawa wedding party consisting of family and friends of family – some of them presumably Trinidadian – Michael feels out of place, remarking, 'Of course they remembered you, but why should you remember them?' (14). Like the story's other major character, Winston Grant, Michael suffers from a kind of racial forgetfulness. As for Winston, 'his skin was a peculiar colour: brown beneath a translucent layer of grey, the colour of long illness or long convalescence' (15): he has the pallor of a winter-faded, brown-skinned man. Winston's very being is suggestive of withered roots. His hands shake 'like twigs' (17) and he is emaciated, 'like a flattened straw' (16). Michael is similarly estranged from his Trinidadian past. When the renowned Trinidadian Calypsonian Sparrow (Francisco Slinger [1933–]) sings, 'One a de women started to beg. He bite she on she chest. He bite she on she leg...' (16), the lyrics refer to a male version of the vampiric fiend that is attacking Winston, but Michael is unable to understand the song's warning: he lives outside of its culture. Winston is also alienated, so that he is driven to ask, 'Who could expect to find a Soucouyant here, in this place, so far from where they usually apportioned death?' (29). Trinidad haunts these *emigrés* who have dared to try to forget their homeland. Winston declares, 'Really, it was just like his parents and their friends to bring a death so bizarre with them from Trinidad' (30). Tellingly, Winston's 'condition had no name, unless you count *mal de pays*' (33), a malaise associated with exile (33). Notably, Michael falls under the Soucouyant's spell after the racial integrity of his family unit has been broken by his father's decision to take up 'with another woman, a white woman with a French accent' (41). In 'The Third Terrace,' a character sharing the same first name and birthdate as the author tells of being a painter whose 'canvasses [*sic*] ended up black from the false lines I drew on them ...' (108), and he exhibits 'two of my "blackened" della Francescas in a school gymnasium' (108). It is amiable to read into these two statements ironic comments on both the tension-fraught black artistic relationship to European culture and on the Black Aesthetic demand that black artists produce 'black' art. If I am right here, it is doubtful that any European-Canadian writer would have bothered to so subtly raise these two concerns. Yet, there are other potential racial codes in the story. An erotic film company is called, leadingly, 'White Films Production Co.' (109), and in one of the films in which the artist participates, namely, 'The Master's Larder' (a possible allusion to slavery), he plays a 'manservant' who is 'costumed in black' (111). Even so, race is never a paramount theme in the tale. Such is Alexis's style. In another short story, 'My Anabasis,' a section title, 'Flight,' alludes perhaps to the title of the second section of Richard Wright's classic African-American novel, *Native Son* (1940). But there is a stronger relationship between that novel and Alexis's 'Metaphysics of Morals,' whose protagonist, Michael, suffers a 'moral quandary' (71) that replicates – and deflates – that of Wright's Bigger Thomas. Having retrieved a glove dropped accidentally on a sidewalk by a sensual, pink-cheeked woman, Michael fails to return it to her because he fears approaching her. His fright, his flight from the woman, and his banal return home mirror, in fine, suggestive satire, the plot movement of Richard Wright's acclaimed novel. In *Native Son*, Bigger smothers a white woman accidentally because he fears that his late-night presence in her bedroom will be misinterpreted by his employers (the woman's parents) as a rape attempt. Alexis's story differs drastically from Wright's novel, but he is astute enough a writer to allow for a teasing correspondence between the two works. Although it is possible to 'out' Alexis as a black writer, the surface racelessness of his fiction betrays him as a ripe candidate for a charge of race treason.[25] Nevertheless, such charges must be complicated by the recognition that 'blackness' and 'Canadianness' are fluid, unstable identities. Thus, one is justified in asking critics of African-Canadian literature to undertake scrupulous research, close readings, and detailed investigation before seconding any of these writers, willy nilly, to either nationalist or assimilationist agendas.

This point returns us to the question of the position of the African-Canadian intellectual. First, the tension between the liberal and nationalist options will not vanish anytime soon, for, as Moses asserts, 'it is probably as true today as it was in the 1850s that all black people harbor some assimilationist daydreams along with black nationalist fantasies' (44). Nevertheless, African-Canadian intellectuals must reject the false 'binary of Black or Canadian' ('Canadianizing' 101), as Sealy has it, and thus the false consciousness that Foster advances, as crystallized in his query 'Can a black person ever fully become a Canadian citizen?' (*Place* 210). Foster's mistake here is that the sentence can too easily be reversed, thus creating second-class black people within the putative black community. To the question posed by Philip, 'how many identities can dance on a maple leaf' (*Frontiers* 17), the only appropriate answer is, as many as possible under the circumstances. To Walcott's thesis that *Black Canadian* should be read 'as name/metaphor for the rhythms of black migration' (126), we must ask, are African Canadians always and only marginals and transients?[26] We cannot accept an unthinking nationalism, either Canadian or black, that would render us 'artistes-tyrannoi' (Sherry 58). Nor can we accept the notion that, as Jamaican-American scholar Orlando Patterson pleads,

'to survive [blacks] must abandon any search for a past, must indeed recognize that they lack any claims to a distinctive cultural heritage, and that the
path ahead lies not in myth making and in historical reconstruction, which are
always doomed to failure, but in accepting the epic challenge of their reality'
(quoted in Sealy 'Canadianizing' 90). This prescription for black progress is a
liberal lie that echoes Rinaldo Walcott's own shouting down of history. I would
not prescribe, though, any reckless nationalization of history, for, as Carl Berger
notes, 'a tradition of racism and a falsified but glorious past ... have always
been the invariable by-products of nationalism' (quoted in Wilson 665). Preferable here is West's notion that 'the future of the Black intellectual lies neither
in a deferential disposition toward the Western parent nor a nostalgic search
for the African one. Rather, it resides in ... insurgent transformation of this
hybrid lineage ...' ('Dilemma' 146). Cruse invites a synthesis, positing that
'American Negro history is basically a history of the conflict between integrationist and nationalist forces in politics, economics, and culture, no matter
what leaders are involved and what slogans are used' (564). Perhaps Cruse is
right that 'American Negro nationalism can never create its own values, find
its revolutionary significance, define its political and economic goals, until
Negro intellectuals take up the cudgels against the cultural imperialism practiced in all of its manifold ramifications on the Negro within American culture' (189). If so, African-Canadian intellectuals must pay heed to apply our
own cultural nationalism responsibly. African-Canadian political scientist V.
Seymour Wilson submits that 'polyethnicity is the nation-state form of the
future, and in Canada we are destined to be more, not less, ethnically and
racially diverse than we now are' (649). Thus, if we mean to have any role in
constructing and interpreting African-Canadian culture, African-Canadian intellectuals will have to become ever more cosmopolitan.

To sum up, neither the liberalism of Benda, Trudeau, and Alexis, nor a
reflex black nationalism – à la Walcott – or Canadian nationalism – à la Grant
and, in one context, Alexis – answer to the complexities of African-Canadian
culture. Rather, we must perform historiographic and sociological analyses of
specific national and regional cultures. To refuse the validity of this approach
is to claim that cultural manifestations such as gospel, *vaudou*, and reggae are
merely spontaneous, *ex nihilo* creations, just gestures of that brand of un-
planned creativity that 'objective' academics too often ascribe to African-heritage cultures, thus reducing our rebellions to riots. A persuasive cultural nationalist scholarship can only rise from a basis of enlightened, X-ray-exact,
critical self-scrutiny.

The point is not that we have committed occasional intellectual treasons, no,
we have not been treasonous enough. It is our God-deemed task to determine
the imperatives of African-Canadian culture (or cultures) and to build economic, political, and cultural institutions that will allow us a measure of au-
tonomy, pride, and independence in our dealings with all other interest groups
in the society. If this work means that we violate conventional notions of the
place of so-called visible minorities in Canadian society, well, *tant pis*. As

Cruse points out, it is our fundamental calling to 'evolve creative and artistic policies that will govern cultural programs, organizations and self-sustained and -administered research institutions' (518), or risk seeing and having our identities continually being defined by others. Either African Canadians are an assembly of miniature nations, or we are nowhere. We must understand that we are creating, for instance, an African-Canadian literature, one that *is* a branch of Canadian literature, but which also maintains definable, Africanist oral/linguistic strategies, as well as a special relationship to song, rhythm, and a specific history. 'If there is no such a thing as a Negro writer or a body of Negro Literature, then, it follows, there is or can be no such thing as a Negro psychology or a distinctly Negro sociology, or a Negro political theory or a particular kind of Negro cultural theory that has relevance to [Canadian] society as regards the Negro situation in [Canada]' (Cruse 247). Because African-Canadian culture exists, its black intellectuals owe it the beguiling gifts of critique and assessment.[27]

None of the above evacuates Benda's thought entirely. His work remains, as Edward Saïd finds, the pristine type of 'a being set apart, someone able to speak the truth to power, a crusty, eloquent, fantastically courageous and angry individual for whom no worldly power is too big and imposing to be criticized and pointedly taken to task' (8). Says Vincent Sherry, 'Benda stands forth as a prophet whose warnings have been confirmed by history' (55). According to Saïd, the work of Benda-like intellectuals like Fanon proves that 'loyalty to the group's fight for survival cannot draw in the intellectual so far as to narcotize the critical sense, or reduce its imperatives, which are always to go beyond survival to questions of political liberation, to critiques of the leadership, to presenting alternatives that are too often marginalized or pushed aside as irrelevant to the main battle at hand' (41). But the work of criticism need not separate the intellectual from his or her community: 'Intellectual work only estranges us from Black communities when we do not relate or share in myriad ways our concerns' (hooks 'Black' 162). One aspect of this sharing must be the recognition that we cannot analyse African-Canadian culture until we apply such scrutiny to ourselves, without flinching, without mercy. We must practise a treason that betrays itself constantly. I turn from Rinaldo Walcott to Derek Walcott: 'To betray philosophy is the gentle treason / of poets ...' ('XII' 22).

Notes

1 This paper originated in three public lectures presented, in chronological order, as (1) the Munroe Beattie Lecture at Carleton University, in Ottawa, Ontario, on 6 February 1998; (2) a Plenary Session co-lecture for the annual meeting of the Association for Canadian and Québécois Literature at the University of Ottawa, on 30 May 1998; and (3) the Third Annual Seagram Lecture at McGill University, in Montréal, Québec, on 19 November 1998. I am thankful for the sharp audience

questions that have sharpened its views. I dedicate this essay to Burnley 'Rocky' Jones, an Africadian community leader and a proud black intellectual who has never shrunk from debate or controversy.

2 Her strange charge reminds me of a situation that American critic Aldon Lynn Nielsen jeers as 'the ludicrous spectacle of one comfortable bourgeois writer denouncing other comfortable bourgeois writers for being comfortably bourgeois' (99).

3 In his history *The Black Jacobins: Toussaint L'Ouverture and the San Domingo Revolution* (1938), James depicts Mulattoes as white-lusting wanna-bes. Worse, they are reactionary, anti-black racists:

> Even while in words and, by their success in life, in many of their actions, Mulattoes demonstrated the falseness of the white claim to inherent superiority, yet the man of colour who was nearly white despised the man of colour who was only half-white, who in turn despised the man of colour who was only quarter white, and so on through all the shades ... (43)

For James, the 'Mulattoes who were masters had their eyes fixed on Paris' (Appendix 394). They supposedly sought white approval, never that of blacks. Although James, *qua* Marxist, means to indict Mulattoes, not on the basis of their 'race' but on the basis of their 'class' (as occasional slaveholders themselves), his language maintains no strict separation between the two identities. Their 'caste,' if one likes, makes them ready traitors in James's history.

4 French Canadians, English Canadians, and African Canadians are not alone in articulating forms of group identity and identification. For instance, Irving Massey, in his 1994 consideration of English-, French-, and Yiddish-Canadian literature, posits – maybe nostalgically – that 'a powerful centripetal communitarianism was the outstanding feature of [Yiddish-speaking Montreal in the 1930s].' This community solidarity was exemplified by 'the hegemony of Yiddish as a lingua franca, which helped to reduce potential conflicts over politics, social class, and religion ...' (48).

5 Trudeau is not categorically opposed to abstract nationalism, or even to the concept of the sovereign state. In 1997, in an interview published in *Cité libre*, he states that 'malgré ses limites, un État souverain peut essayer de corriger les injustices du marché et il doit le faire' (9). In *Toward the Just Society* (1990), Trudeau defended his government's record in part by arguing that it had succeeded in giving the 'Canadian nation ... its very own constitution' with a Charter of Rights and Freedoms, thus laying down 'firm foundations for a national identity' (379). It is not nationalism *per se* that Trudeau detests (as is the case with Benda), but ethnic nationalism. His Pan-Canadianism – like black Pan-Africanism – is a liberal response to 'petty nationalism.' He extols Pan-Canadianism to combat Québécois nationalism. Here it is prudent to cite Lord Acton, one of Trudeau's major philosophical influences, on his opposition to nationalism:

> It overrules the rights and wishes of the inhabitants, absorbing their divergent interests in a fictitious unity; sacrifices their several inclinations and duties to the higher claim of nationality, and crushes all natural rights and all established liberties for the purpose of vindicating itself. (Quoted in Christiano 49)

Trudeau espouses like views in 'New Treason of the Intellectuals,' asserting that the nation-state is 'a kind of magic [that nationalists call] forth to fill in for [a] lack of discipline in pursuing the true ideals' (174).

6 Alexis is not the only African-Canadian Trudeauite. In his novel *Erzulie Loves Shango* (1998), Haitian-Canadian scholar and writer Max Dorsinville ascribes to his Québécoise character Denise Dupuis feelings of dissatisfaction with Québec's 'tribal spirit of conformity':

> She had found the name for it in her readings: 'the wigwam complex.' She agreed with the essayist who had coined the term, Pierre Elliott Trudeau. She had been enlightened by his essay, 'The New Treason of the Clerics.' In it, she had discovered what lay behind the siege mentality of [her town] ... (139)

In *Riot* (1995), Ottawa-born playwright Andrew Moodie presents a character, Alex, who, in his closing speech, rhapsodizes over 'Pierre Trudeau,' who 'was the coolest. We had no idea why, he just was, he was the coolest' (93). Opposing such eulogies, Gérard Étienne, in his novel *La Pacotille* (1991), gives a non-hagiographic vision of P.E.T.: 'un millionnaire arrogant, téméraire, prétentieux qui ne tardera pas à faire un saut en politique fédérale dans le but d'étouffer toute lutte de libération au pays' (71).

7 African-Canadian writer Cecil Foster agrees, here, with Alexis. In his work *A Place Called Heaven: The Meaning of Being Black in Canada* (1996), Foster wonders whether African Canadians 'can have a community without their own heroes and myths, when they must borrow from other societies [i.e., the United States and the Caribbean], rather than venerate and elevate their own' (19). His questioning is sparked by his record of an Afrocentric ceremony in which none of the African 'spirits invited to move among us' – including those of Sojourner Truth, Frederick Douglass, Malcolm X, Nelson Mandela, and Marcus Garvey – would qualify, he realizes, 'as a typical Canadian hero' (17).

8 Paradox afflicts Walcott's claim that 'in Canada, black identities must be rooted elsewhere and that elsewhere is always outside Canada' (122). If true, why should we bother to protest mainstream narratives that construe blackness as an alien quality?

9 The urge to blacklist seemingly 'white-identified' authors like Alexis is suspect. Aldon Nielsen warns, 'Surely there is something deeply wrong with critical definitions that might have the end effect of repressing the reality of a black poet by viewing him and his work as being sited outside of black reality' (16). But Nielsen's proviso is stymied by Frantz Fanon's notion that black – or 'native' – intellectuals must strive to ascend a scale of 'virtue,' escalating from 'the first stage [where] the "native intellectual gives proof that he has assimilated the culture of the occupying power"' (the 'stage' of Alexis), to 'the second phase [where] "we find the native is disturbed; he decides to remember what he is" ... [thus] "creating literature of just-before-the-battle"' (Cliff 27). In the 'third phase, which [Fanon] calls "the fighting phase" ... the writer will "shake the people"' (Cliff 27). Rinaldo Walcott would like to boost Alexis from the Fanonian first to the third phase, but a Nielsenian 'black reality' *must* also include the 'first-phase' stance of an Alexis. In

their respective essays on Alexis's first novel, *Childhood* (1998), critics Leslie Sanders and Peter Hudson upbraid Alexis for writing as if 'race is of no consequence in the Canadian landscape' (Sanders, 'Impossible' 184) and thus contributing to Canada's 'powerfully dehumanizing racism' (Hudson, 'Last' 198). Sanders ignores the unignorable issue of Alexis's liberalism, while Hudson cites his 'conservative, almost reactionary response to questions of race, that is masked in a kind of rational liberalism' ('Last' 197), but never interrogates its rationale. Like Walcott, Sanders and Hudson 'blacklist' Alexis for a supposed evacuation of 'blackness.' Yet, they do not query the ways in which 'blackness' persists in Alexis's works.

10 Emigrants from majoritarian black societies – in Africa and the Caribbean – do not necessarily possess a *race* consciousness. In *The Crisis of the Negro Intellectual* (1967), Harold Cruse alleges that 'West Indians are never so much in love with Caribbean heritage, or never so vehement in defending the West Indian image, as when they are indulging these sentiments from afar in England or North America' (438). Cruse notes that 'most of the West Indians from [Pan-Africanist leader Marcus] Garvey's homeland in Jamaica leave home not to return to Africa but to emigrate to the British Isles' (360). Or, one must add, to Canada or the United States. As for Africans, Cruse argues that those who live in Western societies 'become passionately attached to the ways of the cosmopolitan West, the high standard of living, the creature comforts of the affluent society' (555). Cruse is harsh, but Ghanaian-Canadian writer Henry Martey Codjoe confesses that 'until coming to Canada, the question of my racial identity was not something that I had thought about. After all, I grew up in an all-Black country where the issue of race or racism was not something that was on my mind' (231). Antiguan-born dub poet Clifton Joseph also acknowledges, employing eccentric punctuation, that 'in my case, I didnt learn anything about being Black as an idea/concept/consciousness (in/school) in antigua' (14). Speaking of the experiences of himself and other young West Indian immigrants in Toronto in the mid-1970s, Joseph says, 'We weren't "Black" where we came from in the west indies [*sic*], but in toronto [*sic*] we had to confront the fact that we were seen as "Black," and had to check out for ourselves what this blackness was' (17). I venture that minority-group blacks will face identity conflicts over 'blackness,' while majority-group blacks will struggle primarily around class and religious differences.

11 To be consistent, Walcott should dismiss African-American poet C.S. Giscombe's reasons for his self-identification: 'I'm African-American, a phrase I like because the last 2 syllables of each word are the same & in that I see two near-identical dark faces' (quoted in Nielsen 21).

12 Nationalism always spawns debates over nomenclature; so, admittedly, Walcott's position is nothing new. To give one example, while Benda and Trudeau, in 'dissing' nationalistic intellectuals, like to speak of their 'treason,' African-American theorists – perhaps because of the determining influence of the 'family' trope in their debates – prefer to use less inflammatory terms, such as, in the case of Cruse, *crisis*, or, in that of Cornel West, *dilemma*, as in his essay 'The Dilemma of the Black Intellectual' (1992). But our contemporary duty, to be righteous, cannot credit disputes over labels. Our task is, says Jean-François Lyotard in *Tombeau de*

l'intellectuel (1984), 'séparer i'intelligence de la paranoïa qui a fait la "modernité"' (22). Of Rinaldo Walcott's agonies over wordage, one may quote Alan J. Peacock on Ezra Pound's *cant*: '... the fact that conventional values are turned so precisely on their head is an indication that we are dealing with rhetoric rather than revolt' (97).

13 The distinction even replicates that which pertains to the francophone citizens of Québec, as summed up in Ramsay Cook's portrait of the province's archetypal native sons, the federalist Trudeau and the *indépendantiste* René Lévesque: 'For the *francophone canadien*, Trudeau, Canada was central; for the *Québécois*, Lévesque, Canada was marginal – at best' (356). In this sentence, one could substitute the Canada-identified Alexis for Trudeau, the black-identified Walcott for Lévesque.

14 Fanon sums up this psychology (psychosis?) in one searing image: 'I marry white culture, white beauty, white whiteness. When my restless hands caress those white breasts, they grasp white civilization and dignity and make them mine' (*Black* 63).

15 In her introduction to *Harlem Duet*, Sears offers the following assertions:
    I have a dream. A dream that one day in the city where I live, at any given time of the year, I will be able to find at least one play that is filled with people who look like me, telling stories about me, my family, my friends, my community ... I must write my own work for the theatre. I must produce my own work, and the work of other writers of African descent. (14)

16 Benda tolerates the nationalist feelings of 'the poets, the novelists, the dramatists, the artists' (54), for they 'may be permitted to give passion, even wilful passion, a predominant place in their works' (54). He cannot see why 'they should exclude national passion or the spirit of party from their vibrant material' (50).

17 American sociologist Kevin Christiano shadows Grant's critique of Trudeau's thought, stating that 'the language of liberalism ... is by its nature and design wildly ill-suited to formulating identity, for to accomplish that goal, one must speak of history and destiny in ways that circumvent, if not obliterate, the individual. One must speak, if not mythologically, then at least sociologically' (69). In eschewing such grounded, communal speech, Trudeau and his allies may have supported 'the prospect of a real national community for Canada, [but] on a level so ethereal, so abstracted from common life and experience, as to be more a creature of intellectual debate than a recognizable ground for order' (72).

18 Grant's absorption of views equivalent to Benda's Platonism is apparent in his comment that 'philosophy is always and everywhere the enemy of the opinions of any society, however much philosophers may have to conceal that enmity' ('Northrop' 361).

19 In a 1995 article, 'Signifying Nothing,' Philip states that 'the profound changes [Americanization] that had begun in Canada in the sixties had more to do with the fundamental reorganization of the Canadian political system that George C. [*sic*] Grant described in his brilliant and prescient work, *Lament for a Nation* [1965]' (8).

20 Rinaldo Walcott proposes that 'what is characteristically complex about Brand's work is that it offers no orthodoxies on blackness' (38). Yet, when Brand recalls that 'once a Czech émigré writer, now very popular in the "free world," looked me dead in my Black eyes and explained the meaning of jazz to me' (*Bread* 20), she is

appealing – albeit humorously – to the black nationalist orthodoxy that white folks ain't got no business commenting upon black folks' art. Walcott's analysis tampers, not just with facts, but with truth itself.

21 In a 4 May 1997, newspaper article, 'Black Stars Rising,' Foster, striking a nationalist stance, rebukes me for allegedly stating in my Introduction to my edited anthology *Eyeing the North Star: Directions in African-Canadian Literature* (1997) that 'black Canadian writing is not political' (13). He advises that 'Mr. Clarke probably needs to talk to all those young book buyers and students who are looking for, and finding, very strong political meaning in the books they are reading' (13). His commentary evinces a knowledge of what young, black book buyers seek, which is presumably some homogenized – or harmonized – black nationalist nostrums. However, Foster misrepresents what I did say, not that African-Canadian literature is apolitical, but that it is too various to be enslaved to any single political viewpoint: 'Bluntly, no African-Canadian intellectual has been able to shepherd his or her sistren or brethren along a single ideological path' (Introduction, *Eyeing* xvi).

22 This fact should be better understood. African Canadians have followed a model applicable – historically – to most Canadians; that is to say, seeking reform within established institutions. In his *History of Canadian Political Thought* (1966), G. P. de T. Glazebrook notes that, in the nineteenth-century, 'virtually every political reformer in British North America was ... a believer in the British system of government (as he interpreted it), and realized too that the British parliament and government were the sources of political power' (83).

23 I cannot resist reporting here the inquiry, addressed to me in 1997 by Foster, demanding to know why I think his work displays Toryism. Yet, in his 1998 novel, *Slammin' Tar*, Foster justifies my thesis. His main narrator, Brer Anancy, a spider, is himself a conservative recollection of the African tradition of the fable. But this spider is suspiciously akin to classical Tories. He expresses a craving for authoritarianism, for 'a leader, with a strong, firm hand on the reins' (204). He confesses that 'I am an old-fashioned male, and I like, in most cases, for things to remain they [sic] way they are. I am for known systems and order' (261). He even says, 'Call me a staunch conservative if you like, but I believe there are some tried and tested things with which you just shouldn't mess' (116).

24 Rinaldo Walcott's evasion of historical realities aligns him with Trudeau, for whom, as Christiano declares, 'democratic equality requires the impersonality of universalism, so it effaces history' (48–9). But Walcott not only fails to assess the conservative aspects of African-Canadian history, he is also oblivious to the radical intellectual effort represented by such neglected works as *Let the Niggers Burn!* (1971), an essay collection, edited by Dennis Forsythe, on Montréal's Sir George Williams University Affair of February 1969 (during which black and white students trashed a computer centre to protest the racist grading of black students). He also overlooks *The Black Experience in the White Mind: Meditations on a Persistent Discourse* (1995), a study of racial representations in art, compiled and edited by Roger McTair. Of this pair, Forsythe's text is ascerbically bracing, arguing that the '"Sir George Williams Affair" ... witnessed the escalation of a conflict from a small internal charge of "racism" by six Black students against a Professor ... to a highly

charged collective episode that shook the West Indies, ruffled the world, and boomeranged black consciousness one step further towards a consolidation called "Peoplehood"' (3). Walcott also neglects the incest between radical and Tory postures. Aldon Nielsen notes, in this regard, that African-American poet Amiri Baraka's 'totalizing impulse, which led him first to Cultural Nationalism and then to Marxism, may be of a piece with an odd conservatism that has to see the new as both ancient and derived' (107). Fundamentally, Walcott's analyses of African-Canadian – or Black Canadian – culture(s) refuse to query his own absorption in the polarities of Afro-Caribbean criticism. Glyne A. Griffith affirms that 'the ideological conflicts in West Indian criticism are not merely between a ... formalist and a ... socio-historical approach ...' (112). Rather, 'West Indian theoretical and critical issues simultaneously engage metropolitan theory...' (112). *Black Like Who?* would have been a more cogent book had Walcott explained how his thought reflected – or refuted – metropole-derived ideas. For instance, he calls African-Canadian culture(s) 'rhizomatic,' but never discusses the term's origin in Gilles Deleuze and Felix Guattari, *Le Rhizome* (1976), and its later use in Edouard Glissant's *Le Discours antillais* (1981) and *Poétique de la relation* (1990) as a figure for anti-hierarchical thought.

25 In other stories, too, Alexis satirizes such staples of African diasporic literature as the moment of self-recognition as *black*. For instance, in 'Horse,' the protagonist awakens and recognizes 'my own poor body': 'How homely I was ... Of course, I had realized some time before that I was a negro, but this "niggerness" still surprised me. My hair was like a cone of wool. My mouth hung open and the side of my face was white with spittle' (*Despair* 152). In 'The Road to Santiago de Compostela,' Alexis satirizes the idea of African *otherness* by introducing a presumably African family, the M'Kolos, about whom 'it was rumoured that they'd been cannibals "back where they came from," but, as with all such rumours, this was something of an exaggeration' (*Despair* 221). Ironically, as it turns out, 'The M'Kolos ... "come from" Glencoe [Ontario], which is not known for its man-eaters, and in all their lives they knew only one cannibal' (*Despair* 221).

26 Here Philip would depart from Walcott's black universalism. In *A Genealogy of Resistance and Other Essays* (1997), she insists that 'true poetry – a poetry of truth – depends very much upon ... a rooting in place ...' (58). Philip argues – in terms reminiscent of Alexis – that 'in the absence of such a bond, we remain forever adrift from all lands, all places, wanderers unable to attach ourselves truly to any one place' (*Genealogy* 66).

27 If the culture exists, then so must a modicum of nationalism. 'Like the elephant, nationalism exists, and must be accepted' (Glazebrook 322). So the 'ethnic' critic or artist or intellectual should feel free – and should feel a duty – to engage his or her culture's creativity, to apply judgment. Italian-Canadian critic Antonio D'Alfonso puts it this way:

> For every group of ethnic artists, the battle worth fighting for is the right to produce with their own means of production a body of artistic and theoretical works in such abundance that their sense of ethnicity can no longer be confined by mainstream culture to a matter of 'appropriate content.' What each individual

and collective should seek is the expression of a complex spirit of dignified difference. (19)

No matter what, though, would-be 'guerilla'-scholars must remember, with Vincent Sherry, that 'history will betray *clercs* who intrude into politics' (196).

Canadian Biraciality and Its 'Zebra' Poetics

For Walter M. Borden (1942–)[1]

Preamble

One constant problem for would-be black nationalist intellectuals has been the place – if any – of mixed-race blacks within their 'world visions.' African-Canadian intellectuals have also been driven to some 'perplexion' regarding the 'black' complexion that is not as 'dark' as some desire. Certainly, like all African diasporic writing, African-Canadian literature engages the symbol and the image of the mixed-race black, for this figure violates the sanctity of racial polarities, reminding Africans and Europeans of white-practised violence against enslaved African women. Scholar Richard Newman stresses that since 'slaves were property, like animals or objects, they had no rights, and all black women were sexually available to all white men' (1320). 'Virtually every [U.S.] plantation produced children of mixed race' (Newman 1320). African-American scholar Michelle M. Wright reports that, by the mid-nineteenth century, 'there were increasingly lurid accounts of depraved white slaveholders and brutally exploited black slaves' (843). Another scholar has apparently detailed 'the widespread practice of rape by white slave owners despite the blind eye turned to or outright denial of such actions in the white discourse of the time' (Michelle Wright 850n7). The Canadian experience varied only lightly. Thus, in 1788, the revelation that 'Rev. Daniel Cock, a highly esteemed minister of the Presbyterian Church in Truro, [Nova Scotia,] was the owner of two female slaves excited public feelings and controversy' (Best, in *Fire*, vol. 1, 121). Black Loyalist Lydia Jackson, eight months pregnant, found herself enslaved and brutalized by her white Nova Scotian master, Dr Bulman (Walker, *Black* 50). Historian Robin Winks reports that 'of 573 children of slaves [in Nouvelle-France] for whom there is adequate record, 59.5 percent were born outside any form of marriage, and ... the entry in the registers – *pere* [*sic*] *inconnu* – no doubt covers many white men ...' (11). Winks supposes that 'proximity and temperament [encouraged] interracial sexual relations' in Nouvelle-France (11), but he does not consider the possibility of sexual assaults by the empowered upon the powerless. Nor does he wager that some black females may have been purchased for sexual reasons. Yet, in Nouvelle-France, 'in 1743 Negro women sold for 800 livres ..., while at the same time men cost 400 livres in 1748 ...' (48). Winks holds that women cost more than men did because, while both sexes served as domestics, 'women were more suited to the tasks demanded of them at home' (48). One must imagine, however, that opportunities for white sexual predation – and concomitant expansion of one's slave 'holdings' – did not go unnoticed. Winks affirms that 'at one time sturdy women who might mother a substantial number of slaves would be worth more than males' (49). Most suspiciously, 'in 1769 an auction was held on the beach at Halifax to sell "two hogsheads of rum, three of sugar and two well-grown negro girls, aged fourteen and twelve"' (Winks 28). On the other hand, marriage to white men may have been a desirable option for black women in Nouvelle-France, for, under its laws, 'if a white man took a Negro slave wife, she was freed by the act of marriage' (Winks 7). In other quarters, and in freedom, white-black liaisons formed for, one hopes, reasons of mutual pleasure and esteem. Thus, Alexander Ochterloney, a white leader of the Jamaican Maroons dispensed to Nova Scotia in 1796, 'took five or six of the most attractive Maroon girls to his bed' (Winks 83). At the same time, Nova Scotia governor Thomas Wentworth 'apparently ... took a Negro mistress' (Winks 81). These tragedies and comedies of white-black coupling mandate that mixed-race figures should activate the imaginations of at least some African-Canadian authors. Fascinatingly, though, it is Western Canadian mixed-race blacks who limn, almost fetishistically, the 'zebra' consciousness.

I. Tragedizing the Mulatto

In his finicky account of Euro-American racism and its African-American victims, *An American Dilemma: The Negro Problem and the Modern Democracy* (1944), Swedish sociologist Gunnar Myrdal asserts that 'everybody having a *known* trace of Negro blood in his veins – no matter how far back it was acquired – is classified as a Negro. No amount of white ancestry, except one hundred per cent, will permit entrance to the white race' (113, his italics).[2] Myrdal's findings were not news for blacks, particularly those of mixed-race heritage, some of whom yearned to trace their entire lineage – if only they could – to whites.[3] Because they could not, ambivalence and alienation were their lot.[4] Honeying this agony – this estranging straddling of the colour-line – the one salutary effect of the so-called one-drop rule was to up the potential number of African-American warriors available to fight U.S. apartheid. Relatively light-skinned blacks like W.E.B. Du Bois (1868–1963), Malcolm X (1925–65), and Angela Davis (1944–) were thus able to unite with darker-skinned brethren and sistren like Paul Robeson (1898–1976), Martin Luther King, Jr (1929–68), and Audre Lorde (1934–92) to promote immediate equality for blacks.[5] Simultaneously, the depiction of the 'Tragic Mulatto' in literature and film stressed that the person of mixed race belonged, absolutely, to an inescapable – if, for some, debilitating – *blackness*.[6]

Crucially, the essays of the incisive, Martiniquan-born foe of racialist imperialism, Frantz Fanon (1925–61), branded the mixed-race black as suspect, that
is, as a ready *collaborateur* with white supremacy. Theoretically, but damningly, he or she was the offspring of a black parent who had sought, through
sexual intercourse with a white partner, to experience the disorienting pleasure of a vicarious whiteness. In *Peau noire, masques blancs* (1952), Fanon insists
that when the Martiniquan author Mayotte Capécia announces, in her autobiography, *Je suis Martiniquaise* (1948), her desire to marry a white Frenchman,
she is seeking 'la lactification' (40).[7] Discussing an allegedly recidivist black
male lust for white women, Fanon's persona explains that 'dans ces seins
blancs que mes mains ubiquitaires caressent, c'est la civilisation et la dignité
blanches que je fais miennes' (53). If the joining of black and white is inherently pathological, as Fanon's exhibits excitedly indicate, how can the offspring not voice self-hatred and Negrophobia? With this worry in mind, Fanon
says, of the mixed-race type in Abdoulaye Sadji's *Nini* (1955?), that she 'non
seulement veut blanchir, mais éviter de régresser. Qu'y a-t-il de plus illogique,
en effet, qu'une mulâtresse qui épouse un Noir?' (46). Fanon's tone is unduly,
startlingly, vindictive, as if the desires of an imaginary being indicted, somehow, his actual, racialized masculinity.

Of course, the catalogue of treacherous Creoles or mixed-bloods or mixed-
races or half-breeds or Mulattoes[8] – in New World African literature – is so
long as to be almost convincing. Then again, Mulattoes were susceptible to
accusations of 'race treason' because of their supposed favoured status in the
eyes of whites. Truly, some white theorists of racialism did claim 'Mulattoes'
as 'acceptable' blacks, ones capable of being assimilated. Thus, Count Arthur
de Gobineau (1816–82), in his *Essai sur l'inégalité des races humaines* (1853–5),
allows that, as Michelle Wright witnesses, 'some mullatos [*sic*] could be integrated into white society – including the professional class, eventually obliterating any color distinction whatsoever' (839). Some Mulattoes were eager to
accept a 'place' as 'honorary' whites. In his examination of Juan Francisco
Manzano's *Autobiography of a Cuban Slave* ([1835], 1937), West Indian literary
critic Lloyd King points out that Juan Gualberto Gomez, an eminent Cuban
Mulatto, 'advised his followers to accept a place as second-class citizens and
suppress their own originality: "What do I say to my my people? Let us invent
nothing, let us develop no taste for originality in any sphere of activity, let us
accept the minor role"' ('Some' 23). Demonstrably, Manzano's *Autobiography*
emerges from a 'matrix of victimhood' ('Juan' 28). King urges that Manzano's
masochism stems from an unlucky circumstance: 'Although born a slave, as a
child he was treated by his first mistress almost as if he were white, and he
never quite recovered from his childhood experience' ('Some' 7). Even after he
becomes the property of a vitriolic second mistress, Manzano remains an ei-
ther-or figure, an 'outsider which ever way he turned' and a 'bridge from the
orality of the enslaved's world to a white civilization's codes of writing and
representation' ('Juan' 29). He plays a racial – and scholastic – 'Mulatto.' In his
Autobiography, Manzano lodges two intriguing confessions. First, he describes

himself as his 'mistress's lap-dog' (47), for she has beaten and browbeaten him into submission; even so, 'I loved her in spite of the harshness with which she treated me ...' (59). Secondly, having learned to write poetry, he found that the art, 'in all the crises of my life, provided me verses to suit my situation whether good or bad' (52). Soon, we find Manzano – the intellectual *métis* – writing *chansons* for the charity of his mistress:

> As my mistress had softened towards me, almost without noticing I had also modified my hardness of heart acquired the last time she had condemned me to chains and labour, holding out against writing or being ordered to write. I had forgotten the past and loved her like a mother ... At this time, I wrote many notebooks of [verse] which I sold ... (60)

This idyll sours, for just as Manzano falls for 'a young mulatress about my age ..., the first one to engender in me something I knew not of before, an angelic inclination, a love as if she were my sister' (61), he is beaten – in view of his beloved's home – by his mistress (61). Then, he fears that he will be sent to El Merino, for, there, he will become 'a mulatto among the negroes' (62). Such utterances reinforce the value of Manzano's text as portraying, says King, 'a certain kind of mulatto sensibility, of a conception of the mulatto role in the culture and society of the Hispanic Caribbean' ('Juan' 29).[9]

Regrettably, the abject, pathetic phantom of a Manzano – the Mulatto writer who prefers to draft love notes to perfidious whites rather than anthems for black liberation – hovers over black diasporic literatures. Distressingly, in one of the first texts in the African-Canadian canon, *A Narrative of the Lord's Wonderful Dealings ...* (1785), a captivity narrative, its author, John Marrant (1755–91), prays that 'the black nations may be made white in the blood of the Lamb' (*Fire*, vol. 1, 48). Marrant toys with the imagery of assimilation and bastardy, the damaging inverses of projects of purity.

Unquestionably, such conceptions attract the disdain of liberationist scholars like the African-Trinidadian intellectual C.L.R. James (1901–89). In his masterful history *The Black Jacobins: Toussaint L'Ouverture and the San Domingo Revolution* (1938), James critiques the role of Mulattoes before, during, and after the Haitian Revolution. In the pre-revolutionary period, James declares,

> The advantages of being white were so obvious that race prejudice against the Negroes permeated the minds of the Mulattoes who so bitterly resented the same thing from the whites. Black slaves and Mulattoes hated each other ... The free blacks ... were not many, and so despised was the black skin that even a Mulatto slave felt himself superior to the free black man. The Mulatto, rather than be slave to a black, would have killed himself. (42–3)

In James's imagination, the Mulattoes are Black Girondins, *vendus*, always congenitally prepared to betray or sabotage the black revolt. Thus, we read of 'Candy, who led a band of Mulattoes, [deserting] the blacks and join[ing] the

Commissioners, beginning that Mulatto vacillation which was to have such disastrous consequences in the future' (123). When a time of reaction ensues, James finds that 'property, white and Mulatto, had come together again under the flag of the counter-revolution' (129). When Mulattoes oppose Toussaint L'Ouverture (1743?–1803), the revolutionary leader of black Haiti, it is because he seemed to them 'a traitor to the Republic and a tyrant seeking to establish a black domination. They fought like tigers' (232). For James, *Mulatto* is a practical synonym for *Fifth Columnist*. He warns, 'Mulatto instability lies not in their blood but in their intermediate position in society' (207), that is to say, in their caste.[10]

James's conception that the Mulatto navigates a treacherous 'Middle Passage' between blacks and whites resonates in contemporary African diasporic intellectual discourse. African-American intellectual Harold Cruse (b. 1916) delineates 'the social role of the "mixed-blood Negro," sometimes called the mulatto, and the special racial role he plays as intermediary in interracial cultural affairs (especially in relation to white liberals who favor this Negro type)' (84). Cruse's comment supports a common prejudice. In *The New Colored People: The Mixed-Race Movement in America* (1997), Jon Michael Spencer indicates that mixed-race persons – or 'multiracialists' – remain suspect, given their 'demand for official recognition as a separate racial category' (Azoulay 151). Yet, Spencer's readings of recent U.S. census data show that 'approximately eighty percent of interracial marriages are *not* between Blacks and whites' (Azoulay 151). In her review of Spencer's book, Katya Gibel Azoulay posits that 'for African Americans the multiracial movement – however infuriating – may be less threatening than Spencer speculates' (151). On the one hand, Spencer's statistics provide relief; on the other hand, mixed-race persons are only 'less threatening' than first thought. The implicit problem is that the multiracialists' quest to eradicate 'the fear of miscegenation' and to obtain 'recognition of the complexity of multiple heritage by transcending racial boundaries' may mask 'the desire for a disassociation from black identities' (Azoulay 152). Given their potential for 'shiftiness' – that is, for 'shifting' into and out of categories of blackness and whiteness – Mulattoes represent a risk for investments of black 'trust.' Appropriately, then, Haitian-Canadian writer Max Dorsinville, in his novel *Erzulie Loves Shango* (1998), bids his dark-skinned, African-American protagonist, James Wait, castigate mixed-race blacks:

Mulattoes, High Yellows, whether they were Haitian or American, Jamaican or Martiniquean, were all bastards, literally. They didn't know who they were and hated with passion the visible part of themselves they didn't know when they saw it around them. Their hatred for blacks was worse than that of the most redneck among 'crackers' ... These 'tragic mulattoes' ended up either in an insane asylum or they killed themselves ... Whatever trick they were up to, they would never get what they craved for: a lily white skin. Nothing more tragic than a nigger who is told he is not black enough; or a nigger who is told he is either too white or too black ... 'Tragic mulattoes' were in a rut; they had to choose to get out of it by themselves. Find out on their own who they were and stop asking others for their say and approval ... Whites, in particular, who had a field day toying with them. (164)[11]

They are dismissed in no uncertain terms, and their dismissal is mandated by Wait's preference for the espousal of black racial solidarity.

Sadly, Wait-like, anti-Mulatto sentiments were popularized in the 1920s by the Universal Negro Improvement Association, led by the militant black nationalist Marcus Mosiah Garvey (1887–1940), who viewed mixed-race persons as symbols and sources of racial pollution. When his organization collapsed, Garvey originated the myth, charges African-American political scientist Wilson Jeremiah Moses, 'that middle class blacks, mulattoes, and conservative intellectuals wrecked his plans' (264). This mythology marked Garvey's allegiance to an 'attitude towards miscegenation [that] was worse than an accommodation to racism; it was an invitation to participate in racism, and it was a direct endorsement of laws that were written to dehumanize black people' (267). Yet, Garveyite sentiments pepper Barbadian-Canadian writer Cecil Foster's novel-length fable *Slammin' Tar* (1998). Here the spider-narrator, Brer Anancy, recycles the *canard* that Garvey's enemies were black-hating, light-skinned blacks:

> The fact that he is, as they say, jet black in complexion obviously has a lot to do with [their] spiteful condemnations. I know I will offend some people by saying such things, but ... the truth shall set us free. Yes, I can still recall how their faces all turned red when the Prophet [Garvey] retorted by calling all his detractors *paughy* mulattoes, *perjohnnies* all, white integrationists in half-black skins, an admixture of white and coloured blood, people vainly searching for ... that elusive social equality between the races. (101–2)

Though such statements vend maddening – and damaging – illusions, they are true to Garvey, who was not, moreover, the last Pan-African leader to question Mulatto loyalties. His ideological heir, Malcolm X, was no less wary of mixed-race blacks. In a 1963 interview with Barbadian-Canadian novelist Austin Clarke (b. 1934), X, then still a minister within the Nation of Islam, asked where 'the children of mixed marriages would fit [within a black separatist schema],' gave this answer: 'They are in trouble. The mixed – if you notice, the white man always rejects children of mixed marriages. When you become of mixed blood you're never white but you are always considered non-white' (274). When Clarke questions X about 'the degree of black blood you must have in order to be black' (274), he receives this cold, *Realpolitik* reply:

> Well, as far as we are concerned, as long as we can tell that you have black blood, you are one of our brothers and when you get in that borderline where you can't tell what you are, or it's questionable, then it's best for you to get some papers,

especially nowadays, because you are going into an era today where the color of your skin might. Save your life. (274–5)

(To be fair, prior to his assassination in February 1965, X had evolved – or was evolving – a black socialist *cum* anti-racist sensibility, but some of his adherents still propagate his unreconstructed, pre–1964, *racist* opinions.) White and black racialists agree that, to cite Michelle Wright, 'miscegenation is the antithesis of nation' (847).

Though it has enjoyed a perennial popularity, the ideal of the traitorous mixed-race – or phony – black is not the only *sign* progressive black writers engage. Another standard trope is that of the Mulatto who outdoes dark-skinned blacks in his or her expression of a radical blackness. African-American writer William Wells Brown (1814–84), for whom 'slavery ... had a special anguish' (Takaki 216), embraces this strategy. First, as a child, Brown 'learned from his mother, a slave of "mixed blood" herself, that his father was a white man and his master's half brother' (216). Then, 'as a mulatto, William encountered not only the hostility of [his mistress] but also the resentment of his fellow black slaves' (217). His daughter and biographer, Josephine Brown, explained that 'the nearer a slave approaches an Anglo-Saxon complexion, the more he is abused by both owner and fellow-slaves. The owner flogs him to keep him "in his place," and the slaves hate him on account of his being whiter than themselves' (quoted in Takaki 217). Brown's major heroine, Clotelle, faces a mirror violence in *Clotelle: A Tale of the Southern States* (1864).[12] Here the jealous Mrs Miller, to 'degrade Clotelle and to make her look like the pure-blooded slaves ..., has her servants cut the child's beautiful long hair and forces [her] to work in the hot sun in order to brown her skin. This hideous and barbaric process delights the black servants' (Takaki 224). In writing his novel, Brown elects to sing an inclusive blackness, one expansive enough to infold those of mixed-race heritage.

These archetypes of the Mulatto – both pathetic Judas and potential martyr-subversive – enjoy a steady and pronounced presence throughout African Diasporic literature, from the era of slavery to our era of political decolonization and global cultural homogenization. As crossed – or jinxed – symbols of the meetings of twains that once were 'pure,' the mixed-race writer carries the absolute tint of impurity, of blending, of remembered violence, of treachery – or treason – implicit in the flesh. (Myrdal insists often: 'The question is also raised: Is the the mulatto a deteriorated or an improved Negro?' [106].) Thus, he or she is prevailed upon to champion a black cultural nationalist perspective. Assuredly, there is little room in the radical vanguard for the black artist who 'turns his back on the imperatives of the ethnic culture' (Cruse 296). By any means necessary, too, he or she must avoid girding up an integrationist perspective, for, to do so, as Cruse feels African-American playwright Lorraine Hansberry (1930–65) did, is to imply 'the end of the Negro as a creative Negro being' (281). Thus, Hansberry's *A Raisin in the Sun* (1959) reveals, Cruse alleges, 'the author's own essentially quasi-white orientation through which she visualizes the Negro world' (283). The poltically *black* mixed-race artist must sidestep the regressive act of tying the black working class 'to the chariot of racial integration driven by the Negro middle class' (Cruse 283). Cruse warns that 'in this drive for integration the Negro working class is ... told in a thousand ways that it must give up its ethnicity and become human, universal, full-fledged American' (283).

Cruse's argument is not unique. Born in apartheid South Africa, where he was classified as an 'Indian Coloured' (12), Black Canadian author Azra Daniel Francis plumps for an Afrocentric consciousness and black racial solidarity in poems like 'The Spotted Tongue':

Afrikaner's
Petty spiteful hate
Is hissed
By forked tongue
Of a snake.

But far more venomous
Contaminating
Racist dung
Spits
Black at Black
At Brown at Brown at Black,
From spotted tongue. (77–8)

Francis summons mixed-race – or 'spotted tongue' – people to adopt Pan-Africanism as the choice antidote to white racism. In 'The Peter-Paul Christian Twins,' he advises 'the Indian Christians / In South Africa' that they are 'the blackest of the Black / South Africans' and attacks their supposed 'lust for Whites' (99). In chapter 11 of his novel, *La Pacotille* (1991), Haitian-Canadian writer Gérard Étienne (b. 1936) pictures a woman 'who was of the line of seasoned mulattoes who think black' (110). The potential mixed-race threat to black solidarity must be countered by a conscious articulation of an overarching black nationalism and Pan-Africanism.

This strategy has been the practice in the United States, where, as early as 'the U.S. Census of 1850, the category "Mulatto" appeared' (Azoulay 152), with quadroons and octoroons being 'temporarily added in the 1890 Census' (Azoulay 152). Their mixed-blood status has always been politicized in ways to render them philosophically *noir*, racially *noir*, or culturally (pathologically?) white. The search for a comfortable mixed-race identity presupposes recognizing that 'the racial binary which characterizes the U.S. is ... in terms of culture – a very unstable concept – black, brown, beige, and white Negroes are very American' (Azoulay 153). There is, in the United States, a 'diversity of people of African descent' (Azoulay 153). Yet, racial brownness will continue to be read as racial blackness in U.S. culture.

In Canada, though, mixed-race status is not so automatically, or so clearly, *black*. For one thing, the polychromatic and polyethnic nature of African-heritage populations militates against the production of a single, mass definition of black identity. The irreducible catholicity of Canadian black experience reflects the truth that its communities encompass not only varying ethnic compositions, lengths of residency in Canada, languages, and religions, but also heterogeneous attitudes toward a 'black' identity. Thus, Dorsinville presents Haitian-Canadian Montréalais who eschew any *black* identity:

> Speaking French, they said they were Frenchmen ... Extremely sensitive about the slightest shade of skin color, they were wracked with anxiety at the thought that 'foreigners' did not see eye to eye with them on that issue ... Or else they would really get carried away by the subject of condemning the white world for lumping them together as 'niggers,' they with their abundant variety of skin shades. Speaking English, they cultivated a stilted French accent that would protect them from being mistaken for ordinary 'niggers.' (104)

In contrast, Henry Martey Codjoe, a Ghanaian-Canadian writer, reveals that 'before coming to Canada [from Ghana] I didn't know what it meant or felt to be discriminated against as a Black person or an African. I hadn't developed any kind of Black consciousness' (232).[13] For her part, Barbara Malanka, a Canadian writer of African-American and Franco-Ontarian heritage, states, 'I am uncomfortable being characterised by a single identity ... I am café au lait and warm sweet potato pie, steaming hot grits smothered in maple syrup' (19). In 'Living Out the Winter' (1995), a story set in Guyana, Canadian-born Jamaican writer John Hearne (1926–94) narrates another instance of racial diversity. His protagonist asserts that 'the combination of an East Indian husband willing to be advised by a wife with all the traditions and techniques that the West Indian peasant woman has had to learn ... is not a partnership to be taken lightly' (87).[14] *Sistahs* (1998), a play by Maxine Bailey (a native of England) and Sharon Mareeka Lewis ('a callaloo mix of Trinidadian and Jamaican heritage' [n.pag.]), showcases five African-Canadian women from contrasting backgrounds. Sandra and Rea are Trinidadian; Dehlia is Jamaican; Assata and Cerise are Canadian by birth. In addition, Sandra and Rea are part black, part Indian (South Asian). The exchanges the women share as they prepare 'every body bring something soup' (8) range across their various cultural traditions. Ultimately, as critic Andrea Davis perceives, 'this will not be a Jamaican or Trinidadian soup, an Afro- or Indo-Caribbean soup, but a West Indian soup cooked in a Canadian kitchen from memories of back home and the bitter sweet of now' (280). *Riot* (1997), a play by Andrew Moodie (b. 1967), enacts a fiesta of clashing black identities. Its six characters sketch a dynamically multicultural portrait of blackness:

WENDLE, a student, 20s, from Halifax, Nova Scotia
ALEX, a student, 20s, from Ottawa

HENRY, owner of electrical repair company, 30s, from Uganda
KIRK, a student, late teens, from Kingston, Jamaica
EFFIE, a student, 20s, from Vancouver
GRACE, a student, 20s, born in Jamaica and raised in Montreal, Kirk's sister
(n.pag.)

Meeting in a Toronto house, this sestet discusses 'race,' racism, and black and white Canadianité while the Los Angeles Riot of 1992 unfolds on television and its Toronto echo ripples outside their doors. The group's views compose a kaleidoscope of its members' different ethnicities and regional affiliations.

While such heterogeneity works against the mass promulgation of any popular, anti-Mulatto attitude among African Canadians, another factor destabilizes any monolithic blackness. It is the Canadian state practice of offering bicultural statuses an official – if partial – legitimization, especially the descendants of a historical First Nations-French admixture. Strikingly, the Western Canadian provinces of Manitoba and Saskatchewan coalesced in the late nineteenth-century out of a revolutionary struggle to guarantee the equality of First Nations and Métis groups *vis-à-vis* whites. Though these groups were routed by white settler-state authority, they resisted assimilation and, in recent decades, have resuscitated their rights. The recognition of so-called Métis within Canada's Constitution Act of 1982 allows, potentially, for a legitimization of bicultural status for other mixed-race Canadians.[15] The premium placed upon French-English bilingualism in Canada may also have a spillover effect in terms of racial identification. I sound the Canadian literary theorist Linda Hutcheon, who points to the 'inherent doubleness' of Canadian identity as 'a bilingual yet *multi*cultural nation' (16). The mixed-race writer may feel central to the representation of this socio-political reality, this nation where 'at least for a time, all the non-native inhabitants have felt dual allegiances' (Hutcheon 16).

II. Canadian 'Zebra' Poetics

Canadian black writers of mixed-race heritage have felt – or feel – freer to explore their identity confusions and dislocations, or even to interrogate their *blackness* in ways that may seem strangely abstract – or, worse, stupefyingly compromising – to African-American readers. For instance, the African-Canadian writer Lawrence Hill, the son of an African-American father and a Euro-American mother, opens his *Roots*-like, family saga, historical-novel, *Any Known Blood* (1997), with a scene of black-white coitus calculated to offend all nationalist mythologies of race. The lovers 'saw his erection and one of her breasts profiled on the wall, they watched their own hands joining, and they noticed that the shadows revealed nothing of her whiteness, or his blackness' (xiv). In support of his non-racialist agenda, Hill creates a protagonist, Cane V, who can 'pass' for white – or, rather, for multiple, non-black identities:

I have the rare distinction – a distinction that weighs like a wet life jacket, but that I sometimes float to great advantage – of not appearing to belong to any particular race, but of seeming like a contender for many.[16]

In Spain, people have wondered if I was French. In France, hotel managers asked if I was Moroccan. In Canada, I've been asked – always tentatively – if I was perhaps Peruvian, American, or Jamaican. But I have rarely given a truthful rendering of my origins.

Once, someone asked, 'Are you from Madagascar? I know a man from Madagascar who looks like you.'

I said: 'As a matter of fact, I am. I was born in the capital, Antananarivo. We moved to Canada when I was a teenager.'

Another time, when a man sitting next to me in a donut shop complained about Sikh refugees arriving by boat in Gander, Newfoundland, I said: 'I was born in Canada and I don't wear a turban, but I'm a Sikh. My mother is white, but my father is a Sikh, and that makes me one, too.' The man's mouth fell open. I paid the waitress to bring him twelve chocolate donuts. 'I've gotta go,' I told him. 'But next time you want to run down Sikhs, just remember that one of them bought you a box of donuts!'

I tried it again at the next opportunity. A woman at a party said Moroccans were sexist pigs, so I became a Moroccan. Then I started claiming I was part Jewish, part Cree, part Zulu, part anything people were running down. (1–2)

Eventually, Cane V states he is 'of Algerian origin' (2).[17] His refusal to be pigeonholed mirrors a like reluctance characteristic of some characters in African-American fiction. However, an incorrigible ambivalence about racial identification is, arguably, more common in African-Canadian than in African-American literature. In Canada, brown skin is not always identified with blackness – either as a state of (nationalist) consciousness or as a matter of pigmentation. Hence, Cane V dubs himself 'Zebra Incorporated' (400), a term signifying his dual-race status – and one that recurs in contemporary African-Canadian writing, including in Hill's autobiographical essay 'Zebra: Growing Up Black and White in Canada' (1994). Here Hill recognizes that 'in the United States ... anyone known to have any African ancestry has been defined as Black' (42) and that 'people as light-skinned as I am are frequently identified as Blacks' (43). But this is 'not so in Canada' (43). To resolve his ambiguous racial status in Canada, Hill swears, 'I'm a man of two races' (47). While acknowledging that '"Zebra" ... sounds faintly ridiculous' as a word to describe his racial identity, Hill prefers it to *mulatto*, a word that 'reduces me to half-status – neither Black nor White' (47). Hill accepts his racial duality; he spurns claims that his chosen identity may camouflage the desire surging – to cite Fanon – 'across the zebra striping of my mind ... to be suddenly *white*' (*Black* 63). Rather, Hill's zebra metaphor is, for him, as *avant-garde* as the black panther *sign* was for *that* party of urban African-American Maoists in the late 1960s.

This linking of black-white subjectivities occurs among many other mixed-race African-Canadian writers. Notably, too, many of them live on the Prairies or on the Pacific Coast. Their geographical isolation from larger black communities in Central Canada (mainly Toronto and Montréal) and the old black communities in Atlantic Canada may serve to explain their espousal of a 'zebra' sensibility. Their socio-geographic context provokes, perhaps, their interrogations of racial identity.[18] Clearly, writers like Suzette Mayr (b. 1967), Mercedes Baines, and Wayde Compton (b. 1972) follow Hill in questioning all efforts to impose a uniform understanding of *blackness* – or even of *race*.

In her poetry and fiction, Mayr, the Alberta-born daughter of a West Indian mother and a German father, taxes the reality of falling between heritages or – more positively put – of uniting them within herself. In her chapbook *Zebra Talk* (1991), a title recalling the racial fixations of Hill, Mayr concentrates on the thin reality of race – or skin – in a sequence of mainly untitled poems. Paradoxically, though, the poems establish that the purported fiction of race determines family relations and extra-familial love affairs. In the first segment, a two-page poem, in free verse that eschews almost all punctuation, Mayr's persona fleshes out her genealogy:

> The skin on a drum
> The skin stretched over a moving rib-cage
> The skin stretched and bitten by two other heads on this
> three-headed body
> 2 brothers 1 sister. 3 heads and 1 body
> plus 1 and 1 parents. (2)

Together, the siblings form a three-headed monster whose '(Zebra pelt [is] stretched over a hot and bloody centre)' (2). The skin of the Mulatto generation is stretched over a volcanic core – a history of violence and death. When the speaker considers her two sets of grandparents, she conjures up a stereotypical black grandmother, 'the one who guides our mother / through her nightmares and bathes our live mulatto skin / with her dead mulatto sweat' (3). This grandmother is associated with 'Boiled black-eyed peas and rice' and her graveyard monument is 'made of grass but also sand and the sun that slaps / the faces of blind white tourists' (3). The ensuing poem also connects brown skin with implicit violence. Here the speaker warns that, even under the skirt of a brown-skinned woman, 'there never were never will be never / aren't any obvious tan stripes' (4) that could reveal her 'pure' heritage, a fact that is 'Too bad' (4). Coitus – animalistic, but transformative – resists any biological notice of race. Hence, two lovers – 'Lady' and 'Never-gonna' – meet and mate, playing 'their venus games to a syncopated drum / beat their bodies clamp belly-to-belly like slugs for hours / for hours for hours' (4). Their union is bestial, but not racialized: 'Slugs are not annelids. Their bodies never / were never will be never aren't segmented or striped' (4). After pondering

the lack of racial markers in the act of sex itself, the speaker questions her
father about mixed-race biology (or, better, zoology):

> My father becomes a child when I ask him these questions
> are you a zebra what colour is the pelt underneath
> the white and white stripes of Germany and downtown
> cowtown? He says for him
>
>   easier to be an asshole. (5)

Colliding together these questions, Mayr emphasizes the surrealism of the
effort to separate out the constituents of mixed-race being. The father refuses
to satisfy his daughter's queries, refuses to affix a racial identity to either
Germany or 'cowtown' (Calgary). For him, to assert such an identity is akin to
becoming an 'asshole.' His solution is one of liberal goodwill, that is, erasure:
if we don't concretize racial identities, racism will wither away. But the daughter
persists in her questioning. She deems her father's answer 'the easiest. The
problem [of race] for him is in / his tongue and in his bum if we are to take the
English / idiom literally. But who is we now?' (5). The daughter's rejection of
an 'asshole' answer signifies that she has become a brown (black) girl. The
poem suggests that black racial identity is nothing but a series of questions
regarding origins. The insistent need for this interrogation is what liberal commentators wish to end. But there can be no easy peace. In another poem,
'Love: Heterosexual,' the speaker remembers her lover was 'A man made of
earth' and 'I was coloured earth' (6). But 'Love: Homosexual' sees her conjure
a romantic race consciousness: '[Yvette] kisses / me straight on the mouth
homophobia and all with thick / brown lips and a thick pink tongue. // I
thought that it was through race we were related brown skin / and all but I
couldn't touch her' (7). The speaker's adoration of her would-be lover is all
atmosphere, non-tactile. She had 'thought that by tearing off / her skin I might
find more earth' (7). She finds, though, what she had also found among her
siblings: 'Nothing but / a hot bloody centre' (7) – the same volcano, the same
seething hurt. (This iterated imagery establishes that race colours everything
for the speaker.) But the speaker will not confront this torturous truth: 'The
only way to understand [Yvette] is to love her. To get inside / her. I'll leave it
to a brother' (7). Unable to fathom Yvette's own racial reality, the speaker
posits the phallus of a 'brother' (a word denoting, perhaps, one of the speaker's
own brothers, but also connoting, in slang, any black male) as the only way
'To get inside' Yvette. The thinking here is as sexist as it is self-hating, and
these faults underscore the speaker's agony. 'Love: Heterosexual' is chased by
a poem, whose concerns are the racial markers of 'hair' and the male sex. In
both instances, the speaker refers to her two brothers. One models 'sweet fresh
hair in ringlets' that 'Goes too well with his straight / clamped / lips' (8). In
contrast, the other is *blacker* in every way:

Another the other his brother my brother goes after fat women blonde women all
of them white women. They like his black man charm and the mythical inside of
his pants that his lips promise. Thick and pushy. (9)

The speaker now cycles back to her opening issue: the racial identification of
her family. Its members run the gamut of types: 'Straight clamped lips and a
small white dink and the blackwhite / stripes of mulattoed Zeeebras' (9). *Zebra
Talk*'s final poem is a single typed line, consisting of three sentences, occupying two pages accorded a single page number, 'TEN.' The line reads, 'Mother
chooses not to speak. Does she hear only a stool-pigeon coo from the centre I
try to make her? The centre of what?' (10). The speaker's questioning of her
mother is less confrontational than her address to her father, yet her queries
are fundamentally identical: 'But who is we now?' (5) is not different in kind
from 'The centre of what?' (10). In both cases, the speaker – representative of
the Mulatto generation – seeks to fathom its creation and its meaning. She
fears rejection by a mother who may view her only as stripping away – or
marking with stripes – a dream of racial reconciliation. *Zebra Talk*, with its
surreal imagery, repetitive interrogatives, closed family circle, and evocations
of violence lurking just beneath the surface of love – and skin – dramatizes the
miscommunication that scores black-white discourses.

In her novel *Moon Honey* (1995), Mayr again eyes mixed-race identity – and
dialogues of deafness – in the context of interracial bondings. To do so, she
employs a conceit that fuses the Roman poet Ovid (43 B.C.E.-18 C.E.) with the
American author John Howard Griffin (1920–80): she images a white girl,
Carmen, who metamorphoses into a brown girl. *Moon Honey* reprises a literature of racial transformation. Carmen's white love-interest, Griffin, is an ironic
inversion of John Howard Griffin, whose memoir, *Black Like Me* (1961), treating his experiences as a white man who chemically darkened his skin, shaved
his head, and passed as a black man in the South, sensationalized the just
cause of the Civil Rights Movement in the United States.[19] In *Moon Honey*,
though, it is Carmen who turns black, while Griffin becomes a white voyeur,
lusting after 'exotic' pussy. True: *Moon Honey* emphasizes the magic involved
in altering skin colour, but it also reminds us of the malleableness of racial
identities, for one can be *blackened* or *whitened* into – or out of – them. Canadian scholar Lisette Boily understands that *Moon Honey* 'exposes the notion of
essentialized identity as a papery construction covering the multitude of possible, contextual, and conflicting identities underneath' (165). Mayr's purpose
is, as the epigraph from Ovid suggests, 'to tell of bodies which have been
transformed into shapes of a different kind' (n.pag.). By turning brown, Carmen
is forced to consider her physical alterity, her coloured woman's body. She
ceases to exist as a free-floating, white-identified, unthinkingly racist individual, and connects with the African body and culture she at first disparages
– tellingly – while making love with Griffin beneath the pool table: 'They have
concussive sex in the same room as the wooden inlay picture of three happy
black people, Africans she supposes, with long thin necks, baskets on their

heads, thick red lips and gold hoops in their ears' (1–2). Carmen's use of 'supposes' suggests her denial of any link between blackness and Africanness. For her, black people are only possibly, not really, African. With her 'blackening,' however, Carmen becomes sensitive to the import of racial imagery. When she views a television commercial for Aunt Jemima maple syrup, she 'farts in disgust' (169). She adopts a critical consciousness: 'Aunt Jemima, Uncle Ben, the only black people she sees in the grocery store. Whose Aunt, whose bloody Uncle?' (169). In contrast to how she first perceives the wooden-inlay picture of black people (1–2), she now remembers having 'found a tin plaque in an antique store the other day advertising Piccaninny Freeze ice cream. She used to like antique stores back when she was a white girl, now she walks into antique and collectible stores and all she sees are images of brown people eating watermelons, gobbling fried chicken drumsticks' (169). She is so racially sensitized now that she 'buys the piccaninny plaque because it stabs her in the heart, she wants to weep at the caricature of a naked little black girl trapped on the sheet of tin, her lips thick and red as the watermelon she holds, huge marble eyes, and her skin charcoal black. Carmen wants to take the little girl home with her, protect her, free her' (169). Carmen's sense of identification expands so far as to allow her to notice that, when 'black teenagers [appear] on the TV arrested and hand-cuffed, their heads forced down,' the newscaster says 'something about a "Jamaican posse" in central Alberta' (170). She perceives the racist stupidity animating this supposedly objective claim. She sees the construction, in progress, of crime as a black and foreign plague. Truly, she has developed 'some kind of radar over the past year, her skin sensitive to stereotype' (169).

Prior to her transformation, Carmen is Griffin's 'white gal' – 'Their bones clash rhythmically in the dark, bodies pale and pasted together, a four-legged, two-headed amoeba' (9). Aptly, the agent of Carmen's blackening is her Indo-Canadian boss, Rama. The metamorphosis occurs after Carmen challenges Rama to 'educate me ... Show me where all this racism is, why you're so angry and bitchy all the time. Show me ... [W]e're all the same underneath. Show me the difference. Show me the difference!'(21). Rama obliges, happily:[20]

Three veins in Rama's forehead stretch upward in the shape of a trident. She gives Carmen a *look*, but this time the look pulls apart Carmen's face, peels off Carmen's skin ..., burrows through the layer of subcutaneous fat and splays out her veins and nerves, frayed electrical wires, snaps apart Carmen's muscles and scrapes at Carmen's bones, digs and gouges away Carmen's life.

The colour of Carmen's pink and freckled fingers and forearms deepens, darkens to freckled chocolate brown and beige pink on the palms of her hands. Her hair curls and frizzes, shortens. Hairs dropped into a frying pan kink up around her face, curl into tight balls on the back of her neck. Her skin, covered in a thin layer of dry skin, flakes from where she missed with the skin lotion this morning. Her hair is drier, finer; irises freshly dipped in dark brown cradle her pupils ... Her history is etched out in negative. (22–3)[21]

Significantly, then, Carmen's interaction with Rama is branded, not only by her own racial insensitivity – 'Rama, is a woman, originally from India or somewhere, and so sensitive' (12) – but also by her unvoiced desire for the born-in-Winnipeg Rama, who is, for Carmen, 'the most beautiful woman in the world' (13). The omniscient narrator states that 'Carmen ... has never worked so closely with a coloured person before' (13) and the experience is practically an aphrodisiac: 'Rama even smells different. Spicy or flowery, some strange brown-skin perfume ... Carmen tells Griffin that Rama's skin is like cinnamon, or no, cappuccino. Carmen would like a tan halfway between her own skin colour and Rama's. This would be the perfect colour' (13–14). Apparently, her envy – no doubt, sexual – regarding Rama's pigmentation catalyzes Carmen's yearning for brownness. Thus, Carmen offers two lingering notices of Rama's 'long, shiny fingernail, the inside of her finger pink and the outside dark, coffee-flavoured brown' (16) and of 'her dark brown fingers, her fingernails polished and pinky-brown as sea-shells on a tropical beach' (18). But Rama also possesses the magical 'pigment transforming smell' (14), which, along with her *'look'* (22), serves to darken Carmen's own pigment.[22] Post-metamorphosis, then, Carmen is able to trace Griffin's path through Europe, on a map, with 'her long brown index finger' (60). With her change in colour – or in colour consciousness, Carmen feels herself suddenly to be as lovely as Rama. Once, her stomach would sink in envious dismay whenever Rama approached, her 'long black hair spread fan-like across her shoulders, make-up always dark and perfect' (18). After her change, Carmen finds that 'being a brown girl almost feels like being drunk' (211). By novel's end, she is 'learning to enjoy the taste of the drink, not just an intoxicating cocktail, but an empowering elixir' (212).

Nevertheless, *Moon Honey* is preoccupied with the story of how a once-white woman learns to accept her new, *de facto* 'blackness.' At first, then, Carmen considers herself 'a dark brown ogre, defined by nothing but reflections ... Buried alive in glass' (56). Her self-image improves only when she is able to find and use apt cosmetics, and she becomes 'meticulous with her appearance' (74). But more than cosmetics are needed to prettify Griffin's white-boy attitude toward the Negro Carmen: 'I've never touched black hair, can I touch it? So soft ... Well, you know what they say, says Griffin, as he strokes her black black hair, pushes in her dark brown nipples. Once you sleep with a black, you never go back ... I've always wanted to sleep with a black woman' (26). He even dubs Carmen's skin 'Her *pelt*' (27). Despite Griffin's baroque insensitivity – his callous boorishness and *Playboy* mentality – Carmen still loves him, a fact which seems a betrayal of everything that she learns in the course of the narrative. Her sentimentality is human and real, but also a disconcerting weakness. The novel's terminal line is, thus, anaemic and unconvincing: 'The world is a tidy place' (212). Helpfully, King's observation about the status of the mixed-race woman in slaveholding Cuba may illuminate Carmen's psychology: 'Without property, the mulatto woman could only sell herself as a sex object, led astray by ambition, to be used and discarded by the white man when he was ready for a bride with property and social position' ('Some' 15). Boily judges Mayr's Carmen to resemble 'a living, but compromised version of Bizet's Carmen or the "tragic mulatto" of 19th and early 20th century African American literature' (168).[23] But Mayr's Carmen is neither some stereotypical 'vamp' nor some racially confused albino. Rather, she is the *embodiment* of the question of racial identity.[24]

Mayr's interests are pursued by Mercedes Baines, a Vancouver-based, mixed-race, black woman writer. Her 1997 poem 'Half Baked Zebra Cake,' using inner rhymes, puns, phoneme deconstructions, and pop culture allusions, contests the marginalization of the Mulatto. Baines rejects any link between being a 'half-breed' and being 'half-baked.' Her persona asserts that society views mixed-race blacks as

Not completely cooked
soft on the inside
brown on the outside
Oreo for real
Reverse Doublestuff (132)

She undercuts this vision of presumed Mulatto inadequacy with acerbic humour:

There's a restaurant that sells Zebra Cake
It's a personal favorite
It's very good
    – very moist – very Betty Crocker meets Aunt Jemima in the 90s. I eat it as a
metaphor for devouring myself – kind of a new age mother goddess thing.
I know waiters don't get the joke
perhaps it's really not that funny
as I eat my own derogatory definition with a smile and a chocolate rush. (132)

The stanza shifts between isolated phrases to be savoured in a mouthful – 'It's very good' – and more filling, longer lines. The style accents candidness – or the rhythm of a stand-up comic routine.[25] Despite her sense of humour, Baines is serious about the politics of her self-styling. Her persona understands that the ':mulatto – mule atto / zebra stripes / too light / too dark' is 'really ... an illegal product of two races' (133), or the product of historical violence:

My last name: Baines. A white woman has the same last name.
Says we might be related.
I think: Yeah, your great, great grandfather raped my great,
great grandmother because he owned her.
Not a pleasant thought at a party.
Not very nice thoughts.
I keep it inside – until I feel like puking history on her feet. Then I
just change the subject and
eat more cake. (133)

To assert her right to be, Baines's persona announces, in majuscule letters,

> THE FACE OF THE FUTURE
> GET OVER IT.
> DO WE NEED TO TALK ABOUT IT
> GET OVER IT.
> THE FACE OF THE FUTURE.
> TAKE A LOOK. (133)[26]

She moves from a position of defensiveness to one of, not only opposition to any limiting conception of herself, but one of aggressive proclamation. Her 'LOOK' – really, her colour – will typify 'THE FACE OF THE FUTURE' (133).

This sense of being open to rich possibility, of being a woman who must seek a future free of racial prejudice, marks Baines's 1994 poem 'Brown Child' (dedicated to her mother, Dorise). Its Mother Goose rhythms reinforce the pain of the life sentence that is racism:

> Brown child, mixed child, mulatto child
> Your bloodlines push against each other
> the world will demand you identify with only parts of yourself. (194)

Like Hill and Mayr, Baines raises the issue of whether any primary racial genetic can take precedence over the vitality of the whole being:

> One drop of black blood makes you black
> Octoroon, quadroon, half and half, salt and pepper.
> You cannot carve out parts of yourself
> and put them on top of your dresser
> with your white Barbie and Ken.
> What will your mother say with part of your heart,
> part of your hand bloody on your white dresser?
> Can you cut out your white self?
> Cut out your brown self? (194)

Obviously, this line of questioning would grant unthoughtful Afrocentrists and black cultural nationalists all they would need to expunge Baines from any canon of black literature they care to devise. But Baines defends a holistic definition of her 'zebra' identity by listing body parts of which her persona is consummately more than their sum:

> 'This nose is white, this butt is definitely black, this thick mass of curls nothing
> but black these eyes are white no maybe black no maybe I'm adopted and do not
> belong to either white or black but am a new species.' (194)

This self-assertive prose passage is followed by a stanza that, again in childlike terms, celebrates the persona's mixed-race status:

Warm sun gets your skin closer to your brown self.
Mixed shades of brown/delicious scents and tastes
Honey-warm and sticky
Caramel coated smooth and creamy
Toffee cream
Maple walnut icecream mmmmmmm
Warm sun
Me I'm more like almond sweet and nutty (195)

In this verse, the supposedly 'Tragic Mulatto' is made beautiful. The leaps between lyric and prose-poem elements work toward manifesting bodily and racial satisfaction – or peace – only achieved *via* the terror of self-doubt.

Terror – actual and remembered – motivates Baines's persona. She recalls, in 'Age of Innocence' (1994), that 'I did not always feel this way / I did not always know the reasons for the odd feelings / or the whisperings behind my back or right in my face' (196). However, 'I am no longer in that place. / The brutality of fists and language have raped my mind' (196). The poetic effort to sketch some proud and righteous sense of being is a sharp reaction to incidents of marginalization and exoticization/demonization (those twin engines of terrorism):

I wonder if the bus driver is speaking loudly because she is deaf
or she thinks I don't understand
her tongue lashing between two thin white lips
I wonder if the man talking to me thinks my blackness will wrap
around him and happily fuck out my insatiable sexual
appetite ... or is he just talking to me?
Why do my students ask where I am from
like it is a matter of course I am not from here
an alien in the classroom
If someone calls me exotic one more time
I think I will spit and scream and froth at the mouth ...
then they will really put me away. (197)

Here the 'zebra' poet experiments with a line that hovers between prose and lyric, in a stanza that piles prejudicial incidents pell-mell one atop the other, because there is no difference among these episodes of racism. Fighting back, her persona asks that we acknowledge her 'pain' and 'honor' her 'voice / ... by accepting ... that this is my reality / therefore it is real' (197).

Another Vancouver poet, Wayde Compton, calls himself 'a capital M Mulatto, left-coaster, working class, voodooiste' (8). The son of an African-American father and an European-Canadian mother, Compton revels in his semi-this, semi-that status. His 1996 poem 'Declaration of the Halfrican Nation' indulges in the pleasures of the indefinite, proposing a playful, Mulatto nationalism of the 'Halfrican,' a portmanteau word that sums up – like Baines's food metaphors – the sweetness of half-and-halfness. This wonderful, sprawling free-verse poem executes a dance across consciousness, one that explodes black-and-white definitions:

> hazel's so definitive. is the window
> half open or half closed? is a black
> rose natural? is it indigenous to this
> coast? ... (10)

Opening with a series of interrogatives, the poem fulfils Fanon's 'ultime prière' at the conclusion of *Peau noire, masques blancs*, 'O mon corps, fais de moi toujours un homme qui interroge!' (190). Here the indefinite black-and-white colour – hazel – becomes 'definitive' (10). Compton's persona permits all questions of the Mulatto figure:

> ... one
> friend said she's white except
> for having this brown skin and some–
> times she forgets it until a mirror shatters
> that conclusion casting backward glances side-
> ways, askance processions of belonging, possession. mirrors walk
> on two legs too sometimes, saying hello to you cause
> you are brown
> as we pass ... (10)

The pun on 'pass' is intentional and radical, for it suggests that brown skin allows for a reverse passing – as black, rather than white – even if, as in the case of the persona's friend, the psyche sometimes conceives of its bodily identity as white. As the poem continues, it nicely occupies and displaces the blackest declaration of African-American Africanness written in the twentieth century, namely, Countee Cullen's celebrated, Harlem Renaissance–era poem 'Heritage' (1926). Cullen's poem inquires, memorably,

> *Once three centuries removed*
> *From the scenes his father loved,*
> *Spicy grove, cinnamon tree,*
> *What is Africa to me?* (ll. 7–10)

Compton's version of these lines foregrounds his African *and* British heritages:

> ... what is britannia
> to me? one three continents removed
> from the scenes my mothers loved,
> misty grove, english rose,
> what is britannia to me? (10)

The rewriting is audacious, to say the least, but Compton still has other targets. Thus, he riffs on Fanon's *Black Skin, White Masks* (1965), noting that, due to snow, blacks in Canada are 'black goths with white masks *literally*' (10). Later, his persona comments, 'sometimes I feel like frantz fanon's ghost / is kickin back with a coke and rum having / a good chuckle at all this, stirring in the tears, his work / done, lounging with the spirits' (11). The tone is light, irreverent, even though the persona sometimes feels 'like history got me / by the throat' (11). The poem seeks to establish the reality of the *in-between*:

> ... the best way
> anyone ever referred to me as mixed-race was a jamaican
> woman who said, *I notice you're touched.* to
> me sounded like she meant by the hand of god
> (or the god of hands), and not the tar brush. made me
> feel like a motherless child a long, long way
> from my home ... (11)

The conversational, deliberately informal, style stresses the speaker's sense that his status, because it is open to question, is richly, rewardingly, *open*. The poem's finale makes this point sardonically:

> ... oh, all
> my fellow mixed sisters and brothers let us mount
> an offensive for our state. surely something
> can be put together from the tracts, manifestoes, auto-
> biographies, ten point programs, constitutions, and historical
> claims. I know more than enough who've ex-
> pressed an interest in dying on the wire just for the victory
> of being an agreed-upon proper noun (11)

The poem concludes, naturally, without a stop, that is to say, a period, for the 'Halfrican Nation' can only ever be declared in the poem; its existence is yet to be. Like Mayr and Baines, Compton elects to accept his dual heritage, to struggle for a sense of unity – with other brown folks and black folks – and never to 'diss' or dissolve what he calls in another poem 'the cabal / that is *négritude*' ('JD' 18). In a prose piece titled 'Diamond,' Compton's persona presents brownness as the *sign* of a struggle for racial justice:

> All my friends when I was a kid were mixed like me. Our parents were interracial couples, as they say, and us Civil Rights babies, I guess ... It was still freaky as hell in the early seventies, I imagine, to see a black man and a white woman pushing a pram with a nappy-headed kid flaunting its golden skin to the world. Brazen. (136)

Yes, to be bronze is to be 'Brazen' – is to be an 'Unbroken Yellow' (164), an identity visible only in a mirror.[27]

In the end, these Western Canadian black Métis – Mayr, Baines, Compton[28] – unsettle, like Hill, any easy assertions of a homogeneous African-Canadian identity. In making their deviously deviant art, they call for exactly what African-American poet Jean Toomer (1894–1967) demands in his poem 'The Blue Meridian' (1932, 1970), the realization of a non-racist and non-racialized 'new America / To be spiritualized by each new American' (50). Mayr, Baines, Compton, and Hill dream this progressive vision for Canada. With their voices, these brown Negroes repudiate the perilous notion of a univocal aesthetics of blackness. They uphold the defiant identity espoused by the mother of Lorena Gale – a Montréal-born, Vancouver playwright of African, First Nations, and South Asian heritage:

> 'Keep reaching for the stars and you'll have the universe. We are coloured. And though your skin will seem like a weight around your body, don't let anybody tell you that you aren't beautiful and good. You are the future. You have a right to the future. Don't let anyone take that away from you.' (54)

This literal, *motherhood* statement should brace all black writers – of black, brown, and beige persuasions – to refute the psychological and socio-political violences that are supposedly the province of the rainbow-gorgeously coloured multitudes encompassed by *our* stigmatized *black* minority. Hear here: the only real intolerance is the demand for oneness coupled with the demand for sameness.

While African-Canadian mixed-race writers have challenged puerile categorizations of their complex *selves*, the first major African-Canadian novelist, Austin Clarke, has attacked negative considerations of black racial identity in English-Canadian society for almost five decades. His work requires consideration, for Clarke has chosen to employ one English-Canadian political ideology – namely, Red Toryism – to critique European-Canadian racism. The results are provocative ...

Notes

1 This essay was first presented at the 'Poetic Subjectivity' conference held at the University of South Carolina, in Columbia, South Carolina, on 9 April 1999. I thank African-Canadian poet and scholar Kwame Dawes for having invited my participation. I dedicate this essay to Walter M. Borden, actor, poet, and playwright, who also happens to be a mixed-race, soulfully *black*, Africadian intellectual.

2 Michelle M. Wright asserts that 'although some Southern states actually compiled a series of intricate laws determining whether or not a person was black or white based on intermixture, even those individuals with 1/64 of black blood were still viewed as inferior by society, despite what the law would have allowed' (851n23).

3 An example of this desire in African-American literature is incarnated by Clare Kendry, the protagonist of Nella Larsen's Harlem Renaissance–era novel *Passing* (1929). In the novel, the light-skinned Kendry is married to 'a successful white businessman, who not only believes she is white but deeply dislikes black people' (Frances Foster, 'Passing' 560). Though Kendry soon undertakes a fervent intercourse with other blacks, even engaging in adultery, her life had been, once, a flight away from any black identity.

4 These feelings are bluesily articulated in 'Cross' (1926), a poem by Langston Hughes (1902–67): 'My [white] old man died in a fine big house. / My [black] ma died in a shack. / I wonder where I'm gonna die, / Being neither white nor black?' (62). The speaker bears the cross of a cross-breeding that has left him feeling cross (and double-crossed). These themes also mark Hughes's two-act tragedy *Mulatto* (1935), which treats 'the psychological consequences of miscegenation from the black perspective' (Barksdale 196).

5 American historian Joel Williamson insists that 'the Negro leadership [in the United States] included blacks and mulattoes' (xiv). 'Because the great majority of American Negroes are in fact of mixed ancestry, and because mulattoes and pure blacks came ultimately to fuse their cultural heritages, what begins in the colonial period as mulatto history and culture ends in the twentieth century as Negro history and culture' (xii).

6 Johanna L. Grimes-Williams holds that 'the tragic mulatto is one of the earliest individual character types to appear in African-American literature' (128). She or he is 'physically indistinguishable from whites and often grows up believing that she or he is white. Yet there is an African ancestry, sometimes identified as "a drop of African blood," and upon having such heritage revealed this character is identified as black and treated accordingly' (128). 'These mulatto characters are "tragic" because their racial identification results in personality disintegration and even death' (128).

7 Lola Young challenges Fanon's readings of black women's writings, positing that, in his work, the black woman 'serves as the other of others without sufficient status to have an other of her own' (100).

8 The term *mulatto*, which descends from the Spanish word *mulato* denoting a young mule (Sykes 664), is 'a patently offensive term,' or so argues African-Canadian writer and journalist Charles Saunders ('Mulatto' 32). He states that it 'derives from the beginning of African slavery in the Western Hemisphere, when early Spanish and Portuguese colonists believed that blacks were not human, and the offspring of whites and blacks would be "mulattos" – little mules' (32). Hence, 'the term remains an insult within the context of its modern usage' (32). While I am sympathetic to Saunders's sense of the incurable negativity of *mulatto*, I use it within this essay as a pithy means of identifying persons of black-white admixture (of whatever percentage). Scholar Norman Whitten reports that, in Latin America, '"Mulatto" often signifies "free black" as well as "lightened black"'; but it can also mean '"darkened white," or just plain "darkened"' (258). However, my use of the word is coloured, I hope, by Indo-Scottish-Canadian critic Aruna Srivastava's perceptions that 'race doesn't actually exist ..., [while] knowing equally well,

profoundly, that racism does exist. It does. And that to be mixed-race is to feel it differently' (4). Adjectives like 'mixed-race / mixedblood / halfbreed / mestiza / hybrid / hyphenated' (Srivastava 4) fail to define the feeling. Even *Creole*, a word which can denote 'people of both African and European descent, as well as their racially mixed offspring' (Bennett 528), in Latin America and the Caribbean, is limited. Rarely sounded in Canada, in the United States, it denotes 'almost exclusively' the French-oriented blacks of New Orleans (Bennett 528). The encyclopedia of terms for New World Africans – 'black, negro, mulatto, *negro, zambo, moreno, trigueno, mulato, pardo, negre, preto, cafuso, noire, nengre* – or *libre* (free) ...' (Whitten 258) – as well as other terms specifying degrees of blackness – 'quadroon,' 'octoroon,' 'griffe,' 'sambo,' 'sacatra,' 'mango,' 'mustees,' and 'mestizo' (Williamson xii–xiii), or the dizzying array of terms defined in Guyanese-Canadian writer Bernard Heydorn's 1998 memoir *Longtime Days* (23–4) – is just archaic, anarchic poetastry. The word *miscegenation* is also an invention. It was 'coined by two Democrats in the presidential election campaign of 1864 in an attempt to embarrass and discredit the Republican incumbent running for reelection, Abraham Lincoln' (Newman 1320).

9 In Latin America and the Caribbean, the figure of the Mulatto embodies the war between black consciousness and 'another master symbol of ideology: *blanqueamiento* – somatic, cultural, or ethnic lightening to become increasingly acceptable to those classified and self-identified as "white"' (Whitten 258). This aspiration accepts, perniciously, 'the implicit hegemonic rhetoric of the United States with regard to "white supremacy"' (Whitten 258). 'So strong is antiblack sentiment in Latin America,' contends scholar John Burdick, 'that for much of the region's history, those toward the lighter end of the color spectrum have sought to "bleach" blacks right out of existence ["through amalgamation"]' (1374). Only recently has 'an entire generation of mulattos ... become activists in black consciousness movements' (Burdick 1376). Thomas Skidmore believes that 'whitening is now a kind of contraband idea surviving in popular thought ...' (1992).

10 James's position is rooted in fact. Burdick affirms that 'during every major [Latin American and Caribbean] slave revolt of the nineteenth century mulattos sided with the whites' (1375). Equally important is the truth that 'the planters were haunted by the specter ... of a mulatto-led slave revolution' (Burdick 1375). My difficulty with James's analysis is that he casts practically *all* Mulattoes as sociopolitically regressive, given their in-between 'race' *and* class status. A trace of this attitude shows up in Haitian-Canadian writer Gérard Étienne's deft portrayal of a 'negro' Haitian man, Ben Chalom, who succeeds in seducing a 'mulatto woman,' Guilène, 'the middle-class lady' (121), in chapter 11 of *La Pacotille* (1991). Ben's feelings for Guilène compound lust and revenge. He dreams that, by bedding Guilène, he will achieve 'a victory for the people,' that is to say, 'dirty negroes segregated by dirty mulattoes. Who make it known to the civilized world that a negro cannot straddle the belly of a mulatto woman' (122). Triumphant, he will celebrate 'the exploit of a lone little negro man who has succeeded in eating the ass of a mulatto woman' (122). Ben's love-hate stance toward Guilène is well-nigh Jamesian.

11 The sentiments of Dorsinville's narrator not only parrot those of 'race' men like Marcus Garvey. They are also reminiscent of the Martiniquais author René Maran (1887–1960), whose seminal 'African' novel, *Batouala* (1921), registers this observation:

> Didn't [white colonialists] abandon the children they had by black women? Knowing themselves sons of whites, when these children grew up they wouldn't stoop to associate with negroes. And these white-blacks, good 'boundjou-voukous' that they were, lived a life apart, full of hatred, burning with envy, detested by all, riddled with faults, spiteful and lazy. (76)

In Africa, too, the Mulatto bears a Cain-like brand.

12 This version of *Clotelle* is the third of four published after the original 1854 appearance in 1854 of Brown's *Clotel; or, The President's Daughter*.

13 Codjoe's insight buttresses J. Lorand Matory's contention that 'in the daily lives of most Africans, blackness constitutes neither a barrier nor an admission pass to any particular social rights, and it signals no salient political or cultural identity' (39).

14 Hearne's protagonist states that these unions produced '*douglahs*: big, heavy-boned hybrids with skins the texture and colour of the icing on a chocolate cake, vivid, troubling faces, and coarse, straight hair like the manes of black horses' (86). A female *douglah* character is sexualized so that 'she have enough black in her to give the leg shape and make the breasts stand out strong' (76).

15 Part II of the Constitution Act, 1982, treating the 'Rights of the Aboriginal Peoples of Canada,' establishes in 35.(2) that 'in this Act, "aboriginal peoples of Canada" includes the Indian, Inuit, and Metis peoples of Canada.'

16 Hill's protagonist, Langston Cane V, echoes the unnamed protagonist of *Invisible Man* (1952), the nightmarish novel by African-American writer Ralph Ellison (1914–94). The major difference between them is that Cane V is not seen – often – as black, while the 'invisible man' is a black whose presence – whose existence – is not recognized by whites: 'I am an invisible man. No, I am not a spook like those who haunted Edgar Allan Poe ... I am invisible, understand, simply because people refuse to see me' (3). Cane V's chameleon-like race identity is his 'distinction'; the 'invisible man' is distinguished by his feeling the 'need to convince yourself that you do exist in the real world' (Ellison 4).

17 Cane V is reminiscent of Mahatma Grafton, the light-skinned black hero of Hill's first novel, *Some Great Thing* (1992), who passes, briefly, for Pakistani.

18 Sociologist Jennifer Kelly, in her study of Black Canadian students in a Western Canadian city, reports that 'there is no real geographic concentration of African Canadians in Edmonton. For the most part, the population is interspersed within mixed neighbourhoods' (96). This point applies to all black urban populations on the Canadian Prairies and West Coast.

19 In *Black Like Me*, Griffin records that 'I decided not to change my name or identity. I would merely change my pigmentation and allow people to draw their own conclusions' (5). In contrast, Carmen's *blackening* is the result of a change in racial consciousness. Yet, *Moon Honey* establishes, like *Black Like Me*, that race shades identity in racialized, hierachical societies. Carmen never asks explicitly the same

question as Griffin: 'Do you suppose [whites] 'll treat me as [myself], regardless of my color – or will they treat me as some nameless Negro, even though I am still the same man?' (5). She receives, though, the same answer: 'As soon as they see you, you'll be a Negro and that's all they'll ever want to know about you' (5).

20 Boily's reading of the episode of Carmen's transformation emphasizes her psychological change: 'Carmen ... strips herself of her false whiteness after playing the racist pseudo-liberal boor so well that the mask cracks ... Rama ... is the only one able to perceive the cracked mask' (167).

21 Carmen's metamorphosis recalls a similar passage in Griffin's *Black Like Me*, where, following his successful darkening of his skin so that he can 'pass' as black, he looks in a mirror and spies 'a fierce, bald, very dark Negro':

> The transformation was total and shocking ... I was imprisoned in the flesh of an utter stranger, an unsympathetic one with whom I felt no kinship. All traces of the John Griffin I had been were wiped from existence ... I looked into the mirror and saw reflected nothing of the white John Griffin's past. No, the reflection led back to Africa, back to the shanty and the ghetto, back to the fruitless struggles against the mark of blackness. (11)

Here is another instance of Mayr's 'history ... etched out in negative' (23).

22 The character of Rama represents the execution of another bold unorthodoxy by Mayr, for, in Hindu scripture, Rama is male, a stunningly handsome prince. Moreover, the epic of his adventures, the *Ramayana* (ca. 500 B.C.) exalts 'the ideals of manly devotion to truth' (quoted in Yutang 137–8). In *Moon Honey*, Rama practises a 'womanly' fidelity.

23 The opera *Carmen* (1875) employs, suggests Hugh MacDonald, a tragic figure who blends 'sultry sensuality and fatal bravado' (19). Mayr's Carmen is, at most, tragicomic (she is contemplating a return to Griffin at novel's end), but she is no *femme fatale* who exhibits fatalism. She resembles the operatic heroine of French librettists Henri Meilhac and Ludovic Halévy and French composer Georges Bizet (1838–75) in one way: she is 'always on the margins of life' (quoted in Hutcheon and Hutcheon 191).

24 Mayr continues to explore the peripheries of racial, cultural, and gender belonging. Her second novel, *The Widows* (1998), includes no black characters. The narrative deals with three white German-Canadian women, all sisters.

25 Baines's style supports the wisdom of a passage from Aldon Nielsen's *Black Chant* (1997): '"There should be, of course, a way of speaking about all kinds of Black poetry ...," according to Stephen Henderson. Such a way must be intertextual and polyglot if it is to address itself to what the narrator of Clarence Major's novel *No* describes as "Creolized language, trade language, contact vernacular, *our* thing"' (30).

26 The word 'LOOK' emphasizes the racial politics of the gaze. In *Moon Honey*, it is Rama's *look* that helps a white-identified Carmen to discover her black-brown self. In *Any Known Blood*, Cane V is every ethnicity under the sun to the whites who gaze upon him; it is by researching his family history that he learns to embrace his black heritage. In Baines's poem, her persona mandates that readers – black and white – *see* her difference. Her insistence mirrors the passion of the nameless

protagonist in Ellison's *Invisible Man*, who also craves to be *seen*, recognized, accepted.

27 This poem, printed in reverse, must be placed before a mirror to be read. Its words describe a flame, but also, allegorically, a mixed-race sensibility.

28 Other mixed-race Western Canadian writers who foreground *brownness* include the British-born, Alberta-raised poet Dawn Carter; Alberta poet Ian Samuels (b. 1975); ex-Victoria poet Shane Book (who describes his lineage as 'African-Irish-Chinese-American-Spanish-German-CaribIndian-Canadian-Venezuelan-Scottish-Trinidadian' and his racial category as 'Unsure' [41]); and Vancouver poets Janisse Browning (who hails from southern Ontario) and Andrea Thompson (who has recently relocated to Toronto).

Clarke versus Clarke: Tory Elitism in Austin Clarke's Short Fiction

For Austin Clarke (1934–)[1]

Perusing Austin Chesterfield Clarke's short stories, one catches, now and then, the distinctive odour of the entertaining *and* tawdry James Bond spy adventures authored by British writer Ian Fleming (1908–64). Too, both authors stud their pages with references to pricey autos and shapely women. (Or should that be shapely automobiles and pricey women?) Then there is their mutual attentiveness to high-stakes card games and horse races. (Clarke works *both* species of gambling into his short story 'Give It a Shot' [1987].) Conceivably, if Fleming were still alive, he would make an apt partner for Clarke in one of those racially two-toned, 'buddy' films that Hollywood insists we must have. Think of Fleming, with his tux, Roosevelt-style cigarette holder, and priceless presidential endorsement (from suave J.F.K.), and then think of Clarke, with his (occasional) pinstripes, pipe, and Errol Barrow–style, prime ministerial poise. Perhaps the resemblance has something to do with both writers having a fondness for splendor – and *fascinante* women. Assuredly, Fleming's Bond is constantly sizing up the 'merchandise' in *Moonraker* (1955):

> As she bent over the table her black skirt brushed Bond's arm and he looked up into two pert, sparkling eyes, under a soft fringe of hair ... then she whisked away. Bond's eyes followed the white bow at her waist and the starched collar and cuffs of her uniform as she went down the long room ... He recalled a pre-war establishment in Paris where the girls were dressed with the same exciting severity. (38–9)

In Clarke's 'How He Does It' (1986), the ogling is explicitly commercial:

> ... when the door open, Jesus Christ! the most prettiest, the most best-dress, the most sexiest, the most beautiful Jewish woman from outta Israel and Judea ... was standing up, full in the door, full in the breasts, full in the hips, solid as the best securities in the stock market down Bay Street, and on the loveliest pairs o' legs these two eyes o' mine have ever had the pleasant pleasure tainted with lust to rest on. (217)

Fine loving requires, irreducibly, fine living. Fleming provides, obligingly enough, this gourmet detail:

Bond helped himself to another slice of smoked salmon from the silver dish beside him. It had the delicate glutinous texture only achieved by Highland curers –
very different from the dessicated products of Scandinavia. He rolled a wafer-thin
slice of brown bread-and-butter into a cylinder and contemplated it thoroughly ...
He stirred the champagne with a scrap of toast ... (39–41)

And Clarke models this sartorial moment in 'A Man' (1986):

He was dressed as if he was going to a wedding ..., tall in a long black woollen
winter coat, three-piece-suit usually of dark brown and worsted, and made with a
hint of London's fashion and cut ... and he would climb into the long, expensive
luxury car after flipping back the tails of his winter coat to avoid sitting on them
on the seat. (120).

A mail-order catalogue of the wares retailed in Clarke's *récits* would include,
for starters, a subscription to the *Globe & Mail* (the *haute couture* Toronto daily),
meerschaum pipes, black leather attaché cases, Bally shoes and slippers (also
black), Dom Perignon champagne (Bond sips it too), pinstripe suits (dark blue),
Chanel Number 17, Oxford shoes, Turkish tobacco, dry martinis (another Bond
favourite), Mario Palomino Jamaican cigars, Martini & Rossi vermouth *secco*,
Bombay Gin, and lubricated condoms. These are the rewards of Clarke's *bourgeois* heaven. Fleming's Bond can purchase such items readily (given his government salary, his consummate skill at cards, and his white male privilege),
but Clarke's black immigrant characters are either would-be or used-to-be
aristocrats. Their access to the status symbols of the (WASP) Canadian Establishment is frustrated by a polite, tight, *white-iste* caste system. Occasionally,
they earn their way to the good life (at high personal cost); usually, they lie or
cheat to advance; frequently, they fail, becoming addicts or suicides. In spite
of such social(ist) realism, Clarke launches few polemical assaults on racism.
His writings are not anti-white (though white women attract venom). Rather,
like Fleming, Clarke nudges us toward accepting conservative notions of social class implicit in the admiration of state spectacle and market commodities.
Hence, Clarke's protagonists pursue fine liquors, luxurious habiliments, prized
tobaccos, and envy-spurring accessories (including mates and lovers). Although
their failures (or compromised successes) suggest a critique of racism, their
narratives preserve the *main* determinant of social stratification: class. Clarke
has read his Marx and Fanon (and Fleming?) only as a means of finding a
fresh route into *Burke's Peerage*.

I

Born in Barbados in 1934, Clarke has lived, since 1955, in Canada, where his
first novel, *Survivors of the Crossing*, appeared in 1964. Despite assertions to the
contrary, he was neither the first nor the second African-Canadian novelist,
but the *sixth*, though he was the first to publish a novel *in* Canada.[2] Known
principally for his novels, Clarke has published five collections of short stories,

from his first – and best – collection, *When He Was Free and Young and He Used to Wear Silks* (1971), to his most recent, *There Are No Elders* (1993).[3] The *nouvelles* articulate, against Caribbean and metropolitan Toronto backdrops, yearnings for independence, cultural assertion, masculine agency, and élite acceptance. Though Clarke's black protagonists produce stolid broadsides against empire, nostalgic paeans to lost Island paradises, romantic poems of cultural pride, and wry deconstructions of icy Canadian racism, they are, for all that, defrocked gentry, anxious to assume classy places in Canada's ruling class. Impeccably educated, often of Brahmin backgrounds, they do not emigrate to Canada to become peons or to serve as slaves. Problematically, though, as Clarke posits in his Introduction to *Nine Men Who Laughed* (1986), 'immigrant life' is tantamount to 'slavery' (7). Tragedy – or Juvenalian satire – in Clarke's *oeuvre* requires, then, not the mere event of racism, but rather the bracing plunge into a lower standard of living. This fact explains the curious repetition of a striking *ur*-moment in two of Clarke's texts. In 'If Only: Only If ...,' a 1986 story set in mid-1950s Toronto, the narrator lists the range of stereotypical jobs then open to black men: railway porter, 'a janitor somewhere,' or 'a man who does handout towels in washrooms down Yonge Stree [*sic*], in bars and clubs that don't let-in no black or coloured or Negro men' (100). Six years later, Clarke opened his essay *Public Enemies: Police Violence and Black Youth* (1992) with a like remembrance of Original, Socio-Economic Sin:

> How should I react to the man, ... dressed in a white butler's jacket and black trousers ..., and in the shine of whose shoes I could see, if I had been so disposed, my disappointment and embarrassment? This man, in this sparkling men's room, its four walls of polished white, squared tiles, dwarfed by two white porcelain urinals. In his silent blackness, this man, with a skin polished high as the marble, standing with an ironic dignity handing out white towels to *me* ... (1)

Clarke is moved to confession in this moment of, to employ a phrase from Richard Sieburth, 'uncharacteristic autobiographical explicitness' (53): 'I disappeared before he could extend his hand. I disappeared in order to obliterate the man, his status and his memory from touching and *tainting my status*' (*Public* 1, my italics). Clarke feels such disdain that, though he shares the same colour as the washroom attendant, the latter's abjection renders him an Untouchable. Though Clarke tried to 'obliterate' the man, his spectre haunts characters and narrators who are, with their champagne tastes and beer budgets, the most pronouncedly class conscious of any in Canadian fiction (save for Mordecai Richler's Duddy Kravitz and Dany Laferrière's Vieux). Clarke's *comédiens* are Lears. Though Clarke later embraces the totem of the washroom attendant as his link to the indigenous African-Canadian past, this too-visible man personifies *Failure*.

Perceptively, Clarke's short fiction delineates a Neo-Darwinian struggle in which the geographically displaced become class-misplaced, regardless of their ability, their training, their morality, their pedigree. Whatever their current shabby, shoddy, even, yes, shitty positions here, his protagonists, at home, enjoyed 'aristocratic status' (Introduction 1).[4] In 'They Heard A-Ringing of Bells' (1971), for instance, Sagaboy, stricken with tuberculosis, remembers that, at home, he had dreamt of being *the governor o' the whole blasted West Indies'* (29). In 'If the Bough Breaks' (1993), Caribbean women in a Toronto beauty parlour exclaim, 'Back home, we'd be ruling the roost. We'd be women with men and husbands that make decisions and run things' (22). Enid, the heroine of 'Waiting for the Postman to Knock' (1971), relates the degradation that immigration has wrought:

> I came into this country as a decent middle-class person in Barbados ... [I]t is only in Canada that I am known as a labourer, or a working woman, ... because back home I never lifted a straw in the way of work, for my parents were rich people. We had servants back home. (32)

Now in Canada, Enid awaits eviction from her barren apartment, her hydro and telephone service have been disconnected, and her landlord and creditors harry her relentlessly. Enid's mother declares that, had Enid remained in Barbados, she would be 'a high school mistress, or a doctor or a lawyer, anything but being in that cold, ungodly place, Canada, working for white people and servanting after people who don't know how to treat you as a human being' (37). This theme returns in a Lord Chesterfield–like, advice-to-my-son-abroad, epistolary fiction, 'Letter of the Law of Black' (1992), in which a father, Anthony Barrington St Omer Edgehill, advises his son, now resident in Canada, that 'the colonial is the fact that transcends blackness' (59). His son's colonial roots will permit him to evade the racism of Canadian life. For one thing, he descends from superior stock – and a proven culture.

According to Clarke, it is immigration, that is to say, a precipitous, economic decline, that creates a negative blackness. The apartheid of immigration, its relegation of vast classes of people to poor-paying jobs or no jobs, fosters the postlapsarian 'slave.' Clarke states explicitly, then, that 'the men [in *Nine Men Who Laughed*] are black only because they live in Toronto, in a society which has officially branded them "immigrants" from the West Indies' (Introduction 7). Clearly, Clarke has studied his Fanon, perhaps *Peau noire, masques blancs* (1952), where Fanon theorizes that 'le Noir n'a plus à être noir, mais à l'être en face du Blanc' (90) and that 'le nègre infériorisé va de l'insécurité humiliante à l'auto-accusation ressentie jusqu'au désespoir' (50). The effect of the Manichean division between black and white is to rigidify class categories. Thus, 'on est blanc comme on est riche, comme on est beau, comme on est intelligente' (Fanon, *Peau* 43); blackness is the infernal inverse. One is not born 'black'; blackness is a socio-economic hell into which one is plunged. Hence, the 'I' in Clarke's polemical *cri de coeur, Public Enemies*, is, simultaneously, 'slave, Negro, coloured, black, colonized' (15). Asking rhetorically, 'How long are we to remain immigrants?' (*Public* 19), Clarke demands, in effect, how long are we to remain black, to remain slaves? In *'Black Man in a White Land'* (1967),[5] a frustrating, frank, reckless pamphlet, Clarke, using the pseudonym Ali Kamal Al Kadir Sudan, proposes that 'the black man in a white society is a minority – subhuman' (4–5). Likewise, in 'Letter,' Edgehill instructs his son in how to subvert negative constructs of blackness:

> But if you are seen ... reading Pushkin ..., *they* will say you are an intellectual. Even if they call you a colonial intellectual, as they have a habit of doing, such as black writer, a black artist, or black doctor, it would be different. You would, by this intelligence, be more dangerous to them, and *they* would not be able to despise, or worse still, ignore your presence, and call you a visible minority. (60)

Thus, blackness is fluid, and can be applied – like paint – to anyone who lapses in class and morality. Clarke affirms the unreality of constructed blackness when he unveils his desire 'to discover something which a former black student at Yale University called a "black aesthetic," a black way of seeing black things, a blackening of the consciousness' (Introduction 6). This blackening denotes a sardonic trope. Any group can be or become black – that is to say, low-class or no-class. Hence, the father in 'Letter' warns his son, 'Beware of the lower classes of all races. They spit on you because they grew up spitting on the ground' (61). Likewise, in 'If the Bough Breaks,' one of the women emphasizes the class jealousy that Euro-Canadians project toward their immigrant equals and superiors. When she and her husband buy a new car, she reports, the neighbours stare '"from behind their curtains. We shouldn't have those things. We shouldn't live the way *they* live. We shouldn't"' (20). In the same story, a woman remembers calling an uppity, white security guard a '"nigger-man"' ('If' 13). Whiteness is, then, an unstable *sign*. Clarke – playing Ali – comments, for instance, that 'the black West Indian has been educated by colonialism to think of himself as *a white man*; in more fortunate cases as a black Englishman, or a black Frenchman, or a black Dutchman' (*Black* 8, my italics). White racists presume, wrongly, that *race* ordains excellence (or *not*), but, as Clarke insists, class and heritage determine that quality: 'cultural ancestry is a greater force than ... colour or the branded status of "immigrant"' (Introduction 7). With this thesis, Clarke is equipped to defend class privilege, even as he indicts the operations of racism. Nevertheless, his apology for classism necessitates a repetition of caste-supporting, sexist, white-fostered images of beauty and success.

II

Jean Baudrillard theorizes in *Seduction* (1979, 1990) that 'the strength of the feminine is that of seduction' (7) and that the secret of this irresistible power is its presentation of an alluring absence, or blankness, whose indeterminacy annihilates masculine attempts at definition. Seduction, 'by producing only illusions, obtains all powers' (70). Crucially, Baudrillard aligns this alluring absence with a cinematic whiteness, 'the spectral whiteness of the heavenly stars, after which they [film stars] are so appropriately named' (96). In his short fiction, Clarke agrees, tacitly, with Baudrillard: women, whiteness, and, hence, white women symbolize attractive, glistening surfaces that can entrap and destroy the unwary,[6] meaning, for Clarke, black male immigrants. Thus, Clarke considers the psychological threat posed to self-conscious blackness by the omnipresence of white-supremacist imagery in North American society. Speaking as Ali in 1967, he asserts, 'Because of the contemporary idiosyncrasy of white advertising media, I do not think the white man understands the dignity of the human body as an object of love' (*Black* 6). The pervasiveness of this spectacular whiteness ensures that 'the black man's future in a white society will always be in terms of white society's schizophrenia about blacks' (*Black* 4). Pursuing this argument, Clarke creates protagonists who view white women as symbols of Canada – that is to say, of a vamp who entices 'her' thralls with phony promises of *bourgeois* comfort.[7] Whore-like, the Canadian 'system' encourages 'laughter and seduces the "immigrant"' (Introduction 5). This sexed perception is accented by Clarke's metonymization of Canada as 'this *fucking* system' (Introduction 5, my italics) and by his autobiographical recollection of a female exemplum of white racism. Damnably, she is 'the *person* who confronted me with her prepossessiveness, the woman, the system ... now a microcosm of all the words, bad conclusions and faulty definitions of "immigrant" and ... a metaphor for arrogance' (Introduction 3). He upholds his conflation of *woman* and *system* in the next paragraph: 'She, the attitude, the system, knew my meaning' (Introduction 3).

The Canada-as-white-whore metaphor recurs, then, throughout Clarke's *oeuvre*. In 'Canadian Experience' (1986), the unemployed protagonist, George, a high-school-educated Barbadian immigrant, about to be dislodged from his abysmal room for non-payment of rent, is succoured by a sometime, white actress who shares the same grimy building. Hearing the woman take her shower, George imagines 'the red-faced ugly blackheads painted red at the bottom of the spine' (38), an obvious red-and-white symbol of Canada (given that the blemishes are scarlet *cold* sores). Suitably, she is, *de temps en temps*, a prostitute, for following her shower, she states that she has washed herself 'clean' to attend 'an audition in an hour': 'You never know what directors're going to ask you to do' (39). This cheerless passage ends with the actress, wrapping a towel about herself, but leaving 'the two small nipples of her dropped breasts' bare to 'his undesiring eyes' (40). He resists this temptation, but there is no escape from predatory whiteness. Hence, in contemplating applying for a job in a ritzy bank, George is frightened away by the 'blue eyes ... like ice-water' of a female employee (43). Ashamed of his failure to find work, haunted by his alienation from paradisal Barbados ('where he was born in a smiling field of comfortable pasture land' [47]), the immigrant commits suicide by leaping in front of a subway train. Naturally, the train's 'ugly red' colour recalls the actress's 'red-corpuscle sores' (50–1).

In 'The Motor Car' (1971), Calvin, the protagonist, objectifies the requisite white woman as 'this Canadian thing' (102). She is 'this blasted white woman humbugging him about sex' (103). As Calvin scrimps and saves to buy a Ford Galaxie automobile, so does he plan to acquire the 'Canadian thing' as the perfect accessory for the vehicle. Eventually he succeeds, but, during his triumphant spin, the woman continues, though he has commanded her to stop, to sing along with a calypso playing over the car radio. Thinking angrily to himself, 'Well, who tell she she could talk back to Bajan man like Calvin?' (109), Calvin brakes abruptly, thereby pitching, fatally, the seatbelt-less woman against the windshield. Notably, this killing results after the folksy, omniscient narrator discusses Canadian economic imperialism in Barbados, stating 'they was more *Air Canada* planes all bout Seawell Airport in Barbados in them days that you would have think that Barbados did own *Air Canada*' (95). In truth, it is 'the other way round' (95). Calvin's assault on 'this Canadian thing' is metaphorical revenge for Canada's raping and pillaging of Barbados.

In 'Not So Old, but Oh So Professional' (1993), Max, a bachelor and Caribbean immigrant, who spends his nights shyly ogling a young prostitute, Linda Pearl Mason, accepts her proposal that she visit his downtown Toronto home. As her middle name suggests, Linda's skin exudes 'a porcelain white sheen' (82). After spending a lyrical evening conversing and drinking, in a kind of casual symposium, Max becomes aroused when Linda passes her fingers through her hair:

> She was not caressing herself the way I have seen some women pass their hands over their breasts, squeezing the nipples a little to stimulate them and the eyes of the man watching; or how I have seen some women pass their hands over their thighs, slowly, slowly, rubbing faster and then faster still, and slapping them; or even as I have seen some women pass their fingers through their pubic hair to their vaginas, even opening the lips, and doing little stimulating, destroying things to a man's balance ... She was just drawing her hands through her hair, a natural function, and that naturalness made it more enticing and betraying and seducing. (97)

Max's voyeuristic, pornographic pleasure (or self-seduction) in watching Linda and his resultant, destabilizing *aporia* mirrors the vertigo that a too-prolonged gazing upon a provocative Canada also induces. (The 'system' also does 'little stimulating, destroying things' to Afro-Caribbean immigrants.) Max climaxes under the ministrations of the 'pearly' white Linda while nostalgic dreams of his Island past fill his mind. But, this setting is callous Toronto. And Linda's cash-driven response to his orgasm returns Max sharply to the mean, capitalist world: 'Now you owe me, motherfucker!' (101) Linda is as cold as the glass-sheathed skyscrapers of Bay Street. Clarke's tale allegorizes the Caribbean male's morbid mating dance with the 'albino' widow spider of Canada. For this reason, Linda's siren-like whiteness receives photographerly attention:

> She was wearing white tonight. I have no defense against that color ... For better *and* for worse: white dominates me ... Her breasts were half-covered in white lace,

worked into the top of her outfit, and that too was made of white, soft cotton. It was oppressive, irredeemably seductive ... (88–9)

Linda is 'overpowering' (89), just as the white chill of Toronto's business district, Bay Street, overwhelms the protagonist of 'Canadian Experience.' Too, disillusioningly, given her French-Canadian roots (her true surname is Maisoneuve), Linda is an archetype of Canada's 'two founding peoples.' This fact suggests that no real *rapprochement* is possible between them and newer claimants of Canadian citizenship. Indeed, another white woman, Susan Cole, the protagonist of 'In an Elevator' [1993], voices, eloquently, the basic white supremacist Canadian attitude: '... I was here first, and I work here, and no goddamn immigrant or cleaning woman or black sonofabitch, nobody's gonna make me feel threatened and live like a victim in my own fucking country, province, in my city' (60). Cole offers her frank revelation after recalling that she had consistently been bested, at a top private school in Ontario, by the black daughter of a Barbadian prime minister.

The seductive white female/system/nation tricks, turns tricks on, and fucks black male slaves/colonials/immigrants. 'Her' 'prepossessiveness' (Introduction 3),[8] her ownership of and first claim to commodities that she does not want, ever, to share, engenders in her black vassals desperation (sometimes violent), self-hatred (sometimes suicidal), and, in the best of them, a passionate cunning. Nevertheless, Clarke's imagery revivifies sorry, nasty, stodgy, and flat-out reactionary notions about female sexuality. Khalid Kishtainy writes that the teachings of St Cyprian of Carthage included the influential precept that 'if a woman invited the eyes of men, called forth their sighs and offered them matter for their lust and fuel for the flames of passion, she must be held guilty of their ruin' (Kishtainy 21). It is impossible to differentiate Clarke's figurative language from this ayatollah-like vision. The 'seductiveness' of the Canadian 'system' thus dooms its 'tricked' immigrants. But the dilemma posed by Clarke's sexist imagery is complicated when one recalls that, for Marx, 'prostitution is the most logical career for the capitalist way of life' (Kishtainy 46).[9] If one accepts this insight, then Clarke's moralistic condemnation of whorish (white) women makes no sense. However, Clarke's real target is the seductive nature of capitalism itself, a 'system' that must be regulated by a meritocracy based, scrupulously, on heritage and talent.[10]

If some of Clarke's white female characters are purveyors of dangerous allure, of treacherous – if radiant – promises, black women inspire an alternative constellation of metaphors, involving notions of nurture. A perpetual contest between 'mothers' – the Canadian 'Whore of Babylon' and the pseudo-Anglican 'Mary of Barbados' – occurs in Clarke. The white harlot offers *fausse* enticements; but the poorer, saintlier, black mother calls on her children to preserve their dignity, to strive for advancement (without giving way to rank materialism), and to honour their heritage. Clarke's employment of the Messalina/*mater* trope highlights his conservatism, for a primal division in his work is the split between the love of the Mother Country – a nearly incestuous desire for that country – versus lust for the stepmother, the new country, a passion expressed in terms of desire for material gain at any price. This essentialist difference is exemplified by the Afro-Barbadian mother in 'An Easter Carol' (1971). She is an idealized, earthbound goddess, a neo-Marian figure. Preparing her son to accompany her to church, she declares, 'Christ! boy, you look real good! You look just like a little doctor. Now, I want you to grow up fast, and be a doctor, hear?' (9). The injunction contrasts starkly with the desires expressed and solicited by the gallery of white female characters surveyed above. Instead, in a kind of neo-natal nationalism, the mother incarnates the *voice* of Barbados – the 'motherland' itself – instructing the boy to succeed. If her words do not suffice to spur the boy to achievement, there is her physicality, her seductiveness:

> I looked up at her, so large, so beautiful, so lovely, and so black – a mysterious queen or something, from Africa, with her hair braided neatly and long; with her old white dress which she washed three times a week, clutching to the feminine twists and turns of her full body. She looked at me, and she looked at my thoughts; and she smiled. She drew me close close to her breasts and her rolling soft stomach, where I could feel the love and blood pumping through her body. (10)

Not only does the mother's body bear the usual romanticized, black nationalist inscriptions of Africa, it is also associated with the topography of Barbados: 'I listened to the beautiful mountains and valleys of her surging voice ...' (1). Whiteness, in this story, is redemptive, unthreatening: '... I could see women dressed in the white of angels, white hats, white shoes, as if they were proud to be part of this great resurrection morning, as if they had remained new brides, new virgins, all their lives' ('Easter' 13). Despite such conceptualizations, the figure of the black mother still shades into that of the white whore, for both are *obscure objets de désir*, both pose the threat of psychological castration. In fact, the mother anticipates the white prostitute, Linda, in a crypto-sexual detail: she uses 'Evening-in-Paris perfume' ('Easter' 9), while Linda *is* 'the scent of Evening in Paris, which is just a way of saying that she is overpowering me' ('Not' 89). Even in the paradisal setting of Barbados, then, a woman can menace masculinity, just as Linda imperils Torontonian Max's sense of maleness: '... I was sitting in a house with a woman whose presence in the house was the consequence of the myth that I was a man. Am a man' ('Not' 98). Vertiginously, then, the white whore and the black mother both endanger self-conscious black manhood.

To avoid this trap, Clarke's protagonists – like Max in 'Not' – quest for true masculinity. However, this search is fraught with difficulty. For instance, in '*Black Man in a White Land*,' Clarke, as Ali, argues, 'it is a bit naive to suggest ... that the black man in North American society can ever have a future as a MAN' (3). Clarke's 1973 essay 'Some Speculations As to the Absence of Racialistic Vindictiveness in West Indian Literature' notes the 'emasculating psychological effects of slavery' (169) and suggests that the dream of a redeemed masculinity is now implicated with a regressive *macho* posture:

It seems that the West Indian writer, a man from a society free of the worst
pathologies of racialism, a man from a society into which Black nationalism had to
be imported from American Blacks ..., could do nothing more than couch his
literary expression in the pathology of self-identity and crisis, personal crisis, and
the concept *machismo* (related to the conquest of women) within the social framework of the island in which he lived. (180)

His frustrated aristocrats are, then, tinder for the Revolution, but they also
represent a tired, effete, black macho nationalism. They are men who 'have
forgotten, at that most critical point in their lives, the moment of their *contact*
with hostility [discrimination]'; each 'has forgotten who he is' (Introduction 2).
Later, Clarke returns to this theme, asking whether his fellow and sister African Canadians 'see themselves as victims, and behave as victims of this racism, without remembering and acknowledging that they are men and women'
(*Public* 8). Memory, particularly that anchored in the 'Motherland,' is a guar-
antor of the 'national' soul, a conservative nostrum that George Grant articulates in *Lament for a Nation: The Defeat of Canadian Nationalism* (1965). Therein,
Grant claims, chasteningly, that 'memory is never enough to guarantee that a
nation can articulate itself in the present' (12).[11] This assertion proves
devastatingly true for George in 'Canadian Experience.' His memories of his
privileged life in Barbados – 'eight, healthy, well-fed Barbadians, squinting
because the sun is in their eyes, standing like proprietors in front of a well-
preserved plantation house made of coral stone, covered in vines so thick that
their spongy greenness strangles the windows and the doors' ('Canadian' 47)
– do not preserve him from suicide. Nor do the get-rich-quick schemes of Pat
in 'Give It a Shot' or the 'playerism' of the protagonist of 'A Man' yield viable
supports for a progressive masculinity.

But Clarke is not bereft of such images. For this reason, the masculinist
scopophilia that influences Clarke's depictions of female characters also determines his accounts of spectacles and the accoutrements of wealth and power.
Thus, in 'An Easter Carol,' the boy-narrator records, nearly without irony, the
majestic images of 'the Lord Bishop, with his robes fluttering like the Union
Jack in the breeze ..., the Prime Minister of the island ... and the lords and
ladies of the island, all untitled, but all rich and white' ('Easter' 14). This
admiration of pomp and circumstance is not a unique, narrative oddity. Clarke
exalts the image of then-Ontario lieutenant governor Lincoln Alexander
'adorned in vice-regal raiment, plumed and epauletted in Elizabethan finery
to resemble a Lord of the Fleet' (*Public* 5). Clarke also bemoans the supposed
truth that African Canadians disparage ostentation, 'particularly as that prominence is bestowed by the media and the establishment': 'It is as if we want to
remain, each and every one of us, oppressed ...' (*Public* 5). Oppression is best
countered, in this scheme, by honouring and rewarding the meritorious, especially those who have demonstrably *overcome* oppression: 'He who is now
being lauded and recompensed, and made a chancellor of York University,
Oscar Peterson, was [once] barred from entering the Towne Tavern, because
on his arm was a white woman' (*Public* 13). Derek Walcott is celebrated as

being 'one of our heroes from another discipline, equal in importance to being a first black Mayor, or a first black Lieutenant-Governor: a poet' (*Public* 6). (This comparison is a curious way to toast a Nobel laureate.) In any case, Clarke's admiration for acceptable public figures is akin to his ease with comfortable – and comforting – commodities. Ownership has its privileges. Thus, Clarke distinguishes little between recording the tastes of gourmet food or the aroma of an exquisite cigar or inscribing a woman's body: 'She puts the dress on and runs her hands over her hips, and she smoothes the rich material which covers her luscious body for a moment from my eyes' ('Beggars' 68). Such images figure the pleasure and import of Tory voyeurism, of seeing one's way clear to what one desires.

III

Clarke drafts a political vision riven by contradiction. His critique of racism is blasted by his defence of privilege. One cannot very well exult 'aristocratic status' (Introduction 1) to ward off racism, and then have a character praise a white mistress because 'her movement was aristocratic' ('Man' 144). Sexism compromises Clarke's criticism of Canadian 'prepossessiveness': the depiction of a sluttish society reproduces the hoariest (whoriest?) gender clichés. Worse, Clarke's anti-racist utterances occasion a hint of rebarbative ethnocentrism. In his Ali persona, he proffers this analysis of the state of the Civil Rights Movement, *circa* 1967:

> The Jew is a Jew because WASP (whites in general) say he's a Jew. The same thing is true for the black man, but with greater visciousness [*sic*]. In the civil rights struggle, the Jew is not doing anything to ease the pressure on the Negro: if there were no Negro, there would be a Jew! The bad publicity that the black man gets today can be ascribed to the Jews because they control the communications. (*Black* 4)

There is, here, a fundamentalist ascription to essences, yet, simultaneously, a realization that no true, 'pure' blackness can ever be recovered. To whit: 'the Canadian black man is obsessed with an irrational Negritude: he hates the white man partly because it is fashionable to hate him' (*Black* 3). When one is free from such faddish irrationalities, one can even support one's local police:

> I will admit that the same policemen we sometimes accuse of violent discrimination, make my life safe and secure in a city bordering on the American syndrome of ghettoized crime. [T]his city is still *north* of the border of America and of racism. (*Public* 18)

Ingeniously, perhaps even with opportunistic *élan*, Clarke has always paired assaults on Canadian racism feeling with a strong endorsement of Canadian anti-Americanism. Speaking as Ali, in 1967, he deplores the fact that 'the CA-

NADIAN BLACK ATTITUDE [is] derived from the Black-White clashes in America' (*Black* 2). Twenty-five years later, Clarke was able to allege that one reason for the riot of 4 May 1992 in Toronto was that 'American racism had taken root in Canada in the minds of black Canadians' (*Public* 3). This argument recurs in 'Initiation' (1992), a satire of black radicalism, in which Clarke's *nom de guerre*, Ali Kamal Al Kadir Sudan, is recycled as the *nom de guerre* of a character whose 'real' name is 'Terrence Washington Jefferson Lincoln Lucas, the *Third*' (43). Ironically, Clarke lampoons a character bearing his ex-cognomen for doing what he had once done, namely, play at U.S.-style radicalism in a setting where it could not apply. Toronto, for better or worse, is not Harlem ('Initiation' 29).

Positioning himself, in his short fiction, as a sane, reasonable, good, Tory writer, Clarke upholds *bourgeois* Canadian nationalism; stands by the police; enforces age-old, Puritan attitudes regarding women; regards racism as an American phenomenon (exercising a hazardous influence *only* on Black Canadians); exalts the virtues of good breeding, good living, and good gin; and even subscribes, shamefully, to the tenets of a conspiracy theory. This version of a 'Common Sense Revolution' could be subscribed to, one imagines, by many conservatives, from Ian Fleming to the Canadian prime minister John George Diefenbaker (1895–1979).

For all Clarke's dexterous writing in support of his ideology, though, one must question the efficacy of a literary politics which holds, in stentorian tones, that Utopia is a location where professionals – and other deserving members of the elect, indigenous or immigrant, black or white – can join hands and drink Johnny Walker (gold), tack 'Q.C.' suffixes or 'Hon.' prefixes to their names, and debate the merits of Combermere School versus those of Bishop Strachan (while police club the envious rabble in the streets?). The ideal is not, however, a convincing prescription for societal happiness. Given his status as social satirist, pomp-loving politico, conservative idealist, pissed-off but loyal subject of Elizabeth II, and mild foe of robber-baron capitalism, perhaps Clarke must be classed as Canada's answer to the Indo-Trinidadian-British conservative writer V.S. Naipaul. Yet, despite the blind spots in Clarke's social vision, there is much that is salvageable, commendable too, in his largely sympathetic overview of the (black) immigrant's plight and in his principled, though limited, attacks on the *de facto* caste system which impedes their upward mobility. Clarke's work reminds us that, as scholar Aubrey McPhail has said of the martyred Nigerian writer Kenule Saro-Wiwa, 'every serious writer is, on some fundamental level, a moral writer' (69). Clarke is strikingly so. (Note the fierce, cryptically Christian aesthetics of his Toryism.) Although, his short stories can seem, like those of Saro-Wiwa, 'unsure, unclear, and sometimes morally suspect' (McPhail 84), he knows that 'the technique of honesty is not always utterly simple' (Pound, 'Troubadours' 96). One can read Clarke's fiction with some relish (or perhaps Grey Poupon mustard), and its underlying elitism remains difficult to digest, but it is, nevertheless, a feast of (social) instruction.

Notes

1 This essay was first presented at the conference on 'Race, Gender, and the Construction of Canada' at the University of British Columbia, Vancouver, BC, on
20 October 1995. I am grateful to the audience members for their critiques of its
readings. I dedicate this essay to Austin Clarke, the man himself, with respect.
2 In his thoughtful review of Stella Algoo-Baksh's *Austin C. Clarke: A Biography*
(1994), 'Survivor of the Crossing,' Brian John Busby, relying on a mistaken claim by
Lorris Elliott in *Literary Writing by Blacks in Canada* (1988), states that a novel by
Brian Gypsin, namely, *To Master, a Long Goodnight*, published in New York in 1946,
'is very likely the first black Canadian novel' (11). But, 'Brian Gypsin' was a
misprint for Brion Gysin, a white American writer, whose purported novel is really
a biography. The first African-Canadian novel was, arguably, African-American
writer Martin Robinson Delany's *Blake*, inked in Chatham, Ontario, and serialized
in two magazines between 1859 and 1862. Next in line was Amelia Etta Hall
Johnson, who was born in Canada West (now Ontario) in 1858 and who published
Clarence and Corinne; or, God's Way in Philadelphia, Pennsylvania, in 1890. (Another
potential contender – and Canada West native – Lucretia Newman Coleman
published her novel, *Poor Ben: A Story of Real Life*, in Nashville, Tennessee, in either
1890 or 1891.) Born in Canada West in 1859, William Haslip Stowers co-authored
Appointed: An American Novel with William H. Anderson, and published it under
the pseudonym Sanda, in Detroit in 1894. A fourth novelist, John Hearne, born in
Montréal in 1926, grew up in Jamaica, and published his first novel in London in
1955. The fifth novelist was Jan Carew, a Guyanese native, who published his first
novel, *Black Midas*, in London in 1958 and later acquired Canadian citizenship.

Busby's point that Clarke's 'literary career stretches back farther than [that of]
any other black Canadian' (11) also requires amendment. When Clarke's *Survivors
of the Crossing* appeared in 1964, Gérard Étienne had already published, in his
native Haiti, *six* books of poetry and prose. After arriving in Canada in the early
1960s, he commenced the Canadian phase of his writing career by releasing
another book of poetry in Montréal in 1966. Similarly, Anthony Phelps had
published three books of poetry in Haiti by 1964; he began to issue new poetry and
drama in Montréal in 1966 and 1968. With three Haitian-published texts to his
credit by 1964, Franck Fouché published his drama *Bouki non paradi* in Montréal in
1964, thus becoming the first published African-Canadian playwright. Another
playwright, the Trinidad-born Lennox Brown, began to publish his prize-winning
dramas with the Ottawa Little Theatre in 1965. New Brunswick poet Anna Minerva
Henderson released her book of poems *Citadel* in 1967; while the Jamaican-born
Gershom Williams self-published a novel in Toronto in 1968. Though Clarke was a
fairly isolated figure, *qua* novelist, in *English* African-Canadian literature in the
mid-1960s, he was not the only publishing writer, or the only pioneer, and his
solitude was short-lived. See my 'A Primer of African-Canadian Literature' (pp.
325–38, below) and 'Africana Canadiana: A Select Bibliography of Literature by
African-Canadian Authors' (pp. 339–448, below).

3 The others are, in chronological order, *When Women Rule* (1985), *Nine Men Who Laughed* (1986), and *In This City* (1992).

4 Clarke's black male 'aristocrats' would fit splendidly into this passage in Fleming's *Moonraker*:

> There were perhaps fifty men in the room, the majority in dinner jackets, all at ease with themselves and their surroundings, all stimulated by the peerless food and drink, all animated by a common interest – the prospect of high gambling, the grand slam, the ace pot, the key-throw in a 64 game at backgammon. There might be cheats or possible cheats amongst them, men who beat their wives, men with perverse instincts, greedy men, cowardly men, lying men; but the elegance of the room invested each one with a kind of aristocracy. (43)

Think, for instance, of J.M.G.M.-C. in 'A Man' (1986), or Mr Joshua Miller-Corbaine in 'How He Does It' (1986), or the Jamaican in 'Give It a Shot' (1987), or Anthony Barrington St Omer Edgehill in 'Letter of the Law of Black' (1992). These gentlemen have their flaws, *oui*, but their commitment to elegance mitigates their sins.

5 Stella Algoo-Baksh does not include this pamphlet, an interview with Ali (Clarke) conducted by Nazzam Al Sudan (Marvin X), in the bibliography she compiled for her monograph, *Austin C. Clarke: A Biography* (1994).

6 Here is yet another point where Clarke attains an accidental *entente* with Fleming, who regularly pimps, in his tales, gorgeous – and drop-dead deadly – (white and 'exotic') women.

7 This vision of white woman as vampire also occurs in African-Canadian writer Darius James's campy satirical novel *Negrophobia* (1992). Here the white female protagonist, Bubbles, exclaims, 'Without the vampiric beauty of my whiteness, without the definition of my skin, without my *emblematic significance*, I was presence without appearance, a being without basis, a creature without context – *an invisible* – a colorless network of organs and entrails in translucent casing' (167–8). Her self-definition is resonantly Baudrillardian – and Fanonesque.

8 Note Clarke's utilization of a quasi-economic term as a synonym for 'racism.' His critique of Canadian 'prepossessiveness' – not racism – accents his class concerns.

9 An interesting irony pertains to Clarke's Canada-as-harlot paradigm. Kishtainy points out that 'prostitutes over the centuries were inwardly religious and conservative and were rightly represented in literature with a royalist mentality' (49). This description of the political orientations of prostitutes squares nicely with accounts of Canada that accent its religious, Tory, and monarchical predilections.

10 In this reading, Clarke's characters resemble black knights (or Bond figures?) endangered by Canadian *'belles dames san merci.'* In their existentialist, noble failings, they uphold masculinist and conservative ideals of chivalry. Thus, in 'An Easter Carol' (1971), the Bajan Easter churchgoers consist of women wearing 'the white of angels,' while the men sport 'suits of long ago black, which fitted them like coats of armour' (14).

11 Clarke's disdain for greed aligns him with Canadian Red Toryism, as defined by Grant, who maintains that, in traditional Canadian conservative thought, 'the good life [makes] strict demands on self-restraint' (Grant, *Lament* 70). Hence, in 'The

Motor Car,' Calvin's greed is viewed as a kind of displacement of nature: 'But the bank account was mounting and climbing like a woman belly when she in the family-way' (98).

Harris, Philip, Brand:
Three Authors in Search of Literate Criticism

For Hardial Bains (1939–97)[1]

Criticism is never innocent, for it is the capital means, promises the U.S. African-Americanist Michael Bérubé, of imagining canons and manufacturing literary stars.[2] Though an instrument of empowerment, then, criticism can enact Machiavellian abuses, even when its intellectual force is utilized for pristine purposes. Indeed, one of the awful intoxications of literary theory is that one dreams that one can do socio-political good, dispelling illiberal forces of malice and ignorance, delivering into the illumination of academic discourse entire canons – or communities – which have been consigned to the limbo of marginality.[3] The belief is praiseworthy, and doubly so when it catalyzes joyful political action. Yet, there is something of the missionary position inherent in the posture, especially when an exuberant idealism leads one to champion communities to which one is merely an observer, or a guest, or, perhaps, an interloper, or even, charitably, a missionary. The risk of this seductive address is that one's own thrusting of theory, of notions of interpretation, upon the Other (that obscure object of desire), may render mute the screams, laughter, and shouts of that supposedly beloved Other, that darling community with which the critic-as-missionary conducts intercourse.

Perhaps a process of this sort has been under way in regards to the critical reception of three première African-Canadian poets, all women, all once of Trinidad, all coming into public prominence in Canada in the mid-1980s. Named in birth order, the members of this vital trio – Claire Harris (b. 1937), M. NourbeSe Philip (b. 1947), and Dionne Brand (b. 1953) – all of whom could be described as Afro-Caribbean or as Black Canadian, have been the subjects of numerous interviews, essays, and even a select anthology with an uncritical introduction. They have been well fêted, with Claire Harris receiving the Commonwealth Award for Poetry in the Americas in 1984, the Writers' Guild of Alberta Poetry Prize and the Alberta Culture Poetry Prize in 1986, and a Governor General's Award nomination for poetry in 1993; Philip, the Casa de las Américas Prize for Anglo-Caribbean Poetry, a Guggenheim Fellowship in 1989, and a City of Toronto Arts Award in 1996; and Brand, a nomination for the Governor General's Award for poetry in 1990, a nomination for the Seal Books

/ *Books in Canada* First Novel Award in 1996, the Governor General's Award
for poetry in 1997, and Ontario's Trillium Book Award in 1998. Significantly,
all three writers have built their literary careers in Canada. Harris arrived in
1966, Philip in 1968, Brand in 1970. While they may be claimed as 'Afro-
Caribbean writers in exile' – the tag applied to them by African-Canadian
academic Myriam J.A. Chancy – they may also be considered as primarily
Canadian writers, for all three began to publish *after* emigrating to Canada. In
this materialist *cum* realist sense, their voices have always been Canadian –
though their audiences have seldom cared to consider this fact. Their early
works – on Trinidadian life, Third World and Black revolution, and the unity
of the struggling classes – were published in Toronto and Calgary, which
suggests that their agency as writers has always been implicated with Canadian regionalism as well as with the nation's peculiar and intractable problems related to book publication, distribution, marketing, and sales across its
empire-sized geography.

   The snare that too many critics fall into in writing about this Trinidadian
trio is that, seeking to promote their own sermons against racism, sexism,
imperialism, classism, and homophobia, they either reduce the writers to the
status of sociologists or they empty their work of aesthetic pursuits. The resultant criticism is tedious, inadequate, irrelevant, and – well – insidious.

   The first exhibit in this gallery of errors is 'After Modernism: Alternative
Voices in the Writings of Dionne Brand, Claire Harris, and Marlene Philip'
(1992), an essay by white British academic Lynette Hunter. Hunter places the
three poets outside of a Canadian literary modernism defined as
'postmodernism and neo-romantic surrealism,' both of which 'depend upon
writing towards the conventional expectations of an extant audience' (257).
Unfazed by the polysemous open-endedness of her definitions, Hunter goes
on to argue that 'the stance taken up by these writers acts towards the possibility of writing by interacting with an audience, constructing a stance out of
its social immediacy and historical need' (257). According to Hunter, this Marxian practice 'outlines a different kind of community, not working from con-
ventionally accepted grounds, but a community anchored as such by actual
social problems, and hence a community that will necessarily change' (257).
Though Hunter's rhetoric is coruscatingly opaque, she seems to suggest here
that Harris, Philip, and Brand write, not for a *bourgeois*, complacent, thrill-
seeking audience, but rather for disaffected constituencies, for communities in
turmoil, for congregations of the conquered. By upping the perceived populism of the trio's works, Hunter seeks to dislodge both a post-modernism
which 'can offer a rejection of history and make action on immediate issues
impossible' (258) and a 'Romanticized surrealism encourag[ing] a dislocation
into the private, which invalidates discussion and rejects the social' (258).
Hunter singles out the best-known Anglo-Canadian writers, Michael Ondaatje
(b. 1943) and Margaret Atwood (b. 1939) (262), as exemplars of, respectively,
'ahistorical postmodernism' and 'romanticist individualism / heroics of the
surreal' (260). Against these idols of political evacuation, Hunter sets Harris,

Philip, and Brand as veritable saints of poeticized politics, restoring qualitative urgency and fury to English-Canadian poetry. To Hunter, they are the bards of 'action' (259) and of their realities 'as women, as lovers, wives, mothers, daughters, women at work' (259). They are saints of agency.

Hunter's analysis enacts, I think, a flaky species of 'maternalism.' For one thing, Hunter dispatches with Ondaatje and Atwood too neatly. The supposedly apolitical and ahistorical Ondaatje is the author of 'Pictures from the War' (1968), a bitter, anti–Vietnam War poem, which sights a child, 'its skull drained of liquid / its side unlaced like tennis shoes' (261). Even the assertion that the war pictures are 'Beautiful photography / that holds no morality' (261), while artistically apolitical, accentuates the point that official photographs of governmental atrocities convey, deliberately, a depoliticizing shock.[4] Rightly, Atwood is notorious for trumpeting the cultural anti-Americanism that scores her *Survival: A Thematic Guide to Canadian Literature* (1972) and the feminism that informs her novels and poetry collections, including *Morning in the Burned House* (1995).[5] Neither writer can be written off as a mere exponent of any unthought, liberal individualism. Too, Hunter's privileging of 'community,' 'action,' and a populist orientation conjures up a 'neo-romantic' socialist realism. Hunter admits that 'one of the most effective strategies for this building of story and movement out into social recognition is conventional realism' (279), which, as she also confesses, can become 'reductive' (279). By valuing Harris, Philip, and Brand as exponents of what might be dubbed 'feminist realism,' Hunter imposes a denuded aesthetic on these writers *and* erases political poetry by other Canadian women writers, from Atwood to Erin Mouré (b. 1955). Yet, all of these writers (and others) have been dedicated to women's – and people's – empowerment.[6] Hunter's categories are so much paper.

A further priminery may be located in Hunter's blithe ascription of apoliticality to the mode of the post-modern. Here she should do battle with Marjorie Perloff, who defends experimental, 'pomo' poetry precisely because it permits vaster political agency than the plain Romantic lyric.[7] In *Dance of the Intellect: Studies in the Poetry of the Pound Tradition* (1985), Perloff argues that 'postmodernism in poetry ... begins in the urge to return the material so rigidly excluded – political, ethical, historical, philosophical – to the domain of poetry, which is to say that the Romantic lyric, the poem as expression of a moment of absolute insight, of emotion crystallized into a timeless patterns [*sic*], gives way to a poetry that can, once again, accommodate narrative and didacticism, the serious and the comic, verse *and* prose' (180–1).[8] Perloff even alleges that 'minor poets continue to write neo–Romantic lyric' (181), a charge which could be applied against Harris, Philip, and Brand, for many of their lyrics rely upon direct subjectivity, the personal voice, the lyric 'eye' as lyric 'I.' Consider Brand's epigram 'they think it's pretty / this falling of leaves / something is dying!' ('4' 197). But see also M. NourbeSe Philip's observation, in her essay collection *A Genealogy of Resistance and Other Essays* (1997), that 'in white Canada the kind of poetry which I write has been dismissed as political, with the caveat that poetry cannot be made of politics (this notwithstanding the tradition of their own political poets like Blake, Shelley, and Yeats), particularly politics as it relates to race' (130). Intriguingly, Philip locates the political *in* the Romantic *cum* modernist tradition – 'Blake, Shelley, Yeats' – a fact which should give Hunter some pause. However, Philip may also be aligned with a post-modern aesthetic, as defined by Perloff, for she also notes that the supposed white Canadian aversion to the political 'is but a gossamer-thin cover for not wanting to engage with the issues the poetry raises' (*Genealogy* 130). Moreover, she proclaims that 'postmodernist is another term used to describe my poetry, to which my response is: then the Caribbean was postmodern long before the term was invented' (*Genealogy* 128–9). The base problem with Hunter's definition of the post-modern and the Romantic is that it relies on rhetorical force, on simply asserting that some poets (preferably black women) are just more political than others (the average white man), and that the politically conscious is necessarily the artistically superior.[9] Yet, by finding that post-modernism voids politics, Hunter almost forces Harris, Philip, and Brand into a neo-Romantic camp, a 'be-in' of leftist *Kitsch*.

In Hunter's defence, one can posit that a poet like Mouré is hardly a vulgar realist, for she crafts L=A=N=G=U=A=G=E poetry, while Atwood has written politically structured verse.[10] Yet, this defence must incur the objection that Harris, Philip, and Brand are also, at times, *avant-gardiste*, not communalist, in their poetry, and Philip can even be enlisted as a L=A=N=G=U=A=G=E poet. To adopt Perloff's definition of the movement, Philip's poetry emphasizes 'prominent sound patterning and arcane, or at least "unnatural," diction' (217) and flouts 'established "distinctions" (between essays and lyrics, between prose and poetry, between philosophy and poetry, between theory and practice)' (222). Philip realizes that 'it can be said – has been said – that I write the kind of poetry that can be described as language [*sic*] poetry – kissing cousins with it at least' (*Genealogy* 128). She acknowledges that 'the audience which appears to have self-selected itself for my work is one that is primarily feminist and womanist, comprised of white and Black women from within and without the academy' (*Genealogy* 130–1). This audience is neither grass-roots popular nor working-class, for Philip admits that 'I would very much like to reach a broader cross-section of people, particularly Caribbean and Afrosporic people. That will only happen, however, if and when my work moves into performance' (*Genealogy* 131). She also senses that 'on the surface at least my work does not fit the traditions of Black poetry' (*Genealogy* 129). Philip's confession merits attention, for she underscores the truth that these 'populist' feminists often scribe erudite, densely allusive, intensely intellectual poems, employing fashionable poetic techniques, which is certainly their artistic right, but also certainly *not* populist. Harris also evinces concern about the accessibility of her own work, remarking, 'The problem is one of audience. We all know *for whom* we write; the ambivalence, and it is a dangerous one, lies in *to whom* we write' (quoted in Hunter 279). A prime example of post-modern difficulty occurs, for instance, in Philip's scintillatingly radical poetry collection *She Tries Her Tongue, Her Silence Softly Breaks* (1989). In 'Discourse on the Logic of Language' (Morrell

136–9), she cascades verse sideways down the left-hand margins of the page, conjoins verse and prose, mocks grammars and primers, and jeopardizes any attempt to read the poem in a standard, linear fashion. Philip acknowledges that 'I set out to destroy the lyric voice, the singularity of the lyric voice ...' (*Genealogy* 115). While writing her poem, she had told herself, 'I want to contaminate the poem – fuck the juxtaposition and resonance – poison the purity with that which has already been poisoned – to bring the non-poetic into the poems ...' (*Genealogy* 114–15). (Her series of precepts instances Perloff's aforecited definition of L=A=N=G=U=A=G=E poetry.) Likewise, Harris, in 'Nude on a Pale Staircase' (1984), limns the disintegration of an interracial union by colliding together lyric and prose, each offering a male or female point of view, and disrupting, again, any facile reading.[11]

In fairness, Hunter accepts this truth. She prefers Brand to Harris and Philip, for the former is more given to setting down gospel-strict, feminist accounts of experience than the latter pair. So, Hunter reads Harris as having but gradually evolved a gynocentric position: 'Despite the continual reference to women and to women's experience, the touchstones for event in the early books are often male' (266). Harris's 'masculinity,' so to speak, is signalled by her aggressive utilization of such late-modern poetic techniques as the fractured page evoking different modes of thought, non-linear modes of typography, and a complex, abstract texture. Hunter is not amused. Reading Harris's poem 'Every Moment a Window' (1986), Hunter complains, 'It is as if the White, intellectual, male tradition of verse and poetics gives [the poem's black *female* speaker] a window on reality at the cost of desiccating [*sic*] her ability, her capacity, to experience' (265). Later, Hunter redeems Harris, finding that her poetry, *circa* 1992, now seems aimed 'toward community and authentic voice rather than the opposing dualities of tradition and an essential individual' (269). Ironically, Hunter's critique of Harris bares her own regressive ascription of masculinity to 'intellectual' verse; her stance is, again, 'maternalistic': the white feminist academic telling the black female poet how to write like a *real* black woman. Contradictorily, though, Hunter misses the flagrant interest displayed by Philip and Brand in that most negative of elitist white male modernists, namely, that most notorious *créditiste sociale* Ezra Pound (1885– 1972). Yet, Brand's *Primitive Offensive* (1982) performs a riff on Pound's *Cantos*,[12] while Philip samples Pound's dictum 'MAKE IT NEW' (from his 'Canto LIII') in one essay (*Genealogy* 115) and cites Pound in three others (*Genealogy* 73, 85, 203).[13] Furthermore, Philip admires African-American novelist James Baldwin (1924–87), even addressing a letter to him in one essay (*Genealogy* 138–40). Both Philip and Brand engage in exercises of influence anxiety regarding their home territory's unexcelled English-language poet, Derek Walcott (b. 1930).[14] None of this is to deny the saliency of women writers for Philip and Brand. Still, Hunter's attempt to pillory Harris for relying upon so-called masculinist influences is a species of wilful illiteracy.

As for Philip, Hunter views her work as having undergone an evolution, but one that has not advanced far enough. If Philip's poem 'Cyclamen Girl'

(1986) undertakes 'a study of the way that womanhood can work against the institutions of a White world, how it can be both a preservation from and an opening up into differences from the White world,' if this 'bridge the writer builds for her sisters crosses all races' (Hunter 276),[15] there is yet a peril. 'This poetry trusts to broad cultural and social references of parenthood, authority, childhood, gender, and other metaphors, but in this openness the issue of race and Philip's Black heritage may be passed over' (Hunter 276). Hunter's comment is startlingly arrogant: who has hired her to police Philip's racial consciousness? A short story by Philip, 'Burn Sugar' (1988), wins Hunter's approval. Recalling the style of recipes – which are 'historically grounded in food pathways and economics' (277) – the piece 'extends both the literary and linguistic features of traditional prose out into techniques, strategies, and genres drawn from the topic of a woman's audience and community' (277). The audacity of Hunter's insight is blinding; she seems to be mandating how a black woman writer should write. Furthermore, she never hints at the basic concern of Philip's story: the transmission and transmutation of (Afro-Caribbean woman) consciousness, here figured as 'black cake' (11–19). Hunter is careful to admit 'there will be necessary differences between any position I could take as a White critic and those of these Afro-Caribbean women writers' (258). However, she validates these women only as creators of texts that 'interact with some common historical grounds that bring the possibility of a socially immediate and radically engaging stance to feminism, at the same time as they open the door on the reality of racial difference and the history of problems that it carries' (258). Crucially, the works of Harris, Philip, and Brand 'could address these problems and make possible another discussion within feminism about race' (258). Here Hunter posits a utopian wish – or nostalgia (as suggested by the phrase 'another discussion') – for a racially unified women's movement. The chief duty of Harris, Philip, and Brand is to create works that will rebuild a fractured solidarity, thus reanimating 'a socially immediate and radically engaging stance to feminism' (258).

Predictably, then, of the three writers, Brand fares best in Hunter's economy of feminist realism: 'Politically the most assertive of the three writers discussed here, Brand is poetically the most traditional' (269). Yet, Brand is positioned as having had, like Philip, to evolve, as having abandoned mere 'modernist dislocation' (270) for the shining path of prose – the pursuit of 'the narrative impulse to conventional communication' (272). Still, Hunter adores Brand, for she enacts both 'militant assertiveness' and 'formality of style' (273). There is a risk of didacticism in this approach, but someone has to teach black history to unschooled (or oblivious) whites, who are, Hunter presumes, one of Brand's select audiences: 'Her work is firmly assertive with an anger that readers either immediately recognize or need to make a place for: the necessity of voicing the fears, reactions, rejections that are tied up in the Black experience of Canada's racism' (273).[16]

If Hunter prods Harris, Philip, and Brand to produce more work in the vein of feminist realism, white Canadian academic Carol Morrell is not far behind.

Introducing *Grammar of Dissent: Poetry and Prose by Claire Harris, M. Nourbese Philip, Dionne Brand* (1994), she lauds the trio for their employment of 'three grand strategies in their otherwise highly individual writing projects: they take an essentialist subject-position, they use that subject-position for political intervention, and they startle the reader by interrogating standard English and substituting new usages, often in the Caribbean demotic, for old ones' (10).[17] Morrell differs from Hunter in casting the works of Harris, Philip, and Brand as 'highly individual'; but, like Hunter, she deems these authors spokespersons for women and the African Diaspora. Morrell tells us that 'all three will assert that they speak "for" their history and "on behalf of" their people, especially the women, however distant in time or place' (10). This political ventriloquism allows the writers 'both a community and a coherent sense of self – however fictive or imaginative – from which to act and write' (10). Ideally, the writers try to 'represent a wide variety of women' (12). In opposition to the tendency of retrograde feminists to interpret 'the old feminist rallying cry "the personal is the political" [as] inviting women to concentrate merely on their own personal lives, avoiding involvement with large social and political issues[,] Harris, Philip, and Brand ... understand and apply the phrase in its original meaning' (12). So, these black women writers reveal to middle-class white women the ideational truths of feminism. Here, Morrell's comments echo, eerily, Hunter's endorsement of these three writers as reconstructers of a once-unified feminism. She even submits that these writers will help Canadians to avoid 'a disastrous future of racial conflict' (14). Even so, whereas Hunter lectures Harris, Philip, and Brand on political morality, Morrell expects them to teach others. She praises their status as ethical instructors: 'When these three authors take up the black, feminist, signifying subject-position, they create a new subject-position: they become teachers of the white Canadian literary and political communities' (12).[18] Morrell's declaration also erases, albeit innocently, nine generations of African Canadians who struggled against racism and sexism, long before Harris, Philip, and Brand began to publish their works. Her statement underlines, too, that black women's writing is best validated as a service industry. Maybe no black writer can author anything consequential unless she or he has first obtained a degree in sociology or, better, performed a stint at social work, to establish his or her credentials. Regrettably, Italian-Canadian academic Joseph Pivato buys into this idea: 'In ethnic minority writing we have not only the recuperation of the author, but also the exercise of his or her authority as a voice in and for the community ... When we write about ethnic minority authors we are implicitly recognizing their vital role as voices in their communities' ('Representation' 160). To support this point, Pivato cites Himani Bannerji's study of Brand, using a passage that brands her a *vox populi*: 'To read her poetry is to read not only about her but also about her people. Her identification with their struggles both in the metropole of Canada and in the hinterland of the Caribbean' (quoted in Pivato, 'Representation' 160). This comment recalls the platitudes of Hunter. But with these critical clichés on display, Morrell proceeds to state that the 'eloquent contribution' of Harris, Philip, and Brand to 'literature in Canada is their making their universe visible, persuasive, acceptable' (Introduction 23). Here Morrell's ill-chosen words spark an ill-tempered query: what was the disagreeable condition of African-Canadian women that once rendered their universe 'unacceptable'? Furthermore, what about other African-Canadian women writers, such as Nova Scotia's Maxine Tynes (b. 1949)? Morrell's *de facto* marginalization of 'surplus' Black Canadian women writers reflects her practice of the kinds of bankrupt liberalism that Jewish-Canadian academic Enoch Padolsky excoriates. Multicultural 'Can Lit' fails to generate comprehensive study, he suggests, because once liberal academics pick their 'star' minority-group writers, they treat all others as 'extras': 'Who needs 17 other Mennonite-Canadian writers when there is Rudy Wiebe?' ('Canadian' 377).

Finally, Morrell endorses, implicitly, Brand over Harris, finding that 'Harris's poetry is never straightforwardly life-writing' (Introduction 17), while 'Brand's work is direct political challenge' (Introduction 23). (Here one could be forgiven for thinking that Morrell is juxtaposing Gertrude Stein's *Tender Buttons* [1914] and Karl Marx and Friedrich Engel's *The Communist Manifesto* [1848].) Morrell views Philip as another speaker, like Brand, of orthodox, grounded truths; her work evinces an 'emphatic insistence on the suffering, bleeding yet triumphant female body as the focal point of experience and meaning for women' (Introduction 19). For Morrell, as for Hunter, the standard for literary achievement is a politicized fealty to realism. Brand is, then, loved over Harris and Philip. But both academics refuse to register that all three writers are hardly consistently linear – or realist – in style.

Morrell and Hunter are not renegades, however. The third entry in my gallery of catatonic criticism is an essay by African-Canadian academic Rinaldo Walcott. He joins Morrell and Hunter in praising African-Canadian women writers as definers and defenders of black female subjectivities within a hostile, white, phallocentric space. But he acts out a comedy of exultation, finding that 'Philip's and Brand's poetic works perform the fluid movement between "hegemonic and ambiguously hegemonic discourse" to utter black feminist and lesbian words which write/construct new black and white histories' (100–1). Walcott does not identify these 'new' histories, and he offers no description of how the texts of Philip and Brand intervene 'between' hegemonies. It is just the usual, feel-good rhetoric. However, Walcott seems to plump, implicitly, for the Morrell perspective that Philip and Brand are pedagogues. He exclaims, 'Theirs is not a poetics of victimhood. Instead, Philip and Brand deform and (re)write the laws of the master; and in the process render law-making futile – because of the expressivity and performativity of blackness' (112). This rococo rhetoric does not bother to distinguish a 'poetics of victimhood' from a poetics of – presumably – liberation. Even if accepted at face value, it is deviant. Indeed, if Morrell and Hunter have anything right, it is that Philip and Brand (and – lest we forget – Harris) address the victimizations fostered by racism and sexism. The most cursory glance at their works will turn up images of victimization – as well as narratives of resistance. Think of Philip's 'Discourse on the Logic of Language' – "my father tongue / is a foreign lan lan lang / language / l / anguish / anguish / english / is a foreign anguish' (quoted in Morrell 138). See also Brand's depiction of the self-destruction of the Grenadian Revolution in *Chronicles of the Hostile Sun* (1984): 'after a while, villainy fingers the eyes, / daubs the hills disenchant / and the mouth lies in its roof / like a cold snake' ('Diary – the Grenada Crisis,' quoted in Morrell 212).[19] Then again, how does '(re)writing the laws of the master' serve to cancel law-making? Would not the process of editing such laws constitute an *act* of legislation? Given the confusion inherent in Walcott's slipshod metaphors, it is almost churlish to note his counter-claim that Philip and Brand engage in 'no mere rewriting' (97). His essay is no 'reveille for radicals,' for one would think it is not the task of revolutionaries to edit laws but to abolish them – or to die in the effort. When one of Brand's protagonists, Verlia, leaps to her death at the finale of the novel *In Another Place, Not Here* (1996), it is because her socialist pseudo-paradise – St Vincent (that is, Grenada) – is enduring an irresistible assault by the forces of imperialist reaction (245–7).[20] She accepts the existentialist notion of revolutionary suicide as her escape from the crisis. A 'Jonestown' philosophy propels her death-leap.

Walcott also asserts that Philip, in her poem 'Dream-skins' (1989), 'alters the notion of "bloodcloth" to reclaim it as a *sign* for mature womanhood and to articulate a black female self' (114). Characteristically, he deigns neither to explain what 'bloodcloth' denotes nor to state how, precisely, Philip alters it, for he enjoys luxuriating in the comforts of a hollow sentiment. In contrast, Hunter reads Philip's 'bloodcloth' imagery, with its allusion to mother-child bonding, as an attempt 'to build bridges' between black and white women (276). Walcott's inability to define 'blood cloth' – the 'nation language'[21] term for tampon/binding – obscures what Hunter reveals: this binding 'is not just to constrain and keep in but to provide some security: it is about baby binding, finding voice as the mother's voice teaches the child, but here there are two voices. The painful transition into White language is not, however, simply loss' (276). Hunter's theory that Philip uses 'blood cloth' to indicate an absorption of white language – the bloodiness of that language – contradicts Walcott's sense that Philip's metaphor articulates simply 'a black female self.' But his sentence is so critically vacuous that it neuters any political meaning.

When Walcott declares that Brand 'reworks words like "guerillas" to make them perform the experience and interior life of [a] poem's narrator' (114), he blunders into epistemological catastrophe. He thinks that Brand's 'riffing evokes the idea of guerillas as warriors for justice as well as racist notions of black people being genealogically linked to the ape family' (115). Walcott's sentence is accidentally racist. He uses 'genealogically' where he means to use *genetically*. Too, it is impossible to conceive how Brand's usage of 'guerillas' moves 'beyond the discourses of victimhood to resist amputations and to plot and chart the coordinates of a new exodus, one that's embedded with the possibilities of freedom' (115). This phraseology is grandiose, rotund, and sonorous, but signifies a fatal weakness in Walcott's approach to both Brand and Philip.

He believes they seek 'a new exodus' (115), presumably, from Canada. Yet, to depart the country would be an admission of defeat, not triumph; it would be the physical rendering of a 'poetics of victimhood.' What Walcott is vainly grasping to achieve is an articulation of how the experience of exodus is 'central to the writing of the black diaspora' (96). His formulation is not merely a tautology, but also a myth, for when he posits that Brand and Philip write from 'in-between spaces' (97), he is asserting their at-home Canadianness. For instance, in a book review, Christian Bök observes that Canadian intellectual Arthur Kroker psychoanalyses Canada 'in terms of a humanistic ambivalence toward the post-modern *zeitgeist* of technocratic heteronomy ..., arguing that the imaginative space of the Canadian mind resides in an "*in-between*" ...' (9). If to be 'in-between' is a Canadian predicament, the writing of Philip and Brand is as *Canadian* as it is anything else. Philip herself, in a poem titled 'July Again,' comments that 'the mornings ... / seem always to hesitate ... / caught between neither and nor / like Canada' (quoted in Morrell 123), an analysis stressing Canada's ambivalent identity. Moreover, the themes of Brand and Philip – survival, ambiguity, struggle, etc. – have long been staples of the nation's literature. In fact, Brand's award-winning poetry collection, *Land to Light On* (1997), opens with a sequence titled 'I Have Been Losing Roads,' in which her persona attempts to come to terms with the cold, misogyny, and isolation of northern Ontario (3–17). Here, whether she intends it or not, she echoes another immigrant poet situated in a similar geography: Alexander MacLachlan (1818–96), the nineteenth-century Scottish socialist bard who emigrated to Canada and wrote class-conscious 'dialect' poems in eastern Ontario. She also seems to follow Ovid (43 B.C.E.–18 C.E.), the classical Roman poet exiled to the Ultima Thule of eastern Europe (whose poetry has also influenced Philip).[22]

Sadly, Walcott's thuggish cheerleading reduces Philip and Brand to being perpetual exiles who, nevertheless, come in from the cold to instruct their readers in the techniques of cultural survival without ever really having to confront Canada itself. Luckily for us, Philip and Brand scotch such superficial readings. Thus, Philip deplores the lack of a 'tradition of writing [in Canada] which was in any way receptive to the African writer' (*Genealogy* 71). Brand seeks to accent all the lost histories of this country: 'Something there, written as wilderness, wood, nickel, water, coal, rock, prairie, erased as Athabasca, Algonquin, Salish, Inuit ... hooded in Buxton fugitive, Preston Black Loyalist, railroaded to gold mountain, swimming in *Komagata Maru*' (*Land* 77). One can only wonder what Walcott may make of Philip's identification of Tobago with Cape Breton Island: '[F]or the first time in almost thirty years in this land they call Canada, I am reminded of the love in home. In Cape Breton Island as I witness the heart-stopping beauty that I have only ever seen in Tobago' (*Genealogy* 26). Here a supposed 'exodus' prefaces a homecoming.[23] Philip also sights links between herself and Lucy Maud Montgomery (1874–1942), the 'bard' of Prince Edward Island: 'On a tiny tropical island a little Black girl develops an odd affinity with a red-headed girl ... Prince Edward Island: source of Lucy

Maud Montgomery's writing life. Tobago: source of my own writing life' (*Genealogy* 28).

Where Walcott leaves off, Myriam Chancy begins. In her book *Searching for Safe Spaces: Afro-Caribbean Women Writers in Exile* (1997), she takes up the imagery of exile and exodus in her analysis of Philip and Brand, who she defines as 'displaced Afro-Caribbean writers in Canada' (78). The subtitle of her chapter on Philip, Brand, and Jamaican-Canadian writer Makeda Silvera (b. 1955) fastens them to the topic of 'Women's Dignity in Canadian Exile' (78). Chancy's studies of their work depend mightily on her feelings as a black, Haitian-born, Canadian-raised academic, now installed in the United States. Chancy writes, '... we enact the principles of Afro-Caribbean diasporic feminism in paying attention to those markers of status (race, sex, class, sexuality, and so on), which delimit the quality of our existence in this world, and move more swiftly toward a transformative progress that will better the condition of Black women's lives and of all others concurrently' (91). Her utilization of 'we' is instructive here. She reads Philip and Brand (and Silvera) against the terms of her own uprooting, and displacement, and she is honest about her personal alienation in ways that Walcott – decorative, superficial – is not. There is romanticism here, a sort of feminist Pan-Africanism: 'By focusing on our personal existence and politicizing the parameters of that existence, we actively transform the terms of our exile and bring our alienation to an end' (91). Chancy seeks to palliate her own academic estrangement by proclaiming her participation in the Andersonian 'imagined community' she reconstitutes in her essay. In doing so, she upholds Brand as the paramount articulator of an 'Afro-Caribbean diasporic feminist vision' (117), for the latter 'steadfastly foregrounds and defines the oppression of Afro-Caribbean women as being comprised of homophobia in addition to racism, sexism, and classism' (117). Finally, Brand 'foregrounds an identity of her own making, which encapsulates Black women's history in Canada and in the Caribbean as well as her own history as a displaced Afro-Caribbean artist struggling to survive against the forces of racism, sexism, and homophobia' (119). One can almost imagine Brand heroically donning a helmet, *à la* Chilean Marxist president Salvador Allende (1908–73), and making a quixotic last stand *somewhere*. In comparison, Philip suffers, for she fails 'to illustrate the growth of an explicitly lesbian relationship [in a novel]' (116). To use a Stalinist analogy, Brand is Lenin, Philip only Trotsky. Chancy shuns Philip's novel *Looking for Livingstone: An Odyssey of Silence* (1991), for it makes no 'valuable connections between the presence of racist, sexist, and homophobic oppression in the lives of Afro-Caribbean women in addition to illustrating the difficulties of surviving between the memory of "home" ... and the imposition of assimilation in English cultures ...' (116). Thus, Philip is just not as politically advanced as Brand, which is a pity. (Perhaps Philip should have joined the Communist Party of Canada, Marxist-Leninist, instead of having opted to practise law between 1973 and 1982.)[24] To employ a now familiar trope, if Philip and Brand are 'bridge builders,' Brand is a bridge architect. To Chancy, she 'suggests that bridges can alternatively be built out of understanding for the dis-similarities in our eyes, as each of us struggles to survive in the face of a misogynistic, racist, and homophobic patriarchal world order' (91).

In light of the readings proffered by Hunter, Morrell, and Chancy, Brand has been enshrined as the demi-godhead of justly progressive expressions, with Philip and Harris (or – for Chancy – Silvera) assigned lesser positions – as semi-benighted divines – in this literary trinity. Worrisomely, while Hunter and Morrell save space on their syllabi for Harris, Chancy and Rinaldo Walcott do not. They exclude her from scrutiny, perhaps because her cosmopolitanism implies a watering-down of black and righteous anger. Not radical enough for their tastes, they ignore her – a warning that her literary stock may be losing some scholarly capital.

Harris need not fret. Her work is saluted in a 1996 essay by Euro-Canadian academic Susan Rudy, namely, '"What There Is Teasing beyond the Edges": Claire Harris's Liminal Autobiography.' If some African-Canadian feminist intellectuals have dropped Harris, Euro-Canadian feminist intellectuals have not. Rudy celebrates Harris, then, in stereotypical terms:

> Harris's representation of a black feminist consciousness requires a complex, con- structed, and yet certain ... subjectivity ... She speaks out against the potentially unravelling oppressions of race, gender, and class in contemporary Canada, re- fashioning poetry, narrative, autobiography, and the English language itself in the process. (94–5)

Like her colleagues – Hunter, Morrell, Walcott, and Chancy – Rudy highlights her select member of the Trinidadian-Canadian trinity as representing an ideal politics, thus reducing her to the mouthpiece of, not even identity poli- tics, but *appearance* politics. Rudy identifies Harris as – to note that beloved trope of liberal critics – a racial bridge-builder: 'Reading Harris's work as autobiographical writing, I feel, more overtly than usual, a desire for commu- nication, for social relation with this person writing, for connection across the barriers not only of language but also of racism' (79). Once again, this Black Canadian woman is exalted as a kind of Trudeaumanic liberal, permitting the ensconced academic to feel – more soulfully, more philosophically – the thrill of progressivism.[25]

When Rudy (writing as Susan Rudy Dorscht) reviews Morrell's *Grammar of Dissent*, she expresses a like delight in discovering works that affirm her ide- als: 'I am delighted by the appearance of *Grammar of Dissent* since it will enable me to teach the visceral, intellectual, political work of black, feminist women in Canada' (Review 188). Excitingly, too, Morrell's work 'makes real and available some of the most committed feminist and anti-racist writing and thinking in contemporary Canada. For that reason alone, I know I shall return to it often' (Review 191). So, Rudy lauds Harris, Philip, and Brand for churchly reasons, using them as mascots or talismans, as madonnas of a humane humanism, a bountiful economics, a Just Society. Faced with such neo-medieval holiness, critique may be surrendered.

Intriguingly, Rudy protests Morrell's merely honourable politics by proposing some right honourable politics of her own. She attacks Morrell's breathless assertion that the 'oppositional literature' of Harris, Philip, and Brand shows that literature 'formed from a context, that speaks directly and passionately about the contradictions in our society and its oppression of certain groups, can be also excellent, stunning not only thematically but technically' (Introduction 23). Rudy replies that Morrell's thesis is 'not useful' (Review 189). To Rudy, Morrell believes 'only literature which speaks out against racism, sexism, classism, is formed by its context, that such "oppositional" literature is thematic, and that it is surprising when oppositional work is also "excellent"' (Review 189). For Rudy, Morrell's words 'have the alarming effect of marginalizing the book's contents' (Review 189). Morrell's introduction is so wrong-headed that Rudy calls into question Morrell's feminism by stressing that the scholar who is so patently muddling things is – incredibly – a 'she (yes, "she")' (Review 189). Rudy also rips into Morrell's 'unproblematized use of terms like "outsiders"' (Review 189) to denote 'black, immigrants, women, and lesbians' (Morrell, Introduction 23). Thus, she becomes, exultantly, the political educator that Morrell has failed to be: 'Women with a radical politics – which these anti-racist feminists certainly have – do not speak of themselves as outsiders' (Review 189). Paradoxically, by battling Morrell on this terrain, Rudy also destabilizes Walcott's ascription of an exilic outsiderness or migrant 'in-betweenness' to Philip and Brand.

Though Rudy does not engage explicitly in any ranking exercises, she seems – like Hunter and Chancy – to finger Brand as the stand-out of the trio, that is, if lineation is any guide. She assigns Harris a nine-line paragraph, Philip a ten-liner, but Brand a solid thirteen-liner (exclusive of a nine-line quotation from a poem) (Review 189–90). Despite these telling apportions of space, nothing substantial is said about the writers. We learn that 'Harris's work is nothing short of a gift' (Review 190), that Philip undertakes an 'analysis of racism in Canadian culture' (Review 190), and that Brand 'takes on these issues [of race and "sexualities"] directly' (Review 190). Here is the evacuation of critique, vapidly conducted.

The South Asian–Canadian academic Victor J. Ramraj, in his article 'West Indian–Canadian Writing in English' (1996), also canvasses well-trod territory in his commentary on Harris, Philip, and Brand. Ramraj finds that the three writers 'are fundamentally concerned with past and present abuses, marginalization, and "dehumanizing exclusivity" of the black woman as a colonial in imperial societies and as an immigrant in North American societies' (165). However, he deems Harris the most adept racial bridge-builder, judging that, in *Dipped in Shadow* (1996), a quintet of long poems, Harris 'down-plays ethnic particulars as she explores the lot of women of various racial and ethnic backgrounds' (165). But 'Brand and Philip are far more militant and confrontational than Harris in their writing' (Ramraj 165). 'They make greater use of narratives of slavery and colonization to accentuate the plight of contemporary blacks' (Ramraj 165–6). While they may be more authentic agents of fury than Harris, Ramraj favours Harris's apparent belief that 'in a society with conflicting but interpenetrating cultures it is important to recognize differences as well as commonalities' (165). By taking this stance, Ramraj jeopardizes Padolsky's 'hurrah' that 'Brand's championing of "Black and immigrant working class women and white working class women" clearly shows a bridging that crosses racial categories, without of course denying them' ('Ethnicity' 31). For Ramraj, Harris is the Great Communicator across racial and ethnic divides;[26] for Padolsky, it's Brand; for Hunter, it's Philip – the 'generous' bridge-builder (275), though at the cost of perhaps neglecting her 'Black heritage' (276). These are paltry, prettifying – no, petrifying – findings.

With collaborationist ease, Hunter, Morrell, Walcott, Chancy, Rudy, and Ramraj exalt Harris, Philip, and Brand as standard-bearers of feminism, or anti-racism, or socialism, or anti-imperialism, or anti-homophobia (and, in Brand's case – fortuitously for her – all of the above). By addressing this choice *troika*, white female critics are given leave to talk about 'race'; white male critics (though few to date) are freed to discuss repressed issues (see Padolsky, 'Ethnicity'); black critics are enabled to discuss sexism and homophobia; and exilic 'post-colonial' critics are empowered to focus on the utopia of the lost home and the cold evils of the 'new land.'[27] It is safe to assume that most of the criticism to date on Harris, Philip, and Brand falls into one of these conventional – even conservative, racial 'bridge-building' – paradigms.

Yet, we do Harris, Philip, and Brand a vacuous – but vicious – injustice, and we shortchange the entirety of African-Canadian literature, by elevating this trio to triumvirate status without bothering to ponder their actual poetics. We should also trouble our refusals to engage the work of black male homosexual writers like Nova Scotia's Frederick Ward (b. 1937) and Walter Borden (b. 1942),[28] or the feminist writings of Tynes, who also champions the rights of the physically challenged and who holds, like Brand, a national award – the People's Poet Award (1988). We must rethink our spurning of the work of younger, Canadian-born, black female and male writers – British Columbia's Wayde Compton (b. 1972), Alberta's Suzette Mayr (b. 1967), Québec's Robert Sandiford (b. 1968). (Perhaps, for us, they lack the glittering penumbra of exoticism ...)

Bluntly, much of the criticism of Harris, Philip, and Brand is irrelevant. It is not enough to acclaim them as poets of exodus; no, not when Brand writes about Toronto and northern Ontario, not when Harris centres her writing career in Alberta, not when Philip identifies with *Anne of Green Gables* (1908) (*Genealogy* 28). Nor is it sufficient to rank them according to some scale of political virtue. If an 'Afro-Caribbean diasporic' aesthetic is preferable to any other, what does this option do for (or *to*) indigenous African-Canadian writers? If realism is the only valid mode of literary expression, why should African-Canadian writers attempt other modes? (Perhaps they should be journalists.)

To avoid these intellectual lacunae, we need to shift the terms of the debate. It is no longer enough to applaud a coming to voice of writers from ex-centric locations. We must engage their poetics, their structures, styles, influences; the histories of their textual productions, receptions, and circulations; the literal connections between their theoretical *poesis* and their political *praxis*, if any. When we undertake these analyses of Harris, Philip, and Brand, we will discover the subversively erotic, the effort to reclaim black bodies from inscriptions within white patriarchal and racist/homophobic hegemonies.[29] We will discover that it is their search for a true tongue – a mother tongue – despite all the grammars of imperialism and the primers of subjugation – that enables these writers to create their most authoritative poetry and fiction.[30] We will reveal these truths – unless we are tiring of writing.

Notes

1 This paper was presented at the 14th Biennial Meeting of the Association for Canadian Studies in the United States, in Minneapolis, Minnesota, on 20 November 1997. I dedicate it to Hardial Bains, the late chair of the Communist Party of Canada, Marxist-Leninist, to laud his achingly brilliant polemics and his bracingly seditious text *Communism: 1989–1991* (1991).

2 In his *Marginal Forces / Cultural Centers: Tolson, Pynchon, and the Politics of the Canon* (1992), Michael Bérubé establishes that 'institutional criticism ... involves not only Weberian bureaucracy but also, for all of us in post-Weberian capitalism, the power to keep texts in circulation, to keep them *current* in an economic sense, even if only by teaching them, distributing them, assigning them in courses' (314). The critic serves to assist the consumption and reproduction of texts, and 'we may say that consumption and reproduction *constitute* the existence of texts' (4).

3 U.S. scholar Victor Strandberg complains that leftist critics believe that 'under the high-minded banners of Theory – Feminism, Marxism ..., Race & Ethnic Studies, Queer Theory, anti-Colonial/Imperialism – the study of literature might serve the ends of social justice and liberation, casting off its historic role as a mere aesthetic enterprise' (2). Yet, 'theory [itself] either ... proves untrue, by falsifying actual experience, or it tells me something I already knew: in essence, that sexism, racism, and homophobia are bad' (2). While one cannot 'deny its achievement, most notably [raising] the self-esteem, -understanding, and -empowerment of social victims,' the exulting of Theory '*was* a noble enterprise ..., but not primarily a literary one' (3). His case is central, for too many excellent writers are being cast aside in the name of a censurious moral rectitude. Bérubé points out that the African-American modernist poet Melvin B. Tolson (1898–1966) has been excluded from canonization because of his valorization of 'the avant-garde over against the "kitsch" of mass culture even as he renews the Romantic revolutionary's faith in the power of the avant-garde to transform the masses' (71). The result has been that 'Tolson's white critics' praise him 'for not writing black' (167), while black critics 'sift through Tolson's poems and set aside everything that does not look suffi-

ciently "black"' (177). The work of American poet James Dickey (1923–97) endures like critical furores: 'Dickey's career became – and remains – a battleground between the advocates of criticism that directly foregrounds political and social issues and those who favor aesthetic cricticism that indirectly affirms humanistic values' (Suarez 102). For her part, French Canadianist Marta Dvorak asks that scholars understand 'we need not settle for language being sacrificed to issues' (27).

4 See John Berger's argument that, in photographs of war atrocities, 'the issue of the war which has caused that moment [of photographed obscenity] is effectively depoliticised. The picture becomes evidence of the general human condition. It accuses nobody and everybody' (40).

5 In *Survival*, Atwood asks her readers to 'suppose, for the sake of argument, that Canada as a whole is a victim, or an "oppressed minority," or "exploited." Let us suppose in short that Canada is a colony' (35). She implies that 'the Thirteen Colonies' – that is, the United States – constitutes a new 'Rome' or imperial power (36). In *Morning in the Burned House*, the poem 'Half-Hanged Mary' argues that its subject, Mary Webster, was hanged for supposed witchcraft by men 'excited by their show of hate, / their own evil turned inside out like a glove' (59–60).

6 See, for instance, Mouré's poem 'Miss Chatelaine':
> Finally there are no men between us.
> Finally none of us are passing or failing according to
> *Miss Chatelaine.*
> I wish I could tell you how much I love you,
> my friends with your odd looks, our odd looks,
> our nervousness with each other ...
> Finally I can meet with you & talk this over.
> Finally I can see us meeting, & our true tenderness, emerge. (54–5)

Perhaps Mouré's feminism is not as advanced as Hunter would prefer a white woman's to be.

7 Thus, Perloff obscures the quite political Romantic poets, including William Blake (1757–1827), William Wordsworth (1770–1850), Samuel Taylor Coleridge (1772–1834), Lord Byron (1788–1824), and Percy Bysshe Shelley (1792–1822). Yet, these figures admit no political exhaustion.

8 Here, Perloff voids the comical-political work of a Byron (see his *Don Juan* [1819–24]) or the didactic-narrative work of a Wordsworth (see his *The Prelude* [1798–1839]) in her definition of the Romantic.

9 Strandberg reminds us that for many critics with 'social aims, ... aesthetic values should merit more friendly consideration' (2).

10 For instance, see Mouré's work 'The Acts [10],' a prose poem that scrutinizes the politics of grammar:
> To break down the noun/verb opposition that is a kind of absolutism in the language itself. So that using the words affirms, *no matter what*, the dominant Order. (94)

Seeming to repond to the radical interrogations bruited by M. NourbeSe Philip in her *She Tries Her Tongue, Her Silence Softly Breaks* (1989), Atwood's later 'Marsh Languages' also critiques the construction of language:

Translation was never possible.
Instead there was always only
conquest, the influx
of the language, of hard nouns,
the language of metal,
the language of either/or,
the one language that has eaten all the others. (55)

While Mouré and Atwood are – at times – provocatively *avant-garde* in their perceptions, practices, and preoccupations, they are also – like Harris, Philip, and Brand – *rooted* in the diurnal, the practical reality of political disputation.

11 In the last two scenes of this cinematic poem, the prose 'panning shot' reveals the Indian wife's recognition of her alienation from her white husband's Occidental and *bourgeois* household wealth –

she takes bacon from the microwave empties the dishwasher struggles against the contradictions of grief/rage/pride rising in her like bile (one final act to free her from kinship to the formal contemptuous caricature the shorthand of gaunt eyes and CARE cupped pathos those fly haunted dyings that this evening will spring from screen and newspaper confirming images of grotesque otherness) ... (19)

– while the verse 'shot' – focusing on the breakfasting husband – establishes that his wife has just broken several cups and is 'riding / a pale staircase her / sari / unwrapped and flailing ...' (20). The poem concludes with a 'close-up' of the wife as 'she stoops / picks up a fragment a / handle [of a cup] / curved and sure in her palm / cool perfect / and without feeling' (20). This final image implies both the callousness of the husband (who has commented, about a massacre in India, '*some things / get worse before they get / better*' [20]) and the ebbing of 'feeling' within the marriage.

12 Compare Brand's use of imagistic anaphora in her 'Canto I' –

white of beaten iron and guns
white with the ancestors' praise and
white with the breath of the whites on our land
white as of eyes on sand on humid vastness
white as the tune of fingers, brisk on dry skin
not even pursed hungry lips were as white (quoted in Morrell 185)

– with Pound's allusion-saturated technique in his 'Canto XLV':

With usura hath no man a house of good stone ...
with usura
hath no man a painted paradise on his church wall ...
with usura
seeth no man no Gonzaga his heirs and his concubines ...
with usura, sin against nature,
is thy bread ever more of stale rags ...
with usura the line grows thick ... (57)

Obviously, Brand's interests diverge from those of Pound, and I do not argue that she has only his example in mind. Her use of number-titled lyrics in later books – *No Language Is Neutral* (1990) and *Land to Light On* (1997) – flags an attentiveness to another male poet, Derek Walcott (b. 1930), who also employs this strategy. Brand has acknowledged, in a 1991 interview with Frank Birbalsingh (Brand, 'Dionne' 123), the influences of two male writers – the Cuban Alejo Carpentier (1904–80) and the Guyanese Wilson Harris (b. 1921) – on her writing of *Primitive Offensive* (1982).

13 The sourcing of Pound's dictum kills Hunter's idea that Philip strikes 'a stance different from the modernist directive to "Make it New"' (278).

14 The title of Brand's *No Language Is Neutral* is borrowed from a line in Derek Walcott's 'LII' (1984): 'No language is neutral; / the green oak of English is a murmurous cathedral / where some took umbrage, some peace, but every shade, all, / helped widen its shadow' (72). Brand differs from Walcott in that her socialist vision of history allows for the potential victory of a popular and paradisal revolution. Walcott seems to believe, contrarily, conservatively, that history recycles sameness, so that revolutions become repetitions. In any event, Philip attacks Walcott for his rumoured sexism:

> Over supper the name of a famous, male writer (of African and European heritage) comes up in a discussion, as well as his reputation for sexually harassing women. Arthur, a Jewish American novelist, defends him by saying he is a Great Writer ... But I must ask, and do – very quietly! – 'What does being a great writer have to do with harassing women?' ... The conversation ends with a woman, saying that she had worked for the Great Writer and that he had told her that if he was in a room alone with a woman, he assumed she wanted him. (*Genealogy* 133–4)

Finally, Brand owes an apparent debt to the Chilean Nobel laureate Pablo Neruda (1904–73), for the twin inspirations of his Marxism and his use of catalogues inside the canto form.

15 The trope of 'building bridges' is the *sine qua non* of politically righteous, liberal-identified criticism. Witness: Hunter states that 'Philip's attempts at bridge-building are immensely generous' (275). In her 1996 essay on 'Afro-Canadian Womanist Poetry,' Indian scholar Coomi S. Vevaina comments that 'the fact that we live in a hate-filled world, should not make us regard the hope of building bridges across cultures with cynicism' (134). The trope is such a staple in post-colonial criticism, it suggests that the field is about – in essence – *race relations*. Understandably, then, in the discipline-defining work *The Empire Writes Back: Theory and Practice in Post-Colonial Literatures* (1989), authors Bill Ashcroft, Gareth Griffiths, and Helen Tiffin swear that comparative studies 'drawn between countries or regions across Black and white diasporas ... form important bridges for the discourse of post-colonialism' (20). Such formulations inspire pugnacious questions: who's crossing these bridges and why?

16 Here it appears that Hunter is engaging in the kind of dramatic – or traumatic – imbrication with notions of *négritude* that are germane to post-colonial literature. The sexy fetish of anger represents a newly chic Africanism, one close to the concept of *négritude* developed by the Martiniquan Aimé Césaire (b. 1913) and the Senegalese poet and politician Léopold Sedar Senghor (b. 1906), which was 'the most profound assertion of the distinctive qualities of Black culture and identity' (Ashcroft, et al., 21). Hence, Hunter does not escape the dilemma of this model –

'the adoption of stereotypes which curiously [reflect] European prejudice' (Ashcroft, et al. 21). Surely, the philosophy of *négritude* implies that African-heritage cultures are 'emotional rather than rational' (Ashcroft, et al. 21). In loving Brand's 'anger,' then, Hunter loves a black stereotype. She enters a trap that Jacques Derrida outlines in *Positions* (1982), principally, that 'the heirarchy of dual oppositions always reestablishes itself ...' (41–2). The *spectacle* of Brand's anger enraptures Hunter – like the objective white explorer encountering the display of the native Other's *emotion*. Yet, her true intellectual duty is to remember the requirement for, as Derrida states, 'an interminable analysis' (41–2).

17 Despite her brave naming of 'the Caribbean demotic,' Morrell never interrogates the use of 'nation language' by Harris, Philip, and Brand; nor does she treat any relevant linguist, such as Edouard Glissant, or even J. Edward Chamberlin's *Come Back to Me My Language: Poetry and the West Indies* (1993), a work which appeared a year before Morrell's anthology. Yet, an appeal to Glissant's understanding of demotic black speech is helpful:

> Creole organizes sentences on the mode of machinegun bursts ... [A]ll over the Creole world, the people speak like that ... This introduces a new factor in Creole sentences: speed. Not speed, perhaps, as much as staccato. Another feature is also the fast unrolling of a sentence into a single indivisible word ... Thus the meaning of a sentence is sometimes concealed ... in accelerated nonsense rumbling with sounds. But this nonsense ferries the true meaning while keeping it from the master's ear. (97)

Chamberlin agrees. He mounts this argument regarding Caribbean English:

> In its resistance to appropriation by the center, especially in circumstances where communities feel themselves under siege, local language often paradoxically confirms the marginality against which it is a protest. Images of solidarity and betrayal also become indispensable to the ideology of language in these situations, so that terms like 'nation language,' which [West Indian poet] Kamau Braithwaite (among others) has proposed to represent the authority of local languages (though not necessarily along national lines), carries with it the same political logic of loyalty and treason that we associate with nationality. (*Come* 35)

The style of any marginalized group's language mirrors Andrew Ross's characterization of the rhetoric of French philosopher Jean Baudrillard as 'a vendetta, a highly ritualized feud with culture itself' (214).

18 Morrell's comment echoes Hunter's assertion that 'these writers write about issues I recognize intimately when they write about their position as women, as lovers, wives, mothers, daughters, women at work' (259). Hunter affirms her need to be 'taught' about racial difference by Harris, Philip, and Brand: 'When a familiar common ground like mothers and daughters, which women might expect to remain stable or at least recognizable, is suddenly refracted through racial difference, the effect is often a radical impetus to extend discussion' (259). The idea is treacle that lacerates.

19 The trauma of the implosion of the Grenadian Revolution in 1983 defines Brand's *oeuvre*. The collapse into political chaos, assassinations masquerading as executions, public turmoil, and a lethal U.S. invasion inform her subsequent works. Yet, no one

has tried to contextualize Brand's lyrics on the matter – for instance, 'October 25th, 1983' (1984) – against military accounts such as chapter 11 – 'October 25: The Struggle for Point Salines' – in Major Mark Adkin's *Urgent Fury: The Battle for Grenada* (1989). Yet, the poetry acquires fresh poignancy when read against Adkin's report that, though U.S. Rangers and Special Operations Forces were originally supposed to leave Grenada on 25 October 1983, they had to remain because 'resistance had been heavier than expected, the Cubans and P[eople's] R[evolutionary] A[rmy] were still fighting [U.S. troops].' Moreover, there had been a 'successful PRA counterattack at Beausejour' (223–4). The quality of PRA resistance was such that 'within another three days [of October 25th], no fewer than six battalions of the 82nd [Airborne Division] were in Grenada [as reinforce-ments]. In light of the struggle of many Grenadians – and some Cubans – to repulse the invasion, Brand's defeatist tone in 'October 25th, 1983' marks the death of the Grenadian Revolution *and* the cessation of a dream-sustaining dream:

> america came to restore democracy,
> what was restored was faith
> in the fact that you cannot fight bombers
> battleships, aircraft carriers, helicopter gunships ...
> you cannot fight this with a machete ...
>
> certainly you cannot fight it with dignity ...
> And finally you can only fight it with the silence of your
> dead body. (Quoted in Morrell 217–18)

The U.S. Joint Chiefs of Staff would salute the persona's fatalistic depression. Their post-mortem on the invasion insists it brought quick and thorough victory:

> The surprise airborne assault on Point Salines airfield by the Rangers effectively neutralized Cuban forces at the outset, and led to the capture of several hundred Cubans despite stiff resistance. Capture of Pearls Airport by the Marines, as well as their successful amphibious operation in the vicinity of St. George's on the 25th led to the capture of Fort Frederick, the Grenadian command and control headquarters, the next day. Successful execution of the US plans on the 25th and 26th led to cessation of organized enemy resistance. (Quoted in Adkins 345)

Brand's poem recognizes this history: 'The planes are circling, / the american paratroopers dropping, / later Radio Free Grenada stops for the last time / In the end they sang – / 'ain't giving up no way, / no i ain't giving up no way' (quoted in Morrell 216–17). Though Adkins judges the capture of Radio Free Grenada to have been frivolous, for it could 'easily have been ignored and allowed to fall into U.S. hands when the [invasion] was over' (174), Brand feels differently. For the poet, the silencing of the 'people's' radio station is equivalent to the silencing of revolutionary song and of the prophecy of redemptive revolution itself. The muting of Radio Free Grenada prophesies only the 'silence of your / dead body' (quoted in Morrell 218).

20 Aptly, in Brand's novel, words of antithesis and negation – *no, nothing, nowhere, no one, nobody* – are used recurrently by the protagonists Verlia and Elizete to describe their realities of oppression – sexual, racial, colonial. One also finds a Nerudian emphasis on the elemental metaphor and the catalogue, on political fire and cussing, on the lyricizing of analysis.

21 The Anglo-Caribbean poet Edward Kamau Braithwaite discusses the idea of 'nation language' in his *History of the Voice: The Development of Nation Language in Anglophone Caribbean Poetry* (1984).

22 Brand's use of a number-titled lyric sequence, running from 'I i' to 'III v' (in 'I Have Been Losing Roads'), recalls the titling style of Ovid, as in his 'The Amores,' where the capital Roman numeral refers to the overarching sequence, while the minuscule numeral denotes a specific lyric within the sequence. Philip's nod to Ovid is clear. Her poetic sequence 'And Over Every Land and Sea' (1989) uses quotations 'from Ovid, *The Metamorphoses*, translated by Mary M. Innes' (quoted in Morrell 128). The quotations trigger Philip's project, for her sequence is a Caribbeanization *cum* Canadianization of the Greco-Roman story of Ceres' search for her daughter, Proserpine.

23 In an interview, Philip notes that 'you won't find Canada in my work in that sense of "wilderness," but I think that the work could only have been written here' ('Secrecy' 18).

24 Brand was a member of the Communist Party of Canada, a point underlined in her essay 'Cuba' (1994): 'And then a poet friend of mine said to me one June, "I was so disappointed when I heard that you joined the Communist Party"' (97). As for Philip, before deciding to write full-time, she practised law in Toronto, 'working in the areas of immigration and family law, primarily as a partner in the firm Jemmott and Philip, the first black women's law partnership in Canada' (Rose 911). Brand contributed to the building of socialist Grenada because 'nothing had felt right until getting there ... Why I went there was because I could not live in the uneasiness of conquest and enslavement, and it didn't seem to me that paths with even the merest suggestion of acceptance of these could lead me out' ('Cuba' 96). Likewise, Philip pioneered contemporary black women's law in Canada and practised direct struggle against racism in Toronto, mainly among its white artistic élites (Rose, 'Philip' 912). Chancy would likely classify Brand as being revolutionary and Philip as being *bourgeois*. Yet, Philip's project had the effect of assisting black women where they were living – in Canada – while Brand's efforts were utopian *and* alien. Crucially, though, both writers have striven to help construct a New Eden: all ideological labels are mischievous obfuscation, a chic chicanery.

25 Rudy may also feel a regional affinity for Harris. A professor of English at the University of Calgary, in Alberta, Rudy resides in the same city where Harris has lived since 1966. Moreover, Harris served as the poetry editor of *Dandelion* (1981–9) and was the co-founder and managing editor of *blue buffalo* (1984–7) (Rose, 'Harris' 516). The regional connection between Rudy and Harris merits mention because it proves that literary criticism is a secretion of autobiography. (Thus, Toronto critic Walcott hails Toronto poets Philip and Brand, but not Harris, the Calgarian.) None

of this detracts from the glory of Harris's global interests, her landscape romanticism, her joy in poetry.

26 Ramraj's preference for Harris may also reflect his position as an Albertan professor of English. See note 25.

27 Coomi S. Vevaina recognizes that critics from different cultural communities exhibit contrasting desires when reviewing 'ex-centric' writers. Those 'belonging to the country of their [the immigrant writers'] adoption desire "cultural authenticity" while those from their [the immigrant writers'] original homelands feel that the writers are distorting, even prostituting their culture in order to cash in on the recent interest in ethnic writing' (125).

28 My own regional allegiance is – well – obvious.

29 See Philip's erotic fiction 'Commitment to Hardness' (1992), a hymn to black nationalist heterosexuality: 'That commitment to [penile] hardness belonged to the race – making Ben's cock a part of him and yet not a part of him' (96).

30 Coomi Vevaina acknowledges that 'the female narrators of Dionne Brand, Claire Harris, Lillian Allen, Nourbese Philip, and Afua Cooper locate the missing part of themselves not in the father but in the being and word of their foremothers and mothers' (130). In her 1994 article 'To "Heal the Word Wounded": Agency and Materiality of Language and Form in M. Nourbese Philip's *She Tries Her Tongue, Her Silence Softly Breaks*,' Euro-Canadian scholar Brenda Carr interrogates cogently Philip's challenging exposé of the inherent oppressiveness of English. Carr affirms that 'the graphemic materiality of Philip's text – different type faces, spacing, vertical texts, and multiply juxtaposed texts – further activates the social fact of poetry as labour by poet, typesetter, and reader ...' (75). Carr underlines Philip's 'remembrance' of 'the superimposed scene of sexual and linguistic violation for the Afrosporic female subject' (79). See also the finely nuanced essays 'Figures of Silence and Orality in the Poetry of M. Nourbese Philip' (1996), by David Marriott, and 'En / Gendering Spaces: The Poetry of Marlene Nourbese Philip and Pamela Mordecai' (1996), by Elaine Savory.

No Language Is Neutral:
Seizing English for Ourselves

For You, Close Reader

If black writers feel pressured to prove, practically continuously, their adeptness, their facility, with the imposed canons and grammars of Europe (and its demi-palimpsest, the New World), they also feel a kind of radical joy in subverting these strictures and structures. As African-American critic Houston A. Baker, Jr, professes, black writers practise a 'deformation of mastery,' a quasi-guerilla action represented by the transformation of usually staid literary forms such as the sonnet into salient vehicles of protest (see Gwendolyn Brooks, see Claude McKay) and by the articulation of Afrocentric themes (i.e., our beauty, our triumphalist history, our essential Africanness). Every black writer has had to ask, 'Whose language is it, anyway?'

One can spy this process at work in the verse of the first African poet to 'deform' a European language, Phillis Wheatley, who, after being kidnapped from Senegal and auctioned at Boston at the age of nine, began, precociously, to compose poetry just seven years later. In her book, *Poems on Various Subjects* (1773), Wheatley uses neoclassical couplets and Miltonic diction to attack slavery and to insist on the equality of – assuredly – all Christians. Misread for years as a poet who cared more about salvation than about slavery, she was, in actuality, a ferocious disciple of liberty, a majestic prophetess of abolition:

> I, young in life, by seeming cruel fate
> Was snatch'd from Afric's fancy'd happy seat:
> What pangs excruciating must molest,
> What sorrows labour in my parent's breast?
> Steel'd was that soul and by no misery mov'd
> That from a father seiz'd his babe belov'd:
> Such, such my case. And can I then but pray
> Others may never feel tyrannic sway?

Not only did Wheatley hammer rhyme into a weapon to use against the ungodly traffic in human beings, she also inaugurated the African diasporic literary tradition of speaking some truths cryptically. For instance, her poem

'Goliath of Gath' repeats the biblical story of the giant warrior's slaying by David, but slyly recasts him as a tribune of slavery, one who would demand 'perpetual service from the vanquish'd.' Wheatley also mothered another re-sistive tradition in black literature by naming herself as an 'Ethiope' and 'Afric's muse,' thus assuming the role of spokesperson and doing so with relish and panache. When she claims Terence, the African-born Roman playwright of antiquity, as her inspiration, she creates a link with an earlier African diasporic writer, a custom that others have subsequently followed. Think, here, of Hai-tian-Canadian writer Dany Laferrière's paeans to the late great James Baldwin.

Certainly, John William Robertson, a Virginia slave who absconded, by ship, to Halifax, Nova Scotia, in 1852, continued the convention of using English to speak, not only for himself, but for a subject people. Not satisfied with simple liberty, he craved literacy. Tutored by his employer, a Captain Barry, he soon became an outspoken author, publishing his elegant and mighty booklet, *The Book of the Bible against Slavery*, in 1854. His polemic throws the slaveholders' hypocritical religion back in their bloody, white faces. Southern preachers swore that slavery was sanctioned by God, but Robertson levied a harsh sanc-tion against them, declaring, 'The spirit of Slavery never seeks refuge in the Bible of its own accord ...' If some authors, like Canada's own Thomas Chan-dler Haliburton, painted bucolic visions of slavery, Robertson presented a different story, one of brutality and torture, of 'eyes put out ..., ears cut off ..., flesh branded with hot irons ... and burnt to death over slow fires.' If earlier English writers had chronicled the martyrdoms of saints, Robertson and his like illuminated a whole new slate of candidates for beatification. In Robertson's hands, literacy becomes a shining sword in the struggle for liberation. He knew what Nobel laureate Derek Walcott knows: 'no language is neutral.'

Neutrality is impossible so long as white society continues to construct and configure blackness as the infernal inverse of itself. Since Standard English was thrust upon African diasporic peoples against their wills, it is marvellous justice that, in every exilic African culture, from New Brunswick to New Or-leans, from Jamaica to California, that tongue now meets a different standard. As Trinidadian-Canadian writer M. NourbeSe Philip attests in *She Tries Her Tongue, Her Silence Softly Breaks* (1989), 'the formal standard language was subverted, turned upside down, inside out, and even erased. Nouns became strangers to verbs and vice versa; tonal accentuation took the place of several words at a time; rhythms held sway.' Hear the folk-coloured vocalizations of Jean Toomer and Olive Senior. Our English is, no longer, the master's voice.

Black writers honour the link between being and language, between em-powerment and articulation. They cannot cease to do so. The word is out.

PART TWO

INCURSIONS:
SELECTED REVIEWS

The Complex Face of Black Canada

Review of *Diversity, Mobility and Change: The Dynamics of Black Communities in Canada*, by James L. Torczyner et al. [Montreal]: McGill Consortium for Ethnicity and Strategic Social Planning, 1997.

A few summers ago, VIA Rail offered an enticing 50 per cent fare reduction for foreign visitors to Canada, but did not advertise the bargain, suspecting that it would anger Canadians whose taxes subsidize the corporation. I learned about the scheme while purchasing a ticket in Kingston, Ontario. The agent asked, stealthily, for my passport. I was puzzled. 'What do you mean, my passport?' She then advised me about the discount for foreigners, specifying that my 'American accent' marked me as an eligible passenger. I informed the agent that (as the *très* white beer commercial says) 'I AM CANADIAN.' But it's never been simple to be a black in Canada.

My bloodlines run deep in this country. My father's father was West Indian, but his mother's father came to Nova Scotia from Virginia in 1898. My mother's ancestors – slaves liberated by British forces during the War of 1812 – voyaged to Nova Scotia, from Chesapeake Bay, in 1813. I was born, raised, and educated in Nouvelle-Écosse. I went to Expo 67, I sang along with Ian and Sylvia and the Great Speckled Bird, I wanted Robert Stanfield to win in '72. Either I am Canadian, or the word means nothing.

Then again, the VIA Rail incident was not about accent. Because my colour distinguishes me from most Canadians, most assume that I hail from 'somewhere else.' When someone asks what island I'm from, I reply, 'Cape Breton.' Moreover, Canadians are abysmally ignorant about African-Canadian history. For instance, a Canadian Civil Liberties Association poll, conducted in 1995, found that 83 per cent of Canadians did not know that slavery had been practised in pre-Confederation Canada.

To be black in Canada is, then, an existential experience. A constant interrogation of our belonging inculcates within us, not just the 'double consciousness' that the superb African-American intellectual W.E.B. Du Bois (pronounced 'Do Boyce' in the U.S.) posited for Black Americans, but a 'poly consciousness.' For as our blackness ranges from ivory to indigo hues, our heritages, ethnic allegiances, religions, and languages are also varied. In fact, African Canada, in its gorgeous, explicit diversity, is a microcosm of Canada.

A McGill study published this year provides both the most current demographic information about Canada's black communities and several surprising findings. Although I prefer the terms *African-Canadian* or *Africadian* – they capture the experiences of those from the United States, Africa, and Caribbean – the authors sought to understand the 'black experience' and how blacks fare in Canadian society. *Diversity, Mobility and Change: The Dynamics of Black Communities in Canada* was written by McGill professor of social work James L. Torczyner, along with colleagues Wally Boxhill, Carl James, and Crystal Mulder.

The report is a response to one consequence of African-Canadian diversity: the fact that almost half of us do not identify ourselves as 'Black' on Canadian census documents. True: 43 per cent of African-heritage respondents to the 1991 census listed themselves as French or British, or as Barbadian, Ethiopian, Ghanaian, Haitian, Somali, Jamaican, Guyanese, Trinidadian/Tobagonian, *et cetera*, leading to a serious undercounting of African-heritage Canadians. Boxhill, a former Statistics Canada employee, recast the numbers to count the above groups as black. This means that, as of 1991, there were 504,290 blacks in Canada, not 366,625 as formerly counted.

These figures entail consequences, but, before I discuss them, I want to tease out an issue that seems to have eluded the study's compilers, namely, the reason for the failure of so many African Canadians to call themselves 'Black.' As Boxhill tells us in a fine essay, 'about half of the respondents born in Haiti – and, in all likelihood black – reported that they were French. A similarly high proportion of persons born in Jamaica reported that they were British.' These self-identifications are neither shocking nor disturbing, if we understand that anti-Africanism, the social construct that turns human beings into 'black' and 'white' (in the U.S. and Canada), is not a potent source for identity in Haiti or in Jamaica, the two countries which have contributed the largest numbers of African-heritage immigrants to Canada in the past thirty years. (Torczyner reveals that 44.2 per cent of all black persons in Canada immigrated in the past twenty years.)

As Québec writer Dany Laferrière's 1985 satire *Comment faire l'amour avec un nègre sans se fatiguer* takes uproarious pains to point out, it is only on the North American mainland that a Haitian becomes 'black,' or is expected to subscribe, instantly, to the white-black angst that plagues the white (and white supremacist) majority in the United States and Canada. In black-majority countries, social divisions occur around class and less so around race (though colourism – discrimination by light-skinned blacks against darker-skinned blacks – is a problem). The Barbados-born, African-Canadian writer Austin Clarke, in 1973, described the 'West Indian writer' as 'a man from a society ostensibly free of the worst pathologies of racialism, a man from a society into which Black nationalism had to be imported from American Blacks.' Clarke's comments underline the weirdness of white-versus-black constructs for many Caribbean emigrés. (I will never forget the chaos that ensued when Haiti-born Jean Alfred, a *péquiste* MNA, told a meeting of the now-defunct National Black Coalition of Canada, in Toronto, in May 1979, that he cared more about the liberation of

Québec than he did about 'national black unity.' Conference delegates felt that the black community and its needs should be paramount.)

What all this means is that Canadian blackness is a complex identity, rich with contradictions and fissures. Certainly, the danger in talking about 'Canadian Blacks' is that one can elide the real differences among, say, a Vancouver Rastafarian, an Anjou Sénégalaise, and a 'Scotian' African Baptist. The Torczyner study skirts this problem, but only barely. Torczyner recognizes, in his informative essay, that there are 'unique regional agendas for the various Canadian Black communities.' Still, he tends to take the immigrant black experience, especially in Ontario and Québec (where 86.9 per cent of all 'Blacks' live), as the norm, even arguing that 'Black immigration' will 'determine something of the collective identity of Black persons in Canada.' Yet, the centuries-old African-heritage populations in the Maritimes, Québec, and southwestern Ontario are jealously insisting upon recovering and rejoicing in their histories. Torczyner does state that 'in Halifax, with its long history of Black settlement, more than nine out of ten persons in the Black communities were born in Canada, and the "Caribbean influence" is comparatively low.' But this knowledge does not pervade the study.

Too, once black immigrants have been settled for a long enough period in Canada, they also begin to confront the barriers that white supremacism erects against black achievement in this society, barriers that indigenous African Canadians understand intimately. A Trinidad-born, black scholar-friend told me recently that in celebrating a recent success of his with several Euro-Canadian friends, one of them said, after a few drinks, 'Well, David, you may have won a grant, but I'm still a white man.'

How does the fact that so many blacks identify themselves with where they came from, and not their colour, affect Canada? I foresee a *rapprochement* in which immigrant African Canadians who identify with their homelands establish an affinity with Canadian-born blacks and exchange strategies of resistance to racism, a common denominator of *black* experience. (Black cultures in Canada are diverse, but all black peoples living in this racialized nation-state experience racism.) These strategies include arguing vociferously against injustices and organizing to reduce the incidence of poverty and illiteracy.

The African-Canadian communities, accounting for only 3 per cent of the Canadian population, will have a more difficult time achieving solidarity than African Americans, who comprise 13 per cent of the American population. In Canada, the increasing numbers of second-generation blacks, living now within a white-majority context, have more in common with the experiences of indigenous African Canadians than with an increasingly remote Caribbean 'homeland.' Two writers who wonderfully evoke this sensibility are Montrealer Robert Edison Sandiford, the son of Bajan immigrants, in his short story collection *Winter, Spring, Summer, Fall: Stories* (1995), and also Calgary's Suzette Mayr, the daughter of German and Caribbean immigrants, in her novel *Moon Honey* (1995), in which the protagonist changes – at least psychologically – from white to brown. According to Torczyner, 85 per cent of all African-Canadian children, *circa* 1991, were born in Canada. They are, all of them, *indigenous* African Canadians.

Canada's blacks are primarily an urban people living in Montréal and Toronto. Boxhill reports that some 240,940 blacks live in Toronto, representing 47.8 per cent of the African-Canadian population; another 101,390 blacks live in Montréal, accounting for another 20.1 per cent of the total. Nevertheless, rural black enclaves still exist in Nova Scotia, New Brunswick, southwestern Ontario, and in Alberta and Saskatchewan. Halifax and Vancouver (with its 3.1 per cent of the African-Canadian population, that is, 15,385 souls) are crucial centres in their own right.

Undeniably, the concentration of blacks in Canada's two largest cities grants these populations some political and economic clout. Not unexpectedly, then, Ontario has sent blacks, beginning with Lincoln Alexander, to the House of Commons in every election since 1968; in contrast, the first Africadian (Black Nova Scotian) to enter Parliament, Gordon Earle, was only elected this past spring in Halifax, a city containing just 2.1 per cent of the African-Canadian population (that is, 10,560 souls). Though it was possible to elect a black, Leonard Braithwaite, to the Ontario legislature in 1963, the feat could not be accomplished in the Nova Scotia legislature until 1993, when Wayne Adams won the constituency of Preston (the largest all-black community in Canada).

As well as stressing diversity, Torczyner's review of the census data says much about mobility and adds to knowledge of the social circumstances of African Canadians. His statistics portray relative black success, despite the community's well-founded complaints of job, school, and housing discrimination as well as its justified charges of police brutality *contra* black males. (Two *causes célèbres* include the shooting of Anthony Griffin in Montréal in 1987 and the suffocation of Robert Gentles in Kingston Penitentiary in 1993.)

However, black men fare better educationally and economically in Canada than they do in the United States. Torczyner finds that 'Black men have marginally higher levels of educational attainment than do all men, all women, or Black women in Canada.' The explanation for this fact is, I wager, the premium that Caribbean and African governments place upon education, especially technical and scientific instruction, particularly for males. Searching the National Library of Canada for literary texts by black authors, I have often found, instead, droves of dissertations, in the sciences, by African-born doctoral candidates. The point is well illustrated by St Vincent–born author H. Nigel Thomas in *Spirits in the Dark* (1993), his first novel, in which the male protagonist is groomed for scholastic achievement by male elders in his society. Some 3.5 per cent African-Canadian men have graduate degrees – slightly more than the average of 3.0 per cent for Canadian men as a whole.

Another explanation lies in Canadian immigration policy, which at first favoured admitting only Caribbean women, only as domestics, and only later permitted the admission of black men, but with a bias for professionals. (Torczyner's discovery that there are 20,000 more black women than men in Canada is attributable to federal immigration rules. This point also explains, in part, the higher number of female-led, single-parent households among African Canadians than among Canadians as a whole.)

Furthermore, some Africans who entered Canada as students chose to remain here after they had completed their education. Too, many of the Haitians who fled the Duvalier dictatorships in the 1960s and 1970s represented their nation's intelligentsia. While Torczyner states that 'Black persons in Montreal had the highest rates of educational attainment when compared to Toronto and Halifax,' he may be referring to that fact. Moroever, the Africans who fled apartheid in South Africa, civil wars in Somalia and Ethiopia, and dictatorships in Uganda, Nigeria, and elsewhere tended to be well-educated members of their nations. Canada has gained – deliberately – from an epochal brain drain. One in five African Canadians is enrolled in university or has a bachelor's degree – which, at 20 per cent, is on par with the Canadian population as a whole.

When one examines employment opportunities, a strange paradox emerges. Blacks are as well educated as the average Canadian but suffer higher unemployment (15 per cent compared to the Canadian average of 10 per cent in 1991). Even university education isn't a guarantee of mobility. One in six black persons with a university degree was poor in 1991. While 7 per cent of all Canadians with bachelor's degrees were poor, the statistic for blacks is 17 per cent – the same as Canadians without a university degree. Systemic racism must lie behind these statistics. African Canadians are nearly absent from higher-paying jobs and senior management positions.

Blacks are less likely to be self-employed or supported by investments. Also, there is the depressing summation that 'Black persons in Canada earn less money on average than the Canadian population as a whole' ($20,617 per year or 15 per cent less than the Canadian average of $24,001). These statistics point again to systemic racism. In this regard, I see that a recent Canadian Human Rights Commission report shows that the federal Government has not been as aggressive as the private sector in hiring visible minorities. Only 4.5 per cent of the public service workforce consists of visible minorities, as opposed to 8.8 per cent of the employees of federally regulated companies (such as airlines, banks, radio and television stations, and telephone companies).

Further, despite the positive educational and employment indicators, and the fact that 'members of the Black community are less likely to be dependent on public assistance ...' than is the population as a whole (10.6 per cent compared to 11.4 per cent), almost a third of all African Canadians, some 31.5 per cent of the population, lived below the Canadian poverty line in 1991, including 40 per cent of all African-Canadian children. These rates are appalling. They cry out for remedial action from all levels of government and NGO institutions, but also from the African-Canadian communities themselves. Torczyner's call, in his conclusion, for 'community organizing strategies to promote access to entitlements,' to ensure that eligible families receive mandated public supports, is one place to start. Also valuable is Torczyner's advice that African Canadians develop a 'national Black consensus.' This is easier said than done in a country that must toil to find a consensus on anything. Nevertheless, his promotion of 'a parliament of Black communities in Canada' is intriguing.

Diversity, Mobility and Change begins to answer, for Canada, a challenge that Du Bois issued to American sociologists in 1898 to study the 'Negro problems.' His rhetoric (the language of the day) is problematic, but his insight is valid. We can only truly weld together an African-Canadian people by studying intensively our conditions, from coast to coast to coast, across five and one-half time zones, two official languages, and a hundred ethnicities. Torczyner, Boxhill, James, and Mulder have made a remarkable stride in that direction.

The report isn't perfect. I wish, for instance, that the brief survey of African-Canadian history had referenced a few more texts, including Robin W. Winks's *The Blacks in Canada: A History* (1971), despite its American liberal blindness toward the substantive Canadian difference from the United States, and James Walker's *The West Indians in Canada* (1984). I also wish that ampler precision had been granted figures and dates in the historical essay. (For example, 1,200, not 2,500, Black Loyalists left Nova Scotia for Sierra Leone in 1792.) Discussing Black Canadian economic stats, Torczyner could have referred to Adrienne Shadd's 1987 study of black male employment and wage rates in Ontario and Nova Scotia as well as to Agnes Calliste's 1995 essay on black families in Canada. Peccadilloes and omissions aside, the McGill group merits kudos for taking a nicely wide-angle snapshot of the state of African Canada.

Viewing African Canada

Review of *The Blacks in Canada: A History*, by Robin W. Winks. 2nd ed. Montréal and Kingston: McGill-Queen's University Press, 1997.

To amend Ezra Pound, history is bad news that stays news. The point applies perhaps most vigorously to histories of disenfranchised polities, such as Québec (before 1960, or before 1976), or the First Nations, or Transplanted Africans, especially where constituted as minorities. Robin W. Winks takes this view in his epochal, almost impeccable tome *The Blacks in Canada: A History*, where he opines that African-Canadian history is 'depressing' and 'petty.' Winks lists several reasons for his judgment. Accounting for 3 per cent or less of the Canadian population, African Canadians have been numerically insignificant and, from the perspective of the white majority, economically and culturally insignificant. Disempowered, scattered across a vast expanse, and internally divided by varying religious, ethnic, and linguistic affiliations, African Canadians register in collective celebrations of Canadian identity only as once-upon-a-time, fugitive, U.S. slaves or as generic, Caribbean immigrants. African-Canadian history is a mystery in Canada.

The chief benefit of Winks's substantial volume is that it sets a repressed chronicle before us in clairvoyant detail. Replete with cinematic documentation and exquisite quotations, Winks's text, republished in a second edition in 1997, remains as crucial to scholarship on African Canadians as it did when it first appeared, in 1971. Though other works have revised or elaborated aspects of *The Blacks in Canada*, it is still the most comprehensive treatment of its subject. The 500-page narrative spans three continents, four centuries, and umpteen *régimes*. It is prodigally erudite, prodigiously literary. It is not, alas, persuasive.

The infuriating insufficiency of *The Blacks in Canada* resides in its infelicitous interpretations. A Euro-American liberal, Winks discounts the distinctive context – French, British, and *Tory* – in which blacks had to make their way, first as colonial slaves (in the Maritimes, Nouvelle-France / Lower Canada, and Upper Canada); then as U.S.-born Loyalists and refugees (in the Maritimes), fugitives (in the Canadas), and pioneers (on Vancouver Island and the Prairies); and, lastly, as urban-bound immigrants from the Caribbean, the United States, Africa, and South America. Wedded to the liberalism of a 'rude Jacksonian democracy,' Winks criticizes African Canadians for always seeming 'to be perhaps a generation behind [their] American counterparts' and for lacking 'the cumulative pride, energy, enterprise, and courage that the catalog of individual acts of defiance would lead one to expect.' Canvassing the records of their potential 'sources of strength' – their schools, churches, newspapers, and voluntary societies – Winks finds illiteracy, impoverishment, futility, and self-segregation. In short, Winks's African Canadians are failed African Americans, *sans* shared history, *sans* unity, *sans* leaders, *sans* much hope (lest they unite, somehow, with their sub–49th Parallel sistren and brethren). He even argues that, by seeming quarrelsome and indolent, refugee and fugitive blacks *fostered* white Canadian racism in the nineteenth-century. Sneering declarations like 'Begging ministers, poverty-stricken churches ... all these hurt the Negro in his slow climb toward acceptance' are deplorably abundant. But their prevalence stems from Winks's implicit belief that assimilation is one desirable 'solution' for the 'Canadian Negro problem.'

In his six-page preface (the only new item in the putatively new edition), Winks denies that he believes that 'Blacks themselves, not White racism, were responsible for their unequal position in society.' Damagingly, though, he acknowledges 'the ambiguities of my language and analysis.' He also concedes that one chapter exhibits a faulty understanding 'of Black culture or of economic and class realities.' But his failure is grander than he knows. He misses a prominent intellectual thrust of African Canadians, one that is apparent from 1608 to 1970, namely, the allegiance of many of them to conservatism and to, at least until the 1960s, the (Progressive) Conservative party. Winks ignores this aspect of African-Canadian culture, even though he notes, scrupulously, its hostility to parliamentary reform, its formation of Tory bodies and presses, and its preference for British institutions over Yankee republicanism. Yet, Winks fails consistently to assess the vitality of the conservative ethos for African Canadians, as he does the attractiveness of Canadian anti-Americanism. (Winks feels, for instance, that a 'generalized anti-Americanism ... limited the effectiveness of the [slavery] abolition movement in Canada.') But it is the adherence of African Canadians to classical Canadian values – community, tolerance, order, etc. – that makes them, despite the countervailing forces of white supremacism and their own Pan-Africanism, profoundly un-American.

Winks asserts that Canadian, anti-black racism stems more from 'indifference' than from economic competition, fears of miscegenation, or simple Negrophobia. But his research uncovers multiple instances where legislative and social violence against blacks was prefaced by whites' expressions of concerns over 'race mixing' or class conflict or both. Even so, to describe black-white relations in Canada, Winks must resort to adjectives like 'confused,' 'uncertain,' 'haphazard,' and 'ambivalent.' At all times, official support for African Canadians has tended to resemble regional development programs: inadequate, patronage-riddled, and calculated to win maximum – if ephemeral – political gain. Hence, though hobbling, Canadian anti-black racism has always been lacklustre, lacking the volcanic, fundamentalist energies that animate American phobias. (In British North America, then, slavery withered away because it was economically irrelevant; in the United States, it could only be extirpated through civil war. In Canada, legal racial segregation ended because it became an embarrassment that no government wanted to enforce; in the United States, it fell only through protest and federal policing.) Without realizing it, then, Winks renders a post-modern history, one shaded by irony and contradiction, one that is, therefore, stubbornly Canadian in narrative, however American in its pretensions. Read against himself, Winks reads like Linda Hutcheon.

There's hardly a paragraph in *The Blacks in Canada* that cannot be transformed into a scholarly thesis or academic book, or even into a novel, or poems, or a play. In fact, Winks's text has served as a Holy Bible – that is to say, a source book for ideas – for two generations of African-Canadian writers. (Lawrence Hill's second novel, *Any Known Blood* [1997], makes use of an incident that Winks records.) Perhaps this remains its golden, ironic fate: to assist all the refutations of African-Canadian 'insignificance' now occurring in Canadian literature and in many other fields. The blacks in Canada are at home, renovating it.

The Death and Rebirth of Africadian Nationalism

Review of *Remember Africville*. National Film Board video production.
Dir. Shelagh Mackenzie. 1991.

This paean to the lost Afro–Nova Scotian community of Africville is a cinematic entry in a catalogue of cultural works seeking to rehabilitate the memory of the black-settled, Bedford Basin–located, Halifax village which was bulldozed into rubble and memorabilia between 1964 and 1970. The film depicts the experiences of some of the four hundred Africvillers who were relocated to inner-city public housing, and also provides the reflections of some of their relocators. Moreover, it subtly displays the rise of modern Afro–Nova Scotian (or, to use my word, *Africadian*) nationalism from the ruins of Africville.

In the liner notes accompanying the video, Halifax writer Charles R. Saunders states that 'a 120-year heritage doesn't vanish at the stroke of a pen or the crash of a wrecking ball. Africville's people and their descendants have refused to allow the memory of their community to die.' By permitting exiled Africvillers to recall their former estate, Mackenzie's film revives the community's rural beauty, spirituality, and home feeling – qualities which were assailed by bureaucrats and politicians desiring either to rid Halifax of a so-called 'segregated ghetto' or to hijack precious waterfront property for industrial use. Mackenzie spotlights her strategy by using Halifax lawyer Gus Wedderburn's comment 'I didn't see the flowers' as a refrain to stress the romantic aspects of a village which was condemned, again and again, as a 'slum' before it was finally condemned to die. The film's title hints at the mythopoeic power of memory, which is, itself, the implicit site of Africville: it is no longer a place, but the consciousness of a people.

Mackenzie uses memory to conjure nostalgia but, also, critical hindsight. *Remember Africville* is thus an anthology of second thoughts and revisions that often conflict but which also contribute to the re-membering of a dis-membered community. Archival footage, home movies, and still photos, in both colour and in black-and-white, are spliced together with excerpts from a 1989 conference whose participants review the decisions and circumstances that led to the expulsion of the Africvillers. The film serves up the oral and visual confessions of the removed and their removers.

In this way, *Remember Africville* juxtaposes citizen impotence and city-state power. Specifically, it bares the bankruptcy of a regressive nationalism unable to counter a liberal gospel of progress, a progress in which the poor, and especially the black poor, are viewed unapologetically as retrograde. Africville becomes a ghost town in which the fatal showdown between a rural, conservative religious culture and the urban, liberal welfare state is constantly re-enacted.

Enlivened by apt sounds and images – of African Baptist 'saints' marching joyfully to the placid waters of Bedford Basin to be 'buried in the likeness of Christ,' of women 'styling' for a trusted camera, of homes and gardens bursting into rainbow bloom, of moaning trains and pealing bells, of, in general, the various social rituals and exchanges that produce a collectivity, the film's memories resurrect an Africville its enemies sought to forget. A textured vision of a living, breathing community arises. The long-gone 'slum by the dump' (which the City of Halifax vomited beside Africville in the 1950s) is born again as a vibrant village with its own post office, school, church, and stores. Yet, the bucolic recollections of the martyrs – the witnesses – of Africville are always counterpointed by sharp interrogations of the relocation and its managers.

Carrie Toussaint, a participant in the 1989 forum, pointedly asks repentant officials, 'Did you use Africville for a test? Were [residents] guinea pigs for something new – integration?' Her query is set against the context of the City's failure to provide such necessities as running water, paved roads, and sewers – even though Africvillers paid taxes to the City of Halifax.

Gus Wedderburn expresses dismay at the thought of 'my brothers scavenging on the dump.' However, Eddie Carvery, an exile, insists that the dump was a 'blessing' from which such items as 'windows, boards, nails, furniture, metals, and bottles' could be salvaged and sold. Even so, Wedderburn is allowed the last word: he tells of a family that suffered lead poisoning one Christmas as a result of burning discarded car batteries for heat. By juxtaposing opposing opinions, Mackenzie constructs a moving, dynamic vision of Africville.

There is a villain in this who-done-it, however; namely, John Edward Lloyd, who was mayor of Halifax from 1960 to 1963. In a salvaged interview, Lloyd asserts that 'Africville, obviously, must be redeveloped.' If that utterance cannot be considered Africville's death sentence, there's no such doubt about Lloyd's following words:

Sometimes, some people need to be shown that certain things are not in their own best interests and not in the best interests of their children ... Certainly, you don't coerce people against their will. But should there be violations of minimum [housing] standards, then you have no alternative but to enforce the law.

Lloyd's comments display the Machiavellian paternalism which constitutes the customary response of white authority to what was once bluntly termed the 'Negro Problem.' Moreover, Lloyd's use of the suggestive word *redeveloped* reveals inadvertently the City's schizophrenic approach to the relocation. In their standard 1974 study (revised in 1987 and 1999), *Africville: The Life and Death of a Canadian Black Community*, Donald H. Clairmont and Dennis Magill show that the relocation was a product of mixed motives. Though the City mouthed liberal-welfare platitudes to justify its plan, it also wanted to reclaim Africville's land for industrial infrastructure. While relocation lurched along, knocking down Africville homes like dominoes, the City's desire for land for the construction of access roads to the A. Murray McKay Bridge took priority over the ballyhooed need to better Africvillers' lives. Hence, Clairmont and Magill assert, the relocation was unsuccessful: 'The relocatees were to be major beneficiaries through compensation, welfare payments, and rehabilitative retraining programmes. The major problem with the relocation was that, although rooted in liberal-welfare rhetoric, it failed to achieve its manifest goals' (17).

Lloyd's comments also highlight the arbitrary nature of the Africville relocation. The characterization by Lloyd and others of Africville as a site of 'urban blight' helped make the expulsion of its citizens an acceptable 'final solution.' Clairmont and Magill observe that in 1966, the Chief Justice of the Supreme Court of Nova Scotia described Africville as a 'social problem "created by whites, because time after time, year after year, municipal councils had ignored the problem"' (53). Thus, according to Clairmont and Magill, once relocation became the City's vaunted solution, its implementation was undemocratic because 'there was no meaningful collective [decision-making] participation by Africville residents' (16–17). Africvillers were expected to go – and to go quietly.

But, not all Africvillers went quietly. In her film, Mackenzie pits her subjects' singing anger against the sonorous drone of bureaucracy. Joseph P. Skinner, a community leader, argues cogently for the right of Africvillers to 'redevelop' their property themselves: 'When you own a piece of property, you're not a second-class citizen. When your land is being taken away from you and you ain't offered nothin', then you become a peasant.' Skinner's redevelopment thesis deconstructs Lloyd's formulation. Other residents also emerge as forceful critics: the sorrow-stricken Leon Steed ('I'm tellin' you the God's truth!'), the irrepressible Ruth Johnson (whose vocal resistance continues), the strong-willed Daisy Carvery, and the impassioned Ralph Jones, deacon of the imperilled Seaview United Baptist Church ('This is the testin' time!'). Their bold, plain-spoken opposition to the loss of their homes and way of life gives *Remember Africville* much of its emotional power.

Current critics – and criticisms – of the relocation abound. Mackenzie's film proffers many speakers who denounced the project at the 1989 conference. Says Rev. D.D. Skeir: 'That was prime land; that was important land.' Irvine Carvery, head of the Africville Genealogical Society (AGS), asserts, 'Someone decided that land of Africville would better serve the City as industrial land ...' In the end, Mackenzie's *de facto* documentary affirms the critique of the relocation expressed in Clairmont and Magill by one Africville woman:

> The City didn't do anything to improve Africville. All the City did was to try to
> get it, and they did, in the end. They just did it, too, because we were coloured. If
> they had been white people down there, the City would have been in there assist-
> ing them to build new homes, putting in water and sewers and building the place
> up ... (53)

While the woman's statement fails to appreciate that poor whites would have
been – and, in fact, were – treated in the same manner as Africvillers, her
perception that racism coloured the issue is just. Racism had always threatened the existence of Africville. For one thing, negative perceptions of
Africadians are woven into the tartan of Nova Scotian society. Thus, famed
Bluenose author Thomas Chandler Haliburton's uses of Black English and
black characters in his Sam Slick sketches (1835–36) provide racist stereotypes. In a Nova Scotian travel sketch published in 1828, Joseph Howe, the
'tribune of Nova Scotia,' comments good-naturedly that one is sure to meet, in
a walk around Bedford Basin, 'a goodly bevy of sable beauties, with their
unsophisticated feet, and their woolly heads, adorned, not with "the likeness
of a kingly crown," but with tubs and baskets of fair dimensions, from which,
like so many dingy Pomonas, they have been pouring strawberries down the
throats of citizens ....' Howe goes on to criticize the 'fashion' for reviling 'these
poor devils, – man, woman, and child, for lazyness [sic], and for the heinous
sin of not immediately accustoming themselves to a climate half a dozen degrees colder than it was where they were born.' Howe bids his readers to
'have a little patience, good people, and let the old leaven of ignorance and
idleness work out of these gentlemen of color' (*Western and Eastern Rambles*
[1973] 55–7). Clairmont and Magill underline the persistence of racism in our
time:

> The groundwork for the subordination of the blacks ... in Nova Scotia was laid by
> the early existence of a slave society. Insidious social-psychological concomitants
> of institutionalized oppression included attitudes of white superiority, which re-
> main deeply rooted ... (32)

These attitudes belied the benevolence of liberal-welfare rhetoric that pictured
the relocation as the liberation of Africville residents from a pastoral ghetto. In
truth, Africvillers fell from being proud, rural homeowners to being welfare-
dependent tenants in asphalt hells, from running their own affairs to suffering
the dictates of social workers.

  While racism is one explanation for the City's refusal to extend services to
the black enclave on its northern coast, another is its historical insistence on
viewing the North End and the shores of Bedford Basin as its peninsular
industrial zone, a place where workers, immigrants, social outcasts, and
coloured peoples could be housed, warehoused, and unhoused, as needed.
From this perspective, Africville constituted an unacceptably green oasis amid

a grey, industrial desert. In fact, according to Clairmont and Magill, at various times in its history Africville suffered on its borders 'a large oil plant / storage complex, a bone-mill plant manufacturing fertilizer ... a cotton factory and a rolling mill / nail factory ... a slaughterhouse and a port facility handling coal' (86). They also report that the aforementioned industries were encircled by a 'tar factory, a shoe plant ... another slaughterhouse, several stone-crushing industries, and a foundry' (86). In later years, these enterprises were replaced by a new slaughterhouse, another stone-crushing plant, the provincial Department of Highways work plant and supply depot, the City's Infectious Diseases Hospital and prison, train tracks slitting through the community, and, as final insults, an open-air garbage dump and incinerator (86).

Mackenzie's film, by focusing on Edenic images of Africville's gardens and folkways (accompanied by acoustic guitar and harmonica notes), accents the community's precarious position as a residential green strip in territory regarded by the City as an industrial zone. In 1947, then, Council 'approved the designation of Africville as industrial land,' state Clairmont and Magill (91). As recently as 1991, the year in which *Remember Africville* was released, the AGS fought with Halifax City Council to protect the Africville memorial – Seaview Park – from planned encroachments by a Canadian National Railway service road. Though the AGS won that skirmish, the crisis accents the persistent municipal tendency to view the Africville site as a colony of industry. To this day, Seaview Park – the ghost of Africville – remains the only green space on the Halifax side of Bedford Basin.

While racism and City policies were external causes for the death of Africville, Africvillers and other Africadians did little, it seems, to slow or to try to stop the relocation. Here, *Remember Africville* highlights an insightful 1989 comment offered by Alan Borovoy, head of the Canadian Civil Liberties Association (and, during the 1960s, an adviser to the Halifax Human Rights Advisory Committee, a group which sought to mediate between Africvillers and the City): 'Pressure without reason is irresponsible, but reason without pressure is ineffectual.' Hence, relocation occurred in part because Africvillers lacked any organization which could 'exert pressure on their behalf.'

Borovoy's revelation illuminates the obscured, implicit subject of *Remember Africville:* the death and rebirth of Africadian nationalism. While Mackenzie must be commended for recreating the image of Africville (and for unmasking the dirty politics of urban development), her primary subject can only be inferred after a careful reading of the images and the narrative that compose the film. Interestingly, its very title, *Remember Africville,* echoes the slogan of a more pronounced nationalism, *Je me souviens.*

Surely, Africadians remember Africville because this lost place represented our innocence. Being a microcosm of Africadia, its existence affirmed our mad belief that we could maintain the strange faith of our forebears – the Black Loyalists and Black Refugees – against the divisive incursions of technological, liberal capitalism, the most dynamic and vulgarly progressive ideology of our common era, a materialist creed utterly destructive of local cultures, particularly those rooted in rural and conservative religious traditions.

The destruction of Africville marked the ignoble and total defeat of the first Africadian nationalism – a silent, brooding, glimmering nationalism that represented, not the craving for a nation, but rather, the yearning for a space – a green space – in which the free self could be realized. In her instructive article 'Acadia Rising: The MFU and the New Nationalism' (1992), Sue Calhoun describes a classical Acadian nationalism 'that some considered elitist but that few dared to criticize openly' (7). If Acadie was dominated by, as Calhoun's reading of author Michel Roy implies, 'an elite made of clergy and professionals' which 'opposed any form of popular movement that arose in Acadian society' (7), a similarly regressive conservatism paralyzed Africadian society. In his decidedly negative history *The Blacks in Canada* (1970), Robin Winks argues that a few families dominated the African Baptist Association (ABA) – the central institution of Africadia – creating 'an aristocracy of the faith, and often [holding] the church to more than ordinarily frozen and conservative theological traditions' (346). The refusal to engage in more than token resistance to acts of discrimination, coupled with a failure to evolve a theology to counter the threat posed by modernity, left Africadia defenceless before the gospel of progress, which, by its very nature, could not accept the continued existence of Africville.

Yet, Africadian religious nationalism had not always been backward-looking. When our forebears arrived in Nova Scotia *en masse* in 1783, they were inspired by a proud theology which led them to first escape from the slaveholding Southern colonies, to next join the Crown in its effort to stop the libertarian revolt which would foster the United States, and then to agitate for passage to British North America to avoid the possibility of being re-enslaved after the Yankee triumph. This same, radical religious impulse led a third of the almost 3,400 Black Loyalists in Nova Scotia to leave in 1792 to help establish the West African nation of Sierra Leone. In his splendid account, *The Black Loyalists: The Search for a Promised Land in Nova Scotia and Sierra Leone 1783–1870* (1976), James Walker describes the separatist theology of his subjects:

> As they regarded the more formalised white churches which had segregated them, they noticed that God did not seem to speak to those older churches in quite the same way as he did to them, the blacks. Inevitably, this produced a feeling of being closer to God, of being, in fact, a chosen people, an elite group of Christians whom God regularly visited and whose role it was to preserve the truth of the moment of salvation. (78)

Interestingly, in the Introduction to his annotated 1976 re-issue of Rev. Peter F. McKerrow's original 1895 edition of *A Brief History of the Coloured Baptists of Nova Scotia*, Frank Boyd reports that, when McKerrow urged the dissolution of the ABA in favour of union with the white Maritime Baptist Convention, his proposal was trounced: 'African Baptists wanted to maintain their identity through continued separatism' ('Editor' v). Clairmont and Magill stress that the Church provided 'the basis for whatever genuine black subculture developed' and was 'the base for unity and contact among the isolated black communities' (68). In Africville, too, the Church fostered group identity. Clairmont and Magill state that Seaview United Baptist Church was 'as old as the community itself and embodied much of Africville's sense of historical continuity' (49).

Hence, the fall of Africville sparked a spiritual and cultural identity crisis for Africadians. (Likewise, Calhoun feels that 'a secularization of Acadian society ... resulted in a collective Acadian identity crisis' [7].) The impotence of classical Africadian nationalism in the modern age was starkly revealed by the confrontation between the bulldozers of 'progress' and the frail, wooden walls of Seaview United Baptist Church (organized in 1849, states McKerrow, as 'Campbell Road Church'). The literal collapse of the old church was a signal, especially to the younger generation, that new values had to be asserted to preserve the collectivity against the corrosive effects of secularization and liberal individualism.

The rout of the old Africadian faith cannot be stressed too much. Not only did the 1960s clergy lose one of the churches established by 'the father of the faith,' Rev. Richard Preston, an escaped Virginia slave who came to Nova Scotia after the War of 1812 and organized the ABA in 1854: it also lost the jewel of the hard-won landbase of Africadia. The clergy ceded Africville, with hardly a whimper, to its enemies. Worse still, had other Nova Scotian municipalities wanted to, they could have also seized territory, using the same arguments used to eliminate Africville: calls for integration, better housing, and improved access to municipal services, along with the lack of proper land titles, could have been pointed to (and in some cases could still be pointed to) to justify the uprooting of *every* black homeland in Nova Scotia – from the strategic watershed locale of the Prestons to Tracadie and to Greenville. (Since the 1960s, many black communities – the Prestons, Sunnyville/Lincolnville, the Vale Road, to name a few – have experienced developmental pressures.) Rev. D.D. Skeir, a young minister at the time of the relocation, cites the weakness of mid-1960s Africadia in this comment in *Remember Africville*: '[Blacks] were not sensitive enough to unite to fight this basic denial [of Africvillers' rights].' Yet, the Church itself must bear some of the blame for that apathy: years of accommodationist rhetoric from ABA ministers helped prepare the way for the crucifixion of Africville ...

Africville was lost because we Africadians refused to sufficiently value our right to exist. If we had held fast to our faith, if we had believed in our God, we would have laid our bodies before the bulldozers. Our leaders of the 1960s allowed themselves to be seduced into thinking of Africville as a slum rather than as a potentially strong Africadian community-neighbourhood in a prime location on peninsular Halifax. Had they been strong enough to resist the temptations of 'progress,' Africville might have become the spiritual capital of Africadia, the conscious annunciation of our existence.

In practical terms alone, Africville might have thrived as a black middle-class and working-class section of Halifax. For all those arriving by train, in fact, the village was already the gateway to Halifax. It was even a postal address – 'Africville, Nova Scotia.' Moreover, Africville reconfigured radically the socio-economic geography of Halifax: Africvillers enjoyed their waterside lifestyle in much the same manner as did the white *bourgeoisie* of the North West Arm. Perhaps the village was also, at least in part, what Canadian literary critic John Fraser calls an 'organic community,' that is, a society which 'satisfies the great majority of the people living in it, but does so because it is a model of a well psyche' (see *The Name of Action* 242). The loss of Africville, then, deserves to be mourned.

Yet, there is a time to mourn and a time to cease from mourning. Africville was crucified to pay for the sins of an apostate collective and a faithless leadership: mercifully, however, it took with it to its grave the weary nationalism which had ducked the merciless twentieth century for as long as it could until, finally, the bulldozers, flanked by social workers, arrived to introduce the blacks and their Church to the benefits of modernity. Hence, the death of Africville necessitated its resurrection in folk art (family photos, home movies, stories, songs) and, especially, in the neo-nationalism of the 'militant' Black United Front of the early 1970s. Nova Scotia's own Black Consciousness Movement began, it seems, just as the last vestiges of Africville were being reduced to rubble. Speaking of Acadie in the 1960s, Calhoun observes that 'unlike the elite nationalism which had been rooted in religion and culture, the new nationalism was rooted in a socio-economic analysis of Acadian society' (8). Africadian nationalism experienced a similar metamorphosis. Insurgent intellectuals like Burnley 'Rocky' Jones and partially radicalized pastors like Rev. Dr W.P. Oliver began to articulate a new pride, a collective sense of identity, and the need to empower 'the people.' For instance, Oliver, in his 1986 introduction to George Borden's second volume of poems, *Footprints – Images and Reflections*, a 'Poetic Account of the Black Experience in Nova Scotia,' published in 1993, argues 'the author bears witness of an emerging intellectual reactionary format,' which is itself part of 'a new and novel reaction to dissatisfaction' on the part of Black Nova Scotians (iv). Simultaneously, Africville itself was transformed into a cultural myth, the product of romanticism and nostalgia, a *pays* to mourn, a source for collective rituals, a focus for communal politics ... The Africadian Cultural Renaissance (which Oliver hails) and its conscious nationalism are the dry bones which have put on flesh and walked from the dust of Africville ...

Other Africvilliana

While Acadians remember the *Grand Dérangement* of 1755, so now do Africadians recognize a symbol of their displacement. In his work *In Search of Evangeline: Birth and Evolution of the Evangeline Myth* (1988), historian Carl A. Brasseaux finds that Henry Wadsworth Longfellow used a 'paradise-lost motif' (11) in his epic poem *Evangeline* (1847), which romanticizes the Dispersal.

Frederick Ward's novel-in-Black English, *Riverlisp: Black Memories* (1974), was inspired by his conversations with ex-Africville residents, so that some of his characters also voice a paradise-lost sentiment. Several moving poems on Africville (particularly 'Dialogue #3: Old Man [to the Squatter]') appear in Ward's collection *The Curing Berry* (1983). Charles Saunders has magnificently translated the feel of Africvillers' lives into his brief narrative 'A Visit to Africville' (1989). Singer-songwriter-musician Faith Nolan's debut album is titled, naturally, *Africville* (1986), after the opening song. Poet Maxine Tynes's second volume of poems, *Woman Talking Woman* (1990), features several poems on Africville (including 'Africville Is My Name,' which she partially recites in Mackenzie's film). David Woods's first book of poems, *Native Song* (1990), includes 'Summons,' a lyric dedicated to Africville. The two-volume compilation *Traditional Lifetime Stories: A Collection of Black Memories*, published by The Black Cultural Centre for Nova Scotia (1987–90), holds recollections by several senior citizens of their lives and experiences in Africville. A nationally toured exhibit of Africville memorabilia, *Africville: A Spirit That Lives On*, was organized and first mounted by the AGS and The Art Gallery of Mount Saint Vincent University and associates in 1989. Mackenzie's *Remember Africville* and the coffee-table format text *The Spirit of Africville*, edited by the AGS (1992), are two recent manifestations of the transfiguration of Africville from martyr to myth. See also George Boyd's play *Consecrated Ground* (1999), and hear Joe Sealy's Juno Award–winning jazz CD *Africville Suite* (1996). Africville survives, *lives*, as metaphor.

An Unprejudiced View of Two Africadian Poets

Review of *Woman Talking Woman*, by Maxine Tynes. Lawrencetown Beach, NS: Pottersfield Press, 1990. *Native Song*, by David Woods. Lawrencetown Beach, NS: Pottersfield Press, 1990.

Let us read Maxine Tynes's second book of poems, *Woman Talking Woman*, and David Woods's first, *Native Song*. Both texts bear witness to the explosion of artistic activity occurring among African Nova Scotians – a two hundred-year-old community founded by African-American Loyalists who landed in the then-colony in 1783, fresh from their evacuation from New York City before it was ceded by the British to the revolutionary government of the fledgling United States of America.

Both Tynes and Woods are conscious of racism, and they address its pernicious effects in their works. However, both are *writers* first, and that is how they shall be considered in the balance of this article.

The first principle in Tynes's work is her obvious echoing of the prophetic voice of Allen Ginsberg and, before him, of Walt Whitman. This echoing actually accords her work originality because few Canadian poets have successfully utilized the rhythms and the forms that are associated intimately with Whitman and Ginsberg (and, on a minor level, with Carl Sandburg, Robinson Jeffers, and Fenton Johnson). For one thing, English-Canadian poets tend to draw more from the British and the American formalist traditions rather than from the American populist tradition. Though the form of English-Canadian verse is ostensibly 'free,' the content is often highly intellectual, abstract, allusive. The cultural prejudice against the popular, the common, and the vulgar has resulted in the need by some to stimulate the production of 'accessible' verse. Thus, the People's Poet Award was inaugurated to canonize the postwar Tribune of the People, Milton Acorn, after he was apparently snubbed for a Governor General's Award in 1970 for *I've Tasted My Blood* (1969). Tynes inherited the award subsequently for her first book of poetry, *Borrowed Beauty*, published in 1987.

Tynes's demotic style materializes at once in *Woman Talking Woman*, her second book, a four-part collection consisting of fifty-eight poems and three short stories. 'As the Book Begins,' the opening poem, exhibits both the weaknesses and the strengths of Tynes's pop poet technique. Anaphora is effectively used to build tension and intimacy –

as the book begins
as you read me now
as you turn my pages
as you look through my leaves

but the effect is dissipated by these trite lines:

sample my thoughts
stack up my isms
walk through my present
my past
and my fantasy
measure the depth of my love ...

When one reads such a collection of heartfelt clichés, one wants to drop the book and get on with life. However, Tynes sloughs off the soporifics to render a thoughtful conclusion:

I stand hopeful and afraid, and
move over
and over to your threshold
as the book begins
as you read me now.

The joy and the agony of reading Tynes is due precisely to her stance as people's poet. Her rhetoric (in both senses) is always attractive; but, often, there's more volubility than virtue, more sensationalism than sense, in her work. See, for instance, 'For the Montreal Fourteen Who Lived and Died in the Heartbeat of Woman.' Recited before any audience that appreciates the significance of the date of 6 December 1989 for Canadians, and especially women, this poem would probably bring people to their feet and tears to some eyes. But it's a terrible poem! Tynes fails to humanize the victims of the self-proclaimed misogynist who murdered fourteen women – because they were women. The martyrs remain unseen, unheard, and unsung. Instead, Tynes generates a series of boorish generalities:

for every woman-want denied
                  devalued
                  belittled
                  ignored
                  unanswered

And her conclusion is cold-blooded propaganda:

We raise the heart and hands of sorrow
and of mourning

and of healing
this womanist body politic.

Moreover, if one *thinks* for a second, one begins to wonder how it would be possible to 'raise the heart and hands ... of healing this womanist body politic'? How can one 'raise' healing? The stew of concrete terms and abstractions bubbles up nonsense. When Tynes turns her attention to another 'ism' – racism – her Muse still sounds addled and jaded. Here's an example from 'Racism ... to Raise the Heart Against': 'the hue and cry of racism / tears at every mother's heart.'

As the foregoing examples demonstrate, Tynes's vices are prolixity, an occasional insensitivity to subject, narcissism, and frequent lapses in logic. Yet, she is a significant poet, a good poet, when she manages to fuse rhetoric, rhythm, and reason. A poem like 'Don't Give Me Looks' proves that Tynes can touch her audience with elegant yet powerful lines that, using plain speech and homespun metaphor, rivet attention:

Don't give me looks that put me in my place
that open my mail
that smell me coming and going ...
Don't give me looks full of hell and damn
and who cares? who cares?

In such poems, the poet's personality appears forcefully. And this kind of self-revelation is vital because Tynes's vision is essentially Beat (as befits her worship of Ginsberg). Nowhere is this stance clearer than in her poems on art. In 'I AM,' personality is celebrated as the disclosure of art:

I am a woman who wears
elephants in her ears tonight
and,[sic] a blue-green parrot over her heart;
the rayon jungle flares and flutters
in Gauguin splendour across my breasts
and back.

A fine instance of the same concern occurs in one of the six poems that Tynes has written in homage to a portrait of herself (which graces the cover of the book). 'When the Setting Is my Classroom' is splendid; here is a portion:

then I am all of my Blackest self
artist, darken your palette
black the to and fro of me
make black punctuation
of all of my dimensions
the crook of my arm, a sleek
black comma
we will go on and on and on.

The relentless egotism of such work can be off-putting; then again, one finds the same sin in poets like Whitman and Ginsberg. One must take the gaudy with the bad. But the poem is defensible for its lyricism of a 'black aesthetic.'

To find Tynes at her best, however, one has to turn to poems that integrate the personal and the social. In *Woman Talking Woman*, the supreme poem is unquestionably 'The Call to Tea,' which commemorates the career of Canada's lustrous contralto of the 1940s and 1950s, Portia White, a Black Nova Scotian who died in Toronto in 1968. The poem is a marvel and a triumph. It casts every other poem in the book into shadow. It merits complete quotation; however, a sense of the poet's achievement can be gleaned from the first strophe:

> The call to tea
> a solid knell of the social register
> in old Halifax
> silk moiré
> dank velvet
> crepe and lace splayed across settee
> mahogany and divan
> the shadow of servers
> invisible in stiff black stuff
> laying table
> just so, with the delicacy of
> cucumber, tea-cake and scone
> on porcelain and silver
> filigree of lacy oak leaf shadow
> through a southend Halifax window.

The poem evokes the genteel apartheid of polished Canadian racism, but also the dignity and artistry of White. Its evocative adjectives and implicit critique of class – as well as racial – difference make it a consummate example of Tynes's talent for scrutinizing social scenes.

In terms of her philosophy, Tynes seems to be a crypto-Christian who exults in Creation – the beauty of Nature and the luxury of the senses – and laments and protests the deprivation and alienation that so many of us suffer. The verb *want* recurs incessantly in her work. Her persona *wants* love, justice, adornment, adoration; she yearns for peace and equality. Another favoured word is *heart*. Tynes speaks from the heart in ways that can be conventional and egotistical, but which can also be, at times, compelling and moving. Tynes's career serves – like a lighthouse – as a guide and a warning. In *Woman Talking Woman*, one can revel in the pleasures – but also, alas, the perils – of garrulity.

A native of Trinidad, David Woods came to Nova Scotia in 1972 at the age of twelve. His poetic technique has been shaped noticeably by African-American writers, especially those of the Harlem Renaissance, namely, Langston Hughes, Sterling A. Brown, Jean Toomer, and Claude McKay. Hence, Woods's poems display a belated early modernism. His work is, then, sharply contemporary, for it is the early modernist period to which English-Canadian poets are retreating or advancing (depending on one's point of view) to find 'new' inspiration and ideas. It also differs from the work of Tynes (who, for one thing, seldom employs Black English), for Woods is not interested so much in the 'human' condition as he is in the specific conditions of Black Nova Scotians. While it is easy to open Tynes's book and find poems that are not strictly black-focused, it is rather hard to discover a like detachment in Woods's. His vision is not Beat, but social realist and, at times, absurdist. His stance is that of the frustrated Romantic, yearning for Beauty and Humanity in a world of machines and money and the generalized oppression necessary to keep them moving.

Woods's bleak vision is obvious from the get-go in *Native Song*, a collection of sixty-five poems, divided into five sections. 'Beauty's Eye' (titled 'Beauty As Now' in the Contents) speaks obsessively of beauty, but keeps confronting an ugly, horrific, and violent socio-economic reality. The poem displays both the attractive and the repulsive elements of Woods's technique. He commences with an interesting image – 'I am inside someone / who is beautiful' – but follows it with obfuscating and enervating pop-psych rhetoric:

I look out of his eyes
Feel the vast areas of
his strength
See the horizons of his
possibilities.

Later, he manifests again his gift for plain but powerful imagery –

... ugliness was twisted into
the soul
Till like a tree – I uncovered
my own roots
And shook powerfully in the sun –

and again he cancels the pleasure of the passage with subsequent clichés:

(It was a beautiful feeling
Glowing through the midnight forest
It moved like a magician
Into the dark chambers of my heart.)

Woods continues on to explain that it is love that he inhabits – 'A beautiful palace you trivialize' – and that 'the Sun is Love,' which rouses him finally to realize such beauty that 'the Sun screams.' The idea intrigues but the execution is only intermittently convincing.

Similar flaws beset a better poem, 'Luminere.' The strength of the piece is its deft usage of repetition:

> Praise men and women
> who were slaves,
> Praise their toil and their love-making,
> Praise their defiance and their shameful
> servitude,
> Praise when they bled from whip-wounds,
> and when in courage
> they lifted their feet into flight.

The weakness of 'Luminere' is its reliance upon hackneyed phrases and ideas:

> And praise when they called to God in
> the sky
> And He came down in a burst of glory
> To open a path to freedom before their eyes.

One can also question the endings of lines. Why break a line, for instance, after a preposition ('in / the sky')? Woods seems hazy about the actual *making* – the construction – of poems. This uncertainty would also explain the frustrating mix of august and atrocious lines in his poems and his awful tendency to move from clarity to cliché – as witnessed in 'Declaration':

> I am often sitting in the blue afternoon,
> Staring out of the window
> That opens like a groggy eyelid
> Onto the ruined expanse of human dreams.

One is often called to question the sense of Woods' lines.

The poet is most effective when describing the flawed beauty of the citizens of his demesne. Every poem in the 'Voices' section of his book, with their emphasis on black orality, bears reading, recitation, and remembrance. See 'Love': '"I love that girl so much / My hair getting kinkier."' 'Signs' is also brief and satisfying:

> She blamed it on stomach flu,
> But nine months later –
> Everybody knew.

'My Father' is another pithy, but evocative, poem:

> My father read the Bible
> Each night before he

went to bed,
Then he would down a
shot of whisky
That kicked like a donkey
through his head.
And to this day,
No word of a lie,
No one's sure if it's the religion
or the whisky,
Keeping that old man alive.

Longer but equally well-written 'Voices' poems include 'For Starr Jones,' 'The Hypocrites and the Poet,' and 'Reuben Jones, B.A.' Woods's plain speech condenses energy.

Given Woods's gift for realistic description, some of his longer poems would have benefitted from being trimmed to the true lines. 'The Howl' wins its significance, for instance, from this 'hooking' passage:

I can only be caught – like
frenzied fish,
in the wide net of their definitions,
I can only beat – like fish
at the end of their hooks ...

In other long poems, such as 'For Old Men on Gottingen Street,' Woods plays a Black Nova Scotian Prufrock:

I have considered the cold
press of feet,
Through the banal avenues of city,
And the sad faces of old men
on concrete steps –
Singing out of old guitars ...

Even so, the poems are far too verbose, far too Gothic, to remain consistently and persistently convincing.

Native Song presents a dynamic debut – though Woods still has much to learn about editing, measuring, crafting. His work exudes a rough appeal, a powerful urgency, but is still often as inarticulate as an alarm. He views what the Loyalists called 'Nova Scarcity' as a place where black men are shot and left to bleed to death on highways and black women are abused and exploited by the men they love. And, in concert with his modernism, Woods preaches an anti-modern gospel. His poems are bully pulpits from which the *modern* (a recurrent term of abuse in his work) is denounced and *beauty* (another recurrent word) is extolled. If he can master his material, Woods may become a major poet. However, Woods is already a stunning artist. Eight, full-colour, glossy reproductions of his paintings (oil and pastel, expressionist and realist) appear in *Native Song*; seven are arrestingly beautiful.

The poetic works of Tynes and Woods are middling, but acceptable. Both poets still must embrace ferocious editing, strong line endings, and clear, original imagery. But they have already written a few moving and memorable poems. If one were to rank these poets, Tynes would come before Woods because she commits errors less frequently. Ultimately, both poets are irreplaceable contributors to the newly diversified canon of Canadian poetry.

Reading Ward's 'Blind Man's Blues'

Review of 'Blind Man's Blues,' by Frederick Ward. In *Fire on the Water:
An Anthology of Black Nova Scotian Writing*. Vol. 2. Ed. George Elliott Clarke.
Lawrencetown Beach, NS: Pottersfield Press, 1992, p. 18.

I didn't appreciate the import of Frederick Ward's lyric 'Blind Man's Blues'
when I first read it, in 1986. I'd bought the book that contained it – *The Curing
Berry* (1983) – from a funky, now-defunct Commie *librairie*, Red Herring Books,
on a cool, foggy, Haligonian afternoon, and probably started reading it on a
bus bound for the city's rough, proletarian North End. *The Curing Berry* is,
astonishingly, the only book of poems Ward, an African American, has released. It must be out-of-print because the publisher, Williams-Wallace International of Toronto and Stratford, is out-of-business. No matter: that pioneering, black publisher merits acclaim for having brought Ward's slim, fine book
– and his beautiful poem – into being.

'Blind Man's Blues' is simple, almost irritatingly so. Really, it's eleven (or, if
you split the four-line ninth strophe in half, twelve) unrhymed couplets that
stage a dramatic monologue about backwoods filial love and violent sexual
jealousy. The phrases – or cadences – are accessibly declarative and appeal-
ingly authoritative. The first couplet indicates the general style:

> The best thing in my life
> was a woman named Tjose.

The first line could be Tin Pan Alley cliché. But what redeems it is the piano-
note-like – or singing – fall of each word into its cadenced place. The second
line polishes the meaning of the first, and the position of 'Tjose,' as its clincher,
accents her position as 'the best thing' – even as the word *thing* forces us to
ponder the speaker's objectification – though amiable – of this woman. The
placement of 'Tjose' reinforces the challenge of its pronunciation. Should it
rhyme with *rose* or *rosé*? Of course, if pronounced in the first manner, the
second line will possess – agreeably – the same number of syllables as the first.
If pronounced in the alternative fashion, however, the name will sound more
exotic. But how should the dipthong 'Tj' be pronounced? To sound like 'Ch,'
'Th,' 'J,' or 'H'?

These questions tease out the suave trickiness of Ward's music-based poetic. Born in Kansas City in 1937 and trained as an artist and musician (Ward studied jazz piano with Oscar Peterson), he foregrounds the roles of letter, syllable, and of word position in the dexterous 'orchestrating' of the poetic (or prose) line. Since his emigration to Halifax and Montreal in 1970, Ward's poems and novels have displayed a *proud* absorption of the techniques of James Joyce, William Faulkner, and, above all, two African-American poets, namely Robert Hayden (like Ward an adherent of the Baha'i faith) and Jean Toomer, whose masterpiece, *Cane* (1923), is simultaneously *avant-garde* and roots-based. Ward profits liberally from these geniuses; thus, he writes with peculiar affinity for the linguistic and tonal music of speech, especially Black English, which he scores more sonorously than any other contemporary writer, whether one reads Toni Morrison or the Africadian poet David Woods. 'Times the *blackness* of the line is sounded in Ward's use of a crisp, rich, vernacular utterance, as in the second strophe of 'Blind Man's Blues':

We never had to sneak for nothing
strong woman.

(The second line must not be read as a continuation of the first; rather, it is a choral reflection on the first. Crucially, too, the empty space after *nothing* must be read as a 'rest' – or 'stop.') Or it is sounded in a haiku-like analogy, as in the poem's third strophe:

Put you in mind of a lone bird at dawn
standing without panic in the dew.

(Hear the lush sonic correspondences among Ward's words: the consonance between 'nd' in 'mind' and 'standing'; the alliteration of 'd' in 'dawn' and 'dew'; the inner rhyme between 'you' and 'dew'; the assonance between 'standing' and 'panic'; and the near rhyme between 'lone' and 'dawn.') Or *blackness* is sounded in the biblical parallelism of the fifth strophe's resonant reprising of the first:

The best thing happen to her
were my own papa.

Or perhaps it is sounded in the repetition of details such as the pleasure that the speaker *and* his father derive from coitus with Tjose:

She kissed me so hard
She'd suck a hum from me.
...
And I caught her sucking that same hum from him.

Ward deploys the resources of rhyme and repetition with inexhaustible ingenuity.

'Blind Man's Blues' ends with the revelation that the speaker suspects that Tjose did not want him 'to look on my naked papa like that // She throw'd lye / in my face.' At the same time, though, it was and is a revelation for African-Canadian literature, for, here, Ward liberates a black accent – and frees it to say what it likes.

I don't think I understood this truth in 1986. It's a realization that has only dawned with time, I mean, that period – two decades now – that I have wrought, tussling with trying to get my own musicked, raw, rambunctious, cussing, Nova Scottish (Africadian) voice down – loudly – on paper.

African-Islanders

Review of *Black Islanders: Prince Edward Island's Historical Black Community*, by Jim Hornby. Charlottetown, PEI: Institute of Island Studies, 1991.

While the history of blacks in Ontario, Nova Scotia, and New Brunswick is somewhat known, that of the slave-founded community of Prince Edward Island has been a steady mystery. Fortunately, *Black Islanders: Prince Edward Island's Historical Black Community*, a slim but panoramic history by Jim Hornby, a white lawyer and amateur historian, should increase knowledge of 'African-Islanders,' to use Hornby's term, and, especially, of racism's three faces, namely, 'structural ideology,' 'social discrimination,' and 'personal prejudice.' Effectively, the most poignant aspect of the history of the African-Islanders is their near-disappearance from the Island because of, Hornby writes, 'a combination of out-migration and assimilation.' Therefore, Hornby's text chronicles the rise and fall or, more precisely, the flourishing and withering of the original African-descended Islanders.

Given that the African-Islanders began their history on the red clay soil of Prince Edward Island in 1783 as the chattel of white Loyalists, that their small number (which, says Hornby, 'probably never exceeded two hundred') never escaped the stigma attached to their first, inferior status, and that they have largely vanished without leaving 'much sign of their passing,' it would be tempting to read the text as a kind of elegy for this now invisible and silent community. Like a detective, then, Hornby uses court records, newspaper accounts, folklore, and other matter to reconstruct the lives of African-Islanders, both slave and free. His discussion of Freelove Hazard Allen, Dimbo Suckles, Jupiter Wise, and James MacDonald affirms that, even on the Island, the lives of slaves were difficult, degraded, and often abbreviated. Likewise, Hornby's narrative of the cold-blooded shooting death of a Charlottetown black youth by two white youths, who were unsurprisingly acquitted, illustrates the arresting fact that, despite the numerous instances of blacks being slain on the Island, 'no one has ever been convicted of such a murder.' Negrophobic racism is one of the enduring legacies of PEI slavery.

Hornby's ability to resurrect the dry bones of the African-Islanders is hampered, as he knows, by the absence or loss of their own records. Hence, he is forced to rely upon public papers which, answering to the needs of a white supremacist society, often portray blacks as lawless and violence-prone fools. Hornby recognizes that 'the African-Islanders are, of necessity, seen against the background of their relationships with the larger white community.' He also points out that 'official documents do not take note of kindness, endurance, and love by the Island's blacks.' Hornby foregrounds, nicely, his awareness of the skewing effect of racist notions on the social construction of blackness in general, and of African-Islanders, in particular. He observes the presence of racism in Island place names and folklore, and insists that white supremacy – a belief 'inherited from colonialism and capitalism' – is a stratifying social force.

Black Islanders accents the indelible mark that African-Islanders have left on Island culture, if not so visibly upon its history. Though their community, which came to be centred on the 'Bog' area of the capital, melted away in the 1920s, it was home to the first African-American heavyweight boxing champion (George Godfrey) and other indefatigable athletes. The text recovers a lost history, and does so with sensitivity, insight, humour, and a lucid and critical intelligence.

Another Great Thing

Review of *Any Known Blood*, by Lawrence Hill. Toronto: Harper Collins, 1997.

The anglophone African-Canadian novel, since its modern début in the 1960s, has been typified by Austin Chesterfield Clarke's Horatio Alger burlesques, in which striving West Indian male immigrants often achieve a middle-class lifestyle and respectability, but at the price of losing their authenticity, their 'roots' culture, or, if partially Americanized, their *blackness*. Clarke's fellow Barbadian-Canadian novelist, Cecil Foster, has continued to mine this ground, though with an emphasis on the necessity for black nationalism. In contrast, *In Another Place, Not Here* (1996), the Trinidadian-Canadian novelist Dionne Brand explores protagonists who reject every measure of *bourgeois* success except the ascetic *and* aristocratic pleasures of attempting to secure an anti-capitalist revolution – or to perish, joyously, in its ruins. The Ontario-born, African-Canadian novelist Lawrence Hill has blazed an alternative trail in his fiction, eschewing both the Malcolm Xian bleakness of Clarke and Foster and the Marxist *élan* of Brand. In his first novel, *Some Great Thing* (1992), and in his follow-up, *Any Known Blood* (1997), this son of an African-American immigrant father (who once helmed the Ontario Human Rights Commission) and a Euro-American mother has consistently depicted black male heroes who struggle to build professional careers – to integrate, at least, class-wise, in the 'white' world – but who never lose their pride in their African ancestry. Nor do they ever meet a racist they do not manage either to ridicule or to convert. Hill's novels chronicle black male achievement – with sweat, blood, and tears, yes, but also with wit, spirit, and style.

In *Some Great Thing* (which is, incidentally, one of the few African-Canadian works in English to find its way into French), the protagonist Mahatma Grafton, a mixed-race journalist with a Winnipeg newspaper, combats – i.e., exposes – police brutality, French-English tensions, white racism, black sell-outs, and anti-communist hysteria, but also explores Black Canadian history, journeys to Cameroon, 'wins' a white woman, and scores major scoops. He is insightful, ironic, and indomitable. *Any Known Blood* offers a series of similar protagonists, namely, five generations of Langston Canes – I, II, III, IV, and V. Most of the novel is narrated by Langston Cane v, a mid-1990s, thirty-eight-year-old, who, in seeking to establish a writing career following the loss of his marriage and his Ontario civil servant job, travels to Baltimore, Maryland, from Oakville, Ontario, and back in time, via family interviews and letters, to uncover layer after layer of Cane history. The novel's *pièce de résistance* is, arguably, Langston Cane v's recovery of a journal kept by Langston Cane i, an escaped slave who had lived in Oakville before heading to Harpers Ferry, Virginia, with John Brown, in time to take part in – and to survive – Brown's famous – if failed – assault on the U.S. federal arms depot. The journal reinforces the novel's theme that pluck and luck can allow even a black slave to rise above his circumstances and find love and prosperity. (Thus, Cane i takes one of Brown's daughters for a mate.) By novel's end, then, Cane v has writ, in truth, his novel. His African friend, Yoyo (a character who, like Hélène Savoie and Mahatma Grafton, is imported – incestuously – from *Some Great Thing*), tells him, 'You have to get this published, my friend,' a moment that echoes the writing-will-bring-me-riches-and-fame, self-reflexive conclusion of Dany Laferrière's *Comment faire l'amour avec un nègre sans se fatiguer* (1985). In addition, Cane v finds a voluptuous and willing African-American woman to help him recover from his divorcé woes. *Any Known Blood* is, like *Some Great Thing*, a true *black* comedy.

But it is also, in ways unavailable to the first-generation-immigrant Black Canadian novelists – Clarke, Foster, Brand, et al. – a novel steeped in African–North-American history, both above and below the 49th Parallel. Though Hill is a second-generation African Canadian, his novel's firm models are, fittingly enough, African-American. His arch protagonists carry the names of the chief African-American poet, Langston Hughes, and the signature novel of the Harlem Renaissance, Jean Toomer's *Cane* (1923). The novel's plot seems to shadow that of *The Chaneysville Incident* (1981), a neglected masterpiece by African-American writer David Bradley, whose black protagonist – a professional archivist – retreats from a troubled relationship with a white woman to research his genealogy, specifically that of his slave-liberating ancestors. *Any Known Blood* opens with an allusion to African-American novelist Ralph Ellison's celebrated *Invisible Man* (1952), but also with a signifying difference. While Ellison's protagonist is 'invisible' because whites do not affirm his presence as a black man, Hill's Cane V does not appear to be recognizably black at all (a trait he shares with Hill's Mahatma Grafton):

> I have the rare distinction – a distinction that weighs like a wet life jacket, but that I sometimes float to great advantage – of not appearing to belong to any particular race, but of seeming like a contender for many.
>
> In Spain, people have wondered if I was French. In France, hotel managers asked if I was Moroccan. In Canada, I've been asked – always tentatively – if I was perhaps Peruvian, American, or Jamaican. But I have rarely given a truthful rendering of my origins.

Admittedly, this hesitation around biracial (black-white) identification appears in some African-American texts, but it may be more common in African-Canadian ones. The likely reason is that the paucity of all-black communities in Canada encourages a greater degree of intermarriage than is possible in the United States. In any event, Cane v is a bit of a chameleon, or a mask-wearing Negro. He even describes himself as 'Zebra Incorporated.' Still, a colleague notices, 'You're a revolutionary under that placid exterior,' an observation the narrative verifies.

Then again, the tradition of being a coloured subversive is precisely the family history that Cane v discovers. This 'greatness' is the grandeur of the 'great-great-grandfather,' Cane I – the progenitor of 'a family of people with great accomplishments' – and it is Cane v's destiny to pass it on. Thus, 'there's nothing more humbling than family history.' But it is not until Cane v begins to document it that he can begin to sense that *writing* will be his own contribution to his family's greatness.

Any Known Blood is satirical, hopeful, and, especially in Cane I's journal, masterful. Hill writes with a lyric clarity and a witty lightness that accords all his intimations of grandeur a beautiful and graceful gravity.

Growing Up Black in Alberta

Review of *Pourin' Down Rain*, by Cheryl Foggo. Calgary: Detselig Enterprises, 1990.

In deploring the poverty, illiteracy, and hopelessness which often seem to demarcate those ghettoized and victimized by racism, it is too easy to overlook their assertions of their humanity, their dignity, and their equality. Black Canadians, particularly the indigenous blacks of Nova Scotia and New Brunswick, have too often received such cavalier consideration: the dilapidated housing, the Gothic crime rate, the incidence of suicidal drug addiction and the capitalism-indicting unemployment rate take prominent positions in well-meaning liberal-left studies, while the obsessively tended backyard garden, the unself-conscious charity of neighbours, the restorative passion for religion, and the non-recorded pursuit of self-employment are neglected. A one-sided – and inadvertently racist – portrait of Black Canadians emerges: all is bleak and dreary and, well, *black*, wherever blacks live in numbers. This invidious construction of blackness helped to engineer the destruction of the largely black community of Africville in North End Halifax in the 1960s. City councillors saw shacks; they did not see a functioning community of close families, independent workers, and gorgeous, flourishing gardens.

Cheryl Foggo's *Pourin' Down Rain*, her memoir about growing up female and black in Alberta in the 1950s and 1960s, showcases the richness, the joy, and the love of black family and community life – even in the midst of an often hostile white culture. This book, her first, offers an accidental corrective to the vulgar, depressing interpretations of what it means to live in a black skin in a society that rejects blackness. Though *Pourin' Down Rain* is culturally specific, its scrutinized family possesses universal significance. Its members appear as complete human beings, not cartoonish 'victims.'

Opening her text with a section titled 'Meeting Jim Crow,' Foggo enacts a typical imperative of New World African texts: to reveal the true value of the self in an environment that insists on one's non-value. This discovery figures the maturation of individual consciousness and becomes a point from which white racism can be critically analysed. Hence, as a child, Foggo was only 'minimally aware that racism was a special problem' (5). Still, she admits that 'a fiercely proud mother's constant reassurances cannot protect her Black child from learning, sooner or later, that skin is a badge you will always wear, a form of identification for those in the world who wish to brand you' (5).

Family and community engagement provide consolations and ways, however, for overcoming the debilitating effects of racial ostracism. Intra-communally, then, the beauty of the black person is affirmed. Foggo remembers attractive self-stylings:

> The women wore hats, the men wore long coats and rubber, slip-on covers for their shoes. Some faces were dark and shiny, others were light brown and waxy looking. The teenage boy cousins wore stove-pipe pants and had very lean faces, the girls wore white lipstick over textured mouths. I was in love with these people who were a magnet to the eyes of all who passed them. (1)

Foggo venerates aunts, uncles, grandparents, and parents for the love they demonstrate and the wisdom they impart. One set of grandparents, then, despite the privations they experienced, 'loved each other with what seems to be almost ferocity and the house was filled with a great deal of laughter' (25). The black community church dispenses, not an opiate of otherworldliness, but a tonic of inspiration – as well as spiritual stimulants for music and song. Smartly, Black English appears as a means for the proud, intra-group assertion of black identity. Foggo affirms that her parents' 'normal speech demonstrated to White society that Black Canadians could speak the Queen's English too,' but '"Talkin' Black" to one another, to relatives and trusted Black friends allowed them also to *feel* Black' (18).

Like Carol Talbot in her *Growing Up Black in Canada* (1984), Foggo chronicles, in vignette after vignette, acts of cultural assertion. Her readable, honest, descriptive style grants her observations the pointed quality of truth. *Pourin' Down Rain* helps to demolish the Hobbes-like view of black existence as 'nasty, brutish, and short' and to replace it with a truer – and more positive – view of black life as tested, tried, and, given adequate community solidarity, triumphant. Foggo's work indicates that no analysis of black communities can be considered accurate if it erases the people's passion for liberty, dignity, and beauty. *Pourin' Down Rain* is an admirable contribution to our understanding of how Black Canadians on the Prairies 'made a way out of no way.'

Toward a Black Women's Canadian History

Review of 'We're Rooted Here and They Can't Pull Us Up': Essays in African-
Canadian Women's History, by Peggy Bristow, coord., Dionne Brand,
Linda Carty, Afua P. Cooper, Sylvia Hamilton, and Adrienne Shadd.
Toronto: University of Toronto Press, 1994.

The construction of race relations in Canada has been subject to one overrid-
ing imperative: the need to demarcate, favourably, the Canadian record from
that of the United States. This prerequisite has even tinctured African-Canadian assessments of black white race relations in Canada. For instance, novelist Austin Clarke, while castigating 'polite' Canadian prejudice in his pamphlet *Public Enemies: Police Violence and Black Youth* (1992), feels compelled to
contend that, despite the race-motivated riot of 4 May 1992, Toronto 'is still
north of the border of America and of racism' (18, his italics). Earlier African
Canadians preached like views. In *Folklore from Nova Scotia* (1931), Arthur Huff
Fauset, an African-American anthropologist who toured Nova Scotia in the
mid-1920s, records a black man singing, 'Mr. and Master, don't grieve after
me, / For I cannot be a slave anymore. / I'm beneath the tiding waves or
beneath the lion's paw, / He will growl if you come near the shore' (101), lines
affirming the Anglo-Canadian vision of Britain as stalwart defender of liberty.
There is truth in such notions: British North America was a haven for Black
Loyalists, War of 1812 Black Refugees, fugitive slaves, and freeborn (and freed)
African-Americans bent on slipping the vast, insidious net cast by America's
Fugitive Slave Law of 1850. Yet, the conception of Canada as a racial Utopia
obscures its own legacy of slavery, discrimination, vigorous segregation, and
anti-black immigration laws. (Hence, the racism of *ur*-Canadian figures such
as Thomas Chandler Haliburton, a defender of slavery, inspires scant interrogation.) Too, the image of the benign 'Great White North' transforms the
historical black presence into a new-minted, 'visible' foil for white Canadian
liberality. In short, the thesis of Canadian racial openness and American racist
narrowness permits the whitewashing of Canadian history. (Witness the omission of slave narratives from anthologies of early Canadian literature.)

African-Canadian history is marginalized in Canadian historiography; that
of African-Canadian women is even less detectable. Scholars like Suzanne
Morton ('Separate Spheres in a Separate World: African–Nova Scotian Women
in late-19th-Century Halifax County' [1993]) and Judith Fingard (*The Dark Side
of Victorian Halifax* [1989]) have excavated elements of this history, but black

women themselves are also undertaking the recovery of their narratives, a *praxis* first begun in 1852, when abolitionist author and publisher Mary Ann Shadd Cary exhorted her African North American compatriots to resist slavery and to immigrate to Canada West. Her toils as well as those of other black women in Ontario and Nova Scotia are the focus of '*We're Rooted Here and They Can't Pull Us Up': Essays in African–Canadian Women's History*, a compelling sextet of papers underscoring the long residency of black women in Canada, their assaults on slavery and chauvinism, and their attitudes toward home, Empire, and the Republic. The six writers – volume 'coordinator' Peggy Bristow, Dionne Brand, Linda Carty, Afua P. Cooper, Sylvia Hamilton, and Adrienne Shadd – rebuke 'the common perception that black people were either non-existent in the development of Canada, or only arrived in Canada through recent migration' [3] and seek to stymie 'the endemic racism that fuels the Canadian intellectual tradition' (8). Skimming standard works on Canadian women and Canadian blacks, the authors find the former eschew race, the latter downplay gender. Thus, in their respective submissions, the writers foreground black women, attack the Disneyish illusion of Canadian non-racialism, and mark the centrality of faith in black communal life.

These themes first emerge in filmmaker and writer Hamilton's chronicle of Africadian women. Hamilton establishes that the more than three-century-long black fact in Nova Scotia is ignored in tourist and corporate publicity (14), that slave women were valued as breeders of capital (i.e., children), that black colonists 'set down long roots, intertwined from community to community' (33), that 'the African Baptist Churches were the focus of social, educational, political, economic, and spiritual work' (35), and that Africadian women have scored many nitid achievements. Hamilton offers indelible portraits of indomitable women, but her choppy article merely consolidates available information.

In her unembellished discussion of women and the Underground Railroad, Shadd stresses the special risks incurred by fleeing female slaves. A writer-researcher with an M.A. in sociology, Shadd reviews the Canadian activities of slave liberator Harriet Tubman and instances early Ontario cases of escape and resistance. Her story of the 1837 mass defence of a fugitive who colonial authorities planned to return to the United States (and, thus, to slavery) taps the vivid testimony of Anna Jameson, an English sojourner in Upper Canada:

> One woman had seized the sheriff, and held him pinioned in her arms; another, on one of the artillery-men presenting his piece, and swearing that he would shoot her ..., gave him only one glance of unutterable contempt, and with one hand knocking up his piece, and collaring him with the other, held him in such a manner as to prevent his firing. (Quoted in Shadd 60)

Shadd also notices unpublished data collected by Professor Michael Wayne which suggests that fewer fugitive slaves than hitherto imagined entered Canada West between 1850 and 1861. Shadd points out that 'over 40 per cent of the census-enumerated Black population were Canadian-born in the 1861 census' (64).

The volume's most substantial entry belongs to Bristow, a doctoral candidate in history. Her analysis of black women's lives in Kent County, Ontario, from 1850 to 1865 utilizes 'census data, government reports, city directories, church records, minute books of organizations, correspondence of government officials, personal letters, diaries, newspaper accounts, and secondary sources' (70) and exposes the racism of such officials as Lord Elgin, who feared that the Province of Canada 'might be "flooded with blackies who are rushing across the frontier to escape from the bloodhounds whom the Fugitive Slave Bill has let loose on their track"' (79). Bristow also reveals that a public meeting was organized in Chatham in 1849 to try to prevent the Elgin Association from creating an asylum in Raleigh Township for fugitive slaves (77). The opposition failed, but Bristow's uncovering of such anti-black sentiment explodes proud notions of Canadian tolerance. Scrutinizing black women's lives in the Elgin Settlement, Chatham, and Buxton, Bristow limns their interest in religion and education, their encounters with a hypocritical sexual morality, and their attention to marriage, child-bearing, and work – domestic, agricultural, and service-oriented. She shows us women – particularly the irrepressible Shadd Cary – organizing communities and editing newspapers. Valuably, too, Bristow plumbs the 'race uplift' ideals and anti-Americanism of black women leaders, stating that 'like the overwhelming majority of settlers, but for fundamentally different reasons, they were concerned about the possibility of republican ideas taking hold in British North America' (124). In fact, 'their allegiance to British institutions was fuelled by the legal protection they achieved and in most cases had to struggle for' (124). Bristow's essay – lucid, ludic, encyclopedic – radiates incisive intelligence.

In her slight piece, Afua P. Cooper, a poet and Ph.D candidate in history, sketches the life of teacher and abolitionist Mary Bibb. Cooper cites Bibb's anti-Americanism (in an 1853 letter, she speaks of 'Republican oppression' [151]), but she also accents a central theme of the volume:

> Canada had styled itself as a haven for the oppressed, those Blacks who had fled the United States because of slavery and virulent racism. But on coming to Canada, many Blacks found that the only difference between the new country and the old was that in the new country the law protected ex-fugitives from re-enslavement. (153)

Cooper skirts the intra-community, class-based dissension over whether or not to accept separate (in effect, segregated) schools; rather, she highlights Bibb's successful effort to launch a private establishment.

Writer, filmmaker, and history doctoral candidate Dionne Brand amalgamates oral accounts and standard texts to reconstruct black women's lives in Ontario between 1920 and 1946. Her interviewees – luculent and personable – recall the constant impingement of discrimination upon them as domestics, factory workers, and farmhands. During the Second World War, for instance, they were often assigned the riskiest tasks in munitions plants. Grace Fowler reports, 'I worked on what they call the high explosives side, where you got paid a little extra because you were workin' with dangerous powders' (182). Even so, at war's end, when Black Canadian women were expected to return to domestic work, they resisted this fate. But if they shied from such labour, Brand states, 'their Black Caribbean sisters [did] not' (189). They 'came to Canada to fill the shortages in domestic workers' (189). Here the volume registers an epochal shift in African-Canadian history, as the African-American-descended blacks begin to be both displaced and augmented by incoming Caribbean (and African) blacks. This change lies, however, outside Brand's orbit. She ends by noting the Canadian state's usage of the dubious 'but nevertheless racial distinction between European women imported as "nannies" and Caribbean women imported as "domestics"' (190). Her piece is vibrant, albeit impressionistic.

The tome's last entry charges that the Canadian state has always eyed black women as exploitable labour. For Carty, a sociologist, the state incarnates hegemonic, élite, white male rule to which 'African-Canadians have always been in a relationship of social subordination ...' (197). Stating facts that, while paramount, are expected, she affirms that 'while the government and many white people in early Canada were opposed to the practice of slavery by their next-door neighbour, it was more through self-righteousness than a belief in the equality of peoples' (199). Damningly, too, Canada has admitted blacks primarily as low-wage workers. To wit, since the 1955 commencement of the West Indian Domestic Scheme, Canada 'has continued the practice of importing women from the Caribbean as domestic workers' (220).

In sum, 'We're Rooted Here and They Can't Pull Us Up' augments our understanding of the lives of African-Canadian girls and women, from 1783 to the present, while also demonstrating that Canada's lax embrace, then sloughing off, of slavery did not render its racism any less noxious than the American genre. The authors regret, properly, the absence of articles on Quebec and the West; yet, more attention could also have been given the Maritimes, where, like Nova Scotia, New Brunswick and Prince Edward Island host Africadian populations. Class issues receive but cursory discussion. Moreover, though such scholarship is necessary to produce original insights, only Brand and Bristow make extensive use of primary sources. Finally, the collection is marred by annoying typos ('1880' for '1800' [31], 'fact' for 'face' [159], et cetera), stylistic gaffes (cf. Cooper's love of interrogative sentences), and loose statements (cf. Carty's assertion that, in 1867, Canada became 'an independent, post-colonial state' [196], an utterance that ignores Canada's slow, painful attainment of effective independence). Faults aside, this volume bears witness to an intellectual renaissance in African-Canadian women's historiography.

Love Which Is Insight

Review of *Bread out of Stone*, by Dionne Brand. Toronto: Coach House, 1994.

How can I read Dionne Brand's eleventh book, her essay collection, *Bread out of Stone*, with academic objectivity? I've known my Trinidadian-Canadian 'sister,' this fierce writer, far too long – since 1978 – for that. Her voice – succinct, lyric–'accented,' love-and-anger-tincted – seeps too deeply inside the flesh to allow anyone the luxury of forgetfulness.

Besides, these thirteen essays, subtitled 'recollections sex / recognitions race / dreaming politics,' testify to the bitter gender, racial, and political battles in which she has engaged since the 1960s. A black, lesbian, immigrant, film-maker, university lecturer, writer, and 1990 nominee for the Governor General's Award for Poetry (not necessarily in this order), Brand believes in the struggle for equality.

From the first page, Brand writes – no, *speaks* – with a beguiling, forensic clarity about the issues that seize our attention: 'There's a hit-and-run game of police and drug dealers in my part of [Toronto], from Christie Pits, gaping wide and strewn with syringes, to Lansdowne and Bloor, where my cousin and so many young men and women walk, hustle, dry-eyed, haunted, hungry and busily, toward a fix.' She eulogizes revolutionary Grenada, where she was stationed as a CUSO worker and from where she was evacuated in the wake of the U.S.-led invasion of October 1983. (This experience engendered *Chronicles of the Hostile Sun*, her 1984 book of poems.)

Brand remembers her roots because she must: 'There is never the room that white writers have in never speaking for their whole race, yet in speaking the most secret and cowardly language of normalcy and affirmation, speaking for the whole race.' She recalls the police killings of black men in Toronto, the ugly fallout of the Just Desserts shooting, the 1993 street-corner strip-search of Audrey Smith, the *Show Boat* and 'Writing thru Race' controversies. Never does she flinch from saying what must be said.

Brand exposes the regressive liberalism of writer Neil Bissoondath, federal culture minister Michel Dupuy, and *Globe* columnists Michael Valpy and Robert Fulford, but also the racism of white women, the sexism of black men, and the anti-lesbianism of straights, black and white. Like M. NourbeSe Philip, Brand relishes the role of public intellectual.

One benefit of these essays is their accidental recovery of recent Black Canadian intellectual history. When Brand writes about the importance of Bathurst Street to the development of Toronto's black community and comments on institutions like Wong's Restaurant (which offers, arguably, the best saltfish and ackee in T.O.), on folks like activist Dudley ('Duds') Laws, and refers, probably, to others like the Africadian musician Faith Nolan, she centralizes blacks marginalized by 'our' white society and culture.

But it's Brand's love – erotic, Platonic – for black women that fires this work. When she concentrates on the black female form, this often maligned and banished body, her writing acquires its strongest force – that of eyes seeing for the first time:

> Often when we talk about the wonderful Black women in our lives, ... we forget that apart from learning the elegant art of survival from them, we also learn in their gestures the fine art of sensuality ... Didn't we take in their sweetness, their skinniness, their voluptuousness, their ample arms, their bone-sharp adroitness, their hot darkness; the texture of their skin, its plumminess, its pliancy; their angularity, their style when dancing, their stride across a piece of yard that sets the yard off, their shake as they sense the earth under their feet, their rock, the way they take music in their shoulder, the way they pause and then shimmy and let it roll?

This powerful love, which is insight, charges every word that Brand writes. She *sees*, and she demands to be *seen*, wholly.

Politics isn't everything in these pieces. The natural description in 'Just Rain, Bacolet' is exquisite. Other pieces made me bust my guts laughing.

I chide my 'sister,' though, for her Toronto-centrism and for her statement that the 1970 Sir George Williams affair 'awakened the Black Power movement in Canada.' Black folks in Ontario and in Nova Scotia risked everything in the 1940s and 1950s to win small but impressive victories – integrating schools, cinemas, restaurants, and the nursing profession.

Quibbles aside, *Bread out of Stone* is material, imagistic, moving, memorable, admirable. *Dionne, write again soon.*

The Outraged Citizen-Poet Speaks Out

Review of *A Genealogy of Resistance and Other Essays*, by M. NourbeSe Philip. Toronto: The Mercury Press, 1997.

People of African heritage have borne witness to the truth of their oppression, or their pain, or their angst, in European-controlled polities ever since the first slaves landed in the Americas. Hence, New World Africans laud heroic intellectuals such as philosopher Angela Davis, sociologist W.E.B. Du Bois, historian C.L.R. James, and psychoanalyst Frantz Fanon. Clearly, too, African-American leaders consist now of not only classical religious politicos like Jesse Jackson and Louis Farrakhan, but also of such public intellectuals as Cornel West and bell hooks (*sic*). In English Canada, a corps of black intellectuals has emerged, featuring journalists Cecil Foster and Odida Quamina, filmmakers Clement Virgo and Sylvia Hamilton, and writers André Alexis, Dionne Brand, Austin Clarke, and Charles Saunders. However, the most provocative anglophone African-Canadian intellectual is M. NourbeSe Philip, whose ninth book, *A Genealogy of Resistance and Other Essays*, yields urgent meditations on the political relevancy of language. It is a manifesto of impassioned reason.

Philip rejects the aristocratic notion that intellectuals should have no truck with supposedly vulgar, political passions such as nationalism and feminism. She respects no divide between citizen and poet, thus producing excellent and exacting critiques on social issues ranging from the *Showboat* imbroglio to the Bernardo-Homolka murders. Both notoriety and adulation followed her principled, media *contretemps* with June Callwood and Michael Coren. Even though silence lies at the crux of her poetics, Philip refuses silence. From her first book, *Thorns* (1980), to her Casa de las Americas–winning poetry collection, *She Tries Her Tongue, Her Silence Softly Breaks* (1989), to her first essay collection, *Frontiers* (1992), the Guggenheim Fellow, ex-lawyer, and Tobago-born writer has scorned *Yanqui* and John Bull imperialism, damned Canuck racism, and exulted in the gyno-specific experiences of birth and menstruation, engaging all with a fire-breathing intellectuality.

For Philip, then, the word *genealogy* may denote family record-keeping, but it connotes histories of suffering and legacies of resistance. Biblically, the title essay consecrates historical acts of self-affirmation: 'I shall begin with him. Not with the word. Which was. In the beginning. I shall speak of him who every evening with slow and careful hands brought light to displace the dark-ness.' Audaciously, Philip links her alteration of her own name to the organic instability of the names of all post–Middle Passage blacks: 'Marlene Philip to M. Nourbese Philip. As if we are all somehow uncomfortable in these names; wearing them like strange and foreign clothes that generation after generation we keep changing and adjusting for a better fit.' Her work cancels the danger-ous comfort of amnesia; it demands recognition of the cultural and socio-economic wounds inflicted by slavery and colonialism.

But Philip spurns mere victimology. Rather, she practises a version of *sankofa*, excavating the past to conceive the future. Her analysis of the annual Toronto festival of Caribana is prefaced by her recollection of the efforts of politicos, throughout modernity, to police the movements of festive black bodies. But so what? Diasporic Africans are 'moving and moving and in the moving they throwing out the seeds that defying the holding in the ships crawling across the Atlantic with them and their brothers and sisters.'

Slavery is cited again in Philip's magisterially lucid, reverberatingly sensa-tional essay 'The Absence of Writing,' where she hypothesizes searingly that Creole tongues represent a deliberate Africanization of European languages: 'The formal standard language was subverted, turned upside down, inside out, and even sometimes erased. Nouns became strangers to verbs and vice versa; tonal accentuation took the place of several words at a time; rhythms held sway.'

Swinging between 'word-jazz' lyric and surging prose, and fusing Carib-bean demotic passages with barrister-exact English, Philip's essays attempt a Creole tone. Studying her own poetics, Philips reveals, 'I set out to destroy the lyric voice, the singularity of the lyric voice, and found that poetry had split.' Her essays hammer at this theme: the forging of poetry (and argument) out of an imposed and base language, English – 'this mother of a tongue.' The struggle is noble, for poetry 'is the only activity' that yet resists 'the all-consuming maw of consumerism': a *de facto* defence of the 'gut-busting, tear-jerking, son-of-a-bitch art.'

Philip's would-be-scholarly assertions falter at times. Her claim that, in Canada, 'there was no tradition of writing which was in any way receptive to the African writer,' iterates the irritating, ivory-tower convention that sermons and other folk forms are sub-literary. Her statement that African-Canadian writers have had 'until very recently, nothing to follow, join, or even resist' parallels, ironically, Trinidadian novelist V.S. Naipaul's unthoughtful, 1962 allegation that 'nothing' was created in the West Indies.

Then again, Philip seems philosophically opposed to writing anything that cannot spark opposition. Rather, she wants 'to contaminate the poem – fuck the juxtaposition and resonance – poison the purity with that which has al-ready been poisoned – to bring the non-poetic into the poems ...' *C'est bien.* Long may she 'mess with the lyric ... interrupting and disrupting it'; long may she contest the page, that 'blank space – where the silence is and never was silent.'

PART THREE

SURVEYS

A Primer of African-Canadian Literature

For Lorris Elliott (1932–99)[1]

I

Memorializing his sojourns in the Grand Republic, Matthew Arnold, in his article 'General Grant' (1887), maligns the Yankee desire to craft an indigenous literature: '... we have "the American Walter Scott," "the American Wordsworth"; nay, I see advertised *The Primer of American Literature*. Imagine the face of Philip or Alexander at hearing of a Primer of Macedonian Literature!' (177) Nettled by this seeming provincialism, Arnold wonders, 'Are we to have a Primer of Canadian Literature too, and a Primer of Australian?' (177) For this *echt*-Victorian arbiter of taste, the offshoots of Britain were 'contributories to one great literature – English Literature' (177). To wish otherwise was to engender Frankenstein monsters – newfangled canons not only 'absurd,' but also 'retarding' (177). Though one might like to dismiss Arnold's qualms, his objections to the creation of new literatures are echoed today by every critic who disbelieves that a particularity must insist upon its distinctiveness *vis-à-vis* a 'parent' culture. Thus Arnold's opinion warrants interrogation. In this regard, I think the Italian-Canadian scholar Joseph Pivato undermines Arnold by positing, in *Echo: Essays on Other Literatures* (1994), that 'a distinct culture is vital to the life of a people; it survives beyond language, beyond geography, and beyond political states' (252). In addition, Pivato's annunciation of a tradition and a canon of Italian-Canadian literature in 'The Arrival of Italian-Canadian Writing' (1982) offers a useful model for scholars of other minority or ethnic Canadian communities who seek to affirm and reconceptualize these literatures. Surveying early Italian-Canadian writing, commenting on notable, contemporary figures, and concluding with a 'Selected Bibliography' enumerating significant Italian-Canadian works in the major genres, Pivato ushers, formally, an entire literature into being.

The preparation of histories and bibliographies is a prerequisite for the project of decolonizing sub-national and post-colonial literatures. Howard Palmer prefaces the special bibliographical issue of *Canadian Ethnic Studies* (1973) with the observation that 'bibliography is an extremely important part of any interdisciplinary field,' especially that of 'a relatively new and developing field like ethnic studies' (vii). This insight applies with equal force to the construction of any 'neo' literature, including that I term *African-Canadian*.[2] However, histories of this literature are non-existent, and the extant bibliographies focus mainly on writings *about* rather than *by* African Canadians.

A quick review of a few sample bibliographies underscores the problem. Though *Canadian Ethnic Studies* publishes, annually, a lustrous bibliography of materials related to ethnicity, it seldom identifies their authors' ethnicities. For example, Jay Goldstein's 1980 listing, 'Recent Publications Relating to Canadian Ethnic Studies,' includes G.W. Bancroft's 1979 text *They Came from Abroad: The Immigrant As Teacher in Ontario*, but it does not indicate that George Bancroft is of African descent. Nor does it note the publication, in 1979, of African-Canadian literary works such as Dionne Brand's second book of poems (*Earth Magic*). Lisette Boily's laudable bibliography 'Contemporary Canadian First Nations Writers and Writers of Colour: A Working Bibliography' (1994) foregrounds its interest in ethnic identification, but does not pause to distinguish, say, Southeast Asian authors from Afro-Caribbean ones. Frequently, too, bibliographies of Caribbean, African-American, and African authors fail to cite the occurrence of Canadian (or even the Canadian-born) authors among their entries.[3] In most bibliographies, then, African-Canadian writers and texts are an Ellisonian 'ectoplasmic' presence. One finds them only if one possesses either an extraordinary degree of patience or a sixth sense.

Professor Lorris Elliott of McGill University pioneered an effort to identify African-Canadian writers more than twenty years ago when he began to compile bibliographies of their works. His labours resulted in two publications: a formal bibliography and a 'preliminary survey' of 'black writers in Canada' (to defer to his preferred phraseology). His texts, *The Bibliography of Literary Writings by Blacks in Canada* (1986) and *Literary Writing by Blacks in Canada: A Preliminary Survey* (1988),[4] are masterpieces of detective work. However, neither publication considers historical material, and both exclude francophone writers. Furthermore, Elliott's work illuminates the perils awaiting the bibliographer of black-authored texts.

Introducing his survey, Elliott comments that 'the library holdings of Black Canadian literature were limited, if not nonexistent' (3), a point only slightly less true now than it was in 1988. More problematically, 'the [library] classification system does not distinguish Blacks from other ethnic groups in Canada,' thus making it 'impossible to tell which of the listed Canadian authors were actually Blacks' (*Literary* 3). An exemplary error of this sort occurs when Elliott names one 'Brian Gypsin' as the first African-Canadian novelist (*Literary* 4). But, Brion Gysin (to reproduce his name correctly) was an American of European descent. Moreover, his supposed 'novel,' *To Master, a Long Goodnight: The Story of Uncle Tom, a Historical Narrative* (a title Elliott renders as '*To Master, a Last Good Night*' [*Literary* 4]), published in New York in 1946, is a biography of an African-Canadian hero, Josiah Henson. Yet, accidental appropriations are almost inevitable, especially given that many non-black authors write, with empathetic authority, on black history and expression. Ironically, Elliott was aware of this *aporia*, for he points out that 'it was almost impossible to identify the author of a work as a Black, even when that particular work ... dealt with some particular aspect of the experience of Blacks' (*Literary* 3). Even so, he produced two bibliographies which serve as harbingers of the literature.[5] Elliott established that bibliography is required to transform the phrase 'African-Canadian literature' from rhetoric into fact.

Admittedly, then, a degree of cultural assertiveness informs my construction of an African-Canadian literature. I accept African-American scholar Henry Louis Gates's thesis, in *Figures in Black* (1987), that black literature depicts 'a complex and ironic relation to [its] criticism: allegations of an absence [lead] directly to a presence, [fostering] a literature often inextricably bound in a dialogue with its potentially harshest critics' (26). It is also important to revise well-meant opinions that limit African-Canadian literature to a matter of 'West Indian writers' exploring 'the tensions between "have" and "have-not" nations, and the racial and cultural hostilities that are the residue of British colonialism, as well as the problems faced by the visible immigrants in Canada' (Palmer and Rasporich, 727–8). I want also to contest Elliott's argument that 'there is no real evidence of extensive literary writing by Blacks in Canada before the 1970s' (*Literary* 4). This V.S. Naipaul–like utterance erases the record of the nineteenth century as well as three-quarters of the last one. A literature is, *at least in part*, what its authors wish it to be, and for some time, African Canadians thought it more important to author slave narratives and histories, and to compile hymnals, than to publish plays and poems. This feature of the canon must be investigated and theorized, not categorically dismissed. Even contemporary African-Canadian 'creative' writers utilize forms such as autobiography, history, anthologies, studies, and compilations of essays and interviews. Furthermore, we still know too little about early African-Canadian writing to be able to assess it in any conclusive manner. For this reason, I have included 'non-literary' works, many of them historical, in the bibliography that follows (see 'Africana Canadiana: A Select Bibliography of Literature by African-Canadian Authors,' pp. 339–448, below). It is time now to sketch the species of literature that it manifests.

II

African-Canadian literature has been, from its origins, the work of political exiles and native dissidents. It began in crisis, matured in crisis, and exists in crisis. The first authors in this tradition were Black Loyalists: African Americans who rejected the slavery-sanctifying American Revolution in favour of the British pledge of land and liberty. Settled in the Maritimes (principally in Nova Scotia) in 1783, a third of the original 3,400-strong contingent, intolerant of British North American prejudice, decamped for Sierra Leone in 1792. Among this party, David George, a Baptist minister, and Boston King, a Methodist, published memoirs in 1793 and 1798 respectively. For her part, Susannah

(Susana) Smith, once of Virginia and Nova Scotia, inaugurated the womanist side of African-Canadian literature by writing a letter, dated 12 May 1792, to Sierra Leone's colonial authorities to request soap, noting that 'we [her family] ar not fit to be Sean for dirt [sic]' (Fyfe 24). John Marrant, the most successful author of this period, was an impressed Loyalist and a missionary for the Countess of Huntingdon Connexion (a Calvinist offshoot), whose Narrative of the Lord's Wonderful Dealings with John Marrant, a Black (Now Going to Preach the Gospel in Nova-Scotia), an almost magic realist account of his bucolic captivity among the Cherokee, first published in 1785, enjoyed at least twenty-one print-ings. His text marks the genesis of African-Canadian literature.

Exiles and refugees continued to sculpt the nascent literature during the nineteenth century. Tens of thousands of African Americans settled in British North America – in the Canadas and in British Columbia – prior to the extir-pation of American slavery in 1865. Some 'fugitives,' settlers, and cross-border migrants published abolitionist-oriented texts. One early work was Peter A. Williams's Discourse ... for the Benefit of the Coloured Community of Wilberforce in Upper Canada, published in New York City in 1830. The first major text by an African-Canadian woman, Condition of Colored People, a pamphlet, was pub-lished in Wilmington, Delaware, in 1849 by Mary Ann Shadd, who became one of Canada's first women newspaper editors when she assumed the editorship of the abolitionist Provincial Freeman from Samuel Ringgold Ward in 1853. (Shadd's second text, A Plea for Emigration, or, Notes of Canada West, a tract intended to persuade African Americans to move to southern Ontario, was published in 1852.) Outright anti-slavery agitation is represented by sev-eral major texts, including Josiah Henson's oft-reprinted Life of Josiah Henson, Formerly a Slave, Now an Inhabitant of Canada (1849), which Harriet Beecher Stowe cited, probably fraudulently, as a source for her incendiary abolitionist novel, Uncle Tom's Cabin (1852). Henry Bibb, the founder of Voice of the Fugi-tive, the first black newspaper in Canada, printed his Narrative in 1849. Bibb was also, perhaps, the first African-Canadian publisher, for Minutes and Pro-ceedings of the General Convention, for the Improvement of the Colored Inhabitants, Held by Adjournments in Amherstburg, C.W. [Canada West] was produced by a firm titled Bibb & Holly, of Windsor, Ontario, in 1853. Samuel Ward's Autobi-ography of a Fugitive Negro; His Anti-Slavery Labours in the United States, Canada and England, published in 1855, rips the veil from Upper Canadian racism and devotes ten pages to skewering the pro-slavery and Negrophobic musings of English Canada's most vaunted early writer, Thomas Chandler Haliburton. Compiled by Benjamin Drew, who was white, A North-Side View of Slavery (1856) rates greater attention, for it presents the oral recollections of ex-U.S. slaves who had 'ridden' the Underground Railroad into Canada. Similarly, The Refugees from Slavery in Canada West: Report to the Freedmen's Inquiry Com-mission (1864), written by Samuel Gridley Howe, another white, contains ver-batim statements by African-American ex-slaves in Canada West. In his 1861 work, Osborne Perry Anderson presents a sympathetic account of John Brown's precipitous raid upon a U.S. arms depot at Harpers Ferry, Virginia. Slave narratives were penned by Moses Roper (1838), Lewis and Milton Clarke (1845–

6), Thomas Smallwood (1851), Theophilus Austin Steward (1856), and by Jermain Wesley Loguen (1859). The strangest work in this genre is a booklet, *The Book of the Bible against Slavery*, inked by John William Robertson, an ex-Virginia slave, and issued in Halifax in 1854. This curious text, one of the few slave narratives to debut in Canada, employs a pungently Dantean style: 'The Spirit of Slavery never seeks refuge in the Bible of its own accord ... Its asylum is its sepulchre, its city of refuge the city of destruction ...' (quoted in George Elliott Clarke, *Fire*, vol. 1, 58). After the demise of American slavery, liberated African Americans who had taken refuge in Canada recalled their sojourns in memoirs such as those by Israel Campbell (1872) and John Malvin (1879).

To fully reconstruct early African-Canadian literature, one must, I think, patriate some African-American writers to Canada, mainly on the basis of their one-time Canadian residency. Roper, Bibb, Ward, Steward, Malvin, Campbell, the Clarkes, Anderson, Loguen, and Williams, though they spent most of their lives in the United States, are (as I presumed above) eminent candidates for African-Canadian canonization. To be frank, my strategy here affirms the Franco-Ontarian critic René Dionne's intuition in *La Littérature régionale aux confins de l'histoire et de la géographie: Étude* (1993) that '... une littérature régionale possède déja un corpus d'oeuvres au moment où ses promoteurs la proclament comme un domaine littéraire particulier' (38). Acadian literature lays claim to American poet Henry Wadsworth Longfellow, the author of *Evangeline: A Tale of Acadia* (1847), though he never set foot in Nova Scotia or Acadie. African-Canadian literature must exhibit just as wide a compass.

Three creative writers, in particular, should be inducted into the canon: Noah Calwell Cannon, James Madison Bell, and Martin Robinson Delany. Cannon, a Delaware native, spent the last six years of his life in Canada (1844–50), becoming, retroactively, Canada's first black poet, for his work *The Rock of Wisdom*, which appeared in 1833. Bell, an Ohio native, also spent six years in Canada (1854–60), publishing his first text in 1862 and his *Poetical Works* in 1901. Delany is, I urge, the first African-Canadian novelist. His well-known fiction 'Blake; or, The Huts of America,' serialized in the *Anglo-African Magazine* (and its successor, the *Weekly Anglo-African*) between 1859 and 1862, was written, states Paul Gilroy, in Chatham, Ontario, where Delany dwelt from 1856 to 1859 (27).[6]

Two other African-American writers deserve provisional – or 'honorary' – status in the African-Canadian canon: William Still and Arthur Huff Fauset. Still's *The Underground Railroad* (1872), a miscellany of primary information relating to the famous slavery-escape network, is rich with Canadian lore. Fauset's *Folklore from Nova Scotia* (1931) is a singular compendium of Africadian (Black Nova Scotian) folklore, the result of a research trip to Nova Scotia that the author, an anthropologist, undertook in 1926.

When early African-Canadian writers were not assaulting slavery, they were organizing churches and protesting against racism. In Nova Scotia, African Baptist ministers published collections of spirituals and hymns, church histories, minutes, and the occasional sermon, producing most of the Africadian literature in circulation up to 1975. One of the most substantial of these works was Antiguan native Peter E. McKerrow's *History of the Coloured Baptists of Nova Scotia* (1895), probably the first text published by a Caribbean-born writer in Canada.[7] Born in 1846, Halifax's William Harvey Goler, an ex-bricklayer, earned a doctorate in divinity from Lincoln University in 1881, became a leader of the African Methodist Episcopal Church, served as president of Livingstone College in Salisbury, North Carolina, from 1894 to 1916, and published sermons and speeches; his first work appeared in 1884. An ex-Mississippian, John Clay Coleman, who graduated from Toronto's Victoria College in divinity in 1895, published in that city in 1898 a 128-page book, *The Jim Crow Car; or, Denouncement of an Injustice Meted Out to the Black Race*, condemning the racial segregation and lynchings then pandemic in the South. Born in Toronto in 1858, Amelia E. Hall Johnson published a Sunday-school novel, *Clarence and Connie; or, God's Way*, in Philadelphia in 1890.

Returning to early secular writers, I should mention that the British Columbia–born attorney A.B. Walker issued the first African-Canadian literary journal, *Neith*, in Saint John, New Brunswick, during 1903–4. U.S.-born William H.H. Johnson published an autobiography *cum* history in Vancouver in 1904. The Toronto-born Mrs M.E. Lampert, asserts Ann Wallace, published two poems, *Hymn to the New Year* and *My Dreams*, 'in the United States around 1868,' thus becoming, perhaps, the first African-Canadian woman poet (8).[8] A native of Drummondsville (now Niagara Falls), Ontario, the famed composer R. Nathaniel Dett issued, in 1911, his book of poems, *The Album of a Heart*. In 1916 and in 1918, a now-forgotten Windsor, Ontario, native, Theodore Henry Shackelford, issued two collections of Negro dialect poems (*cum* Wordsworthian ballads) in Philadelphia. Another Ontarian, Matthew George Matthews saw his two-volume *Wit, Wisdom and Philosophy* printed in 1915 and 1925. In 1927, Dett, ensconced in Hampton Institute in Virginia, published a landmark compilation of spirituals, *Religious Folk-Songs of the Negro*, his signal contribution to the Harlem Renaissance.

A place in the canon must also be reserved for Canadian-born authors who made their names in the Caribbean. John Hearne is the most prominent of this group. Born in Montreal in 1925, he published his novels and short stories in London and Jamaica, beginning in 1955. Another writer, Hugh Doston Carberry, born in Montreal in 1921, published his first book, *A West Indian in London*, in 1950.

Even a cursory survey of early African-Canadian literature renders untenable the position, *à la* Elliott, that it is only a recent invention. But the contemporary period, commencing in the 1960s, requires elaboration.

III

I would need another book to chronicle, in depth, the development of African-Canadian literature since 1960. I will restrict myself to a few tentative observations.

1. The exile tradition persists. Haitian and Anglo-Caribbean emigrés – specifically from Trinidad, Barbados, and Jamaica – have become major voices in the literature. Dionne Brand, Claire Harris, Theresa Lewis, David Woods, Nalo Hopkinson, Nigel Darbasie, and André Alexis hail from Trinidad; M. NourbeSe Philip grew up in Tobago; Austin Clarke and Cecil Foster are Bajan *hombres*; Makeda Silvera, Olive Senior, Ayanna Black, Bernadette Dyer, Pamela Mordecai, vernacular poet Louise Bennett ('Miss Lou'), reggae poet Patrick Arthurs ('St Patrick'), and several dub poets – Lillian Allen, Afua Cooper, Devon Haughton, and Ahdri Zhina Mandiela – are all Jamaica natives. Other Caribbean-rooted writers include poet Clifton Joseph and essayist Althea Prince, both formerly of Antigua; poet, novelist, and scholar Jan Carew, born in Guyana; and novelist H. Nigel Thomas, once of St Vincent.

The first African-Canadian published play *in English, The Captive,* was penned by the Trinidad-born Lennox Brown and published in 1965. However, the first ever African-Canadian published play was the work of a francophone, Franck Fouché, who published a version of Sophocles' *Oedipus Rex* in his native Haiti in 1958 and a play in Creole, *Bouki nan paradi,* in his adopted Montréal in 1964. Other Haitian-Canadian writers number, not just Gérard Étienne and Anthony Phelps and – that *enfant terrible* – Dany Laferrière, but also Émile Ollivier, Roland Morisseau, Sonia-Pascale, Jacqueline Beaugé-Rosier, Stanley Péan, and Liliane Dehoux, to name *only* a few.

African-American natives also continue to contribute to the literature. Notable figures include the early 'Black Atlanticist' Alma Norman, who, born in the United States in 1930, was educated in Montréal, and published her sole book of poems, *Ballads of Jamaica,* in Jamaica in 1964. But one must also cite David Pinson (whose *Studies in Black and White,* a suite of maudlin poems on a doomed Negro-Québécoise love affair, appeared in 1966); Frederick Ward, a Montreal-and-Nova-Scotia-based, jazz-influenced, masterful scripter of lyrical poems, screenplays, dramas, and fiction; Charles R. Saunders, a Halifax novelist and amateur historian; Ernesto Cuevas, an overlooked, Ottawa short-story writer; Toronto poet Charles C. Smith, who edited the vital African-Canadian anthology *sad dances in a field of white* (1985); and southwestern Ontario's Charlotte Bronté Perry, a composer of histories and poetry. Michigan native Christopher Paul Curtis, a children's book writer, has won the John Newbery Medal, the most prestigious award the United States bestows on juvenile literature. (His work is so appreciated in the United States that he was invited to read at the inauguration of President George W. Bush in 2001.) Born in Missouri, Daniel G. Hill produced, in 1981, an oft-cited history of black settlers in Ontario. Another African American, E. Curmie Price, published a fine book of poems in British Columbia in 1970. An African-American woman, Zainab Amadahy, has published a work of science fiction with Sister Vision Press. Finally, New Jersey native son Rubin 'Hurricane' Carter, a one-time resident of Canada, may be accorded status in the African-Canadian canon, thanks to his searing memoir *The Sixteenth Round* (1974).

The South African poet Arthur Nortje, who spent two and a half years in Toronto and British Columbia, *may be* the first African-born, African-Canadian writer in English.[9] For one thing, his book, *Dead Roots* (1973), published post-humously in London, reflects his Canadian sojourn. The first Anglo-African native to publish *in* Canada, however, was another South African, Harold Head, whose only book of poems appeared in 1974. Interestingly, Head also edited the *third* African-Canadian anthology, *Canada in Us Now: The First Anthology of Black Poetry and Prose in Canada* (1976), which followed Montreal native Camille Haynes's *Black Chat* (1973) and Liz Cromwell's *One out of Many* (1975). Other vital South Africans include Rozena Maart, Rayda Jacobs, and Archie Crail. Malawi native Paul Tiyambe Zeleza has been publishing fiction since 1976. Ghana native Kwame Dawes won Britain's prestigious Forward Poetry Prize in 1994 for the best first collection. Miguna Miguna, a Kenyan exile, has issued four titles since his arrival in Canada in 1988. Ken Wiwa, a native of Nigeria, published an important memoir in 2001. The Ugandan-born playwright George Seremba won acclaim for *Come Good Rain* (1994). Epah Fonkeng, another playwright, hails from Cameroon (the linguistic inverse of Canada). Tanzanian-Canadian writer Tololwa M. Mollel has received many honours for his children's books. A native of Ethiopia, Nega Mezlekia issued his acclaimed *Notes from the Hyena's Belly: Memories of My Ethiopian Boyhood* in 2000. Francophone African writers include Makombo Bamboté (formerly of the Central African Republic), Joseph Nnadi (once of Niger), and Maguy Kabamba and Pius Nkashama (both of the former Zaire).

A few writers have come to Canada from the African Diaspora to the United Kingdom, including award-winning playwright and anthologist Djanet Sears, short-story writer Hazelle Palmer, film critic Cameron Bailey, playwright Maxine Bailey, and highly praised memoirist Rachel Manley. But fiction writer Tessa McWatt, raised in Québec, now uses London, England, as her base.

2. As the foregoing (not exhaustive) catalogue suggests, African-Canadian literature is a heterogeneous and polyglot discourse – a medley of accents. Still, it mirrors the standard Canadian regional variations, a fact critics have ignored. West Coast African-Canadian writers, like Christopher James, David Odhiambo, Wayde Compton, Janisse Browning, and (formerly) Andrea Thompson, compose *avant-garde* works. (See, also, Peter Hudson's beautiful 'little magazine,' *diaspora*.) Across the Prairies, the mode is either crisply ironic – see anything by Suzette Mayr and Ian Samuels – or coolly realistic – see Archie Crail, Cheryl Foggo, and Nigel Darbasie. Ontario offers a cornucopia of traditions and styles. Québec's writers treat linguistic and racial divides – Michel Adam, Francklin Allien, Darius James, and, spectacularly, Dany Laferrière and Stanley Péan. Tanya Evanson and Robert Edison Sandiford are two young anglophone 'Québécois' who explore this territory. (An Ontario native, Lawrence Hill addresses the identical dialectics in his novel *Some Great Thing* [1992].) East Coast writers veer toward high classical modes (see Anna Minerva Henderson), traditional verse (George A. Borden), nitty-gritty realism (Saunders and Woods), and populism (1988 Milton Acorn People's Poet Award winner Maxine Tynes). In Acadien literature, there is the singular voice of Gérard Étienne.

3. 'Indigenous' African-Canadian writers from British Columbia, Alberta, southern Ontario, and the East Coast have tended to craft community histories, memoirs, and autobiographies. See, for instance, Velma Carter's vignettes of African-Albertan history; Foggo's memoir about Calgary's black community in the 1950s and 1960s; Willa Dallard's reminiscences of rural black life in Alberta and Saskatchewan from 1910 to the 1970s; Carol Talbot's study of Windsor, Ontario, in the 1960s; Karen Shadd-Evelyn's celebration of Buxton, Ontario; Stephen Hubbard's biography of Toronto's first black politician and deputy mayor, William Peyton Hubbard; Rella Braithwaite's honourings of women; Gwendolyn and John Robinson's records of Chatham, Ontario; Dorothy Shadd Shreve's analyses of 'AfriCanadian' religion; the genealogical researches of Hilda Dungy; Calvin Ruck's chroniclings of the struggles of Black Canadian servicemen in the First World War; Carrie Best's autobiography; Pearleen Oliver's Africadian church and community histories; and any work bearing the imprint of the Black Cultural Centre of Nova Scotia. Other 'indigenous' community writers employ their knowledge of their history in creative writing. See, for example, Lorena Gale's play *Angélique* (2000), a critique of slavery in historical Nouvelle-France and of domestic labour in present-day Québec, or try Compton's *49th Parallel Psalm* (1999), a verse treatment of 'Black Pacific' history.

4. Given the reluctance of mainstream Canadian publishers to handle black writers (until recently), small – and alternative – presses have produced much of the literature. Contemporary African-Canadian literature was ushered into being, beginning in the mid-1960s, by a constellation of presses around Toronto and Montréal, with major presses publishing the few, and small presses publishing the 'mass.' Austin Clarke's first two novels were published by Toronto-based McClelland and Stewart, in 1964 and 1965 respectively; in contrast, Fouché's first 'Canadian' play was apparently self-published. Étienne's first 'Canadian' work appeared with Montréal's miniscule Éditions L'Ésterel in 1966, while Phelps's first such work appeared with Holt, Rinehart et Winston, also in 1966. Lennox Brown's plays were issued by the Ottawa Little Theatre, another small enterprise, in 1965 and 1966; but Raymond Spence published a novel with Putnam of New York in 1969. These writers and others released works in the 1960s, but it was in the mid-1970s that a mini-explosion in publication occurred. In Toronto, Ann Wallace's WACACRO published the first anthology of Black Canadian women's writing (1975), while Harold Head's Khoisan Artists produced Liz Cromwell's own poetry (1975) and Brand's first chapbook (1978). Head's anthology, *Canada in Us Now* (1976), and Charles Roach's sole poetry text (1977) were carried by NC Press.

Montréal was, though, the site of the 'real' action. Here, Leo Bertley's Bilongo Publishers launched the 'Africadian Renaissance' by producing Gloria Wesley-Daye's sole chapbook of poems in 1975. Another Montreal press, Mondiale, produced poetry by the Jamaica-born Hopeton Anderson (1975) and Nova Scotia's Peter A. Bliss Bailey (1975). For a brief, shining period, from 1975 to

1979, there were more African-Canadian titles available in French than in English. Francophone presses like Egyptian-born Antoine Naaman's Éditions Naaman and Nouvelle Optique outperformed their anglophone counterparts. Éditions Naaman saw into print works by Claude Pierre (1974), Raymond Chassagne (1976), Liliane Dehoux (1976), Maurice Jacques (1977 and 1979), an anthology edited by Ghislaine Rey (Charlier) (1978), work by Roger Pereira (1977), an essay by Carl Prezeau (1977), and work by Yves Antoine (1979). Nouvelle Optique published Anthony Phelps (1976), Franck Fouché (1976), Jean-Richard Laforest (1978), Maximilen Laroche (1978), Serge Legagneur (1978), Gérard Étienne (1979), and Roland Morisseau (1979).

Toronto regained some momentum in the late 1970s and early 1980s when a triumvirate of essential presses was established: Ann Wallace's Williams-Wallace, Makeda Silvera's Sister Vision Press, and the collective enterprise Domestic Bliss. Williams-Wallace introduced Canadians to NourbeSe Philip (1980), Lorris Elliott (1982), Claire Harris (1984), and Ernesto Cuevas (1986), and published nearly all of Brand's work between 1982 and 1988. Sister Vision Press has added depth, texture, and lustre to Canadian literature. Its roster of authors features Brand (1983), Ahdri Mandiela (1985), Djanet Sears (1990), Althea Prince (1993), and Pamela Mordecai (1993). Domestic Bliss covered the politicized raps of Lillian Allen (1982), Devon Haughton (1983), and Clifton Joseph (1983). Women's Press and Kids Can Press were also pivotal in establishing anglo African-Canadian literature.

On the Québec front, a phalanx of vital publishers emerged in the 1980s, including Horace Goddard's AFO Enterprises, Kauss Éditeurs, Éditions du CIDIHCA (Centre internationale de documentation et d'information haïtienne, caraïbéene et afro-canadienne), Humanitas – Nouvelle Optique, VLB, and Triptyque. In Atlantic Canada, Goose Lane Editions (publisher of Claire Harris, Pamela Mordecai, and Kwame Dawes), Gynergy Press (publisher of M. NourbeSe Philip), Pottersfield Press (publisher of Maxine Tynes, David Woods, and Charles Saunders), and the Black Cultural Centre of Nova Scotia began to publish black writers in the mid-1980s. Currently, the new small presses championing African-Canadian texts include Toronto's Insomniac Press and Mercury Press, Hamilton's Capricornus, Montréal's Typo, and Vancouver's Raincoast Books, Arsenal Pulp Press, and Mother Tongue. Gradually, across the country, other presses, new and old, large and small, are drafting African-Canadian writers for their lists.

5. Despite my last assertion, self-publication remains a critical necessity for many Black Canadian writers. From Peter McKerrow in 1895 to Toronto's 'Black Katt' (Robert O. Brown) in 1995, self-publishing has been an honourable way of putting one's work before the public. Crucially, Anna Henderson, of Saint John, New Brunswick, brought out her set of Miltonic poems, *Citadel*, in 1967, when she was eighty, thereby producing probably the first *complete* collection of poems by an African-Canadian woman. Authored by Mairuth Sarsfield, a native of Montréal, *No Crystal Stair* became, in 1997, the first novel in a century to be published by an indigenous, African-Canadian woman. Had

it not been for Gershom Williams's solo effort of 1968, Austin Clarke would have remained the sole, published-in-Canada, anglo African-Canadian novelist from 1964 until 1974, when Truman Green and Frederick Ward both released novels.

6. Foreign presses also helped bring African-Canadian literature into being, with the most important ones being located in London, New York, Paris, Kingston (Jamaica), and, *oui, certainement*, Port-au-Prince. Make no mistake, the Haitian contribution to our literature is immense, brilliant, *très riche*. Scholars must consider the centrality of a 'foreign' journal, *Haiti Littéraire*, founded in part by Anthony Phelps, Serge Legagneur, Davertige (Villard Denis), and Roland Morisseau, to the modernization of African-Canadian literature.

7. Poetry has been the medium of choice for African-Canadian writers, though fiction, particularly short fiction, has gained in popularity over the past two decades. Dionne Brand received the 1997 Governor General's Award for Poetry and Ontario's Trillium Award, for her book *Land to Light On* (1997).[10] M. NourbeSe Philip won a Guggenheim Fellowship for her manuscript for *She Tries Her Tongue, Her Silence Softly Breaks*. On the francophone side, Joël Des Rosiers won the 1999 Grand Prix du livre de Montréal and the Prix du Festival international de la poésie 2000, for his book *Vétiver* (1999), which was also nominated for a Governor General's Award. (Des Rosiers was nominated for the same award in 1990, for his book *Tribu*.) In the genre of fiction, the long-serving Austin Clarke has received the Casa de las Americas Prize (1980) and the W.O. Mitchell Literary Prize (1999). His novel *The Question* was a Governor General's Award nominee in 2000. André Alexis's *Childhood* (1998) received a flood of awards, while Stanley Péan is a household name in Québec. African-Canadian writers have also invaded the field of children's literature, with Lillian Allen, Pamela Mordecai, the prolific C. Everard Palmer, Richardo Keens-Douglas, Christopher Paul Curtis, whose books have won a Newbury Honor Award and the John Newbery Medal, and, another champion in the genre, author Tololwa Mollel – whose book *The Orphan Boy* (1990) was recognized for its illustrations – all producing worthy work. In addition, Cheryl Foggo was nominated for a Governor General's Award for Children's Literature in 1997. Essays and socio-political meditations occupy a prominent place in the African-Canadian canon, with significant titles by Dionne Brand, M. NourbeSe Philip, Austin Clarke, George Dei, Cecil Foster, Makeda Silvera, Wilson Head, Carol Aylward, Daniel Hill, Vincent D'Oyley, Odida Quamina, Carl James, Adrienne Shadd, Paul Dejean (or, as he is known in Haitian Creole, Pòl Dejan), Georges Anglade, Claude Moïse, Cary Hector, and Émile Ollivier. Histories and memoirs have also proven to be popular forms. See, in this regard, Pearleen Oliver; Peggy Bristow (as coordinator); and Charles Saunders. British-born, Jamaica-raised, African-Canadian writer Rachel Manley received the 1997 Governor General's Award for her memoir, *Drumblair: Memories of a Jamaican Childhood* (1996), while the Ethiopian-Canadian author Nega Mezlekia received the same honour in 2000 for his *Notes from the Hyena's Belly*. One fiction genre that has attracted notable African-Canadian participation is

sci-fi/fantasy, with titles by Saunders, Zainab Amadahy, Stanley Péan, and Nalo Hopkinson, who won the Warner Aspect First Novel contest for her manuscript for *Brown Girl in the Ring* (1998). The one literary mode that lags behind the others – in terms of publication – is drama. Yet Franck Fouché, Lennox Brown, Anthony Phelps, Lorris Elliott, Walter Borden, Djanet Sears, Archie Crail, Ahdri Mandiela, Diana Braithwaite, George Boyd, George Seremba, Lorena Gale, Pamela Mordecai, Andrew Moodie, and André Alexis have all produced strong plays. In addition, Sears won the 1998 Governor General's Award for Drama for her play *Harlem Duet* (1997), while Boyd was nominated for this prize in 2000 for *Consecrated Ground* (1999). Playwrights Canada Press has published more African-Canadian drama than any other publisher. However, one must remember that, only a few years ago, in the mid-1990s, Sister Vision Press held that honour.

8. Translations from one official language into the other are rare. The only African-Canadian writer who is nearly fully accessible in the 'other' language is Laferrière (who has also been translated into Dutch, Italian, Spanish, and Korean). Austin Clarke, Dionne Brand, Claire Harris, Frederick Ward, and NourbeSe Philip have no titles translated into French (though Clarke's novel *Amongst Thistles and Thorns* [1965] is available in Russian [1972], his memoir *Growing Up Stupid ...* (1980) is available in Spanish [1980], and his *The Question* [1999] first appeared in Italian [1996]; and NourbeSe Philip's novel *Harriet's Daughter* [1988] is available in German [1993] as is a work by Harris [1996]). Jan Carew's novels have been translated into German (1959, 1961, 1965), Portuguese (1961, 1971), Russian (1963), Georgian (1966), Japanese (1981, 1983), and Spanish (1983). John Hearne's work is available in Swedish, German, Portuguese, and Russian. Olive Senior has work available in Dutch (1992) and German (1996). Suzette Mayr's *The Widows* (1998) also exists in German (1999). André Alexis's *Childhood* has been issued in French, Danish, Finnish, Dutch (all in 1998), German, and Japanese (both in 2000). Darius James's unique, surrealist novel *Negrophobia* (1992), has been translated for Paris and for Tokyo (both in 1995); Richardo Keens-Douglas's children's books have appeared in French and in Spanish. Shamefully, no work by Roland Morisseau or Jacqueline Beaugé-Rosier has been Englished. Émile Ollivier has one title in English. Gérard Étienne has one title in Portuguese and one in German. Not one of Anthony Phelps's texts is available in English, but one of them can be read in Spanish. Perhaps because his novel treats linguistic tensions in Manitoba, Lawrence Hill's *Some Great Thing* (1992) was published in French translation by a Franco-Manitoban press in 1995. Foster's novel *No Man in the House* (1991), and his essay *Distorted Mirror: Canada's Racist Face* (1991), have both been rendered in French (in 1995 and 1991 respectively). C. Everard Palmer has also seen one of his books transfigured into French, but Tololwa Mollel has published books in Xhosa and Afrikaans, and one of his titles, *Matembezi Msituni* (1987), is available only in his native Swahili. Happily, the Brazilian-born, Portuguese-language writer Assar-Mary Santana saw her novel *Boléro*

published in French in 1994 and in English in 1997. To put it mildly, more translations are essential.

9. Though African-Canadian serials are generally ephemeral, they are also serially replenished. Toronto has been well served by a host of journals and newspapers over the past thirty years, including the important intellectual publications *Black Images* (1972–5), whose first editor was none other than Lennox Brown; *Spear* (1971–?), once edited by the indomitable J. Ashton Brathwaite (Odimumba Kwamdela), and *The Harriet Tubman Review* (1981–?), whose editors included Dionne Brand, Clifton Joseph, and Makeda Silvera. *The Word*, founded in 1991, has been a crucial instrument of community dialogue and debate. Anglo Montréal saw the birth and too-soon demise of a wonderful black-oriented magazine *The Black i* (1972–3), edited briefly by Clarence S. Bayne, an important figure in black theatre circles in the city. *Focus Umoja* fared somewhat better, lasting from 1974 to 1978. *Kola*, a literary magazine now edited by Horace Goddard, is still publishing after a decade and more, while *Community Contact* serves as the source of community news. In Halifax, recent African-Canadian serials of note include *The Rap* (1986–8), a black community newspaper with a 'punk' design, and *Black to Business* (1997–), a current magazine edited by Rustum Southwell. One of the most important little magazines was *Caribe*, edited by Harold Marshall, and published roughly twice a year, from 1979 to 1991, in Winnipeg. The pages of these publications and others must be carefully surveyed to recover the early writings and perspectives of contemporary African-Canadian writers.

IV

To conclude, African-Canadian literature has had a long history – but also a more recent efflorescence. It is a distinctive canon, for it draws upon a variety of cultural (and 'national') traditions, accents, and languages. Though I have not discussed themes in this survey, the literature worries identity issues surrounding race, gender, class, language, religion, and region. Perhaps its most persistent quality has been its tendency to appropriate the 'colonial' and to transubstantiate it into native forms ...

Notes

1 In my Acknowledgments on pp. vii–x, I thank many of the scholars and writers who assisted with the compilation of 'Africana Canadiana: A Select Bibliography of Literature by African-Canadian Authors.' Now I would like to dedicate this essay and the bibliography to Dr Lorris Elliott (1932–99), a McGill University professor who pioneered the serious study of African-Canadian literature.

2 In this essay, the term *African-Canadian* denotes indigenous writers, immigrant writers, and sometime resident writers.

3 This point carries a personal resonance for me, for, though the matrilineal side of my family has lived in Nova Scotia since 1813, I turn up (with the New York–born poet Charles C. Smith) as a 'Canadian-based poet of Caribbean origin' in VèVè A. Clark's bibliography of Caribbean writers. See *Callaloo* 13.3 (Summer 1990): 572.

4 A French translation was produced in 1990: *Production littéraire des Noirs du Canada: Étude préliminaire* ([Ottawa]: Multiculturalisme et Citoyonneté Canada / Multiculturalism and Citizenship Canada).

5 Elliott tried to identify authors accurately by supplementing library excursions with visits to 'bookstores, community leaders, and writers,' a procedure he found 'effective, though time-consuming and costly' (3). He also found that 'the most rewarding method of gathering information proved to be writing and telephoning directly to people with an interest in the area' (3). I have followed his methodology, but I have also attempted, whenever possible, to verify authors's racial (and national) identities by searching for their work, or references to their work, in black community newspapers, journals, and other serials, by scouring black-focused anthologies and bibliographies, and by inspecting 'suspect' books or other texts.

6 The issue of whom should be considered the first African-Canadian novelist is contentious. In 1988, Lorris Elliott awarded the title to Brion Gysin (Elliott's 'Brian Gypsin'), who was American, not Canadian, and Celtic-Swiss in ancestry, not African, and whose 1946 'novel' was, in reality, a biography. Still, at least five other contenders for the crown remain: Delany, Amelia Etta Hall Johnson, Lucretia Coleman, William Haslip Stowers, and Austin Clarke. Johnson, who was born in Canada West in 1858, authored *Clarence and Corinne; or, God's Way*, which appeared in Philadelphia in 1890. Coleman, who was also born in Canada West, published her only novel, *Poor Ben*, in Nashville, Tennessee, in either 1890 or 1891. Stowers, yet another Canada West baby (born in 1859), published, with William H. Anderson (under the pseudonym of 'Sanda'), their novel, *Appointed: An American Novel*, in Detroit, Michigan, in 1894. Clarke can rightly bear the title of being the first African-Canadian writer to publish a novel *in* Canada, namely, his 1964 work, *The Survivors of the Crossing*. In summary, then, Delany has the claim by residency, Johnson, Coleman, and Stowers have it by birth, and Clarke has it by place of publication.

7 McKerrow is the first *published* African-Canadian writer of Caribbean origin. However, Sir James Douglas (1803–77), the Caribbean-born (in British Guiana) mixed-race governor of British Columbia (1858–64), kept a journal (1840–65). The Vancouver Public Library published his 1841 journal in 1965. See Wayde Compton, ed., *Bluesprint* (298, 309).

8 Possibly, M.E. Lampert is M.E. Lambert, who edited *St. Matthew's Lyceum Gazette* in Detroit. See I. Garland Penn, *The Afro-American Press and Its Editors* (1891, 1969).

9 John William Nyakatura, a Ugandan, published, in the Bunyoro tongue, in Quebec in 1947, a history of Uganda's Bunyoro-Kitara people. An English translation appeared in New York in 1973.

10 My own narrative lyric suite, *Execution Poems* (2000, 2001), received the 2001 Governor General's Award for Poetry.

Africana Canadiana:
A Select Bibliography of Literature by African-Canadian Authors, 1785–2001, in English, French, and Translation

Authors

Abdi, Hassan. b. Somalia.
- *Somalia: By the Nozzles of the Guns*. Toronto: Spearhead Graphics and Printing Intl, 1993. [history]

Abdias, Nebardoum Derlemari. [1967–]. b. Chad.
- *Cri sonore*. Montréal: Éditions d'Orphée, 1987. [poetry]

Abucar, Mohamed Hagi. b. Somalia.
- *Struggle for Development: The Black Communities of North and East Preston and Cherry Brook, Nova Scotia, 1784–1987*. [Cherry Brook, NS: The Black Cultural Centre of Nova Scotia, 1988.] [prose]
- *Italians*. Tantallon NS: Four East Publications, 1991. [prose]

Adam, Michel. [1945–]. b. Haiti.
- *Vers-de-terre: (anté-poésie)*. Montréal: Les Éditions Dérives, 1976. [poetry]
- *La Longue Nuit des petits exécutants*. Montréal: Éditions des Idées, 1983. [fiction]

Adams, Micheline. b. Trinidad.
- [et al.] *Affinities*. By Windsor [ON] Printmaker's Forum. [Windsor, ON]: Windsor Printmaker's Forum, 1993. [poetry and prints]

Adekoya, Prince Kay-ode.
- *World without a Mirror: What You Need to Know*. [Vancouver?]: n.p., 1999. [history]

Africa, John.
- *The Present Condition of Blacks in Toronto*. Toronto: Cross-Cultural Communications Centre, 198? [essay]

Agnant, Marie-Célie. [1953–]. b. Haiti.
- *Balafres*. Montréal: Éditions du CIDIHCA, 1994. [poetry]
- *La Dot de Sarah*. Montréal: Éditions du remue-ménage, 1995, 2000. [fiction]
- Trad. avec Guy Romer. *Poème de Santiago*. [By] Tito Alvarado. [Montréal]: Éditions d'Orphée, 1995. [poetry]
- *Le Silence comme le sang*. Montréal: Éditions du Remue-Ménage, 1997. [short fiction]
- *Le Noël de Maite*. Montréal: Hurtubise HMH, 1999. [juvenile]
- *Alexis d'Haïti*. Montréal: Hurtubise HMH, 1999. [juvenile]

- *Alexis, fils de Raphaël*. Montréal: Hurtubise HMH, 2000. [juvenile]
- *Le Livre d'Emma*. Montréal: Les Éditions du Remue-Ménage; Port-au-Prince: Les Éditions Mémoire, 2001. [fiction]

Akili, Wanda Leffler. b. Alberta.
- with Velma Carter. *The Window of Our Memories*. St. Albert's, AB: B.C.R. Society of Alberta, 1981. [history]

Akwani, Obi O. [1958–]. b. Ghana.
- *Winning Over Racism*. Ottawa: Achama Communications, 1995. [prose]

Alexander, Winston M. b. Tobago.
- *The Joy, the Sorrow and Denn*. New York: Vantage Press, 1974. [fiction]

Alexandre, Jerry. b. Québec?
- *The Words of a Philanthropist*. Montréal: Jerry Alexandre, 2000. [poetry]
- *Why My Tears Drop*. Montréal: Jerry Alexandre, 2001. [poetry]

Alexis, André. [1957–]. b. Trinidad.
- *Despair, and Other Stories of Ottawa*. Toronto: Coach House, 1994. Rpt. Toronto: McClelland & Stewart, 1998; New York: H. Holt, 1999. Rpt. *The Night Piece*. London: Bloomsbury, 1999. [short fiction]
- *Childhood*. Toronto: McClelland & Stewart, 1998. [fiction]
- *Enfance*. Trans. Émile Martel. Montréal: Éditeur Fides, 1998. [fiction]
- *Barndom*. Trans. Per Vadmand. Kbenhavn [Copenhagen]: Forlaget Viva, 1998. [fiction]
- *De kamers van Mijn Jeugd*. Trans. Marianne Gossije. Breda, Nederland: Uitgeverij de Geus, 1998. [fiction]
- *Lapsuus*. Trans. Irmeli Ruuska. Porvoo [Finland]: W. Soderstrom, 1999. [fiction]
- *Lambton Kent: A Play*. Toronto: Gutter Press, 1999. [drama]
- *Kindheit*. Trans. Henning Ahrens. Munchen: Claassen, 2000. [fiction]
- *Shonen jidai*. Trans. Yoshiki Obayashi. Tokyo: DHC, 2000. [fiction]

Allain, Carol. [1962–]. b. England.
- and Rosamund Elwin, eds. *Getting Wet: Tales of Lesbian Seductions*. Toronto: Women's Press, 1992. [anthology]

Allen, Lillian. [1951–]. b. Jamaica.
- *Rhythm an' Hard Times*. Toronto: Domestic Bliss, 1982. [poetry]
- *If You See Truth: Poems for Children and Young People*. Toronto: Verse to Vinyl, 1990. [juvenile]
- *Why Me?* Toronto: Well Versed Publications, 1991. [juvenile]
- *Nothing But a Hero*. Toronto: Women's Press, 1992. [juvenile]
- *Women Do This Every Day: Selected Poems*. Toronto: Women's Press, 1993. [poetry]
- *Psychic Unrest*. Toronto: Insomniac Press, 1999. [poetry]

Alleyne, Vanessa. [1968–]. b. Trinidad.
- *There Were Times I Thought I Was Crazy: A Black Woman's Story of Incest*. Toronto: Sister Vision Press, 1997. [memoir]

Allien, Francklin. b. Haiti.
- *O Canada, mon pays, mes amours*. Paris: Pensée universelle, 1977. [fiction]

Amadahy, Zainab. [1956–]. b. United States.
- *The Moons of Palmares*. Toronto: Sister Vision Press, 1997. [fiction]

Anderson, Abbott. [1933–]. b. Jamaica.
- *The Strafed Artery.* Toronto: Advent Publishing Co. 197? [poetry]
- *Psalms of Babylon.* Toronto: Advent Publishing Co., 1972. [poetry]
Anderson, Ho Che.
- *King.* Seattle: Fantagraphic Books, 1993. [comic book biography of Martin Luther King]
- *The No-Boys Club.* Toronto: Groundwood, 1998. [juvenile]
Anderson, Hopeton A. [Hope]. [1950–]. b. Jamaica.
- *Out of the Woods.* Montreal: Dawson College Press, 1970. [poetry]
- *Buck Mount.* Montreal: Mondiale Pub., 1975. [poetry and drama]
- and David Phillips, eds. *The Body.* North Vancouver: Tatlow House, 1979. [anthology]
- *Slips from Grace.* Toronto: Coach House Press, 1987. [poetry]
Anderson, Osborne Perry. [1830–72]. b. United States.
- *A Voice from Harper's Ferry. A Narrative of Events at Harper's Ferry; with Incidents Prior and Subsequent to Its Capture by Captain Brown and His Men.* Boston: [Osborne Anderson], 1861. [memoir]
Anderson, W[olseley]. W[ellington]. [1930–]. b. Guyana?
- *Manpower and Training into the 1980s in Guyana.* 5 vols. Georgetown, Guyana: n.p., 1978. [prose]
- ed. *Caribbean Orientations: A Bibliography of Resource Materials on the Caribbean Experience in Canada.* Toronto: The Organization for Caribbean Canadian Identities (OCCI) and Williams-Wallace Publishers, Inc., 1985. [bibliography]
- and Rudolph W. Grant. *The New Newcomers: Patterns of Adjustment of West Indian Immigrant Children in Metropolitan Toronto Schools.* Toronto: Canadian Scholars' Press, 1987. [prose]
- et al., eds. *Education and Social Change: An Interdisciplinary Reader.* Toronto: Canadian Scholars' Press, 1989. [compilation]
- *Caribbean Immigrants: A Socio-Demographic Profile.* Toronto: Canadian Scholars' Press, 1993. [prose]
Andre, Irving W. b. Dominica.
- and Gabriel J. Christian. *In Search of Eden: The Travails of a Caribbean Mini State.* Upper Marlboro, MD; Brampton, ON; Roseau, Dominica: Pond Casse Press, 1992. [prose]
- *Distant Voices: The Genesis of an Indigenous Literature in Dominica.* Brampton, ON: Pond Casse Press, 1995. [prose]
Anglade, Édouard. [1944–]. b. Haiti.
- *Nom de code, Mao: Parcours du premier policier haïtien à Montréal.* Montréal: Éditions du CIDIHCA, 1995. [memoir]
Anglade, Georges. [1944–]. b. Haiti.
- *L'Espace haïtien.* Montréal: Presses de l'Université de Québec, 1974. [prose]
- *La Géographie et son enseignement: Lettre ouverte aux professeurs.* Montréal: Presses de l'Université de Québec, 1976. [prose]
- *Mon pays d'Haïti.* Port-au-Prince: Éditions de l'Action sociale; [Montréal]: Presses de l'Université de Québec, 1977. [prose]
- *Atlas critique d'Haïti.* Montréal: Département de géographie, Université du Québec à Montréal; Centre de recherches caraïbes de l'Université de Montréal, 1982. [atlas and prose]

- *Espace et liberté en Haïti*. Montréal: Groupe d'études et de recherches critiques d'espace, Département de géographie, Université du Québec à Montréal; Santiago: Universidad catòlica Madre y Maestra, 1982. [maps]
- *Hispaniola*. Montréal: Groupe d'études et de recherches critiques d'espace, Département de géographie, Université du Québec à Montréal, 1982. [prose]
- *Éloge de la pauvreté*. Montréal: Éditions ERCE, 1983. [prose]
- [et al.] *Pouvoir noir en Haïti: L'Explosion de 1946*. Mont-Royal, QC: V&R, 1988. [prose]
- *Cartes sur table*. 3 vols. Port-au-Prince: Éditions H. Deschamps; Montréal: Études et recherches critiques d'espace, 1990. [prose]
- *Les Blancs de mémoire: Lodyans*. Montréal: Éditions Boréal, 1999. [short fiction]
- *Leurs jupons dépassent: Lodyans*. [Montréal]: Éditions du CIDIHCA, 2000. [short fiction]

Anonymous.
- 'The Coloured Inhabitants of Vancouver Island.' Ed. Philip S. Foner. *B.C. Studies* 8 (Winter 1970–1): 29–33. [This article reprints 'an anonymous Black's impression of Victoria (BC) in the mid-1860s.' See Crawford Kilian, *Go*, 176]

Anthony, Terence. [1968–]. b. Ontario.
- *Shadowtown* 1.1. Plymouth, MI: Iconographix Books, 1992. [comic book]
- *Shadowtown: Black Fist Rising* 1.1-3. New Westminster, BC: Madheart Productions, 1994. [comic book]

Antoine, Yves. [1941–]. b. Haiti.
- *La Veillée: Poèmes*. [Port-au-Prince]: Imprimerie Serge L. Gaston, [1964]. [poetry]
- *Fleurs d'ébène*. Port-au-Prince: Imprimerie Serge Gaston, 1965. [poetry]
- *Témoin oculaire*. Port-au-Prince: Imprimerie Serge Gaston, 1970. [poetry]
- *Au Gré des heures*, suivi de *Horizon fantôme*. Port-au-Prince: Presses Nationales d'Haiti, 1972. [poetry]
- *Les Sabots de la nuit*. Québec: Gasparo, 1974. [poetry]
- *Alliage*. [Hull, QC: Imprimerie Gasparo, ltée, 1978.] [poetry]
- *Alliage: Poésie et prose*. Sherbrooke, QC: Éditions Naaman, 1979. [poetry and prose]
- *Chants de la toundra*. Sherbrooke, QC: Éditions Naaman, 1985. [poetry]
- *Libations pour le soleil: Poésie et prose*. Sherbrooke, QC: Éditions Naaman, 1985. [poetry and prose]
- *Sémiologie et personnage romanesque chez J.S. Alexis*. Montréal: Éditions Balzac, 1994. [prose]
- *Polyphonie: Poésie*, précédée de *Jeu de miroirs*. Ottawa: Les Éditions du Vermillion, 1996. [poetry]
- *Inventeurs et savants noirs*. Paris and Montréal: Éditions L'Harmattan, 1998. [prose]

Appelt, Pamela G.
- *Citizenship, Culture, and the Black Community*. Dartmouth, NS: Black Cultural Centre for Nova Scotia, 1988. [prose]

Armstrong, Bromley L. [1926–]. b. Jamaica.
- with Sheldon Taylor. *Bromley: Tireless Champion for Just Causes: Memoirs*. Pickering, ON: Vitabu Publishing, 2000. [biography]

Arthurs, Patrick [St Patrick]. [1939–]. b. Jamaica.
- *Soul Revolution*. New York: Exposition, 1975. [poetry]

- *Babylon Overboard: Inspired through Emperor Haile Selassie I*. Toronto: Salt & Pepper Pub., 1994. [poetry]

Augustin, Joseph. [1921–]. b. Haiti.
- *Profil culturel haïtien I: Le Meurtri, le marron, l'anti-sorcier*. Montréal: Centre interculturel Monchanin, 1983. [prose]

Aylward, Carol A. b. Nova Scotia?
- *Canadian Critical Race Theory: Racism and the Law*. Halifax, NS: Fernwood Press, 1999. [prose]

Badoe, Adwoa. b. Ghana.
- *Crabs for Dinner*. Toronto: Sister Vision, 1995. [juvenile]
- *The Queen's New Shoes*. Toronto: Women's Press, 1998. [juvenile]
- *The Pot of Wisdom: Ananse Stories*. Toronto: Douglas & McIntyre, 2001. [juvenile]

Badr, Ibrahim H. [1950–]. b. Sudan.
- [et al.] *De paroles en figures: Essais sur les littératures africaines et antillaises*. Comps. Christiane Ndiaye et Josias Semujanga. Montréal: Harmattan, 1996. [compilation]
- *Jean Giono: L'Esthétique de la violence*. New York: Peter Lang, 1998. [prose]

Baganda, Usutha [pseud. of Ralph Campbell]. [1942–]. b. Trinidad.
- *Collections*. Toronto: Westindian Theatre Toronto Publishers, 1982. [poetry]

Bailey, Cameron. [1963–]. b. England.
- Essay. In *The Night Has a Thousand Eyes: Adrian Piper, Ramona Ramlochand*. Ottawa: Ottawa Art Gallery, 2000. [exhibition catalogue]

Bailey, Maxine. [1959–]. b. England.
- and Sharon Lewis. 'Sistahs.' *Canadian Theatre Review* 83 (Summer 1995): 52–68. [drama]
- and Sharon Lewis. *Sistahs*. Toronto: Playwrights Canada Press, 1998. [drama]
- and Sharon Lewis. 'Sistahs.' In Sears, ed., *Testifyin'*, Vol. 1. (2000), 277–329. [drama]

Bailey, Peter A. [Bliss]. [1953–]. b. Nova Scotia.
- *This Is My Song*. Montreal: Mondiale, 1975. [poetry]
- *Going Black Home*. Montreal: Concordia and Dawson College, 1978. [poetry]
- *To the Sky This Time*. Montreal: Upshaw Publishing House, 1993. [poetry]

Bamboté, Makombo [Pierre]. [1932–]. b. Central African Republic.
- *La Poésie est dans l'histoire*. Paris: P.J. Oswald, [1960]. [poetry]
- *La Salamandre*. 1964. [short fiction]
- *Les Randonnées de Daba de Quadda à Bangui*. Paris: Éditions La Farandole, 1966; Abidjan: N.E.A., 1983. [juvenile]
- *Daba's Travels from Quadda to Bangui*. Trans. John Buchanan-Brown. [New York]: Pantheon Books, 1970. [juvenile]
- *Princesse Mandapu: Roman*. Paris: Présence Africaine, [1972]. Rpt. *Princesse Mandapu*. [Paris]: Nathan-poche, 1987. [fiction]
- *Technique pour rien; suivi de Civilisation des autres*. Paris: Librairie Saint-Germain-des-Pres, 1973. [poetry]
- *Journal d'un paysan de l'Afrique centrale*. Paris: Éditions Saint-Germain-des-Prés, 1974. [short fiction]
- *Les Nouvelles de Bangui*. Montréal: Presses de l'Université de Montréal, 1980. [short fiction]

- *Coup d'état nègre: Récit.* [Montréal]: Humanitas Nouvelle optique, 1987. [fiction]
- *Que ferons-nous après la guerre, ou, Éloge de l'animisme: Poèmes à diverses dimensions.* Brossard, QC: Humanitas, 1998. [poetry]
- *Chant funèbre pour un héros d'Afrique: Poésie.* Outremont, QC: Lanctôt, 1999. [poetry]

Bancroft, George W. b. Guyana.
- *A Survey of Criticisms, Comments and Suggestions Concerning Adult Education in London, Ontario, 1966.* [London, ON]: London Council for Adult Education, [1966]. [prose]
- *The Immigrant As Teacher in Ontario.* [Toronto]: Ontario Ministry of Education, 1974. [prose]
- [ed.] *Outreach for Understanding: A Report of the Intercultural Seminar Program Conducted in Toronto between 1973 and 1975.* Toronto: Ministry of Culture and Recreation, Multicultural Development Branch, 1977; [Toronto: Multicultural Development Branch, 1978.] [prose]
- *They Came from Abroad: The Immigrant As Teacher in Ontario.* Toronto: Guidance Centre, Faculty of Education, University of Toronto, 1979. [prose]
- [ed.] *The Novice and the Newcomer: Student Teachers' Perspectives on Multiculturalism and Education.* London, ON: Third Eye, 1982. [prose]
- and Dorothy A. Wills, and Cecille M. De Pass. *The Civic Participation of Visible Minorities in Canadian Society: Framework and Issues for Research and Analysis.* [Ottawa]: Policy and Research, Multiculturalism Sector, Multiculturalism and Citizenship Canada, 1990. [report]

Bansfield, Anthony. [1963–]. b. Québec?
- ed. *The N'x Step: Hochelaga and the Diasporic African Poets: A Collection of Performance Poetry by a Montreal-based Black Writers Group.* Montreal: RevWord Press, 1995. [anthology]

Banton, Gertie.
- *What Is Love: A Collection of Thoughts and Poems.* Owings Mills, MD: Watermark Press; Toronto: n.p., 1991. [poetry]
- *The Imaginary Flight to Nowhere: A Collection of Thoughts and Poems.* Toronto: n.p., 1994. [poetry]

Barnard, Denise. b. Antigua?
- *some tings lie so deep.* Toronto: Gargoyle Press, 1995. [short fiction]

Barrow, Anthony T. [1969–]. b. Manitoba?
- *De Madman Cometh.* Winnipeg: Village Ruff Productions, 1998. [poetry]

Bartholomew, Lloyd E.N. [1938–]. b. Guyana.
- *Peaceful Contemporary Expressions.* Burlington, ON: ACTWRITE, 1985. [poetry]

Bastien, Elliott. [1941–]. b. Trinidad.
- *A Nancy Story.* Pt Cumana, Trinidad: E. Bastien, 1981. [short fiction]

Bauld, Florence L. [Florence Smith-Bauld]. [1938?–]. b. Nova Scotia.
- *Bear River: Untapped Roots, Moving Upward.* Dartmouth, NS: Florence L. Bauld, 1997. [history and memoir]

[Beal, William S. A.] [1865–1968]. b. United States.
- *Billy: The Life and Photographs of William S. A. Beal.* By Robert Barrow and Leigh Hambly. Winnipeg: Vig Corps Press, 1988. [photographs].

Beaugé-Rosier, Jacqueline. [1932–]. b. Haiti.
– *Climats en marche*. Port-au-Prince: Imprimerie des Antilles, 1962. [poetry]
– *À vol d'ombre*. Port-au-Prince: Imprimerie Serge Gaston, 1966. [poetry]
– ed. *La Ville /collaborateurs et collaboratrices*. Hull, QC: [Beaugé-Rosier et al.], 1980.
   [anthology].
– *Les Cahiers de la mouette*; poèmes suivis de *Tranché pour toi; Léila ou La déracinée: Deux
   nouvelles*. Sherbrooke, QC: Éditions Naaman, 1983. [poems and short fiction]
– *D'Or vif et de pain: Textes poétiques*. Regina: Éditions Louis Riel, 1992. [poetry]
Bell, James Madison. [1826–1902]. b. United States.
– *A Poem*. San Francisco: S.F. Sterett, 1862. [poetry]
– *A Poem Entitled the Day and the War, Delivered January 1, 1864, at Platt's Hall by
   J. Madison Bell at the Celebration of the First Anniversary of President Lincoln's Emancipa-
   tion Proclamation*. San Francisco: Agnew and Deffebach, 1864. [poetry]
– *An Anniversary Poem Entitled the Progress of Liberty, Delivered January 1st, 1866, at Zion
   Church at the Celebration of the Third Anniversary of President Lincoln's Emancipation
   Proclamation*. San Francisco: Agnew and Deffebach, 1866. [poetry]
– *A Poem, Entitled the Triumph of Liberty, Delivered April 7, 1870, at Detroit Opera House,
   by J. Madison Bell, on the Occasion of the Grand Celebration of the Final Ratification of the
   Fifteenth Amendment to the Constitution of the United States*. Detroit: Printed by the
   Tunis Steam Printing Co., 1870. [poetry]
– *The Poetical Works of James Madison Bell*. Lansing, MI: Wynkoop, Hallenbeck,
   Crawford Co., 1901. [poetry]
– *The Poetical Works of James Madison Bell*. [With a Biography by Bishop Benjamin
   William Arnett.] Lansing, MI: Wynkoop, Hallenbeck, Crawford Co., 1901. [poetry]
Bennett, Louise Simone [Mrs Eric Coverley; Miss Lou.] [1919–]. b. Jamaica.
– *Jamaican Dialect Verses*. Comp. George Bowen. Kingston, JA: Herald, 1942. [poetry]
– *Jamaican Humour in Dialect*. Kingston, JA: Kingston Press Association, 1943.
   [poetry]
– [et al.] *Anancy Stories and Dialect Verse*. N.p.: n.p., 1945; Kingston, JA: Pioneer Press,
   1950; new series, Kingston, JA: Pioneer Press, 1957. [prose and poetry]
– *M's' Lulu Sez: Jamaican Dialect Poems*. Kingston, JA: Gleaner, Co., Ltd, 1949. [poetry]
– *Laugh with Louise, a Pot-Pourri of Jamaican Folklore, Stories, Songs and Verses*. Kingston,
   JA: City Printery, 1961. [prose and poetry]
– *Jamaica Labrish: Jamaica Dialect Poems*. Ed. Rex Nettleford. Kingston, JA: Sangster's
   Book Stores, 1966. [poetry]
– *Anancy and Miss Lou*. Kingston, JA: Sangster's Book Stores, 1979. [folktales and
   songs]
– ed. *Mother Goose / Jamaica Muddah Goose*. Kingston, JA: Friends of the Jamaica School
   of Art Association, 1981. [traditional rhymes]
– *Selected Poems*. Ed. Mervyn Morris. Kingston, JA: Sangster's Book Stores, 1982; rev.
   ed., 1983. [poetry]
Benz, Brenda. b. Jamaica.
– *As It Is: Straight Talk about Important Matters*. [Toronto?]: [n.p.?] 2000. [essays]
Berrouët-Oriol, Robert. [1951–]. b. Haiti.
– *Lettres urbaines: Poèmes*; suivi de *Le Dire-à-soi (du rapport à la langue)*. Montréal:
   Triptyque, 1986. [poetry]

Bertley, Leo W. [1934–]. b. Trinidad.
- *Black Tiles in the Mosaic.* [Pierrefonds, QC: L.W. Bertley], 1974. [history]
- *Montreal's Oldest Black Congregation: Union Church, 3007 Delisle Street.* Pierrefonds, QC: Bilongo Publishers, 1976. [history]
- *Canada and Its People of African Descent.* Pierrefonds, QC: Bilongo Publishers, 1977. [history]
Best, Carrie M. [1903–2001]. b. Nova Scotia.
- *That Lonesome Road: The Autobiography of Carrie M. Best.* New Glasgow, NS: Clarion, 1977. [autobiography]
Bibb, Henry. [1815–54]. b. United States.
- *Narrative of the Life and Adventures of Henry Bibb, an American Slave, Written by Himself.* New York: n.p., 1849; Salem, NH: Ayer Company Publishers, 1991. [autobiography]
Bishop, Henry. b. Nova Scotia.
- and Frank Boyd. *A Black Community Album before 1930.* Halifax, NS: Art Gallery, Mount Saint Vincent University, 1983. [catalogue of photo exhibition]
Black, Ayanna [Marjorie Black]. b. Jamaica.
- *No Contingencies.* Toronto: Williams-Wallace, 1986. [poetry]
- In Dôre Michelut et al. *Linked Alive: Sets of Renga.* [Laval, QC]: Éditions Trois, [1990]. [poetry]
- ed. *Voices: Canadian Writers of African Descent.* Toronto: HarperPerennial, 1992. [anthology]
- ed. *Fiery Spirits: Canadian Writers of African Descent.* Toronto: HarperPerennial, 1995. [anthology]
- ed. *Fiery Spirits and Voices: Canadian Writers of African Descent.* Toronto: HarperPerennial, 2000. [anthology]
Black Katt [Robert O. Brown].
- *Black Katt Book of Poetry Vol. 1: The One That Brings Bad Luck.* Toronto: Black Katt Entertainment Co., 1995. [poetry]
Blackman, Margot. b. Barbados.
- comp. *Bajan Proverbs.* Montreal: [Margot Blackman], 1982. [prose]
Blizzard, Flora Helena [Flora (Blizzard) Francis]. [1932–].
- *West Indians in Canada: A Selective Annotated Bibliography.* Guelph, ON: [University of Guelph Library], 1970. [bibliography]
- [as Flora Francis]. *A Black Canadian Bibliography.* Ottawa: Pan-African Publications, 2000. [bibliography]
Boncy, Ralph. b. Haiti.
- [et al.] *La Chanson d'Haïti:Tome 1 (1965–1985).* Montréal: Éditions du CIDIHCA, 1992. [prose]
Book, Shane. [1970–]. b. Peru.
- *Forgetting the Rest Beyond Blue.* Victoria: Smoking Lung Press, 1997. [poetry]
- with Susan B. Rich and Linda Jarkesy, *The Rella Lossy Poetry Award, 1999.* San Francisco: The Poetry Center and American Poetry Archives, 2000. [poetry]
Borden, Edwin Howard. [1869–1953]. b. Nova Scotia.
- *Are the Baptists Waning?* [A professor, preacher, and author, Borden reputedly

published 'several books,' but his bibliography is as obscure as his life. See Donna
Byard Sealey, *Colored Zion* (2001), 215–17, listed below.]
Borden, George A. [1935–]. b. Nova Scotia.
– *Canaan Odyssey: A Poetic Account of the Black Experience in North America*. Dartmouth,
  NS: Black Cultural Centre for Nova Scotia, 1988. [poetry]
– *Footprints – Images and Reflections (History in Poetry)*. Cherrybrook, NS: Black
  Cultural Centre for Nova Scotia, 1993. [poetry]
– *A Mighty Long Way! ... from Africa to Africadia*. Dartmouth, NS: G.A.B. Consulting,
  2000. [poetry]
Borden, Walter M. [1942–]. b. Nova Scotia.
– 'Tightrope Time: Ain't Nothin' More Than Some Itty Bitty Madness between
  Twilight and Dawn.' *Callboard* 34.2 (Sept. 1986): 8–81. [drama]
– 'Tightrope Time: Ain't Nothin' More Than Some Itty Bitty Madness between
  Twilight and Dawn.' In Sears, ed., *Testifyin'*, Vol. 1 (2000), 471–554. [drama]
Boxill, [Herman Francis] Anthony. [1935–]. b. Barbados?
– *V.S. Naipaul's Fiction: In Quest of the Enemy*. Fredericton, NB: York Press, 1983.
  [prose]
Boyd, Frank Stanley, Jr. [1943–]. b. Nova Scotia.
– ed. *McKerrow: A Brief History of the Coloured Baptists of Nova Scotia, 1783–1895*. By
  Peter E. McKerrow. 1895. Halifax, NS: Afro Nova Scotian Enterprises, 1976. [photo-
  graphs and notes, 3.1–3.32; history]
– and Henry Bishop. *A Black Community Album before 1930*. Halifax, NS: Art Gallery,
  Mount Saint Vincent University, 1983. [photo exhibition booklet]
Boyd, George Elroy. [1952–]. b. Nova Scotia.
– 'Consecrated Ground: A Teleplay.' In George Elliott Clarke, ed., *Fire on the Water:
  An Anthology of Black Nova Scotian Writing*, Vol. 2 (1992), 98–109. [excerpt of unpub-
  lished television drama]
– *Two, By George!* La Have, NS: Stage Hand Publishers, 1996. [drama: two plays:
  Consecrated Ground and *Gideon's Blues*]
– *Consecrated Ground*. Winnipeg: Blizzard Publishing, 1999. [drama]
Boyd, Georgia.
– and Carol Tremaine [Carol Talbot]. *The Saga of Anne-Marie Weems, Fugitive Girl of 15*.
  Rexdale, ON: Identity Black Canada, 1977. [juvenile]
Braithwaite, Daniel. [1927–]. b. Nova Scotia.
– *The Banning of the Book 'Little Black Sambo' from the Toronto Public Schools 1956*.
  Toronto: Overnight Typing and Copy Co., 1978. [history]
Braithwaite, Diana [Diana Braithwaite-Spence]. [1957–]. b. Ontario.
– [as Diana Braithwaite-Spence]. *Babylon Down*. Toronto: OISE, 1974. [poetry]
– *Martha and Elvira: A One-Act Play*. Toronto: Sister Vision, 1993. [drama]
Braithwaite, Lawrence [Ytzhak]. [1963–]. b. British Columbia?
– *Wigger*. Vancouver: Arsenal Pulp Press, 1995. [fiction]
– *Ratz Are Nice (PSP)*. Los Angeles: Alyson Publications, 2000. [fiction]
Braithwaite, Rella. b. Ontario.
– with Enid D'Oyley, comps. *Women of Our Times*. Toronto: Canadian Negro Women's
  Association for the National Congress of Black Women, 1973. [history]

- comp. and ed. *The Black Woman in Canada*. West Hill, ON: n.p., 1976. [history]
- and Tessa Benn-Ireland. *Some Black Women: Profiles of Black Women in Canada*. Toronto: Sister Vision, 1993. [history]
- and Eleanor Joseph. *Some Black Men: Profiles of Over 100 Black Men in Canada*. Scarborough, ON: Marlon Press, 1999. [biographies]

Brand, Dionne. [1953–]. b. Trinidad.

- *'Fore Day Morning*. Toronto: Khoisan Artists, 1978. [poetry]
- *Earth Magic*. Toronto: Kids Can Press, 1979. Rpt. *Earth Magic: Poetry for Young People*. Toronto: Sister Vision, [1983, 1993]. [juvenile]
- *Primitive Offensive*. Toronto: Williams-Wallace International, 1982. [poetry]
- *Winter Epigrams and Epigrams to Ernesto Cardenal in Defence of Claudia*. Toronto: Williams-Wallace, 1983, 1984. [poetry]
- *Chronicles of the Hostile Sun*. Toronto: Williams-Wallace, 1984. [poetry]
- and Krisantha Sri Bhaggiyadatta. *Rivers Have Sources, Trees Have Roots*. Toronto: Cross-Cultural Communication Centre, 1986. [prose]
- *Sans Souci and Other Stories*. Stratford, ON: Williams-Wallace, 1988; Toronto: Women's Press, 1989; New York: Firefly Books, 1989. [short fiction]
- et al. *Sight Specific: Lesbians and Representation*. Toronto: A Space, 1988. [compilation]
- *No Language Is Neutral*. Toronto: Coach House, 1990. Rpt. Toronto: McClelland & Stewart, 1998. [poetry]
- with Lois De Shield and the Immigrant Women's Job Placement Centre. *No Burden to Carry: Narratives of Black Working Women in Ontario, 1920s–1950s*. Toronto: Women's Press, 1991. [history]
- *Bread out of Stone*. Toronto: Coach House, 1994. Rpt. Toronto: McClelland & Stewart, 1998; Toronto: Vintage Canada, 1998. [essays]
- with Peggy Bristow, coord., et al. *'We're Rooted Here and They Can't Pull Us Up': Essays in African-Canadian Women's History*. Toronto: University of Toronto Press, 1994. [history]
- *In Another Place, Not Here*. Toronto: Alfred A. Knopf Canada, 1996; Toronto: Vintage Canada, 1997; New York: Grove Press, 1997. [fiction]
- *Land to Light On*. Toronto: McClelland & Stewart, 1997. [poetry]
- *At the Full and Change of the Moon*. Toronto: Alfred A. Knopf Canada, 1999; New York: Grove Press, 1999; London: Granta Books, 1999. Rpt. Toronto: Vintage Canada, 2000. [fiction]
- *A Map to the Door of No Return: Notes to Belonging*. Toronto: Doubleday Canada, 2001. [essays]
- *Thirsty*. Toronto: McClelland & Stewart, 2002. [poetry]

Brathwaite, Keren S.

- ed. *Stories from Life: The Transitional Year Programme Collection of Short Fiction*. Toronto: Canadian Scholars' Press, 1987. [anthology]
- and Carl James, eds. *Educating African Canadians*. Toronto: James Lorimer & Co., 1996. [compilation]

Breyfogle, Donna.
- and Marion Dwoaszek, comps. *Blacks in Ontario: A Select Bibliography, 1965–1976.*
  No. 8. Toronto: Ontario Ministry of Labour, Research Library, 1977. [bibliography]
Brissett, Linda. [194?–]. b. Jamaica.
- *In Fields of Dreams and Other Poems.* New York: Carlton Press, 1992; 2nd ed.,
  Hamilton, ON: Briss Books, 2001. [poetry]
- *Sunshine in the Shadows.* New York: Vantage Press, 1993. [poetry]
- *Give Us This Day.* Hamilton, ON: Briss Books, 1995. [poetry]
- *Carols of Christmases Past.* Hamilton, ON: Briss Books, 1996. [short fiction]
- *Linda's Culinary Cuisines: A Touch of Jamaican Cooking.* Hamilton, ON: Briss Books,
  1999. [cookbook]
- *Naked Frailties.* Hamilton, ON: Briss Books, 1999. [short fiction, poetry, prose]
- *Canadianizing Jamaican Patois: A Book of Jamaican Patois Poems.* Hamilton, ON: Briss
  Books, 2001. [poetry]
Bristow, Peggy.
- coord., with Dionne Brand, et al. *'We're Rooted Here and They Can't Pull Us Up':
  Essays in African Canadian Women's History.* Toronto: University of Toronto Press,
  1994. [history]
Brown, Lennox John. [1934–]. b. Trinidad.
- 'The Captive: Snow Dark Sunday.' *Ottawa Little Theatre*, Ranking Play Series 2,
  Catalogue No. 43, September 1965. [drama]
- 'Jour ouvert (or Daybreak).' *Ottawa Little Theatre*, Ranking Play Series 2, Catalogue
  No. 56, 1966. [drama]
- 'The Meeting.' *Ottawa Little Theatre*, Ranking Play Series 2, Catalogue No. 56,
  October 1966. Rpt. in *Performing Arts in Canada* 7.4 (Winter 1970). [drama]
- 'I Have to Call My Father.' *Drama & Theatre* 8.2 (Winter 1969).
- *A Ballet behind the Bridge.* New York: Negro Ensemble Theatre, 1972. [drama]
- 'Devil Mas'.' In *Kuntu Drama: Plays of the African Continuum.* Ed. Paul Carter
  Harrison. New York: Grove Press, 1974. [drama]
- 'The Trinity of Four.' In *Caribbean Rhythms: The Emerging English Literature of the West
  Indies.* Ed. James T. Livingstone. New York: Washington Square Press, 1974. [drama]
- [et al.] *Cultural Crisis.* Ed. William Doyle-Marshall. Toronto: Calypso Hous, 1981.
  [prose]
- *The Twilight Dinner and Other Plays.* Vancouver: Talonbooks, 1981. [drama]
Brown, Paola. b. United States?
- *Address Intended to Be Delivered in the City Hall, Hamilton, February 7, 1851, on the
  Subject of Slavery.* [In his *Narrative of the Life of Thomas Smallwood* (1851), Smallwood
  charges that Brown's text is plagiarized from African-American author David
  Walker's *Appeal* (1829).] Hamilton, ON: [Paola Brown], 1851. [prose]
Brown, Paul Fehmiu [Paul Fehmiu-Brown]. [1940–]. b. Nova Scotia.
- *Ces Canadiens oubliés.* 2 vols. Sainte-Thècle, QC: Éditions Aquarius, 1981. Rpt. Saint-
  Léonard, QC: Éditions Publishing 5 Continents, 1998. [fiction]
- *En commençant par la fin: Récit biographique.* Sainte-Thècle, QC: Éditions Aquarius,
  1981. [fiction]

– [avec] Monique La Grenade-Meunier. *Blacks in Québec Society, Past and Present*. [Québec]: Ministère des affaires internationales, de l'immigration et des communautés culturelles / Ministère de l'éducation, 1995. [history]
– [avec] Monique La Grenade-Meunier. *La Présence des noirs dans la société québécoise d'hier et d'aujourd'hui*. [Québec]: Ministère des affaires internationales, de l'immigration et des communautés culturelles / Ministère de l'éducation, 1995. [history]
– *Appel du sang*. Saint-Léonard, QC: Éditions Publishing 5 Continents, 1998. [fiction]
– *Inventeurs et héros noirs*. Saint-Léonard, QC: Éditions Publishing 5 Continents, 1998. [non-fiction]
– *Marie-Josèphe-Angélique: Montréal, Québec 21 juin 1734*. Saint-Léonard, QC: Éditions Publishing 5 Continents, 1998. [fiction]
Brown, Rosemary. [1930–]. b. Jamaica.
– *Being Brown: A Very Public Life*. Toronto: Random House, 1989. Rpt. Ballantine Books, 1990. [autobiography]
Browne, Joan. b. Jamaica.
– *South Western Nova Scotia Black Communities*. Halifax, NS: Institute of Public Affairs, 1978. [study]
Browning, Janisse [Gloria Janisse Browning-Leveque]. [1965–]. b. Ontario.
– co-ord. *Some Johnson Family Stories: From Slavery to Present*. Amherstburg, ON: The North American Black Historical Museum, 1993. [interview transcripts]
– *BikerTrucker*. Vancouver: Wave7 Press, 1994. [poetry]
Bryant, Maurice. b. Guyana?
– *Roots, Resistance, and Redemption: The Rise of Rastafari*. Ottawa: African Story Press, 1997. [history]
Bunyan, H[ector]. Jay [Hijay]. b. Guyana.
– 'Thy Creature Blues.' In George Seremba et al., eds, *Beyond the Pale* (1996), 112–15. [drama]
– *Prodigals in a Promised Land*. [1981]. Toronto: PUC Play Service, 2000. [drama]
– 'Prodigals in a Promised Land.' In Sears, ed., *Testifyin'*, Vol. 1 (2000), 143–214. [drama]
Cadet, Maurice. [1933–]. b. Haiti.
– *Turbulences*. Jonquière, QC: Éditions Sagamie / Québec, 1989. [poetry]
– *Chalè piman: Pwezi kreyòl (poèmes creoles)*. Alma, QC: Éditions Le Signet, 1990. [poetry]
– *Haute dissidence*. Trois-Rivières, QC: Écrits des Forges, 1991. [poetry]
– *Sortilège sonore*. [Dans] *La Littérature et la vie au collégial*. Mont-Royal, QC: Modulo Éditeur, 1991. 14–17. [poetry]
– *Itinéraires d'un enchantement*. Trois–Rivières, QC: Écrits des Forges, 1992. [poetry]
– *Réjouissances*. Trois-Rivières, QC: Écrits des Forges, 1994. [poetry]
– *L'Illusoire éternité de l'été*. Montréal: Les Écrits des Forges, 1996. [poetry]
– *Cocorico pour un combat royal*. Port-au-Prince, Haïti; Montréal: Éditions Mémoire, Ozo Éditions graphiques, 1998. [poetry]
– [et al.] *Compère Jacques Soleil: Hommage à Jacques Stephen Alexis*. Montréal: Planète rebelle, 1998. [short fiction]

- *Ondes vagabondes*. [Trois-Rivières, QC]: Écrits des Forges, 1998. [poetry]
- *Tambour battant*. Montréal: Éditions du CIDIHCA, 1999. [poetry]
- *À voix basse*. Trois-Rivières, QC: Écrits des Forges, 2001. [poetry]

Callender, Ophelia. [1937–]. b. Barbados.
- *The Orphan Within*. Montreal: Laureson Press (Mtl Ltd), 1995. [poetry]
- *Passing for Gold: A Collection of Poems*. Montreal: Laureson Press, 1996. [poetry]

Calliste, Agnes [Miranda]. [1944–].
- and George J. Sefa Dei, eds. *Anti-Racist Feminism: Critical Race and Gender Studies*. Halifax, NS: Fernwood, 2000. [compilation]
- and George J. Sefa Dei, eds. *Power, Knowledge, and Anti-Racism Education: A Critical Reader*. Halifax, NS: Fernwood, 2000. [compilation]

Cambridge, Vibert C. [1942–]. b. British Guiana [Guyana].
- *Historical Perspectives*. Toronto: WACACRO, n.d.
- *Excuse Me! May I Offer Some Interpretations*. Toronto: WACACRO Production, 1975. [poetry]

Campbell, Israel. [d. 1872]. b. United States.
- *An Autobiography. Bond and Free: or Yearnings for Freedom, from My Green Brier House. Being the Story of My Life in Bondage, and My Life in Freedom*. Philadelphia: Israel Campbell, 1872. [autobiography]

Camper, Carol. b. Ontario.
- ed. *Miscegenation Blues: Voices of Mixed Race Women*. Toronto: Sister Vision Press, 1994. [anthology]

Cannon, Noah Calwell W. [1796–1850]. b. United States.
- *Interesting Hymns. (In the Rock of Wisdom; An Explanation of the Sacred Scriptures, by the Rev. N. C. Cannon [a Man of Color] to Which Are Added Several Interesting Hymns.)* New York, 1833. [prose and verse]
- *Truth. Instruction to Youth. Seek Ye after Knowledge*. Reprinted by James Nelson. Rochester, NY: C.S. McConnell & Co., 1843. [prose]

Carberry, H[ugh]. D[oston]. [1921–]. b. Québec.
- with Dudley Thomas. *A West Indian in England*. 1950. [prose]
- *It Takes a Mighty Fire*. Ed. Edward Baugh. Kingston, JA: Ian Randle Publishers, 1995. [poetry]

Carew, Jan R[ynveld]. [1920–]. b. Guyana.
- *Streets of Eternity*. Georgetown, Guyana, 1952. [poetry]
- *Black Midas*. London: Secker & Warburg, 1958; [paperback] London: Ace Books, 1959; Nendeln: Kraus-Thompson Ltd, 1971; London: Longman Group, 1980, 1967. Rpt. *A Touch of Midas*. New York: Coward-McCann, 1958. Rev. ed. *Black Midas*. [London]: Longman, 1969. [Adapted for schools by Sylvia Wynter.] [fiction]
- *The Wild Coast*. London: Secker & Warburg, 1958; Nendeln: Kraus-Thompson Ltd, 1971; Trinidad: Longman Caribbean, 1983; London: Longman Group, 1983. [fiction]
- *Schwartzer Midas*. Munchen: List Verlag, 1959. [fiction]
- *The Last Barbarian*. London: Secker & Warburg, 1961. [fiction]
- *O Midas Negro*. Lisboa: Editoria Ulisseia, 1961. [fiction]
- *Wilde Kuste*. Munchen: List Verlag, 1961. [fiction]

- *Prikosnoveniya Midaca*. Moskva: Gosudarstvenoye Isdatelstvo 'Hudodjestvenoy Literaturi,' 1963. [fiction]
- *Moscow Is Not My Mecca*. London: Secker & Warburg, 1964. Rpt. *Green Winter: A Novel*. New York: Stein and Day, 1965; [paperback] New York: Berkley Pub. Co., 1966. Rpt. *Winter in Moscow*. New York: Avon Books, 1967. [fiction]
- *Moskau ist Nicht Mein Mekka*. Munchen: List Verlag, 1965. [fiction]
- *Cernyj Midas*. Trans. N. Gudzabidze. Tbilisi, Union of Soviet Socialist Republics: Sabcota Sakartvelo, 1966. [fiction]
- *Invierno Verde*. Rio de Janeiro: Distribuidora Record, 1971. [fiction]
- *The Third Gift*. Boston: Little, Brown, 1972, 1974. [juvenile]
- *The Caribbean Writer and Exile*. Evanston, IL: Northwestern University, 1976. [essay]
- *Children of the Sun*. Boston: Little, Brown, 1976, 1980. [juvenile]
- *Save the Last Dance for Me: And Other Stories*. London: Longman, 1976. [short fiction]
- *Stranger Than Tomorrow: Three Stories of the Future*. London: Longman, 1976. [juvenile]
- *Children of the Sun*. Japanese ed. Tokyo: Hopy Shoppan Publishers, 1981. [fiction]
- *Dark Night, Deep Water*. Harlow, UK: Longman, 1981. [fiction?]
- *Deadman's Creek: Two Stories*. Harlow, UK: Longman, 1981. [short fiction]
- *House of Fear: Two Stories*. Harlow, UK: Longman, 1981. [short fiction]
- *Sea Drums in My Blood*. Port of Spain: Diego Martin, 1981. [poetry]
- *Midas Negro*. La Habana: Casa de Las Americas, 1983. [fiction]
- *The Third Gift*. Japanese ed. Tokyo: Hopy Shoppan Publishers, 1983. [fiction]
- *Grenada: The Hour Will Strike Again*. Prague: International Organization of Journalists, 1985. [history]
- *Fulcrums of Change: Origins of Racism in the Americas and Other Essays*. Trenton, NJ: Africa World Press, 1988. [essays]
- 'Black Horse, Pale Rider.' In *Roots and Blossoms: African-American Plays for Today*. Troy, MI: Bedford Publishers, 1991. [drama]
- *Ghosts in Our Blood: With Malcolm X in Africa, England, and the Caribbean*. New York: Lawrence Hill Books, 1994. [prose]
- *The Rape of Paradise: Columbus and the Birth of Racism in the Americas*. New York: A&B Books, 1994. [history]

Carnegie, Herb. [1919–]. b. Ontario.
- with Robert Payne. *A Fly in a Pail of Milk: The Herb Carnegie Story*. Oakville, ON: Mosaic Press, 1997. [autobiography]

Carter, Leah Suzanne. [1973–]. b. Alberta.
- with Velma Carter. *The Window of Our Memories, Volume II: The New Generation*. St Albert, AB: The Black Cultural Research Society of Alberta, 1990. [history]

Carter, Levero (Lee). b. Alberta.
- with Velma Carter. *The Black Canadians: Their History and Contributions*. Edmonton: Reidmore Books, 1989; rev. ed., 1993. [history]

Carter, Rubin 'Hurricane.' [1937–]. b. United States.
- *The 16th Round: From Number 1 Contender to Number 45472*. Toronto: Macmillan of Canada, 1974. Rpt. Toronto: Penguin Books Canada, 1991. [memoir]

Carter, Velma. [1912–]. b. Alberta.
- and Wanda Leffler Akili. *The Window of Our Memories*. St. Albert, AB: B.C.R. Society of Alberta, 1981. [history]
- and Levero (Lee) Carter. *The Black Canadians: Their History and Contributions*. Edmonton: Reidmore Books, 1989; rev. ed, 1993. [history]
- and Leah Suzanne Carter. *The Window of Our Memories, Volume II: The New Generation*. St Albert, AB: The Black Cultural Research Society of Alberta, 1990. [history]
Carty, Linda Eugenie. [1952–].
- ed. *And Still We Rise: Feminist Political Mobilizing in Contemporary Canada*. Toronto: Women's Press, 1993. [compilation]
- with Peggy Bristow, coord., et al. *'We're Rooted Here and They Can't Pull Us Up': Essays in African-Canadian Women's History*. Toronto: University of Toronto Press, 1994. [history]
Carvery, Valerie. b. Nova Scotia.
- and Verna Thomas. *Report on the Halifax Jamaica Women's Exchange Project*. [Ottawa]: CMHC, [1990]. [prose]
Case, Frederick Ivor. [1939–]. b. Guyana.
- [with Carol A. Thomas]. *Aimé Césaire: Bibliographie*. Toronto: Manna Pub., 1973. [bibliography]
- *La Cité idéale dans 'Travail' d'Émile Zola*. Toronto: University of Toronto Press, 1974. [essay]
- *Racism and National Consciousness*. Toronto: Plowshare Press, 1979. [essay]
- *The Crisis of Identity: Studies in the Guadeloupean and Martiniquan Novel*. Sherbrooke, QC: Éditions Naaman, 1985. [essay]
- [dir.], et al. *Études Afro-Canadiennes: Guide pédagogique, cycle intermédiaire*. [Toronto]: Ontario, Ministère de l'éducation, 1988. [guide]
- et al., [eds.] *Black Studies: A Resource Guide for Teachers*. Toronto: Ontario, Ministry of Education, 1988. [guide]
Casisi, Kofi [pseud. of Cecil Cummins]. [1938–]. b. Barbados.
- *No Apologies*. Scarborough, ON: World Heritage Publications, 1996. [poetry]
Caudeiron, Daniel. [1942–]. b. Venezuela.
- *Folklore of Dominica*. Dominica: Arts Council, 1972. [prose]
- ed. *Dominican Short Stories*. Vol. 1. Dominica: Arts Council, 1973. [anthology]
- *Poems, 1962–1973*. Dominica: Arts Council, 1973. [poetry]
- *More about Me*. Toronto: Black Theatre Canada, 1977. [photocopied drama]
- *A Few Things about Us*. Toronto: Black Theatre Canada, 1978. [photocopied drama]
Cham, Serge. [1946–]. b. Haiti.
- *La Petite Louve blessée*. Gatineau, QC: S. Cham, 1991. [juvenile]
- *Chroniques de l'espoir: Écrits patriotiques, 1991–1996*. Gatineau, QC: Éditions du Regard neuf, [1996?]. [essays]
Chancy, Myriam J[osèphe]. A[imée]. [1970–]. b. Haiti.
- *Framing Silence: Revolutionary Novels by Haitian Women*. New Brunswick, NJ: Rutgers University Press, 1997. [prose]

– *Searching for Safe Spaces: Afro-Caribbean Women Writers in Exile*. Philadelphia: Temple University Press, 1997. [prose]

Charles, Bernadette M. b. Grenada.

– *Slave Spirit Speaks*. Montreal: n.p., 1993. [poetry]

Charlier, Ghislaine [Ghislaine Rey]. [1918–]. b. Haiti.

– [as Ghislaine Rey], réd. *Anthologie du roman haïtien de 1859 à 1946*. Sherbrooke, QC: Éditions Naaman, [1978?] [anthology]

– *Julie Maurer: Mémoires d'une affranchie: roman*. Montréal: Éditions du Méridien, 1989. [fiction]

Chassagne, Raymond. [1924–]. b. Haiti.

– *Mots de passe: Poèmes*. Sherbrooke, QC: Éditions Naaman, 1976. [poetry]

– *Incantatoire*. Port-au-Prince: Éditions Regain, 1996. [poetry]

Chuck, Dominic F. [1932]. b. Trinidad.

– *Small Miracles in My Life: Personal Life Experiences*. Mississauga, ON: Agnel Pub., 1999. [autobiography]

Civil, Jean. [1932–]. b. Haiti.

– *Entre deux pays: Recueil de poèmes*. Sherbrooke, QC: Les Éditions Sherbrooke, 1979. [poetry]

– comp. *Petit album des auteurs des Cantons de l'Est*. Saint-Elie d'Orford, QC: Association des auteurs des Cantons de l'Est, 1980. [authors' directory]

– *Au bout l'abîme*. Sherbrooke, QC: Les Éditions la Margelle, 1985. [poetry]

Clarke, Austin C[hesterfield]. [Tom]. [1934–]. b. Barbados.

– *Pensamientos*. N.p.: n.p., 1950. [poetry]

– *The Survivors of the Crossing*. Toronto: McClelland & Stewart; London: Heinemann, 1964. [fiction]

– *Amongst Thistles and Thorns*. Toronto: McClelland & Stewart; London: Heinemann, 1965; Toronto: McClelland & Stewart, 1974, 1984. [fiction]

– *The Meeting Point*. Toronto: Macmillan; London: Heinemann, 1967; Boston: Little, Brown, 1972. Rpt. Toronto: Vintage Canada / Random House Canada, 1998. [fiction]

– [Unidentified trans.] Moskva: Mollodaia gvardia, 1972. [fiction]

– [as Ali Kamal Al Kadir Sudan, pseud.] Ali Kamal Al Kadir Sudan: '*Black Man in a White Land*.' Interviewed by Nazzam Al Sudan [pseud. of Marvin X (Marvin E. Jackmon)]. Burlington, ON: Al Kitab Sudan, 1967. [interview]

– *The Confessed Bewilderment of Dr. Martin Luther King and the Idea of Non-Violence As a Political Tactic*. Burlington, ON: T. Watkins, 1968. [essay]

– *When He Was Free and Young and He Used to Wear Silks*. Toronto: Anansi, 1971; Boston: Little, Brown, 1973. [short fiction]

– *Storm of Fortune*. Boston: Little, Brown, 1973. Rpt. Toronto: Vintage Canada / Random House Canada, 1998. [fiction]

– *The Bigger Light*. Boston: Little, Brown, 1975. Rpt. Toronto: Vintage Canada / Random House Canada, 1998. [fiction]

– *The Prime Minister*. Don Mills, ON: General, 1977; London: Routledge & K. Paul, 1978; Markham, ON: Paperjacks, 1978. Toronto: Exile Editions, 1994. [fiction]

– *Growing Up Stupid under the Union Jack: A Memoir*. Toronto: McClelland & Stewart, 1980; La Habana: Casa de las Americas, 1980. Rpt. Toronto: Vintage Canada / Random House Canada, 1998. [memoir]

- *When Women Rule: Stories.* Toronto: McClelland & Stewart, 1985. [short fiction]
- *Nine Men Who Laughed.* Markham, ON: Penguin, 1986. [short fiction]
- *Proud Empires.* London: Gollancz, 1986. Rpt. Markham, ON: Viking / Penguin, 1988. [fiction]
- *In This City.* Toronto: Exile Editions, 1992. [short fiction]
- *Public Enemies: Police Violence and Black Youth.* Toronto: HarperCollins, 1992. [essay]
- *There Are No Elders.* Toronto: Exile Editions, 1993. [short fiction]
- *A Passage Back Home: A Personal Reminiscence of Samuel Selvon.* Toronto: Exile Editions, 1994. [memoir]
- *The Austin Clarke Reader.* Ed. Barry Callaghan. Toronto: Exile Editions, 1996. [compilation]
- *The Question.* Trans. Isabella Maria Zoppa. Turin: University of Turin, La Rosa, Centro per lo Studio delle Letterature e delle Culture delle Aree Emer Geni, 1996. [fiction]
- *The Origin of Waves.* Toronto: McClelland & Stewart, 1997. [fiction]
- *Pig Tails 'n' Breadfruit: Rituals of Slave Food.* Toronto: Random House Canada, 1999; Toronto: Vintage Canada, 2000; New York: New Press, 2000; Kingston, JA: Ian Randle Publishers, 2000. [memoir]
- *The Question.* Toronto: McClelland & Stewart, 1999. [fiction]
- 'When He Was Free and Young and He Used to Wear Silks.' In Sears, ed., *Testifyin'*, Vol. 1 (2000), 381–438. [drama]
- *The Polished Hoe.* Toronto: Thomas Allen Publishers, 2002. [fiction]
Clarke, George Elliott. [1960–]. b. Nova Scotia.
- *Saltwater Spirituals and Deeper Blues.* Porter's Lake, NS: Pottersfield Press, 1983. [poetry]
- *Whylah Falls.* Winlaw, BC: Polestar Press, 1990; 2nd ed., Vancouver: Polestar Books, 2000. [poetry]
- ed. *Fire on the Water: An Anthology of Black Nova Scotian Writing.* 2 vols. Lawrencetown Beach, NS: Pottersfield Press, 1991–2. [anthology]
- *A Lifetime of Making: Ralph and Ada Cromwell.* Halifax, NS: Mount Saint Vincent University Art Gallery, 1992. [essay]
- *Provençal Songs.* Ottawa: Magnum Book Store, 1993. [poetry]
- *Lush Dreams, Blue Exile: Fugitive Poems, 1978–1993.* Lawrencetown Beach, NS: Pottersfield Press, 1994. [poetry]
- with J.A. Wainwright et al., eds. *Border Lines: Contemporary Poems in English.* Toronto: Copp Clark, 1995. [anthology]
- ed. *Eyeing the North Star: Directions in African-Canadian Literature.* Toronto: McClelland & Stewart, 1997. [anthology]
- *Eyeing the North Star: Perspectives of African-Canadian Literature.* Ambassador's Lecture Series. [No. 19]. Washington, DC: Canadian Embassy / Ambassade du Canada, 1997. [essay]
- 'Beatrice Chancy: A Libretto in Four Acts.' *Canadian Theatre Review* 96 (Fall 1998): 62–77. [libretto]
- *Beatrice Chancy.* Victoria, BC: Polestar Books, 1999. [verse-drama]
- guest ed. *The Dalhousie Review.* Special Africadian Issue. 77.2 (Summer 1997) [1999]. [journal]

– *Treason of the Black Intellectuals?* Working Paper of the Third Annual Seagram Lecture Presented on 4 November 1998. Montreal: McGill Institute for the Study of Canada, 1999. [essay]

– *Whylah Falls: The Play.* Toronto: Playwrights Canada Press, 1999; 2nd edition, 2000. [drama]

– *Execution Poems.* Wolfville, NS: Gaspereau Press, 2000, 2001. [poetry]

– *Gold Indigoes.* Durham, NC: Carolina Wren Press, 2000. [poetry]

– 'Whylah Falls: The Play.' In Sears, ed., *Testifyin'*, Vol. 1 (2000), 215–76. [drama]

– *Africadian History: An Exhibition Catalogue.* Wolfville, NS: Gaspereau Press, 2001. [poetry]

– *Blue.* Vancouver: Raincoast / Polestar Books, 2001. [poetry]

– *Odysseys Home: Mapping African-Canadian Literature.* Toronto: University of Toronto Press, 2002. [prose]

Clarke, Lewis Gerrard. [1812–97]. b. United States.

– *Narrative of the Sufferings of Lewis Clarke, during a Captivity of More Than Twenty-Five Years among the Algerines of Kentucky, One of the So-called Christian States of North America, Dictated by Himself.* Boston: D.H. Ela, 1845. [autobiography]

– and Milton Clarke. *Narratives of the Sufferings of Lewis and Milton Clarke, Sons of a Soldier of the Revolution, during a Captivity of More Than Twenty Years among the Slave-Holders of Kentucky, One of the So Called Christian States of North America.* Boston: B. Marsh, 1846. [autobiography]

Clarke, Milton. b. United States.

– with Lewis Clarke. *Narratives of the Sufferings of Lewis and Milton Clarke, Sons of a Soldier of the Revolution, during a Captivity of More Than Twenty Years among the Slave-Holders of Kentucky, One of the So Called Christian States of North America.* Boston: B. Marsh, 1846. [autobiography]

Clarke, Sheryl. [1965–]. b. Jamaica.

– *Soul Searching: On Finding Intimacy in Relationship.* Toronto: Sheryl Clarke & Associates, 1999. [prose]

Clayton, Willard Parker. [1921–]. b. Nova Scotia.

– *Pearls from Patmos: Studies in The Book of Revelation.* Hantsport, NS: n.p., 1982. [essays]

– *Whatever Your Will, Lord: A Brief History Written in Commemoration of the 139th Anniversary of Emmanuel Baptist Church, Upper Hammonds Plains, Nova Scotia.* Hantsport, NS: Lancelot, 1993. [history]

Clements, Chrystal. b. Nova Scotia.

– *Adrian Piper: A Retrospective.* Halifax, NS: Mount Saint Vincent University Art Gallery, 2000. Pamphlet. [prose]

Coker, Anthony. b. Trinidad.

– and Kim Robinson. *Climax.* Montreal: n.p., 1976. [poetry]

Colas, Justin L. [1930–]. b. Haiti.

– *Mosaïques.* Chicoutimi, QC: Éditions Le Progrès du Saguenay, 1969. [poetry]

– *Port ensablé.* Desbiens, QC: Éditions du Phare, 1970. [fiction]

Cole, J.

– *The Africa School of Thoughts.* 1991. Brampton, ON: J. Cole, 1994. [poetry]

Coleman, J[ohn]. Clay. [1876–]. b. United States.
– *The Jim Crow Car; or, Denouncement of Injustice Meted Out to the Black Race*. Toronto: Hill, 1898. [prose]
Coleman, Lucretia Newman. b. Canada West. [Ontario]
– *Poor Ben: A Story of Real Life*. Nashville, TN: A.M.E. Sunday School Union, 1890. [fiction]
Compton, Wayde. [1972–]. b. British Columbia.
– *49th Parallel Psalm*. Vancouver: Advance / Arsenal Pulp Press, 1999. [poetry]
– ed. *Bluesprint: Black British Columbian Literature and Orature*. Vancouver: Arsenal Pulp Press, 2002. [anthology]
Cooper, Afua [Ava Pamela]. [1957–]. b. Jamaica.
– *Breaking Chains*. Toronto: Weelahs Publications, 1984. [poetry]
– *The Red Caterpillar on College Street*. Toronto: Sister Vision, 1989. [juvenile]
– *Memories Have Tongue*. Toronto: Sister Vision, 1992. [poetry]
– with Peggy Bristow, coord., et al. *'We're Rooted Here and They Can't Pull Us Up': Essays in African-Canadian Women's History*. Toronto: University of Toronto Press, 1994. [history]
– ed. *Utterances and Incantations: Women, Poetry and Dub*. Toronto: Sister Vision Press, 1999. [anthology]
– ed. *African Canadian Historical Biographies*. Toronto: Afua Cooper, [2001?]. [CD-ROM format biographies]
Coward, Curtis. [1957–]. b. Nova Scotia.
– and Tony Seed. *The Kids' Baseball Book*. Halifax, NS: New Media Publications, 1994. [prose]
Cox, Rita. [1939–]. b. Trinidad.
– and Marjorie Fleming. *The Pre-School Story Hour: A Handbook on Planning and Programming for Pre-School Groups*. Toronto: Toronto Public Libraries, 1973. [training manual]
– *How Trouble Made the Monkey Eat Pepper*. Toronto: Kids Can Press, 1977. [folktale]
– *Checklist of the West Indian Collection*. Toronto: Parkdale Library, 1978. [bibliography]
– and Ann Gagnon. *Multicultural Programming*. Ottawa: Canadian Library Association, 1989. [prose]
Crail, Archie. [1948–]. b. South Africa.
– *Exile*. Winnipeg: Blizzard Publishing, 1990. [drama]
– *The Bonus Deal*. Regina: Cocteau, 1992. [short fiction]
Creider, Jane Tapsubei. b. Kenya.
– *Two Lives: My Spirit and I*. London: Women's Press, 1986. [autobiography]
– *A Grammar of Nandi*. 1989. [grammar]
– *The Shrunken Dream*. Toronto: Women's Press, 1992. [fiction]
Cromwell, Edith. b. Nova Scotia.
– *Inglewood: My Community*. [Bridgetown, NS?]: n.p., 1994. [history]
Cromwell, Liz [Eliza Clark Cromwell]. [1934–]. b. Trinidad.
– *Canadian Jungle Tea: Poems*. Toronto: Khoisan Artists, 1975. [poetry]
– ed. *One Out of Many: A Collection of Writings by 21 Black Women in Ontario*. Toronto: WACACRO Productions, 1975. [anthology]

– assoc. ed. *Title Unknown: Writings by Ontario Women* [for] *International Women's Year.* Ed. Judith Merril. Toronto: n.p., 1975. [anthology]
– *Awake Sweet Agony.* Toronto: WACACRO, 1976. [poetry?]
– ed. *Talking Dragline: Poems.* Linden, Guyana: Guyana Mining Enterprise Limited, Cultural Development Unit, 1978. [anthology]
– ed. *The River Between.* Linden, Guyana: Linden Mining Enterprise Limited, Cultural Development Unit, 1979. [anthology]
Cruz, Maria Carmen Corinne. [1974–]. b. Puerto Rico.
– *Pride and Resistance.* N.p.: Maria Cruz, 1999. [poetry]
– *The Mac Truck Rages On.* [Toronto]: M.C.C. Cruz, [2000?] [poetry]
Cudjoe, Vera. b. Trinidad.
– with Robin Breon. *The Story of Mary Ann Shadd.* Toronto: Carib-Can Publishers, Inc., 1988. [juvenile]
– with Robin Breon. *The Story of John Ware.* Toronto: Carib-Can Communications Inc., 1994. [juvenile]
Cuevas, Ernesto R. [1923–]. b. United States.
– *Some Friends of Mine: Short Stories.* Toronto: Williams–Wallace, 1986. [short fiction]
Cummins, Willis. [1937–]. b. Trinidad.
– *Calypsos, Symphonies, and Incest.* Toronto: Arawak Publishing House, 1974. [essays]
Curtis, Christopher Paul. [1953–]. b. United States.
– *The Watsons Go to Birmingham – 1963: A Novel.* New York: Delacorte Press, 1995. Rpt. Bantam Doubleday Bell Books, 1997. [juvenile]
– *Bud, Not Buddy.* New York: Delacorte Press, 1999. [juvenile]
Dallard, Willa Reese (Bowen). [1897–1988]. b. United States.
– *Memories of My Father: The Late Willis Bowen of Amber Valley, Alberta.* [Prelate, SK: n.p., 1978.] [memoir]
Damour, Alix. b. Haiti.
– *Pages blanches et un poème pris en otage.* Port-au-Prince: Éditions Damour, 1980. [poetry]
Daniel, Earl. [1963–]. b. Jamaica.
– *Overlaugh: A Rich Blend of Caribbean and North American Humour.* Montreal: n.p., 1992. [narratives]
Darbasie, Nigel. [1950–]. b. Trinidad.
– *Last Crossing: Poems.* Edmonton: Nidar Communications Inc., 1988. [poetry]
– *A Map of the Island.* Edmonton: University of Alberta Press, 2001. [poetry]
Dauphin, Claude. [1949–]. b. Haiti.
– *Brit kolobrit introduction méthodologique* suivi de *30 chansons enfantines haïtiennes recueillies et classées progressivement en vue d'une pédagogie musicale aux Antilles.* Sherbrooke, QC: Éditions Naaman, 1981. [prose and music]
– *Musique du vaudou: Fonctions, structures et styles.* Sherbrooke, QC: Éditions Naaman, 1986. [prose]
– *Rousseau, musicien des Lumières.* Montréal: Louise Courteau, éditrice, inc., 1992. [prose]

Davertige [Villard Denis]. [1940–]. b. Haiti.
- *Idem.* Port-au-Prince: Imprimérie Théodore, 1962. Rpt. *Idem et autres poèmes.* Paris: Pierre Seghers, 1964. Rpt. *Idem.* Montréal: Nouvelle Optique, 1983. [poetry]
Davis, Selwyn. b. Trinidad.
- *Selected Slips.* Toronto: Williams-Wallace International, 1980. [poetry]
Dawes, Kwame [Senu Neville]. [1962–]. b. Ghana.
- *Progeny of Air.* London: Peepal Tree, 1994. [poetry]
- *Prophets.* London: Peepal Tree, 1995. [poetry]
- *Resisting the Anomie.* Fredericton, NB: Goose Lane Editions, 1995. [poetry]
- *Jacko Jacobus.* London: Peepal Tree, 1996. [poetry]
- *Requiem: A Lament for the Dead.* London: Peepal Tree, 1996. [poetry]
- *Shook Foil: A Collection of Reggae Poems.* London: Peepal Tree, 1997. [poetry]
- ed. *Wheel and Come Again: An Anthology of Reggae Poetry.* Fredericton, NB: Goose Lane Editions, 1998. [anthology]
- *Natural Mysticism: Towards a New Reggae Aesthetic in Caribbean Writing.* Leeds: Peepal Tree, 1999. [prose]
- *Midland.* Fredericton: Goose Lane Editions, 2001; Athens, OH: Ohio University Press, 2001. [poetry]
- *Talk Yuh Talk: Interviews with Anglophone Caribbean Poets.* London: University Press of Virginia, 2001. [interviews]
De Haarte, Norma. [1933–]. b. Guyana.
- *Guyana Betrayal.* Toronto: Sister Vision Press, 1991. [fiction]
- *Mr. Jimmy: The Blackpudding Man.* Weston, ON: De Haarte, 1997. [poem and history]
De Verger, Jean-Claude. [1939–]. b. Haiti.
- *Haïti: Vive la démocratie!: Par l'union qui fait la force: Nouveau contrat social ou un nouveau projet de societé pour Haïti.* Val-d'Or, QC: D'ici et d'ailleurs, 1994. [prose]
Deen, Faizal. [1968–]. b. Guyana.
- *Land without Chocolate: A Memoir.* Toronto: Wolsak and Wynn, 1999. [poetry]
Dehoux, Liliane Dévieux. [1942–]. b. Haiti.
- *L'Amour, oui. La Mort, non: Roman Haïtien.* Sherbrooke, QC: Éditions Naaman, 1976. [fiction]
Dei, George J[erry]. Sefa. [1954–]. b. Ghana.
- *Hardships and Survival in Rural West Africa.* Dakar, Senegal: CODESRIA, 1992. [study; also published in French translation in 1993]
- with Leilani Holmes et al. *Drop Out or Push Out: The Dynamics of Black Students' Disengagement from School: A Report.* [Toronto]: Ontario Institute for Studies in Education, 1995. [report]
- *Anti-Racism Education: Theory and Practice.* Halifax, NS: Fernwood Publishing, 1996. [prose]
- et al. *Reconstructing 'Dropout': A Critical Ethnography of the Dynamics of Black Students' Disengagement from School.* Toronto: University of Toronto Press, 1997. [compilation]
- and Agnes Calliste, eds. *Anti-Racist Feminism: Critical Race and Gender Studies.* Halifax, NS: Fernwood, 2000. [compilation]

– and Agnes Calliste, eds. *Power, Knowledge, and Anti-Racism Education: A Critical Reader*. Halifax, NS: Fernwood, 2000. [compilation]
– [et al.] *Removing the Margins: The Challenges and Possibilities of Inclusive Schooling*. Toronto: Canadian Scholars' Press, 2000.
– with Budd L. Hall and Dorothy Goldin Rosenburg, eds. *Indigenous Knowledges in Global Contexts: Multiple Readings of Our World*. Toronto: OISE/UT Book and University of Toronto Press, 2000.
– et al. *Inclusive Schooling: A Teacher's Companion to 'Removing the Margins.'* Toronto: Canadian Scholars' Press, 2002. [prose]
Dejean, Paul [Pòl Dejan]. [1931–]. b. Haiti.
– [et] Iv Dejan. *Evanjil dimanche ak fèt*. Issy-les-Moulineaux: Imprimerie St-Paul, 1962. [prose]
– *Problèmes d'alphabétisation en Haïti*. Paris: n.p., 1963. [cyclostyled text]
– [avec] Iv Dejan. *4 ti liv evanjil yo*. Port-au-Prince: Éditions Henri Deschamps, 1967. [prose]
– *Les Haïtiens au Québec*. Montréal: Presses de l'Université du Québec, 1978. [prose]
– *The Haitians in Quebec*. Trans. Max Dorsinville. Ottawa: Tecumseh Press, 1980. [prose]
– *Le Racisme dans l'industrie du taxi à Montréal: Deux mémoires à la Commission des droits de la personne du Québec*. [Québec (Province): n.p.], 1983; rpt. Montréal: Eben-Ezer, 1984. [prose]
– *Florilège de lutte et d'espèrance: 18 mars-18 juin 1986*. Montréal: n.p., 1986. [cyclostyled text]
– [et] Iv Dejan. *Yon konstitisyon, pur ki sa, pou ki moun?* Pòtoprens: Enprimri Wodrigèz, 1986. [prose]
– *Konstitisyon Repiblik d Ayiti 1987*. Pòtoprens: n.p., 1987. [prose]
– *Ochan pou Pèp Ayisyen. 7 fevriye pap peri!* Pòtoprens: Enprimri Wodrigèz, 1987. [prose]
– *Prélude à la liberté*. Port-au-Prince: Imprimerie Rodriguez, 1987. [prose]
– *Survol des tentatives d'alphabétisation en Haiti par les services gouvernementaux (1943–1988)*. Port-au-Prince: GARE, 1987. [history]
– *Dans la tourmente. Interlude douloureux. Premier et deuxième mouvements. Mars 1987-avril 1989*. Port-au-Prince: n.p., 1990. [prose]
– *D'Haïti au Québec*. Montréal: CIDIHCA, 1990. [prose]
– *Ki sa gouvènman peyi a janm fè ant 1943 ak 1988 pou l regle koze pa konn li ak pa konn ekri ann Ayiti?* Pòtoprens: Le Natal, 1990. [prose]
– [trad.] *Constitution de la République d'Haïti / Konstitisyon Repiblik d Ayiti 29 mas 1987*. Port-au-Prince: Éditions Henri Deschamps, 1991. [prose]
– [avec CIDIHCA]. *Haïti, un an après le coup d'État*. Montréal: CIDIHCA, 1992. [history]
– *Haïti: Alerte, on tue!* Montréal: CIDIHCA, 1993. [history]
– *Haïti: L'Inélucable retour*. Montréal: Éditions du CIDIHCA, 1994. [prose]
– *Willy Romélus: L'Évêque-courage*. La Salle, QC: Éditions Hurtubise HMH, 1995. [history and biography]
Dejean, Yves. [1927–]. b. Haiti.
– *Comment écrire le créole d'Haïti / 1980*. Outremont, QC: Collectif Paroles, 1980. [guide]

Delany, Martin Robinson. [1812–85]. b. United States.
- *Eulogy on the Life and Character of the Rev. Fayette.* Pittsburgh: Benj. Franklin Peterson, 1847. [prose]
- *The Condition, Elevation, Emigration, and Destiny of the Colored People of the United States Politically Considered.* Philadelphia, 1852. [prose]
- *The Origin and Objects of Ancient Free Masonry; Its Introduction into the United States and Legitimacy among Colored Men. A Treatise Delivered before St. Cyprian Lodge, No. 13, June 24th, A. D. 1853 – A. L. 5853.* Pittsburgh: W.S. Haven, 1853. [prose]
- 'Blake; or, The Huts of America.' In *The Anglo-African Magazine* and *Weekly Anglo-African* (1859; 1861–2). Rpt. *Violence in the Black Imagination: Essays and Documents.* 1972. Expanded Edition. Ed. Ronald T. Takaki. New York: Oxford University Press, 1993. 103–214. [fiction]
- *Official Report of the Niger Valley Exploring Party.* New York: Thomas Hamilton, 1861. [prose]
- *To the Students of Wilberforce University* ... Charleston: Republican Book and Job Office, 1870. [prose]
- *Principia of Ethnology: The Origin of Races and Color, with an Archeological Compendium of Ethiopian and Egyptian Civilization, from Years of Careful Examination and Enquiry.* Philadelphia: Harper & Brother, 1879. [prose]

Déluy, José. [1946–]. b. Haiti.
- *Hilarité et morosité.* N.p.: J. Déluy, 1973. [poetry]
- *Maitre Maçon.* Montréal: Cercle littérature ésotérique, 1975. [poetry]
- *Le Vent tourne: Poésie.* Montréal: Éditions Déluy, [1992]. [poetry]

Des Rosiers, Joël. [1951–]. b. Haiti.
- *Métropolis Opéra: Poèmes.* Montréal: Triptyque; Grenoble: La Vague à l'ame, 1987. [poetry]
- *Tribu: Poésie.* Montréal: Éditions Triptyque, 1990. [poetry]
- *Savanes: Poème.* Montréal: Triptyque, 1993. [poetry]
- *Théories caraïbes: Poétique du déracinement: Essai.* Montréal: Triptyque, 1996. [essay]
- *Vétiver: Poèmes.* Montréal: Triptyque, 1999. [poetry]
- *Métropolis Opéra;* suivi de *Tribu: Poésie.* Montréal: Triptyque, 2000. [poetry]

Deschausay, Sonia E.
- *What's a Memory?* Nashville: James C. Winston Pub.; Montreal: Winston–Derek Publishers Group, Inc., 1995. [juvenile]
- *Qu'est-ce que c'est la mémoire?* Trans. Pierre-Yves Bezzaz. Montréal: Winston–Derek Publishers Group, Inc., 1995. [juvenile]

Dett, R[obert]. Nathaniel. [1882–1943] b. Ontario.
- *The Album of a Heart.* Jackson, TN: Mocowat-Mercer / Lane College, 1911. [poetry]
- *Religious Folk-Songs of the Negro As Sung at Hampton Institute.* Hampton, VA: Hampton Institute Press, 1927. [compilation]
- *The Dett Collection of Negro Spirituals.* N.p.: Hall and McCrealy, 1936. [compilation]
- *The Collected Piano Works of R. Nathaniel Dett.* Evanston, IL: Summy-Birchard Co., 1973. [music]

Diallo, Amadou Mouctar. [1945–]. b. Mali?
- *La Verité à cacher.* [Saint-Hubert, QC: A.M. Diallo, 1994?] [prose]

Diallo, Lamine. b. Sénégal.
- *Atelier-discussion sur l'interculturalisme.* Sudbury, ON: Programme Apprenons ensemble [et] le Centre Franco-Ontarien de ressources en alphabétisation, 1996. [prose]
Diallo, Yaya. [1946–]. b. Mali?
- *Profil culturel africain: Témoinage de Yaya Diallo.* Montréal: Centre interculturel Monchanin, 1985. [prose]
- [and Mitchell Hall]. *The Healing Drum: African Wisdom Teachings.* Rochester, VT: Destiny Books, 1989. [prose]
Dialo, Boubacar.
- *Plus jamais ça!* Laval, QC: Beauchemin, [1999?]
Dorsinville, Max. [1943–]. b. Haiti.
- *Caliban without Prospero: Essay on Québec and Black Literature.* Erin, ON: Press Porcépic, 1974. [essay]
- *Le Pays natal: Essais sur les littératures du Tiers-Monde et du Québec.* [Dakar]: Nouvelles Éditions africaines, 1983. [essays]
- [réd.] *Accords perdus: Roman.* Par Roger Dorsinville. Montréal: CIDIHCA, 1987. [edited novel by Roger Dorsinville]
- *Solidarités: Tiers-Monde et littérature comparée.* Montréal: Éditions du CIDIHCA, 1988. [prose]
- *James Wait et les lunettes noires: Roman.* [Montréal]: Éditions du CIDIHCA, 1995. Rpt. and trans. *Erzulie Loves Shango.* [Montréal]: Éditions du CIDIHCA, 1995. [fiction]
Douglas, Debbie.
- et al., eds. *Ma'-ka: Diasporic Juks: Contemporary Writing by Queers of African Descent.* Toronto: Sister Vision Press, 1997. [anthology]
Douglas, James. [1803–77]. b. British Guyana.
- *Fort Victoria Correspondence Outward, July 13, 1840–May 24, 1841.* Victoria: British Columbia Provincial Archives. [letters]
- *James Douglas in California, 1841; Being a Journal of a Voyage from the Columbia to California.* Vancouver: Vancouver Public Library's Press, 1965. [journal]
- *Journal of James Douglas, 1843. Including Voyage to Sitka and Voyage to the North-West Coast.* Victoria: British Columbia Provincial Archives. [journal]
- *Despatches and Correspondence Transmitted to the House of Assembly in Governor Douglas' Message 3rd September 1863.* Victoria: Daily Chronicle, 1863. [letters]
- *Travel Diary of 1864–1865.* Victoria: British Columbia Provincial Archives. [journal]
Douglas, Rosie [Roosevelt Douglas]. [d. 2000]. b. Barbados.
- *Chains or Change: Focus on Dominica.* N.p.: n.p., 1972. [prose]
- *Canada's Racist Immigration Policy.* Toronto: Pathfinder Press, 1975. [essay]
Douglas, Stephen. b. Trinidad.
- *Historic Hangings in the Chadee Gang.* [Toronto: S. Douglas,] 2000. [poetry]
Douyon, Emerson. [1929–]. b. Haiti.
- [réd.] *Culture et développement en Haïti / Symposium Haïti.* Montréal: Leméac, 1972. [prose]
- [invité]. *La Victime.* [Par] Roger Citerné [entrevue]. Montréal: Service des transcriptions et dérivés de la radio, Maison Radio-Canada, 1976. [interview transcript]

- *Certains aspects de l'application des techniques psychologiques en pays sous-développé.* N.p.: n.p., 197–? [prose]
- [et] André Normandeau. *Justice et communautés culturelles?* Laval, QC: Éditions du Méridien, 1995. [prose]

Douyon, Frantz. [1938–]. b. Haiti.
- *Sortir du Marasme: Réflexions pour une croissance économique durable en Haïti.* Montréal: CIDIHCA, 1997. [prose]

Downes, Marguerite [Peggy] A. b. Nova Scotia.
- *Military and Music: Personal Reflections.* Dartmouth, NS: Black Cultural Centre of Nova Scotia, 1990. [memoir]

Doyle-Marshall, William. [1944–]. b. Trinidad.
- *Who Say?* Port of Spain: W. Doyle-Marshall, 1977. [poetry?]
- *Messenger of My Spirit: A Collection of Poems.* Toronto: Calypso Pub. House, 1980. [poetry]
- ed. *Cultural Crisis: A Look at Cultural Impacts in Canada, the Caribbean and England.* Toronto: Calypso Hous, 1981. [compilation]
- *A Mandate for Educating African-Canadians.* Toronto: Calypso Hous, 1994. [essay]

D'Oyley, Enid F[rederica]. b. Jamaica.
- and Rella Braithwaite, comps. *Women of Our Times.* Toronto: Canadian Negro Women's Association for the National Congress of Black Women, 1973. [history]
- *A Sample Checklist of Latin American and Caribbean Material Published in Canada.* N.p.: n.p., 1977. [bibliography]
- *Between Sea and Sky.* Toronto: Williams-Wallace Productions Intl, 1979. [juvenile]
- *Animal Fables and Other Tales Retold.* Toronto: Williams-Wallace, 1982. Rpt. Animal Fables and Other Tales. Stratford, ON: Williams-Wallace, 1988. [folktales]
- *The Bridge of Dreams.* Toronto: Williams-Wallace, 1984. [fiction]

D'Oyley, Vincent [Roy]. [1927–]. b. Jamaica.
- *Jamaica: Development of Teacher Training through the Agency of the Lady Mico Charity from 1835 to 1914.* [Toronto]: Department of Educational Research, Ontario College of Education, University of Toronto, 1964. [history]
- *Technical Manual for the Canadian Tests: Statistical Data on the Carnegie Study Tests of Academic Aptitude and Achievement in Grades 8, 9, and 10 in Ontario Schools and Grades 7 and 8 in Toronto Schools.* [Toronto]: Department of Educational Research, Ontario College of Education, University of Toronto, 1964. [study]
- *Testing: The First Two Years of the Carnegie Study, 1959 to 1961; Analysis of Scores by Course, Sex, and Size of Municipality.* [Toronto]: Department of Educational Research, Ontario College of Education, University of Toronto, 1964. [study]
- *Annotated Bibliography of Literature Related to the Tests Constructed by the Department of Educational Research, Ontario College of Education, University of Toronto.* Toronto: Ontario Ministry of Education, 1965. [bibliography]
- *Comparative Study of Post-Secondary Achievement and Attitudes of Students from Traditional and Credit System High Schools.* Toronto: Ontario Ministry of Education, 1973. [study]
- with Sybil Everesta Wilson. *Teacher Internships as an Adventure: Can It Be a Replanning*

Strategy in Jamaica? Toronto: Department of Educational Planning, Ontario Institute
for Studies in Education, 1973. [study]
- ed. *Black Students in Urban Canada.* Toronto: Ministry of Culture and Recreation,
1976. [compilation]
- *The Impact of Multi-Ethnicity on Canadian Education.* Toronto: Urban Alliance on Race
Relations, 1977. [prose]
- *Black Presence in a Multi-Ethnic Canada.* Vancouver: Centre for the Study of Curriculum and Instruction, University of British Columbia, 1978; abridged ed., Vancouver:
Centre for the Study of Curriculum and Instruction, University of British Columbia,
1982. [prose]
- ed. *Domestic Violence: Issues and Dynamics.* Toronto: Ontario Institute for Studies in
Education, 1978. [compilation]
- ed. *Perspectives on Race, Education and Social Development: Emphasis on Canada.*
Vancouver: Centre for the Study of Curriculum and Instruction, University of
British Columbia, 1978. [compilation]
- [Chairman, British Columbia Multicultural Conference, 1979, Vancouver, BC].
Conference Proceedings: Toward a Provincial Multicultural Policy: [held at] *Hotel
Vancouver, Vancouver, B.C., April 3rd & 4th, 1979.* N.p: n.p., 1979. [report]
- and Reginald Murray, eds. *Development and Disillusion in Third World Education, with
Emphasis on Jamaica.* Toronto: Ontario Institute for Studies in Education, 1979.
[compilation]
- and Stan M. Shapson and Anne Lloyd, eds. *Bilingualism and Multiculturalism in
Canadian Education.* [Vancouver]: Centre for the Study of Curriculum and Instruc-
tion, (University of British Columbia), 1982. [compilation]
- *Perspectives on Race, Education and Social Development: Emphasis on Canada.*
Vancouver: Centre for the Study of Curriculum and Instruction, University of
British Columbia, 1982. [conference papers]
- and Douglas Ray, eds. *Human Rights in Canadian Education.* Dubuque, IA: Kendall /
Hunt Pub Co., 1983. [compilation]
- and Stan Shapson, eds. *Bilingual and Multicultural Education: Canadian Perspectives.*
Clevedon, Avon: Multilingual Matters, 1984. [compilation]
- and Aziz Khaki. *Progress towards Equality: Action Plan of the National Symposium on
Progress towards Equality, September 16–18, 1988, Vancouver, B.C.* Vancouver: Committee for Racial Justice, 1989. [prose]
- and Stan Shapson, eds. *Innovative Multicultural Teaching.* Toronto: Kagan and Woo,
1990. [compilation]
- and Adrian Blunt and Ray Barnhardt, eds. *Education and Development: Lessons from
the Third World.* Calgary: Detselig Enterprises, 1994. [compilation]
- ed. *Innovations in Black Education in Canada.* By National Council of Black Educators
of Canada. Toronto: Umbrella Press, 1994. [compilation]
- with Carl E. James, eds. *Re/visioning: Canadian Perspectives on the Education of Africans
in the Late Twentieth Century.* North York, ON: Captus Press, 1998. [compilation]
Drew, Benjamin. [1812–1903]. b. United States.
- comp. *A North-Side View of Slavery; The Refugee; or, The Narratives of Fugitive Slaves in
Canada Related by Themselves; with an Account of the History and Condition of the Colored*

Population of Upper Canada. Boston: John P. Jewett, 1856. Rpt. Toronto: Prospero
  Books, [Drew was Euro-American, but the narratives are by African Americans in
  Canada.] [compilation]
Dungy, Hilda. [1906–]. b. Ontario.
– *Planted by the Waters: A Genealogy of the Jones-Carter Family*. Wallaceburg, ON:
  Standard, 1975. [history]
– *Planted by the Waters: A Family History of the Jones-Carter Family*. Rev. ed.
  Wallaceburg, ON: Standard, 1977. [history]
Dyer, Bernadette. b. Jamaica.
– *Of Earth and from the Sky*. Whitby, ON: The Plowman, 1989. [poetry]
– *Pej: And Other Poems*. Whitby, ON: The Plowman, 1989. [poetry]
– *Villa Fair*. Vancouver: Beach Holme Publishers, 2000. [short fiction]
Edmonds, Pamela. [195?–]. b. Quebec.
– with Anthony Joyette. *Black Body: Race, Resistance, Response*. Halifax, NS: Dalhousie
  Art Gallery, 2001. [art show catalogue]
Edwards, Haskell G. [1936–].
– *The Immigrant Family: Framework for Adaptation and Excellence*. West Hill, ON: We
  Care Associates, 1992. [prose]
Elliott, Lorris. [1932–99]. b. Tobago.
– *Coming for to Carry: A Novel in Five Parts*. Toronto: Williams-Wallace, 1982. [fiction]
– and Wesli Riy-Ves. *Rocking in Paradise*. Montreal: Centaur Theatre Company, 1984.
  [musical script / drama]
– 'How Now Black Man: Part 4 – the Final Act.' In Lorris Elliott, ed., *Other Voices:
  Writings by Blacks in Canada* (1985), 65–76. [drama]
– ed. *Other Voices: Writings by Blacks in Canada*. Toronto: Williams-Wallace, 1985.
  [anthology]
– 'The Trial of Marie-Joseph Angelique: Negress and Slave.' In Lorris Elliott, ed., *Other
  Voices: Writings by Blacks in Canada* (1985), 55–65. [drama]
– comp. *The Bibliography of Literary Writings by Blacks in Canada*. Toronto: Williams-
  Wallace, 1986. [bibliography]
– comp. *Literary Writing by Blacks in Canada: A Preliminary Survey*. Ottawa: Department
  of the Secretary of State, 1988. [bibliography]
– comp. *Production littéraire des Noirs du Canada: Étude préliminaire*. [Ottawa]:
  Multiculturalisme et Citoyonneté Canada / Multiculturalism and Citizenship
  Canada, 1990. [bibliography]
Ellis, Keith. [1935–].
– *El Arte narrativo de Francisco Ayala*. Madrid: Gredos, 1964. [prose]
– ed. *La Cabeza del cordero*. By Francisco Ayala. Englewood Cliffs, NJ: Prentice-Hall,
  [1968]. [short fiction]
– comp. *El Ensayo y la critica literaria en Iberoamerica: Memoria del XIV Congreso
  Internacional de Literatura Iberoamericana, Universidad de Toronto, Toronto, Canada,
  24–28 de Agosto de 1969*. Toronto: University of Toronto Press, 1970. [conference
  papers]
– *Critical Approaches to Ruben Dario*. Toronto: University of Toronto Press, 1974. [prose]
– *Cuba's Nicolas Guillen: Poetry and Ideology*. Toronto: University of Toronto Press,

1983. Rpt. and trans. *Nicolas Guillen: poesia e ideologie: perfil libre*. Cuidad de la
Habana: Union de Escritores y Artistas de Cuba, 1987. [prose]

– trans. *Mirrors of War: Literature and Revolution in El Salvador*. Ed. Gabriela Yanes
[et al.]. Toronto: Between the Lines, 1985. [prose]

– ed. and trans. *New Love Poetry: In Some Springtime Place: Elegy*. Trans. of *Nueva Poesia
de amor: en algun sitio de la primavera: elegia*. By Nicolas Guillen. Toronto: University
of Toronto Press, 1994. [poetry and prose]

– *The Role of Science in Cuban Culture / El papel de la ciencia en la cultura Cubana*.
Toronto: York Medical, 1995. [prose]

Elwin, Rosamund. [1955–].

– and Michele Paulse. *Asha's Mums*. Toronto: Women's Press, 1990. [juvenile]

– and Michele Paulse. *The Moonlight Hide-&-Seek Club in the Pollution Solution*. Toronto:
Women's Press, 1992. [juvenile]

– with Carol Allain, eds. *Getting Wet: Tales of Lesbian Seductions*. Toronto: Women's
Press, 1992. [anthology]

– and Karen X. Tulchinsky, eds. *Tangled Sheets: Stories and Poems of Lesbian Lust*.
Toronto: Women's Press, 1995. [anthology]

– ed. *Countering the Myths: Lesbians Write about the Men in Their Lives*. Toronto:
Women's Press, 1996. [anthology]

– ed. *Tongues on Fire: Caribbean Lesbian Lives and Stories*. Toronto: Women's Press, 1997.
[anthology]

Estigène, Eugène Bénito. [194?–]. b. Haiti.

– *Mémoire de l'iris*. Ottawa: Les Éditions du Vermillon, 1998. [poetry]

– *Mémoire d'une nuit à genoux*. Ottawa: Les Éditions David, 2001. [poetry]

Étienne, Gérard [Vergniaud]. [1936–]. b. Haiti.

– *Au milieu des larmes*. Port-au-Prince: Togiram Presse, 1960. [poetry]

– *Plus large qu'un rêve*. Port-au-Prince: Éditions Dorsainvil, 1960. [poetry]

– *La Raison et mon amour*. Port-au-Prince: Les Presses Port-au-princiennes, 1961.
[poetry]

– *Essai sur la négritude*. Port-au-Prince: Éditions Panorama, 1962. [essay]

– *Gladys*. Port-au-Prince: Éditions Panorama, 1963. [poetry]

– *Le Nationalisme dans la littérature haïtienne*. Port-au-Prince: Éditions Lycée Pétionville,
1964. [essay]

– *Lettre à Montréal*. Montréal: Éditions L'Ésterel, 1966. [poetry]

– 'Vous n'êtes pas seul.' *Lettres et écritures*. Janvier 1969. 6–12. [drama]

– *Dialogue avec mon ombre*. Montréal: Éditions Francophones du Canada, 1972. [poetry]

– *Le Nègre crucifié: Récit*. Montréal: Éditions Francophones du Canada et Nouvelle
Optique, 1974; [Genève, Suisse]: Métropolis, 1989; Montréal: Éditions Balzac, 1994.
[fiction]

– *Un Ambassadeur macoute à Montréal*. Montréal: Éditions Nouvelle Optique, 1979.
[fiction]

– *Cri pour ne pas crever de honte*. Montréal: Éditions Nouvelle Optique, 1982. [poetry]

– *Une Femme muette*. Montréal: Éditions Nouvelle Optique; Paris: Éditions Silex, 1983.
[fiction]

– *Una Mulher Calada*. Trans. Zila Bernd. Federal do Rio Grande do Sol [Brazil]: Editora
da Universidada, 1987. [fiction]

– *La Reine Soleil levée: Récit.* Montréal: Éditions Guérin-Littérature, 1987; [Genève, Suisse]: Métropolis, 1989. [fiction]
– *Der Aufstand Der Sonnenkönigen.* Trans. G. Walkerlin Induni. Hanovre und Amden: Shönbach Verlag, 1990. [fiction]
– *La Pacotille: Roman.* Montréal: Éditions l'Héxagone, 1991. [fiction]
– *La Charte des crépuscules (oeuvres poétiques, 1960–1980).* Moncton, NB: Éditions d'Acadie, 1993. [poetry]
– *La Question raciale et raciste dans le roman québécois: Essai d'anthroposémiologie.* Montréal: Les Éditions Balzac, 1995. [prose]
– avec François Soeler. *La Femme noire dans le discours littéraire haïtien: Éléments d'anthroposémiologie.* Montréal: Balzac-le Griot, 1998. [prose]
– *L'Injustice! Désinformation et mépris de la loi.* Brossard, QC: Humanitas, 1998. [essay]
– *La Romance en do mineur de Maître Clo.* Montréal: Balzac, 2000. [fiction]
– *Vous n'êtes pas seul.* Montréal: Balzac Éditeur, 2001. [fiction]
Etienne, Gerry [Shafiq, pseud.]. b. Dominica.
– *Crossroads Cant.* Ed. Joe Blades. Fredericton: Broken Jaw Press, 1997. [poetry]
Evans, Doris. b. Nova Scotia.
– and Gertrude Tynes. *Telling the Truth: Reflections: Segregated Schools in Nova Scotia.* Hantsport, NS: Lancelot Press, 1995. [history]
Evanson, Tanya. [1972–]. b. Québec.
– *Blood In, Blood Out: A Universal Preparation.* Montreal: Mother Tongue Media, 1996. [poetry]
– *word class animal.* Montreal: Mother Tongue Media, 1997. [poetry, essay]
– *Throwing Skin: South American Poems 1997–1998.* Vancouver: Mother Tongue Media, 1999. [poetry, short fiction, journal]
– *Cut of Buddha/The Vancouver Eloquence.* Vancouver: Mother Tongue Media, 2000. [poetry]
Farmer, Bonnie. [1959–]. b. Nova Scotia.
– 'Irene and Lillian Forever.' In *Escape Acts: Seven Canadian One-Acts.* Ed. Colleen Curran. Montréal: NuAge Editions, 1992. 10–29. [drama]
– [et al.] *Success: Grade 5 Activity Book, English As a Second Language.* Dir. Lama'a Habbouche Yammine. Montréal: Guérin, 1998, 2000. [textbook]
– [et al.] *Success: Grade 5 Answers and Pedagogical Notes.* Montréal: Guérin, 1998. [prose]
Fauset, Arthur Huff. [1899–1983]. b. United States.
– comp. *Folklore from Nova Scotia.* New York: American Folk-Lore Society, 1931. [Fauset was African-American, but most of this lore is by Africadians.]
Felj, Claudy [Jean-Claude Felix]. [1952–]. b. Haiti.
– *L'Automne du condor: Prose et poésie.* Montréal: Kauss, 1983. [prose and poetry]
Ffrench, Robert. [1959–]. b. Nova Scotia.
– *Black Canadian Achievement: Out of the Past into the Future: An Introductory Learning Guide.* Dartmouth, NS: Pride Communications, 1994. [textbook]
– *In Our Time: An Introductory Learning Guide.* Dartmouth, NS: Black Star Books, 1996. [textbook]
Foggo, Cheryl. b. Alberta.
– *Pourin' Down Rain.* Calgary: Detselig Enterprises Ltd, 1990. [memoir]
– *One Thing That's True.* Toronto: Kids Can Press, 1997. [juvenile]

– *I Have Been in Danger*. Regina: Coteau Books, 2001. [juvenile]
Fonkeng, Epah Francis. b. Cameroon.
– *Still Searching*. Yaounde: [Fonkeng], 1985. [poetry]
– *The Captive*. Ottawa: [Fonkeng], 1990. [drama]
Ford-Smith, Honor [Maria]. [1951–]. b. Jamaica.
– ed. *Lionheart Gal: Life Stories of Jamaican Women*. By Sistren. London: Women's Press, 1986; Toronto: Sister Vision Press, 1987. [compilation]
– *Ring Ding in a Tight Corner: A Case Study of Funding and Organizational Democracy in Sistren, 1977–1988*. Ed. Linzi Manicom. Toronto, ON: Women's Program, ICAE, 1989. [prose]
– *My Mother's Last Dance and Other Poems*. Toronto: Sister Vision Press, 1997. [poetry]
Forsythe, Dennis. b. Jamaica.
– ed. *Let the Niggers Burn! The Sir George Williams University Affair and Its Caribbean Aftermath*. Montréal: Our Generation Press / Black Rose Books, 1971. [anthology]
– ed. *Black Alienation, Black Rebellion*. Washington, DC: College and University Press, 1975. [anthology]
– *Rastafari for the Healing of the Nation*. Kingston, JA: Zaika Publications, 1983. [prose]
Foster, Cecil. [1954–]. b. Barbados.
– *Distorted Mirror: Canada's Racist Face*. Toronto: HarperCollins, 1991. [essay]
– *Miroir déformant: Le Visage raciste du Canada*. Trans. Maryvon Delano. Toronto: HarperCollins, 1991. [essay]
– *No Man in the House*. Toronto: Random House, 1991; New York: Ballantine Books, 1992, 1994; Toronto: Vintage Books, 1993. [fiction]
– *Pas d'homme à la maison*. Trans. Marie-Hélène Sabard. Paris: Médium, 1995. [fiction]
– *Caribana: The Greatest Celebration*. Toronto: Random House, 1995; New York: Ballantine Books, 1995. [prose]
– *Sleep On, Beloved*. Toronto: Random House, 1995; New York: Ballantine Books, 1995. [fiction]
– *A Place Called Heaven: The Meaning of Being Black in Canada*. Toronto: HarperCollins, 1996. [prose]
– *Island Wings: A Memoir*. Toronto: HarperCollins, 1998; Toronto: HarperPerennial, 1998. [memoir]
– *Slammin' Tar*. Toronto: Random House, 1998. Rpt. Toronto: Vintage Canada, 1999. [fiction]
– *Dry Bone Memories: A Novel*. Toronto: Key Porter Books, 2001. [fiction]
Fouché, Franck. [1915–78]. b. Haiti.
– *Message*. Port-au-Prince: Nemours Telhomme, 1946. [poetry]
– *Un fauteuil dans un crâne*. In *Optique*. Haiti, 1957. [drama]
– *Oedipe Roi*. Port-au-Prince: n.p., 1958. [drama]
– *Les Lambis de la Sierra*. Trans. Nicholas Guillen. Moscow, 1960. [poetry]
– *Symphonie en noir majeur: Poeme pour Roussan Camille in memoriam*. Port-au-Prince: Art Graphique Presse, 1962. [poetry]
– *Bouki nan paradi*. Montréal: n.p., 1964. [drama]
– *Guide pour l'étude de la littérature haïtienne*. Port-au-Prince: Éditions Panorama, 1964. [guide]

- *Yerma*. [Creole version of play by Garcia Lorca.] [Dans] *Optique*. Haiti, 1965. [drama]
- *Bouki au paradis: Pièce folklorique en quatre mensonges, une vérité et six tableaux*. Trans. Jacqueline Fouché. [Dans] *L'Haïtien*. Montréal: Les Éditions de Saint-Marie, 1968. [drama]
- *Trou de dieu*. [Dans] *Théâtre vivant*, 4. Montréal: Holt, Rinehart et Winston, 1968. 45–80. [drama]
- *Général Baron-la-Croix: ou, Le Silence masqué: tragédie moderne en 2 calvaires, 28 stations et une messe en noir et rouge*. [Montréal]: Leméac, 1974. [drama]
- *Vodou et théâtre pour un nouveau théâtre populaire*. Montréal: Éditions Nouvelle Optique, 1976. [essay]

Francis, Azra Daniel. b. South Africa.
- *Pinocchio's Canadian Adventure: A One-Act Play for Children*. Windsor, ON: Windsor Italo-Canadian Culture Centre, 1986. [drama]
- *Josiah Henson: A Documentary Drama*. Windsor, ON: Windsor Italo-Canadian Culture Centre, 1988. [drama]
- *Notes on Voice for Speech and Acting*. Toronto: Canadian Scholars' Press, 1995. [prose]
- *Growing Up Brown in White Apartheid South Africa* with *The Spotted Tongue*. New York: Vantage Press, Inc., 1998. [memoir and poetry]
- *Five Plays on Apartheid*. Windsor, ON: Kabkort Publishers, 1999. [drama]
- *Nine Plays on Intercultural Conflict*. Windsor, ON: Kabkort Publishers, 1999. [drama]

Francis, Samuel B. [1922–]. b. Montserrat.
- *Me! And Who Am I?* Montreal: Société de belles lettres Guy Maheux, 1977. [poetry]

François, James. b. Jamaica.
- and Althea Tolliver. *From Africville to New Road: How Four Communities Planned Their Development*. Dartmouth, NS: Watershed Joint Action Committee / Black United Front, 1983. [study]

François, Ruben [pseud. Black Snowgoat]. [1945–75]. b. Haiti.
- *Confessions – One Blues and Rapssodies of a Black Immigrant*. Montreal: [François], n.d. [poetry]
- *My Soul in Tears and Other Collected Poems*. Montreal: Spare Change? Press, 1972. [poetry]
- *The Scavengers and Other New Collected Poems*. Montreal: Spare Change? Press, 1972. [poetry]

Fraser, J[oyce]. C[armen]. [pseud. Haile Telatra Edoney]. b. Guyana.
- [as Haile Telatra Edoney]. *Cry of the Illegal Immigrant*. [Toronto]: [Third World Books and Crafts], 1979? [autobiography].
- *Cry of the Illegal Immigrant*. Toronto: Williams-Wallace Productions International, 1980. [autobiography]

Frederick, Rawle. [1945–]. b. Trinidad.
- *Transatlantic Cargo*. Montreal: Work-Study Institute, Black Writers' Workshop, [1973]. [poetry]
- *The Vendor of Dreams and Other Stories*. Devonshire, Bermuda: Bermuda Writers' Collective, 1992. [short fiction]

French, Joan. b. Jamaica.
- *Wid Dis Ring*. Toronto: Sistren Research [and Sister Vision Press], 1987. [history]

Fuertès, Serge. [1943–]. b. Haiti.
– [Dans] *En Passant: Poésies de Serge Fuertès, Pierre Pelletier, Georges Tissot*. Hull, QC: n.p., 1975. [poetry]
Fyfe, Christopher.
– ed. *'Our Children Free and Happy': Letters from Black Settlers in Africa in the 1790s*. Edinburgh: Edinburgh University Press, 1991. [Fyfe is British, but this edited work consists of letters by 'Nova Scotians,' that is, the Black Loyalists who settled in Sierra Leone following their exodus from Nova Scotia in 1792. It yields a letter by Susannah – or Susana – Smith, perhaps the first African-Canadian woman writer.]
Gairey, Harry. [1898–]. b. Ontario.
– *A Black Man's Toronto, 1914–1980: The Reminiscences of Harry Gairey*. Ed. Donna Hill. Toronto: Multicultural History Society of Ontario, 1981. [autobiography]
Gale, Lorena. [1958–]. b. Québec.
– co-ed. *Taking the Stage: Selections from Plays by Canadian Women*. Ed. Cynthia Zimmerman. Toronto: Playwrights Canada Press, 1994. [anthology]
– 'Writing "Angélique."' *Canadian Theatre Review* 83 (Summer 1995): 20–3. [essay and drama excerpt]
– 'Angelique.' In *Another Perfect Piece: Monologues from Canadian Plays*. Ed. Tony Hamill. Toronto: Playwrights Canada Press, 1995. 64–6. [drama]
– 'And What of This Yearning?' *Canplay* 12.5 (Sept.–Oct. 1995): 6–7. [drama]
– 'Angelique.' In George Seremba, et al., eds., *Beyond the Pale* (1996), 212–15. [drama]
– *Angélique*. Toronto: Playwrights Canada Press, 2000. [drama]
– *Je me souviens: Memories of an Expatriate Anglophone Montréalaise, Québécoise Exiled in Canada*. Vancouver: Talonbooks, 2001. [drama]
Garnier, Eddy. [1949–]. b. Haiti.
– *Plaie rouillée: Monologue en vers*. Ottawa: Les Éditions du Vermillion, 1987. [poetry]
– *Éclats de bourgeons: Yon bann tikal boujon*. Québec: Éditions du Loup de gouttière, 1993. [poetry]
– *Adieu bordel, bye bye vodou: Roman*. Hull, QC: Vents d'ouest, 1994. [fiction]
– *En balise d'île Mémoire / Ginen-m an chalkalis*. Ripon, QC: Écrits des Hautes-Terres, 1998. [poetry in French and in Haitian Creole]
– *Vivre au noir en pays blanc*. Hull, QC: Vents d'ouest, 1999. [fiction]
Garraway, Garbette A.M.
– *Accomplishments and Contributions: A Handbook on Blacks in British Columbia*. Vancouver: Black Theatre West, 1990. [biographies]
Gauthier, LaFlorya. [1929–]. b. United States.
– *Whispers in the Sand*. Columbus, MS: Genesis Press, 1996. [fiction]
– *The Romance Writer's Handbook and Cassette: How to Organize and Outline Your Romance Novel*. St Didace, QC: GNW Systemed, 1998. [guide and audio cassette]
– *Guide pour l'écrivain de romans d'amour: Comment organiser et préparer votre roman d'amour*. [St Didace, QC: GNW Systemed, 1998.] [guide and audio cassette]
Gaye, Jerome. [1925–]. b. Sierra Leone.
– *Caught between Two Forces*. Toronto: Zebra Books, 1976. [fiction]
George, David. [c.1743–1810]. b. British America [United States]
– 'An Account of the Life of Mr. David George, from Sierra Leone in Africa; Given by

Himself in a Conversation with Brother John Rippon of London, and Brother Pearce of Birmingham.' *Baptist Annual Register* 1 (1790–3): 473–84. [autobiography]
- 'An Account of the Life of Mr. David George, from Sierra Leone in Africa; Given by Himself in a Conversation with Brother Rippon of London, and Brother Pearce of Birmingham.' 1793. Rpt. in *Unchained Voices: An Anthology of Black Authors in the English-Speaking World of the 18th Century.* Ed. Vincent Carretta. Lexington, KY: University Press of Kentucky, 1996. 333–50. [autobiography]

George, Hudson F[rancis]. [1954–]. b. Grenada.
- *Caribbean Child.* [Toronto]: [H.F. George], 1983. [poetry]
- *Blood in Grenada.* [Toronto]: [H.F. George], 1984. [poetry]
- *Migos in Exile.* [Toronto]: [H.F. George], 1984. [poetry]
- *People's Power.* [Toronto]: [H.F. George], 1986. [poetry]
- *At the Mountain Looking at the Fountain.* [Toronto]: H.F. George, 1989. [poetry]
- *Family Confusion.* [Toronto]: H.F. George, 1992. [drama]
- *Open Your Eyes.* [North York, ON]: H.F. George, 1997. [poetry]
- *Sufferers in Heaven Hiding from Hell.* [North York, ON: The author], 1997. [poetry]

Gibbs, Mifflin Wistar. [1823–1915]. b. Pennsylvania.
- *Shadow and Light: An Autobiography with Reminiscences of the Last and Present Century.* Washington, DC: n.p., 1902. New York: Arno Press, 1968. Rpt. *Shadow and Light.* Lincoln, NB: University of Nebraska Press, 1995. [autobiography]

Gibson, Ethel L. [1888–]. b. Nova Scotia.
- *My Journey through Eternity: An Autobiography.* Dartmouth, NS: Black Cultural Centre for Nova Scotia, 1988. [autobiography; title *should* read 'My Journey *to* Eternity']

Gillard, Denise. [1961–]. b. Nova Scotia.
- *Music from the Sky.* Vancouver: Douglas & McIntyre, 2001. [juvenile]

Gipson, Joella H[ardeman]. b. Ontario.
- ed. *Impetus, the Black Woman: Proceedings of the Fourth National Congress of Black Women of Canada / Nouvel essor, la femme noire: Procédure du quatrième Congrès nationale des femmes noires du Canada.* Windsor, ON: National Congress of Black Women of Canada, 1978. [report]
- [and] L. Carey Bolster, and H. Douglas Woodburn. *Consumer and Career Mathematics.* Toronto: Gage Pub., 1980. [textbook]
- [and] L. Carey Bolster, and H. Douglas Woodburn. *Consumer and Career Mathematics: Solution Key.* Canadian ed. Toronto: Gage Pub., 1981. [textbook]

Gladwell, Malcolm. [196?–]. b. Ontario.
- *The Tipping Point: How Little Things Make a Big Difference.* New York: Little, Brown, 2000. [prose]

Glaze, Avis Elane. [1948–]. b. Jamaica.
- *Career Aspirations and Expectations of Ontario Girls.* Toronto: [Ontario Ministry of Education] Queen's Printer for Ontario, 1979. [study]
- with Ken Alexander. *Towards Freedom: The African-Canadian Experience.* Toronto: Umbrella Press, 1996. [history]

Goddard, Horace I[shmael]. [1947–]. b. Barbados.
- *Rastaman: Poems for Leonta.* St-Laurent, QC: AFO Enterprises, 1982. [poetry]

- *The Long Drums*. St-Laurent, QC: AFO Enterprises, 1986. [poetry]
- ed. *A Common Tongue*. St-Laurent, QC: AFO Enterprises, 1987. [interviews with African and Caribbean writers]
- *The Awakening; and, Song of the Antilles*. St-Laurent, QC: AFO Enterprises, 1988. [poetry]
- *A Dog Named Sputnik*. St-Laurent, QC: AFO Enterprises, 1993. [juvenile]
- *Phoebus and the Crow*. St-Laurent, QC: AFO Enterprises, 1993. [juvenile]
- *Paradise Revisited*. Tennessee: Scythe Publications, 1997. [fiction]

Goler, William Harvey. [1846–]. b. Nova Scotia.
- *In Memory of Rev. Matthew Alston*. Greensboro, NC: Thomas, Reece & Co., 1884. [prose]
- *The Funeral Sermon over the Body of Rev. J.C. Price, D.D., President of Livingstone College. Delivered in Huntington Hall, Livingstone College, Friday, October 28, 1893*. [Salisbury, NC]: Livingstone Press, [1893?] [prose]
- *Addresses of Dr. W.H. Goler, President of Livingston College, N.C., at the 120th Anniversary of the Pennsylvania Society for Promoting the Abolition of Slavery, the Relief of Free Negroes Unlawfully Held in Bondage and for Improving the Condition of the African Race*. N.p.: n.p., 1895. [prose]
- *Report of President of Livingstone College, Located at Salisbury, N.C., to the General Conference Assembled at Philadelphia, May 6, 1908*. Philadelphia: Davis Printing Co., [1908?] [prose]

Goodison, Lorna. b. Jamaica.
- *Tamarind Season*. Kingston, JA: Institute of Jamaica, 1980. [poetry]
- *Selected Poems*. Ann Arbor: University of Michigan Press, 1992. [poetry]
- *To Us, All Flowers Are Roses*. Chicago: University of Illinois Press, 1995. [poetry]
- *Guinea Woman: New and Selected Poems*. Manchester, UK: Carcanet Press, 2000. [poetry]
- *Travelling Mercies*. Toronto: McClelland & Stewart, 2001. [poetry]

Gousse, Edgard [Edgardjsthgousse]. [1950–]. b. Haiti.
- *Antilles – 2, Croisade pour un paradis-nègre: Poèmes*. [Montréal: Edgard Gousse, 1981.] [poetry]
- [as Edgardjsthgousse]. *Cieux verts pour la diaspora: Poème*. [Montréal]: Edgardjsthgousse, 1981. [poetry]
- *Mémoires du vent*. Montréal: Éditions du Noroît, 1993. [poetry]
- *La Sagesse de l'aube: Poème*. Montréal: Triptyque, 1997. [poetry]

Govia, Francine. [1949–].
- and Helen Lewis, comps. *Blacks in Canada in Search of the Promise: A Bibliographic Guide to the History of Blacks in Canada*. Edmonton: Harrambee Centres Canada, 1988. [bibliography]

Graham, Pat. b. Manitoba.
- and Darryl Stevenson, eds. *The Black Experience in Manitoba: A Collection of Memories*. Winnipeg: The Winnipeg School Division No. 1 and the IDEA Centre, 1993. [compilation]

Green, Adam S. b. United States.
- *The Future of the Canadian Negro: A Paper Read before the African Baptist Association, Halifax, N.S., Monday Evening, Sept. 5, 1904*. Truro, NS: Adam S. Green, 1904. [essay]

Green, Truman. [1945–]. b. British Columbia.
- *A Credit to Your Race: A Novel*. Tsawwassen, BC: Simple Thoughts Press, 1974. [fiction]
Grizzle, Stanley G[eorge]. [1918–]. b. Ontario.
- *Discrimination, Our Achilles Heel*. [Ottawa: Queen's Printer, 1961.] [prose]
- *Distinctions injustes: Notre talon d'Achille?* [Ottawa: Imprimeur de la Reine, 1961.]
  [prose]
- [et al.] *Universality of Human Rights and the Black Experience: A Collection of Speeches*.
  Dartmouth, NS: Black Cultural Centre for Nova Scotia, 1989. [compilation]
- *My Name's Not George: The Story of the Brotherhood of Sleeping Car Porters in Canada:
  Personal Reminiscences of Stanley G. Grizzle*. With John Cooper. Toronto: Umbrella
  Press, 1997. [autobiography]
Hamalengwa, Munyonzwe. b. Zambia.
- *Thoughts Are Free: Prison Experience and Reflections on Law and Politics in General*.
  Toronto: Africa in Canada Press, 1991. [prose]
Hamilton, Sylvia. [1950–]. b. Nova Scotia.
- with Peggy Bristow, coord., et al. *'We're Rooted Here and They Can't Pull Us Up':
  Essays in African-Canadian Women's History*. Toronto: University of Toronto Press,
  1994. [history]
Hamilton-Dauda, Lucille.
- *How the Weeping Willow Got Its Name*. Ottawa: Boyd McRubie Communications Inc.,
  1992. [juvenile]
Harding, Winston.
- *Icons Reaching Out: Poetry and Prose on Some of Our Most Interesting People*. Toronto:
  Full House, 1998. [poetry and prose]
Harris, Amah. b. Jamaica.
- *Anansi and His Mission to Happiness*. Toronto: Black Theatre Canada, 1978. [photo-
  copied drama]
- *Anansi's Rescue in the Ant Kingdom*. Toronto: Black Theatre Canada, 1978. [photocop-
  ied drama]
Harris, Claire. [1937–]. b. Trinidad.
- *Fables from the Women's Quarters*. Toronto: Williams-Wallace, 1984; Fredericton:
  Goose Lane Editions, 1995. [poetry]
- *Translation into Fiction*. Fredericton: Fiddlehead Poetry Books and Goose Lane
  Editions, 1984. [poetry]
- *Travelling to Find a Remedy*. Fredericton: Fiddlehead Poetry Books and Goose Lane
  Editions, 1986. [poetry]
- *The Conception of Winter*. Stratford, ON: Williams-Wallace, 1989; Fredericton: Goose
  Lane Editions, 1995. [poetry]
- *Drawing Down a Daughter*. Fredericton: Goose Lane Editions, 1992. [poetry]
- with Edna Alford, eds. *Kitchen Talk: Contemporary Women's Prose and Poetry*. Red
  Deer, AB: Red Deer College Press, 1992. [anthology]
- *Dipped in Shadow*. Fredericton: Goose Lane Editions, 1996. [poetry]
- *Dreams and Mirrors: Träume und Spiegel*. Osnäbruck: OBEMA, 1996. [prose?]
- *She*. Fredericton: Goose Lane Editions, 2000. [poetry]
Haughton, Devon. b. Jamaica.
- *Roots an' Culture*. Toronto: Domestic Bliss, 1983. [poetry]

Haynes, Camille. b. Québec.
- ed. *Black Chat: An Anthology of Black Poets*. Montreal: Black and Third World Students Association, Dawson College, 1973. [anthology]
Head, Harold [pseud. Morena Kichwa]. [1936–]. b. South Africa.
- [as Morena Kichwa]. *Bushman's Brew*. Toronto: Goathair Press, 1974. [poetry]
- ed. *Canada in Us Now: The First Anthology of Black Poetry and Prose in Canada*. Toronto: NC Press, 1976. [anthology; it is the *third*, not the 'first']
Head, Wilson A. [1914–93]. b. United States.
- *Urban Need in Canada 1965: A Case Report on the Problems of Families in Four Canadian Cities*. Ottawa: Canada Welfare Council, 1965. [prose]
- *Poverty: A Major Issue Confronting Canadians*. [Ottawa: National Liberal Federation, 1969.] [one of a series of papers prepared by members of a Task Force on Poverty for presentation to the Harrison Liberal Conference]
- *Partners in Information: A Study of Community Information Centres in Ontario*. [Toronto: Department of the Provincial Secretary and Citizenship, 1971.] [prose]
- *The Black Presence in the Canadian Mosaic: A Study of Perceptions and the Practice of Discrimination against Blacks in Metropolitan Toronto*. Toronto: Ontario Human Rights Commission, 1975. [prose]
- *National Black Coalition of Canada*. [Toronto: n.p., 1979.] [prose]
- *Exploratory Study of the Attitudes and Perceptions of Minority and Majority Health Care Workers*. [Toronto]: [Ontario Human Rights Commission, Race Relations Division], 198? [study]
- *Adaptation of Immigrants: Perceptions of Ethnic and Racial Discrimination: An Exploratory Study*. [Downsview, ON]: York University, 1980;
- *Adaptation of Immigrants: Perceptions of Ethnic and Racial Discrimination*. [Toronto]: York University, 1981. [prose]
- and Don Clairmont. *Discrimination against Blacks in Nova Scotia: The Criminal Justice System: Research Study*. Prepared for the Royal Commission on the Donald Marshall, Jr, Prosecution. [Halifax, NS]: The Commission, 1989. [study]
- and Don Clairmont. *Discrimination against Blacks in Nova Scotia: The Criminal Justice System*. Prepared for the Royal Commission on the Donald Marshall Jr, Prosecution. [Halifax, NS]: The Commission, 1990. [prose]
- *A Life on the Edge: Experiences in 'Black and White' in North America: Memoirs of Wilson Head*. Toronto: Dr Wilson Head Institute, 1995. [memoir]
Hearne, John [pseud. John Morris]. [1926–94]. b. Québec.
- *Voices under the Window*. London: Faber and Faber, 1955, 1973; London and Boston: Faber and Faber, 1985. [fiction]
- *A Stranger at the Gate*. London: Faber and Faber, 1956; Jamaica: Collins and Sangster, 1970. [fiction]
- *Faces of Love*. London: Faber and Faber, 1957. Rpt. *Eye of the Storm*. Boston: Little, Brown, 1958. [fiction]
- *The Autumn Equinox*. London: Faber and Faber, 1959. Rpt. *Autumn Equinox*. New York: Vanguard, 1961 [fiction]
- *Land of the Living*. London: Faber and Faber, 1961; New York: Harper & Row, 1962. [fiction]

- with Rex Nettleford. *Our Heritage*. [Mona, JA]: Department of Extra-mural Studies, University of the West Indies, 1963. [prose]
- [*A Stranger at the Gate*.] Russian translation. 1969. [fiction]
- [and Morris Cargill, together as John Morris]. *Fever Grass*. London: Collins, 1969; London: Fontana Books, 1970. [fiction]
- [and Morris Cargill, together as John Morris]. *The Candywine Development*. London: Collins, 1970; London: Fontana Books, 1971. [fiction]
- [and Morris Cargill, together as John Morris]. *The Checkerboard Caper*. New York: Citadel, 1975. [fiction]
- ed. *Carifesta Forum: An Anthology of Twenty Caribbean Voices*. Kingston, JA: Carifesta 76, 1976. [anthology]
- ed. *The Search for Solutions: Selections from the Speeches and Writings of Michael Manley*. Oshawa, ON: Maple House Publishing Company, 1976. [compilation]
- *The Sure Salvation*. London: Faber and Faber, 1981, 1985; New York: St Martin's Press, 1982. [fiction]
- [et al.] *Testing Democracy through Elections*. Ed. Marie Gregory. Kingston, JA: Bustamante Institute, 1985. [prose]

Hector, Cary. b. Haiti.
- [avec] Claude Moïse, Émile Ollivier. *1946–1976: Trente ans de pouvoir noir en Haïti*. Lasalle, QC: Collectif Paroles, 1976. [history]

Henderson, Anna Minerva. [1887–1987]. b. New Brunswick.
- *Citadel*. Fredericton: [Henderson], 1967. [poetry]

Henry, Gale.
- *Granny and Me*. Toronto: Women's Press, 1994. [juvenile]
- *Grandpa's Garden*. Toronto: Women's Press, 1995, 1997. [juvenile]

Henry, Keith S[tanley]. [1936–]. b. Barbados.
- *The Formative Influences in Earlier Twentieth Century African Responses to America*. Buffalo, NY: Council on International Studies, State University of New York at Buffalo, 1976. [history]
- *Black Politics in Toronto since World War One*. Toronto: Multicultural History Society of Ontario, 1981. [history]

Henson, Jim. b. United States.
- *Broken Shackles*. [Oshawa, ON?], 1889. Rpt. as *Broken Shackles: Old Man Henson from Slavery to Freedom*. Ed. Peter Meyler. Toronto: Natural Heritage Books, 2001. [autobiography, narrated to John Foster Jr, who published under the pseudonym, Glenelg]

Henson, Josiah. [1789–1883]. b. United States.
- *Life of Josiah Henson, Formerly a Slave, Now an Inhabitant of Canada, Narrated by Himself*. Boston: A.D. Phelps, 1849. [autobiography, narrated to Sam Eliot]
- *The Life of Josiah Henson, Formerly a Slave. As Narrated by Himself*. London: Charles Gilpin, Bishopsgate without; Edinburgh: Adam and Charles Black; Dublin: James Bernard Gilpin, 1852. [autobiography]
- *Truth Stranger Than Fiction: Father Henson's Story of His Own Life*. Boston: A.D. Phelps, 1849. Rpt. *Truth Stranger Than Fiction: Father Henson's Story of His Own Life*. Boston: J.P. Jewett; Cleveland: H.P.B. Jewett, 1858. [autobiography]

- *'Uncle Tom's Story of His Life': An Autobiography of the Rev. Josiah Henson (Mrs. Harriet Beecher Stowe's 'Uncle Tom'), from 1789 to 1876*. London: Christian Age, 1876. [biography, authored by John Lobb]
- *The Young People's Illustrated Edition of 'Uncle Tom's Story of His Life' (from 1789 to 1877)*. London: Christian Age Office, 1877. [biography, authored by John Lobb]
- *Uncle Tom's Story of Himself*. London, 1877. [authored by Lobb?]
- *Wirkliche Lebensgeschichte des Onkels Tom in Frau Beecher-Stowe's 'Onkel Tom's Hutte.'* Trans. Marie Schweiker. Cincinnati: Hitchcock & Walden, 1878. [biography]
- *'Truth Is Stranger Than Fiction.' An Autobiography of the Rev. Josiah Henson (Mrs. Harriet Beecher Stowe's 'Uncle Tom'), from 1789–1879*. Boston: B.B. Russell, 1879. [authored by Lobb?]
- *An Autobiography of the Rev. Josiah Henson ('Uncle Tom'), From 1789 to 1881*. London, ON: Schuyler, Smith, 1881. [authored by Lobb?]
- *Father Henson's Story of His Own Life*. New York: Corinth Books, 1962. ['autobiography']
- *The Life of Josiah Henson, Formerly a Slave*. [Dresden, ON: Uncle Tom's Cabin & Museum, 1965]. ['autobiography']
- 'An Autobiography of the Reverend Josiah Henson.' In *Four Fugitive Slave Narratives*. Reading, MA: Addison-Wesley Pub. Co., [1969]. [authored by Lobb?]

Heydorn, Bernard L[eon]. [1945–]. b. British Guiana [Guyana].
- *A Report on the Teaching of Reading and Language Arts to Slow Learners in the High School*. Toronto: Ontario Teachers' Federation, [1974]. [report]
- *Song of the West Indies*. St Augustine, TT: n.p., 1986. [poetry]
- *Heydorn Elementary Learning Profile, Grade 1–Grade 8*. Newmarket, ON: Learning Improvement Centre Inc., 1993. [test booklets]
- and Vivienne Niles Heydorn. *Dialect and/or Cultural Interference in Language Arts*. [Newmarket, ON: Learning Improvement Centre Inc.], 1993. [study]
- *Walk Good Guyana Boy*. Newmarket, ON: Learning Improvement Centre Inc., 1994. [short fiction]
- *Carnival Girl*. Newmarket, ON: Learning Improvement Centre Inc., 1996. [fiction]
- *Longtime Days*. Newmarket, ON: Learning Improvement Centre Inc., 1998, 1999. [memoir]

Heydorn, Malcolm W. [1940–]. b. British Guiana [Guyana].
- *Guyana at the Millennium Crossroads: A Psychosocial Perspective*. Ancaster, ON: M & L Counselling, 2000. [prose]

Heydorn, Vivienne N[iles]. [1946–].
- with Bernard Heydorn. *Dialect and/or Cultural Interference in Language Arts*. [Newmarket, ON: Learning Improvement Centre Inc.], 1993. [study]

Hill, Dan. [1954–]. b. Ontario.
- *Comeback*. Toronto: McClelland & Stewart / Bantam, 1983. [fiction]

Hill, Daniel G[rafton]. [1923–]. b. United States.
- *Negroes in Toronto, 1793–1865*. N.p.: n.p., 1963. [history]
- and Harold H[erbert]. Potter. *Negro Settlement in Canada, 1628–1965: A Survey*. [Ottawa: n.p.], 1966. [report presented to the Royal Commission on Bilingualism and Biculturalism]

- *Human Rights in Canada: A Focus on Racism.* [Ottawa: Canadian Labour Congress, 1977.] [prose]
- *Les Droits de la personne au Canada: Regard sur le racisme.* [Ottawa]: Congrès du travail du Canada, [1977?] [prose]
- *Study of Mind Development Groups, Sects, and Cults in Ontario: A Report to the Ontario Government.* [Toronto: Office of the Special Advisor, 1980.] [prose]
- *The Freedom-Seekers: Blacks in Early Canada.* Agincourt, ON: Book Society of Canada, 1981; Don Mills, ON: Stoddart, 1992. [history]
- *Regionalization – the Ontario Experience.* Edmonton: International Ombudsman Institute, 1986. [prose]
- and Marvin Schiff. *Human Rights in Canada: A Focus on Racism.* [Ottawa]: Canadian Labour Congress and the Human Rights Research and Education Centre, University of Ottawa, [1986]. [prose]
- and Marvin Schiff. *Human Rights in Canada: A Focus on Racism.* 2nd ed. Distributed with *Moving beyond Racism: Worship Resources and Background Materials.* Comp. by Division of Mission in Canada. [Toronto]: The United Church of Canada, [1987]. [prose]

Hill, Lawrence. [1957–]. b. Ontario.
- *Some Great Thing.* Winnipeg: Turnstone, 1992. [fiction]
- *Trials and Triumphs: The Story of African Canadians.* Toronto: Umbrella Press, 1993. [juvenile]
- *De grandes choses: Roman.* Trans. Robert Paquin. Saint-Boniface, MB: Les Éditions du Blé, 1995. [fiction]
- *Women of Vision: The Story of the Canadian Negro Women's Association, 1951–1976.* Toronto: Umbrella Press, 1996. [history]
- *Any Known Blood.* Toronto: HarperCollins; New York: Morrow, 1997. [fiction]
- *Black Berry, Sweet Juice: On Being Black and White in Canada.* Toronto: HarperFlamingo Canada, 2001. [prose]

Hill, Peter B[ernard]. [1945–]. b. Guyana.
- *The Bacoo.* Toronto: VanderHill Publishing, 1998. [fiction]
- *Vietnam and Other Reflections.* West Hill, ON: VanderHill Publishing, 1998. [poetry]

Hinds, Michael. [1954–].
- and Tony Castrilli. *The Spirit of Egypt in America.* Ed. Shadrock. Toronto: Fifth Ribb Publishing, 1995. [prose]

Holas, W[ilma]. P[atricia]. b. Grenada.
- *Millennium Minds: One Hundred Black Canadians.* Ottawa: Pan-African Publications, 2000. [prose]

Homer, Randolph Augustus. [1929–]. b. British Guiana [Guyana].
- *Blood River.* St-Laurent, QC: AFO Enterprises, 1988. [short fiction]

Hooks, Gwen. [1920–]. b. United States.
- *The Keystone Legacy: Reflections of a Black Pioneer.* Edmonton: Brightest Pebble Pub. Co., 1997. [memoir]

Hopkinson, Nalo. b. Trinidad.
- *Brown Girl in the Ring.* New York: Warner Books, 1998. [fiction]
- *Midnight Robber.* New York: Warner Books, 2000. [fiction]

- ed. *Whispers from the Cotton Tree Root: Caribbean Fabulist Fiction.* Montpelier, VT: Invisible Cities Press, 2000. [anthology]

Hopkinson, Slade [Abdur-Rahman Hopkinson]. [1934–]. b. Guyana.

- *The Four and Other Poems.* Barbados: Advocate Co., 1954. [poetry]
- *The Onliest Fisherman: A Medium-Length Play.* Port of Spain, TT: U.W.I. Extra Mural Department, 1967. [drama]
- *The Madwoman of Papine: Poems.* [Georgetown, Guyana]: Ministry of Education and Social Development, Curriculum Development Centre, 1976. [poetry]
- [as Abdur-Rahman Hopkinson]. *The Friend: Poems.* [Georgetown, Guyana]: Ministry of Education and Social Development. Curriculum Development Centre, 1976. [poetry]
- [as Abdur-Rahman Hopkinson]. *Snowscape with Signature: Poems, 1952–1992.* Leeds: Peepal Tree, 1993. [poetry]

Hosein, Clyde. [1940–]. b. Trinidad.

- *The Killing of Nelson John and Other Stories.* London: London Magazine Press, 1980. [short fiction]

Howe, Samuel Gridley. [1801–76]. b. United States.

- *The Refugees from Slavery in Canada West: Report to the Freedmen's Inquiry Commission.* Boston: Wright and Potter, 1864. [Howe was European-American, but his text includes many verbatim narratives by African Americans in Canada.]

Hubbard, Stephen L[angton]. [1961–]. b. Ontario.

- *Against All Odds: The Story of William Peyton Hubbard, Black Leader and Municipal Reformer.* Toronto: Dundurn Press, 1987. [biography]

Hudson, Karen. b. Nova Scotia.

- *The Jamaica Maroons and Twentieth Century Caribbean Immigration to Nova Scotia.* Cherrybrook, NS: Black Cultural Centre for Nova Scotia, 1990. [prose]

Huie, Bari. b. Jamaica.

- ed. *The Ketch-Up Book: A Collection of Jamaican Words and Phrases.* Scarborough, ON: Bargergol, 1993. [prose]
- ed. *Tell Mi fi True: A Collection of Jamaican Proverbs.* Scarborough, ON: Bargergol, 1993. [prose]

Husbands, Sybil. [1915–]. b. Guyana.

- *Serenity: Inspirational Poems.* Brampton, ON: Bald Eagle Press, 1994. [poetry]

Hyppolite, Michel-Ange. [1953–]. b. Haiti.

- *Anba-lakay: (pwezi kreyòl).* [Montréal?]: Êditions Nèg'bossal, [1984?]. [poetry]
- *Atlas/Leksik zo mounn.* Rivière des Prairies, QC: Edisyon Koukouy, 1989. [anatomical charts]
- *Zile nou: pwezi = Nôtre île = Our Island.* [Ontario]: Edisyon Production Koukourouj, 1995. [poetry]

I Shaka. [pseud.?] b. Jamaica.

- *The Word.* Toronto: I Shaka, 1983. [poetry]

Ifill, Lionel L. [1937–]. b. Trinidad?

- prep. *Readings in Canadian Economic Issues.* [Ottawa]: Media Algonquin, 1975. [prose]

Ishmael, John A. [1939–]. b. Guyana.

- *The Black Bug: The Genetic Bomb Has Arrived.* Winnipeg: National Publishing, 1991. [fiction]

- ed. *Constitutional Rights for Children: Turning the System Upside Down*. Winnipeg: National Publishing, 1992. [compilation]
Issajenko, Angella [Angella Taylor]. [1958–]. b. Jamaica.
- as told to Martin O'Malley and Karen O'Reilly. *Running Risks*. Toronto: Macmillan of Canada, 1990. [autobiography]
Iton, Richard. [1961–]. b. Québec.
- *Solidarity Blues: Race, Culture, and the American Left*. Chapel Hill, NC: University of North Carolina Press, 2000. [prose]
Jackson, Richard [L.] [1937–]. b. United States.
- et al. *Latin American and Caribbean Studies: An Exploratory Report with Recommendations for Carleton University*. Ottawa: Carleton University, [1972]. [report]
- *The Black Image in Latin American Literature*. Albuquerque: University of New Mexico Press, 1976. [prose]
- *Black Writers in Latin America*. Albuquerque: University of New Mexico Press, 1979. [prose]
- *The Afro-Spanish American Author: An Annotated Bibliography of Criticism*. New York: Garland, 1980. [prose]
- *Black Literature and Humanism in Latin America*. Athens, GA: University of Georgia Press, 1988. [prose]
- *The Afro-Spanish American Author II: The 1980s*. West Cornwall, CT: Locust Hill Press, 1989. [prose]
- *Black Writers and the Hispanic Canon*. New York: Twayne Publishers, 1997. [prose]
- *Black Writers and Latin America: Cross-Cultural Affinities*. Washington, DC: Howard University Press, 1998. [prose]
Jacob, Bianca.
- 'Man You Mus'.' In George Seremba et al., eds, *Beyond the Pale* (1996), 38–53. [drama]
Jacobs, Rayda. b. South Africa.
- *The Middle Children*. Ed. Charis Wahl. Toronto: Second Story Press, 1994. [short fiction]
Jacques, Maurice. [1939–]. b. Haiti.
- *Le Fils bâtard*. 1965. [drama]
- *Les Ancêtres du Messie*. 1968. [drama]
- *Nuit coloniale ou Cendres des marrons*. 1968. [drama]
- *Le Miroir: Poésie*. Sherbrooke, QC: Éditions Naaman, 1977. [poetry]
- *L'Ange du diable: Conte haïtien*. Sherbrooke, QC: Éditions Naaman, 1979. [short fiction]
- *Les Voix closes: Florilège*. Sherbrooke, QC: Éditions Naaman, 1980. [poetry]
James, Carl E. [1952–]. b. Jamaica.
- [et al.] *Losers and Winners: The Pursuit of Equality and Social Justice in Higher Education*. Toronto: Butterworths, 1982. [prose]
- [et al.]. *The Pursuit of Equality: Evaluating and Monitoring Accessibility to Post-Secondary Education in Ontario*. Toronto: Ministry of Education / Ministry of Colleges and Universities, 1982. [prose]
- [et al.] *What Jobs Pay: The Complete Guide to Careers and Salaries in Canada*. Edmonton: Hurtig, 1984. [guide]

- *Seeing Ourselves: Exploring Race, Ethnicity and Culture*. Oakville, ON: Instructional and Human Resource Development, Sheridan College, 1989; rev. ed., Toronto: Thompson Educational Publishing, Inc., 1995; 2nd ed., 1999. [prose]
- *Making It: Black Youth, Racism and Career Aspirations in a Big City*. Oakville, ON: Mosaic Press, 1990. [prose]
- *Career Equity for Youth*. Toronto: Guidance Centre, Ontario Institute for Studies in Education, 1993. [prose]
- and Adrienne Shadd, eds. *Talking about Difference: Encounters in Culture, Language and Identity*. Toronto: Between the Lines, 1994. Rpt. *Talking about Identity: Encounters in Race, Ethnicity, and Language*. Toronto: Between the Lines, 2001. [compilation]
- with Keren S. Brathwaite, eds. *Educating African Canadians*. Toronto: James Lorimer & Co., 1996. [compilation]
- ed. *Perspectives on Racism and the Human Services Sector: A Case for Change*. Toronto: University of Toronto Press, 1996. [compilation]
- with James L. Torczyner, et al. *Diversity, Mobility and Change: The Dynamics of Black Communities in Canada*. [Montreal]: McGill Consortium for Ethnicity and Strategic Social Planning, 1997. [report]
- with Vincent D'Oyley, eds. *Re/visioning: Canadian Perspectives on the Education of Africans in the Late Twentieth Century*. North York, ON: Captus Press, 1998. [compilation]
- ed. *Experiencing Difference*. Halifax, NS: Fernwood, 2000. [compilation]
James, Christopher. [1948–].
- *Rhapsody of the Satanic Dancer*. Vancouver: n.p., 1969; Berkeley, CA: Directions Press, 1970. [poetry]
- *Gilma Stein*. Vancouver: Gastown Saloon, 1970. Rpt. *Gilma Stein: A Novel Song*. Vancouver: West Coast Publications, 1970. [poetry and drama excerpt]
- 'and we are as one to be'; 'and the celestial;' 'the raving of hamlet'; and 'theme of winter.' N.p.: n.p., 1971. [mimeographed folio of poetry]
- *Two Sides*. [Toronto]: C. James, 1971. [poetry]
James, Darius. b. United States.
- *Negrophobia: An Urban Parable: A Novel*. New York: Carol Publishing Group / Citadel Press, 1992. [fiction]
- *Négrophobia*. Trans. ? Paris: L'Incertain, 1995. [fiction]
- *Nigurophobia*. Trans. Yamagata Hiroo. Tokyo: Hakusuisha, 1995.
- *That's Blaxploitation!: Roots of the Baadasssss 'tude (rated X by an all-whyte jury)*. New York: St Martin's / Griffin, 1995. [prose]
Jean, Fayolle S. b. Haiti.
- *Tenue de ville: Poésie*. Montréal: Cimage Québec, 1991. [poetry]
Jean, Michaëlle. [1957–]. b. Québec?
- coord. et réd. *La Sexualité blessée: Étude sur la violence sexuelle en milieu conjugal*. [Par] Regroupement provincial des maisons d'hébergement et de transition pour femmes victimes de violence. Montréal: Le Regroupement, 1987. [report]
Jean-Baptiste, Alfred. [1959–]. b. St. Lucia.
- *Caribbean English and the Literacy Tutor: Tutor's Kit*. Toronto: Toronto ALFA Centre, 1995. [prose with audio cassette]

Jean-Charles, Dary. [1950–]. b. Haiti.
- *Haïtianeiges*. Montréal: Édition Lagomatik, [1992?] [poetry]
- [et] Mozart-F. Longuefosse, Lenous Suprice. *Pages triangulaires: Poésie*. Montréal: Éditions des Intouchables, 1994. [poetry]
- *Encres brûlées: Poèmes*. Montréal: Humanitas, 1997. [poetry]
  L'Îlerrant: Poèmes. Brossard, QC: Humanitas, 2000. [poetry]
Jean-Pierre, Julio. [1940–]. b. Haiti.
- *Les Gens simples*. Montréal: Kauss, 1983. [poetry]
- *La Route de la soif*. [Montréal: Éditions Le Lambi, 1983.] [poetry]
- *L'Éternité provisoire: Poèmes*. Suivi de *Un simple geste d'amitié, un texte de Fernand Philipe-Auguste, écrit en hommage à Julio Jean-Pierre*, d'apres *les poèmes de la Route de la soif et Les Gens simples*. [Montréal-Nord, QC]: Éditions Le Lambi, 1994. [poetry]
Jing-Shin, I. [pseud. of Hugh B. Jones].
- *In Black and White*. Toronto: In Black and White, 1996. [prose]
Joachim, Sébastien. [1933–]. b. Haiti.
- *Le Français au collège: Une voie pour l'autoperfectionnement assisté*. Montréal: Presses de l'Université du Québec, 1978. [prose]
- *Le Nègre dans le roman blanc: Lecture sémiotique et idéologique de romans français et canadiens 1945–1977*. Montréal: Presses de l'Université de Montréal, 1980. [prose]
Johnson, Amelia E[tta]. Hall. [1858–1922]. b. Canada West [Ontario].
- *Clarence and Corinne; or, God's Way*. Philadelphia: American Baptist Publication Society, 1890. [fiction]
- *The Hazeley Family*. Philadelphia: American Baptist Publication Society, 1894. [fiction]
- *Martina Meriden; or, What Is My Motive?* Philadelphia: American Baptist Publication Society, 1901. [fiction]
Johnson, Kirk. [1973–]. b. Nova Scotia.
- with David Widgington. *Montréal Up Close: A Pedestrian's Guide to the City*. Montréal: Cumulus Press, 1998. [prose]
- *Companion Pieces*. Montréal: Cumulus Press, 1999. [poetry]
Johnson, Ruth. [1929–]. b. Jamaica.
- *Hospital Interpreting Services: The Use of Staff Volunteers at Toronto General*. Toronto: Multicultural Development Branch, [1977]. [prose]
- *Our Memories of Anansi: Collected for Anansi for All People Week, April 17–23, 1978*. [Toronto]: Teaching Aids, 1978. [compilation]
- coll., and Enid Lee, ed. *CORE: Stories and Poems Celebrating the Lives of Ordinary People Who Call Toronto Their Home*. Toronto: CORE, 1982. [compilation]
Johnson, William H.H. [1839–1905]. b. Indiana.
- *The Horrors of Slavery*. Vancouver: [n.p.], 1901. Rpt. *The Life of Wm. H.H. Johnson: From 1839–1900, and The New Race*. Vancouver: Bolam & Harnett, 1904. [prose]
Johnston, Leonard [Lenny]. b. Jamaica.
- *The Thoughts of Lenny*. Toronto: [Leonard Johnston], 1991. [aphorisms]
Johnstone, P[aul]. A[nthony]. [1931–89]. b. Jamaica.
- and David States. *Cultural Sensitization and the Black Community of Nova Scotia*. Halifax, NS: Nova Scotia Department of Education, 1981. [prose]

- *Being Black in the Family of Man*. Halifax, NS: Black Cultural Society, 1982. [prose]
- *The Life and Thoughts of Tony Johnstone*. Ed. Trevor Philips. Halifax, NS: Four East, 1991. [compilation]

Jonassaint, Jean. [1950–]. b. Haiti.
- [dir.] *Manu script*. [Par] Montfaucon Research Center. Montréal: Éditions Dérives, [1981?] [collage]
- *La Déchichure du (corps) texte et autres brèches*. Montréal: Nouvelle Optique; Paris: Dérives, 1984. [essays and poetry]
- *Le Pouvoir des mots, les maux du pouvoir: Des romanciers haïtiens de l'exil*. Paris: Éditions de l'Arcantère; Montréal: Presses de l'Université de Montréal, 1986. [prose]
- ed. *Frankétienne, écrivain haïtien*. [Montréal] *Dérives*. 53/54. 1986/1987. [prose]

Jones, Bernice.
- *The Adventures of Tom, the Cat Next Door*. Toronto: Lugus Publications, 1993. [juvenile]

Jones, Jocelyn [Ed]. [1944–].
- *Thundering Voices: An Extraordinary Reference Book That Is Not Only Useful but Fascinating to Read*. Scarborough, ON: [Jones], 1997. [aphorisms]
- *Voices for the Millennium*. Scarborough, ON: [J.E. Jones], 2000. [aphorisms]

Joseph, Clifton. [1957–]. b. Antigua.
- *Metropolitan Blues*. Toronto: Domestic Bliss, 1983. [poetry]

Joseph, Eleanor. b. Barbuda.
- and Rella Braithwaite. *Some Black Men: Profiles of Over One Hundred Black Men in Canada*. Scarborough, ON: Marlon Press, 1999. [biographies]

Joseph, Jean–Serge. b. Haiti.
- [et] Éternel Victor. *Haïti en péril*. Montréal: Kauss Éditeurs, 1988. [prose]

Joseph, Oni [Ingrid Windsor Joseph]. [196?–]. b. Québec.
- *Lyrically Imbalanced*. Ottawa: Onistudio, 2001. [poetry]

Joyette, Anthony T[revor]. [1949–]. b. St Vincent.
- *The Germination of Feeling: A Collection of Twenty-four Poems*. St Laurent, QC: n.p., 1980. [poetry]
- ed. *Vincentian Poets, 1950 to 1980*. St-Laurent, QC: AFO Enterprises, 1990. [anthology]
- with Pamela Edmonds. *Black Body: Race, Resistance, Response*. Halifax, NS: Dalhousie Art Gallery, 2001. [art show catalogue]

Jubal, Jahleel Hilkiah.
- *The Blatant Principles of Absolute Truth*. Toronto: Arawak Publishing House, 1980. [poetry]

Juste-Constant, Vogly [Voegeli]. [1946–]. b. Haiti.
- *Symphonie en do 'bourrique': Roman*. Montréal: Éditions des Quatre libertés, 1988. [fiction]

K., King. b. Antigua.
- *Rainbow Chase*. New York: Vantage, 1992. [juvenile]

Kabamba, Maguy. [1960–]. b. Zaire.
- *La Dette coloniale: Roman*. Montréal: Humanitas, 1995. [fiction]

Kasozi, A[bdu]. B[asajjabaka]. K[awalya]. [1942–]. b. Uganda.
- *The Integration of Black African Immigrants in Canadian Society: A Case Study of Toronto CMA, 1986.* Toronto: Canadian-African Newcomer Aid Centre of Toronto, 1988. [study]
- [et al.] *The Social Origins of Violence in Uganda, 1964–1985.* Montreal: McGill-Queen's University Press, 1994. [prose]
Kauss, Saint-John [John Nelson]. [1958–]. b. Haiti.
- *Autopsie du jour.* Port-au-Prince: Éditions Choucoune, 1979. [poetry]
- *Chants d'homme pour les nuits d'ombre.* Port-au-Prince: Éditions Choucoune, 1979. [poetry]
- *Hymne à la survie et deux poèmes en mission spéciale.* Port-au-Prince: Éditions Damour, 1980. [poetry]
- *Au Filin des coeurs.* [Montréal]: Éditions Nelson, [1981]. [poetry]
- *Ombres du Quercy: Poèmes.* Montréal: Éditions Nelson, 1981. [poetry]
- *Entre la parole et l'écriture.* Montréal: Les Éditions Nelson, 1982. [essay]
- *Zygoème, ou Chant d'amour dans le brouillard.* Montréal: Kauss Éditeurs, 1983. [poetry]
- *Twa degout: pwezi kreyol.* Port-au-Prince: Éditions Choucoune; Montréal: Kauss, 1984. [poetry]
- *La Danseuse exotique*, précedé de *Protocole ignifuge.* Port-au-Prince: Éditions Choucoune, 1987. [poetry]
- *Chansons de sang pour une suzeraine.* Port-au-Prince: Éditions Choucoune, 1989. [poetry]
- *Pages fragiles: Poèmes.* Montréal: Humanitas Nouvelle Optique, 1991. [poetry]
- *Testamentaire: Poèmes.* Montréal: Humanitas Nouvelle Optique, 1993. [poetry]
- *Territoires: Poèmes.* Montréal: Humanitas, 1995. [poetry]
- *Tarâmul copilarei / Territoire de l'enfance: Poemes in româneste de Andrei Stoiciu.* Montréal: Humanitas; Bucuresti: Editura Libra, 1996. [poetry in French, with Romanian translations by Stoiciu]
Kauss, Saint-Valentin [Valentino Nelson]. [1959–]. b. Haiti.
- *Du Sommet de la pente douce au pied de la pente raide.* Montréal: Éditions Cercle littérature ésotérique, 1980. [poetry]
- *Au Verso de mes déchirures.* Montréal: Les Éditions Nelson, 1981. [poetry]
- *Gants du lendemain: Poésies '80.* Montréal: Éditions Nelson, 1981. [poetry]
- *-et puis dans sa fureur, le vent: Poèmes 82.* Montréal: Kauss, 1983. [poetry]
- *Mille et une nuits de grève intérieur.* Port-au-Prince: Éditions Choucoune, 1989. [poetry]
- *Oracles du visible: Poèmes.* Montréal: Humanitas / Nouvelle Optique, 1992. [poetry]
- *Cinq grandes stances par-dessus bord jetées.* Montréal: Humanitas, 1996. [poetry]
Keens-Douglas, Richardo. b. Grenada.
- 'Once upon an Island.' In *Take Five: The Morningside Dramas.* Ed. Dave Carley. Winnipeg: Blizzard Publishing, 1991. 97–126. [drama]
- *The Nutmeg Princess.* Toronto: Annick, 1992. [juvenile]
- *Le Mystère de l'île aux Épices.* Trans. Raymonde Longval. Toronto: Editions Annick, 1992. [juvenile]

– *El misterio de la Isla de las Especias*. Trans. Shirley Langer. [Toronto]: Annick, 1992. [juvenile]
– *La Diablesse and the Baby: A Caribbean Folktale*. Toronto: Annick, 1994. [juvenile]
– *La Diablesse et le bébé: Un conte traditionnel des Caraïbes*. Trans. Christiane Duchesne. Toronto: Annick, 1994. [juvenile]
– *Freedom Child of the Sea*. Toronto: Annick, 1995. [juvenile]
– 'Obeah Man.' In *Another Perfect Piece: Monologues from Canadian Plays*. Ed. Tony Hamill. Toronto: Playwrights Canada Press, 1995. 69–70. [drama]
– *Grandpa's Visit*. Toronto: Annick Press, 1996. [juvenile]
– *The Miss Meow Pageant*. Toronto: Annick Press, 1998. [juvenile]
– *Mama God, Papa God: A Caribbean Tale*. London: Tradewind Books, 1999. [juvenile]
– *The Nutmeg Princess*. Toronto: Playwrights Canada Press, 2000. [drama]
– *The Trial of the Stone: A Folktale*. Toronto: Annick, 2000. [juvenile]
Kelly, Jenny. b. Jamaica.
– *Under the Gaze: Learning to Be Black in White Society*. Halifax, NS: Fernwood, 1998. [prose]
Kennedy, Cyril J.
– *The Gift*. Montreal: Mondiale, 1981. [poetry]
Kester, Norman G. [1962–]. b. South Africa.
– *From Here to District Six: A South African Memoir with New Poetry, Prose and Other Writings*. Toronto: District Six Press, 2000. [memoir, poetry, prose]
Khenti, Akwatu. b. Jamaica.
– *The African Canadian Heritage in Historical Perspective*. [N.p.: n.p., 1996?] [prose]
King, Boston. [c.1760–1802]. b. British America [United States].
– 'Memoirs of the Life of Boston King, a Black Preacher, Written by Himself during His Residence at Kingswood School.' *Methodist Magazine* 21 (1798): 105–10, 157–61, 209–13, 261–5. [autobiography]
– 'Memoirs of the Life of Boston King, a Black Preacher, Written by Himself, during His Residence at Kingswood-School.' 1798. Rpt. in *Unchained Voices: An Anthology of Black Authors in the English-Speaking World of the 18th Century*. Ed. Vincent Carretta. Lexington, KY: University Press of Kentucky, 1996. 351–68. [autobiography]
Kly, Y[ussuf]. N[aim]. [1935–]. b. United States.
– *The U.S. Human Rights Foreign Policy, the Black Minority in the U.S., and International Law*. Lévis, QC: International Academic Press, [1979]. [prose]
– *International Law and the Black Minority in the U.S*. Ottawa and Atlanta, GA: Clarity Press, 1985; 1990. [essay]
– *The Black Book: The True Political Philosophy of Malcolm X (El Hajj Malik El Shabazz)*. Ottawa and Atlanta, GA: Clarity Press, 1986. [prose and poetry]
– *The Anti-Social Contract*. Atlanta, GA: Clarity Press; Windsor, ON: Clarity International, 1989. [prose]
– [et al.] *Overcoming Systemic Discrimination against Aboriginal People in Saskatchewan: Brief to the Indian Justice Review Committee and the Métis Justice Review Committee, November 1991*. Regina: Prairie Justice Research, School of Human Justice, University of Regina, 1992. [prose]

- *A Popular Guide to Minority Rights.* Regina: International Human Rights Association of American Minorities, 1995. [prose]
- *Societal Development and Minority Rights.* Regina: Clarity Press, 1997; Atlanta, GA: Clarity Press, 1997. [prose]

Kofie, Martha. [1967–]. b. Québec.
- with Nancy Chong and Kwanza Msingwana. *Only Mountains Never Meet: A Collection of Stories by Three New Writers.* Toronto: Well Versed Publications, 1993. [short fiction]

Kom, Ambroise. [1946–]. b. Cameroun.
- *Le Harlem de Chester Himes.* Sherbrooke, QC: Éditions Naaman, 1978. [essay]
- dir. *Dictionnaire des oeuvres littéraires négro-africaines de langue française: Des origines à 1978.* Sherbrooke, QC: Éditions Naaman; Paris: ACCT, 1983. [guide]
- dir. *Mélanges: Littérature négro-africaine de langue française.* Rabat, Morocco: Diffusion Laporte, Libraririe aux Belles Images, 1984. [guide]
- *George Lamming et le destin des Caraïbes.* LaSalle, QC: Didier, 1986. [essay]
- *Éducation et démocratie en Afrique: Le temps des illusions.* Paris: L'Harmattan, 1996. [prose]

Ku-soonogo [pseud.] b. Jamaica.
- *From Nigeria with Love.* Brampton, ON: Bazba Theatrical Players Inc., 1993. [poetry]

Kuwabong, Dannabang. [1955–]. b. Ghana.
- *Echoes from Dusty Rivers.* Hamilton, ON: Capricornus Enterprises, 1999. [poetry]

Kwamdela, Odimumba [John Ashton Brathwaite]. [1942–]. b. Barbados.
- *A Black British Soldier.* Toronto: 21st Century Book, 1969; rev. ed., Toronto: 21st Century Press, 1969; 2nd ed., Brooklyn, NY: Kibo Books, 1986. Rev. ed. *Black British Soldier.* Brooklyn, NY: Kibo Books, 1999. [memoir]
- *Soul in the Wilderness.* Toronto: 21st Century Book, 1970, 1977; rev. ed., Brooklyn: Kibo Books, 1993. [memoir]
- *Niggers ... This Is CANADA: C-old A-nti N-iggers A-nd D-efinitely A-merican.* Toronto: 21st Century Book, 1971. Rpt. *Niggers ... This Is Canada.* New York: Kibo Books, 1986. [fiction]
- *The Grassroots Philosopher.* Toronto: 21st Century Book, 1972. 2nd. ed. Brooklyn, NY: Kibo Books, 1992. [poetry]
- *The Prophet Next Door / Children of Africa: Thirty Sure Steps to Black Freedom.* Brooklyn, NY: Kibo Books, 1981, 1992. [poetry]
- *Raining Ruins and Rockstones.* Brooklyn, NY: Kibo Books, 1981, 1992. [short fiction]
- *Blood-Boiling Black Blues.* Brooklyn, NY: Kibo Books, 1983. 2nd ed. Brooklyn, NY: Kibo Books, 1989. [poetry]
- *Black British Soldier / Niggers ... This Is Canada.* Brooklyn, NY: Kibo Books, 1986. [combined edition of previously separately issued works / memoir and short fiction]
- *Back to Penny Hole Forever.* Brooklyn, NY: Kibo books, 1997. [memoir and short fiction]
- *Searching Soul Down Inna Southern Africa.* New York: Deep Roots Books, 1998. [memoir]
- *Soul Surviving Up in Canada.* New York: Deep Roots Books, 1998. [memoir]

L'Abbé, Sonnet. b. Alberta?

– *A Strange Relief.* Toronto: McClelland & Stewart, 2001. [poetry]

Laferrière, Dany. [1953–]. b. Haiti.

– *Comment faire l'amour avec un nègre sans se fatiguer: Roman.* Montréal: VLB, 1985; Paris: P. Belfond, 1989; Paris: Éditions J'ai lu, 1990. [fiction]

– *How to Make Love to a Negro: A Novel.* Trans. David Homel. Toronto: Coach House, 1987; London: Bloomsbury, 1991. [fiction]

– *Éroshima.* Montréal: VLB, 1987; Montréal: Éditions Typo, 1998. [fiction]

– *Eroshima.* Trans. David Homel. Toronto: Coach House, 1991. [fiction]

– *Konsten att älska med en neger utan att bli utmattad.* Trans. Tony Andersson. Stockholm: Tidens Förlag, 1991. [fiction]

– *L'Odeur du café: Récit.* Montréal: VLB, 1991; Montréal: Typo, 1999. [fiction]

– *Eroshima.* Trans. Chris van de Poel. Belgium: Kritak, 1992; Holland: Goossens, 1992. [fiction]

– *Le Goût des jeune filles: Roman.* Montréal: VLB, 1992. [fiction]

– *Vrijen Met Een Neger Tot Je Zwart Ziet.* Trans. Chris van de Poel. Belgium: Kritak, 1992; Holland: Goossens, 1992. [fiction]

– *An Aroma of Coffee.* Trans. David Homel. Toronto: Coach House, 1993. [fiction]

– *Cette grenade dans la main du jeune nègre est-elle une arme ou un fruit?: Roman.* Montréal: VLB, 1993. Rpt. Montréal: Typo, 2000. [fiction]

– [*L'Odeur du café: Récit.*] Trans. Korea: Inner World Publishing Co., 1994. [fiction]

– *Chronique de la dérive douce.* Montréal: VLB, 1994. [poetry]

– *Dining with the Dictator.* Trans. David Homel. Toronto: Coach House, 1994. [fiction]

– *Why Must a Black Writer Write about Sex?* Trans. David Homel. Toronto: Coach House, 1994. [fiction]

– [et al.] *Dialogue d'île en île, de Montréal à Haiti: Dialogue épistolaire entre Jacques Godbout et Émile Ollivier, Monique Proulx et Dany Laferrière, Paul Chamberland et Serge Legagneur, Jacques Brault et Jean-Richard Laforest.* [Montréal]: Éditions du CIDIHCA, 1996. [prose]

– *Pays sans chapeau.* Outremont, QC: Lanctôt, 1996, 1999. Rpt. [St-Laurent, QC]: Édition du Club Québec loisirs, [1997?] [fiction]

– *La Chair du maître.* Montréal: Lanctôt éditeurs, 1997. [fiction]

– *Le Charme des après-midi sans fin.* [Outremont, QC]: Lanctôt, 1997. Rpt. Paris: Le Serpent à plumes, 1998. [fiction]

– *Como hacer el amor con un negro sin cansarse.* Trans. Lluis Maria Todo. Barcelona: Ediciones Destino, 1997. [fiction]

– *Down among the Dead Men.* Trans. David Homel. Toronto: Douglas & McIntyre, 1997. [fiction]

– *A Drifting Year.* Trans. David Homel. Toronto: Douglas & McIntyre, 1997. [fiction]

– *Le Cri des oiseaux fous: Roman.* Outremont, QC: Lanctôt, 2000; Paris: Le Serpent à plumes, 2000. Rpt. [St-Laurent, QC]: Édition du club Québec loisirs, [2000]. [fiction]

– *J'écris comme je vis.* [Interviewed by Bernard Magnier.] Outremont, QC: Lanctôt, 2000; Lyon: La passe du vent, 2000. [interview transcript]

– *Je suis fatigué.* Outremont, QC: Lanctôt, 2001. [prose]

Laforest, Jean-Richard. [1940–]. b. Haiti.

– *Insoupçonne.* Port-au-Prince: Librairie indigène, 1960. [prose]

- *Le Divan des alternances.* Montréal: Nouvelle Optique, 1970. [poetry]
- [et al.] *Dialogue d'île en île, de Montréal à Haiti: Dialogue épistolaire entre Jacques Godbout et Émile Ollivier, Monique Proulx et Dany Laferrière, Paul Chamberland et Serge Legagneur, Jacques Brault et Jean-Richard Laforest.* [Montréal]: Éditions du CIDIHCA, 1996. [prose]
- *Poèmes de la terre pénible.* Montréal: Équateur, 1998. [poetry]

Langford, F.R. [d. 1915]. b. United States.
- comp. *A Call from Zion: Jubilee Songs and Old Revival Hymns.* Weymouth, NS: n.p., 1882. [compilation]

Laroche, Maximilien. [1937–]. b. Haiti.
- *Haïti et sa littérature.* [Montréal]: AGEUM, 1963. [essay]
- *Portrait de l'Haïtien.* [Dans] *L'Haïtien.* Montréal: Éditions de Saint-Marie, 1968. [essay]
- réd. *Le Temps des Lilas.* [Par] Marcel Dubé. Montréal: Leméac, 1969. [prose]
- *Marcel Dubé.* Montréal: [Fides, 1970]. [essay]
- *Le Miracle et la métamorphose: Essai sur les littératures du Québec et d'Haïti.* Montréal: Éditions du Jour, [1970]. [essay]
- *Deux études sur la poésie et l'idéologie québécoises.* Québec: Institut supérieur des sciences humaines, Université Laval, 1975. [essay]
- *L'Image comme Echo: Essais sur la littérature et la culture haïtiennes.* Montréal: Éditions Nouvelle Optique, [1978]. [essay]
- *Le Romancero aux étoiles et l'oeuvre romanesque de Jacques-Stéphen Alexis.* Paris: Éditions Fernand Nathan, 1978. [prose]
- *La Littérature haïtienne: Identité, langue, réalité.* [Montréal]: Leméac, 1981. [essay]
- *Trois études sur 'Folie' de Marie Chauvet.* Québec: GRELCA, 1983. [essay]
- et al. *Anthologie de la nouvelle poésie créole: Caraïbe, Océan Indien: Koute pou tan! Akout pou tande!* Coord. Lambert Félix Prudent. [Paris]: Éditions Caribéenes, 1984. [anthology]
- *L'Avènement de la littérature haïtienne.* Sainte-Foy, QC: GRELCA, 1987. [essay]
- *Contribution à l'étude du réalisme merveilleux.* [Sainte-Foy, QC]: GRELCA / Université Laval, 1987. [essay]
- *Le Patriarche, le marron et la dossa: Essai sur les figures de la gémellité dans le roman haïtien.* Sainte-Foy, QC: GRELCA, 1988. [essay]
- [réd.] *Tradition et modernité dans les littératures francophones d'Afrique et d'Amérique: Actes du colloque tenu à l'Université Laval, le 5 mars 1988.* Sainte-Foy, QC: GRELCA, 1988. [compilation]
- *La Découverte de l'Amérique par les Américaines: Essais de littérature comparée.* Sainte-Foy, QC: GRELCA, 1989. [essays]
- *La Double Scène de la représentation: Oraliture et littérature dans la Caraïbe.* Sainte-Foy, QC: GRELCA, 1991. [essays]
- [avec] H. Nigel Thomas, Euridice Figueiredo. *Juan Bobo, Jan Sot, Ti Jan et Bad John: Figures littéraires de la Caraïbe.* Sainte-Foy, QC: GRELCA, 1991. [essays]
- *Dialectique de l'américanisation.* [Sainte-Foy, QC]: GRELCA, 1993. [essay]
- *Sémiologie des apparences.* Sainte-Foy, QC: GRELCA, 1994. [essay]
- [dir.] *Bibliographie d'Haïti 1994.* Sainte-Foy, QC: GRELCA, 1995. [bibliography]
- *Hier: analphabètes, aujourd'hui: autodidactes, demain: lettrés.* Sainte-Foy, QC: GRELCA, 1996. [essay]

– *Bizango: Essai de mythologie haïtienne*. Sainte-Foy, QC: GRELCA, 1997. [essay]
Lawrence, Correena. [1976–]. b. Nova Scotia.
– with Grace May Lawrence and Daniel Lawrence. *Reflections to the Third Power*. Ed. Jacqueline Zena Lawrence. Digby, NS: Grace May Lawrence, 1989. [poetry and fiction]
Lawrence, Daniel. [1951–]. b. Nova Scotia.
– with Grace May Lawrence and Correena Lawrence. *Reflections to the Third Power*. Ed. Jacqueline Zena Lawrence. Digby, NS: Grace May Lawrence, 1989. [poetry and fiction]
Lawrence, Grace May. [1928–]. b. Nova Scotia.
– with Daniel Lawrence and Correena Lawrence. *Reflections to the Third Power*. Ed. Jacqueline Zena Lawrence. Digby, NS: Grace May Lawrence, 1989. [poetry and fiction]
Lawrence, Trevor. b. Jamaica.
– *Hey Lickle Bwoy*. Rosenort, MB: Prairie View Press, 1996. [poetry]
Leclair, Didier. [196?–]. b. Québec.
– *Toronto, je t'aime*. Ottawa: Les Éditions du Vermillon, 2000. [fiction]
Legagneur, Serge. [1937–]. b. Haiti.
– *Textes interdits*. Montréal: Éditions de l'Estérel, 1966. [poetry]
– *Textes en croix*. Montréal: Éditions Nouvelle Optique, [1978]. [poetry]
– *Le Crabe*. Montréal: Ésterel, 1981. [poetry]
– *Inaltérable*. Saint-Lambert, QC: Éditions du Norôit, 1983. [poetry]
– *Textes muets*. Saint-Lambert, QC: Éditions du Norôit, 1987; Toulon: Table rase, 1987. [poetry]
– *Glyphes*. Montréal: Équateur, 1989. [poetry]
– [et al.] *Dialogue d'île en île, de Montréal à Haiti: Dialogue épistolaire entre Jacques Godbout et Émile Ollivier, Monique Proulx et Dany Laferrière, Paul Chamberland et Serge Legagneur, Jacques Brault et Jean-Richard Laforest*. [Montréal]: Éditions du CIDIHCA, 1996. [prose]
– *Poèmes choisis, 1961–1997*. Montréal: Éditions du Norôit, 1997. [poetry]
Leslie, Lincoln D. [1952–].
– *In the Minds of Many*. [Lachine, QC?]: n.p., 1987. [poetry]
– *Fact between a Thin Line*. [Lachine, QC]: U.S.V.I. Productions, 1990. [poetry]
Levene, Desmond Lloyd. b. Jamaica.
– *The Other Side: Rastaman Vibrations*. Downsview, ON: Black Fan Publishing, 1988. [fiction]
Lewis, Ray. [1910–]. b. Ontario.
– As told to John Cooper. *Shadow Running: Ray Lewis, Canadian Railway Porter and Olympic Athlete*. Toronto: Umbrella Press, 1999. [memoir]
Lewis, Sharon [Mareeka]. [1965–]. b. Ontario.
– and Maxine Bailey. 'Sistahs.' *Canadian Theatre Review* 83 (Summer 1995): 52–68. [drama]
– and Maxine Bailey. *Sistahs*. Toronto: Playwrights Canada Press, 1998. [drama]
– 'Poverty and Love – Indigo.' In *Mercury Retrograde and Other Stories by Women*. By Camille Hernandez-Ramdwar, Sharon Mareeka Lewis, et al. Toronto: Sister Vision, 1999. 30–57. [short fiction]

- and Maxine Bailey. 'Sistahs.' In Sears, ed., *Testifyin'*, Vol. 1 (2000), 277–329. [drama]

Lewis, [Thelma] Theresa. b. Trinidad.
- *Caribbean Folk Legends*. Stratford, ON: Williams-Wallace, 1989; Trenton, NJ: Africa World Press, 1990. [traditional tales]
- *Things Elusive*. Stratford, ON: Williams-Wallace, 1990. [poetry]
- *The Yarn Spinner*. Stratford, ON: Williams-Wallace Publishers, 1992. [poetry]

Lochan, Dick. [1948–]. b. Jamaica?
- *'Doh Make Joke': Caribbean Dialect*. Scarborough, ON: We Lingo Publications, 1987. [poetry]
- *'Fuh True?': Dialect Writings of Dick Lochan*. Scarborough, ON: We Lingo Publications, 1989. [poems and stories]

Loeffelholz, Joycelyn [Joycelyn Loeffelholz-Rea]. b. Jamaica.
- *Portraits*. Ottawa: Commoners' Publishing Society, 1988. [poetry]
- *The Evolution*. Ottawa: Boyd McRubie Communications, 1989. [poetry]
- *Snakes, Ladders, and Skyways: A Book of Poems and Illustrations*. Ottawa: Legas, 1993. [poetry]
- *Island Interlude: A Memoir*. Ottawa: LEGAS, 1998. [memoir]
- [as Joycelyn Loeffelholz-Rea]. *Looking Forward at the Past: A History of the Unitarian Congregation of Ottawa*. Ottawa: LEGAS, 1999. [history]

Loguen, J[ermain]. W[esley]. [1814–72]. b. United States.
- *The Rev. J.W. Loguen, As a Slave and As a Freeman: A Narrative of Real Life*. Syracuse, NY: J.G.K. Truair & Company, Printers, 1859. [autobiography]

Longuefosse, Mozart-F. b. Haiti.
- [et] Dary Jean-Charles, Lenous Suprice. *Pages triangulaires: Poésie*. Montréal: Éditions des Intouchables, 1994. [poetry]

Lopez, Basil. b. Jamaica.
- *The New Jamaica: Poems*. Kingston, JA: [Basil Lopez], 1966. [poetry]
- *On Top of Blue Mountain*. [Spanish Town, JA: B. Lopez], 1976. [poetry]
- *Easy Street*. Ed. Lorna Nembhard. Kingston, JA: JAMAL, 1981. [short fiction]
- *Only As the Wind Blows*. Bramalea, ON: Bazba Theatrical Players Inc., 1987. [short fiction]

Lopez, Sandra. [1957–]. b. Trinidad.
- 'BCAACP [British Columbia Association for the Advancement of Colored People] Summer Project 1976: A Report of the History of the Association from 1958–1975.' [Vancouver?], unpublished, 1976. [report]
- *The U Factor: Weight Management Program*. Toronto: Key Porter Books, 1990. [prose]

Louis, Michel Salmador. [1939–]. b. Haiti.
- [et al.] *Les Femmes de la CUQ en mutation?: Un essai préliminaire sur la dynamique du changement chez la femme québécoise*. [Sainte-Foy, QC: Centre integré d'études sociales], 1981. [prose]
- *Pour la germination des graines: Poèmes en français et en créule*. Sherbrooke, QC: Éditions Naaman, 1982. [poetry]
- *Syndiques, syndicat, syndicalisme au STTELF: Principes d'un essai sur l'évolution et la contre-évolution du mouvement syndicaliste québécois*. [Sainte-Foy, QC: Centre integré d'études sociales], 1982. [prose]

- *Ateliers de sensibilisation aux relations interculturelles pour les employées et employés de la ville de Québec: Cahier du participant.* [Sainte-Foy, QC: IRFIQ et al., 1994. [prose]
- [avec Lidia Boloz]. *Immigration et travail au feminin dans la Communauté urbaine de Québec: Le Cas des Polonaises.* Sainte-Foy, QC: IRFIQ, 1994. [prose]
- [et Pierre Toussaint]. *Regards de jeunes sur le racisme: Des Dessins qui parlent.* Sainte-Foy, QC: IRFIQ, 1996. [juvenile]

Louis-Jean, Antonio. [1941–]. b. Haiti.
- *La Crise de possession et la possession dramatique.* Ottawa: Les Éditions Leméac, 1970. [prose]

Luc, Jean [pseud. of Yves Montas]. [1930–]. b. Haiti.
- *Structures économiques et lutte nationale populaire en Haïti.* Montréal: Éditions Nouvelle Optique, 1976. [prose]

Lumu, N[ehemia]. B[osa]. E[ryani]. [1911–]. b. Uganda.
- *Development of the African Youth of Today and Tomorrow.* Toronto: Lumu Graphics, 1991. [prose]

Maart, Rozena. [1962–]. b. South Africa.
- *Talk about It!* Stratford, ON: Williams-Wallace, 1990. [poetry]
- *The Absence of Knowledge of White Consciousness in Contemporary Feminist Theory, or Consciousness, Knowledge and Morality.* Toronto: Awomandla, 1999. [essay]
- *Talk about It!: From District 6 to Lavender Hill.* Toronto: Awomandla! Publishers, 2000. [prose]

Magloire, Adéline [Adéline Magloire Chancy]. [1932–]. b. Haiti.
- *Le Mal de vivre.* Port-au-Prince: Éditions du Verseau, 1968. [fiction]
- *Autopsie in vivo. Le Sexe mythique.* Port-au-Prince: Éditions du Verseau, 1975. [fiction, preceded by essay]
- [as Adéline Magloire Chancy]. *L'Analphabétisme chez les femmes immigrantes haitiennes.* Montréal: Librairie de l'Université de Montréal, [1981]. [prose]
- [as Adéline Magloire Chancy]. *La Gramè = Grammaire créole.* Montréal: Meizon d'Ayiti, 1982. [prose]
- [as Adéline Magloire Chancy]. *Faut-il nommer le racisme?* [Montréal: CIDIHCA, 1986.] [prose]

Magloire, Hébert. [1911–]. b. Haiti.
- *Actualité de Jacques Romain: Le Christ noir.* N.p.: n.p., [1975]. [prose]
- *Pour que le jour se lève sur la rosée: Cahier des textes francophones.* Montréal: Societé de belles-lettres G. Maheux, 1976. [prose]

Magloire-Castille. b. Haiti.
- *Des Larmes de sang: Prose et poésie.* Montréal: Kauss, 1982. [poetry and prose]

Maguire, Dianne [Elizabeth Dianne Rose Kelvin Maguire]. [1947–]. b. Jamaica.
- *Dry Land Tourist.* Toronto: Sister Vision Press, 1991. [short fiction]

Malvin, John. [1795–1880]. b. United States.
- *A Narrative Containing an Authentic Account of his fifty years' struggle in the state of Ohio in behalf of the American slave, and the equal rights of all men before the law without reference to race or color; forty-seven years of said time being expended in the city of Cleveland.* Cleveland, OH, 1879. [autobiography]

- *North into Freedom: The Autobiography of John Malvin, Free Negro, 1795–1880.* Cleveland, OH: Press of Western Reserve University, 1966.

Mandiela, Ahdri Zhina. b. Jamaica.
- *'Speshal Rikwes.'* Toronto: Sister Vision, 1985. [poetry]
- *Dark Diaspora – in Dub: A Dub Theatre Piece.* Toronto: Sister Vision, 1991. [drama]
- *'dark diaspora ... in dub.'* In Sears, ed., *Testifyin'*, Vol. 1 (2000), 439–70. [drama]

Manigat, Max. b. Haiti.
- *Haïtiana 1991–1995: Bibliographie haïtiane.* Montréal: Éditions du CIDIHCA, 1997. [bibliography]

Manley, Rachel [Rachel Manley Drummond]. [1947–]. b. England.
- *Prisms.* Kingston, JA: Hyde, Held and Blackburn Ltd, 1972. [poetry]
- *Poems 2.* [Wildey, Barbados: Coles Printery], 1981. [poetry]
- ed. *Edna Manley: The Diaries.* London: Andre Deutsch, 1989. [prose]
- *A Light Left On.* Leeds: Peepal Tree Press, 1992. [poetry]
- [as Rachel Manley]. *Drumblair: Memories of a Jamaican Childhood.* Toronto: Alfred A. Knopf Canada, 1996; Kingston, JA: Ian Randle Publishers, 1996. Rpt. Toronto: Vintage Canada, 1997. [memoir]
- [as Rachel Manley]. *Slipstream: A Daughter Remembers.* Toronto: Alfred A. Knopf Canada, 2000. [memoir]

Manning, William H[arry]. b. Jamaica.
- *The Doyen of Vere.* Richmond Hill, ON: LTL Enterprizes [*sic*], 1991. [biography]
- *My Name Is Eva: A Biography of Eva Smith.* Toronto: Natural Heritage Books / The Collector's Choice, 1995. [biography]

Mansa.
- [Untitled]. In *Mercury Retrograde and Other Stories by Women.* By Camille Hernandez-Ramdwar, Mansa et al. Toronto: Sister Vision, 1999. 58–85. [short fiction and poetry]

Marcelline, Ashley. b. Trinidad.
- *Ashley Marcelline's Black Film and Video Guide.* Thornhill, ON: Black Cinema Network, 1994. [guide]

Mariamour, Jean-Hubert [pseud. of Jean-Hubert Papailler]. [1916–]. b. Haiti.
- *Fleurs d'ombre et paillettes d'écumes.* Laprairie, QC: Séminaire des Saints-Apôtres, 1954. [prose and poetry]
- *Coup d'ailes.* Montréal: Imprimerie Saint-Joseph, 1956. [poetry]
- *Le Bicolore, symbole de l'Unité nationale.* Port au Prince, 1959. [essay]
- *Les Laboureurs de la mer.* [Québec?], 1959. [fiction]

Marrant, John. [1755–91]. b. British America [United States].
- *A Narrative of the Lord's Wonderful Dealings with John Marrant, a Black (Now Going to Preach the Gospel in Nova-Scotia) Born in New-York, in North America.* London: Gilbert and Plummer, 1785. [autobiography]
- *A Funeral Sermon Preached by the Desire of the Deceased, John Lock; The Text Chosen by Himself, from the Epistle of St. Paul to the Phillipians, Chap. I. Ver. 21.* N.p.: n.p., 1787. [bound with *Journal*, 1790, below]
- *A Sermon Preached the 24th day of June, 1789, Being the Festival of Saint John the Baptist, at the Request of the Right Worshipful the Grand Master Prince Hall, and the Rest of the*

Brethren of the African Lodge of the Honorable Society of Free and Accepted Masons in Boston. Boston: The Bible & Heart, 1789. Rpt. in *Black Atlantic Writers of the Eighteenth Century: Living the New Exodus in England and the Americas*. Ed. Adam Potkay and Sandra Burr. New York: St Martin's Press, 1995. 106–22. [prose]

- *A Journal of the Rev. John Marrant, from August the 18th, 1785, to the 16th of March, 1790. To Which are Added Two Sermons*. London, 1790. [autobiography]
- *A Narrative of the Life of John Marrant, of New York in North America Giving an Account of His Conversion When Only Fourteen Years of Age* ... Halifax, NS: Printed at the office of J. Nicholson & Co., 1808, 1812, 1813, 1815. [autobiography]
- *A Narrative of the Lord's Wonderful Dealings with John Marrant, a Black (Now Going to Preach the Gospel in Nova-Scotia), Born in New-York, in North-America*. 1785. Rpt. in *Black Atlantic Writers of the Eighteenth Century: Living the New Exodus in England and the Americas*. Ed. Adam Potkay and Sandra Burr. New York: St Martin's Press, 1995. 75–105. [autobiography]
- *A Narrative of the Lord's Wonderful Dealings with John Marrant, a Black (Now Going to Preach the Gospel in Nova-Scotia), Born in New-York, in North-America*. [...] 4th edition. London: Printed for the Author, by R. Hawes, No. 40, Dorset-Street Spitalfields, [1785]. Rpt. in *Unchained Voices: An Anthology of Black Authors in the English-Speaking World of the 18th Century*. Ed. Vincent Carretta. Lexington, KY: University Press of Kentucky, 1996. 110–33. [autobiography]

Mars, Frantz. [1951–]. b. Haiti.
- *Trajectoire poétique*. Montréal: Éditions Déluy, [1988]. [poetry]
- *Les Fruits de la passion: Poèmes*. [Montréal]: Edisyon Lagomatik, 1990. [poetry]
- *Paroles intimes: Poèmes*. Montréal: Humanitas, 1995. [poetry]

Marshall, Harold. b. Barbados.
- *Full Fathom Five*. Barbados: n.p., 1973. [poetry]

Martin, W[inston]. L[loyd]. [Stan]. [1942–]. b. Jamaica.
- *Loyalty and Integrity*. Hamilton, ON: Capricornus Enterprises, 1996. [autobiography]
- *Murder in Jamaica*. Hamilton, ON: Capricornus Enterprises, 1997. [fiction]
- *Jewels of the Bahamas*. Hamilton, ON: Capricornus Enterprises, 2000. [fiction]

Mathieu, Marie-Soeurette. [1949–]. b. Haiti.
- *Lueurs*. [N.p.: n.p.,] 1971. [poetry]
- [as M. Soeurette Mathieu Résilard]. *Poèmes d'autrefois et Fêlures*. [Anjou]: l'auteur, [1976]. [poetry]
- *Lueurs; et, Quinze poèmes d'éveil*. Montréal: Édition Lagomatik, 1991. [poetry]
- *Pagaille dans la ville*. Montréal: Humanitas, 1995. [fiction]
- *Ardéméé: Poèmes*. [Montréal]: Humanitas, [1997?] [poetry]
- *L'Amour en exil*. Montréal: Éditions du CIDIHCA, 2000. [fiction]

Matthews, Matthew George. [1878–]. b. Ontario.
- *Matthews' Famous Stories and Work*. Windsor, ON: W.T. Jacques & Sons, [1915]. [memoir]
- *Wit, Wisdom and Philosophy: The World As I See It*. Books 1 and 2. Ottawa: Department of Agriculture, 1915–25. [prose]

Mayr, Suzette. [1967–]. b. Alberta.
- *Zebra Talk*. Calgary: disOrientation Press, 1991. [poetry]

- *Moon Honey*. Edmonton: NeWest Press, 1995. [fiction]
- *The Widows*. Edmonton: NeWest Press, 1998. [fiction]
- *Drei Witwen und ein Wasserfall: Roman*. Trans. Christine Struh and Ursula Wulfekamp. München: Schneekluth, 1999. [fiction]

Mazebedi, Judge. [1970–]. b. Botswana.
- *Chicken Cries Out*. Hamilton, ON: Meckler & Deahl, 1995. [poetry]

McFarlane, Courtney.
- et al., eds. *Ma'-ka: Diasporic Juks: Contemporary Writing by Queers of African Descent*. Toronto: Sister Vision Press, 1997. [anthology]

McIntyre, D[anny]. [1950–2001]. b. New Brunswick.
- *The Black United Front: A New Approach*. Halifax, NS: Maritime School of Social Work, Dalhousie University, 1976. [study]
- *The Political Economy of Racism and Its Effect on Blacks in Nova Scotian Labour Force*. Halifax, NS: Maritime School of Social Work, Dalhousie University, 1976. [report]

McKerrow, Peter [Evander]. [1841–1906]. b. Antigua.
- *A Brief History of the Coloured Baptists of Nova Scotia, and Their First Organization as Churches, A.D. 1832*. Halifax, NS: Nova Scotia Printing Company, 1895. [history]
- *McKerrow. A Brief History of the Coloured Baptists of Nova Scotia, 1783–1895*. Ed. Frank Stanley Boyd, Jr. Halifax, NS: Afro Nova Scotian Enterprises, 1976. [history]

McLean, Dirk. [1956–]. b. Trinidad.
- and Brenda Kamino, eds. *Talent over Tradition: A Transcript of the First National Symposium on Non Traditional Casting*. Toronto: Canadian Actors' Equity Association, 1992.
- 'Encore.' In George Seremba et al., eds, *Beyond the Pale* (1996), 100–10. [drama]
- *Steel Drums and Ice Skates*. Vancouver: Douglas & McIntyre, 1997. [juvenile]
- *The Presence of Spirits*. Toronto: Marabella Press, 1999. [poetry]
- *Play Mas': A Carnival ABC*. Toronto: Tundra Books, 2000. [juvenile]

McNeilly, Pat. [1945–].
- with Rustin Oree. *Caiso, Caiso: A Cultural Handbook on Calypso and Soca: The Story of Calypso Brought to Life*. Mississauga, ON: ROZ Pub., 1993. [history]

McTair, Roger. b. Trinidad.
- *The Chain: A Play in One Act*. Port of Spain, TT: U.W.I. Extra Mural Department, 1979. [drama]
- ed. *Winter Epigrams and Epigrams to Ernesto Cardinal in Defense of Claudia*. By Dionne Brand. 1983. 2nd ed. Toronto: Williams-Wallace, 1984. [poetry]
- comp. and ed. *The Black Experience in the White Mind: Meditations on a Persistent Discourse*. [Toronto]: Roger McTair, 1995. [essay]

McWatt, Tessa. [1959–]. b. Barbados.
- *Out of My Skin*. Toronto: Riverbank Press, 1998. [fiction]
- *Dragons Cry*. Toronto: Riverbank Press, 2000. [fiction]

Meeks, Brian. [1953–]. b. Canada.
- *Caribbean Revolutions and Revolutionary Theory: An Assessment of Cuba, Nicaragua, and Grenada*. London: Macmillan Caribbean, 1993. [prose]

Mékoulnodji, Priscille. b. South Africa?
- *Indifférence*. [Montréal]: Éditions d'Orphée, 1995. [fiction]

Melekin, Embaye. b. Ethiopia.

- *Ab * yssinia Shall Rise!* [Downsview, ON]: Embaye Melekin, 1996. [fiction/prose]
- *Manifestations: Mysteries Revealed: An Account of Bible Truth and the Book of Mormon Prophecies.* [North York, ON]: E. Melekin, 2000. [prose]

Mensah, Joe Rockson. b. Ghana.

- *Trials and Tribulations of a Man.* New York: Vantage Press, 1991. [autobiography]

Mezlekia, Nega. [1958–]. b. Ethiopia.

- *Notes from the Hyena's Belly: Memories of My Ethiopian Boyhood.* Toronto: Penguin, 2000. [memoir]
- *The God Who Begat a Jackal.* Toronto: Penguin, 2001. [fiction]

Middleton, Joyce Shadd. [1943–]. b. Ontario.

- [et al.] *Something to Hope For: The Story of the Fugitive Slave Settlement, Buxton, Canada West.* [North Buxton, ON: Buxton National Historic Site & Museum, 2000.] [history]

Miguna, Miguna. b. Kenya.

- *Disgraceful Osgoode.* Toronto: AV Publications, 1994. [essays]
- *Songs of Fire.* Toronto: AV Publications, 1994. [poetry]
- *Afrika's Volcanic Song.* Toronto: AV Publications, 1995. [poetry]
- *Toes Have Tales.* Toronto: AV Publications, 1995. [fiction]

Moïse, Claude. [1932–]. b. Haiti.

- [et] Charles Manigat, Émile Ollivier. *Haiti: quel développement?: Propos sur 'L'enquête ...' de Jean-Jacques Honorat.* Montréal: Collectif paroles, 1975. [prose]
- [et] Cary Hector, Émile Ollivier. *1946–1976: Trente ans de pouvoir noir en Haïti.* Lasalle, QC: Collectif Paroles, 1976. [history]
- *Constitutions et luttes de pouvoir en Haïti: 1804–1987.* Montréal: Éditions du CIDIHCA, 1988. [history]
- *Constitutions et luttes de pouvoir en Haïti. Tome II: De l'occupation étrangère à la dictature macoute (1915–1987).* Montréal: Éditions du CIDIHCA, 1990. [history]
- [et] Émile Ollivier. *Repenser Haiti: Grandeur et misère d'un mouvement démocratique.* Montréal: Éditions du CIDIHCA, 1992. [essay]
- *Une constitution dans la tourmente: Le Nouveau Régime politique haïtien et la crise nationale, 1987–1993.* Montréal: Éditions Images, [1994].
- *Le pouvoir législatif dans le système politique haïtien: Un Aperçu historique.* Montréal: Éditions du CIDIHCA, 1999. [essay]

Mollel, Tololwa M[arti]. b. Tanzania.

- *Matembezi Msituni.* Dar es Salaam, Tanzania: Press and Publicity Centre, 1987. Swahili. [juvenile]
- *Rhino's Boy.* New Zealand: Outriggers Publishers, 1988. [juvenile]
- *The Orphan Boy.* Toronto: Oxford University Press, 1990. Rpt. *The Orphan Boy: A Maasai Story.* New York: Clarion Books, 1991. Rpt. *The Orphan Boy.* Toronto: Stoddart, 1995. [juvenile]
- *Rhinos for Lunch and Elephants for Supper! A Maasai Tale.* Toronto: Oxford University Press, 1991; New York: Clarion Books, 1992; Toronto: Stoddart [1994]. [juvenile]
- *The Princess Who Lost Her Hair.* [N.p.]: Troll Books, 1992. [juvenile]
- *A Promise to the Sun: An African Story.* Toronto: Little, Brown & Co., 1992; Forestweg, South Africa: Anansi-Uitgewers, 1993. [juvenile]

– *The King and the Tortoise*. Toronto: Lester Publishing Co; New York: Clarion Books, 1993. [juvenile]
– [*Rhinos for Lunch and Elephants for Supper!*] Afrikaans ed. Trans. Z. Ellis. Durbanville, South Africa: Garamond Uitgewers, 1993. [juvenile]
– [*Rhinos for Lunch and Elephants for Supper!*] Xhosa ed. Trans. Syney S. Zotwana. Durbanville, South Africa: Garamond Uitgewers, 1993. [juvenile]
– *The Flying Tortoise: An Igbo Tale*. Toronto: Oxford University Press, 1994; New York: Clarion Books, 1995. [juvenile]
– *Big Boy*. Toronto: Stoddart; New York: Clarion, 1995. [juvenile]
– *Ananse's Feast: An Ashante Tale*. New York: Clarion Books, 1997. [juvenile]
– *Dume's Roar*. Toronto: Stoddart Kids, 1997. [juvenile]
– *Kele's Secret*. Toronto: Stoddart, 1997. [juvenile]
– *Kitoto the Mighty*. Toronto: Stoddart, 1997. [juvenile]
– *Subira Subira*. New York: Clarion Books, 2000. [juvenile]
Montague, Masani. b. Jamaica.
– *Dread Culture: A Rastawoman's Story*. Toronto: Sister Vision, 1994. [fiction]
Moodie, Andrew. [1967–]. b. Ontario.
– 'Riot.' In George Seremba et al., eds, *Beyond the Pale* (1996), 164–8. [drama]
– *Riot*. [Winnipeg]: Scirocco, 1997. [drama]
– *A Common Man's Guide to Loving Women*. [Winnipeg]: Scirocco, 1999. [drama]
– 'Riot.' In Sears, ed., *Testifyin'*, Vol. 1 (2000), 1–78. [drama]
– *The Lady Smith*. Winnipeg: Blizzard Pub., 2000. [drama]
Moore, Donald. [1891–]. b. Barbados.
– *Don Moore: An Autobiography*. Toronto: Williams-Wallace, 1985. [autobiography]
Moore, Myreah. [1958–] b. British Columbia.
– *Dating in the Nineties*. New York: HarperCollins? [1999?]. [prose]
– and Jodie Gould. *Date like a Man (to Get the Man You Want)*. New York: HarperCollins, 2000. [prose]
Mordecai, Pamela Claire [Pamela Hitchens]. [1942–]. b. Jamaica.
– and Mervyn Morris, eds. *Jamaica Woman: An Anthology of Fifteen Jamaican Women Poets*. Kingston, JA: Heinemann Caribbean, 1980; London: Heinemann, 1985. [anthology]
– with R. Fagan, R. White, and C. Battick, eds. *Confrontation: An Anthology of Poems*. [Kingston, JA]: School of Education Teaching Section, 1981. [anthology]
– ed. *From Our Yard: Jamaican Poetry since Independence*. Kingston, JA: Institute of Jamaica Publications, 1987. [anthology]
– *Story Poems: A First Collection*. London: Ginn & Co. Ltd., 1987. [poetry]
– with Grace Walker Gordon. *Sunsong 1: An Anthology of Poetry for Secondary Schools*. Essex, England: Longman, 1987. [anthology]
– with Grace Walker Gordon. *Sunsong 2: An Anthology of Poetry for Secondary Schools*. Essex, England: Longman, 1987. [anthology]
– *Report on UNESCO Workshop to Review Innovative Strategies and Measures to Develop and Extend Integrated Early Childhood Education in Jamaica for Age Group Birth to Six Years*. N.p.: UNESCO, 1988. [report]
– and Betty Wilson. *Her True-True Name: An Anthology of Women's Writing from the Caribbean*. London: Heinemann, 1989. [anthology]

- *Journey Poem*. Kingston, JA: Sandberry Press, 1989. [poetry]
- *Sun Rhymes First ABC Colouring Book*. Kingston, JA: Sandberry Press, 1989. [juvenile]
- *Sun Rhymes First 123 Colouring Book*. Kingston, JA: Sandberry Press, 1989. [juvenile]
- *Don't Ever Wake a Snake: Poems and Stories for Children*. Kingston, JA: Sandberry Press, 1992. [juvenile]
- with Martin Mordecai. *Learn, Stretch, Reach: The North Coast Project for Training Basic School Teachers*. Kingston, JA: BVLF/CECE, 1993. [report]
- with Grace Walker Gordon. *Sunsong Tide Rising: An Anthology of Poetry for Secondary Schools*. Essex, England: Longman, 1993. [anthology]
- *De Man: A Performance Poem*. Toronto: Sister Vision, 1995. [dramatic poetry]
- *Ezra's Goldfish and Other Story Poems*. Kingston, JA: National Book Development Council, 1995. [poetry]
- *Certifiable*. Fredericton: Goose Lane Editions, 2001. [poetry]
Morgan, Dwayne.
- *Straight from the Roots*. [Toronto?]: Tropicana C.S.O., 1995. [poetry]
- *The Revolution Starts Within*. Toronto: Up from the Roots, 1996. [poetry]
- *Long Overdue*. Toronto: Up from the Roots, 1999. [poetry]
- *The Man behind the Mic*. Toronto: Up from the Roots, 2002. [poetry]
Morgan, Lincoln. [1941–]. b. Trinidad.
- *Everyday Poems for You and Me*. Montréal: G. & L. Morgan Publishing, 1996. [poetry]
Morisseau, Roland. [1933–]. b. Haiti.
- *Cinq poèmes de reconnaissance*. Port-au-Prince: Imprimerie Théodore, 1961. [poetry]
- *Germination d'espoir*. Port-au-Prince: Imprimerie N.A. Théodore, 1962. [poetry]
- *Clef du soleil*. Port-au-Prince: Éditions Les Araignées du soir, 1963. [poetry]
- *La Chanson de Roland: Poèmes 1960–1970*. Montréal: Éditions Nouvelle Optique, 1979. [poetry]
- *La Promeneuse au jasmin*. Montréal: Éditions Guernica, 1988. [poetry]
- *Poésie (1960–1991): Chanson de Roland* suivi de *Raison ensanglantée* et *La Promeneuse au jasmin*. Montréal: Les Éditions Guernica Inc., 1993. [poetry]
Morrison, Glen E. [1938–]. b. Jamaica.
- *Racism and Discrimination*. Hamilton, ON: Capricornus, 1999. [memoir]
Morrison-Reed, Mark D. [1949–]. b. United States.
- *Black Pioneers in a White Denomination*. Boston: Skinner House Books, 1984. [history]
Moseley, Romney M. [1943–92] b. United States?
- *No Longer Strangers: Ministry in a Multicultural Society: A Report to the Anglican Church of Canada*. Toronto: Anglican Book Centre, 1993. [prose]
Moses, Wellington Delaney. [1815–90]. b. England.
- 'Diaries.' Public Archives of British Columbia, Victoria, unpublished, 1869–89.
Motion [pseud. of Wendy Brathwaite]. [1970]. b. Ontario.
- *Motion in Poetry: Elements of Mine*. [Toronto]: blacklist and motionlive.ent, 2000. [poetry]
- *Motion in Poetry*. Toronto: Women's Press, 2002. [poetry]
Mougnan, Moïse N'Djekornondé. [1966–]. b. Chad.
- *Des Mots à dire*. Montréal: Éditions d'Orphée, [1987]. [poetry]

– *Le Rhythme du silence*. Montréal: Éditions d'Orphée, [1987]. [poetry]

Mpala, Ras Kagiso.

– *Escaped Convicts: Of Mental Slavery and the Prison Mentality* [with audiotape *Movements in Peace*]. Ottawa: Afrikan Resurrection Productions, 1995. [poetry]

Msingwana, Kwanza. [1961–].

– with Nancy Chong and Martha Kofie. *Only Mountains Never Meet: A Collection of Stories by Three New Writers*. Toronto: Well Versed, 1993. [short fiction]

Murray, Xanet L.

– ed. *Directory of Black Volunteer Organizations*. [Scarborough, ON]: [People's Volunteer Connection], 1997. [directory]

Nah-ee-lah. [pseud.?]

– *Time to Let Go*. Montréal: Yah Ga Yah Productions, 2001. [poetry pamphlet]

Niang, Sada. [1953–].

– with Simeon Waliaula Chilungu, eds. *African Continuities / L'Héritage africaine*. Toronto: Terebi, 1989. [essay compilation]

Nissré, Abebe. b. Ethiopia.

– *Démegnayé Mannew* [Who Is My Killer Enemy?] Toronto: n.p., 1991. [novel written in the Ge'ez script of the Amharic language]

Nkashama, Pius Ngandu. [1946–]. b. Zaïre.

– *La Délivrance d'Ilunga*. Paris: Pierre Jean Oswald, 1977. [drama]

– *La Littérature africaine écrite en langue française: La Poésie, le roman, le théatre*. Issy-les-Moulineaux: Les Classiques africains, 1979. [prose]

– [as Elimane Bakel, pseud.] *Bonjour Monsieur le Ministre*. Paris: Silex, 1983. [drama]

– *Le Fils de la tribu: Roman*; suivi de *La Mulatresse Anna*. Dakar: Nouvelles éditions africaines, 1983. [(short?) fiction]

– *La Malédiction*. Paris: Silex, 1983. [(short?) fiction]

– [réd.] *Littératures africaines de 1930 à nos jours*. Paris: Silex, 1984. [anthology]

– *Le Pacte de sang*. Paris: L'Harmattan, 1984. [(short?) fiction]

– avec B. Magnier. *L'Afrique noire en poésie*. Paris: Gallimard, 1985. [prose]

– *La Mort faite homme*. Paris: L'Harmattan, 1986. [(short?) fiction]

– *Vie et moeurs d'un primitif en Essonne quatre-vingt-onze*. Paris: L'Harmattan, 1987. [(short?) fiction]

– *Les Étoiles écrasées*. Paris: Publisud, 1988. [(short?) fiction]

– *Écritures et discours littéraires en Afrique: Études sur le roman africain*. Paris: Harmattan, 1989. [prose]

– *Églises nouvelles et mouvements réligieux*. Paris: L'Harmattan, 1990. [prose]

– *Les Années littéraires en Afrique: 1912–1987*. Paris: L'Harmattan, 1991. [prose]

– *Des mangroves en terre haute*. Paris: L'Harmattan, 1991. [(short?) fiction]

– *L'Empire des ombres vivantes*. Carnières, Belgium: Lansman, 1991. [drama]

– *Les Enfants du lac Tana*. [Dans] *Enfance, enfance* ... En collaboration avec R. Belamri et E. Mazigi. LaSalle, QC: Hurtubise HMH, 1991. [juvenile]

– *Un Jour de grand soleil*. Paris: L'Harmattan, 1991. [(short?) fiction]

– *Littératures et écritures en langues africaines*. Paris: L'Harmattan, 1992. [prose]

– *Négritude et poétique: Une Lecture de l'oeuvre critique de Léopold Sédar Senghor*. Paris: L'Harmattan, 1992. [prose]

– *Un Matin pour Loubène.* LaSalle, QC: Hurtubise HMH, 1993. [juvenile]
Nkembé, Théo. b. Senegal.
– *Père Clément Cormier: Fondateur en Acadie.* Moncton: n.p., 1974. [biography]
Nnadi, Joseph Emmanuel. b. Niger.
– *Visions d'Afrique dans l'oeuvre de Baudelaire.* Yaoundé: Éditions CLE, 1980. [prose]
– *The Humanities in Contemporary Nigerian Education: Relevance and Methodological
     Options.* Eha-Amufu: College of Education, 1987. [prose]
– *Les Négresses de Baudelaire.* Saint-Boniface, MB: Les Éditions des Plaines, 1994. [prose]
Norman, Alma. [1930–]. b. United States.
– *Ballads of Jamaica.* Kingston: n.p., 1964; rev. ed., London: Longmans, Green and Co.
     Ltd, 1967; 2nd rev. ed., St Andrew, JA: Twin Guinep, 2000. [poetry]
Nortje, Arthur. [1942–70]. b. South Africa.
– *Dead Roots.* London: Heinemann, 1973. [poetry]
– *Lonely against the Light.* A special issue of *New Coin* (9.3–4 [September 1973]).
     [poetry]
– *Anatomy of Dark: Collected Poems of Arthur Nortje.* Ed. Dirk Klopper. Pretoria, South
     Africa: Unisa Press, 2000. [poetry]
Nyakatura, J[ohn]. W[illiam]. [1895–]. b. Buyaga [Uganda].
– *Abakama ba Bunyora Kitara.* St Justin, QC: W.-H. Gagne, 1947. [history]
– *Aspects of Bunyoro Customs and Tradition.* Trans. Zebiya Kwamya. Nairobi: East
     African Literature Bureau, [1970]. [prose]
– *Anatomy of an African Kingdom: A History of Bunyoro-Kitara.* Trans. Teopista
     Muganwa. New York: NOK Publishers, 1973. Trans. of *Abakama ba Bunyoro Kitara.*
     St Justin, QC: W.-H. Gagne, 1947. [history]
Nzegwu, Nkiru. b. Nigeria.
– *Figures héroiques: Sculptures africaines de la Collection Justin et Elisabeth Lang.*
     [Kingston, ON]: Agnes Etherington Art Centre, [1988?] [art show catalogue]
– *Celebrating African Identity: Politics and Icon of Representation (Rites to Passage) June
     27–August 1, 1992.* Toronto: CAN-BAIA and A Space Gallery, 1992. [art show
     catalogue]
– *The Creation of the African-Canadian Odyssey, June 26–Sept. 7, 1992.* Toronto: The
     Power Plant – Contemporary Art at Harbourfront, 1992. [art show catalogue]
O'Brien, Randy. [194?–]. b. Tobago.
– *My Epitaph.* Mississauga, ON: Words and Music International, 1996. [poetry, short
     fiction, essays]
Odhiambo, David Nandi. [1965–]. b. Kenya.
– [et al.] *mouth to mouth.* Vancouver: Panarchy Press, 1995. [poetry]
– 'afrocentric.' In George Seremba et al., eds, *Beyond the Pale* (1996), 200–10. [drama]
– *Diss/ed banded nation.* Victoria, BC: Polestar Book Publishers, 1998. [fiction]
Oguntebi, Samuel Oladele. [1929–]. b. Nigeria.
– *Son of Orokoko: Memoirs of Chief S.O. Oguntebi.* Edmonton: Fisher House Publishers,
     2000. [memoir]
Olema, Debhonvapi. b. Zaïre.
– [et al.] *De paroles en figures: Essais sur les littératures africaines et antillaises.* Comps.
     Christiane Ndiaye et Josias Semujanga. Montréal: Harmattan, 1996. [compilation]

Oliver, Don [Hon. Donald H. Oliver]. [1938–]. b. Nova Scotia.
- *Men Can Cook Too!* Hantsport, NS: Lancelot Press, 1981. [prose]
- [as Hon. Donald H. Oliver, Senator]. *The Fourth Dr. Abdul Qaiyum Lodhi Memorial Lecture, March 20, 1998.* Fredericton, NB: Atlantic Human Rights Centre, St Thomas University, 1998. [prose]
Oliver, Jules. b. Nova Scotia.
- *Final Report on the Problem of Unemployment for the Negro.* Halifax, NS: Nova Scotia Human Rights Commission, 1969. [report]
Oliver, Leslie H. b. Nova Scotia.
- *'Family Ties': Seventh Anniversary Lecture of the Black Cultural Society.* [Cherrybrook, NS]: Black Cultural Centre for Nova Scotia, 1990. [essay]
Oliver, Pearleen. [1917–]. b. Nova Scotia.
- *A Brief History of the Colored Baptists of Nova Scotia, 1782–1953. In Commemoration of Centennial Celebrations of the African United Baptist Association of Nova Scotia.* Halifax, NS: [African United Baptist Association of Nova Scotia], 1953. [history]
- *A Root and a Name.* Lower Sackville, NS: n.p., 1977. [history]
- *One of His Heralds: A Sketch from the Life of Agnes Gertrude Waring.* Lower Sackville, · NS: n.p., n.d. [history]
- *An Historic Minority: The Black People of Nova Scotia, 1781–1981.* Dartmouth, NS: n.p., 1981. [history]
- *A Tribute to the Black Loyalists of Nova Scotia 1783–1983.* Dartmouth, NS: Society for the Protection and Preservation of Black Culture in Nova Scotia, 1983. [history]
- *From Generation to Generation: Bi-Centennial of the Black Church in Nova Scotia, 1785 – a Synopsis – 1985.* [Cherrybrook, NS: Black Cultural Centre for Nova Scotia, 1985.] [history]
- *Song of the Spirit: 150th Anniversary, Beechville United Baptist Church.* Hantsport, NS: Lancelot Press, 1994. [history]
Oliver, W[illiam].P[early]. [1912–86]. b. Nova Scotia.
- *A Brief Summary of Nova Scotia Negro Communities.* Halifax, NS: Nova Scotia Department of Education, 1964. [mimeograph]
- *Education in the Black Communities in Nova Scotia.* Halifax, NS: Nova Scotia Department of Education, 1974. [prose]
Ollivier, Émile. [1940–]. b. Haiti.
- [et] Charles Manigat, Claude Moïse. *Haïti: Quel développement?* Montréal: Collectif paroles, 1975. [essay]
- [et] Cary Hector, Claude Moïse. *1946–1976: Trente ans de pouvoir noir en Haïti.* Lasalle, QC: Collectif Paroles, 1976. [history]
- *Paysage de l'aveugle: Roman.* Montréal: Éditions Pierre Tisseyre, 1977. Rpt. *Paysage de l'aveugle* suivi de *Le Vide huilé.* Montréal: Cercle du livre de France, 1977. [fiction]
- *Mère-solitude: Roman.* Paris: Albin Michel, 1983. [fiction]
- *La Discorde aux cent voix: Roman.* Paris: Albin Michel, 1986. [fiction]
- *Mother Solitude.* Trans. David Lobdell. Ottawa: Oberon, 1989. [fiction]
- réd. *La Marginalité silencieuse.* Montréal: CIDIHCA, 1991. [essays]
- et al. *La Marginalité silencieuse: Matériaux pour des pratiques d'alphabétisation auprès des publics migrants.* Montréal: CIDIHCA, 1991. [guide]

- *Passages: Roman.* Montréal: Éditions de l'Héxagone, 1991. Rpt. Saint-Laurent, QC: Edition du Club Quebec loisirs, 1992. [fiction]
- [et] Claude Moïse. *Repenser Haïti: Grandeur et misères d'un mouvement démocratique.* Montréal: Editions du CIDIHCA, 1992. [prose]
- *Les Urnes scellées.* Paris: Albin Michel, 1995. [fiction]
- [et al.] *Compère Jacques Soleil: Hommage à Jacques Stephen Alexis.* Montréal: Planète rebelle, 1998. [short fiction]
- *Mille Eaux: Récit.* [Paris]: Gallimard, 1999. [autobiography]

O'Ree, Willie. [1935–]. b. New Brunswick.
- with Michael McKinley. *The Autobiography of Willy O'Ree: Hockey's Black Pioneer.* Toronto: Somerville House, 2000. [autobiography]

Oree, Rustin. [1947–].
- with Pat McNeilly. *Caiso, Caiso: A Cultural Handbook on Calypso and Soca: The Story of Calypso Brought to Life.* Mississauga, ON: ROZ Pub., 1993. [history]

Osei, Victor A[mbrose]. [1943–].
- *How to Be a Successful Immigrant: We're Here, What Do We Do Now?* Scarborough, ON: Suxexes Book, 1990. [prose]

Osopher, Negrophil [pseud.?] [1942–]. b. Jamaica.
- *Renditions of an Arawak: Poems.* Toronto: n.p., [1973?] [poetry]

Palmer, C[yril]. Everard. [1930–]. b. Jamaica.
- *The Broken Vessel.* Kingston, JA: Pioneer Press, 1951, 1960; Kingston, JA: Heinemann, 1982. [juvenile]
- *The Adventures of Jimmy Maxwell.* [Kingston, JA]: Jamaica Publ. Branch, Ministry of Education, 1962. [juvenile]
- *A Taste of Danger.* [Kingston, JA]: Jamaica Publ. Branch, Ministry of Education, 1963. [juvenile]
- *The Cloud with the Silver Lining.* London: André Deutsch, 1966; New York: Pantheon, 1967; Harmondsworth: Penguin, 1973; London: Macmillan Caribbean, 1987, 1989. [juvenile]
- *Big Doc Bitteroot.* London: André Deutsch, 1968; Indianapolis: Bobbs-Merrill, 1971; London: Macmillan, 1992. [juvenile]
- *The Sun Salutes You.* London: André Deutsch, 1970; Indianapolis: Bobbs-Merrill, 1971; London: Macmillan, 1984, 1986–93. [juvenile]
- *The Hummingbird People.* London: André Deutsch, 1971; Sunbury-on-Thames, England: Nelson Caribbean, 1979. [juvenile]
- *Baba and Mr. Big.* Indianapolis: Bobbs-Merrill, 1972; London: Collins, 1974; London: André Deutsch, 1974; London: Macmillan, 1992, 1994. [juvenile]
- *The Wooing of Beppo Tate.* London: André Deutsch, 1972; Kingston, JA: Nelson Caribbean, 1979. [juvenile].
- *A Cow Called Boy.* London: André Deutsch, 1973; London: Macmillan, 1985. [juvenile]
- *My Father, Sun-Sun Johnson.* London: André Deutsch, 1974; London: Macmillan, 1984. [juvenile]
- *A Dog Called Houdini.* London: André Deutsch, 1978; Richmond Hill, ON: Scholastic-TAB Publications, 1980; Richmond Hill, ON: Scholastic Canada, 1991. [juvenile]

- *Beppo Tate and Roy Penner: The Runaway Marriage Brokers: Two Stories*. London: André Deutsch, 1980. [juvenile]
- *Crab Hunt. The Rescue. Ordeal at Sea. The Fife-Man*. Kingston, JA: Ministry of Education, Youth and Sports, 1980. [juvenile]
- *Houdini, Come Home*. London: André Deutsch, 1981. [juvenile]
- *Houdini, le chien*. Trans. François Renaud. Richmond Hill, ON: Scholastic Canada, 1991. [juvenile]

Palmer, Hazelle. [1959–]. b. England.
- *Tales from the Gardens and Beyond*. Toronto: Sister Vision, 1995. [short fiction]
- ed. '*– But Where Are You Really From? Stories of Identity and Assimilation*. Toronto: Sister Vision Press, 1997. [compilation]

Paris, Cherry M. b. Nova Scotia.
- *An Unclouded Day: A Brief Account of the Black Loyalists*. [Digby, NS]: [Paris,] 1983. [history]
- [et al.] *Universality of Human Rights and the Black Experience: A Collection of Speeches*. Dartmouth, NS: Black Cultural Centre for Nova Scotia, 1989. [compilation]
- *Windsor Plains United Baptist Church: A Brief History*. [Windsor, NS]: [Windsor Plains United Baptist Church], 2001. [history]

Paris, Peter J. [1933–]. b. Nova Scotia.
- *Black Leaders in Conflict: Joseph H. Jackson, Martin Luther King Jr., Malcolm X, Adam Clayton Powell Jr*. New York: Pilgrim Press, 1978. Rev. ed. *Black Religious Leaders: Conflict in Unity*. Louisville, KY: Westminster / John Knox Press, 1991. [prose]
- *The Social Teaching of the Black Churches*. Philadelphia: Fortress Press, 1985. [prose]
- with Douglas A. Knight, eds. *Justice and the Holy: Essays in Honor of Walter Harrelson*. Atlanta, GA: Scholar's Press, 1989. [compilation]
- *The Moral, Political and Religious Significance of the Black Churches in Nova Scotia*. Cherrybrook, NS: Black Cultural Centre for Nova Scotia, 1989. [prose]

Parisien, Jean-Éric. [1944–]. b. Haiti.
- *Nadeige: Récit*. Sherbrooke, QC: Éditions Naaman, 1981. [fiction]

Parker, Raymond L. [1936–]. b. Nova Scotia.
- *Beyond the Dark Horizon*. Cherrybrook, NS: Black Cultural Centre for Nova Scotia, 1987. [fiction; originally a drama]

Paulse, Michele. [1958–].
- and Rosamund Elwin. *Asha's Mums*. Toronto: Women's Press, 1990. [juvenile]
- and Rosamund Elwin. *The Moonlight Hide-&-Seek Club in the Pollution Solution*. Toronto: Women's Press, 1992. [juvenile]

Payne, Alicia.
- 'Don't Call Me That.' In *Word Up: The Bi-Monthly Newsletter of Canadian Artists' Network: Black Artists in Action* [Toronto] 5.6 (Dec. 1996): 12–15. [drama]
- 'The Troubleshooter.' In George Seremba et al., eds, *Beyond the Pale* (1996), 170–6. [drama]

Péan, Stanley. [1966–]. b. Haiti.
- *La Plage des songes et autres récits d'exil: Huit Nouvelles fantastiques*. Montréal: Éditions du CIDIHCA, 1988. Rpt. *La Plage des songes et autres récits d'exil*. [Saint-Laurent, QC]: BQ, 1998. [short fiction]

- *Le Tumulte de mon sang: Roman*. Montréal: Québec/Amérique, 1991. Rpt. Montréal: La Courte échelle, 2001. [fiction]
- *Sombres allées et autres endroits peu hospitaliers: Treize Excursions en territoire de l'insolite*. Montréal: Voix du Sud / Éditions du CIDIHCA, 1992. [short fiction]
- 'Blues en rouge sur blanc.' *Meurtres à Québec: Nouvelles*. [Par] Hugues Corriveau et al. Québec: L'instant même, 1993. [short fiction]
- *L'Emprise de la nuit*. Montréal: Éditions de la Courte échelle, 1993. [juvenile]
- *L'Automne sauvage*. [N.p.]: Trécarré, 1994. [juvenile]
- *La Mémoire ensanglantée*. Montréal: Éditions de la Courte échelle, 1994. [juvenile]
- *Treize Pas vers l'inconnu: Nouvelles fantastiques*. Saint-Laurent, QC: Éditions Pierre Tisseyre, 1996. [juvenile]
- *Zombi Blues*. Montréal: Éditions de la Courte échelle, 1996. [fiction]
- *L'Appel des loups*. Montréal: Éditions de la Courte échelle, 1997. [juvenile]
- *Quand la bête est humaine*. Montréal: La Courte échelle, 1997. [juvenile]
- [et al.] *Compère Jacques Soleil: Hommage à Jacques Stephen Alexis*. Montréal: Planète rebelle, 1998. [short fiction]
- *Un Petit Garçon qui avait peur de tout et de rien*. Montréal: La Courte échelle, 1998. [juvenile]
- *Noirs Désirs*. Montréal: Leméac, 1999. [short fiction]
- *Le Temps s'enfuit*. Montréal: La Courte échelle, 1999. [juvenile]
- *Toute la ville en jazz*. [Montréal]: Éditions Trait d'union, 1999. [history of Montreal International Jazz Festival]
- *La Nuit démasque*. Montréal: Planète rebelle [et] Éditions du CIDIHCA, 2000. [short fiction]
- *Planète culture: Les Bonnes Adresses culturelles dans Internet*. Montréal: Éditions rebelle, 2000. [prose]

Pereira, Roger. [1932–]. b. Haiti.
- *Les Galops de dune*. Sherbrooke, QC: Éditions Naaman, 1977. [poetry]

Perry, Charlotte Bronté. [1910–]. b. United States.
- *The Long Road: The History of the Coloured Canadian in Windsor, Ontario, 1867–1967*. Windsor, ON: Sumner Printing & Publishing Co., 1967; 2nd ed., 1969. [history]
- *One Man's Journey: Roy Prince Edward Perry, 1905–1972*. Windsor, ON: Sumner Press, 1982. [history]

Peterson, Carlisle John. [1956–].
- *The Destiny of the Black Race*. Toronto: Lifeline Communications, 1991. [prose]

Phelps, Anthony. [1928–]. b. Haiti.
- *Présence: Poème*. Port-au-Prince: Art graphique presse, [1949?] [poetry]
- *Été: Poème*. Port-au-Prince: N.A. Théodore, 1960. [poetry]
- *Éclats de silence: Poèmes*. Port-au-Prince: n.p., 1962. [poetry]
- [et al.] *Il était une fois une main*. [Dans] *Image et Verbe*. Montréal: Ive, 1966. [poetry]
- *Points cardinaux*. Montréal: Holt, Rinehart et Winston, 1966. [poetry]
- *Le Conditionnel*. Montréal: Holt, Rinehart et Winston, 1968, 1970. [drama]
- *Mon pays que voici*, suivi de *Les Dits du fou-aux-cailloux*. Paris: Pierre-Jean Oswald, 1968. [poetry]
- *Et moi je suis une île*. Montréal: Leméac, 1973. [juvenile]

- *Moins l'infini: Roman haïtien*. Paris: Les Éditeurs français réunis, 1973. [fiction]
- *Mémoire en Colin-Maillard: Roman*. Montréal: Éditions Nouvelle Optique, 1976. Rpt. [Montréal]: Éditions du CIDIHCA, 2001. [fiction]
- *Motifs pour le temps saisonnier: Poèmes*. Paris: Pierre-Jean Oswald, 1976. [poetry]
- *Mon pays que voici ... suivi de Les Dits du fou-aux-cailloux*. Honfleur, France: P.J. Oswald, 1978. [poetry]
- *La Bélière Caraïbe*. Montréal: Nouvelle Optique; [La Habana]: Casa de las Americas, 1980. [poetry]
- *Même le soleil est nu*. Montréal: Nouvelle Optique, 1983. [poetry]
- *Haïti!Haïti!: Roman*. En collaboration avec Gary Klang. Montréal: Libre Expression, 1985. [fiction]
- *Este es mi país*. Trans. Monica Mansour. Mexico: J. Boldo i Climenti, 1987. [poetry]
- *Orchidée nègre*. La Habana: Casa de las Americas, 1985; Montréal: Triptyque, 1987. [poetry]
- *Les Doubles Quatrains mauves*. Port-au-Prince: Éditions Mémoire, 1995. [poetry]
- *Immobile Voyageuse de Picas et autres silences: Poèmes*. Montréal: Éditions du CIDIHCA, 2000. [poetry]

Philip, M[arlene]. Nourbe[S]e. [1947–]. b. Tobago.
- *Thorns*. Toronto: Williams-Wallace, 1980. [poetry]
- *Salmon Courage*. Toronto: Williams-Wallace, 1983. [poetry]
- *Harriet's Daughter*. Toronto: Women's Press; Oxford: Heinemann, 1988; Portsmouth, NH: Heinemann, 1992; Toronto: Women's Press, 2000. [fiction]
- *She Tries Her Tongue, Her Silence Softly Breaks*. Charlottetown, PEI: Ragweed, 1989; London: The Women's Press, 1993. [poetry]
- *Looking for Livingstone: An Odyssey of Silence*. Stratford, ON: Mercury, 1991. [fiction]
- *Frontiers: Essays and Writings on Racism and Culture, 1984–1992*. Stratford, ON: Mercury, 1992. [prose]
- *Harriet und Schwarz Wie Ich*. Trans. Nina Schindler. Kevelaer, Germany: Anrich, 1993. [fiction]
- *Showing Grit: Showboating North of the 44th Parallel*. Toronto: Poui Publications, [1993]. [essay]
- *The Redemption of Al Bumen (a Morality Play): A Play in One Act*. Incl. with *Showing Grit: Showboating North of the 44th Parallel*. 2nd ed. Toronto: Poui Publications, 1993. [drama]
- *Caribana:African Roots and Continuities: Race, Space and the Poetics of Moving*. Toronto: Poui Publications, 1996. [essay]
- 'Coups and Calypso.' In George Seremba et al., eds, *Beyond the Pale* (1996), 8–14. [drama]
- *A Genealogy of Resistance and Other Essays*. Toronto: The Mercury Press, 1997. [essays]
- *Coups and Calypsos*. Toronto: PUC Play Service, 2000. [drama]
- 'Coups and Calypsos.' In Sears, ed., *Testifyin'*, vol. 1 (2000), 79–142. [drama]
- *Coups and Calypsos*. [Toronto]: Mercury Press, 2001. [drama]

Phillips, Nathan. [1923–]. b. Trinidad?
- *A Voice from the Bush: Stories, Observations and Thoughts in Verse and Dialogue*. [Greenfield Park, QC]: N. Phillips, 1989. [poetry]
- *African Identity in Crisis: The Possible Answer*. [Montreal]: N. Phillips, 1990. [prose]

- *The Caribbean Alive: Stories in Verse, Dialogue and Prose*. Greenfield Park, QC: Nathan Phillips, 1991. [short fiction and poetry]
- *Play Pan: The Quick and Easy Method*. Greenfield Park, QC: Nathan Phillips, 1991. [prose]
- *Chukwuma Nwankwo: A Caribbean Story*. Greenfield Park, QC: N. Phillips, 1993. [juvenile]
- *The Caribbean Journey: A Celebration*. Montreal: P. Nathan, 1995. [juvenile?]

Phillips, Trevor. b. Jamaica.
- *On Eagle's Wings: A Testimony of Faith and Friendship*. Halifax, NS: World Eagle Press Association, 1997. [sermons]

Pierre, Claude. [1941–]. b. Haiti.
- *À Haute voix et à genoux*. N.p.: n.p., 1965. [poetry]
- *Coucou rouge*. N.p.: n.p., 1973. [poetry]
- *Tourne ma toupie*, suivi de *Oeil*. Sherbrooke, QC: Éditions Naaman; New York: French & European Publications, 1974. [poetry]
- *Arc en neige*. [Quebec (Province): Pierre, 1983.] [poetry]
- *Huit poèmes infiniment*. Sainte-Cécile-de-Masham, 1983. [poetry]
- *Le Coup de l'étrier: Textes poétiques*. Ottawa: Éditions du Vermillon, 1986. [poetry]
- [comme Klod Pye]. *Crues*. Ottawa: Éditions du Vermillon, 1986. [poetry]
- *Doencens et de soufre*. Ottawa: Éditions du Vermillon, 1986. [poetry]
- *Présentation de Gouverneurs de la Rosée*. [N.p.: n.p., 1987.] [prose]
- [et] Jean-Guy Paquin. *C'est un grand arbre qui nous unit: Poésie*. Montréal: VLB, 1988. [poetry]
- *Le Voyage inventé*. Pétion-Ville, Haiti: Éditions Pleine-Plage, 1998. [poetry]

Pierre-Charles, Gérard. [1928–]. b. Haiti.
- *L'Économie haïtienne et sa voie de developpement*. Paris: G.P., Maisonneuve et Larose, 1967. [essay]
- *Haïti: Radiografia de una dictadura*. México: Editorial Nuestro Tiempo, 1969. [history]
- *Problemas dominico-haitianos y del Caribe*. México: Universidad Nacional Autonoma de México, 1973. [prose]
- *Radiographie d'une dictature: Haïti et Duvalier*. Montréal: Éditions Nouvelle optique, 1973. [history]
- *Sociologia de la Opresion*. Santiago de Chile: n.p., 1973. [prose]
- *Haïti: La Crisis ininterrumpida, 1930–1975*. La Habana: Casa de las Americas, 1978. [history]
- *Génesis de la Revolucion Cubana*. 3rd ed. México: Siglo Veintiuno Editores, 1980. [history]
- *El Caribe contemporàneo*. México D.F.: Siglo Veintiuno Editores, 1981; 4th ed., 1987. [essay]
- *El Pensiamento Sociopolitico Moderno en el Caribe*. México: Instituto de Investigaciones Sociales, UNAM: Fondo de Cultura Economica, 1985. [prose]

Pinson, Dave. b. United States.
- *Studies in Black and White*. New York: Vantage, 1966. [poetry]

Pitter, Jay. [1971–]. b. Jamaica.
- *Alone with Myself*. Toronto: n.p., 1991. [poetry]

Pleasant, Juanita [Juanita Ann Pleasant-Wilburn]. b. Nova Scotia.
- *Reflections from the Heart*. Kentville, NS: Reflections Publishing, 1997; 2nd ed., 1999. [poetry]
- *Bear River's Finest*. [Kentville, NS]: [Juanita Pleasant], 1998. [juvenile]
- *My Valley Heritage*. [Kentville, NS]: Reflections Publishing, 1999. [poetry]
- *The Swissair 111 Disaster at Peggy's Cove*. [Kentville, NS]: Reflections Publishing, 1999. [poetry]
- *'I Never Knew': Part 1*. [Kentville, NS]: Reflections Publishing, 2000. [poetry and prose]
Prezeau, Carl. [1934–]. b. Haiti.
- *Gestion socio-économique et gouvernement des hommes: Essai sur l'équilibre social et réflexions sur la societé américaine*. Sherbrooke, QC: Éditions Naaman, 1977. [essay]
- *Agir pour être Dieu: La Pause bouddhique*. Sherbrooke, QC: Éditions Cogito, 1993. [prose]
- *L'Apprenti Dieu et le temps de l'Esprit: Essai sur l'identité de l'être humain*. Sherbrooke, QC: Éditions Cogito, 1993. [prose]
- *Le Subtil Effet-plafond de la verité: Essai sur l'évolution humaine*. Sherbrooke, QC: Éditions Cogito, 1993. [prose]
- *Virage vers la prosperité au pays du marron: Des Propositions d'action pour un enjeu moderne*. Sherbrooke, QC: Éditions Cogito, 1994. [prose]
- *Échec à la guerre et à la pauvreté: Perspectives nouvelles et contemporaines*. Sherbrooke, QC: Éditions Cogito, 1995. [prose]
- *L'Ultime Dessein de Dieu*. Sherbrooke, QC: Éditions Cogito, 1995. [prose]
- *La Démocratie du capital et la santé collective: Nouvelles Perspectives sur le devenir collectif*. Sherbrooke, QC: Éditions Cogito, 1999. [prose]
Price, E. Curmie. [1940–]. b. United States.
- *The State of the Union*. Surrey, BC: Sono Nis Press, 1970. [poetry]
Prince, Althea [Althea Veronica Trotman]. [1945–]. b. Antigua.
- *How the East Pond Got Its Flowers*. Toronto: Sister Vision, 1991. [juvenile]
- *How the Starfish Got to the Sea*. Toronto: Sister Vision, 1992. [juvenile]
- *Ladies of the Night and Other Stories*. Toronto: Sister Vision, 1993. [short fiction]
- *Being Black: Essays*. Toronto: Insomniac Press, 2001. [essays]
- *Loving This Man*. Toronto: Insomniac Press, 2001. [fiction]
Prince, Bryan. [1952–]. b. Ontario.
- [et al.] *Something to Hope For: The Story of the Fugitive Slave Settlement, Buxton, Canada West*. [North Buxton, ON: Buxton National Historic Site & Museum, 2000.] [history]
Procope, Mervyn [Kenneth]. [1942–]. b. Barbados?
- *Energy = Mercy Squared: Poems*. Toronto: Toussaint Publications, [1966]. [poetry]
Prophète, Jean L. [pseud., Max Dollarge]. b. Haiti.
- *Index de Max Dollarge / Les Vieux Cahiers de Jean L. Prophète*. Montréal: Éditions du CIDIHCA, 1997. [prose]
Providence, Tien. b. St Vincent.
- *The Dancer*. Kingstown, St Vincent: n.p., 1983. [drama]
- *Street Life*. Kingstown, St Vincent: n.p., 1985. [drama]
- *The Collection: A Selection of Short Stories*. [Agincourt, ON: n.p., 1989.] [short fiction]

– 'Blues for My Grandfather.' In George Seremba et al., eds, *Beyond the Pale* (1996), 128–33. [drama]

Quamina, Odida T. b. Guyana.
– *Mineworkers of Guyana: The Making of a Working Class*. London: Zed Books, 1987; Scarborough, ON: Edan's Publishers, 1988. [history]
– *All Things Considered: Can We Live Together?* Toronto: Exile Editions, 1996. [prose]

Renaud, Alix Joseph. [1945–]. b. Haiti.
– *Le Troc mystèrieux, carte-poème*. Genève, Suisse: Éditions Poésie Vivante, 1970. [poetry]
– *M. de Vastey*. N.p.: n.p., 197?. [drama]
– *Carème*. [Paris]: Éditions Saint-Germain-des-Prés, 1972. [poetry]
– *De ma fenêtre*. Québec: Zyx, 1974. [poetry]
– *Extase exacte*. Paris: Pensée universelle, 1976. [poetry]
– *Grâces: Poème de chevet*. [Lévis, QC: Éditions de l'Erbium, 1979.] [poetry]
– *Le Mari: Nouvelles*. Sherbrooke, QC: Éditions Naaman, [1980?] [short fiction]
– *Dictionnaire de l'audiophonie: – de la machine à gravure à la salle d'écoute / Audio Dictionary: – from the Recording to the Listening Room*. Paris: Nathan; Montréal: CEDIC, Ville-Marie, 1981. [prose]
– *Dix Secondes de sursis: Nouvelles*. Marseilles: Éditions Le Temps parallèle; Sainte-Foy, QC: Éditions Laliberté, 1983. [short fiction]
– *Merdiland*. Marseilles: Éditions Le Temps parallèle, 1983. [fiction]
– *À corps joie*. Montréal: Nouvelle Optique, 1985. Rpt. Montréal: Éditions Balzac, 1994. [fiction]
– *Snesnob: Nouvelle*. Sainte-Foy, QC: Éditions de l'Erbium, 1987. [short fiction]
– *Vocabulaire des additifs alimentaires / Vocabulary of Food Additives*. Ottawa: Secretariat d'État du Canada / Department of the Secretary of State of Canada, 1990. [prose]
– 'Exanoïa.' [Dans] *Sol: Nouvelles*. [Par] Guy Bouchard et al. Montréal: Les Éditions Logiques, 1991. 187–242. [short fiction]
– *Douce-amère = Dulcamara*. Québec: Éditions du Loup de gouttière, 1992. [poetry]
– *Pale kreyol: Manuel d'apprentissage du creole à l'usage des francophones*. Québec: Garneau-international, 1994. [prose]
– [et al.] *Compère Jacques Soleil: Hommage à Jacques Stephen Alexis*. Montréal: Planète rebelle, 1998. [short fiction]
– *Tande kreyòl la byen*. Québec: Garneau-International, 1998. [Haitian Creole manual and audio cassette]
– *Ovation*. Montréal: Planète rebelle, 1999. [short fiction]

Richardson, E.A.
– *Brief Historical Sketch of the British Methodist Episcopal Church*. N.p.: n.p., [1860?–1930?]. [history]

Roach, Charles. [1933–]. b. Trinidad.
– *Root for the Ravens: Poems for Drum and Freedom*. Toronto: NC Press, 1977. [poetry]

Roach, Kiké [Kikélola Roach]. [1970–]. b. Ontario.
– with Judy Rebick. *Politically Speaking*. Vancouver: Douglas & McIntyre, 1996. [transcribed dialogues]

Robb, Ralph [pseud., Sylvester Young]. [1961–]. b. Britain.
- *What Goes Around*. Cork, Ireland: Black Amber Books, 1999. [fiction]
Robbins, Arlie C[lara]. [1922–]. b. Ontario.
- *Legacy to Buxton*. North Buxton, ON: A.C. Robbins, [1983]. [history]
- *Prince Hall Masonry in Ontario, 1852–1933*. N.p.: n.p., 1994. [history]
Robbins, Vivian. b. Ontario.
- *Musical Buxton*. Buxton, ON: n.p., 1970. [history]
Robertson, Angela. [1967–]. b. Canada.
- and Enakshi Dua, eds. *Scratching the Surface: Canadian Anti-Racist Feminist Thought*. Toronto: Women's Press, 1999. [compilation]
Robertson, John William. b. United States.
- *The Book of the Bible against Slavery*. Halifax, NS: [Robertson], 1854. [autobiography]
Robinson, Gwendolyn S. [1932–]. b. Ontario.
- and John W. Robinson. *Seek the Truth: A Story of Chatham's Black Community*. Chatham, ON: n.p., 1989, 1994, 1996. [history]
Robinson, John W. [1926–]. b. Ontario.
- with Gwendolyn S. Robinson. *Seek the Truth: A Story of Chatham's Black Community*. Chatham, ON: n.p., 1989, 1994, 1996. [history]
Robinson, Kim. b. Jamaica.
- and Anthony Coker. *Climax*. Montreal: n.p., 1976. [poetry]
Roper, Moses. [1816–]. b. United States.
- *A Narrative of the Adventures and Escape of Moses Roper, from American Slavery with an Appendix Containing a List of Places Visited by the Author in Great Britain and Ireland and the British Isles, and Other Matter*. London: Darton, Harvey and Darton, 1838; Brantford, ON: T. Lemmon & Sons, 1849. [autobiography]
Roy, Lynette. [1942–]. b. Jamaica?
- *Brown Girl in the Ring: Rosemary Brown – a Biography for Young People*. Toronto: Sister Vision, 1992. [juvenile]
- *The Kindergarten Companion*. Uxbridge, ON: Orchid Communications, 1998. [prose]
- *Glenn Gould: The Genius and His Music: A Biography for Young People*. Ed. Hanna Miller. Toronto: [Roy], 1999. [juvenile]
- *Maureen Forrester: Canada's Charming Contralto: A Biography for Young People*. Ed. Hanna Miller. Toronto: [Roy], 1999. [juvenile]
- *Three Caribbean Women in Canadian Politics: A Biography for Young People*. Ed. Hanna Miller. Toronto: [Roy], 1999. [juvenile]
Ruck, Calvin W[oodrow]. [1925–]. b. Nova Scotia.
- *Canada's Black Battalion: No. 2 Construction, 1916–1920*. Halifax: Society for the Protection and Preservation of Black Culture in Nova Scotia, 1986. Rpt. *The Black Battalion: 1916–1920: Canada's Best Kept Military Secret*. Halifax: Nimbus Pub., 1987. [history]
- [et al.] *Universality of Human Rights and the Black Experience: A Collection of Speeches*. Dartmouth, NS: Black Cultural Centre for Nova Scotia, 1989. [compilation]
Ruggles, Clifton. [1940s–1997]. b. Québec.
- and Olivia Rovinescu. *Outsider Blues: A Voice from the Shadows*. Halifax, NS: Fernwood Publishing, 1996. [essays]

Russell, Hilary [Anna]. [1947–]. b. Jamaica.
- *All that Glitters: A Memorial to Ottawa's Capitol Theatre and Its Predecessors*. In *Canadian Historic Sites / Lieux historiques canadiens*. Ottawa: [Indian and Northern Affairs / Affaires indiennes et du Nord], 1975. [history]
- *Tout ce qui luit: Hommage au cinéma Capitol d'Ottawa et à ses prédécésseurs*. Dans *Lieux historiques canadiens*. Ottawa: [Parcs Canada / Parks Canada], 1980. [history]
- *Annotated Illustrations of Domestic Activities in Canada, ca. 1840–1920: A Description of the Project and a Classification Scheme*. [Ottawa]: Parks Canada, 1981. [prose]
- *Illustrations annotées des activités domestiques au Canada, ca 1840–1920: Une Description du projet et un schema de classification*. [Ottawa]: Parcs Canada, 1981. [prose]
- *Double Take: The Story of the Elgin and Winter Garden Theatres*. Toronto: Dundurn Press, 1989. [history]
- comp. *A Bibliography Relating to African Canadian History*. [Ottawa]: Historical Research Branch, National Historic Sites Directorate, 1990. [bibliography]
Sadlier, Rosemary. b. Ontario.
- *Leading the Way: Black Women in Canada*. Toronto: Umbrella Press, 1994. [biography]
- *Mary Ann Shadd: Publisher, Editor, Teacher, Lawyer, Suffragette*. Toronto: Umbrella Press, 1995. [juvenile]
- *Tubman: Harriet Tubman and the Underground Railroad: Her Life in the United States and Canada*. Toronto: Umbrella Press, 1996. [juvenile]
Sadu, Itah. [1961–]. b. Barbados.
- *How the Coconut Got Its Face*. Toronto: Carib-Can Publishers, Inc., 1988. [juvenile]
- *Christopher, Please Clean Up Your Room!* Richmond Hill, ON: Scholastic Canada, 1993; Buffalo, NY: Firefly, [1996]. [juvenile]
- *Name Calling*. Toronto: Well Versed Publications, 1992; Toronto: Women's Press, 1994. [juvenile]
- *Christopher Changes His Name*. Richmond Hill, ON: Scholastic Canada, 1996; Buffalo, NY: Firefly Books, 1998. [juvenile]
Saint-Charles, Jean. [1948–]. b. Haiti.
- *Affiches: Poésie*. Montréal: Éditions Rada, 1986. [poetry]
- *Phase: Poésie*. Montréal: Éditions Rada, 1986. [poetry]
- *Figures*. [Montréal]: Éditions Rada, 1987. [poetry]
- *Digues*. [Montréal]: Éditions Rada, 1991. [poetry]
- *Miroirs*. [Montréal]: Éditions Rada, 1991. [poetry]
Saint-Fleur, Henry. [1958–]. b. Haiti.
- *Transhumance: Poésie*. Montréal: Éditions du CIDIHCA, 1994. [poetry]
Samuels, I[an]. L. [1975–]. b. Alberta?
- *Fuga: Being a Selection from the Historical Document on the Nature of Slaves*. Calgary: housepress, 1998. [poetry]
- *Cabra*. Calgary: Red Deer Press, 2000, 2001. [poetry]
Sandiford, Keith A[rlington]. P[atrick]. [1936–]. b. Jamaica.
- *Great Britain and the Schlesweig-Holstein Question, 1848–64: A Study in Diplomacy, Politics, and Public Opinion*. Toronto: University of Toronto Press, 1975. [history]
- *Cricket and the Victorians*. Aldershot, UK: Scholar Press; Brookfield, VT: Ashgate Publishing Company, 1994. [history]

– and Earle H. Newton. *Combermere School and the Barbadian Society.* Jamaica: The Press UWI, 1995. [history]

– *Cricket Nurseries of Colonial Barbados: The Elite Schools, 1865–1966.* Kingston, Jamaica: The Press, University of the West Indies, 1998. [history]

Sandiford, Robert Edison. [1968–]. b. Québec.

– *Winter, Spring, Summer, Fall: Stories.* Montreal: Empyreal Press, 1995; Montreal: The Independent Press and Empyreal Press, 1999. [short fiction]

– *Attractive Forces.* New York: Amerotica – NBM, 1997. [adult comic book]

Santana, Assar-Mary. [1952–]. b. Brazil.

– *Boléro.* Trans. Suzanne Grenier. Montréal: Éditions du Remue-ménage, 1994. [fiction]

– *Boléro: A Novel.* Trans. Louise Hinton and Suzanne Grenier. Toronto: Women's Press, 1997. [fiction]

– *Récit de la saleté en attendant un bon bain.* Trans. Suzanne Grenier. Montréal: Éditions du Remue-ménage, [1997?] [fiction]

Saptel, Bonaventure F. [1960–].

– *Dying by Pieces and Other Rituals.* Toronto: Buzzard Press, 1998. [poetry]

Sarsfield, Mairuth Hodge. b. Québec.

– with Marcia Brown and Maria Otarola, eds. *Six Women from the South Discuss Gender in the Development Process / Six Femmes du Sud discutent du genre dans le processus de développement.* By/Par Asha Kambon et al. Ottawa: Match International Centre, 1993. [prose]

– ed. *Voices of Young Women / Voix de jeunes femmes.* Ottawa: Match International Centre, 1996. [prose]

– *No Crystal Stairs: A Novel.* Norval, ON: Moulin Publishing Limited, 1997; Toronto: Stoddart, 1998. [fiction]

Saunders, Charles R. [1946–]. b. United States.

– *Imaro.* New York: Daw Books, 1981. [fiction]

– *Imaro II: The Quest for Cush.* New York: Daw Books, 1984. [fiction]

– *Imaro III: The Trail of Bohu.* New York: Daw Books, 1985. [fiction]

– *La Route du Cush: Imaro II.* Trans. Michel Pagel. Paris: Garancière, 1986. [fiction]

– 'A Visit to Africville.' In *Africville: A Spirit That Lives On.* Exhibition catalogue. Halifax, NS and Dartmouth, NS: The Art Gallery, Mount Saint Vincent University et al., 1989. 5–21. [short fiction]

– *Sweat and Soul: Saga of Black Boxers from the Halifax Forum to Caesar's Palace.* Hantsport, NS: Lancelot Press; Dartmouth, NS: The Black Cultural Centre for Nova Scotia, 1990. [history]

– *Share and Care: The Story of the Nova Scotia Home for Colored Children.* Halifax, NS: Nimbus, 1994. [history]

– *Black and Bluenose: The Contemporary History of a Community.* Lawrencetown Beach, NS: Pottersfield Press, 1999. [prose]

Scobie, Carver Milton. b. Trinidad.

– *Memory's Song of an Island: A Grenadian Anthology.* [N.p.: n.p., 1969.] [poetry]

– *Upbeat: Drums, Drums, Drums.* Mayaro, TT: P.N.M. Publishing Co., 1973. [poetry]

– *Ancient: Folk Verses.* Toronto: Norran Press, 1997. [poetry]

- *Mausica Teachers College: 1962(65)–(67)1979, Looking Back*. Toronto: Norran Press, [1997?] [poetry]
- *Splinters Embedded: Right Justification*. Toronto: Norran Press, [1997?] [poetry]
Scott, Gilbert H. b. Jamaica.
- *Cultural Pluralism, Multiculturalism and Community Development*. Dartmouth, NS: Black Cultural Centre of Nova Scotia, 1987. [prose]
- et al. *Universality of Human Rights and the Black Experience: A Collection of Speeches*. Dartmouth, NS: Black Cultural Centre for Nova Scotia, 1989. [compilation]
Seaforth, Sybil. [1935–]. b. Jamaica.
- *Growing Up with Miss Milly*. [Hamilton, ON: n.p.], 1988. [fiction]
- *A Boundary for Vimal*. [Hamilton, ON: n.p.], 1996. [fiction]
- *Voyage to Sandy Bay*. [Hamilton, ON: n.p.], 1997. [fiction]
- *In Silence the Strands Unravel*. Hamilton, ON: Capricornus Enterprises, 1999. [fiction]
Sealey, Donna [Lee] Byard. b. Nova Scotia.
- *Colored Zion: The History of Zion United Baptist Church and the Black Community of Truro, Nova Scotia*. [Dartmouth, NS: Donna Byard Sealey, 2001.] [history]
Sears, Djanet. [1959–]. b. England.
- *Afrika Solo*. Toronto: Sister Vision, 1990. [drama]
- 'Who Killed Katie Ross? A True Tragedy in One Act.' In *Taking the Stage: Selections from Plays by Canadian Women*. Ed. Cynthia Zimmerman. Toronto: Playwrights Canada Press, 1994. 234–45. [drama]
- 'The Madwoman and the Fool: A Harlem Duet.' In George Seremba et al., eds, *Beyond the Pale* (1996), 144–9. [drama]
- *Harlem Duet*. [Winnipeg]: Scirocco Drama, 1997, 1998. [drama]
- 'Harlem Duet.' In Sears, ed., *Testifyin'*, vol. 1 (2000), 555–632. [drama]
- ed. *Tellin' It Like It Is: A Compendium of African Canadian Monologues for Actors*. Toronto: PUC Play Service, 2000. [anthology]
- ed. *Testifyin': Contemporary African Canadian Drama*. Volume 1. Toronto: Playwrights Canada Press, 2000. [anthology]
Sekyi-Otu, Ato. [1965–]. b. Ghana.
- *Fanon's Dialectic of Experience*. Cambridge, MA: Harvard University Press, 1996. [prose]
Semujanga, Josias. [1956–]. b. Rwanda.
- *Configuration de l'énonciation interculturelle dans le roman francophone*. [Québec]: Nuit blanche, 1996. [prose]
- [avec] Christiane Ndiaye, comps. *De Paroles en figures: Essais sur les littératures africaines et antillaises*. Par Amadou Koné et al. Montréal: Harmattan, 1996. [compilation]
- [et al.] *De paroles en figures: Essais sur les littératures africaines et antillaises*. Comps. Christiane Ndiaye et Josias Semujanga. Montréal: Harmattan, 1996. [compilation]
Senior, Olive. [1941–]. b. Jamaica.
- *The Message Is Change*. Kingston, JA: Kingston Publishers, 1972. [prose]
- *Once Upon a Time in Jamaica*. Ed. Officers of the Ministry of Education. Kingston, JA: Ministry of Education; Jamaican Tourist Board, 1977. [tales]
- *First in Jamaica*. Ed. Officers of the Ministry of Education. Kingston, JA: Ministry of Education; Jamaican Tourist Board, 1978. [tales]

- *Peenie Wallies and Silk Cotton Trees*. Ed. Officers of the Ministry of Education. Kingston, JA: Ministry of Education; Jamaican Tourist Board, 1978. [tales]
- *The Queen of Kingston and Other People*. Ed. Officers of the Ministry of Education. Kingston, JA: Ministry of Education; Jamaican Tourist Board, 1978. [tales]
- *A-Z of Jamaican Heritage*. Kingston, JA: Heinemann Educational Books (Caribbean), 1983. [prose]
- *Talking of Trees*. Kingston, JA: Calabash Publications, 1985. [poetry]
- *Summer Lightning and Other Stories*. Harlow, UK: Longman, 1986. [short fiction]
- *The Arrival of the Snake-Woman and Other Stories*. Harlow, UK: Longman, 1989. [short fiction]
- *Working Miracles: Women's Lives in the English-Speaking Caribbean*. London: J. Curry; Bloomington: Indiana University Press, 1991. [prose]
- *Zomerweerlicht*. Trans. Marie Luyten. The Hague, Netherlands: Ambo/Novib, 1992. [short fiction]
- *Gardening in the Tropics: Poems*. Toronto: McClelland & Stewart, 1994; Newcastle upon Tyne: Bloodaxe Books, 1995. [poetry]
- *Discerner of Hearts*. Toronto: McClelland & Stewart, 1995. [short fiction]
- *Das Erscheinen der Schlangenfrau*. Trans. Wolfgang Binder. Frankfurt, Germany: Dipa Verlag, 1996. [short fiction]

September, Dee. b. South Africa.
- *Making Waves*. Toronto: Unfinished Monument Press, 1979. [poetry]

Seremba, George Bwanika. [1958–]. b. Uganda.
- *Come Good Rain*. Winnipeg: Blizzard Publishing, 1993. [drama]
- with Yvette Nolan and Betty Quan, eds. *Beyond the Pale: Dramatic Writing from First Nations Writers and Writers of Colour*. Toronto: Playwrights Canada Press, 1996. [anthology]
- 'Napoleon of the Nile.' In George Seremba et al., eds, *Beyond the Pale* (1996), 72–9. [drama]
- [et al.] *Along Human Lines: Dramas from Refugee Lives*. Winnipeg: Blizzard, 2000. [drama]
- 'Come Good Rain.' In Sears, ed., *Testifyin'*, vol. 1 (2000), 329–80. [drama]

Shackelford, Theodore Henry. [1888–1923]. b. Ontario.
- *Mammy's Cracklin' Bread, and Other Poems*. Philadelphia: Press of I.W. Klopp Company, 1916. [poetry]
- *My Country and Other Poems*. Philadelphia: Press of I.W. Klopp Company, 1918. [poetry]

Shadd, Adrienne Lynn. [1954–]. b. Ontario.
- and Carl E. James, eds. *Talking about Difference: Encounters in Culture, Language and Identity*. Toronto: Between the Lines, 1994. Rpt. *Talking about Identity: Encounters in Race, Ethnicity, and Language*. Toronto: Between the Lines, 2001. [compilation]
- with Peggy Bristow, coord., et al. *'We're Rooted Here and They Can't Pull Us Up': Essays in African-Canadian Women's History*. Toronto: University of Toronto Press, 1994. [history]

Shadd, Mary A[nn]. [Mary Ann Shadd Cary]. [1823–93]. b. United States.
- *Condition of Colored People*. Pamphlet. Wilmington, DE: n.p., 1849. [prose]

– *A Plea for Emigration; or, Notes of Canada West; in its moral, social, and political aspect; with suggestions respecting Mexico, West Indies, and Vancouver's Island, for the information of colored emigrants.* Detroit: G.W. Pattison, 1852. [prose]
– *A Plea for Emigration, or, Notes of Canada West.* 1852. Ed. Richard Almonte. Toronto: The Mercury Press, 1998. [prose]
Shadd, Ruth Ann. [1945–]. b. Ontario.
– *Breaking Loose: A History of African-Canadian Dance in Southwestern Ontario 1900–1955.* Windsor, ON: Preney Print & Litho Inc., 1995. [history]
Shadd-Evelyn, Karen. [1958–]. b. Ontario.
– *I'd Rather Live in Buxton.* Toronto: Simon & Pierre Publishing, 1993. [memoir]
– [et al.] *Something to Hope For: The Story of the Fugitive Slave Settlement, Buxton, Canada West.* [North Buxton, ON: Buxton National Historic Site & Museum, 2000.] [history]
Shadrock [pseud.?] [1940–].
– *The Truth, the Lie, and the Bible: Christianity Exposed with All Its Naked Lies ...* Ed. Reggie Andalcio and Sandy McIntyre. Toronto: Fifth Ribb Publishing, 1990. Rpt. *The Truth, the Lie, and the Bible: Bible Companion ...* Toronto: Fifth Ribb Publishing, 1992, [1994], 1995. [prose]
– *The Forgotten Israelites: God's Chosen People, Another Bible Companion.* Toronto: Fifth Ribb Publishing, 1991. [prose]
– ed. *The Word, the Israelites, and the Damned.* Toronto: Fifth Ribb Publishing, 1993. [essay compilation]
– ed. *The Spirit of Egypt in America.* By Michael Hinds and Tony Castrilli. Toronto: Fifth Ribb Publishing, 1995. [prose]
Shirley, James R. [1944–]. b. United States.
– *Jim Shirley Returns: The Art of James R. Shirley.* Ed. Ingrid Jenkner. Halifax, NS: Mount Saint Vincent University Art Gallery, 2000. [booklet]
Shreve, Dorothy Shadd. [1909–]. b. Ontario.
– *Pathfinders of Liberty and Truth: A Century with the Amherstburg Regular Missionary Baptist Association.* Merlin, ON: Merlin Standard, 1940; N.p.: n.p., 1990. [history]
– *The AfriCanadian Church: A Stabilizer.* Jordan Station, ON: Paideia Press, 1983. [history]
'Sierra Leone Settlers' Letters: 1791–1800.' In *Black Writers in Britain, 1760–1890.* [Ed.] Paul Edwards and David Dabydeen. Edinburgh University Press, 1991. [Letters by ex-Nova Scotians: Thomas Peters; David Edmon; Susana Smith; David George et al. (a petition); Cato Perkins; Isaac Anderson; James Liaster; Luke Jordan; Nathaniel Snowball; James Robertson, et al. (a petition).]
Silvera, Makeda. [1955–]. b. Jamaica.
– *Silenced: Caribbean Domestic Workers Talk with Makeda Silvera.* Toronto: Sister Vision, 1983. Rpt. *Silenced: Talks with Working Class West Indian Women about Their Lives and Struggles as Domestic Workers in Canada.* Toronto: Williams-Wallace, 1984; rev. ed. Toronto: Sister Vision, 1989, 1995. [prose, interviews]
– ed. *Fireworks: The Best of Fireweed.* Toronto: Women's Press, 1986. [anthology]
– *Growing Up Black: A Resource Manual for Black Youth.* Toronto: Sister Vision, 1989. [manual]
– and Nila Gupta, eds. *The Issue Is 'Ism: Women of Colour Speak Out.* Toronto: Sister Vision, 1989. [anthology: a reprint of *Fireweed: A Feminist Quarterly* 16 (1983), an issue focusing on women of colour]

- ed. *Piece of My Heart: A Lesbian of Colour Anthology*. Toronto: Sister Vision, 1991. [anthology]
- *Remembering G and Other Stories*. Toronto: Sister Vision Press, 1991. [short fiction]
- ed. *The Other Woman: Women of Colour in Contemporary Canadian Literature*. Toronto: Sister Vision, 1992. [interviews]
- *Her Head a Village and Other Stories*. Vancouver: Press Gang Publishers, 1994. [short fiction].
- and C. Allyson Lee, eds. *Pearls of Passion: A Treasury of Lesbian Erotica*. Toronto: Sister Vision Press, 1994. [anthology]
- et al., eds. *'Ma'-ka: Diasporic Juks: Contemporary Writing by Queers of African Descent*. Toronto: Sister Vision Press, 1997. [anthology]
- and Stephanie Martin, eds. *Sapodilla: The Sister Vision Book of Lesbian Poetry*. Toronto: Sister Vision Press, 1999. [anthology]
- *Maria's Revenge*. Vancouver: Press Gang Publishers, 2000. [fiction]
- *The Heart Does Not Bend*. Toronto: Random House Canada, 2002. [fiction]
Skinner, Bette. b. Nova Scotia.
- coord. *Black Community Profile: A Survey of the Black Population of New Glasgow, Nova Scotia, Summer 1973*. [Halifax, NS]: Nova Scotia Human Rights Commission, 1973. [study]
Smallwood, Thomas. [1801–83?]. b. United States.
- *A Narrative of Thomas Smallwood (Coloured Man): Giving an Account of His Birth, the Period He Was Held in Slavery, His Release and Removal to Canada, etc.: Together with an Account of the Underground Railroad*. Toronto: Printed for the author by James Stephens, 1851. [autobiography]
- *A Narrative of Thomas Smallwood (Coloured Man)*. 1851. Ed. Richard Almonte. Toronto: The Mercury Press, 2000. [autobiography]
Smith, Charles [C.] [1953–]. b. United States.
- ed. *The Teeth of the Whirlwind: Poems by* [Lillian] *Allen* ... [Dionne] *Brand* ... [Clifton] *Joseph* ... [Charles C.] *Smith*. Toronto: Black Perspectives, 1984. [anthology]
- ed. *sad dances in a field of white*. Toronto: Is Five Press, 1985. [anthology]
- *Partial Lives*. Toronto: Williams-Wallace, 1987. [poetry]
Smith, Craig. [1961–]. b. Nova Scotia.
- with Quenta Tynes and Cecil Wright, eds. *Journey: African Canadian History Study Guide*. Yarmouth, NS: Southwest Nova African Canadian Cultural Awareness Project and Human Resources Development Canada, 2000. [history]
Smith, Fernando C[arol]. [1951–]. b. Antigua.
- with Keithlyn B. Smith. *To Shoot Hard Labour: The Life and Times of Samuel Smith, an Antiguan Workingman, 1877–1982*. Scarborough, ON: Edan's Publishers, 1986, 1988. [transcribed autobiography]
Smith, Keithlyn B[yron]. [1938–]. b. Antigua.
- and Fernando C. Smith. *To Shoot Hard Labour: The Life and Times of Samuel Smith, an Antiguan Workingman, 1877–1982*. Scarborough, ON: Edan's Publishers, 1986, 1988. [transcribed autobiography]
Sonia-Pascale. b. Haiti.
- [avec] Gilles Gauthier. *Plan de nègre: Récit*. Montréal: VLB, 1994. [autobiography]

Spence, Christopher M[ichael]. [1962–]. b. Ontario.
- *The Skin I'm In: Racism, Sports and Education.* Halifax, NS: Fernwood Publishing, 1999. [prose]
Spence, Lily Agnes. [1932–]. b. St Lucia.
- *The Whirring Windmills: A Complete Collection of Poems; and An Iouanaloaon Mermaid's Tale: (A Narrative Poem).* Burnaby, BC: Morning Star Press, 1997. [poetry]
Spence, Raymond. b. Ontario?
- *Nothing Black but a Cadillac: A Novel.* New York: G.P. Putnam's Sons, 1969. Rpt. *Nothing Black but a Cadillac.* New York: Putnam, 1986. [fiction]
States, David ['Skip']. b. Nova Scotia.
- with Anthony Johnstone. *Cultural Sensitization and the Black Community of Nova Scotia.* Halifax, NS: Nova Scotia Department of Education, 1981. [prose]
States, W[ellington]. N[aey]. [1877–1927]. b. Nova Scotia.
- comp. *Hymns Sung at the Services.* Halifax, NS: n.p., 1903. [compilation]
Stephens, Kwame. [1961–].
- *Accra! Accra!: Poems about Modern Afrikans.* Toronto: KS.COM, 1998. [poetry]
Stevenson, Byron.
- [and] Jacqueline A.Wilson, Veronica Sullivan. *Caribbean Carnival Canadian Style: A History Souvenir Special and a Guide to Happenings.* Toronto: Afro-Caribbean Alternative Secondary School Committee, 1986. [history and guide]
Stevenson, Darryl. b. Manitoba.
- and Pat Graham, eds. *The Black Experience in Manitoba: A Collection of Memories.* Winnipeg: The Winnipeg School Division No. 1 and the IDEA Centre, 1993. [compilation]
Steward, [Theophilus] Austin. [1794–1860]. b. United States.
- *Twenty-Two Years a Slave, and Forty Years a Freeman; Embracing a Correspondence of Several Years, While President of Wilberforce Colony.* Rochester, NY: Alling & Cory, 1856. Rpt. *Twenty-Two Years a Slave, and Forty Years a Freeman; Embracing a Correspondence of Several Years, While President of Wilberforce Colony, London, Canada West.* Rochester, NY: William Alling, 1857; 4th ed. Canandaigua, NY: [Steward], 1867. [autobiography]
- 'Twenty-Two Years a Slave, and Forty Years a Freeman.' In *Four Fugitive Slave Narratives.* Reading, MA: Addison-Wesley Pub. Co., [1969]. [autobiography]
Stewart, Douglas.
- et al., eds. *Ma'-ka: Diasporic Juks: Contemporary Writing by Queers of African Descent.* Toronto: Sister Vision Press, 1997. [anthology]
Stewart, H.U. b. Ontario?
- *Historical Sketches of the William St. Baptist Church.* N.p.: n.p., 1948. [history]
Still, William. [1821–1902]. b. United States.
- *The Underground Rail Road: A Record of the Facts, Authentic Narratives, Letters, etc., Narrating the Hardships, Hair-breadth Escapes and Death Struggles of the Slaves in Their Efforts for Freedom and Related by Themselves, and Others, or Witnessed by the Author; Together with Sketches of Some of the Largest Stockholders, and Most Liberal Aiders and Advisers, of the Road.* Philadelphia: Porter and Coates, 1872. Rev. ed. *Underground Railroad Records, With a life of the Author, narrating the hardships, hair-breadth escapes,*

and death struggles of the slaves in their efforts for freedom; together with sketches of some of the eminent friends of freedom, and most liberal aiders and advisers of the road. Philadelphia: William Still, 1886. [history]

Stowers, William (Walter?) Haslip [pseud., Sanda]. [1859–]. b. Canada West [Ontario].

– and William H. Anderson. *Appointed: An American Novel.* Detroit: Anderson and Stowers, 1894. [fiction]

Sudan, Nazzam Al [pseud. of Marvin X (Marvin E. Jackmon)]. [1944–]. b. United States.

– *Ali Kamal Al Kadir Sudan: 'Black Man in a White Land.'* Burlington, ON: Al Kitab Sudan, 1967. [interview with Ali Kamal Al Kadir Sudan, pseud. of Austin Clarke]

– *Muslims and Vietnam: A Position Paper.* [Burlington, ON: Al Kitab Sudan Publications], 1967 [prose]

– *Sudan Rajuli Samia / Black Man Listen.* Burlington, ON: Al Kitab Sudan Publications, 1967. [poetry]

– [as Marvin X]. *Love and War.* [Castro Valley, CA: Black Sparrow Press]?, 1995. [poetry]

– [as Marvin X (Jackmon)]. *Somethin' Proper: The Life and Times of a North American African Poet.* Castro Valley, CA: Black Sparrow Press, 1998. [autobiography]

– [as Marvin X]. *After Difficulty, Ease: New Poems.* Castro Valley, CA: Black Sparrow Press, 1998. [poetry]

Sullivan, Veronica.

– [and] Jacqueline A.Wilson, Byron Stevenson. *Caribbean Carnival Canadian Style: A History Souvenir Special and a Guide to Happenings.* Toronto: Afro-Caribbean Alternative Secondary School Committee, 1986. [history and guide]

– *Gem Activity Book: Discovering Black Scientists and Inventors.* [Scarborough, ON]: Carib-Can Publishers, 1986. [juvenile]

– *Gem Activity Book: Uncovering Black Scientists and Inventors.* [Scarborough, ON: Carib-Can Publishers, 1987.] [juvenile]

– *Discovering Kwanzaa.* Toronto: C.C. Communications, 1991. [juvenile]

– *Discovering Kwanzaa 2.* Toronto: C.C. Communications, 1991. [juvenile]

Suprice, Lenous [pseud., Nounous]. b. Haiti.

– *Reverrant: Poèmes; suivi de Journal intime.* [Montréal]: Édition Lagomatik, 1990. [poetry]

– *Bwamitan.* Montréal: Édition Lagomatic, 1993. [poetry]

– *Faits divers: Poésie.* Montréal: CIDIHCA, 1994. [poetry]

– [et] Dary Jean-Charles, Mozart-F. Longuefosse. *Pages triangulaires: Poésie.* Montréal: Éditions des Intouchables, 1994. [poetry]

– *En enjambant le vent: Poèmes (1990–1995).* Montréal: Humanitas, 1997. [poetry]

– *L'Île en pages: Poèmes.* Brossard, QC: Humanitas, [1998?] [poetry]

– *Rouge cueillaison: Poèmes.* Brossard, QC: Humanitas, 2000. [poetry]

Sutton, James W[inford]. [1916–]. b. Nevis.

– *A Testimony of Triumph: A Narrative of the Life of James Sutton and Family in Nevis and St. Kitts, 1920–1940.* Scarborough, ON: Edan's Publishers, 1987. [biography]

– *Our Love Prevailed (Narrative of the Life of James Sutton and Family in St. Kitts, Nevis, Anguilla, West Indies, during the 1940's and 1950's.)* Scarborough, ON: Sutton Publishing, 1990. [biography]

- *A Testimony of Triumph: A Narrative of the Life of James W. Sutton and Family in St. Kitts-Nevis-Anguilla, 1920s–1940s, and of the Social, Economic, and Political Development of the Islands during the Period.* Rev. ed. Scarborough, ON: Sutton Publishing, 1996. [biography]

Sydney, Elliott N.
- *Celebrating Black Scientists and Inventors.* Toronto: Village Books, 1992. [juvenile]

Talbot, Carol [Ann] [Carol Tremaine]. b. Ontario.
- [as Carol Tremaine] and Georgia Boyd. *The Saga of Anne-Marie Weems, Fugitive Girl of 15.* Rexdale, ON: Identity Black Canada, 1977. [juvenile]
- *Growing Up Black in Canada.* Toronto: Williams-Wallace, 1984, 1989. [memoir]

Tardieu-Dehoux, Charles. [1947–]. b. Haiti.
- *Cabanons.* Montréal: Éditions de l'Albatross, 1967. [poetry]
- *Sang de bêtes, Ventre d'hommes.* [Dans] *L'Haïtien.* Montréal: Les Éditions de Sainte-Marie, 1968. [poetry]
- *L'Évaluation et l'orientation des étudiants immigrants haïtiens à Montréal.* N.p.: [C. Tardieu-Dehoux], 1977. [prose]
- and Esmerelda Thornhill, eds. *Final Report on the Aspirations and Expectations of the Quebec Black Community with Regard to Education.* By Black Community Working Group on Education. Montréal: n.p., 1978. [report]

Taylor, Patrick D[avid]. M[ichael]. [1953–]. b. Barbados.
- *The Narrative of Liberation: Perspectives on Afro-Caribbean Literature, Popular Culture, and Politics.* Ithaca, NY: Cornell University Press, 1989. [prose]
- with Harry P. Diaz and Joanna W.A. Rummens, eds. *Forging Identities and Patterns of Development in Latin America and the Caribbean.* Toronto: Canadian Scholars' Press, 1991. [prose]

Taylor, Sheldon. b. St. Kitts.
- *Many Rivers to Cross: Four Hundred Years: African-Canadian History.* Toronto: Multicultural History Society of Ontario, 1992. [exhibition catalogue]
- with Bromley Armstrong. *Bromley: Tireless Champion for Just Causes: Memoirs.* Toronto: Vitabu Publishing, 2000. [biography]

Théodore, Oriol. [1942–]. b. Haiti.
- *L'Idéologie blanche et l'aliénation des Noirs: Essai.* Montréal: Kauss Éditeurs, 1983. [prose]
- *Une philosophie pour une république.* Montréal: Kauss Éditeurs, 1984. [prose]

Thomas, Carolyn G. [194?–]. b. Nova Scotia.
- ed. *Reflections: The East Preston United Baptist Church on Its 150th Anniversary.* Hantsport, NS: Lancelot Press, 1996. [history]

Thomas, H. Nigel. [1947–]. b. St Vincent.
- *From Folklore to Fiction: A Study of Folk Heroes and Rituals in the Black American Novel.* New York: Greenwood Press, 1988. [prose]
- [et] Maximilien Laroche, Euridice Figueiredo. *Juan Bobo, Jan Sot, Ti Jan et Bad John: Figures littéraires de la Caraïbe.* Sainte-Foy, QC: GRELCA, 1991. [essays]
- *Spirits in the Dark.* Concord, ON: Anansi, 1993; London: Heinemann, 1994. [fiction]
- *How Loud Can the Village Cock Crow? Stories.* Saint-Laurent, QC: AFO Enterprises, 1996. [short fiction]

- *Moving through Darkness.* Saint-Laurent, QC: AFO Enterprises, 1999. [poetry]
- *Behind the Face of Winter.* Toronto: TSAR, 2001. [fiction]
Thomas, Owen A[ndrew]. [1962–]. b. Ontario?
- *Niagara's Freedom Trail: A Guide to African-Canadian History on the Niagara Peninsula.* Thorold, ON: The Niagara Region Tourist Council, 1994; 2nd. rev. ed., [Thorold, ON]: The Corporation, 1996. [history]
Thomas, Ven L. b. Trinidad.
- *Singing in Steel: Poems on the Steelband.* Toronto: Creative Crew, 1983. [poetry]
- *The Rainbow Rastas.* Scarborough, ON: Venn Educational Products, 1994. [juvenile]
Thomas, Verna. [1935–]. b. Nova Scotia.
- with Joyce Ross and Mary Glasgow. *The Meeting at the Well: A Brief History Written in Commemoration of the East Preston Ladies Auxiliary 69th Anniversary.* East Preston, NS: The Auxiliary, 1987. [history]
- and Valerie Carvery. *Report on the Halifax Jamaica Women's Exchange Project.* [Ottawa]: CMHC, [1990]. [prose]
- *Invisible Shadows: A Black Woman's Life in Nova Scotia.* Halifax, NS: Nimbus, 2001. [autiobiography]
Thompson, Andrea. [1967–]. b. Ontario.
- *Fire Belly.* Vancouver: Pink Flamingo Works, 1997. [poetry]
- *Eating the Seed.* Victoria, BC: Ekstasis Editions, 1999. [poetry]
Thornhill, Esmerelda Mary-Anne. [1948–]. b. Québec?
- and Charles Tardieu-Dehoux, eds. *Final Report on the Aspirations and Expectations of the Quebec Black Community with Regard to Education.* By Black Community Working Group on Education. Montréal: n.p., 1978. [report]
- *Le Revers de la médaille: Des Oublis de l'histoire.* Montréal: Commission des droits de la personne du Québec, 1982. [history]
- *So Often against Us, So Seldom for Us: Being Black and Living with the Canadian Justice System.* Montréal: Commission des droits de la personne du Québec, [1989?]. [report]
- [avec Monique Lortie et Nicole Pothier]. *Février, c'est le mois de l'histoire noire!* [Montréal]: Commission des droits de la personne du Québec, [1993]. [history]
Tolliver, Althea. b. Nova Scotia.
- and James A. François. *From Africville to New Road: How Four Communities Planned Their Development.* Dartmouth, NS: Watershed Joint Action Committee / Black United Front, 1983. [study]
Tolliver, Lynn [Orrin Lynn Tolliver, Jr]. [1950–]. b. United States.
- *Everybody Reads Lynn Tolliver Jr.* Victoria, BC: Trafford Pub., 1996. [prose]
- *O.J. Simpson: The Official No Affiliation Reference Guide.* Victoria, BC: Trafford Pub., 1996. [prose]
- *Dialogue.* Victoria, BC: Trafford Pub., 1997. [poetry and prose]
- *Prenuptial: The Rough Draft.* Victoria, BC: Trafford Pub., 1997. [guide]
- *The Best of Lynn Tolliver Jr.* Victoria, BC: Trafford Pub., 1998. [prose]
- *When You Wish upon a Star: A Spoof on the President's* [Clinton's Lewinsky] *Controversy.* Victoria, BC: Trafford Pub., 1998. [prose]
- *Movie Concepts, Sitcom Presentations.* Victoria, BC: Trafford Pub., 2000. [guide]

– *Prenuptial: The Paperback*. Victoria, BC: Trafford Pub., 2000. [guide]
– *To E or Not to E: A Collection of Short Poems and Theories*. Victoria, BC: Trafford Pub.,
   2000. [poetry and prose]
Touré, Babakar Pierre. b. Ivory Coast.
– avec Renée Bouque. *L'Image des groupes ethniques dans les médias québécois*. [Québec]:
   Association des travailleurs immigrants et québécois, 1987. [report]
Toussaint, Eddy.
– avec Eva von Gencsy. *Standard de la Féderation des loisirs-danse du Québec pour
   l'enseignement du jazz*. [Montréal: Féderation des loisirs-danse du Québec], 1972.
   [guide]
Trotz, D. A[lissa]. [1968–]. b. Ontario.
– with Linda Peake. *Gender, Ethnicity and Place: Guyanese Women's Identities*. London:
   Routledge, 1999. [prose]
Troy, William. b. United States.
– *Hair-Breadth Escapes from Slavery to Freedom*. Manchester, England: W. Bremner, 1861.
   [autobiography]
Tucker, Ernest.
– *Underworld Dweller*. New York: Rivercross Publishing, 1994. [fiction]
Tudor, Beverley Ethelina. [1950–]. b. Barbados.
– *The Faithful Donkey and Other Poems*. [St-Laurent, QC: AFO Enterprises, 1992.]
   [juvenile]
Tulloch, Headley. [1934–]. b. Jamaica?
– *Black Canadians: A Long Line of Fighters*. Toronto: NC Press, 1975. [history]
Tynes, Gertrude. b. Nova Scotia.
– with Doris Evans. *Telling the Truth: Reflections: Segregated Schools in Nova Scotia*.
   Hantsport, NS: Lancelot Press, 1995. [history]
Tynes, Maxine. [1949–]. b. Nova Scotia.
– *Borrowed Beauty*. Porters Lake, NS: Pottersfield, 1987. [poetry]
– *Woman Talking Woman*. Porters Lake, NS: Pottersfield, 1990. [poetry]
– *Save the World for Me*. Lawrencetown Beach, NS: Pottersfield, 1991. [juvenile]
– *Door of My Heart*. Lawrencetown Beach, NS: Pottersfield, 1993. [poetry]
Tynes, Quenta. [1969–]. b. Nova Scotia.
– with Craig Smith and Cecil Wright, eds. *Journey: African Canadian History Study
   Guide*. Yarmouth, NS: Southwest Nova African Canadian Cultural Awareness
   Project and Human Resources Development Canada, 2000. [history]
Uhindu-gingala, Ginganj.
– *Terre des autres*. Montréal: Des Éditions d'Orphée, 1990. [poetry]
VanDyke, Janice [Janice Banigan]. [1942–]. b. Ontario.
– *Like the Leaves*. Windsor, ON: Sumner Printing and Publishing Co. Ltd, 1972.
   [juvenile]
Victor, Éternel. b. Haiti.
– [avec] Jean-Serge Joseph. *Haïti en péril*. Montréal: Kauss Éditeurs, 1988. [prose]
Villefranche, Marjorie [Marjorie Brès]. b. Haiti.
– et al. *L'Expérience ti pye zoranj monte ...* Outremont, QC: Grafik Universel, 1989.
   [juvenile]

– *Vwazen, vwazen: kaye egzèsis*. Montréal: Les Éditions du CIDIHCA, 1993. [guide]
Walcott, Rinaldo. [1965–]. b. Barbados.
– *Black Like Who? Writing Black Canada*. Toronto: Insomniac Press, 1997. [prose]
– ed. *Rude: Contemporary Black Canadian Cultural Criticism*. Toronto: Insomniac Press, 2000. [essays]
Walcott, Roderick. [1930–]. b. Saint Lucia.
– *Harrowing of Benjy*. Kingston, JA: Caribbean Plays Edition, 1958. [drama]
– *Albino Joe*. Port of Spain, TT: Caribbean Plays Edition, U.W.I., 1966. [drama]
– *Shrove Tuesday March: A Play of the Steel Band*. Port of Spain, TT: Caribbean Plays Edition, 1966; Mona, JA: U.W.I., Extra-Mural Studies, [1966]. [drama]
– *A Flight of Sparrows*. Port of Spain. TT: Caribbean Plays Edition, U.W.I., 1967. [drama]
– *Malfinis or the Heart of a Child*. Port of Spain, TT: Caribbean Plays Edition, U.W.I., 1967. Rpt. *Malfinis, or, The Heart of a Child: A Trial in Purgatory*. St Augustine, TT: U.W.I., Extra-Mural Studies, 1981. [drama]
– 'Cul-de-sac: A Play (excerpts).' In *A Shapely Fire: Changing the Literary Landscape*. Ed. Cyril Dabydeen. Oakville, ON: Mosaic Press, 1987. 139–75. [drama]
Walker, A.B. b. British Columbia.
– *The Negro Problem; or, The Philosophy of Race Development from a Canadian Standpoint*. Atlanta, [1890?] [prose]
– *A Message to the Public*. Saint John, NB: n.p., [1903?] [prose]
Wallace, Ann P. b. Jamaica.
– ed. *Daughters of the Sun, Women of the Moon: Poetry by Black Canadian Women*. Stratford, ON: Williams-Wallace, 1991. [anthology]
– with J.A. Wainwright et al., eds. *Border Lines: Contemporary Poems in English*. Toronto: Copp Clark, 1995. [anthology]
Wallace, Marie Stark. [1867–1966]. b. British Columbia.
– 'Notes made by Maria Albertina Stark (afterwards Mrs. Wallace) from the recollections of her mother, Sylvia Stark, who was born a slave in Clay County, Missouri, and settled on Salt Spring Island, with her husband, Louis Stark, and family in the year 1860, as homesteaders.' Victoria, BC: Provincial Archives, unpublished. [See Crawford Kilian, *Go*, 181.] [biography]
Wallen, Thelma J. b. Québec.
– *Multiculturalism and Quebec: A Province in Crisis*. Stratford, ON: Williams-Wallace Publishers, 1991. [essay]
Walls, Bryan E. b. Ontario.
– *The Road That Led to Somewhere*. Windsor, ON: Olive Publishing Co., 1980. [fiction]
Walters, Ewart. b. Jamaica.
– ed. *Jamaican Canadians: A Commitment to Excellence*. Toronto: Jamaican-Canadian Association, 1987. [biographies]
– *Resistance and Vision: The Making of Jamaica's National Heroes*. Ottawa: Boyd McRubie Communications, Inc., 1997. [history]
Ward, Frederick. [1937–]. b. United States.
– *Poems*. Albuquerque: Duende, 1964. [poetry]
– ed. *Anthology of Nine Baha'i Poets*. Detroit: n.p., 1966. [anthology]

- ed. *Present Tense*. Halifax, NS: New Options School, 1972. [anthology]
- *Riverlisp: Black Memories*. Montreal: Tundra Books, 1974. [fiction]
- *Nobody Called Me Mine: Black Memories*. Montreal: Tundra Books, 1977. [fiction]
- *A Room Full of Balloons*. Montreal: Tundra Books, 1981. [fiction]
- *The Curing Berry*. Toronto: Williams-Wallace, 1983. [poetry]

Ward, Samuel Ringgold. [1817–66]. b. United States.

- *Autiobiography of a Fugitive Negro; His Anti-Slavery Labours in the United States, Canada and England*. London: J. Snow, 1855. [autobiography]
- *Reflections of the Jordan Rebellion*. 1866. [memoir?]

Watkis, Evadne L. b. Jamaica.

- *Seh Wah?? Poetry in Jamaican Dialect (Patois)*. [Toronto: n.p., 1990?] [poetry]

Watson, Edward A[nthony]. [1936–]. b. Jamaica.

- *Out of the Silent Stone and Other Poems*. Red Hills, JA: Bruckings House, 1976. [poetry]
- *A Study of Selected English Critical Terms from 1650 to 1800: A Constellation*. New York: Peter Lang, 1987. [study]
- and E.W. Ducharme. *Literary Criticism: Ten Approaches: An Introductory Reader*. Toronto: Canadian Scholars' Press, 1990. [prose]

Watson, G. Llewellyn. b. Jamaica.

- *Social Theory and Critical Understanding*. Washington, DC: University Press of America, 1982. [prose]
- ed. *Black Society in the New World: Essays in Comparative Sociology*. Lexington, MA: [?], 1986. [compilation]
- *Dilemmas and Contradictions in Social Theory*. Lanham, MD: University Press of America, 1987. [prose]
- and Aubrey W. Bonnett, eds. *Emerging Perspectives on the Black Diaspora*. Lanham, MD: University Press of America, 1990. [compilation]
- [with] Janet P. Sentner. *Feminism and Women's Issues: An Annotated Bibliography and Research Guide*. New York: Garland Publishing, 1990. [bibliography]
- *Jamaican Sayings: With Notes on Folklore, Aesthetics, and Social Control*. Tallahassee, FL: Florida A&M University Press, 1991. [prose]

Watson, Norbert. b. Jamaica.

- *The Metaphor Lays Barren*. [Toronto]: n.p., 1986. [poetry]
- *Lyrics and Shorter Poems*. Toronto: [Watson], 1987. [poetry]

Wèche, Mérès. b. Haiti.

- *L'Onction du St-Fac ou Au-delà de Mais Gate*. [Trois-Rivières, QC]: n.p., 1980. [fiction]

Wesley-Daye, Gloria [Gloria Anne Wesley-Desmond]. [1948–]. b. Nova Scotia.

- *To My Someday Child*. Pierrefonds, QC: Bilongo Publications, 1975. [poetry]

Westmaas, Rupert H.D. [193?–]. b. British Guiana [Guyana].

- *'101' Rupert's Rhymes: Entertainment for Ordinary Folk Who Enjoy Controversial, Philosophical, and Humorous Rhymes, Including Love*. [Gloucester, ON: Rupert H.D. Westmaas, 1988.] [poetry]

White, Melville A. [1959–]. b. Jamaica.

- *Oh, Mel! Love Rhapsodies and Blues: A Love Joint*. [Toronto]: Mello Orange, 2001. [poetry]

White, Michael. [1941–].
– *The Voice of the Seed: A Collection of Poems and Songs.* Pickering, ON: Ruminech Publishing House, 1994. [poetry]
Whyte, Thomas Henry. b. United States.
– *Poetical Inspiration.* Toronto: Rowen Press, 1934. [poetry]
Williams, Dorothy W. b. Québec.
– *Blacks in Montreal, 1628–1986: An Urban Demography.* Cowansville, QC: Éditions Yvon Blais, 1989. [history]
– *The Road to Now: A History of Blacks in Montréal.* Montréal: Véhicule Press, 1997. [history]
– *Les Noirs à Montréal: Essai démographique urbaine.* Trans. Pierre DesRuisseaux. Montréal: VLB Éditeur, 1998. [history]
Williams, Gershom Antonio. [1936–]. b. Jamaica.
– *The Native Strength.* Toronto: n.p., 1968. [fiction]
– *A Hero for Jamaica: A Novel of the Living Legend of Marcus Garvey.* New York: Exposition Press, 1973. [fiction]
Williams, Peter A. Jr. [1780–1840]. b. British America [United States].
– *An Oration on the Abolition of the Slave Trade, Delivered in the African Church, in the City of New York, January 1, 1808.* New York: Samuel Wood, 1808. [prose]
– *A Discourse Delivered on the Death of Captain Paul Cuffee, before the New York African Institution, in the A.M.E. Zion Church, October ?1, 1817.* New York: B. Young & Company, 1817, 1818. [prose]
– *Discourse Delivered in St. Philip's Church, for the Benefit of the Coloured Community of Wilberforce in Upper Canada, on the Fourth of July, 1830.* New York: G.F. Bunce, 1830. [prose]
Wilson, Jacqueline A.
– [and] Veronica Sullivan, Byron Stevenson. *Caribbean Carnival Canadian Style: A History Souvenir Special and a Guide to Happenings.* Toronto: Afro-Caribbean Alternative Secondary School Committee, 1986. [history and guide]
Wilson, Trevor. [1957–].
– *Diversity at Work: The Business Case for Equity.* New York and Toronto: John Wiley & Sons, 1996. [prose]
– *Diversity at Work: The Business Case for Equity.* With case studies by Mary Ann Sayers. Toronto: John Wiley & Sons, 1997. [prose]
Wilson, Victor-Emmanuel Roberto. [1928–] b. Haiti.
– *Légende Arrawak: Poème en vers libres et en six tableaux.* Québec: V.-E.R. Wilson, [1973]. Rpt. *Aguanamo, Légende Arrawak: Poème en vers libres et en six tableaux.* Québec: Éditions Garneau, 1974. [poetry]
– *Le Général Alexandre Dumas: Soldat de la liberté.* Ste-Foy, QC: Éditions Quisqueya-Québec, [1977]. [biography]
– *Simon Bolivar: Vu par un citoyen du Québec.* [La Prairie, QC]: Éditions M. Broquet, 1983. [biography]
– *L'Extraordinaire odyssée: Christophe Colomb, 1492–1992.* Ste-Foy, QC: Éditions Quisqueya-Québec, 1991. [prose]

Wilson, V[incent]. Seymour. [1937–]. b. Trinidad.
– with J.E. Hodgetts et al. *The Biography of an Institution: The Civil Service Commission of Canada, 1908–1967*. Montreal: McGill-Queen's University Press, 1972. [prose]
– and G. Bruce Doern. *Issues in Canadian Public Policy*. [Toronto]: Macmillan of Canada, 1974. [textbook]
– with J.E. Hodgetts et al. *Histoire d'une Institution*. Québec: Les Presses de l'Université Laval, 1975. [prose]
– *Canadian Public Policy and Administration: Theory and Environment*. Toronto: McGraw-Hill Ryerson, 1980. [textbook]
– *Fiscal Federalism and Constitutional Concerns: The Case of Canada*. Canberra: Fiscal Federalism Centre, Australian National University, 1992. [monograph]
– with C.E.S. Franks, co-ed., et al. *Canada's Century: Governance in a Maturing Society, Essays in Honor of J. Meisel*. Montreal: McGill-Queen's University Press, 1994. [essays]
– with J.R. Mallory. *The Structure of Canadian Government*. Toronto: Oxford University Press, 1997. [prose]
– *Value for Many: The Institute of Public Administration of Canada, 1947–1997*. Toronto: Institute of Public Administration of Canada / Institut d'administration publique au Canada, 1997. [prose]
Wiwa, Ken. [1968–]. b. Nigeria.
– *In the Shadow of a Saint*. Toronto: Alfred A. Knopf Canada, 2000. [memoir]
Wms-Forde, Bily.
– *Requiem for a Black American Capitalist*. New York: Troisième Canadian, 1975. [fiction]
Woods, David A. [1959–]. b. Trinidad.
– *Native Song: Poetry and Paintings*. Lawrencetown Beach, NS: Pottersfield, 1990. [poetry]
Wright, Cecil. [1955–]. b. Nova Scotia.
– with Craig Smith and Quenta Tynes, eds. *Journey: African Canadian History Study Guide*. Yarmouth, NS: Southwest Nova African Canadian Cultural Awareness Project and Human Resources Development Canada, 2000. [history]
Yayeh, Qes Asres. [1903–]. b. Ethiopia.
– *Traditions of the Ethiopian Jews*. Thornhill, ON: Kibur Asres, 1995. [prose]
Zapparoli, David. b. Ontario?
– *Our Views of Struggle*. [Toronto]: Gallery 44, [1992]. [photo exhibit catalogue]
– *Regent Park: The Public Experiment in Housing*. Toronto: The Market Gallery, 1999. [photo exhibit catalogue]
Zeleza, [Paul] Tiyambe. [1955–]. b. Malawi.
– *Night of Darkness and Other Stories*. Limbe, Malawi: Popular Publications, 1976. [short fiction]
– *Smouldering Charcoal*. Oxford: Heinemann, 1992. [fiction]
– *A Modern Economic History of Africa*. [Dakar, Senegal]: CODESRIA, 1993. [history]
– *The Joys of Exile: Stories*. Toronto: Anansi, 1994. [short fiction]
– *Maasai*. New York: Rosen Pub. Group, 1994. [juvenile]
– *Akamba*. New York: Rosen Pub. Group, 1995. [juvenile]
– *Mijikenda*. New York: Rosen Pub. Group, 1995. [juvenile]

Corporate Authors

African Canadian Caucus.
- *Justice Reform and the Black Community of Nova Scotia: The Case of Donald Marshall, Jr.* Halifax, NS: The African-Canadian Caucus of Nova Scotia, 1992. [booklet]
African Canadian Community Health Care Coalition.
- *The Ujima Parent Handbook.* Toronto: [African Canadian Community Health Care Coalition], 1995. [handbook]
African Methodist Episcopal Church.
- *Church Review.* 1895–6. [includes biographies of church leaders]
Africville Genealogy Society.
- *The Spirit of Africville.* Halifax, NS: Formac, 1992. [history and historical fiction]
Afro-American Progressive Association.
- *Harambee: Let's Pull Together.* Montreal: n.p., [1977?] [prose]
Afro-Canadian Caucus.
- *Afro-Canadian Caucus Response to: Information on Implementation of Marshall Royal Commission Recommendations.* Halifax, NS· Afro-Canadian Caucus, 1992. [prose]
AME Church in the Province of Canada.
- *Minutes of the Sixteenth Annual Conference.* Chatham, ON: AME Church in the Province of Canada, 1865. [report]
Amherstburg, Ontario, Convention.
- *Minutes and Proceedings of the General Convention, for the Improvement of the Colored Inhabitants, Held by Adjournments in Amherstburg, C.W. [Canada West] June 16th and 17th, 1853.* Windsor, ON: Bibb & Holly, 1853. [report]
Anglo-African Mutual Improvement and Aid Association of Nova Scotia.
- *Constitution and By-Laws of the Anglo-African Mutual Improvement and Aid Association of Nova Scotia.* Halifax, ca. 1842. [constitution]
Art Gallery, Mount Saint Vincent University.
- *Africville: A Spirit That Lives On.* Halifax, NS: Art Gallery, Mount Saint Vincent University, Black Cultural Centre for Nova Scotia, Africville Genealogy Society, and National Film Board, Atlantic Centre, 1989. [exhibition catalogue]
- *A Lifetime of Making: Ralph and Ada Cromwell.* Halifax, NS: Art Gallery, Mount Saint Vincent University, 1992. [exhibition catalogue]
Association haïtienne des travailleurs du taxi.
- *Enquête sur les travailleurs haïtiens de l'industrie de taxi à Montréal.* Montréal: n.p., 1982. [report]
- *La Situation des travailleurs noirs dans l'industrie du taxi.* Montréal: n.p., 1983. [report]
Bilalian Development Association of Nova Scotia.
- *A Contemporary Profile of Blacks in the Economic Structure of Nova Scotia and Related Policy Recommendations.* [Halifax, NS: Bilalian Development Association of Nova Scotia, 1981.] [report]
Black Business Consortium Society.
- *Black Business Consortium Society Directory.* [Halifax, NS: Black Business Consortium Society, 1982.] [directory]

Black Business Initiative: Report of the Task Force. [Halifax, NS]: Atlantic Canada Oppor-
   tunities Agency, 1995. [report]
Black Community Steering Committee Report to the North York Board of Education. Toronto:
   n.p., 1985. [report]
Black Community Working Group on Education.
– *Final Report on the Aspirations and Expectations of the Quebec Black Community with
   Regard to Education.* Ed. Charles Tardieu-Dehoux and Esmerelda Thornhill.
   Montréal: n.p., 1978. [report]
Black Cultural Centre for Nova Scotia.
– *Traditional Lifetime Stories: A Collection of Black Memories.* 2 vols. Cherrybrook, NS:
   The Black Cultural Centre for Nova Scotia, 1987–90. [compilation]
– comp. *Three Nova Scotian Black Churches: African Orthodox* [by] *Joyce Ruck, African
   Methodist Episcopal* [by] *Edward Matwawana, Disney Chapel / Rose of Sharon Assembly*
   [by] *Carolyn Smith (A Collection of Historical Essays).* Cherrybrook, NS: Black Cultural
   Centre for Nova Scotia, 1990. [history]
– *Juba'Lee: A Celebration of Black Culture in Nova Scotia.* Cherrybrook, NS: The Black
   Cultural Centre for Nova Scotia, 2000. [souvenir program]
Black Culture in the Maritimes. Halifax, NS: Curriculum Department, Halifax District
   School Board, [1990]. [historical sketches and biographies]
The Black Girls.
– *Black Girl Talk.* Toronto: Sister Vision, 1995. [anthology]
Black Heritage in Bertie Township, Welland County. St Catharines, ON: Ontario Genea-
   logical Society, Niagara Peninsula Branch, 1993. [history]
Black Heritage in Grantham Township, Lincoln County. St Catharines, ON: Ontario
   Genealogical Society, Niagara Peninsula Branch, 1993. [history]
Black Learners Advisory Committee.
– *Instructions and Information Concerning Tendering the Research Project.* Halifax, NS:
   Black Learners Advisory Committee, 1991. [guide]
– *BLAC Report on Education: Redressing Inequality, Empowering Black Learners.* 3 vols.
   Halifax, NS: Black Learners Advisory Committee, 1994. [report]
Black Loyalist Heritage Society.
– *The Black Loyalist Heritage Project.* Shelburne, NS: Black Loyalist Heritage Society,
   [1999]. [report]
The Black Man in Nova Scotia: Teach-In Report. Antigonish, NS: St Francis Xavier
   University, 1969. [report]
Black Oral History. [Halifax, NS: Nova Scotia Department of Advanced Education and
   Job Training, 1991.] [school workbook]
Black Theatre Canada.
– *Black Theatre Canada in Perspective.* [Toronto: Black Theatre Canada, 1980.]
   [history]
– *Black Theatre Canada: 10th Anniversary Production: A Caribbean Midsummer Night's
   Dream.* N.p.: n.p., [1983]. [account]
The Black Trade and Business Directory. Toronto: East-West Business Agency, [1976].
   [directory]

Black United Front of Nova Scotia.
- *Annual Progress Report.* April 1971-March 1972. Halifax, NS: Black United Front of
   Nova Scotia, 1972. [report]
- *Black United Front Report of Housing Survey of Black Communities in Nova Scotia.*
   Halifax, NS: Black United Front, 1973.
Black Youth Television Workshop. Montreal: Mondiale Publishers, 1974. [report]
*Blacks in British Columbia: A Catalogue of Information and Sources of Information Pertaining
   to Blacks in British Columbia.* Victoria, BC: Victoria Black People's Society, 1978.
   [catalogue]
British Columbia Association for the Advancement of Colored People.
- 'Black Community Survey.' [Vancouver?], unpublished, 1971. [report]
Brotherhood of Sleeping Car Porters.
- *Regional Conference ... Brotherhood of Sleeping Car Porters.* Montreal, 1945. [report]
Canada. Department of Labour.
- *Towards Racial Understanding: A Catalogue of Material on Racial Discrimination.* Ottawa:
   Department of Labour, 1962. [bibliography]
Canadian Artists Network – Black Artists in Action.
- *Celebrating African Identity.* Toronto: Canadian Artists Network – Black Artists in
   Action, 1992. [conference catalogue]
Canadian Jubilee Singers.
- *Songs Sung by the Famous Canadian Jubilee Singers.* Hamilton, ON: n.p., 189?–.
   [compilation]
Canadian League for the Advancement of Colored People.
- *Report for 1932 and Appeal for 1933.* London, ON, [1933?]
- *Tenth Annual Appeal of the Executive Board.* London, ON, 1934. [Other annual reports
   were published at least to 1940.]
Caribbean Conference Committee.
- *West Indian Nation in Exile.* Montreal: n.p., 1967. [report]
Commissioners for the West Indies, British Guiana, and British Honduras.
- *Location List: West Indian Students in Canada, 1961–62.* Montreal, 1961. [directory]
Congress of Black Women.
- *Report of the Second National Congress of Black Women.* [Montreal?]: n.p., [1975?]
   [Conference report, November 8–10, Sheraton Mt Royal Hotel]
Cross-Cultural Communication Centre.
- *Bibliography of Centre's Resources on Immigrant Women in Canada and Their Countries of
   Origin.* Toronto: Cross-Cultural Communication Centre, 1978. [mimeographed
   bibliography]
*'La Culture noir vue par Charles Biddle' ou l'histoire parfois sortie de l'ombre de l'une des plus
   diversifiées de nos communautés.* Montréal: Maison de la culture Marie-Uguay, 1991.
   [texts accompanying an exhibition]
De Poonani Possee.
- *Da Juice! A Black Lesbian Thang.* Toronto: Fireweed, 1995.
Directory of British Columbia Black Owned Businesses and Services. Vancouver: British
   Columbia Black Action Coalition, 1994. [directory]

Draw It Black Artists' Collective.
- *Draw It Black.* Ed. Buseje Bailey. Toronto: Draw It Black Artists' Collective, 2000. [booklet of artists' work]
Equatoria Collection.
- *An Open Book: A Listing of Books, Films, and Stories about People of Colour (for Concerned Teachers, Parents, and the Children of Canada).* Ottawa: Equatoria Collection, 1995. [bibliography]
First Baptist Church.
- *First Baptist Church: Celebrating Our 160th Anniversary, 1826–1986.* Toronto: [First Baptist Church], 1986. [history]
Heritage 83: Celebrating 125 Years of Black History in British Columbia. N.p.: Black Historical and Cultural Society of British Columbia, 1983. [history]
Highland African Methodist Episcopal Church.
- *Souvenir Booklet: The Old and the New.* Amherst, NS: Highland African Methodist Episcopal Church, 1973. [history]
Jamaican-Canadian Association.
- *Jamaican Canadians: A Commitment to Excellence.* Ed. Ewart Walters. Toronto: Jamaican-Canadian Association, 1987. [biographies]
Journal of Proceedings of the Fifty-Third Session of the Ontario A.M.E. [African Methodist Episcopal] Church Conference of 1937. Chatham, ON: n.p., 1937.
Journal of Proceedings of the Forty-Fourth Session of the Ontario Annual Conference (A.M.E. [African Methodist Episcopal]). Hamilton, ON: n.p., 1928.
Les Journées Africaines et Créoles 1997. Montréal: Vues d'Afrique, 1997. [exhibition guide]
Justin Coward Memorial Society.
- *Justin Coward Memorial Basketball Tournament 2000.* Dartmouth, NS: Justin Coward Memorial Society, 2000. [program]
La Maison d'Haïti.
- [avec] Carrefour internationale. *Femmes haïtiennes.* Montréal: La Maison d'Haïti [avec] Carrefour internationale, 1980. [prose]
- [avec] Comité de femmes Nègres. *Fanm poto mitan / Femmes immigrantes haïtiennes.* Montréal: La Maison d'Haïti [avec] Comité de femmes Nègres, 1982. [prose]
Minutes and Proceedings of the General Convention for the Improvement of the Coloured Inhabitants of Canada. Held in Amherstburg in the First Baptist Church; June 16 and 17, 1853. N.p.: Bibb and Holly, [1853].
Minutes of the Forty-Second Session of the Nova Scotian Annual Conference of the A.M.E. [African Methodist Episcopal] Church. N.p.: n.p., 1925.
Montreal Black Communities Demographics Project.
- *The Evolution of the Black Community of Montreal: Change and Challenge.* By James L. Torczyner and Sharon Springer et al. Montréal: McGill Consortium for Ethnicity and Strategic Social Planning – Montreal Black Communities Demographics Project, 2001. [study]
National Black Coalition of Canada.
- *A Key to Canada.* 5 vols. Montréal: National Black Coalition of Canada, 1975–6. [guidebook and history]

- *The National Black Awards of Canada: National Black Awards for the Years 1973, 1974, 1975.* N.p.: National Black Coalition, 1976. [report]

National Council of Black Educators of Canada.
- *Innovations in Black Education in Canada.* Ed. Vincent D'Oyley. Toronto: Umbrella Press, 1994. [essays]

National Gallery of Canada.
- *People of African Descent: An Historical Presence, Works of Art from the National Gallery of Canada: Teacher's Manual and Slide Kit.* Ottawa: National Gallery of Canada, Education and Public Programs, 2000. [kit]

Negro Theatre Guild.
- *The Negro Theatre Guild Presents 'Emperor Jones' by Eugene O'Neill.* Montreal: n.p., [194?]. [drama program]

New Glasgow Black Gala Homecoming Committee.
- *New Glasgow Black Gala Homecoming: Church and Community Groups, August 11–18, 2000.* New Glasgow, NS: New Glasgow Black Gala Homecoming Committee, 2000.

New Music Notes: A Canadian Showcase of Rising Stars. [Toronto]: The Four Seasons Festivals Ontario and The Black Cultural Arts Project of Ontario, 1989/90. [articles]

Nova Scotia Advisory Group on Race Relations.
- *Report.* Halifax: Nova Scotia Advisory Group on Race Relations, 1991.

Nova Scotia Alliance of Black Organizations.
- *A Plan of Action for Progress in the Black Community – Balance of the 1980's.* Halifax, NS: [Nova Scotia Human Rights Commission], 1983. [agenda for Provincial Human Rights Conference, held at Dalhousie University, 13–14 May 1983]

Nova Scotia Human Rights Commission.
- *Pictorial on Black History: Nova Scotia.* [Halifax, NS: Nova Scotia Human Rights Commission, 1973.] [Researchers: Ainsley Crawley and Lois Symonds.] [history]
- *Visible Minorities in Nova Scotia: A Call for Equality.* By Eleanor Elms, Evelyn Jackson, and Chief Richard MacEwen. Halifax, NS: Nova Scotia Human Rights Commission, 1973. [report]
- *Focus: Lucasville, Hammond Plains, and Cobequid Road.* Halifax, NS: Nova Scotia Human Rights Commission, 1974. [study]
- *Textbook Analysis: Nova Scotia.* Halifax, NS: Nova Scotia Human Rights Commission, 1974. [study]

Ontario Black History Society and The City of Toronto.
- *Black History in Early Ontario: A Travelling Exhibition.* Toronto: Market Gallery, 1981. [a photograph exhibit catalogue]

[Ontario] Groupe d'étude sur les relations entre la police et les minorités raciales.
- *Rapport du Groupe d'étude sur les relations entre la police et les minorités raciales.* [Toronto]: [Gouvernment d'Ontario] Le Groupe d'étude, 1992. [report]

Ontario Human Rights Commission.
- *A Brief Pictorial History of Blacks in Nineteenth Century Ontario.* Toronto: Ontario Human Rights Commission, 1972. [history]

Ontario Ministry of Culture and Recreation.
- *Papers on the Black Community.* Toronto: Ministry of Culture and Recreation, 1976. [essay compilation]

- *Intercultural Seminars: Blacks*. Toronto: Ontario Ministry of Culture and Recreation, Multicultural Development Branch, [1978?] [booklet]
- *Ontario Ethnocultural Profiles: Black Canadians*. Toronto: Ontario Ministry of Culture and Recreation, Multicultural Development Branch, [1979]. [booklet]
Ontario Ministry of Education.
- *Afro-Canadian Studies*. Toronto: Ontario Ministry of Education, 1968. [guide]
[Ontario] Race Relations and Policing Force.
- *The Report of the Race Relations and Policing Task Force*. [Toronto]: [Government of Ontario] The Task Force, 1989, 1992. [report]
Our Roots 2: Personal and Family Histories from the OAC Stephen Leacock Black History Class, 1994. Agincourt, ON: History Department, Stephen Leacock Collegiate Institute (Scarborough Board of Education), 1994. [compilation]
Our Roots 3: Personal and Family Histories from the OAC Stephen Leacock Black History Class, 1995. Ed. Peta-Gaye Domville, et al. Toronto: Mudpie Press, 1997. [compilation]
Petition of the Coloured People at Preston. 1840–45. Public Archives of Nova Scotia. Box – Crown Lands – Peninsula of Halifax.
Petition [to Governor James Douglas against Segregationist Behaviour in British Columbia]. 'Signed on behalf of Two hundred and Sixty colored residents.' [Signatories included Wellington Delany Moses.] Victoria, BC, 1861. [See Kilian, *Go*, 124.]
Progress: An Official Record of the Achievements of the Coloured Race up to August, Windsor, ON: Emancipation Celebration, July 31–August 1,2, 1948. [history]
Project of Quebec Blacks for a Better Education.
- *What You Should Know about Your Children and Their School*. Montreal: Quebec Blacks for a Better Education, [1971]. [booklet]
PRUDE.
- *The Invisible Minorities: Employment Equity Research Project Saint John, New Brunswick*. Prepared by Donna Spalding. Saint John, NB: PRUDE (Pride of Race, Unity, Dignity, Education), Inc., 1999. [study]
Quebec Board of Black Educators.
- *Some Missing Pages: The Black Community in the History of Quebec and Canada: Primary and Secondary Source Materials*. [Québec]: Ministère de l'éducation, Services à la communauté anglophone, Direction des politiques et des projets, 1996. [teaching guide]
Rasambleman Fanm Ayisyèn à Montréal.
- *Femmes haïtiennes*. Montréal: Rasambleman Fanm Ayisyèn à Montréal, 1976. [prose]
Report of the Convention of the Coloured Population, Held at Drummondsville, Aug., 1847. Toronto: Printed at the Banner Office, 1847. [report]
Sant Na Rive.
- *Alphabétiser en créole: L'Expérience d'alphabétisation au Bureau de la communauté chrétienne des Haïtiens de Montréal*. Québec: Ministère de l'Éducation du Québec, 198?.
Secretary of State.
- *Prejudice and Discrimination: A Study Guide*. Ottawa: Secretary of State, 1975. [guide]
'Senior Citizens' of Upper Hammonds Plains.
- *Early Pioneers: A Heritage of Faith and Courage*. Hammonds Plains, NS: ['Senior Citizens' of Upper Hammonds Plains], 1978. [history]

Sharp-Pen Associates.
- *Anansi and the Seeds*. Toronto: Sharp-Pen Associates, [198?]. [comic book]
Shelburne County Cultural Awareness Society.
- *Birchtown Archaeological Survey (1993): The Black Loyalist Settlement of Shelburne County, Nova Scotia, Canada*. Laird Niven, comp. Lockeport, NS: Roseway Publishing Company, 1994. [survey]
Souvenir Program: St. Phillip A.M.E. [African Methodist Episcopal] Church, Saint John, N.B., 1859–1959. Saint John, NB, 1959. [history]
Souvenir Programme, 1926–1965, 40th Anniversary Banquet Honoring Reverend Charles Este. Montreal, 1965. [history]
Toronto Board of Education.
- *Pepper Pot*. Toronto: Language Study Centre, Toronto Board of Education, 1978. [report]
- *Final Report of Sub-committee on Race Relations*. Toronto: Toronto Board of Education, 1979. [report]
- *Consultative Committee on the Education of Black Students in Toronto Schools*. Toronto: Toronto Board of Education, 1987. [report]
Toronto Negro Business and Professional Men's Association.
- *Writings of Professor Fred Landon on the Canadian Negro, 1918 – *. [Toronto]: Toronto Negro Business and Professional Men's Association, 196?. [bibliography]
Union Congregational Church.
- *65th Anniversary Program, 1907–1972*. Montreal: Union Congregational Church, 1972. [history]
Wilberforce Lyceum Education Society ...
- *Constitution and By-Laws*. Amherstburg, ON: Wilberforce Lyceum Education Society for Moral and Mental Improvement, Cannonsburg, Township of Colchester, 1850. [constitution]
Windsor Council on Group Relations.
- *How Does Our Town Add Up after Ten Years?* Windsor, ON: n.p., 1957. [report]
Windsor Interracial Council.
- *How Does Our Town Add Up?* Windsor, ON: Sumner Printing and Publishing, 197?. [report]

Primary Anthologies

Alford, Edna, and Claire Harris.
- eds. *Kitchen Talk: Contemporary Women's Prose and Poetry*. Red Deer, AB: Red Deer College Press, 1992.
Allain, Carol, and Rosamund Elwin.
- eds. *Getting Wet: Tales of Lesbian Seduction*. Toronto: Women's Press, 1992.
Anderson, Hope, and David Phillips.
- eds. *The Body*. North Vancouver: Tatlow House, 1979.
Bansfield, Anthony.
- ed. *The N'x Step: Hochelaga and the Diasporic African Poets: A Collection of Performance Poetry by a Montreal-based Black Writers Group*. Montreal: RevWord Press, 1995.

Beaugé-Rosier, Jacqueline.
– *La Ville /collaborateurs et collaboratrices*. Hull, QC: [Beaugé-Rosier et al.], 1980.
Black, Ayanna.
– ed. *Voices: Canadian Writers of African Descent*. Toronto: HarperPerennial, 1992.
– ed. *Fiery Spirits: Canadian Writers of African Descent*. Toronto: HarperPerennial, 1995.
– ed. *Fiery Spirits and Voices: Canadian Writers of African Descent*. Toronto: HarperPerennial, 2000.
The Black Girls.
– *Black Girl Talk*. Toronto: Sister Vision, 1995.
Brand, Dionne.
– et al. *Sight Specific: Lesbians and Representation*. Toronto: A Space, 1988.
Brathwaite, Keren S.
– ed. *Stories from Life: The Transitional Year Programme Collection of Short Fiction*. Toronto: Canadian Scholars' Press, 1987.
Camper, Carol.
– ed. *Miscegenation Blues: Voices of Mixed Race Women*. Toronto: Sister Vision Press, 1994.
Carretta, Vincent.
– ed. *Unchained Voices: An Anthology of Black Authors in the English-Speaking World of the 18th Century*. Lexington, KY: University Press of Kentucky, 1996.
Clarke, George Elliott.
– ed. *Fire on the Water: An Anthology of Black Nova Scotian Writing*. 2 vols. Lawrencetown Beach, NS: Pottersfield Press, 1991–2.
– with J.A. Wainwright, et al., eds. *Border Lines: Contemporary Poems in English*. Toronto: Copp Clark, 1995.
– ed. *Eyeing the North Star: Directions in African-Canadian Literature*. Toronto: McClelland & Stewart, 1997.
Compton, Wayde.
– ed. *Bluesprint: Black British Columbian Literature and Orature*. Vancouver: Arsenal Pulp Press, 2002.
Cooper, Afua.
– ed. *Utterances and Incantations: Women, Poetry and Dub*. Toronto: Sister Vision Press, 1999.
Cromwell, Liz.
– ed. *One Out of Many: A Collection of Writings by Twenty-one Black Women in Ontario*. Toronto: WACACRO Productions, 1975. [the second anthology of African-Canadian writers]
– assoc. ed. *Title Unknown: Writings by Ontario Women* [for] *International Women's Year*. Ed. Judith Merril. Toronto: n.p., 1975.
Dabydeen, Cyril.
– ed. *A Shapely Fire: Changing the Literary Landscape*. Oakville, ON: Mosaic, 1987.
Davies, Carole Boyce, and Molara Ogundipe-Leslie.
– eds. *Moving beyond Boundaries: International Dimensions of Black Women's Writing*. Vol. 1. Washington Square, NY: New York University Press, 1995.

Dawes, Kwame.
– ed. *Wheel and Come Again: An Anthology of Reggae Poetry*. Fredericton, NB: Goose Lane Editions, 1998.
Douglas, Debbie.
– et al., eds. *'Ma'-ka: Diasporic Juks: Contemporary Writing by Queers of African Descent*. Toronto: Sister Vision Press, 1997.
Elliott, Lorris.
– ed. *Other Voices: Writings by Blacks in Canada*. Toronto: Williams-Wallace, 1985.
Elwin, Rosamund.
– ed. *Tongues on Fire: Caribbean Lesbian Lives and Stories*. Toronto: Women's Press, 1997.
Espinet, Ramabai.
– ed. *Creation Fire: A CAFRA Anthology of Caribbean Women's Poetry*. Toronto: Sister Vision, 1990.
Fyfe, Christopher.
– ed. *'Our Children Free and Happy': Letters from Black Settlers in Africa in the 1790s*. Edinburgh: Edinburgh University Press, 1991. [This text consists of letters by 'Nova-Scotians,' i.e., the Black Loyalists who settled in Sierra Leone following their exodus from Nova Scotia in 1792. It yields a letter by Susannah Smith, perhaps the first African-Canadian woman writer.]
Hamel, Réginald, John Hare, Paul Wyczynski.
– eds. *Dictionnaire des auteurs de langue française en Amérique du Nord*. Montréal: Éditions Fides, 1989.
Haynes, Camille.
– ed. *Black Chat: An Anthology of Black Poets*. Montreal: Black and Third World Students Association, Dawson College, 1973. [the *first* anthology of African-Canadian writers]
Head, Harold.
– ed. *Canada in Us Now: The First Anthology of Black Poetry and Prose in Canada*. Toronto: NC Press, 1976. [the *third* anthology of African-Canadian writers]
Hopkinson, Nalo.
– ed. *Whispers from the Cotton Tree Root: Caribbean Fabulist Fiction*. Montpelier, VT: Invisible Cities Press, 2000.
Hutcheon, Linda, and Marion Richmond.
– eds. *Other Solitudes: Canadian Multicultural Fictions*. Toronto: Oxford University Press, 1988.
Joyette, Anthony.
– ed. *Vincentian Poets, 1950 to 1980*. St-Laurent, QC: AFO Enterprises, 1990.
Martin, Stephanie.
– with Makeda Silvera, eds. *Sapodilla: The Sister Vision Book of Lesbian Poetry*. Toronto: Sister Vision Press, 1999.
McFarlane, Courtney.
– et al., eds. *Ma'-ka: Diasporic Juks: Contemporary Writing by Queers of African Descent*. Toronto: Sister Vision Press, 1997.

Mordecai, Pamela.
- and Mervyn Morris, eds. *Jamaica Woman: An Anthology of Fifteen Jamaican Women Poets*. Kingston, JA: Heinemann Caribbean, 1980; London: Heinemann, 1985.
- ed. *From Our Yard: Jamaican Poetry since Independence*. Kingston, JA: Institute of Jamaica Publications, 1987.
- and Betty Wilson, eds. *Her True-True Name: An Anthology of Women's Writing from the Caribbean*. London: Heinemann, 1989.
Morrell, Carol.
- ed. *Grammar of Dissent: Poetry and Prose by Claire Harris, Marlene Nourbese Philip, Dionne Brand*. Fredericton: Goose Lane, 1994.
Nkashama, Pius Nkanda.
- [réd.] *Littératures africaines de 1930 à nos jours*. Paris: Silex, 1984.
Palmer, Hazelle.
- ed. *'... But Where Are You Really From?': Stories about Identity and Assimilation in Canada*. Toronto: Sister Vision Press, 1997.
Potkay, Adam, and Sandra Burr.
- eds. *Black Atlantic Writers of the Eighteenth Century: Living the New Exodus in England and the Americas*. New York: St Martin's Press, 1995.
Rey, Ghislaine [Ghislaine Charlier].
- réd. *Anthologie du roman haïtien de 1859 à 1946*. Sherbrooke, QC: Éditions Naaman, [1978?]
Ripley, C. Peter.
- ed. *The Black Abolitionist Papers. Vol. 2: Canada, 1830–1865*. Chapel Hill: University of North Carolina Press, 1986.
Sears, Djanet.
- ed. *Tellin' It Like It Is: A Compendium of African Canadian Monologues for Actors*. Toronto: PUC Play Service, 2000.
- ed. *Testifyin': Contemporary African Canadian Drama*. Volume 1. Toronto: Playwrights Canada Press, 2000.
'Sierra Leone Settlers' Letters: 1791–1800.' In *Black Writers in Britain, 1760–1890*. [ed.] Paul Edwards and David Dabydeen. Edinburgh: Edinburgh University Press, 1991. [letters by ex-Nova Scotians: Thomas Peters; David Edmon; Susana Smith; David George, et al. (a petition); Cato Perkins; Isaac Anderson; James Liaster; Luke Jordan; Nathaniel Snowball; James Robertson et al. (a petition)]
Silvera, Makeda.
- ed. *Fireworks: The Best of Fireweed*. Toronto: Women's Press, 1986.
- and Nila Gupta, eds. *The Issue Is 'Ism: Women of Colour Speak Out*. Toronto: Sister Vision, 1989. [a reprint of *Fireweed: A Feminist Quarterly* 16 (1983), an issue focusing on women of colour]
- ed. *Piece of My Heart: A Lesbian of Colour Anthology*. Toronto: Sister Vision, 1991.
- ed. *The Other Woman: Women of Colour in Contemporary Canadian Literature*. Toronto: Sister Vision, 1992. [interviews]
- and C. Allyson Lee, eds. *Pearls of Passion: A Treasury of Lesbian Erotica*. Toronto: Sister Vision Press, 1994.

– et al., eds. *'Ma'-ka: Diasporic Juks: Contemporary Writing by Queers of African Descent*. Toronto: Sister Vision Press, 1997.

– and Stephanie Martin, eds. *Sapodilla: The Sister Vision Book of Lesbian Poetry*. Toronto: Sister Vision Press, 1999.

Smith, Charles [C.]

– ed. *The Teeth of the Whirlwind: Poems by* [Lillian] *Allen* ... [Dionne] *Brand* ... [Clifton] *Joseph* ... [Charles C.] *Smith*. Toronto: Black Perspectives, 1984.

– ed. *sad dances in a field of white*. Toronto: Is Five Press, 1985.

Stewart, Douglas.

– et al., eds. *Ma'-ka: Diasporic Juks: Contemporary Writing by Queers of African Descent*. Toronto: Sister Vision Press, 1997.

Vera, Yvonne.

– ed. *Opening Spaces: An Anthology of Contemporary African Women's Writing*. Oxford: Heinemann, 1999.

Wainwright, J.A., George Elliott Clarke et al., eds.

– *Border Lines: Contemporary Poems in English*. Toronto: Copp Clark, 1995.

Wallace, Ann P.

– ed. *Daughters of the Sun, Women of the Moon: Poetry by Black Canadian Women*. Stratford, ON: Williams-Wallace, 1991.

– with J.A. Wainwright et al., eds. *Border Lines: Contemporary Poems in English*. Toronto: Copp Clark, 1995.

Ward, Frederick.

– ed. *Anthology of Nine Baha'i Poets*. Detroit: n.p., 1966.

– ed. *Present Tense*. Halifax, NS: New Options School, 1972.

Primary Bibliographies and Associated Sources

Algoo-Baksh, Stella.

– 'Selected Bibliography.' In *Austin C. Clarke: A Biography*. Toronto: ECW Press; Barbados, Jamaica, Trinidad and Tobago: The Press of the University of the West Indies, 1994. 218–30.

Anderson, W.W.

– ed. *Caribbean Orientations: A Bibliography of Resource Materials on the Caribbean Experience in Canada*. Toronto: The Organization for Caribbean Canadian Identities (OCCI) and Williams-Wallace Publishers, Inc., 1985.

Bell, Dorothy.

– comp., et al. *Canadian Black Studies Bibliography*. [London, ON]: n.p., 1971.

Bertley, Leo W.

– *Canada and Its People of African Descent*. Pierrefonds, QC: Bilongo Publishers, 1977.

Black Culture in the Maritimes. Halifax, NS: Curriculum Department, Halifax District School Board, [1990].

Blacks in British Columbia: A Catalogue of Information and Sources of Information Pertaining to Blacks in British Columbia. Victoria, BC: Victoria Black People's Society, 1978.

Blacks in Canada: Representative Source Material. Halifax: Dalhousie University Library Bibliographies, 1970.

Blizzard, Flora Helena [Flora (Blizzard) Francis].

– *West Indians in Canada: A Selective Annotated Bibliography*. Guelph, ON: [University of Guelph Library], 1970.

– [as Flora Francis]. *A Black Canadian Bibliography*. Ottawa: Pan-African Publications, 2000.

Boily, Lisette.

– comp. 'Contemporary Canadian First Nations Writers and Writers of Colour: A Working Bibliography.' *West Coast Line* 28.1–2 (1994): 303–18.

Breyfogle, Donna, and Marion Dwoaszek

– comps. *Blacks in Ontario: A Select Bibliography, 1965–1976*. No. 8. Toronto: Ontario Ministry of Labour, Research Library, 1977.

Brundage, Donald H[azen].

– *West Indian Literature: A Selected Bibliography*. [Toronto]: OISE Staff Study, 197–?.

Canadian Griots Tour across Canada. [Ottawa: Department of Canadian Heritage Canada and Canadian Alliance of Black Educators, 1997.] [brochure with bibliography]

Chamberlin, J. Edward.

– 'Selected Bibliography: Contemporary West Indian Poetry in English, Anthologies of West Indian Poetry, Selected Regional and National Anthologies.' In *Come Back to Me My Language: Poetry and the West Indies*. Toronto: McClelland & Stewart, 1993. 295–303.

Clarke, George Elliott.

– 'Africana Canadiana: A Primary Bibliography of Literature by African-Canadian Authors, 1785–1996, in English, French, and Translation.' *Canadian Ethnic Studies* 28.3 (1996): 106–209.

– ed. 'Selected Works.' In *Fire on the Water: An Anthology of Black Nova Scotian Writing*. Vol. 1. Lawrencetown Beach, NS: Pottersfield Press, 1991. 173–7.

Communiqué: Canadian Studies 3.1 (Oct. 1976). [special bibliographic issue on multiculturalism]

Compton, Wayde.

– 'A Bibliography of Black British Columbian Literature and Orature.' In *Bluesprint: Black British Columbian Literature and Orature*. Ed. Wayde Compton. Vancouver: Arsenal Pulp Press, 2002. 297–302.

Cox, Rita.

– *Checklist of the West Indian Collection*. Toronto: Parkdale Library, 1978.

Cross-Cultural Communication Centre.

– *Bibliography of Centre's Resources on Immigrant Women in Canada and Their Countries of Origin*. Toronto: Cross-Cultural Communication Centre, 1978.

D'Oyley, Enid F.

– *A Sample Checklist of Latin American and Caribbean Material Published in Canada*. N.p.: n.p., 1977.

Dumond, Dwight Lowell.

– *A Bibliography of Antislavery in America*. Ann Arbor: University of Michigan Press, 1961.

Elliott, Lorris.
- comp. *The Bibliography of Literary Writings by Blacks in Canada*. Toronto: Williams-Wallace, 1986.
- comp. *Literary Writing by Blacks in Canada: A Preliminary Survey*. Ottawa: Department of the Secretary of State, 1988.
- *Production littéraire des Noirs du Canada: Étude préliminaire*. [Ottawa]: Multiculturalisme et Citoyonneté Canada / Multiculturalism and Citizenship Canada, 1990.
Ellison, Curtis W., and E.W. Metcalf, Jr.
- *William Wells Brown and Martin R. Delany: A Reference Guide*. Boston: G.K. Hall & Co., 1978.
Emera, Alix.
- 'Bibliographie de la littérature haïtian.' In *Notre Librairie*. 132. *Littérature haïtienne: De 1960 à nos jours*. Paris: CLEF, 1998. 186–204.
Feuerwerker, Natania.
- *Gérard Étienne: Profil professionnel et bibliographie jusqu'au 1er janvier 1996*. [Moncton, NB: n.p., 1996.]
Forte, Nick G., and Gabriele Scardellato.
- *A Guide to the Collections of the Multicultural History Society of Ontario*. Toronto: Multicultural History Society of Ontario, 1992.
Govia, Francine, and Helen Lewis.
- comps. *Blacks in Canada in Search of the Promise: A Bibliographic Guide to the History of Blacks in Canada*. Edmonton: Harambee Centres Canada, 1988.
Heath, Leila.
- 'Black Ink: An Historical Critique of Ontario's Black Press.' *Fuse* 11.182 (Summer 1987): 20–7.
Hills, Theo L.
- comp. *Caribbean Topics: Theses in Canadian University Libraries*. Montreal: Centre for Developing–Area Studies, 1973.
Hubbard, Lorraine D.
- 'Black Theatre in Canada: A Decade of Struggle.' *Polyphony: The Bulletin of the Multicultural History Society of Ontario* 5.2 (Fall/Winter 1983): 57–66.
Jain, Sushil Kumar.
- *The Negro in Canada: A Select List of Primary and Secondary Sources for the Study of the Negro Community in Canada from the Earliest Times to the Present Days*. Regina: Regina Campus Library, University of Saskatchewan, 1967.
Jonassaint, Jean.
- 'Les Productions littéraires haïtiennes en Amérique du Nord (1969–1979).' *Études littéraires* 13.2 (1980): 313–33.
- ed. 'Littératures haïtiennes II.' *Mot pour mot* 12 (1983).
Keith, Russell.
- 'Black Journalism: A Rich Canadian Heritage.' *Black Images* 1.1 (Jan. 1972): 10–11.
Kilian, Crawford.
- Bibliography. In *Go Do Some Great Thing: The Black Pioneers of British Columbia*. By Crawford Kilian. 1978. Vancouver: Douglas & McIntyre, 1980. 173–81.

Krestensen, K.
- *The Negro in Canada: Material Held in the Library*. Toronto: Ontario Department of Labour Library, 1972.
Laroche, Maximilien.
- [dir.] *Bibliographie d'Haïti 1994*. Sainte-Foy, QC: GRELCA, 1995.
Malycky, Alexander.
- 'University Research on Negro Canadians. A Preliminary Check List of Theses.' *Canadian Ethnic Studies* 5.1–2 (1973): 225–7.
Manigat, Max.
- *Haïtiana 1991–1995: Bibliographie haïtiane*. Montréal: Éditions du CIDIHCA, 1997.
Moreau, Bernice M.
- 'Black Nova Scotian Literature: A Select Bibliography.' *Journal of Education* [Halifax, NS] 400 (April 1987): 46–50.
Ngatia, Therese.
- 'The Blacks in Canada: A Selective Annotated Bibliography.' Edmonton, University of Alberta, Faculty of Library Science, 1984.
Ontario. Department of Labour. Human Rights Commission.
- *Selected Reading List – the Negro in Canada*. Toronto: Department of Labour, Human Rights Commission, 1970.
Ontario Multicultural Development Branch.
- *Papers on the Black Community*. Toronto: Ministry of Culture and Recreation, 1976.
Porter, Dorothy B.
- *North American Negro Poets: A Bibliographical Checklist of Their Writings, 1760–1944*. Hattiesburg, MS: The Book Farm, 1945.
Ripley, C. Peter.
- ed. *The Black Abolitionist Papers. Vol. 2: Canada, 1830–1865*. Chapel Hill: University of North Carolina Press, 1986.
Rowan, Carl T.
- 'Negroes in Canada.' *Ebony* 15 (Aug. 1960): 98–106.
Russell, Hilary.
- comp. *A Bibliography Relating to African Canadian History*. [Ottawa]: Historical Research Branch, National Historic Sites Directorate, 1990.
Sears, Djanet.
- 'Naming Names: Black Women Playwrights in Canada.' In *Women on the Canadian Stage: The Legacy of Hrotsvit*. Ed. Rita Much. Winnipeg: Blizzard Publishing, 1992. 92–103.
Simpson, Donald George.
- *Negroes in Ontario from Early Times to 1870: A Bibliography*. London, ON: University of Western Ontario, 1971.
Stevenson, Darryl, Pat Graham, and Linda McDowell.
- eds. and comps. *The Black Experience in Manitoba*. Winnipeg: Communications Department of Winnipeg School Division No. 1, 1993.
Walker, James W. St G.
- *Identity: The Black Experience in Canada*. Ed. Patricia Thorvaldson. [Toronto]: The Ontario Educational Communications Authority [and] Gage Educational Publishing Ltd, 1979.

- *A History of Blacks in Canada: A Study Guide for Teachers and Students.* Hull, QC: Minister of State, Multiculturalism, 1980.
- *Précis d'histoire sur les Canadiens de race noire: Sources et guide d'enseignement.* Hull, QC: Ministre d'État, Multiculturalisme, 1980.
- 'Allegories and Orientations in African-Canadian Historiography: The Spirit of Africville.' *Dalhousie Review* [special Africadian issue] 77.2 (Summer 1997): 155–77.

Serials

Abstract. [A 'Hip Hop'-oriented magazine.] Ed. Mansa. [Toronto?], 1992–7.
Africa Speaks: The Voice of the Coloured Man in Canada. Monthly. Ed. Carl H. Woodbeck. Toronto. Vols 1–13, 1949–68; vols 4–10, 1969–75.
African Echo / Echo africain. Quarterly. Gatineau, QC. 1987.
African Heritage Month. Annual supplement. *Daily News.* Ed. Charles R. Saunders. Halifax, NS. February 1996–.
African Messenger, The. Monthly. Toronto: A. Teka, 1991–.
African-Nova Scotian Worker. Monthly. Ed. Andrea David. Halifax, NS. October 1996–.
African Oracle, The. Monthly. [Toronto.] 1992–?
African Voice. Montreal: African Progressive Study Group, 1973.
African Xpress. Monthly. Ed. Bayo Phillips. Toronto: Mohammed Olemoh, 1996–.
Africanadian Journal. Monthly. Ed. Jane Bintu. Toronto, 1996.
Afrikan Voices. Ed. Miguna Miguna. [Toronto.] 198?–.
Afrique tribune. Biweekly. Ed. Pierre Adjété. Montréal: Afrique Pagel International, Inc., 1994–.
AfriQuébec: Magazine d'éducation au développement. Annual. Ottawa: Regroupement Afriquébec, 1991–.
Afro-Beacon. Monthly. Toronto. [ca. 1939–45.]
Afro-Can. Montreal: Negro Community Centre, 1982–.
Afro-Can Communications. Montreal: Negro Community Centre, 1981–2.
Afro-Canada Journal. Montreal.
Afro-Dawson. Montreal: Black and Third World Student Affairs of Dawson College, 1972.
Afro News: The Voice for the Black Community, The. Ed. Michelle Lee Williams. Aldergrove, BC: Black Theatre West, 1986–.
Akili. Quarterly. Ed. Sheldon Taylor. North York, ON: Centre for African-Canadian Studies, 1993–5.
Al Kitab Sudan. [Monthly dedicated to 'Third World Writing.'] Burlington, ON: As-Salaam-Alaikum, 1967.
Annual Report. Elgin Association. Vols 1–8. 1851–6.
Appeal of the Canadian League for the Advancement of Colored People. Annual. London, ON. 1924–40.
At the Crossroads: A Journal for Women Writers of African Descent; At the Crossroads: Black Women's Art Magazine. Ed. Karen Miranda Augustine. Toronto: Another Dark Art production, 1992–.
Atlantic Advocate. Halifax, NS. Vol.1-ca. 5. 1915–20.
Atlantic Black Journal, The. Halifax, NS: African People's Intercommunal Communications Service, 1973–4, 1980.

BAM News. [Barbados Association of Montreal.] Montreal: Barbados House, 1977.

Bantu. Ed. Charles C. Smith and Lillian Allen. Toronto. 1984.

Beyond Black Magazine. Ed. Jacqueline Lawrence. Ottawa. 1989–90.

Black: Journal of Black Expression, The. Ottawa. 1972–3.

Black Action Party, Inc., The. Bi-weekly. Montreal: Black Information Service, 1972.

Black and Third World Student Affairs. Montreal: The Black and Third World Student Affairs Department of Dawson College, 1973–?

Black Canadian Magazine. Ed. Tricia Hylton. Brampton, ON. July 1999–.

Black Express. Monthly. Ed. Charles Husbands. Halifax, NS. 1981–2.

Black Focus. Ed. Basil Mortley. Black Focus Co-Op. Halifax, NS. Fall 1995-Fall 1996; Spring 1999–.

Black Historical Calendar. Annual (irregular). Afro-Caribbean Association of Manitoba. Winnipeg. 1973–4, 1981–2, 1986–91, 1994–.

Black History Month. Annual supplement. *Daily News*. Ed. Charles R. Saunders. Halifax, NS. February 1991–5.

Black Horizons. Halifax, NS: Black United Front of Nova Scotia. 1983.

Black i: A Canadian Journal of Black Expression, The. Ed. Carl A. Taylor [1972], Clarence S. Bayne [1973]. Kyap Enterprises, Ltd. Montreal. 1.1 (March 1972)-2.1 (Summer 1973).

Black Images: A Critical Quarterly of Black Culture. Quarterly. Ed. Lennox Brown [1972], Jojo Chintoh [1972–5]. Toronto. 4 vols. 1972–5.

Black Insight. Weekly. Black Research and Action Committee. Halifax, NS. 1.1–1.3. 6–21 July 1971.

Black Liberation News. Monthly. Ed. George Dash. Black Liberation Front of Canada. Toronto. 1.1 (July 1969)-2.2 (Feb. 1970).

Black Loyalist, The. Newsletter. Shelburne, NS: The Black Loyalist Heritage Society, 1998–.

Black Male: The Brothers Reaching Out Society Newsletter. Quarterly. Halifax: The Brothers Reaching Out Society, 1997–.

Black Pages Directory. Annual directory. Toronto: BlackPages Canada Inc., 1991–.

Black Pages / Pages noires. Annual directory. Montreal: Black Pages. 1989–.

Black Time. Halifax, NS. 1976.

Black to Business. Quarterly. Ed. Rustum Southwell. Halifax: Black Business Initiative, 1997–.

Black Voice. Toronto: Black Youth Organization, June 1970–?

Black Voice, The. Montreal: Côte des Neiges Project, 1972–4.

Black Voice, The. Ottawa: Raymond Grant, 1997–?

Black Voices. Quarterly. Ed. Charlene Cadogan [1994]; Noreen Basso [1995]. Toronto: Robert Richards, 1994–?

Black Voices. Book catalogue. Ed. Donna Boyce, Anna McKinnon. Toronto: Alison Bailey Communications, 1996–.

BRIC News. Monthly. Black Resources Information Centre. Toronto. May 1976-July 1977.

British American, The. [Ontario.] March 1845.

British Columbia Association for the Advancement of Coloured People Quarterly. Vancouver. 1966–72.

British Lion, The. Ed. Charles A. Johnson. Hamilton, ON, 1881–92. [published as *The American Eagle* in New York City]

Bulletin Maison d'Haïti. Montreal: Centre communitaire haïtien, 1976–?

BYCAP: Black Youth Community Action Project. Toronto. April 1977.

Cacique: English Language Arts and Culture Magazine of Montreal. Semi-Annual. Ed. Anthony Joyette. Montreal: Ligue Canadienne des Artiste Noir [sic], 2000–.

Canada-West Indies Magazine. Montreal. 1959.

Canadian Cricketer, The. Ed. Ahmad Saidullan. Toronto. 1972–94?

Canadian Negro, The. Monthly (irregular). Ed. Ray Greenidge [1953–4], John E. White [1953–6], Donald Carty [1953–6?], Jean Daniels [1956–7?]. Toronto: Canadian Negro Publishing Association, 1953–7.

Canadian Observer. Ed. J.R.B. Whitney. Toronto. 1914–19.

Caribana Lights. Official Magazine of Caribana. Ed. William Doyle-Marshall. Toronto: Horace Gooden, 1989.

Caribbean, The. Monthly. Ed. Audley Cummings and Eric Olson. Toronto. 1964–70?

Caribbean Business News: The Quarterly Magazine of the Caribbean Business Community Toronto. 1980s?

Caribbean Chronicle. Monthly. Ed. Darryl Dean. Toronto. July 1967–?

Caribe. Thirdly. Ed. Harold Marshall. Winnipeg: Black Creative Writers, 1979–91; 1993.

Carnival Toronto Magazine. Ed. Norman Murray. Toronto. July 1988.

Clarion, The. Biweekly. Ed. Carrie Best. New Glasgow, NS. 1946–9.

Colours: Canada's Urban Lifestyle Magazine. Toronto. 1997?–.

Communicant. Edmonton. ca. 1984?

Community Contact. Monthly. Ed. Egbert Gaye. Montréal. 1986–.

Concrete Magazine Online. www.neocom.ca/~majestic. 1996. [internet publication]

Contrast. Weekly. Ed. Olivia Grange-Walker and Al W. Hamilton. Toronto. 1969–91.

Coppertone: The Canadian Negro Magazine. Ed. Denfield Grant. Halifax, NS: Grant Print Publishers, Dec. 1966–1967.

Cotopaxi. Ed. Jan Carew. Toronto. 1968.

Dawn of Tomorrow, The. Ed. James F. Jenkins [1920–32], Christine Jenkins [1932–75?]. London, ON: Canadian League for the Advancement of Colored People, 1920–75?

Diaspora. Ed. Peter Hudson. Vancouver. 1993–4.

Drum. Monthly. Ed. Nick Van der Graaf. Ottawa: Harmedia Corp., 1992–.

Ebo Voice. Ed. Austin Clarke. Toronto. 1965–7.

Ebony Express News, The. Monthly. Ed. Charles Husbands. Halifax, NS. January 1979–June 1981.

8th of June. Anonymous. 4 issues. Halifax, NS. 1986.

Ember. Bimonthly. Ed. Katherine Walker Alleyne. Toronto: Alleyne Communications Ltd, 1991–.

ÉQOH du futur. Monthly. Ed. Yves-Gérard François. Montréal: Édition des Québécois d'Origine Haïtienne, 1994–.

Excellence. [See Flora Francis, *A Black Canadian Bibliography*, p. 32.] 1986–?

Expression. Montreal: Negro Citizenship Association of Montreal, 1965–9.

Fana Amharic Magazine. Toronto. 1990. [issued in Ge'ez script]

Focus Umoja. Monthly. Ed. Euton Jarvis. Montreal: Black Community Central Administration of Quebec, 1974–8.

Free Lance, The. Ed. E.M. Packwood. Montreal. 1934–41.

[Black] *Georgian, The*. A single, special issue of *The Georgian* produced by black students. Sir George Williams University. Montréal. 28 January 1969.

Grasp. Ed. Walter Borden [1976–8]. Black United Front of Nova Scotia. Halifax, NS. Aug. 1970-Dec. 1977; Mar. 1978–1983?

Habari Kijiji [Village News]. Ed. Dorothy Wills. Montreal: National Black Coalition of Canada, 1975.

Harambee Mosaic: The Official Publication of the Ottawa Black People's Association. [Ottawa: The Association. 197?–6.]

Harriet Tubman Review: A Journal of Literary and Political Writings. Ed. Dionne Brand, Clifton Joseph, Maresa Masini, Makeda Silvera, and Elaine Thompson. Toronto: Black Communications Exploration, 1981–?

In Focus. Jamaican-Canadian Association. Toronto. Monthly, Sept. 1985-Nov. 1987; bimonthly, Nov. 1987–.

In Other Words: Literary Quarterly. Ed. Nicole Curling. Markham, ON, [1994].

I-Rastafacts. Ed. Sister Y Marie. Vol. 1. (Summer 1994). Toronto: The Rastafari Progressive Organization and Harambee Publishing House, 1994.

Islander, The. Toronto. 1973-[still publ. in 1979.]

Jembere. Ed. Sam Getachew. Ottawa. September 1995–.

Jet Journal, The. Monthly. Ed. Percy Paris. Halifax, NS: Paris Enterprises Co., Ltd, 1984–Oct. 1985.

Jump Magazine: 'Carnivaltoronto.' Annual. Ed. Millicent Redway. Toronto: Lynrod Douglas, 1995–?

Kola: A Black Literary Magazine. Ed. Anthony Joyette [1987–2000], Horace I. Goddard [2000–]. Montreal: The Black Writers' Guild, 1987–.

Literary Gazette. Ed. Harvey Travis. Buxton, ON: Buxton Literary Society, 1915.

Minutes. Amherstburg Baptist Association. 1841–77.

Minutes and Proceedings of the Annual Conferences of the African Methodist Episcopal Church. Canada District. 1853, 1855, 1856.

Minutes of Occasional Meetings of the Members and Trustees. Wesleyan Methodist Church (Coloured). Toronto. 1864–83.

Minutes of the African Baptist Association of Nova Scotia. 1854–1918.

Minutes of the African United Baptist Association of Nova Scotia. 1919–.

Montreal Oracle, The. Ed. Oswald Bartolo. Montreal: Ronald Joseph, 1976–7.

Negro Citizen, The. Biweekly. Ed. Carrie Best. New Glasgow, NS: Clarion Publishing Co., 1949–50?

Negro Directory. Annual? Ed. Esther Hayes. Toronto. 1966–?

Neith: A Magazine of Literature, Science, Art, Philosophy, Jurisprudence, Criticism, History, Reform, Economics. Ed. A.B. Walker. Saint John, NB. Vol. 1, no. 1-vol. 1, no. 5 (Feb. 1903-Jan. 1904).

Nouvelles Alkebu-Lan Newsletter. Ed. Daniel K. Kabasele. Châteauguay, QC. 1987–?

NuBeing International. Quarterly. Ed. Nicole James. Ottawa: NuBeing International, 1997–.

Outcome, The. Montreal. 1935.

Possibilitiis [sic]: *Literary Arts Magazine.* Ed. Maureen Henry. Ottawa. 1993–5; 1997–.

Preserver, The. Quarterly (irregular). Cherrybrook, NS: Society for Protection and Preservation of Black Culture in Nova Scotia, 1980–.

Pride: Canada's National Caribbean and African Canadian Voice. Weekly. Ed. Michael Van Cooten. Scarborough, ON: Pride Communications Inc., 1983–.

Provincial Freeman, The. Ed. Samuel Ringgold Ward [1853], Mary Anne Shadd [Cary] [1853-ca. 1857]. Chatham, ON. 1853–ca. 1857.

Provincial Monitor, The. Ed. Regina James. Dartmouth, NS. 1993–4.

Rap, The. Ed. George Elliott Clarke [Dec. 1986–Sept. 1987], Charles R. Saunders [Oct. 1987–April 1988]. Halifax, NS: Black United Front of Nova Scotia and Fine Print Publications, Dec. 1986–April 1988 [?]

Reach th' People. Black Theatre Canada. Toronto. 1.1. 1984–?

Reaching Out: A Journal of Black Women Together. Toronto? 1979.

La Revue Noire. Monthly. Drummondville, QC: Les Éditions noires, 1992–.

Sankofa News. Quarterly. Ed. Charles Quist-Adade. Windsor, ON: Sankofa Communications Network, 1994–.

Share: Canada's Largest Ethnic Newspaper. Weekly. Ed. Arnold Auguste. Toronto. 1978–.

Soca Hits 1994. Ed. Alvin C. Daniell. Toronto: A.T.C. Heirs Promotions, [1994].

Spear: Canadian Magazine of Truth and Soul. Monthly. Ed. J. Ashton Braithwaite [1971–], Danny Gooding [197?–1974], Sam Donkoh [1974–7], Arnold Auguste [1977–]. Toronto: Spear Publications, 1971–8; Willowdale, ON: Spear Communications, 1983–?

Spectrum, The. Monthly. Ed. Ewart Walters. Managing ed. Merle Walters. Ottawa: Boyd-McRubie Communications Inc., 1984–.

Straight Up: Youth Magazine. Co-ord. Egbert Gaye. Youth Initiative Project, Community Contact, and the Association of Black Human Services Workers. Montreal: Summer 1996–.

Summer Programme. Annual. Montréal: Universal Negro Improvement Association (Montreal Division), 1935–9.

Talking Drum: Official Newsletter of the African Canadian Association of British Columbia, The. Ed. Dan Kashagama. Vancouver, 1986–.

Talking Drums. Weekly. Ed. Duke V. Vanderpuije. Toronto. 17 Dec. 1975–16 June 1976.

taloua: magazine de la jeune femme. Quarterly. Réd. Léonie Tchatat. Toronto. 1.1 (jan. 2002)–.

Third World Forum. Montreal: Afro-Asian Latin American People's Solidarity Committee, 1974–?

Third World News. Toronto. 1976?

Thunder. Managing ed. Dudley Laws. Toronto: Black Action Defence Committee, 1996.

Tiger Lily: Journal by Women of Colour. Toronto: Williams-Wallace Publishers, 1986; Stratford, ON: Earthtone Women's Magazine, 1987–9?

True Royalist and Weekly Intelligencer. Ed. Rev. A.R. Green. Windsor, ON. 1860–1.

Uhuru: Black Community News Service. Biweekly. Ed. Wantumi Bumboko, Leroy Butcher, and Norman Gyles. Montreal. 1969–75.

Uhuru: Canadian-African News. Biweekly. Toronto: Uhuru Communications, 1985–.
Ujamaa 1996–1997 Black Business Directory. Ottawa. 1996.
Ujima: Collective Work and Responsibility. Semi-annual. Montreal. 1995–.
Umoja: Black Dialogue. Ed. Clarence S. Bayne. Montreal: National Black Coalition, 1969–72.
Uprising International. Ed. Ras Leon Saul. Toronto: Uprising International Newspaper Co., 1992–.
Voice of the Fugitive. Biweekly. Ed. Henry Bibb. Sandwich, [ON]. 1851–3.
West Indian News. Monthly? Ed. Tanya Hume. Toronto. April–Nov. 1967. [superseded by *West Indian News Observer*]
West Indian News Observer. Monthly. Ed. W.S. Richardson. Toronto. April 1967-Jan. 1969. [superseded by *Contrast*]
Witt [West Indian Theatre Toronto] *News: Caribbean Community Newsletter.* Toronto. 1982.
Word: Toronto's Black Culture Magazine, The. Monthly. Ed. Phillip Vassell. Toronto. 1991–.
Word Up: The Bi-Monthly Newsletter of Canadian Artists' Network: Black Artists in Action. Bi-monthly. Toronto: Canadian Artists' Network: Black Artists in Action (CAN: BAIA), 1992–9.

Special Issues and Supplements

Border/Lines: Canada's Magazine of Cultural Studies 29/30 (Fall 1993): special double issue, 'Race to Representation.'
Callaloo: A Journal of African-American and African Arts and Letters 15.2 (Spring 1992): 'Haiti: The Literature and Culture: A Special Issue, Part I'; 15.3 (Summer 1992): 'Haiti: The Literature and Culture: A Special Issue, Part II.'
Canadian Literature 95 (Winter 1982): Caribbean issue.
Canadian Theatre Review 83 (Summer 1995): Black theatre in Canada / African-Canadian theatre. Guest ed. Angela Lee.
Canadian Women's Studies 14.2 (Spring 1994): 'Racism and Gender.'
Chemins critiques 2.4. CIDIHCA.
Communiqué: Canadian Studies 3:1 (Oct. 1976): special bibliographic issue on multiculturalism.
Dalhousie Review, The, 77.2 (Summer 1997): special Africadian issue. Guest ed. George Elliott Clarke.
Descant 101 (Summer 1998): 'The Canadian Caribbean.' Guest ed. Roger McTair.
Essence 24.6 (Oct. 1993): 'Special Travel Section: Canada's Black Presence.'
Fireweed: A Feminist Quarterly 16 (1983): 'Women of Colour.' [Rpt. as *The Issue Is 'Ism: Women of Colour Speak Out,* ed. Nila Gupta and Makeda Silvera (Toronto: Sister Vision, 1989)]
Fireweed: A Feminist Quarterly 23 (Summer 1986): 'Canadian Women Writers.'
Fuse. 16.5–6 (Summer 1993): special double issue on cultural appropriation.
International Review of African American Art, The, 10.1 (1992): special issue on African-Canadian art and culture.
Lettres québécoises 66 (1992): supplement: 'De l'autre littérature québécoise. Autoportrait(s).'

Literary Review, The, (Summer 1992): special issue on the poetry of Caribbean women.

Mix: The Magazine of Artist-Run Culture 22.3 (Winter 1996/97): Black Pacific; disappearing histories of the black Pacific; contemporary black art in Vancouver.

Mot pour mot 12 (1983): 'Littératures haïtiennes II.' Ed. Jean Jonassaint.

Notre Librairie 132. Paris: CLEF, 1998. *Littérature haïtienne: De 1960 à nos jours.*

Prairie Fire: A Canadian Magazine of New Writing 21.4 (2001): special issue: 'Race Poetry, Eh?' Ed. Ashok Mathur.

Prism International 22.4 (1984): [an issue juxtaposing West African and African-Canadian writers].

Revue noire 25 (juin-juil.-août 1997): 'African Canada.'

West Coast Line: A Journal of Contemporary Writing and Criticism 28.1–2 (1994): 'Colour. An Issue.'

West Coast Line: A Journal of Contemporary Writing and Criticism 31.1 (Spring/Summer 1997): 'North: New African Canadian Writing.' Ed. Peter Hudson.

Secondary Bibliographies Consulted

African Books Collective Ltd. *New and Recent Titles on African Literature and Languages.* [ABC Subject Catalogues, no. 1.] Oxford: African Books Collective Ltd, 1996.

African-Canadian Educators: A 1996 Calendar. [Ed.] Wilma Patricia-Holas. Ottawa: Betterworld Publications, 1996.

Alston, Sandra, and Karen Evans, eds. *A Bibliography of Canadiana: Being Items in the Metropolitan Library Relating to the Early History and Development of Canada.* 2nd Supplement. Volume 3. 1850–67. Toronto: Metropolitan Toronto Library Board, 1986.

Arata, Esther Spring, and Nicholas John Rotoli. *Black American Playwrights, 1800 to the Present: A Bibliography.* Metuchen, NJ: The Scarecrow Press, Inc., 1976.

Arata, Esther Spring, et al. *More Black American Playwrights: A Bibliography.* Metuchen, NJ: The Scarecrow Press, Inc., 1978.

Asein, S.O. 'West Indian Poetry in English, 1900–1970: An Annotated Bibliography.' *Black Images* 1.1 (Jan. 1972): 12–15.

Balutansky, Kathleen M., et al. 'Studies in Caribbean and South American Literature: An Annotated Bibliography, 1990.' *Callaloo* 15.1 (Winter 1992): 199–313.

– 'Studies in Caribbean and South American Literature: An Annotated Bibliography, 1991–1992.' *Callaloo* 16.4 (Fall 1993): 931–1033.

Bibliographic Guide to Black Studies: 1993. New York: G.K. Hall & Co., 1994.

Books on Canada: Canadian Studies / Livres sur le Canada: Études canadiennes. Ottawa: Association for the Export of Canadian Books / Association pour l'exportation du livre canadien, 1995–2001.

Campbell, Dorothy W. *Index to Black American Writers in Collective Biographies.* Littleton, CO: Libraries Unlimited, Inc., 1983.

Canadian Ethnic Studies [annual bibliography of publications relating to Canadian ethnic studies]. 1976–.

Canadian Ethnic Studies 5.1–2 (1973): special bibliographic issue.

Canadian Studies Programme, Mount Allison University. *A Preliminary Checklist of Nineteenth Century Canadian Poetry in English.* Sackville, NB: Canadian Studies Programme, Mount Allison University, 1976.

CARICOM Bibliography. Vols. 1–10. Georgetown, Guyana: Caribbean Community Secretariat, Information and Documentation Section, 1977–89.

Christian, Barbara. *Black Women Novelists: The Development of a Tradition, 1892–1976*. Westport, CT: Greenwood Press, 1980.

Clark, Edward. *Black Writers in New England: A Bibliography, with Biographical Notes, of Books by and about Afro-American Writers Associated with New England in the* 'Collection of Afro-American Literature.' Boston: National Park Service, 1985.

Clark, VèVè A., et al. 'Studies in Caribbean and South American Literature: An Annual Annotated Bibliography, 1988.' *Callaloo* 12.4 (Fall 1989): 741–847.

– 'Studies in Caribbean and South American Literature: An Annual Annotated Bibliography, 1989.' *Callaloo* 13.3 (1990): 556–697.

Coates, Carrol F. 'The Haitian Intellectual Scene: Creative Writers, Essayists, and Visual Artists.' *Callaloo* 15.3 (Summer 1992): 863–73.

Dance, Daryl Cumber. *Fifty Caribbean Writers: A Bio-Bibliographical Critical Sourcebook*. New York: Greenwood Press, 1986.

Decosta-Willis, Miriam, Reginald Martin, and Roseann P. Bell, eds. *Erotique Noire: Black Erotica*. New York: Doubleday, 1992.

Department of Labour. Economics and Research Branch. *Discrimination in Employment: A Selected Annotated Bibliography*. Ottawa: Department of Labour, Economics and Research Branch, 1970.

Dictionary Catalog of the Arthur B. Spingarn Collection of Negro Authors. 2 vols. Washington, DC: Howard University Library, 1970.

Dumond, Dwight Lowell. *A Bibliography of Antislavery in America*. Ann Arbor: University of Michigan Press, 1961.

Dyck, Ruth, comp. 'Ethnic Folklore in Canada: A Preliminary Survey.' *Canadian Ethnic Studies* 7.2 (1975): 90–101.

Edwards, Paul, and David Dabydeen. *Black Writers in Britain: 1760–1890*. Edinburgh: Edinburgh University Press, 1991.

Fenwick, M.J. *Writers of the Caribbean and Central America: A Bibliography*. 2 vols. New York: Garland Publishing, 1992.

Foster, M. Marie Booth. *Southern Black Creative Writers, 1829–1953: Bibliographies*. New York: Greenwood Press, 1988.

French, William P., Michel J. Fabre, Amritjit Singh, and Geneviève E. Fabre. *Afro-American Poetry and Drama, 1760–1975: A Guide to Information Sources*. Detroit: Gale Research Company, 1979.

Fulford, Robert, David Godfrey, and Abraham Rotstein, eds. *Read Canadian: A Book about Canadian Books*. Toronto: James Lewis & Samuel, 1972.

Glikin, Ronda. *Black American Women in Literature: A Bibliography, 1976 through 1987*. Jefferson, NC: McFarland & Company, Inc., Publishers, 1989.

Gregorovich, Andrew, comp. *Canadian Ethnic Groups Bibliography*. Toronto: Queen's Printer, Ontario, 1972.

Gregorovich, Andrew, and Gabriele Scardellato. *A Bibliography of Canada's Peoples, Supplement 1, 1972–1979*. Toronto: Multicultural History Society of Ontario, 1993.

Hatch, James V., and Omanii Abdullah, comps. and eds. *Black Playwrights, 1823–1977: An Annotated Bibliography of Plays*. New York: R.R. Bowker Company, 1977.

Helly, Denise, [et] Anne Vassal. *Romanciers immigrés: Biographies et oeuvres publiées au Québec entre 1970 et 1990*. Québec: Institut québécois de discours et sociocritique des textes (CIADEST), 1993.

Herdeck, Donald E., ed., et al. *Caribbean Writers: A Bio-Bibliographical-Critical Encyclopedia*. Washington, DC: Three Continents Press, Inc., 1979.

Horning, Lewis Emerson, and Lawrence J. Burpee. *A Bibliography of Canadian Fiction (English)*. Toronto: William Briggs, 1904.

Humphries, Jill, comp. *Who's Who in the League of Canadian Poets: Directory of Members and Books in Print 1995/96*. Toronto: The League of Canadian Poets, 1995.

– *Who's Who in the Playwrights Union of Canada: A Directory of Members 1995/96*. Toronto: Playwrights Union of Canada, 1995.

Ingles, Ernest Boyce, ed. and comp. *Bibliography of Canadian Bibliographies*. 3rd ed. Toronto: University of Toronto Press, 1994.

Institute of Jamaica, Jamaica, West Indies. *The Jamaican National Bibliography: 1964–1974*. Millwood, NY: Kraus International Publications, 1981.

International Poetry Review 20.2 (Fall 1994): Voix du Québec / Voices of Québec.

Jackson, Blyden. *A History of Afro-American Literature: Volume I, The Long Beginning, 1746–1895*. Baton Rouge: Louisiana State University Press, 1989.

Jacques, Ruxl-Léonel. 'Bibliographie / Bibliography.' *Canadian Ethnic Studies* 18.2 (1986): 178–82. [focuses on Québec]

Jamaican National Bibliography. [6 vols.] Kingston, JA: Institute of Jamaica, West India Reference Library, 1976–8; National Library of Jamaica, Institute of Jamaica, 1980–2.

Jordan, Casper LeRoy, comp. *A Bibliographical Guide to African-American Women Writers*. Westport, CT: Greenwood Press, 1993.

Kellner, Bruce, ed. *The Harlem Renaissance: A Historical Dictionary for the Era*. 1984. New York: Methuen, 1987.

Koskie, Mary Patricia. *Selective Bibliography of Ethnic Groups in Canada*. Toronto: Social Sciences Department, Metropolitan Toronto Library, 1980.

Lajmi, Nouri, coord. *Répertoire: Les Journalistes des communautés ethnoculturelles du Québec*. [Québec]: Centre d'études sur les médias, 1995.

Lang, Robert, coord. ed., et al. *Contemporary Canadian Authors*. Volume 1. Toronto: Gale Canada, 1996.

Library Company of Philadelphia. *Afro-Americana 1553–1906: Author Catalog of the Library Company of Philadelphia and the Historical Society of Pennsylvania*. Boston: G.K. Hall & Co., 1973.

Lindfors, Berth, and Reinhard Sander. *Dictionary of Literary Biography, Vol. 117: Twentieth-Century Caribbean and Black African Writers*. First Series. Detroit: Gale Research Inc., 1992.

– *Dictionary of Literary Biography, Vol. 125: Twentieth-Century Caribbean and Black African Writers* Second Series. Gale Research Inc., 1994.

– *Dictionary of Literary Biography, Vol. 157: Twentieth-Century Caribbean and Black African Writers*. Third Series. Gale Research Inc., 1996.

Literary Publications Supported by Multiculturalism Canada / Publications littéraires subventionnés par Multiculturalisme Canada. [1971–84.] Ottawa: Minister of Supply and Services Canada / Ministre des Approvisionnements et Services Canada, 1985.

Mallea, J.R. 'Canadian Cultural Pluralism and Education: A Select Bibliography.' *Canadian Ethnic Studies* 8.1 (1976): 81–8.

Margolies, Edward, and David Bakish. *Afro-American Fiction, 1853–1976: A Guide to Information Sources*. Detroit: Gale Research Company, 1979.

Matthews, Geraldine A., et al. *Black American Writers, 1773–1949: A Bibliography and Union List*. Boston: G.K. Hall & Co., 1975.

Matthews, William, comp. *Canadian Diaries and Autobiographies*. Berkeley: University of California Press, 1950.

McClain, Paula Denice. *Alienation and Resistance: The Political Behaviour of Afro-Canadians*. Palo Alta, CA: R and E Research Associates, 1979.

McLaren, Duncan. *Ontario Ethno-Cultural Newspapers, 1835–1972: An Annotated Checklist*. Toronto: University of Toronto Press, 1973.

Miska, John, comp. *Ethnic and Native Canadian Literature, 1850–1979: A Bibliography of Primary and Secondary Materials*. Lethbridge, AB: Microform Biblios, 1980.

Morrison, James H. *A Common Heritage: An Annotated Bibliography of Ethnic Groups in Nova Scotia*. Halifax, NS: International Education Centre, Saint Mary's University, 1984.

Murray, Rudy G. 'A Bibliography of Caribbean Novels in English.' *Black Images* 1.1 (Jan. 1972): 23–5.

Nakamura, Joyce, ed. *Contemporary Authors: Autobiography Series, Volume 16*. Detroit: Gale Research Inc., 1992.

National Union Catalog: Pre–1956 Imprints. London: Mansell Information Publishing Limited, 1971.

Obradovic, Nadezda, ed. *African Rhapsody: Short Stories of the Contemporary African Experience*. New York: Anchor Books, 1994.

Page, James A., and Jae Min Roh, comps. *Selected Black American, African, and Caribbean Authors: A Bio-Bibliography*. Littleton, CO: Libraries Unlimited, 1985.

Penn, I. Garland. *The Afro-American Press and Its Editors*. Springfield, MA: Willey & Co., 1891. Rpt. New York: Arno Press and the New York Times, 1969.

Perron, J. *Bibliographie des thèses et mémoires sur les communautés culturelles et l'immigration*. Montréal: Ministère des Communautés culturelles et de l'immigration, 1983.

Peterson, Bernard L., Jr. *Contemporary Black American Playwrights and Their Plays: A Biographical Directory and Dramatic Index*. New York: Greenwood Press, 1988.

Primus, Wilma. 'A Bibliography of Haitian Literature: 1900–1972.' *Black Images* 2.1 (Spring 1973): 43–59.

Racine, Daniel L. 'French West Indian Poetry from 1900 to 1970: A Panoramic View with a Selective Bibliography.' *Black Images* 2.3–4 (Autumn/Winter, 1973): 37–43.

Recent Publications Supported by Multiculturalism and Citizenship Canada / Publications récentes subventionnées par Multiculturalisme et Citoyonneté Canada. [1984–91.] [Ottawa]: Minister of Supply and Services Canada / Ministre des Approvisionnements et Services Canada, 1992.

Redmond, Eugene B. *Drumvoices: The Mission of Afro-American Poetry, a Critical History*. Garden City, NY: Anchor Books, 1976.

Resource Guide of Publications Supported by Multiculturalism Programs 1973–1992 / Guide des publications subventionnés par les programmes du multiculturalisme 1973–1992.

[Comp. Daniel Woolford.] Ottawa: Minister of Supply and Services Canada / Ministre des Approvisionnements et Services Canada, 1993.

Rhodenizer, Vernon Blair. *A Handbook of Canadian Literature*. Ottawa: Graphic, 1930.

Rowell, Charles H., and Mohamed B. Taleb-Khyar, comps., et al. 'Studies of African Literatures: An Annual Annotated Bibliography, 1988.' *Callaloo*. 12.4 (Fall 1989): 848–914.

Rush, Theressa Gunnels, Carol Fairbanks Myers, and Esther Spring Arata. *Black American Writers Past and Present: A Biographical and Bibliographical Dictionary*. 2 vols. Metuchen, NJ: The Scarecrow Press, Inc., 1975.

Sherman, Joan R., ed. *African-American Poetry of the Nineteenth Century: An Anthology*. Urbana, Il.: University of Illinois Press, 1992.

Shockley, Ann Allen. *Afro-American Women Writers, 1746–1933: An Anthology and Critical Guide*. Boston: G.K. Hall, 1988.

Spadoni, Carl, and Judy Donnelly. *A Bibliography of McClelland and Stewart Imprints, 1909–1985: A Publisher's Legacy*. Toronto: ECW Press, 1994.

Spradling, Mary Mace, ed. *In Black and White: A Guide to Magazine Articles, Newspaper Articles, and Books Concerning More Than 15,000 Black Individuals and Groups*. 3rd ed. 2 vols. Detroit: Gale Research Company, 1980.

– *In Black and White: A Guide to Magazine Articles, Newspaper Articles, and Books Concerning More Than 6,700 Black Individuals and Groups*. Supplement. Detroit: Gale Research Company, 1985.

Staton, Frances M., and Marie Tremaine, eds. *A Bibliography of Canadiana: Being Items in the Public Library of Toronto, Canada, Relating to the Early History and Development of Canada*. Toronto: The Public Library, 1934.

Tait, Terence D., ed. *Black and White in North America: Selected Sources*. Toronto: McClelland and Stewart, 1970.

Thibault, Claude. *Bibliographia Canadiana*. Don Mills, ON: Longman Canada Limited, 1973.

Thomas, Joy, comp. 'A Select Bibliography of West Indian Literature.' In *See Me Yah!: Working Papers on the Newly-Arrived West Indian Child in the Downtown School*. Comp. Anne-Marie Stewart. Toronto: Language Study Centre, Toronto Board of Education, 1977. 106A–128.

– 'Fourteen West Indian Writers.' In *See Me Yah! Working Papers on the Newly-Arrived West Indian Child in the Downtown School*. Comp. Anne-Marie Stewart. Toronto: Language Study Centre, Toronto Board of Education, 1977. 129–45.

Tlili, Najwa. *Répertoire des femmes d'images de l'Afrique francophone*. Montréal: Vues d'Afrique, 1994.

Trinidad and Tobago National Bibliography. Vol. 7–13. St Augustine, TT: Central Library of Trinidad and Tobago and The University of the West Indies Library, 1981–7.

Union des Écrivains québécois. *Dictionnaire des écrivains québécois contemporains*. Montréal: Québec/Amérique, 1983.

Wagner, Anton, ed. *The Brock Bibliography of Published Canadian Plays in English, 1766–1978*. Toronto: Playwrights Press, 1980.

Walmsley, Anne. *The Caribbean Artists Movement, 1966–1972: A Literary and Cultural History*. London: New Beacon Books, 1992.

Watters, Reginald Eyre. *A Checklist of Canadian Literature and Background Materials: 1628–1960.* 2nd ed. Toronto: University of Toronto Press, 1972.

Weiss, Allan Barry. *A Comprehensive Bibliography of English-Canadian Short Stories, 1950–1983.* Toronto: ECW Press, 1988.

Wharton-Lake, Beverly D., comp. *Creative Literature of Trinidad and Tobago – A Bibliography.* Washington, DC: Columbus Memorial Library, Organization of American States, 1988.

Winks, Robin W. *The Blacks in Canada: A History.* 1971. Montreal: McGill-Queen's University Press, 1997.

Writers' Development Trust, Prairie Work Group. *The Immigrant Experience: A Resource Guide for the Teaching of Canadian Literature.* Toronto: Writers' Development Trust, 1977.

Yellin, Jean Fagan, and Cynthia D. Bond. *The Pen Is Ours: A Listing of Writings by and about African-American Women before 1910: With Secondary Bibliography to the Present.* New York: Oxford University Press, 1991.

Young, Judy. 'Canadian Literature in the Non-Official Languages: A Review of Recent Publications and Work in Progress.' *Canadian Ethnic Studies* 14.1 (1982): 138–49.

Sites Visited

Amistad Research Center, Tulane University (New Orleans), Bibliothèque nationale du Québec (Montréal), Black Cultural Centre for Nova Scotia (Cherrybrook, NS), Carleton University (Ottawa), Caron Librairie (Montréal), Dalhousie University (Halifax, NS), A Different Booklist (Toronto), Duke University (Durham, NC), Legislative Library (Fredericton, NB), Librairie Pantoute (Québec), Library of Congress (Washington, DC), Metropolitan Toronto Reference Library (Toronto), National Library of Barbados (Bridgetown, Barbados), National Library of Canada (Ottawa), National Library of Trinidad and Tobago (Port of Spain, TT), Public Archives of Nova Scotia (Halifax, NS), Queen's University (Kingston, ON), Roy States Collection, Rare Book Room, McGill University (Montreal), Third World Books (Toronto), University of New Brunswick (Fredericton, NB), University of Ottawa (Ottawa), University of Toronto (Toronto), University of the West Indies (Cave Hill, Barbados), and University of the West Indies (St Augustine, Trinidad).

WORKS CITED

Note: Most texts by African-Canadian writers appear in 'Africana Canadiana: A Select Bibliography of Literature by African-Canadian Authors' (pp. 339–448, above). The African-Canadian texts cited here are mainly individual poems, short stories, and essays.

Abraham, Arthur. 'Bangura, J.A.' Entry. *Dictionary of African Biography*. Volume 2: Sierra Leone–Zaire. Ed. L.H. Ofosu-Appiah. Algonac, MI: [The Encyclopaedia Africana], 1979.

Abrahams, Roger D. *Singing the Master: The Emergence of African American Culture in the Plantation South*. New York: Pantheon-Random, 1992.

Acorn, Milton. *I've Tasted My Blood: Poems 1956 to 1968*. [Toronto]: Ryerson Press, [1969].

Adkins, Major Mark. *Urgent Fury: The Battle for Grenada*. New York: Lexington / Macmillan, 1989.

Afrique Tribune. 'À L'Horizon.' 2.33 (1–14 mars 1996): [16].

Afro News, The. [Vancouver, B.C.] 10.3 (March 1996): 1–20.

Alexander, Elizabeth. '"Can you be BLACK and look at this?": Reading the Rodney King Video(s).' In *Black Male: Representations of Masculinity in Contemporary American Art*. Ed. Thelma Golden. New York: Whitney Museum of Modern Art, 1994. 91–110.

Alexander, Ken, and Avis Glaze. *Towards Freedom: The African Canadian Experience*. Toronto: Umbrella Press, 1996.

Alexis, André. 'Borrowed Blackness.' *This Magazine* 28.8 (May 1995): 14–20.

– 'Crossroads.' *This Magazine* 30.5 (March/April 1997): 30–5.

Algoo-Baksh, Stella. *Austin C. Clarke: A Biography*. Toronto: ECW Press; Barbados, Jamaica, Trinidad and Tobago: The Press of the University of the West Indies, 1994.

Almonte, Richard. Introduction. *A Narrative of Thomas Smallwood (Coloured Man)*. 1851. Ed. Richard Almonte. Toronto: The Mercury Press, 2000. 9–20.

– '"Treason in the Fort": Blackness and Canadian Literature.' In Rinaldo Walcott, ed., *Rude*, 11–25.

Anderson, Benedict. *Imagined Communities: Reflections on the Origin and Spread of Nationalism*. 1983. Rev. ed. London: Verso, 1991.

Anderson, Debra L. *Decolonizing the Text: Glissantian Readings in Caribbean and African-American Literatures*. New York: Peter Lang, 1995.

Andrews, William L., et al., eds. *The Oxford Companion to African American Literature*. New York: Oxford University Press, 1997.

Appiah, Kwame Anthony. 'Ethnicity and Identity in Africa: An Interpretation.' In Appiah and Gates, eds, *Africana*, 703–5.

– 'Pan-Africanism.' In Appiah and Gates, eds, *Africana*, 1484–6.

– 'Race: An Interpretation.' In Appiah and Gates, eds, *Africana*, 1574–80.

Appiah, Kwame Anthony, and Henry Louis Gates, Jr, eds. *Africana: The Encyclopedia of the African and African American Experience*. New York: Basic Civitas Books, 1999.

Aquin, Hubert. *Trou de mémoire*. Montréal: Le Cercle du Livre de France, Ltée, 1968.

Arnold, Matthew. 'General Grant.' *Murray's Magazine* 1 (Jan.-Feb. 1887): 130–44, 150–66. Rpt. in *The Last Word*. Vol. 11 of *The Complete Prose Works of Matthew Arnold*. 11 vols. Ed. R.H. Super. Ann Arbor: University of Michigan Press, 1977. 144–79.

Aronowitz, Stanley. 'Double Bind: America and the African Diaspora.' *Transition* 69 (Spring 1996): 222–35.

Ashcroft, Bill, Gareth Griffiths, and Helen Tiffin. *The Empire Writes Back: Theory and Practice in Post-Colonial Literatures*. 1989. London: Routledge, 1993.

Atwood, Margaret. 'Half-Hanged Mary.' Poem. In *Morning in the Burned House*. Toronto: McClelland & Stewart, 1995. 58–69.

– 'Marsh Languages.' Poem. In *Morning in the Burned House*. Toronto: McClelland & Stewart, 1995. 54–5.

– *Survival: A Thematic Guide to Canadian Criticism*. Toronto: House of Anansi Press, 1972.

Azoulay, Katya Gibel. Review of *The New Colored People: The Mixed-Race Movement in America*. By Jon Michael Spencer. *African American Review* 33.1 (Spring 1999): 151–3.

Baines, Mercedes. 'Age of Innocence.' Poem. *West Coast Line* 28.1–2 (Spring/Fall 1994): 196–7.

– 'Brown Child.' Poem. *West Coast Line* 28.1–2 (Spring/Fall 1994): 194–5.

– 'Half-Baked Zebra Cake.' Poem. *West Coast Line* 31.1 (Spring/Summer 1997): 132–3.

Bains, Hardial. *Communism: 1989–1991*. [Toronto]: Ideological Studies Centre, 1991.

Baker, Houston A., Jr. *Afro-American Poetics: Revisions of Harlem and the Black Aesthetic*. Madison, WI: University of Wisconsin Press, 1988.

– 'America's War on Decency and a Call to the Mall: Black Men, Symbolic Politics, and the Million Man March.' *Black Renaissance / Renaissance Noire* 1.1 (Fall 1996): 70–82.

– *Modernism and the Harlem Renaissance*. Chicago: University of Chicago Press, 1987.

Baldwin, James. *Another Country*. 1960. New York: Dell, 1978.

Bansfield, Anthony. Introduction. *The N'x Step: Hochelaga and the Diasporic African Poets: A Collection of Performance Poetry by a Montreal-based Black Writers Group*. Ed. Anthony Bansfield. Montreal: RevWord Press, 1995. 4–5.

Barker, Siobhan R.K. 'the "whole" truth: nothing but "images."' *Diaspora* 1.2 (Fall 1994): 14–16.

Barksdale, Richard K. 'Miscegenation on Broadway: Hughes's *Mulatto* and Edward Sheldon's *The Nigger*.' In *Critical Essays on Langston Hughes*. Ed. Edward J. Mullen. Boston: G.K. Hall, 1986. 191–9.

Barlow, Julie. 'This and That.' *This Magazine* 29.5 (Dec./Jan. 1996): 4.

Barnes, LaVerne. *The Plastic Orgasm*. 1971. Richmond Hill, ON: Simon & Schuster of Canada, 1973.

Baudrillard, Jean. *Seduction*. Trans. Brian Singer. Montréal: New World Perspectives, 1990. Trans. of *De la séduction*. Paris: Éditions Galilée, 1979.

Bayliss, John F. 'Ghettoization and Black Literature.' In *The Black Writer in Africa and the Americas*. Ed. Lloyd W. Brown. Los Angeles: Hennessey & Ingalls, Inc., 1973. 69–84.

Beaton, Virginia, and Stephen Pedersen. *Maritime Music Greats: Fifty Years of Hits and Heartbreak*. Halifax, NS: Nimbus, 1992.

Benda, Julien. *The Betrayal of the Intellectuals*. Trans. Richard Aldington. Boston: The Beacon Press, 1955. Trans. of *La Trahison des clercs*. Paris: Éditions Bernard Grasset, 1927. First pub. as *The Treason of the Intellectuals*. Trans. Richard Aldington. New York: William Morrow & Company, Inc., 1928.

– 'Dialogues à Byzance.' *La Revue blanche*. 1898.

Bengtsson, Elna. *The Language and Vocabulary of Sam Slick I*. Upsala Canadian Studies. Ed. S.B. Liljegren. Copenhagen: Ejnar Munksgaard; Upsala, Swe.: A.-B. Lundequistska Bokhandeln, 1956.

Bennett, Eric. 'Creoles.' In Appiah and Gates, eds, *Africana*, 528–9.

Berger, John. *About Looking*. New York: Pantheon, 1980.

Bernstein, Michael André. 'History and Textuality in Ezra Pound's *Cantos*.' In Korn, ed., *Pound*, 15–22.

Bérubé, Michael. *Marginal Forces / Cultural Centers: Tolson, Pynchon, and the Politics of the Canon*. Ithaca, NY: Cornell University Press, 1992.

Best, Carrie M. *That Lonesome Road*. Excerpt. In George Elliott Clarke, ed., *Fire*, Vol. 1, 118–28.

Black, Ayanna, ed. Foreword. *Voices: Canadian Writers of African Descent*. Toronto: HarperCollins, 1992. xi–xiii.

Black Cultural Centre for Nova Scotia. *Traditional Lifetime Stories: A Collection of Black Memories*. 2 vols. Cherrybrook, NS: The Black Cultural Centre for Nova Scotia, 1987, 1990.

Black Cultural Centre for Nova Scotia and The Canadian Broadcasting Corporation. *Lord You Brought Me a Mighty Long Way: An African Nova Scotian Musical Journey*. Compact Disc. Cherrybrook, NS and Halifax, NS: The Black Cultural Centre for Nova Scotia and The Canadian Broadcasting Corporation, 1997.

Black to Business. [Halifax, NS.] 16 (Spring 2001): 14.

Blake, William. 'The Garden of Love.' Poem. 1794. In *The Norton Anthology of Poetry: Revised*. Ed. Alexander W. Allison et al. 1970. New York: W.W. Norton & Company, Inc., 1975. 554.

Bogle, Donald. Introduction. *A Separate Cinema: Fifty Years of Black Cast Posters*. By John Kisch and Edward Mapp. New York: The Noonday Press, 1992. xiii–xxxiii.

Boily, Lisette. comp. 'Contemporary Canadian First Nations Writers and Writers of Colour: A Working Bibliography.' *West Coast Line*. 28.1–2 (1994): 303–18.

– Review of *Moon Honey*. By Suzette Mayr. *West Coast Line* 31.1 (Spring/Summer 1997): 164–8.

Bök, Christian. 'No Pomo Promo: Linda Hutcheon and *The Canadian Postmodern.*'
   Paragraph 17.1 (Summer 1995): 5–11.
Book, Shane. [Bio.] *Absinthe* 9.2 (1996): 41.
Borden, George. 'A Race Defaced.' Poem. In George Borden, *Canaan*, 3.
– 'To My Children I Bequeath.' Poem. 1988. In George Elliott Clarke, ed., *Fire*, Vol. 1,
   166–7.
Boudreau, Raoul. 'Poetry As Action.' Preface. In Cogswell and Elder, eds and trans.,
   Unfinished, xvii–xxvii.
– 'Une Poésie qui est un acte.' In Cogswell and Elder, eds, *Rêves*, 7–20.
Bowering, George. 'Pharoah [sic] Sanders, in the Flesh.' Poem. In *The Jazz Poetry
   Anthology*. Ed. Sascha Feinstein and Yusef Komunyakaa. Bloomington, IN: Indiana
   University Press, 1991. 16–17.
Boyd, Frank Stanley, Jr, ed. 'Editor to Reader.' In *McKerrow: A Brief History of the
   Coloured Baptists of Nova Scotia (1783–1895)*. Rev. ed. of Peter E. McKerrow, *A Brief
   History of the Coloured Baptists of Nova Scotia and Their First Organization as Churches,
   A.D. 1832*. 1895. Halifax, NS: Afro-Nova Scotian Enterprises, 1976. iii–vii.
Boyd, George Elroy. *Shine Boy*. Program for play. Halifax, NS: Neptune Theatre, 1988.
   [n.pag.]
Bradley, David. *The Chaneysville Incident*. New York: HarperCollins, 1981.
Braithwaite, Edward Kamau. *History of the Voice: The Development of Nation Language in
   Anglophone Caribbean Poetry*. London: New Beacon, 1984.
Brand, Dionne. 'Canto I.' Poem. 1982. In Morrell, ed., *Grammar*, 184–5.
– 'Cuba.' In Brand, *Bread*, 85–99.
– 'Diary – the Grenada Crisis.' Poem. 1984. In Morrell, ed., *Grammar*, 211–14.
– 'Dionne Brand: No Language Is Neutral.' Interview. By Frank Birbalsingh. In
   Frontiers of Caribbean Literature in English. Ed. Frank Birbalsingh. London: Macmillan
   Education Ltd, 1996. 120–37.
– '4.' Poem. 1983. In Morrell, ed., *Grammar*, 197.
– 'I Have Been Losing Roads.' Poem. 1997. In Brand, *Land*, 3–17.
– 'October 25th, 1983.' Poem. 1984. In Morrell, ed., *Grammar*, 216–18.
Brasseaux, Carl A. *In Search of Evangeline: Birth and Evolution of the Evangeline Myth*.
   Thibodaux, LA: Blue Heron Press, 1988.
Bristow, Peggy. '"Whatever you raise in the ground, you can sell it in Chatham": Black
   Women in Buxton and Chatham, 1850–65.' In Bristow et al., *'We're*, 69–142.
Brown, Lennox. 'A Crisis: Black Culture in Canada.' *Black Images* 1.1 (Jan. 1972): 4–8.
Brown, Lloyd W. 'Beneath the North Star: The Canadian Image in Black Literature.'
   Dalhousie Review 50.3 (1970): 317–29.
Browne, Robin. 'Mystory.' Poem. In Bansfield, ed., 8–9.
Bryant, M. Darrol. 'The Barren Twilight: History and Faith in Grant's Lament.' In
   George Grant in Process: Essays and Conversations. Ed. Larry Schmidt. Toronto:
   Anansi, 1978. 110–19.
Brydon, Diana. 'Commonwealth or Common Poverty?: The New Literatures in
   English and the New Discourse of Marginality.' *Kunapipi* 11.1 (1989): 1–16.
Burdick, John. 'Myth of Racial Democracy in Latin America and the Caribbean: An
   Interpretation.' In Appiah and Gates, eds, *Africana*, 1374–6.

Burnside, Scott, and Alan Cairns. *Deadly Innocence*. New York: Warner Books, 1995.

Busby, Brian John. 'Survivor of the Crossing.' *Literary Review of Canada* 4.6 (June 1995): 11–12.

Byerman, Keith. 'An Introduction: Is There Race in This Writing? African American Fiction Today.' *American Book Review* (Nov.-Dec. 1999): 1.

Byron, George Gordon, Lord. *Don Juan*. [1819–24]. London: J. Lane, 1926.

Calhoun, Sue. 'Acadia Rising: The MFU and the New Nationalism.' *New Maritimes* Jan./Feb. (1992): 6–13.

Cantwell, Robert. *Bluegrass Breakdown: The Making of the Old Southern Sound*. Urbana, IL: University of Illinois Press, 1984.

Capécia, Mayotte. *Je suis Martiniquaise*. Paris: Corréa, 1948.

Carr, Brenda. 'To "Heal the Word Wounded": Agency and Materiality of Language and Form in M. Nourbese Philip's *She Tries Her Tongue, Her Silence Softly Breaks*.' *Studies in Canadian Literature* 19.1 (1994): 72–93.

Cartwright, John R. *Politics in Sierra Leone 1947–1967*. Toronto: University of Toronto Press, 1970.

Chamberlin, J. Edward. 'The Canadian Caribbean *Descant*, an Introduction.' *Descant* 101 (Summer 1998): 7–10.

– *Come Back to Me My Language: Poetry and the West Indies*. Toronto: McClelland & Stewart, 1993.

Champagne, Dominic. *La Cité interdite: Théatre*. Montréal: VLB Éditeur, 1992.

Chandler, Nahum Dimitri. 'The Economy of Desedimentation: W.E.B. DuBois and the Discourses of the Negro.' *Callaloo* 19.1 (Winter 1996): 78–93.

– 'The Figure of the X: An Elaboration of the Du Boisian Autobiographical Example.' In *Displacement, Diaspora, and Geographies of Identity*. Ed. Smadar Lavie and Ted Swedenburg. Durham, NC: Duke University Press, 1996. 235–72.

Chase, Preston. 'After the Love.' 1996. Novella. TS. Unpublished novella in the author's possession.

Cheney-Coker, Syl. 'Absurdity.' Poem. 1980. In Cheney-Coker, *The Graveyard*, 17.

– *The Blood in the Desert's Eyes: Poems*. London: Heinemann, 1990.

– 'Cheney-Coker, Syl 1945–.' Entry. In *Contemporary Authors*. Vol. 101. Ed. Frances C. Locher. Detroit: Gage Research Co., 1981. 114.

– 'Cheyney-Coker, Syl' [sic]. Entry. In *Contemporary Poets*. Ed. Thomas Riggs. Detroit: St James Press, 1996. 156–7.

– *Concerto for an Exile*. London: Heinemann, 1973.

– 'Concerto for an Exile.' Poem. 1973. In Cheney-Coker, *The Graveyard*, 20.

– 'Cotillion.' Poem. In Cheney-Coker, *Blood*, 12–13.

– 'Freetown.' Poem. 1973. In Cheney-Coker, *The Graveyard*, 16.

– *The Graveyard Also Has Teeth*, with *Concerto for an Exile: Poems*. London: Heinemann, 1980.

– 'He Falls, the Invertebrate Man.' Poem. In Cheney-Coker, *The Graveyard*, 91.

– 'Hydropathy.' Poem. 1973. In Cheney-Coker, *The Graveyard*, 7–8.

– *The Last Harmattan of Alusine Dunbar*. London: Heinemann, 1990.

– 'Misery of the Convert.' Poem. 1973. In Cheney-Coker, *The Graveyard*, 30–2.

– 'Obelisk.' Poem. 1973. In Cheney-Coker, *The Graveyard*, 33.

- 'The Traveller.' Poem. 1973. In Cheney-Coker, *The Graveyard*, 5–6.
Chesnutt, Charles W. *The House behind the Cedars*. 1900. New York: Collier-Macmillan, 1969.
Chiasson, Herménégilde. 'Eugénie Melanson.' Poem. In Cogswell and Elder, eds, *Rêves*, 46–7.
- 'Rouge.' Poem. In Cogswell and Elder, eds, *Rêves*, 50–1.
Chintoh, Jojo. 'Lennox Brown: A Black Canadian Dramatist.' Interview. *Black Images* 1.1 (Jan. 1972): 28–9.
Chinweizu, Onwuchekwa Jemie, and Ihechuckwu Madubuike. *The Decolonisation of African Literature*. Vol. 1. Washington, DC: Howard University Press, 1983.
Chisholm, Alistair. 'Sierra Leone.' In Appiah and Gates, eds, *Africana*, 1705–9.
Chittick, V.L.O. 'Books and Music in Haliburton.' *Dalhousie Review* 38 (Summer 1958): 207–21. Rpt. in *On Thomas Chandler Haliburton: Selected Criticism*. Ed. Richard A. Davies. Ottawa: Tecumseh, 1979. 168–85.
Christiano, Kevin J. *Pierre Elliott Trudeau: Reason before Passion*. Toronto: ECW Press, 1994.
Clairmont, Donald H. 'Moving People: Relocation and Urban Renewal.' In *The Spirit of Africville*. Ed. The Africville Genealogical Society. Halifax, NS: Maritext / Formac, 1992. 53–76.
Clairmont, Donald H., and Dennis William Magill. *Africville: The Life and Death of a Canadian Black Community*. Toronto, 1974.
Clarke, Austin. 'Beggars.' In Austin Clarke, *Elders*, 63–80.
- 'Canadian Experience.' In Austin Clarke, *Nine*, 31–51.
- 'The Cradle Will Fall.' In Austin Clarke, *Elders*, 142–67.
- 'An Easter Carol.' 1971. In Austin Clarke, *When He Was Free*, 1–15.
- 'Give It a Shot.' In *A Shapely Fire: Changing the Literary Landscape*. Ed. Cyril Dabydeen. Oakville, ON: Mosaic, 1987. 37–59.
- 'How He Does It.' In Austin Clarke, *Nine*, 205–25.
- 'If the Bough Breaks.' In Austin Clarke, *Elders*, 9–28.
- 'In an Elevator.' In Austin Clarke, *Elders*, 46–62.
- 'Initiation.' In Austin Clarke, *In This City*, 25–54.
- Introduction. In Austin Clarke, *Nine*, 1–7.
- 'Letter of the Law of Black.' In Austin Clarke, *In This City*, 55–74.
- 'A Man.' In Austin Clarke, *Nine*, 117–52.
- 'The Motor Car.' 1971. In Austin Clarke, *When He Was Free*, 90–111.
- 'Not So Old, but Oh So Professional.' In Austin Clarke, *Elders*, 81–101.
- 'Some Speculations As to the Absence of Racialistic Vindictiveness in West Indian Literature.' In *The Black Writer in Africa and the Americas*. Ed. Lloyd W. Brown. Los Angeles: Hennessey & Ingalls, Inc., 1973. 165–94.
- 'They Heard A-Ringing of Bells.' In Austin Clarke, *When He Was Free*, 16–29.
- 'Waiting for the Postman to Knock.' In Austin Clarke, *When He Was Free*, 30–50.
Clarke, George Elliott. 'Addendum to Bartlett: A Letter from George Elliott Clarke (September 5, 2000).' *Elizabeth Bishop Society of Nova Scotia: Newsletter* 7.2 (Fall 2000): 2–3.
- 'Confession.' In George Elliott Clarke, ed., *Fire*, Vol. 1, [9].

- 'An Interview with Rocky Jones: The Politics of Passion.' In *Toward a New Maritimes*. Ed. Ian McKay and Scott Milsom. Charlottetown, PEI: Ragweed, 1992. 25–30.
- Introduction. In George Elliott Clarke, ed., *Eyeing*, xi–xxviii.
- Introduction. In George Elliott Clarke, ed., *Fire*, Vol. 1, 11–29.
- 'Must We Burn Haliburton?' In *The Haliburton Bi-centenary Chaplet: Papers Presented at the 1996 Thomas Raddall Symposium*. Ed. Richard A. Davies. Wolfville, NS: Gaspereau Press, 1997. 1–40.
- 'Reading, 'riting, 'rithmetic and racism.' *Atlantic Insight* 11. 9 (1989): 5–7.
- 'White Niggers, Black Slaves: Slavery, Race and Class in T.C. Haliburton's *The Clockmaker*.' *Nova Scotia Historical Review* 14.1 (1994): 13–40.

Clayton, Willard Parker. *Whatever Your Will, Lord: A Brief History Written in Commemoration of the 139th Anniversary of Emmanuel Baptist Church, Upper Hammonds Plains, Nova Scotia*. Hantsport, NS: Lancelot, 1984.

Cleaver, Eldridge. *Soul on Ice*. 1968. New York: Dell / Ramparts, 1970.

Clemens, Samuel [pseud., Mark Twain]. *Adventures of Huckleberry Finn*. 1884. *The Norton Anthology of American Literature*. 3rd ed. Ed. Nina Baym et al. New York: W.W. Norton, 1989. 1170–358.

- *The Adventures of Tom Sawyer*. Toronto: Belford Bros., 1876.

Cliff, Michelle. 'Telling It on the Mountain.' *The Nation* 266.17 (11 May 1998): 24–30.

Coalfleet, Pierre [pseud. of Frank Cyril Davison]. *Solo*. 1923. New York: G.P. Putnam, Knickerbocker Press, 1924.

Codjoe, Henry Martey. 'Black Nationalists Beware! You Could Be Called a Racist for Being "Too Black and African."' In *Talking about Difference: Encounters in Culture, Language and Identity*. Ed. Carl E. James and Adrienne Shadd. Toronto: Between the Lines Press, 1994. 231–5.

Cogswell, Fred, and Jo-Anne Elder, trans. and eds. *Rêves inachevés: Anthologie de poésie acadienne contemporaine*. Moncton, NB: Éditions d'Acadie, 1990.

- eds. *Unfinished Dreams: Contemporary Poetry of Acadie*. Fredericton, NB: Goose Lane Editions, 1990.

Coleman, Daniel. *Masculine Migrations: Reading the Postcolonial Male in 'New Canadian' Narratives*. Toronto: University of Toronto Press, 1998.

Compton, Wayde. 'Declaration of the Halfrican Nation.' Poem. *Absinthe* 9.2 (1996): 10–11.
- 'Diamond.' Poem. In Compton, *49th*, 136–41.
- 'JD.' Poem. In Compton, *49th*, 18–19.
- ['The Unbroken Yellow.'] In Compton, *49th*, 164.

Connelly, Marc. *The Green Pastures*. Play. New York: Farrar and Rinehart, 1929.

Connor, John, and M.V. Marshall. *Three-Five Mile Plains Study: Socio Economic Indicators*. Wolfville, NS: Acadia University, 1965.

Constitution Act, 1982. [Canada.]

Cook, Mercer. 'Some Literary Contacts: African, West Indian, Afro-American.' In *The Black Writer in Africa and the Americas*. Ed. Lloyd W. Brown. Los Angeles: Hennessey & Ingalls, Inc., 1973. 119–40.

Cook, Ramsay. '"I never thought I could be as proud ...": The Trudeau-Lévesque Debate.' In *Towards a Just Society: The Trudeau Years*. Ed. Thomas S. Axworthy and Pierre Elliott Trudeau. Markham, ON: Viking / Penguin, 1990. 342–56.

Cooper, Afua P. 'Black Women and Work in Nineteenth-Century Canada West: Black Woman Teacher Mary Bibb.' In Bristow et al., 'We're, 143–70.

– 'Redemption Dub: ahdri zhina mandiela and the Dark Diaspora.' In Sears, ed., Testifyin', Vol. 1 (2000), 441–4.

Cooper, Frederick. 'Decolonization in Africa: An Interpretation.' In Appiah and Gates, eds, Africana, 571–82.

Cozzens, Frederick S. Acadia; or, A Month with the Blue Noses. New York: Derby & Jackson, 1859.

Craig, Terrence. Racial Attitudes in English-Canadian Fiction, 1905–1980. Waterloo, ON: Wilfrid Laurier University Press, 1987.

Cruse, Harold. The Crisis of the Negro Intellectual. 1967. New York: Quill, 1984.

Cullen, Countee. 'Heritage.' Poem. 1925. In American Negro Poetry. Ed. Arna Bontemps. New York: Hill and Wang, 1963, 1964. 83–6.

Dabydeen, David. 'On Not Being Milton: Nigger Talk in England Today.' In Crisis and Creativity in the New Literatures in English. Ed. Geoffrey Davis and Hena Maes-Jelinek. Amsterdam: Rodopi, 1990. 61–74.

Dalby, David. 'The African Element in Black American English.' Ed. Courtney Cazden et al. The Function of Language in the Classroom. New York: Teachers College-Columbia University Press, 1972.

– Black through White: Patterns of Communication in Africa and the New World. Hans Wolff Memorial Lecture. Bloomington, IN: Indiana University Press, 1969.

D'Alfonso, Antonio. In Italics: In Defense of Ethnicity. Toronto: Guernica Editions, 1996.

Dandurand, Anne. The Cracks. Trans. Luise von Flotow. Stratford, ON: Mercury, 1992. Trans. of Un Coeur qui craque. Montréal: [XYZ Éditeur?], 1991.

Dantin, Louis [pseud. of Eugène Seers]. 'Chanson javanaise.' In Louis Dantin: Sa Vie et son oeuvre. By Gabriel Nadeau. Manchester, NH: Les Éditions Lafayette, 1948. 140–5.

– Fanny. Trans. Raymond Y. Chamberlain. Montreal: Harvest House Ltd, 1974. Trans. of Les Enfances de Fanny. Montréal: Le Cercle du Livre de France, Ltée, 1951.

Davies, Gwendolyn. Studies in Maritime Literary History. Fredericton, NB: Acadiensis, 1991.

Davis, Andrea. 'Healing in the Kitchen: Women's Performance As Rituals of Change.' In Sears, ed., Testifyin', Vol. 1 (2000), 279–80.

Davis, C. Mark. 'Recent Black Maritime Studies.' Acadiensis 23.2 (1994): 148–54.

Davis, Kay. Fugue and Fresco: Structures in Pound's Cantos. [Orono, ME]: National Poetry Foundation, 1984.

Davis, Ursula Broschke. Paris without Regret: James Baldwin, Kenny Clarke, Chester Himes, and Donald Byrd. Iowa City: University of Iowa Press, 1986.

Dawes, Kwame. '360 Degrees Black: A Conversation with Lillian Allen.' Interview. West Coast Line 31. 1 (Spring/Summer 1997): 78–91.

Deleuze, Gilles, and Félix Guattari. Le Rhizome: Introduction. Paris: Éditions de Minuit, 1976.

Derrida, Jacques. Positions. Trans. Alan Bass. Chicago: University of Chicago Press, 1982.

Deverell, Rita Shelton. 'Reflections of a Black Antigone: Cross-Cultural Encounters Are Frightening to Some People.' Tiger Lily 6 (1990): 21–6.

Dillard, J.L. *Black English: Its History and Usage in the United States*. 1972. New York: Vintage-Random, 1973.

– 'The History of Black English in Nova Scotia – a First Step.' *Revista Interamericana Review* 2.4 (Winter 1973): 507–20.

– 'The West African Day-Names in Nova-Scotia.' *Names* 19 (1971): 257–61.

Dion-Levesque, R. 'Louis Dantin.' In *Fanny*. By Louis Dantin [pseud. of Eugène Seers]. Trans. Raymond Y. Chamberlain. Montreal: Harvest House Ltd, 1971. 1–3.

Dionne, René. *La Littérature régionale aux confins de l'histoire et de la géographie: Étude*. Sudbury, ON: Prise de Parole, 1993.

'Divine, Father.' Entry. In Appiah and Gates, eds, *Africana*, 604–5.

Donnell, Alison, and Sarah Lawson Welsh, eds. *The Routledge Reader in Caribbean Literature*. London: Routledge, 1996.

Dover, Cedric. *American Negro Art*. New York: New York Graphic Society, 1960.

Du Bois, W.E.B. *Black Reconstruction in America*. 1935. New York: Russell & Russell, 1962.

– *Dusk of Dawn: An Essay Toward an Autobiography of a Race Concept*. 1940. New York: Schocken Books, 1968.

– *The Souls of Black Folk*. 1903. New York: Viking Penguin, 1989.

Dudek, Louis. 'Poetry in Canada.' 1962. In *In Defence of Art: Critical Essays and Reviews*. By Louis Dudek. Ed. Aileen Collins. Kingston, ON: Quarry Press, 1988. 160–2.

Dvorak, Marta. 'Yes, but Is It Literature?' *Commonwealth* 18.1 (1995): 22–30.

Eke, Maureen N. 'The Novel: *Sozaboy: A Novel in Rotten English*.' In *Ken Saro-Wiwa: Writer and Political Activist*. Ed. Craig W. McLuckie and Aubrey McPhail. Boulder, CO: Lynne Rienner Publishers, 2000. 87–106.

Eldridge, Michael. '"Why Did You Leave There?": Lillian Allen's Geography Lesson.' *Diaspora* 3.2 (1994): 169–83.

Ellison, Ralph. *Invisible Man*. 1952. New York: Vintage International / Random House, 1995.

Étienne, Gérard. 'La Pacotille.' Trans. Keith Louis Walker. [A translation of chapter 11 of *La Pacotille* (Montréal: Éditions de L'Héxagone, 1991).] In Ayanna Black, ed., *Fiery*, 100–24.

Fairburn, Laura. *Endless Bay: A Novel*. Stratford, ON: The Mercury Press, 1994.

Fanon, Frantz. *Black Skin, White Masks*. 1965. Trans. Charles Lam Markmann. New York: Grove, 1967. Trans. of *Peau noire, masques blancs*. Paris: Éditions de Seuil, 1952.

– *Peau noire, masques blancs*. 1952. Paris: Éditions du Seuil, 1971.

Farmer, Clarence. *Soul on Fire*. New York: Belmont Books, 1969.

Fauset, Arthur Huff, comp. *Folklore from Nova Scotia*. New York: American Folk-Lore Society, 1931.

– Introduction. *Folklore from Nova Scotia*. New York: American Folk-Lore Society, 1931. vii-xi.

Fee, Margery. 'The Signifying Writer and the Ghost Reader: Mudrooroo's *Master of the Ghost Dreaming* and *Writing from the Fringe*.' *Australian and New Zealand Studies in Canada* 8 (Dec. 1992): 18–32.

Fergusson, C.B. *A Documentary Study of the Establishment of Negroes in Nova Scotia between the War of 1812 and the Winning of Responsible Government*. Publication no. 8. Halifax, NS: Public Archives of Nova Scotia, 1948.

Filmakers Library. Catalogue. *Deep River / Strong Currents: Films and Videos about the African-American, Afro-Caribbean and African Experience.* New York: Filmakers Library, [1996].

Fingard, Judith. *The Dark Side of Victorian Halifax.* Lawrencetown Beach, NS: Pottersfield, 1989.

Fitz, Earl E. *Rediscovering the New World: Inter-American Literature in a Comparative Context.* Iowa City: University of Iowa Press, 1991.

Fleming, Ian. *Moonraker.* 1955. London: Pan Books Ltd, 1964.

Forbes, Allen. 'De Secon Comin.' Poem. *Absinthe* 9.2 (1996): 59.

Forsythe, Dennis, ed. *Let the Niggers Burn! The Sir George Williams University Affair and Its Caribbean Aftermath.* Montreal: Our Generation Press / Black Rose Books, 1971.

Foster, Cecil. 'A Long Sojourn.' Interview. By Donna Nurse. *Books in Canada* 24.6 (Sept. 1995): 18–21.

Foster, Frances Smith. 'Passing.' In *The Oxford Companion to African American Literature.* Ed. William L. Andrews et al. New York: Oxford University Press, 1997. 560–1.

Francis, Azra Daniel. 'The Peter-Paul Christian Twins.' Poem. In Daniel Francis, *Growing,* 99–100.

– 'The Spotted Tongue.' Poem. In Daniel Francis, *Growing,* 77–8.

Fraser, John. *The Name of Action.* Cambridge: Cambridge University Press, 1982.

– *Violence in the Arts.* London: Cambridge University Press, 1974.

Frazier, E. Franklin. *Black Bourgeoisie: The Rise of a New Middle Class in the United States.* 1957. New York: Collier / Macmillan, 1965.

Fukuyama, Francis. 'The End of History?' *The National Interest* (Summer 1989): 3–18.

Fyfe, Christopher, ed. *'Our Children Free and Happy': Letters from Black Settlers in Africa in the 1790s.* Edinburgh: Edinburgh University Press, 1991.

Gaggi, Silvio. *Modern/Postmodern: A Study in Twentieth Century Art and Ideas.* Philadelphia: University of Pennsylvania Press, 1989.

Gale, Lorena. 'Where Beauty Sits.' In Hazelle Palmer, ed., '... But', 51–4.

Garneau, Michel. *Héliotropes: Théâtre.* Montréal: VLB Éditeur, 1994.

Gates, Henry Louis, Jr. *Figures in Black: Words, Signs, and the 'Racial' Self.* New York: Oxford University Press, 1987.

– *The Signifying Monkey: A Theory of Afro-American Literary Criticism.* New York: Oxford University Press, 1988.

Gates, Henry Louis, Jr, and Nellie Y. McKay, gen. eds. *The Norton Anthology of African American Literature.* New York: W.W. Norton, 1997.

Genovese, Eugene D. 'By Way of a Dedication ...' *In Red and Black: Marxian Explorations in Southern and Afro-American History.* By Eugene D. Genovese. New York: Random House, 1971. v–vi.

Gilroy, Paul. *The Black Atlantic: Modernity and Double Consciousness.* Cambridge, MA: Harvard University Press, 1993.

Giscombe, C.S. *Into and Out of Dislocation.* New York: Farrar, Strauss, Giroux, 2000.

Glassco, John, ed. Introduction. *The Poetry of French Canada in Translation.* Toronto: Oxford University Press, 1970. xvii–xxvi.

Glazebrook, G.P. de T. *A History of Canadian Political Thought.* Toronto: McClelland & Stewart, 1966.

Glissant, Edouard. *Le Discours antillais*. Paris: Éditions de Seuil, 1981.

– 'Free and Forced Poetics.' In *Ethno Poetics: A First International Symposium*. Ed. Michael Benamou and Jerome Rothenberg. Boston: Alcheringa / Boston University, 1976. 95–111.

– *Poétique de la relation*. [Paris]: Gallimard, 1990.

Goldsmith, Oliver. *The Rising Village*. 1825; 1834. Ed. Gerald Lynch. London, ON: Canadian Poetry, 1989.

Goldstein, Jay. 'Recent Publications Relating to Canadian Ethnic Studies.' *Canadian Ethnic Studies* 12.3 (1980): 171–6.

Grant, George P. Introduction. *Lament for a Nation: The Defeat of Canadian Nationalism*. Toronto: McClelland & Stewart, 1970. vii–xii.

– *Lament for a Nation: The Defeat of Canadian Nationalism*. 1965. Toronto: McClelland & Stewart, 1970.

– 'Northrop Frye (1912–91).' In *The George Grant Reader*. Ed. William Christian and Sheila Grant. Toronto: University of Toronto Press, 1998. 357–61.

– 'Pierre Trudeau.' In *The George Grant Reader*. Ed. William Christian and Sheila Grant. Toronto: University of Toronto Press, 1998. 102–7.

– *Technology and Empire: Perspectives on North America*. Toronto: House of Anansi, 1969.

Grayson, J. Paul, and Deanna Williams. *Racialization and Black Student Identity at York University*. [North York, ON]: Institute for Social Research, York University, 1994.

Greene, Graham. *The Heart of the Matter*. 1948. London: Penguin Books, 1971, 1978.

Griffin, John Howard. *Black Like Me*. 1961. Boston: Houghton Mifflin, 1977.

Griffin-Allwood, Philip G.A. 'The Reverend James Thomas and "union of all God's people": Nova Scotian African Baptist Piety, Unity and Division.' *Nova Scotia Historical Review* 14.1 (1994): 153–68.

Griffith, Glyne A. 'Veiled Politics in West Indian Criticism.' *Kunapipi* 15.2 (1993): 104–12.

Grimes-Williams, Johanna L. 'Character Types.' In *The Oxford Companion to African American Literature*. Ed. William L. Andrews et al. New York: Oxford University Press, 1997. 127–30.

Gunew, Sneja. 'Foreword: Speaking to Joseph.' In *Echo: Essays on Other Literatures*. By Joseph Pivato. Toronto: Guernica Editions Ltd, 1994. 7–31.

Gysin, Brion. *To Master, a Long Goodnight: The Story of Uncle Tom, a Historical Narrative*. New York: Creative Age Press, 1946.

Haley, Alex. *Roots*. Garden City: Doubleday, 1976.

Haliburton, Thomas Chandler. *The Clockmaker; or, The Sayings and Doings of Sam Slick, of Slickville*. [First Series.] Halifax: Howe, 1836.

– *The Clockmaker; or, The Sayings and Doings of Samuel Slick, of Slickville*. Second Series. London: Bentley; Halifax, NS: Howe, 1838.

– *The Clockmaker; or, The Sayings and Doings of Samuel Slick, of Slickville*. Third Series. London: Bentley, 1840.

– *An Historical and Statistical Account of Nova-Scotia*. 2 vols. Halifax, 1829.

Hall, Stuart. 'Ethnicity and Politics: An Interpretation.' In *Appiah and Gates*, eds, *Africana*, 705–8.

Hamilton, Sylvia. 'Naming Names, Naming Ourselves: A Survey of Early Black Women in Nova Scotia.' In Bristow et al., *'We're*, 13–40.

– 'November Tea.' Poem. In *Daughters of the Sun, Women of the Moon: Poetry by Black Canadian Women*. Ed. Ann Wallace. Stratford, ON: Williams-Wallace, 1991. 48.

Hamilton, Wayn. Letter to the author, 29 September 1997. 1–2. TS in the possession of the author.

Hansberry, Lorraine. *A Raisin in the Sun*. [1959.] New York: The New American Library / Signet, [1966?]

– *To Be Young, Gifted and Black: Lorraine Hansberry in Her Own Words*. Adapted by Robert Nemiroff. Englewood Cliffs, NJ: Prentice-Hall, Inc., 1969.

Harper, Philip Brian. 'Nationalism and Social Division in Black Arts Poetry of the 1960s.' *Critical Inquiry* 19.2 (Winter 1993): 234–55.

Harris, Claire. 'Every Moment a Window.' Poem. In Claire Harris, *Travelling to Find a Remedy*, 7–17.

– 'Nude on a Pale Staircase.' Poem. 1984. In Claire Harris, *Fables*, 9–20.

Harris, Eddy L. *South of Haunted Dreams: A Ride through Slavery's Old Back Yard*. New York: Simon & Schuster, 1993.

Harris, Frederick Wheelock. 'The Black Population of the County of Annapolis.' [1920.] In *The Romance of Old Annapolis Royal Nova Scotia*. [Ed. and comp.] Charlotte Isabella Perkins. 1925. Annapolis Royal, NS: Historical Association of Annapolis Royal, 1985. 60–8.

Hatlen, Burton. 'Ezra Pound and Fascism.' In Korn, ed., *Pound*, 145–72.

Hauge, Hans. 'George Grant's Critique of Frye.' In *Essays in Canadian Literature*. Ed. Jorn Carlsen and Bengt Streijffert. Lund, Sweden: Nordic Association for Canadian Studies, 1987. 61–70.

Head, Harold. Introduction. In Herald Head, ed., *Canada*, 7–12.

Hearne, John. 'Living Out the Winter.' In Ayanna Black, ed., *Fiery*, 72–99.

Hébert, Jacques, and Pierre Elliott Trudeau. *Two Innocents in Red China*. Trans. I.M. Owen. Toronto: Oxford University Press, 1968. Trans. of *Deux Innocents en Chine rouge*. Montréal: Les Éditions de l'homme, 1961.

Hémon, Louis. *Maria Chapdelaine*. 1914. Paris: A. Fayard, 1928.

Henderson, Mae G. '"Where, by the Way, Is This Train Going?": A Case for Black (Cultural) Studies.' *Callaloo* 19.1 (Winter, 1996): 60–7.

Henry, Charles P. *Culture and African American Politics*. Bloomington, IN: Indiana University Press, 1990.

Henry, Frances. 'Black Music in the Maritimes.' *Canadian Folk Music Journal* 3 (1975): 12–13.

– *Forgotten Canadians: The Blacks of Nova Scotia*. Don Mills, ON: Longman Canada Limited, 1973.

Hill, Lawrence. 'Zebra: Growing Up Black and White in Canada.' In Carl James and Adrienne Shadd, eds, *Talking*, 41–7.

Hill, Patricia Loggins, et al., eds. '"Go Down, Moses, Way Down in Egypt's Land": African American History and Culture, 1619–1808 ...' In *Call and Response: The Riverside Anthology of the African American Literary Tradition*. Boston: Houghton Mifflin, 1998. 1–27.

Hodges, Graham Russell, ed. *The Black Loyalist Directory: African-Americans in Exile after the American Revolution*. New York and London: Garland Publishing, Inc., in association with the New England Historic Genealogical Society, 1996.

– Introduction. In Graham Russell Hodges, ed., *The Black Loyalist Directory*, xi-xlvii.

Homel, David. 'How to Make Love with the Reader ... Slyly.' Introduction. *How to Make Love to a Negro*. By Dany Laferrière. Trans. David Homel. Toronto: Coach House, 1987. 7–10.

hooks, bell. [pseud. of Gloria Watkins]. 'Black Women Intellectuals.' In *Breaking Bread: Insurgent Black Intellectual Life*. By bell hooks and Cornel West. Toronto: Between the Lines, 1991. 147–64.

– *Yearning: Race, Gender, and Cultural Politics*. Toronto: Between the Lines, 1990.

hooks, bell, and Cornel West. *Breaking Bread: Insurgent Black Intellectual Life*. Toronto: Between the Lines, 1991.

Hornby, Jim. *Black Islanders: Prince Edward Island's Historical Black Community*. Charlottetown, PEI: Institute of Island Studies, 1991.

Howard, Hilda G. [pseud., Hilda Glynn-Ward]. *The Writing on the Wall*. Vancouver: Vancouver Sun, 1921. Rpt. Toronto: University of Toronto Press, 1974.

Howe, Joseph. *Western and Eastern Rambles: Travel Sketches of Nova Scotia*. ['Western Rambles,' *Novascotian* (July-Oct. 1828); 'Eastern Rambles,' *Novascotian* (Dec. 1829-Oct. 1831).] Ed. M.G. Parks. Toronto: University of Toronto Press, 1973.

Hudson, Peter. 'Editor's Note: In the Country of the Snow Blind.' *West Coast Line* 31.1 (Spring/Summer 1997): 5–6.

– 'The Last Days of Blackness: André Alexis Gets Over.' In Rinaldo Walcott, ed., *Rude*, 189–99.

– 'Primitive Grammars.' Book review. *Sulfur* 44 (Spring 1999): 193–5.

Hughes, Langston. 'Cross.' Poem. 1926. In *American Negro Poetry*. Ed. Arna Bontemps. New York: Hill and Wang, 1963, 1964. 62.

– 'Harlem.' Poem. 1951. In *The Langston Hughes Reader: The Selected Writings of Langston Hughes*. New York: George Braziller, 1958. 123.

– 'Mother to Son.' Poem. 1922, 1926. In *The Dream Keeper and Other Poems*. New York: Alfred A. Knopf, 1932, 1986. 73.

– *Mulatto*. 1935. In *Five Plays by Langston Hughes*. Ed. Webster Smalley. Bloomington: Indiana University Press, 1963. 1–35.

Hunter, Lynette. 'After Modernism: Alternative Voices in the Writings of Dionne Brand, Claire Harris, and Marlene Philip.' *University of Toronto Quarterly* 62.2 (Winter 1992/93): 256–81.

Hutcheon, Linda. *Splitting Images: Contemporary Canadian Ironies*. Toronto: Oxford University Press, 1991.

Hutcheon, Linda, and Michael Hutcheon. *Opera: Desire, Disease, Death*. Lincoln, NB: University of Nebraska Press, 1996.

Ibrahim, Awad El Karim M. '"Hey, ain't I Black too?": The Politics of Becoming Black.' In Rinaldo Walcott, ed., *Rude*, 109–36.

Insell, Celeste. 'Defining an Aesthetic: African-Canadian Playwrights in Vancouver.' *Canadian Theatre Review* 83 (Summer 1995): 39–42.

Jackson, Blyden. *A History of Afro-American Literature, Volume 1: The Long Beginning, 1746–1895*. Baton Rouge, LA: Louisiana State University Press, 1989.

Jacobs, Diane. 'On Becoming a Black Canadian.' Poem. *Kola* 8.2 (1996): 71–2.

James, C.L.R. Appendix. *The Black Jacobins: Toussaint L'Ouverture and the San Domingo Revolution*. 1938. New York: Vintage, 1963. 391–418.

– *The Black Jacobins: Toussaint L'Ouverture and the San Domingo Revolution*. 1938. New York: Vintage, 1963.

Jennings, Nicholas. 'Some Like It Hot: Canadians Warm to the Sizzling Sounds of Homegrown Latin Music.' *Words & Music* 3.3 (March 1996): 12–13.

Jobb, Dean. *Shades of Justice: Seven Nova Scotia Murder Cases*. Halifax: Nimbus, 1988.

Johnson, Anne. 'Preface.' In *Three Nova Scotian Black Churches*. By Joyce Ruck et al. Cherrybrook, NS: Black Cultural Centre for Nova Scotia, 1990. [n.pag.]

Johnson, James Weldon. *God's Trombones: Seven Negro Sermons in Verse*. New York: The Viking Press, 1927.

Johnson, Lemuel. 'The Brigadier-General's Dance.' Poem. In *Highlife for Caliban*. Trenton, NJ: Africa World Press, 1995. 10.

Jones, Burnley A. 'Rocky.' 'Uncrowned King.' Interview. By George Elliott Clarke. *New Works* [Halifax, NS] (May 1986): 5–6.

Jones, Gayl. *Liberating Voices: Oral Tradition in African American Literature*. Cambridge, MA: Harvard University Press, 1991.

Joseph, Clifton. 'Recollections: A Seventees [*sic*] Black RAP.' Introduction. In *Being Black*. By Althea Prince. Toronto: Insomniac Press, 2001. 13–21.

Joyette, Anthony. Editorial. *Kola* 8.1 (1996): 5.

Kayman, Martin. 'Ezra Pound and Science: Phenomenon and History.' In Korn, ed., *Pound*, 37–51.

Kellner, Bruce, ed. *The Harlem Renaissance: A Historical Dictionary for the Era*. New York: Methuen; London: Routledge & Kegan Paul, 1987.

Kelly, Jennifer. '"Experiences with the white man": Black Student Narratives.' *Canadian Ethnic Studies*. 30.2 (1998): 95–113.

Kilian, Crawford. *Go Do Some Great Thing: The Black Pioneers of British Columbia*. 1978. Vancouver: Douglas & McIntyre, 1980.

King, Boston. 'Memoirs of the Life of Boston King, a Black Preacher, Written by Himself, during His Residence at Kingswood-School.' 1798. Excerpt. In George Elliott Clarke, ed., *Fire*, Vol. 1., 49–56.

King, Lloyd. 'Juan Francisco Manzano.' In *The Autobiography of a Cuban Slave*. By Juan Francisco Manzano. Trans. Lloyd King. St Augustine, TT: Lloyd King, n.d. 27–9.

– 'Some Literary Intellectuals and Slavery in Cuba.' In *The Autobiography of a Cuban Slave*. By Juan Francisco Manzano. Trans. Lloyd King. St Augustine, TT: Lloyd King, n.d. 1–26.

King, Martin Luther, Jr. *Conscience for Change: Massey Lectures, Seventh Series*. Toronto: Canadian Broadcasting Corporation, 1967.

Kishtainy, Khalid. *The Prostitute in Progressive Literature*. London: Alison & Busby, 1982.

Klein, A.M. 'Political Meeting.' Poem. 1948. In *The Collected Poems of A.M. Klein*. Toronto: McGraw-Hill Ryerson, 1974. 306–8.

Knight, Claudette. 'Black Parents Speak: Education in Mid-Nineteenth-Century Canada West.' In *Race and Gender in the Northern Colonies*. Ed. Jan Noel. 1997. Toronto: Canadian Scholars' Press, 2000. 257–76.

Korn, Marianne, ed. *Ezra Pound and History*. [Orono, ME]: National Poetry Foundation, 1985.

– Preface. In Korn, ed., *Pound*, 7–11.

Kristiansen, Erik. 'Time, Memory, and Rural Transformation.' *New Maritimes* (March/ April 1990): 22–7.

– 'Time, Memory and Rural Transformation: Rereading History in the Fiction of Charles Bruce and Ernest Buckler.' 1990. In *Contested Countryside: Rural Workers and Modern Society in Atlantic Canada, 1800–1950*. Ed. Daniel Samson. Fredericton, NB: Acadiensis Press, 1994. 225–56.

Lantagne, Suzanne. *Et autres histoires d'amour ...: Nouvelles*. Québec: Éditions de L'instant même, 1995.

Larsen, Nella. *Passing*. 1929. New York: Penguin Putnam Inc., 1997.

LeBlanc, Raymond Guy. 'Je suis acadien.' Poem. In Cogswell and Elder, eds, *Rêves*, 144–5.

Lee, Angela. Editorial. 'Black Theatre in Canada / African-Canadian Theatre.' *Canadian Theatre Review* 83 (Summer 1995): 3.

Legault, Josée. *L'Invention d'une minorité: Les Anglos-Québécois*. Montréal: Boréal, 1992.

Léger, Dyane. 'Lesbiennes latentes.' Poem. In Cogswell and Elder, eds, *Rêves*, 163–9.

Lester, Julius. *Fallen Pieces of the Broken Sky*. New York: Arcade, 1990.

Levine, Lawrence W. *Black Culture and Black Consciousness: Afro-American Folk Thought from Slavery to Freedom*. New York: Oxford University Press, 1977.

– Preface. In Lawrence Levine, *Black Culture*, ix–xiv.

Lewis, David Levering. *W.E.B. Du Bois: Biography of a Race, 1868–1919*. New York: Henry Holt, 1993.

Logan, John Daniel. *Thomas Chandler Haliburton*. Ed. Lorne Albert Pierce. Makers of Canadian Literature. Toronto: Ryerson, 1923.

Longchamps, Renaud. 'Génies, étonnez-moi!' *Nuit blanche* 58 (déc. 1994, jan., fév. 1995): 16–17.

Longfellow, Henry Wadsworth. *Evangeline: A Tale of Acadie*. 1847. Mount Vernon, NY: The Peter Pauper Press, [1947].

Lovell, John, Jr. *Black Song: The Forge and the Flame, the Story of How the Afro-American Spiritual Was Hammered Out*. New York: Macmillan, 1972.

Lubiano, Wahneema. 'Mapping the Interstices between Afro-American Cultural Discourse and Cultural Studies: A Prolegomenon.' *Callaloo* 19.1 (Winter 1996): 68–77.

Lyotard, Jean-François. *Tombeau de l'intellectuel et autres papiers*. Paris: Éditions Galilée, 1984.

MacDonald, Hugh. 'The Shock of Sensuality in the Raw: The Critical Fortunes of "Carmen."' Liner Notes. *Georges Bizet: Carmen*. Philips Classics Productions, 422 366–2, 1989. 17–22.

Mackenzie, Shelagh, dir. *Remember Africville*. National Film Board video production. 9191–086. 1991.

Major, Clarence. *No*. New York: Emerson Hall, 1973.

Malanka, Barbara. 'A Gem of Great Price.' In Hazelle Palmer, ed., '... But,', 17–19.

Mandiela, Ahdri Zhina. 'Ahdri Zhina Mandiela: Encountering Signposts.' Interview. By Angela Lee. *Canadian Theatre Review* 83 (Summer 1995): 5–8.

– 'An Interview with Ahdri Zhina Mandiela: The True Rhythm of the Language.' In *The Other Woman: Women of Colour in Contemporary Canadian Literature*. Ed. Makeda Silvera. Toronto: Sister Vision Press, 1995. 80–92.

Mannette, J.A. 'My Dearest Child.' In Rinaldo Walcott, ed., *Rude*, 49–68.

- '"Revelation, Revolution, or Both": Black Arts As Cultural Politics.' Lecture presented at the conference '400 Years: African Canadian History,' Multicultural History Society of Ontario, Toronto, June 1990. TS. In the possession of the author.

- '"Strangers in Our Homeland": To be Black in Nova Scotia.' *Cape Breton Post* (15 Aug. 1991): 5.

Manzano, Juan Francisco. *Autobiography of a Cuban Slave*. [1835], 1937. Trans. Lloyd King. St Augustine, TT: Lloyd King, n.d.

Mao Tse-Tung [Mao Zedong]. *Four Essays on Philosophy*. 1966. Peking [Beijing]: Foreign Languages Press, 1968.

Maran, René. *Batouala: A True Black Novel*. Trans. Barbara Beck and Alexandre Mboukou. Washington, DC: Black Orpheus Press, 1972. Trans. of *Batouala*. Paris: Éditions Albin Michel, 1921, 1938.

Marcuse, Herbert. *An Essay on Liberation*. 1969. Harmondsworth: Pelican Books, 1973.

Margolis, Edward. 'The Letters of Richard Wright.' In *The Black Writer in Africa and the Americas*. Ed. Lloyd W. Brown. Los Angeles: Hennessey & Ingalls, Inc., 1973. 101–18.

Marrant, John. *A Narrative of the Lord's Wonderful Dealings with John Marrant, a Black, (Now Going to Preach the Gospel in Nova-Scotia) Born in New-York, in North-America*. Excerpt. In George Elliott Clarke, ed., *Fire*, Vol. 1., 40–8.

Marriott, David. 'Figures of Silence and Orality in the Poetry of M. Nourbese Philip.' In *Framing the Word: Gender and Genre in Caribbean Women's Writing*. Ed. Joan Anim-Addo. London: Whiting & Birch Ltd, 1996. 72–85.

Martin, Waldo. 'Black Consciousness in the United States.' In Appiah and Gates, eds, *Africana*, 253.

Marx, Karl, and Friedrich Engels. *The Communist Manifesto*. 1848. Trans. Samuel Moore. 1888. Harmondsworth: Penguin Books, 1967, 1977.

Massey, Irving. *Identity and Community: Reflections on English, Yiddish, and French Literature in Canada*. Detroit: Wayne State University Press, 1994.

Mathieu, Sarah-Jane. Review of *Towards Freedom: The African Canadian Experience*. By Ken Alexander and Avis Glaze. *Canadian Ethnic Studies* 30.2 (1998): 169–70.

Matory, J. Lorand. 'Afro-Atlantic Culture: On the Live Dialogue between Africa and the Americas.' In Appiah and Gates, eds, *Africana*, 36–44.

Matthews, John. *Tradition in Exile: A Comparative Study of Social Influences on the Development of Australian and Canadian Poetry in the Nineteenth Century*. Toronto: University of Toronto Press, 1962.

McCurdy, Howard. *House of Commons Debates*. 33rd Parliament. Vol. 13. (26 May–5 July 1988): 17153–4.

McHenry, Elizabeth. 'Literature, African American.' In Appiah and Gates, eds, *Africana*, 1171–5.

McKerrow, Peter Evander. *A Brief History of the Coloured Baptists of Nova Scotia, and Their First Organization As Churches, A.D. 1832*. Excerpt. In George Elliott Clarke. ed., *Fire*, Vol. 1, 65–70.

McLachlan, Alexander. *The Emigrant, and Other Poems*. Toronto: Rollo & Adam, 1861.

McNaught, Kenneth. *The Pelican History of Canada*. 1969. Harmondsworth: Pelican, 1978.

McPhail, Aubrey. 'The Short Fiction: *A Forest of Flowers* and *Adaku and Other Stories.'* In *Ken Saro-Wiwa: Writer and Political Activist.* Ed. Craig W. McLuckie and Aubrey McPhail. Boulder, CO: Lynne Rienner Publishers, 2000. 69–86.

Micheaux, Oscar, dir. *The Brute.* Micheaux Film Corporation. 1920.

– *Within Our Gates.* Micheaux Film Corporation. 1920.

'Minute Book[,] Number Three District of the African United Baptist Association of Nova Scotia (Commencing May, 1965) (to Sept. 1966).' [1966.] MS. E. Clark Wright Archives, Acadia University, Wolfville, NS.

Minutes of the African United Baptist Association of Nova Scotia [101st Session and 102nd Session]. Halifax, NS: African Baptist Association of Nova Scotia, 1955.

Minutes of the African United Baptist Association of Nova Scotia [114th and 115th Sessions]. New Glasgow, NS: African Baptist Association of Nova Scotia, 1968.

'Minutes of the District No. 4 Sessions of the African United Baptist Association (Oct. 1949–1956, May).' 1956. MS. E. Clark Wright Archives, Acadia University, Wolfville, NS.

Minutes of the Eighth Session of the African Baptist Association of Nova Scotia. Halifax, NS: African Baptist Association of Nova Scotia, 1861.

Minutes of the Fifty-Eighth and Fifty-Ninth Annual Sessions [1911–12] *of the African Baptist Association of Nova Scotia ...* Halifax, NS: African Baptist Association of Nova Scotia, 1912.

Minutes of the Twenty-Fourth Session of the African Baptist Association of Nova Scotia. Halifax, NS: African Baptist Association of Nova Scotia, 1877.

Moisan, Clément. *A Poetry of Frontiers: Comparative Studies in Quebec/Canadian Literature.* Victoria, BC: Press Porcépic, 1983.

Montégut, Émile. 'Un Humoriste Anglo-Américaine. Haliburton.' *Revue des Deux Mondes* 5 (1850): 731–48. Rpt. in 'Extracts from Selected Contemporary Reviews / Critical Essays.' Trans. Frank Ledwidge. In *On Thomas Chandler Haliburton: Selected Criticism.* Ed. Richard A. Davies. Ottawa: Tecumseh, 1979. 72–9.

Moodie, Andrew. 'The King and I.' *This Magazine* 30.5 (March/April 1997): 18–22.

Moodie, Susanna. *Roughing It in the Bush; or, Life in Canada.* 1852. Toronto: McClelland & Stewart, 1989.

Morley, Margaret W. *Down North and Up Along.* New York: Dodd Mead, 1900.

Morrell, Carol, ed. *Grammar of Dissent: Poetry and Prose by Claire Harris, Marlene Nourbese Philip, Dionne Brand.* Fredericton: Goose Lane, 1994.

– Introduction. In Carol Morrell, ed., *Grammar,* 9–24.

Morrison, Toni. *Playing in the Dark: Whiteness and the Literary Imagination.* The William E. Massey Lectures in the History of American Civilization 1990. Cambridge, MA: Harvard University Press, 1992.

– *Song of Solomon.* New York: Alfred A. Knopf, 1977.

Morton, Suzanne. 'Separate Spheres in a Separate World: African–Nova Scotian Women in late-19th-Century Halifax County.' *Acadiensis* 22.2 (Spring 1993): 61–83.

Moses, Wilson Jeremiah. *The Golden Age of Black Nationalism, 1850–1925.* 1978. New York: Oxford University Press, 1988.

Mouré, Erin. 'The Acts [10].' Poem. In *Furious*. Toronto: House of Anansi, 1988. 94.

– 'Miss Chatelaine.' Poem. In *Furious*. Toronto: House of Anansi, 1988. 54–5.

Murphy, Emily. *The Black Candle*. Toronto: T. Allen, 1922.

Myrdal, Gunnar. *An American Dilemma: The Negro Problem and the Modern Democracy*. New York: Harper & Brothers, 1944.

Nélligan, Émile. *Poésies complètes: 1896–1899*. 1989. [Montréal]: Bibliothèque québécoise, 1991.

Nepveu, Pierre. 'Le Poème québécois de l'Amérique.' In *Intérieurs du Nouveau Monde: Essais sur les littératures du Québec et des Amériques*. By Pierre Nepveu. [Montréal]: Boréal, 1998.

– 'Quebec Culture and Its American Moods.' Paper. Canadian Studies Center, Duke University, Durham, North Carolina, 10 April 1995. TS. In the possession of the author.

Newman, Richard. 'Miscegenation.' In Appiah and Gates, eds, *Africana*, 1320.

Newton, Norman. 'Classical Canadian Poetry and the Public Muse.' 1972. In *Colony and Confederation: Early Canadian Poets and Their Background*. Ed. George Woodcock. Vancouver, BC: University of British Columbia Press, 1974. 7–23.

Nielsen, Aldon Lynn. *Black Chant: Languages of African-American Postmodernism*. Cambridge: Cambridge University Press, 1997.

Nightingale, Marie. *Out of Old Nova Scotia Kitchens: A Collection of Traditional Recipes of Nova Scotia and the Story of the People Who Cooked Them*. Halifax, NS: Petheric, 1970.

Nixon, Rob. 'Pipe Dreams: Ken Saro-Wiwa, Environmental Justice, and Microminority Rights.' In *Ken Saro-Wiwa: Writer and Political Activist*. Ed. Craig W. McLuckie and Aubrey McPhail. Boulder, CO: Lynne Rienner Publishers, 2000. 109–25.

Njami, Simon. 'Canada: L'Invention de l'identité.' *Revue Noire* 25 (juin-juil.-août 1997): 4–5.

– *Traces of Identity*. Pamphlet. Trans. Susan Kealey. Toronto: Gallery 44 / Centre for Contemporary Photography, 1997.

Nolan, Faith. *Africville*. Recording. [Toronto]: Multicultural Women In Concert, 1986.

Nortje, Arthur. *Dead Roots*. London: Heinemann, 1973.

Oliver, Pearleen. 'Mini Historical Note: Toil and Tears.' In *Dedication of New Church and Multi-Purpose Centre*. Bulletin. Beechville, NS: Beechville United Baptist Church, 29 April 1979.

– 'Report of Official Organizer, Ladies Auxiliary, to the African United Baptist Association of Nova Scotia, Convening at Cherry Brook on August 15–17, 1981.' In *Annual Minutes of the African United Baptist Association of Nova Scotia: 128th Sessions*. Halifax, NS: African Baptist Association of Nova Scotia, 1984. 32.

– *A Root and a Name*. 1977. Excerpt. In George Elliott Clarke, ed., *Fire*, Vol. 1, 136–44.

Oliver, W.P. Introduction. *Footprints – Images and Reflections (History in Poetry)*. By George Borden. Cherrybrook, NS: The Black Cultural Centre for Nova Scotia, 1993. iii–vi.

– 'The Negro in Nova Scotia.' Excerpt. 1949. In George Elliott Clarke, ed., *Fire*, Vol. 1, 129–35.

Ondaatje, Michael. *Coming Through Slaughter*. Toronto: House of Anansi Press, 1976.

– 'Pictures from the War.' Poem. *Queen's Quarterly* 75.2 (Summer 1968): 261.

Ovid. 'The Amores.' In *The Erotic Poems*. Trans. Peter Green. Harmondsworth: Penguin, 1982. 85–165.

Pachai, Bridglal. *Beneath the Clouds of the Promised Land: The Survival of Nova Scotia's Blacks, Volume II: 1800–1989*. Halifax, NS: The Black Educators Association of Nova Scotia, 1990.

Padolsky, Enoch. 'Canadian Ethnic Minority Literature in English.' In *Ethnicity and Culture in Canada: The Research Landscape*. Ed. J.W. Berry and J.A. Laponce. Toronto: University of Toronto Press, 1994. 361–86.

– 'Ethnicity and Race: Canadian Minority Writing at a Crossroads.' In *Literary Pluralities*. Ed. Christl Verdun. Toronto: Broadview Press / Journal of Canadian Studies, 1998. 19–36.

– '"Olga in Wonderland": Canadian Ethnic Minority Writing and Post-Colonial Theory.' *Canadian Ethnic Studies* 28.3 (1996): 16–28.

Palmer, Howard. 'Preface.' *Canadian Ethnic Studies* 5.1–2 (1973): vii.

Palmer, Tamara J., and Beverly J. Rasporich. 'Ethnic Literature.' In *The Canadian Encyclopedia*. Vol. 2. 1985. 2nd ed. Edmonton: Hurtig Publishers, 1988. 725–8.

Parkinson, Frank Merryman. 'The Republic of Sierra Leone.' *The Black Express* [Halifax, NS] 4.1 (Jan. 1982): 11.

Peacock, Alan J. 'Pound and Propertius: The Limitations of an Historical Persona.' In Korn, ed., *Pound*, 83–98.

Pellerin, Suzanne. 'La Cité des interdits.' Poem. *International Poetry Review* 20.2 (Fall 1994): 44, 46.

Penn, I. Garland. *The Afro-American Press and Its Editors*. Springfield, MA: Willey & Co., 1891. Rpt. New York: Arno Press and the New York Times, 1969.

Perloff, Marjorie. *Dance of the Intellect: Studies in the Poetry of the Pound Tradition*. Evanston, IL: Northwestern University Press, 1985.

Petesch, Donald A. *A Spy in the Enemy's Country: The Emergence of Modern Black Literature*. Iowa City, IA: University of Iowa Press, 1989.

'Petition of the Coloured People at Preston.' 1840–5. Public Archives of Nova Scotia. Box – Crown Lands – Peninsula of Halifax.

Philip, M. Nourbese [M. NourbeSe Philip]. 'The Absence of Writing or How I Almost Became a Spy.' In Philip, *She Tries Her Tongue*, 10–25.

– 'And Over Every Land and Sea.' Poem. 1989. In Morrell, ed., *Grammar*, 128–35.

– 'Blackness Repossessed.' Letter. *This Magazine* 29.2 (Aug. 1995): 2–3.

– 'Burn Sugar.' In *Imagining Women*. Ed. The Second, Second Story Collective. Toronto: Women's Press, 1988. 11–19.

– 'Commitment to Hardness.' 1992. In George Elliott Clarke, ed., *Eyeing*, 95–8.

– 'Cyclamen Girl.' Poem. *Fireweed* 23 (Summer 1986): 112–13.

– 'Discourse on the Logic of Language.' Poem. 1989. In Morrell, ed., *Grammar*, 136–9.

– 'Dream-skins.' Poem. 1989. In Morrell, ed., *Grammar*, 131–3.

– 'July Again.' Poem. 1983. In Morrell, ed., *Grammar*, 122–3.

– 'Meditations on the Declension of Beauty by the Girl with the Flying Cheek-bones.' In George Elliott Clarke, ed., *Eyeing*, 93–4.

– 'The Other Gates and Slavery's Blame Game.' *Word* 8.9 (Dec. '99–Jan. '00): 29.

– 'Secrecy and Silence.' Interview. By Barb Carey. *Books in Canada* 20.6 (Sept. 1991): 17–21.
– 'Signifying Nothing.' *Border/Lines* 36 (1995): 4–11.
Phillips, Claude S. 'Political Instability in Independent States.' In *The African Political Dictionary*. Santa Barbara, CA: ABC-Clio Information Services, 1984. 208–13.
Pinckney, Darryl. 'Magic of James Baldwin.' *New York Review of Books* 65.18 (19 Nov. 1998): 64–74.
Pivato, Joseph. 'The Arrival of Italian-Canadian Writing.' *Canadian Ethnic Studies* 14.1 (1982): 127–37.
– *Echo: Essays on Other Literatures*. Toronto: Guernica Editions, Inc., 1994.
– 'Representation of Ethnicity As Problem: Essence or Construction.' In *Literary Pluralities*. Ed. Christl Verdun. Toronto: Broadview Press / Journal of Canadian Studies, 1998. 152–61.
Poplack, Shana. Introduction. *The English History of African American English*. Ed. Shana Poplack. Malden, MA: Blackwell, 2000. 1–32.
Poplack, Shana, and Sali Tagliamonte. 'African American English in the Diaspora: Evidence from Old-line Nova Scotians.' *Language Variation and Change* 3 (1991): 301–39.
Poteet, Lewis J. *The Second South Shore Phrase Book: A Nova Scotia Dictionary*. Hantsport, NS: Lancelot, 1985.
Potkay, Adam. Introduction. *Black Atlantic Writers of the Eighteenth Century: Living the New Exodus in England and the Americas*. Ed. Adam Potkay and Sandra Burr. New York: St Martin's Press, 1995. 1–20.
Pound, Ezra. 'Canto XLV.' Poem. In *Selected Cantos of Ezra Pound*. 1934–70. New York: New Directions, 1970.
– 'Canto LIII.' Poem. In *Selected Poems of Ezra Pound*. 1926–57. New York: New Directions, 1957.
– 'Troubadours: Their Sorts and Conditions.' In Pound, *Walking*, 87–98.
– *A Walking Tour in Southern France: Ezra Pound among the Troubadours*. Ed. Richard Sieburth. New York: New Directions, 1992.
Préfontaine, Yves. *This Desert Now*. Trans. Judith Cowan. Montreal: Guernica Editions Inc., 1993. Trans. of *Le Désert maintenant*. [Trois-Rivières]: Les Écrits de Forges, 1987.
Prieto, Claire, and Sylvia Hamilton, dirs. *Black Mother, Black Daughter*. National Film Board. 1990.
Prince, Mary. *The History of Mary Prince, a West Indian Slave, Related by Herself*. 1831. Ed. Moira Ferguson. Ann Arbor: University of Michigan Press, 1987, 1993.
Pringle, Ian. 'The Concept of Dialect and the Study of Canadian English.' *Queen's Quarterly* 90.1 (Spring 1983): 100–21.
Radwanski, George. *Trudeau*. Toronto: Macmillan, 1978.
Ramraj, Victor J. 'West Indian-Canadian Writing in English.' *International Journal of Canadian Studies* 13 (Spring 1996): 163–8.
Razack, Sherene H. Introduction. *Looking White People in the Eye: Gender, Race, and Culture in Courtrooms and Classrooms*. Toronto: University of Toronto Press, 1998, 1999. 3–22.
Reed, Ishmael. *Flight to Canada*. New York: Random House, 1976.

Reid-Pharr, Robert F. 'It's Raining Men: Notes on the Million Man March.' *Transition* 69 (Spring 1996): 36–49.

Roberts, George O. *The Anguish of Third World Independence: The Sierra Leone Experience.* Washington, DC: University Press of America, Inc., 1982.

Robertson, Allen B. 'Book Reviews.' *Nova Scotia Historical Review* 15.2 (1995): 148–61.

– *Tide and Timber: Hantsport, Nova Scotia 1795–1995.* Hantsport, NS: Lancelot Press, 1996.

Robertson, John William. *The Book of the Bible against Slavery.* 1854. Excerpt. In George Elliott Clarke, *Fire*, Vol. 1 (1991), 58–64.

Robertson, Marion: *The Chestnut Pipe: Folklore of Shelburne County.* Halifax, NS: Nimbus, 1991.

Rose, Marilyn. 'Harris, Claire.' In *The Oxford Companion to Canadian Literature.* 2nd ed. Ed. Eugene Benson and William Toye. Don Mills, ON: Oxford University Press Canada, 1997. 515–6.

– 'Philip, Marlene Nourbese.' *The Oxford Companion to Canadian Literature.* 2nd ed. Ed. Eugene Benson and William Toye. Don Mills, ON: Oxford University Press Canada, 1997. 911–12.

Rosenberg, Neil V. 'Ethnicity and Class: Black Country Musicians in the Maritimes.' *Journal of Canadian Studies* 23.1–2 (Spring/Summer 1988): 138–56.

Ross, Andrew. 'Baudrillard's Bad Attitude.' In *Seduction and Theory: Readings of Gender, Representation, and Rhetoric.* Ed. Dianne Hunter. Champaign, IL: University of Illinois Press, 1989. 214–25.

Royer, Jean. *Introduction à la poésie québécoise: Les Poètes et les oeuvres des origines à nos jours.* [Montréal]: Bibliothèque québécoise, 1989.

Rudy, Susan [Susan Rudy Dorscht]. Review of *Grammar of Dissent: Poetry and Prose by Claire Harris, M. Nourbese Philip, Dionne Brand*, ed. Carol Morrell. *Canadian Ethnic Studies* 29.1 (1997): 188–91.

– '"What There Is Teasing beyond the Edges": Claire Harris's Liminal Autobiography.' *Essays on Canadian Writing* 60 (Winter 1996): 78–99.

Sadji, Abdoulaye. *Nini: Mulâtresse du Sénégal.* [In] *Trois Écrivains noirs. Présence africaine* 16. [1955?]

Saïd, Edward W. *Representations of the Intellectual.* 1994. New York: Vintage / Random House, 1996.

Saillant, John. '"Wipe Away All Tears from Their Eyes": John Marrant's Theology in the Black Atlantic, 1785–1808.' *Journal of Millennial Studies* 1.2 (Winter 1999). www.mille.org/journal/.html

Sanders, Leslie. 'Blackness Repossessed.' Letter. *This Magazine* 29.2 (Aug. 1995): 2.

– 'Impossible to Occupy: André Alexis's Childhood.' In Rinaldo Walcott, ed., *Rude*, 169–87.

Sandiford, Keith A. *Measuring the Moment: Strategies of Protest in Eighteenth-Century Afro-English Writing.* Selinsgrove: Susquehanna University Press, 1988.

Sanger, Peter. Editorial. *Elizabeth Bishop Society of Nova Scotia: Newsletter* 8.1 (Spring 2001): 1–2.

Saul, John Ralston. *Reflections of a Siamese Twin: Canada at the End of the Twentieth Century.* Toronto: Penguin Books Canada, 1998.

Saunders, Charles. '"Mulatto" an Offensive Term – Regardless of Etymology.' *Sunday Daily News* [Halifax, NS] (18 Dec. 1994): 32.

– 'N.S. Has Link to Sierra Leone.' *Daily News* [Halifax, NS], 10 April 1994. Rpt. in Saunders, *Black* (1999), 167–8.

– 'Standing Tall, Walking Proud: Black Arts in Nova Scotia.' *The International Review of African American Art* 10.1 (1992): 12–17.

– 'A Visit to Africville: Summer, 1959.' In *Africville: A Spirit That Lives On*. Catalogue. Halifax, NS: The Art Gallery, Mount Saint Vincent University; The Africville Genealogical Society; The National Film Board, Atlantic Centre; Cherrybrook, NS: The Black Cultural Centre for Nova Scotia, 1989. 5–15.

Savory, Elaine. 'En / Gendering Spaces: The Poetry of Marlene Nourbese Philip and Pamela Mordecai.' In *Framing the Word: Gender and Genre in Caribbean Women's Writing*. Ed. Joan Anim-Addo. London: Whiting & Birch Ltd, 1996. 12–27.

Sealey, Donna Byard. 'Edwin Howard Borden: Lone Star Legend.' In 'Black History Month: February 1994.' Supplement. *Daily News* [Halifax, NS] (Feb. 1994): 18.

Sealy, David. '"Canadianizing" Blackness: Resisting the Political.' In Rinaldo Walcott, ed., *Rude*, 87–108.

– 'Talking B(l) ack.' In *Border/Lines* 36 (April 1995): 12–16.

Sealy, Joe. *Africville Suite*. Recording. [Toronto]: Sea Jam Recordings, 1996.

Seers, Eugène [pseud., Louis Dantin]. *Fanny*. Trans. Raymond Y. Chamberlain. Montreal: Harvest House Ltd, 1974. Trans. of *Les Enfances de Fanny*. Montréal: Le Cercle du Livre de France, Ltée, 1951.

Sellman, James Clyde. 'Black Nationalism in the United States.' In Appiah and Gates, eds., *Africana*, 255–7.

Shadd, Adrienne. '"Where Are You *Really* From?": Notes of an "Immigrant" from North Buxton, Ontario.' In Carl James and Adrienne Shadd, eds, *Talking*, 9–15.

Shange, Ntozake [b. Paulette Williams]. *for colored girls who have considered suicide / when the rainbow is enuf*. 1977. New York: Bantam Books, 1981.

Sherry, Vincent. *Ezra Pound, Wyndham Lewis, and Radical Modernism*. New York: Oxford University Press, 1993.

Sicari, Stephen. *Pound's Epic Ambition: Dante and the Modern World*. SUNY Series, The Margins of Literature. [Ed.] Mihai I. Spariosu. Albany, NY: State University of New York Press, 1991.

Sieburth, Richard. Introduction. In Pound, *Walking*, vii-xxi.

Siegfried, André. *The Race Question in Canada*. 1907. Ed. Frank Underhill. Toronto: Macmillan, 1978. Trans. of *La Canada, les deux races: Problèmes politiques contemporains*. Paris: Librairie Armand Colin, 1906.

'Sierra Leone.' In *Africa Year Book and Who's Who 1977*. London: Africa Journal Limited, 1976. 761–8.

Skidmore, Thomas. 'Whitening.' In Appiah and Gates, eds, *Africana*, 1991–2.

Smith, Roch. 'Voices of Québec Poetry – at Home in a Diverse World.' *International Poetry Review: Voix du Québec / Voices of Quebec* 20.2 (Fall 1994): 6–15.

Smith, Sandra. *Affirming Minority Rights: A Modern Perspective*. Toronto: New Magazine Pub. Co., 1995.

Smith, T. Watson. 'The Loyalists at Shelburne.' *Nova Scotia Historical Society Collections* 6 (1888): 67–89.

Snead, James A. 'Repetition As a Figure of Black Culture.' In *Out There: Marginalization and Contemporary Cultures*. Ed. Russell Ferguson, Martha Grever, Trinh T. Minh-ha, and Cornel.West. New York: New Museum of Contemporary Art; Cambridge, MA: MIT Press, 1990. 213–30.

Söderlind, Sylvia. *Margin/Alias: Language and Colonization in Canadian and Québécois Fiction*. Toronto: University of Toronto Press, 1991.

Souster, Raymond. 'Death Chant for Mr. Johnson's America.' In *The New Romans: Candid Canadian Opinions of the U.S.* Ed. Al Purdy. Edmonton: M.G. Hurtig Ltd, 1968. 65–9.

Spadoni, Carl. Editor's Introduction. '*My Recollection of Chicago*' and '*The Doctrine of Laissez Faire.*' By Stephen Leacock. Ed. Carl Spadoni. Toronto: University of Toronto Press, 1998. vii-xxxix.

Spectrum, The [Ottawa]. 'Caucus Will Give Blacks United Voice, Organizers Say.' 14.4 (April-May 1997): 8.

– 'Census Lists 43% Fewer Blacks.' 14.4 (April-May 1997): 1.

Spencer, Jon Michael. *The New Colored People: The Mixed-Race Movement in America*. New York: New York University Press, 1997.

Srivastava, Aruna. 'From the HypheNation Collective.' *Absinthe* 9.2 (1996): 4–5.

Stein, Gertrude. *Tender Buttons: Objects, Food, Rooms*. 1914. New York: Gordon Press, 1972.

Stewart, J.J. 'Early Journalism in Nova Scotia.' *Nova Scotia Historical Society Collections* 6 (1888): 91–122.

Story, Alan. 'Black Renaissance in the Arts.' *Atlantic Insight* 5.7 (1983): 39–41.

Stowe, Harriet Beecher. *Uncle Tom's Cabin; or, Life among the Lowly*. 1852. New York: Modern, 1948.

Strandberg, Victor. 'The Value of Surplus Theory.' Editorial. *The Faculty Forum* [Duke University, Durham, NC] 10.5 (Jan. 1999): 1–3.

Suarez, Ernest. *James Dickey and the Politics of the Canon: Assessing the Savage Ideal*. Columbia, MO: University of Missouri Press, 1993.

Sullivan, Martin. *Mandate '68*. Toronto: Doubleday, 1968.

Sykes, J.B., ed. *The Concise Oxford Dictionary of Current English*. 7th ed. Oxford: Clarendon Press, 1982, 1986.

Tagliamonte, Sali, and Jennifer Smith. 'Old *Was*, New Ecology: Viewing English through the Sociolinguistic Filter.' In *The English History of African American English*. Ed. Shana Poplack. Malden, MA: Blackwell, 2000. 141–71.

Takaki, Ronald T. *Violence in the Black Imagination: Essays and Documents*. New York: G.P. Putnam's Sons, 1972.

Taylor, Charles. *Reconciling the Solitudes: Essays on Canadian Federalism and Nationalism*. Montreal and Kingston, ON: McGill-Queen's University Press, 1993.

Taylor, Clyde. 'One in a Million.' *Black Renaissance / Renaissance Noire* 1.1 (Fall 1996): 82–101.

– 'We Don't Need Another Hero: Anti-Theses on Aesthetics.' In *Blackframes: Critical*

Perspectives on Black Independent Cinema. Ed. Mbye B. Cham and Claire Andrade-Watkins. Cambridge, MA: MIT, 1988. 80–5.

Thomas, Lorenzo. 'Marvin X ...' In *Afro-American Writers after 1955: Dramatists and Prose Writers*. Vol. 38. *Dictionary of Literary Biography*. Ed. Thadious M. Davis and Trudier Harris. Detroit: Gale Research Company, 1985. 177–84.

Thomson, Colin A. *Born with a Call: A Biography of Dr. William Pearly Oliver, C.M.* Cherrybrook, NS: Black Cultural Centre for Nova Scotia, 1986.

Toomer, Jean. 'The Blue Meridian.' 1932, 1970. Poem. In *The Collected Poems of Jean Toomer*. Ed. Robert B. Jones and Margery Toomer Latimer. Chapel Hill: University of North Carolina Press, 1988. 50–75.

– 'Box Seat.' In Toomer, *Cane*, 59–69.

– *Cane*. 1923. New York: W.W. Norton & Company, 1988.

– 'Prayer.' Poem. In Toomer, *Cane*, 70.

Torczyner, James L., et al. *Diversity, Mobility and Change: The Dynamics of Black Communities in Canada*. [Montreal]: McGill Consortium for Ethnicity and Strategic Social Planning, 1997.

Trehearne, Brian. *Aestheticism and the Canadian Modernists: Aspects of a Poetic Influence*. Montreal and Kingston, ON: McGill-Queen's University Press, 1989.

Trudeau, Pierre Elliott. *Against the Current: Selected Writings 1939–1996*. Toronto: McClelland & Stewart, 1996.

– 'The Asbestos Strike.' Trans. James Boake. In Trudeau, *Against the Current*, 42–66. Trans. of 'La Grève de l'amiante.' 1956. First published as 'The Asbestos Strike.' In *The Asbestos Strike*. Toronto: James, Lewis & Samuel, 1974.

– 'Deuxième entretien avec Pierre Elliott Trudeau.' [Interview.] Max and Monique Nemni. *Cite libre* 25.2 (mars-avril 1997): 7–14.

– *The Essential Trudeau*. Ed. Ron Graham. Toronto: McClelland & Stewart, 1998.

– *Federalism and the French Canadians*. Trans. Patricia Claxton. Toronto: Macmillan, 1968. Trans. of *Le Fédéralisme et la société canadienne-française*. Montréal: Éditions HMH, Ltée, 1967.

– *Le Fédéralisme et la société canadienne-française*. Montréal: Éditions HMH, Ltée, 1967.

– *Memoirs*. Toronto: McClelland & Stewart, 1993.

– 'New Treason of the Intellectuals.' Trans. Patricia Claxton. In Trudeau, *Against the Current*, 150–81. Trans. of 'La Nouvelle Trahison des clercs.' *Cité libre* 46 (avril 1962): 3–16. First published as 'New Treason of the Intellectuals.' In *Federalism and the French Canadians*. Trans. Patricia Claxton. Ed. John T. Saywell. Toronto: Macmillan, 1968.

– 'The Values of a Just Society.' Trans. Patricia Claxton. In *Towards a Just Society: The Trudeau Years*. Ed. Thomas S. Axworthy and Pierre Elliott Trudeau. Markham, ON: Viking / Penguin, 1990. 357–85.

Trudel, Marcel. *L'Ésclavage au Canada français*. Montréal: Les Éditions de l'horizon, 1960.

Tynes, Maxine. 'Africville Spirit.' Poem. In Tynes, *Woman*, 60.

– 'Cashiers at the Supermarket.' Poem. In Tynes, *Woman*, 25.

– 'The Profile of Africa.' Poem. In George Elliott Clarke, ed., *Fire*, Vol. 1 (1991), 74.

Ullman, Victor. *Look to the North Star*. Boston: Beacon Press, 1969.

Vallières, Pierre. *Le Devoir de résistance*. Montréal: VLB Éditeur, 1994.

– *White Niggers of America: The Precocious Autobiography of a Quebec 'Terrorist.'* Trans. Joan Pinkham. New York: Monthly Review, 1971. Trans. of *Nègres blancs d'Amérique: Autobiographie précoce d'un 'terroriste' québécois*. Montréal: Éditions Parti pris, 1968.

Vastel, Michel. *The Outsider: The Life of Pierre Elliott Trudeau*. Trans. Hubert Bauch. Toronto: Macmillan, 1990. Trans. of *Trudeau le québécois*. Montréal: Éditions de l'Homme, 1989.

Vennin, Loic. 'Les AfroAcadiens.' *Le Ven' d'est* [Petit-Rocher, N-B] (hiver 94–5): 16–17.

Vevaina, Coomi S. 'Whose Voices Are These Anyway? The Creation of "Imaginary Homelands" in Afro-Canadian Womanist Poetry.' *International Journal of Canadian Studies / Revue internationale d'études canadiennes* 19 (Spring / printemps 1999): 125–36.

Virgo, Clement, dir. *Rude*. 1995.

Walcott, Derek. 'XII.' Poem. In *Midsummer*. London: Faber and Faber, 1984. 22.

– 'LII.' Poem. In *Midsummer*. London: Faber and Faber, 1984. 72.

– 'The Muse of History.' 1974. In *The Routledge Reader in Caribbean Literature*. Ed. Alison Donnell and Sarah Lawson Welsh. London: Routledge, 1996. 354–8.

Walcott, Rinaldo. '"Who is she and what is she to you?" Mary Ann Shadd Cary and the (Im)possibility of Black/Canadian Studies.' In Rinaldo Walcott, ed., *Rude*, 27–47.

Walker, Alice. *The Color Purple*. 1982. New York: Pocket Books, 1985.

Walker, David. *Appeal to the Colored Citizens of the World*. 1829. Ed. Herbert Aptheker. New York: Humanities Press, 1965.

Walker, James W. St G. 'African Canadians.' In *The Encyclopedia of Canada's Peoples*. Ed. P.R. Magocsi. Toronto: University of Toronto Press, 1999. 139–76.

– *The Black Loyalists: The Search for a Promised Land in Nova Scotia and Sierra Leone 1783–1870*. 1976. Toronto: University of Toronto Press, 1992.

– 'Canada.' In Appiah and Gates, eds, *Africana*, 360–5.

– *'Race,' Rights and the Law in the Supreme Court of Canada: Historical Case Studies*. [Toronto and Waterloo, ON]: The Osgoode Society for Canadian Legal History and Wilfrid Laurier University Press, 1997.

– *The West Indians in Canada*. Ottawa: Canadian Historical Association, 1984.

Wallace, Ann, ed. Introduction. In Ann Wallace, ed., *Daughters*, 5–9.

Walmsley, Anne. *The Caribbean Artists Movement, 1966–1972: A Literary and Cultural History*. London: New Beacon Books Ltd, 1992.

Ward, Frederick. 'Blind Man's Blues.' Poem. 1983. In George Elliott Clarke, ed., *Fire*, Vol. 2 (1992), 18.

– 'Dialogue #3: Old Man (to the Squatter).' Poem. 1983. In George Elliott Clarke, ed., *Fire*, Vol. 2 (1992), 19–20.

Watts, Richard. 'Literature, French Language, in Caribbean.' In Appiah and Gates, eds, *Africana*, 1182–3.

'WCC's Head Tells of Aid for Caribbean.' *Caribbean Contact* 5.4 (July 1977): 24.

Wesley-Desmond, Gloria [Wesley-Daye]. 'Back Alley Tramp.' Poem. 1975. In George Elliott Clarke, ed., *Fire*, Vol. 2 (1992), 66–7.

West, Cornel. 'Cornel West Interviewed by bell hooks.' In *Breaking Bread: Insurgent Black Intellectual Life*. By bell hooks and Cornel West. Toronto: Between the Lines Press, 1991. 27–58.

- 'The Dilemma of the Black Intellectual.' In *Breaking Bread: Insurgent Black Intellectual Life*. By bell hooks and Cornel West. Toronto: Between the Lines Press, 1991. 131–46.

Wheatley, Phillis. 'An Answer to the *Rebus*, by the Author of These Poems.' In Wheatley, *Poems on Various Subjects*, 124.

- *Poems on Various Subjects, Religious and Moral*. London: A. Bell, 1773.

White, Hayden. 'The Burden of History.' 1966. In *Tropics of Discourse: Essays in Cultural Criticism*. Baltimore: Johns Hopkins University Press, 1978, 1985. 27–50.

Whitten, Norman. 'Blackness in Latin America and the Caribbean: An Interpretation.' In Appiah and Gates, eds, *Africana*, 257–60.

Wilhelm, James J. *Dante and Pound: The Epic of Judgment*. Orono, ME: National Poetry Foundation and the University of Maine Press, 1974.

Williams, Stephen, dir. *Soul Survivor*. 1995.

Williams, William Carlos. 'The Red Wheelbarrow.' Poem. 1923. In *The Norton Anthology of American Literature*. 3rd ed. (shorter). Ed. Nina Baym (et al.) New York: W.W. Norton, 1989. 1777.

Williamson, Joel. Preface. *New People: Miscegenation and Mulattoes in the United States*. Baton Rouge: Louisiana State University Press, 1995. xi–xiv.

Wilson, V. Seymour. 'The Tapestry Vision of Canadian Multiculturalism.' *Canadian Journal of Political Science / Revue canadienne de science politique* 26:4 (Dec./déc. 1993): 645–69.

Winks, Robin W. *The Blacks in Canada: A History*. 1971. Montreal and Kingston, ON: McGill-Queen's University Press, 1997.

Woods, David. 'Bidii (The Flight).' Poem. In David Woods, *Native*, 18.

- 'Epitaph.' Poem. In George Elliott Clarke, ed., *Fire*, Vol. 2 (1992), 143–5.

- 'Love.' Poem. In David Woods, *Native*, 51.

- 'Native Song.' Poem. In David Woods, *Native*, 102.

Wordsworth, William. *The Prelude*. [1798–1839.] Ed. E.E. Reynolds. London: Macmillan, [1932].

Wright, Michelle M. 'Nigger Peasants from France: Missing Translations of American Anxieties on Race and the Nation.' *Callaloo* 22.4 (1999): 831–52.

Wright, Richard. *Eight Men*. 1960. New York: Thunder's Mouth Press, 1987.

- 'The Man Who Was Almost a Man.' In Wright, *Eight Men*, 11–26.

- *Native Son*. New York: Harper and Brothers, 1940.

- *White Man, Listen!* Garden City: Doubleday, 1957.

Wynter, Sylvia. 'The Poetics and the Politics of a High Life for Caliban.' Afterword. *Highlife for Caliban*. By Lemuel Johnson. Trenton, NJ: Africa World Press, 1995. 85–110.

X, Malcolm. 'Austin Clarke / Malcolm X.' Interview. 1963. By Austin Clarke. In *The Austin Clarke Reader*. Ed. Barry Callaghan. Toronto: Exile Editions, 1996. 264–76.

- *The Autobiography of Malcolm X*. With Alex Haley. 1965. New York: Ballantine Books, 1972.

Yeats, W.B. 'The Second Coming.' 1921. In *Modern British Literature*. Ed. Frank Kermode and John Hollander. Oxford: Oxford University Press, 1973. 192.

Young, Lola. 'Missing Persons: Fantasising Black Women in *Black Skin, White Masks*.' In *The Fact of Blackness: Frantz Fanon and Visual Representation*. Ed. Alan Read. London and Seattle: Institute of Contemporary Arts and Bay Press, 1996. 86–101.

Yutang, Lin, ed. *The Wisdom of China and India*. New York: Random House, 1942.

Zahar, Renate. *Frantz Fanon: Colonialism and Alienation*. Trans. Willfried F. Feuser. New York: Monthly Review Press, 1974. Trans. of *Kolonialismus und Entfremdung*. Frankfurt: Europäische Verlagsanstalt, 1969.

INDEX

Note: This index catalogues personages – primarily authors – and pertinent agencies cited in the main body of the text, up to page 338. It does not canvass titles, concepts, or the appended bibliographies, spanning pages 339 to the end.

COLOPHON

Odysseys Home: Mapping African-Canadian Literature was typeset in 10 pt. Palatino on a 12 pt. leading. Hermann Zapf created this Old Face font in the late 1950s and named it after Giambattista Palatino, a master of stylish, classic calligraphy from the era of Leonardo da Vinci.